Treat this book with care and

It should become part of your personal and professional library. It will serve you well at any number of points during your professional career.

FIFTH EDITION

HERBERT J. CHRUDEN
Professor of Business Administration
California State University, Sacramento

ARTHUR W. SHERMAN, Jr.
Professor of Psychology
California State University, Sacramento

G80

Published by
SOUTH-WESTERN PUBLISHING CO.

CINCINNATI WEST CHICAGO, ILL. DALLAS PELHAM MANOR, N.Y.
PALO ALTO, CALIF. BRIGHTON, ENGLAND

ISBN: 0-538-07800-6

Library of Congress Catalog Card Number: 74-76897

1 2 3 4 5 6 7 8 **K** 3 2 1 0 9 8 7 6

Printed in the United States of America

Preface

Since 1959, when the first edition of this book was published, the body of knowledge relating to personnel management has continued to expand and to change as a result of research and developments that have occurred within the field. Furthermore, technological and social progress together with changing economic conditions and legislation also have had influential effects upon the organizational environment within which people work and upon the management of personnel. Perhaps most significant of the more recent developments has been the growing trend among employers to recognize their social responsibilities and obligations and to administer their personnel programs in a manner that will enable them to meet such obligations. More attention, for example, is being focused upon the recruitment and employment of minority groups, such as women and blacks, and upon retraining and reassigning employees who otherwise would have to be terminated. Finally, there has been a growing recognition of the importance of designing jobs to better fit human needs and capabilities. As a result, it has been a major objective of the authors to include in this fifth edition a large portion of new material relating to this progress and change, thus necessitating an extensive revision of its contents.

Because it provides the foundation for the contemporary theory and practices relating to the management of people, more than half of the content of this book is devoted to behavioral science, in terms of both theory and application. Thus, behavioral science is considered in the context of managing the human resources within an organization as a part of the total management system. Major attention also is devoted to the basic personnel processes that are involved in the procurement, development, and maintenance of these human resources, including those relating to the selection, training, motivation, and remuneration of employees and in maintaining relations with their unions. These processes are discussed not only from the standpoint of research and experience in the field of management but also in terms of what is considered to be sound practice in the light of contemporary behavioral science theories.

In order that students may continue to have the opportunity to apply contemporary theories and principles of personnel management, some new discussion problems and questions are included at the end of the chapters; and at the end of the book are 14 cases, seven of which are new. Additional opportunities to apply the theories and principles may be found in the authors' *Practical Study Experiences in Personnel Management,* Fifth Edition, a project book designed to provide students with a variety of experiences similar to those that they are likely to find on the job. The project book and *Readings in Personnel Management,* Fourth Edition, a compilation of selected journal articles that provide elaboration on the theories and principles discussed in this book, have been designed to correlate closely with the material in this fifth edition of the text.

Although recognition is given throughout this book to the role of the personnel department in the administration of the personnel program and the processes relating to it, the major emphasis is upon the role of departmental supervisors, managers, and their superiors in the management of subordinate personnel according to the objectives and policies of the personnel program of the organization. Consequently, it is the desire of the authors to provide material that will be useful and relevant to the needs of those individuals who may occupy positions of management responsibility, presently or in the future, rather than to focus on the needs of those who may occupy positions in a personnel department.

In preparing the manuscript for this fifth edition, the authors have drawn not only upon the current literature in the personnel field but also upon the current practices of organizations that have furnished information and illustrations relating to their personnel programs. The authors are indebted to the leaders in the field who have developed the available heritage of information and practices of personnel management and who have influenced the authors through their writings and personal associations. The authors have also been aided, particularly in the preparation of discussion problems and cases, by students in their classes, by former students, by the participants in the management development programs with which they have been associated, by personnel managers, and by their colleagues. In particular the authors would like to express their appreciation to James A. Adler, Elizabeth Arnold, Frank Davis, Pallo Defteros, W. R. Donaldson, C. C. Firch, Jr., Dr. Irving Herman, Barbara Marino, John E. Mills, Bob Rodman, Donald E. Porritt, Richard F. Schlecht, Anthony D. Sciara, Verne M. Sellin, J. W. Sindall, Richard T. Soderberg, Francis G. Stoffels, James D. Strickler, and Chuck Stuart for their contributions. As in the past, our wives—Marie Chruden and Leneve Sherman—have not only contributed in many ways to the development of this revision but they have made the entire task more pleasant and rewarding through their continued enthusiasm and support. Their many contributions are gratefully acknowledged.

Herbert J. Chruden

Arthur W. Sherman, Jr.

Contents

PART ONE THE PERSONNEL MANAGEMENT SYSTEM

PART SIX REMUNERATION AND SECURITY

PART SEVEN ASSESSMENT AND RESEARCH

CASES

The Personnel Management System

The Role of Personnel Management

The efficiency with which any organization can be operated will depend to a considerable measure upon how effectively its personnel can be managed and utilized. Every manager, therefore, must be able to work effectively with people and to resolve satisfactorily the many and varied problems that the management of these people may entail. Effective personnel management requires the development of a program that will permit employees to be selected and trained for those jobs that are most appropriate to their developed abilities. Moreover, it requires that employees be motivated to exert their maximum efforts, that their performances be evaluated properly for results, and that they be remunerated on the basis of their contributions to the organization.

Although managers and supervisors in the past often were arbitrary and autocratic in their relations with subordinates, today this type of leadership increasingly is being rejected. The present generation of employees is more enlightened and better educated than were preceding ones. Today's employees demand more considerate treatment and a more sophisticated form of leadership. Furthermore, because of the protection that is afforded to them by their unions and by government legislation or because their skills are in short supply, many groups of employees are in a position to demand and obtain more favorable employment conditions and treatment.

Since the activities of most organizations today are becoming more and more complex in nature, the managers in these organizations are required to have greater technical competency than was formerly the case. In addition, they must possess a better understanding of human behavior and of the processes by which personnel can be managed effectively. Fortunately, a growing body of knowledge relating to human behavior and to management systems and processes is being accumulated from experience and research which can be of assistance to the manager in developing better relations with subordinates. Personnel management is able to borrow from many of the more basic disciplines and to apply the contributions of these disciplines to the improvement of the personnel program. The contributions that have been derived from these disciplines will be covered in the discussion of the various processes of personnel management in this and the chapters that follow.

THE NATURE OF PERSONNEL MANAGEMENT

There are certain basic processes to be performed, general principles and rules to be observed, as well as tools, techniques, and methods to be utilized in the management of personnel in any organization regardless of its type, purpose, or the qualifications of its personnel. This fact holds true whether the organization is a business, government, research, military, educational, or some other type of organization. Since all organizations, regardless of their size, functions, or objectives, must operate with and through people, the management of such organizations basically is a process of managing people. Any manager or supervisor who is responsible for the work of others in an organization therefore must engage in personnel management and in the various processes, such as training, motivating, and counseling, that this responsibility entails. The primary function of the personnel department staff, on the other hand, is to provide managers with service and assistance that they may require in managing subordinates more effectively and in accordance with established personnel policies and procedures.

The Organizations to be Managed

Because the ability to earn a profit is essential to their continued survival, and because profits serve as a primary motive for their existence, business organizations generally were among the first to take action to bring labor and other operating costs under control, and also the first to be subject to union pressures and government regulations. As a result of these conditions, personnel programs tended to be developed earlier and more fully by business than by other types of organizations. In recent years the need for effective personnel management, however, also has become critical in the nonprofit organizations. Most organizations in the public sector, for example, have had to expand their services and the size of their work forces and to bargain with employee unions demanding higher wages and fringe benefits, while at the same time they have been forced to operate under increasing budgetary restrictions. School districts, hospitals, colleges, and private foundations also have encountered similar experiences which have required them to devote more attention to personnel management. Even opera and symphony orchestra associations, and union organizations themselves, have encountered their share of personnel problems as their employees have unionized and made demands for increased financial benefits and for greater participation in policy making.

While business organizations may encounter certain personnel problems that differ from those in the nonprofit organizations, they also have many problems in common with them. Most of the knowledge that has been accumulated in the field, therefore, generally is just as applicable to the management of personnel in a hospital, a state highway department, or the United States Postal Service as it is to a store, a bank, or a steel mill. As a result of this fact, the tendency is to make less and less distinction between personnel management in terms of its specialized application to a particular type of organization. Personnel management and the process that it entails can be adapted and utilized to serve the needs of all organizations.

The Work Force to be Managed

Personnel management in the past was concerned more with the management of blue-collar workers in the factory than with white-collar workers in the office. The reason for this fact was that the plant rather than the office provided the major source of a company's employment and labor costs. Cost reduction programs involving the use of time and motion study and other industrial engineering techniques to establish performance standards, simplify work methods, and generally improve efficiency were introduced first in the plant. It was in this area of the organization rather than in the office, furthermore, where workers first organized and bargained collectively. The need to achieve greater efficiency and maintain some type of workable relationship with the employees and their union representatives thus helped to stimulate the development of formal personnel programs to perform such processes as selection, training, supervision, and grievance handling and labor relations more effectively.

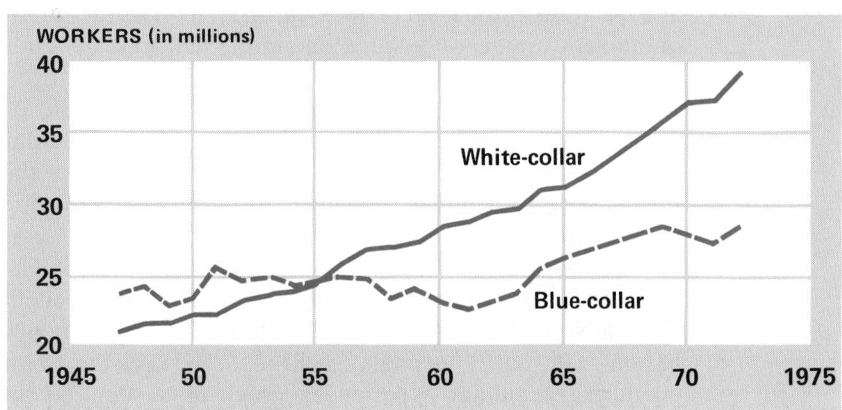

Source: U.S. Department of Labor, Bureau of Labor Statistics, "Employment Outlook for Tomorrow's Jobs," *Occupational Outlook Handbook,* 1974-1975 edition, Reprint Bulletin 1785-1 (Washington, D.C.: U.S. Government Printing Office), p. 5.

Figure 1-1 TRENDS IN WHITE-COLLAR AND BLUE-COLLAR EMPLOYMENT

Increasing White-Collar Work Force. Since the mid-1950s, as Figure 1-1 indicates, the white-collar workers in the labor force have outnumbered the blue-collar ones, and their numbers are continuing to increase at a proportionately greater rate. While the demand for workers in the plant has been declining as the result of automation and other work-saving devices, the demand for white-collar workers has been growing because of increases in the number of technical, clerical, and administrative positions being required within an organization. The work forces of organizations such as banks, insurance companies, and administrative agencies of the government, furthermore, are comprised almost entirely of white-collar personnel. Thus, it can be seen from Figure 1-2 that the organizations which will have the greatest employment growth during the next two decades are for the most part those that employ largely white-collar personnel.

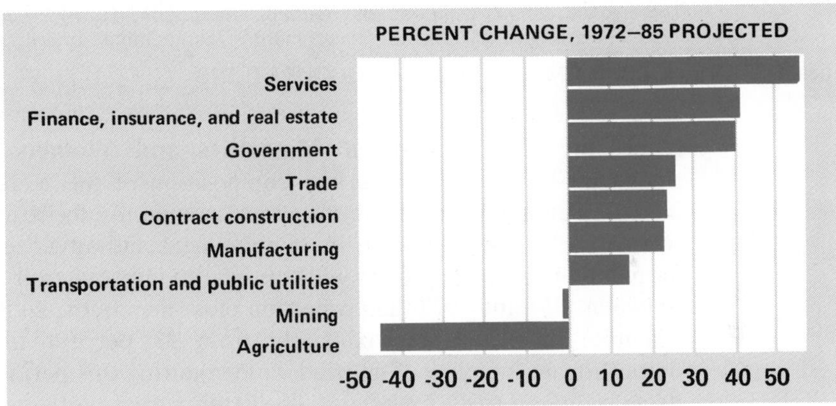

Source: U.S. Department of Labor, Bureau of Labor Statistics, "Employment Outlook for Tomorrow's Jobs," *Occupational Outlook Handbook,* 1974-75 edition, Reprint Bulletin 1785-1 (Washington, D.C.: U.S. Government Printing Office), p. 3.

Figure 1-2 PROJECTED CHANGES IN EMPLOYMENT BY INDUSTRY

As Figure 1-3 indicates, the greatest growth will be in technical and professional employment where the majority will be college graduates, and many also will possess a master's degree or even a doctorate. Most of the personnel employed in sales or clerical work generally will possess at least a high school education and many will have completed some work in college or even be college graduates. The growth of employment opportunities in jobs requiring higher levels of education and training will necessitate a more sophisticated and participative style of personnel management that will permit employees to exercise a greater role in decision-making processes. Better communication also will be required to satisfy the desires of these employees to know what is going on in the organization and where they stand regarding their performance and progress within it.

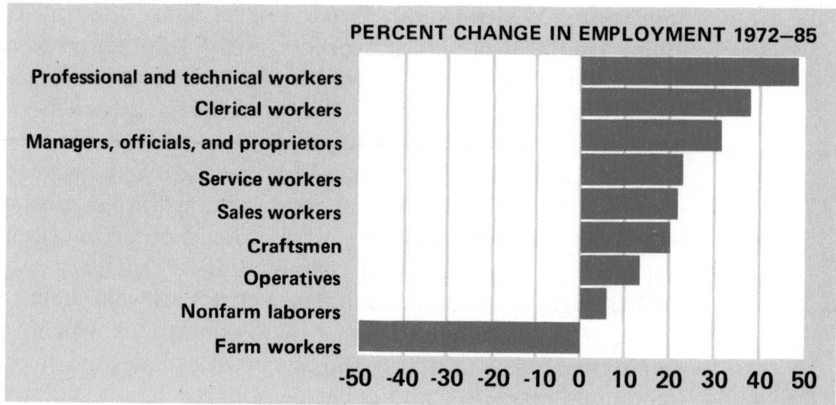

Source: U.S. Department of Labor, Bureau of Labor Statistics, "Employment Outlook for Tomorrow's Jobs," *Occupational Outlook Handbook,* 1974-75 edition, Reprint Bulletin 1785-1 (Washington, D.C.: U.S. Government Printing Office), p. 6.

Figure 1-3 CHANGES IN EMPLOYMENT BY OCCUPATIONS

Increasing Employment of Minorities and Women. One of the most significant future changes in the composition of the work force will be the increased employment of minorities and women. As the result of legislation and affirmative action programs, the employment and advancement opportunities for members of these groups will continue to improve as it has in recent years. Between 1961 and 1973 the proportion of women in the civilian labor force, for example, increased approximately from 33 percent to 40 percent. The proportionate increase of married women during this period was even greater, rising from 32.7 to 41.2 percent.[1] The latter increase reflects the greater number of younger married women with children, many of preschool age, who have entered the labor force and who hold full-time, year-round positions.[2] It also serves to refute many of the stereotypes concerning the role of women in employment situations.

THE EVOLUTION OF PERSONNEL MANAGEMENT

Although personnel management has been recognized formally as a field of functional specialization and practice for little more than a half century, its roots are embedded deeply in the past. Personnel management has been necessary as long as there have been groups of people organized to achieve common goals. Individuals responsible for leading and managing organizations, even centuries ago, for example, were confronted with the need to provide some type of training, motivation, leadership, and remuneration for their personnel if only on a hit-or-miss basis. Gradually, however, improvements

[1] "Married Women in the Labor Force," *Statistical Bulletin,* Vol. 55 (New York: Metropolitan Life, August, 1974), p. 9.

[2] *Ibid.*

were required to be made in the performance of these personnel processes. Many of these improvements were in response to specific needs or pressures that arose as the result of military, economic, or social crises, but more often improvements tended to evolve slowly over long periods of time.

Early Developments in the Field

Some of the earliest developments relating to personnel management occurred during the period of the Middle Ages. It was during this period that free employment relationships upon which contemporary personnel relations are based began to emerge. The growth of towns and villages provided a new demand for goods and services as well as employment for those seeking to escape their positions as serfs within the feudal system. Skilled artisans organized into guilds which established controls and regulations pertaining to their respective trades.[3] These guilds were the forerunner of today's employer associations and helped to provide standards of craftsmanship and the foundation for apprenticeship training that many craft unions still require of individuals seeking to enter a trade. Since the opportunity for journeymen to establish their own shops was limited, many of them were forced to continue to work for other master craftsmen and, as a result, began to form yeomanry guilds which resembled the contemporary trade union.

Until the Industrial Revolution most goods were manufactured in small shops or in the home by handicraft methods of production. The Industrial Revolution stimulated the growth of factories as the result of the availability of capital, free labor, power-driven equipment, improved production techniques, as well as the growing demand for manufactured goods. The factory system thus permitted goods to be manufactured more cheaply than had been possible in homes and small shops. The system with its specialization of work, however, brought about new problems in the area of human relations through the creation of many unskilled and repetitive jobs in which the work often tended to be monotonous and unchallenging as well as unhealthy and hazardous. Unlike the craftsman, who enjoyed some degree of economic security by virtue of having a marketable skill, factory workers lacked security and had little power to improve their situations because they could be replaced easily by other individuals who could be trained quickly to perform their jobs.

Developments in America

Originally manpower, along with money, machinery, and materials, was regarded by employers as constituting one of the factors necessary for the production of goods and services. Employees thus tended to be regarded mainly as a commodity to be employed at the lowest wage possible and discarded when their services no longer could be utilized profitably. Since it

---

[3] Cyril Curtis Ling, *The Management of Personnel Relations* (Homewood, Illinois: Richard D. Irwin, Inc., 1965), pp. 21-23.

was the employer who held the position of power, employees usually were forced to accept their conditions of employment on a "take it or leave it" basis. The need for income and the inability to find another job, let alone better employment conditions, prevented those who were employed from going elsewhere.

Improvement of Employment Conditions. Prior to the middle of the last century, there were no laws to guarantee the individual or collective bargaining rights of employees. Until the Commonwealth *v.* Hunt decision of 1842, their attempts to organize and to bargain collectively with employers were considered, under the existing common law, to constitute a criminal act of conspiracy.

The gradual extension of voting privileges and free education to all citizens helped workers to become more effectual politically. Through their ability to muster public support for their cause, workers gradually were able to gain the passage of legislation that offered them some degree of protection. State laws regulating hours of work for women and children were among the earliest forms of labor legislation to be enacted in this country. As time passed protective legislation was extended to cover hours of work for male labor, working conditions affecting employee health and safety, and compensation payments for injuries suffered through industrial accidents. This legislation, together with the worker's collective bargaining achievements, eventually helped to bring about substantial improvements in employment conditions.

The Emergence of Large-Scale Enterprise. It was not until the introduction of mass production methods that full advantage was gained from the developments that had been introduced by the Industrial Revolution. Mass production was made possible through the production and assembly of standardized parts and by the development of the corporate form of enterprise in which ownership was vested among many individual stockholders. Thus, instead of taking an active hand in the management of the enterprise, this function was delegated by the stockholders to the new and expanding group of professional managers.

The growth of large-scale manufacturing operations also was made possible through the further improvement of production techniques and laborsaving machinery and equipment. Although these developments increased worker productivity, they also led to increases in overhead costs and wage rates. Consequently, more attention had to be devoted to the problem of utilizing the production equipment, facilities, and labor more efficiently. Furthermore, in addition to being mechanized, the operations of many jobs were simplified to the point that the same work cycle was repeated by a worker hundreds of times a day. These repetitive type operations, however, permitted any time savings resulting from increased effort or improved work methods on the part of a worker to multiply very rapidly.

The Scientific Management Movement. By the beginning of this century, rising labor and overhead costs had forced management to devote more effort to achieving greater production efficiency through the improvement of work methods and the development of standards by which employee efficiency could be judged. Such efforts led to the scientific management movement during the early part of this century, which had a definite impact upon personnel management. The movement helped to stimulate the use of new personnel management tools with which to measure and to motivate employee productivity. However, it also created human relations problems for managers to resolve.

Taylor's Approach to Personnel Management. The scientific management movement was stimulated by the contributions of Frederick W. Taylor, who often has been referred to as the father of scientific management. Among his contemporaries who also contributed to the movement were such leaders as Frank and Lillian Gilbreth, Henry L. Gantt, Harrington Emerson, and Harry Hopf. Taylor believed that work could be systematically analyzed and studied by using the same scientific approach as that followed by the researchers in the laboratory.[4] In his words, scientific management constituted "the substitution of exact scientific investigation and knowledge for the old individual judgment or opinion, either of the workman or the boss, in all matters relating to the work done in the establishment."[5] Thus, Taylor relied upon time studies as a basis for establishing the methods and standards for performing a job, for training and supervising employees in the use of the proper methods, and for evaluating their work.

Taylor also believed that scientific management offered the best means for increasing the productivity and the earnings of the workers and for providing higher profits for owners and lower prices for customers. He regarded accurate performance standards, based upon objective data gathered from time studies and other sources, as constituting an important personnel management tool for rewarding the superior workers and for eliminating the inefficient ones. Furthermore, he believed that financial incentives, which permit workers to earn more by working harder and more efficiently, represented the best form of employee motivation. This concept was in sharp contrast to the prevailing practice, which has never disappeared completely, of attempting to gain more work from employees by threatening them with punishment including the loss of their jobs.

Taylor's Views on the Planning Function. Perhaps most important was Taylor's recognition that efficiency was also dependent upon good planning. However, as contrasted to today's prevailing philosophy of job enrichment in which workers are given the opportunity to participate in planning and decision making, Taylor believed that the planning function was primarily the responsibility of management. Although his approach may have been somewhat autocratic in comparison with today's emphasis upon soliciting

---

[4] See Chapter 23 for a detailed résumé of the scientific approach to problem solving.

[5] Frederick W. Taylor, "What Is Scientific Management?" as reprinted in Harwood F. Merrill (Editor), *Classics in Management* (New York: American Management Association, 1960), p. 80.

employee participation and contributions, it was progressive in terms of the practices used by management at the time. In the area of personnel management, Taylor helped management to recognize the fact that employees differed in their abilities and that many of them through lack of proper job placement and training did not have the opportunity to make maximum use of their abilities to the detriment of themselves and their employers.

Developments in Industrial Psychology. The development of personnel management into a professional field was aided by the knowledge and research contributions from industrial psychology as it emerged as a field of study.

Contributions of Pioneer Industrial Psychologists. One of the best known of the pioneers in industrial psychology was Hugo Münsterberg whose book, *Psychology and Industrial Efficiency,* published in 1913, called attention to the contributions that psychology as a field of study could render in the areas of employment testing, training, and efficiency improvement. Many other psychologists who followed his example made notable contributions to personnel management. Among them are Walter Dill Scott, recognized for his early work in the selection of salesmen and for his classic book in personnel management with Clothier and Spriegel; J. McKeen Cattell, noted for his test development activities and efforts in establishing The Psychological Corporation (1921); and Walter Van Dyke Bingham, author of books in interviewing and aptitude testing and later chief psychologist for the War Department. Professors and researchers in American universities whose early work has contributed substantially to the present efforts include A. T. Poffenberger of Columbia, Harold E. Burtt of Ohio State, Arthur W. Kornhauser of Chicago, and Morris S. Viteles of Pennsylvania.

Psychological Journals and Research. G. Stanley Hall, the first president of the American Psychological Association (1892), was among those who recognized the need for a journal that would focus on the applications of psychology to industry. He founded the *Journal of Applied Psychology* in 1917 that shortly was taken over by J. P. Porter. The *Journal of Applied Psychology* and *Personnel Psychology,* which largely grew out of the early efforts of Bingham, are the leading psychological journals devoted to the dissemination of literature in the personnel and industrial fields. Psychological research stimulated by World War I and again in World War II has helped to bring about further advances in psychological testing, in performance appraisal techniques, and in learning theory. In more recent years research and training centers have made significant progress in the areas of sensitivity training, group dynamics, personnel assessment, and organizational behavior. Currently in all types of organizations the contributions of industrial and organizational psychology are being utilized to achieve more effective results in the management of personnel.

Functional Specialization in Personnel Management

Toward the beginning of this century, personnel management began to develop as a field of specialization in its own right. Its growth was aided by the new knowledge being generated at that time from the scientific management movement and from the field of industrial psychology. The welfare and the union movements that were gaining momentum by the end of the 1800s also helped to stimulate the need to formalize personnel management.

Initial Personnel Functions. Initially the functions of personnel management, which generally were limited largely to hiring, firing, and timekeeping, were handled by each supervisor. As production methods became more complicated and work loads increased, supervisors ceased to have time to engage in keeping payroll and other personnel records. Consequently, these responsibilities were assigned to a clerk in the department who became one of the first "personnel specialists." This initial function in some instances was enlarged to include certain responsibilities for employment and eventually other personnel functions.

The welfare movement during the 1800s helped to focus public attention on the conditions under which many workers and their families were forced to exist. It also encouraged some employers to become more concerned about the economic welfare of their own employees.[6] This concern led to the creation of the position of welfare secretary in some organizations, a position which constituted one of the beginnings of the personnel department and was concerned with providing cultural, educational, or recreational facilities for employees as well as financial, medical, housing, and similar forms of assistance.[7] Many of the persons who were appointed as welfare secretaries, as might be expected, had backgrounds in philanthropic or social work. Some agencies such as the YMCA, furthermore, established programs for the purpose of training people to become welfare secretaries.[8] The influence of the welfare secretary approach to personnel management continued to exist to some degree until the depression of the 1930s and probably was a factor in attracting, among others, certain individuals to the field who "liked people and wanted to help them."

Personnel as a Departmental Function. Although the personnel functions existed earlier in the form of an employment or welfare activity, the personnel department did not emerge until about 1912. In 1915 the first college personnel course consisting of a training program for employment managers was offered by the Tuck School at Dartmouth College, and by 1919 at least twelve colleges were offering training programs in personnel management.[9] By the beginning of the 1920s, therefore, the field of personnel management had become fairly well established as had personnel departments in many of the larger companies and governmental organizations. These departments were established for the purpose of coordinating personnel activities and assisting managers and supervisors in the management of their personnel.

---

[6] Actually, as Ling points out, the welfare movement can be traced back to the feudal manor and the guild systems of the Middle Ages during which time provisions were made for maintaining the well-being of the system's less fortunate members. Ling, *op. cit.*, pp. 54-70.

[7] Henry Eilbirt, "The Development of Personnel Management in the United States," *Business History Review*, Vol. 33, No. 3 (Autumn, 1959), pp. 345-364.

[8] Ling, *op. cit.*, p. 80.

[9] Eilbirt, *op. cit.*, pp. 10-11.

The growth in the status of personnel departments within organizations is due in no small measure to the contributions that have been made by researchers and practitioners who helped pioneer the field. Early leaders, such as Whiting Williams, Walter Dill Scott, Walter V. Bingham, Ordway Tead, and others, contributed to knowledge in the field as a result not only of their observations and experiences but also of their ability to communicate this knowledge through their writings and speeches. These leaders, by advancing the professionalization of personnel work, helped the services of the personnel specialist to become accepted more by line managers and made personnel work more attractive as a career.

Development of the Personnel Functions

As the benefits to be derived from the personnel functions became more widely recognized and accepted, the scope of personnel programs expanded. The programs began to evolve from being merely recordkeeping or employment functions to ones covering all phases of personnel management. Personnel specialists were employed to assist managers with such activities as training; wage, salary and fringe benefit administration; and labor relations.

Personnel Selection. Originally the selection of an employee was based on little more than a decision reached as a result of face-to-face contact. Eventually various types of tests were utilized to provide additional evidence upon which the selection might be based. With the establishment of the Civil Service Commission in 1883, the federal government became one of the first organizations to attempt to select and promote employees on an objective basis. By developing competitive examination procedures for hiring job applicants, the Commission provided a foundation for various types of employment tests that were used in the decades that followed. However, it was not until a critical need developed for more effective selection tools during World War I that such tests began to receive widespread usage. Thus, the Army Alpha and Beta tests were constructed for the purpose of screening personnel for military assignments. Experience with the use of these tests for measuring intelligence encouraged the construction of various other tests for measuring job knowledge, aptitude, interest, and personality that were used increasingly by government and industry.

In recent years, because of civil-rights legislation, the focus of attention in the selection process has been upon increasing the employment of women and minorities and improving their advancement opportunities within the organization. In order to accomplish these results and to improve the recruiting process, organizations currently are devoting more attention to predicting and preparing for their staffing needs through better personnel planning. These planning activities are directed not only toward achieving the required staff but also toward the reduction of labor costs.[10]

---

[10] Charles J. Coleman, "Personnel: The Changing Function," *Public Personnel Management,* Vol. 2, No. 3 (May-June, 1973), p. 187, as reprinted in Herbert J. Chruden and Arthur W. Sherman, Jr., *Readings in Personnel Management* (4th ed.; Cincinnati: South-Western Publishing Company, 1976), pp. 34-46.

Training. Training was another personnel activity that was emphasized by both industry and government during World Wars I & II. Experience and knowledge gained in the field of training during these wars did much to make companies aware of their potential contributions with the result that training has become an important division of the personnel department. Since the late 1940s, training programs have broadened into personnel development programs covering all phases of growth and development of personnel at all levels within an organization. These programs also are receiving greater attention as evidenced by the fact that two thirds of the personnel managers contacted in one survey reported giving top priority to them in their personnel planning.[11]

Wage and Salary Administration. Although the scientific management movement led to the creation of various types of engineered incentive systems, it was not until the middle 1920s that an objective system of job evaluation for determining basic hourly wage rates was developed. Among some of the first job evaluation systems were those originated during the middle 1920s by Merril R. Lott and Eugene Benge. Although these systems were developed initially for jobs below the management level, other systems subsequently have been created for management positions.

Fringe Benefits. By the 1920s certain benefits and services began to be provided for employees by some companies as a part of their personnel programs. One of these services, employee counseling, made use of the growing body of knowledge being acquired from the fields of psychology and psychiatry. Other benefits initiated included employee health and recreation, paid holidays, vacation, sick leave, and paid life insurance. Many of these benefits, which often were installed in a spirit of benevolent paternalism, were eliminated during the 1930s. As the result of employee and union demands rather than employer generosity, most of these benefits were reintroduced on an even larger scale starting with World War II.

Labor Relations. The passage of the Wagner Act in 1935 forced many private employers to bargain collectively with unions representing their employees. In more recent years employees of federal, state, and local government agencies and of educational and other nonprofit organizations also have resorted to unionization. They have sought to bargain collectively with their employers and, in some instances, have resorted to strike activity in an effort to gain improvements in employment conditions. Labor relations thus has become an important function of personnel management in most types of organizations. Whether or not labor costs can be kept from becoming excessive, and whether or not strikes, slowdowns, or other disruptions can be avoided depends upon how effectively an employer is able to bargain with the union. Members of top management, therefore, have tended to take a more active role in bargaining and in resolving grievances with the union.

Personnel Research. By the 1920s the need for greater knowledge concerning human behavior based upon objective evidence led to greater emphasis being

[11] *Ibid.*

placed upon personnel research. Some of the early research studies were directed toward determining the effects that working conditions, such as hours of work and periods of rest, might have upon fatigue and worker productivity.

The famous Hawthorne Study was initiated to research this subject. As this study progressed, however, it was discovered that the social environment could have an equal if not a greater effect upon productivity than the physical one. Conducted by Mayo, Roethlisberger, and Dickson in the late 1920s, the study represented a pioneering endeavor in what has come to be referred to as the field of behavioral science.[12] The study revealed the influence that the informal work group can have upon the productivity of employees and upon their response to such factors as supervision and financial incentives. Also, it represented the beginning of nondirective counseling with employees.

CONTEMPORARY DEVELOPMENTS IN PERSONNEL MANAGEMENT

The existence of labor strife as well as a level of low morale and efficiency in many companies following World War II stimulated efforts to improve employee cooperation and to promote better mutual understanding. It also caused a greater emphasis to be placed upon employee communication and participation programs and upon the improvement of human relations. The organization of training programs to help managers and supervisors better understand and motivate subordinates constituted the primary efforts to improve these relations. The programs encouraged the use of participative leadership techniques in the supervision of personnel and sought to help managers acquire greater insight into the causes of their own personalities and their effects upon the behavior of subordinates. Managers also have been aided in developing a greater awareness of the reactions of others to them by participating in laboratory type sensitivity courses. This type of training, which was pioneered by the National Training Laboratory for Group Development, is now being provided by various universities and consulting organizations throughout the nation.

Attempts to induce employees to cooperate and to exert their maximum efforts have created renewed interest in financial incentive plans in organizations. Unlike those of a few decades ago, incentive plans today provide employees with the opportunity to participate in decisions affecting their work as well as their income. Some of these plans permit the incentive payments to be deferred in order to provide funds for retirement, as well as an income tax shelter. Private pension plans have increased rapidly in number since 1948 following a Supreme Court ruling that they were a legitimate subject for collective bargaining. The vast majority of the larger companies now provide a pension plan for their employees; and the small enterprises, as the result of union pressure and the competition for good personnel, are rapidly being forced to do likewise.

---

[12] F. Roethlisberger and W. J. Dickson, *Management and the Worker* (Cambridge, Massachusetts: Harvard University Press, 1939).

Contributions of the Behavioral Sciences

The field of personnel management utilizes the contributions derived from many academic areas including economics, law, mathematics, industrial engineering, and management. More important, however, are those disciplines that comprise what has come to be known as the behavioral sciences. Behavioral sciences are interdisciplinary in nature and embrace several academic disciplines, the most important of which are psychology, sociology, and anthropology. Social economics, political science, linguistics, and education are also considered to be a part of these sciences.[13] Some of the principal characteristics of the behavioral sciences, according to Rush, are those listed in Figure 1-4.[14]

Nature of Behavioral Science. The unifying concern of behavioral science is to bring about the interaction of the disciplines that comprise it for the purpose of studying human behavior in its social or cultural setting. As Rush indicates,

CHARACTERISTICS OF A CONTEMPORARY BEHAVIORAL SCIENCE

1. It is an applied science.
2. It is normative and value centered.
3. It is humanistic and optimistic.
4. It is oriented toward economic objectives.
5. It is concerned with the total climate or milieu.
6. It stresses the use of groups.
7. It is aimed at participation.
8. It is concerned with development of interpersonal competence.
9. It views the organization as a total system.
10. It is an ongoing process to manage change.

Figure 1-4 CHARACTERISTICS OF A CONTEMPORARY BEHAVIORAL SCIENCE

[13] Harold M. F. Rush, *Behavioral Science: Concepts and Management Application*, Personnel Policy Study No. 216 (New York: National Industrial Conference Board, 1969), p. 2.

[14] *Ibid.*

however, this unifying concern does not necessarily imply agreement among these disciplines in the acceptance of some common theory of human nature. In fact, widespread disagreement on the subject exists among behavioral science disciplines just as it does within each of them. Behavioral science is seen not as a neatly defined theory of human behavior but rather as an approach to the study of it that places equal emphasis upon behavior and upon science.[15] As Rush explains:

> Generally, the study of behavior follows the outline of scientific method, which implies the development of a systematic theory and an experimental plan for testing the theory. As these tests or investigations are carried out, new hypotheses are evolved, and these, in turn, are tested under controlled conditions. Furthermore, the behavioral sciences, in their investigations, generally follow the three fundamental steps of scientific method: research, development, and application. Unlike the biological and physical sciences, the behavioral sciences have a more difficult time in following rigidly the rules of scientific method because the subject of their inquiry is more variable. Simply, people and their environment are forever changing.[16]

In contrast to the more limited fields and methodical approaches of scientific management and human relations, behavioral science takes a much broader approach. It is concerned with all aspects of the total work environment and its effects upon employee behavior, particularly as it concerns productivity. Thus, while behavioral science, like scientific management, is concerned with improving employee efficiency, it seeks to improve efficiency by discovering and making improvements within the work environment that are necessary and not merely by improving work methods, establishing work standards, or using similar engineering techniques. Furthermore, it does not reject the human relations movement's concern for good morale within an organization. However, it does reject what is considered to be the insincere and manipulative approach that has characterized human relations in some organizations with its emphasis upon creating a happy work force. Behavioral science instead seeks to develop better interpersonal or human relations by improving communications and by creating a social climate that will permit each member to gain recognition and satisfaction through contributions to the organization. It recognizes that high productivity among employees is the result of the many conditions that go to make up the total environment of the organization rather than just morale-building efforts.

Limitations of Behavioral Science. As in the case of the movements that preceded it, there is the risk that the behavioral science movement may be looked upon as the panacea for all of the human relations problems that confront modern organizations. While the field of behavioral science is helping to provide new knowledge and insights that can be utilized in managing personnel, it still is in its infancy. In spite of the research that has been

[15] *Ibid.*, p. 6.
[16] *Ibid.*, p. 2.

conducted to date, there is a great deal more to be learned in terms of understanding and predicting human behavior.

Since the body of knowledge supporting the field of personnel management will be expanding rapidly, it is essential for those in the field to keep abreast of the research and writings that are rapidly being contributed to it. Unfortunately the volume of articles on behavioral science being published makes it difficult to remain current in the field. A considerable amount of scanning and sifting of the literature is necessary, therefore, in order for those articles that represent original findings or thinking on the subject to be separated from the others. Another difficulty is that many of the studies upon which conclusions regarding human behavior are based leave something to be desired in terms of research design and control of variables. Before accepting any research conclusions about human behavior, one should determine the quality of the research since the mere publication of these conclusions does not necessarily mean that they are valid or have wide application.

Challenges Confronting Personnel Management

Organizations today, like the larger society of which they are a part, are confronted with many critical challenges. These challenges are the result of various internal and external forces that are being exerted upon these organizations. Such forces include those of an economic, technological, and social nature, as well as the projected dominance of younger age groups in the labor force.

Economic Forces. One of the greatest challenges in our society today is that created by the forces of inflation which continually erode the purchasing power of income and savings. Inflation concerns personnel management directly because any wage increases that are not accompanied by corresponding increases in productivity can have a detrimental effect upon the nation's economy. Substantial wage increases can also result in many employees pricing their services out of the market. For example, increasing numbers of people have turned to "do-it-yourself" projects in order to avoid the rising cost of employing someone to provide the work services for them. Inflation, furthermore, can complicate planning for retirement benefits since it erodes the purchasing power of the funds that once were considered to constitute an adequate pension benefit.

Efforts to curb inflation through credit restrictions and tighter money can have the short-term effect of forcing a reduction in the number of persons employed by an organization. Personnel management thus must cope with both the causes and results of inflation. On the one hand, managers must offer resistance to union demands for excessive wage increases that will serve to aggravate inflationary trends. On the other, they must try to minimize layoffs during recessionary periods when steps are taken by the government to curb inflation. As yet no federal government administration has succeeded in solving the problem of controlling inflation without creating unemployment.

Technological Forces. Another challenge to personnel management is that created by the growth of automation and computerization in organizations. This growth has resulted in the elimination of many jobs, particularly those of a routine nature, and it has forced changes to be made in the duties of many remaining jobs. Particularly affected is middle management in organizations where computers, by facilitating a greater centralization of control, are reducing the number of jobs needed at this level. Furthermore, many persons who remain in those middle management positions are endangered by professional obsolescence.[17]

When jobs are eliminated as a result of technological innovations, an organization usually feels morally obligated to try and place in other jobs those employees who have been technologically displaced. However, many of the jobs eliminated are those which previously provided employment for persons who have little skill and training, thereby creating some significant problems for society since there are fewer jobs available which these persons are capable of performing. As a result of automation, personnel management also often is faced with the problem of providing employees the opportunities to compensate for loss of job satisfaction that may occur when automation reduces the duties and challenges of their jobs.

Social Forces. In contemporary society pressures from various groups can directly affect the decisions of personnel management. These include pressures from groups representing the racial and religious minorities, the women's liberation movement, economically disadvantaged persons, as well as members of the radical fringes, to mention a few. Members of these groups are demanding the opportunity to become more directly involved in the policy-making decisions affecting their welfare as well as in the opportunity to improve their economic and social status. Women and members of racial minorities, for example, are becoming better organized and able to exert sufficient economic and political pressures to secure the elimination of the discriminative practices that previously have limited their employment and advancement opportunities in many organizations. Having experienced success in gaining the removal of some discriminatory barriers as a result of both voluntary action by employers and compulsory legislation, these groups can be expected to increase their efforts to bring about the end of any remaining practices that are perceived to be discriminatory. Employers thus are faced with the necessity of insuring that their personnel programs do in fact provide equal opportunity for all persons and are not just something that looks good on paper.

Most important, personnel management must endeavor through education and communication to strive toward changing managers' attitudes and prejudices that may underlie some discriminatory practices. Adjustments also must be made in various recruitment, selection, training, motivational, and supervisory practices so that any cultural differences of disadvantaged groups that in the past have presented a barrier to their employment can be identified and resolved in the future.

---

[17] William Carp, "Management in the Computer Age," *Data Management* (December, 1970).

A Younger Labor Force. Another major challenge to personnel management is that presented by the changes that are occurring in the composition of this nation's labor force. As Figure 1-5 reveals, the labor force during the next two decades will be composed of persons the majority of whom will be much younger than previously has been the case. There will be almost as many persons in the 25 to 34 age group as in all the other age groups combined. As a result, a substantial increase in the number of jobs at the entering level will be required to meet the employment needs of young persons who possess relatively little experience. Competition among them for employment and advancement opportunities is likely to be much more vigorous than it has been previously because of the greater numbers comprising their age group.

Source: U.S. Department of Labor, Bureau of Labor Statistics, "Employment Outlook: Tomorrow's Jobs," *Occupational Outlook Handbook,* 1970-71 edition, Reprint Bulletin 1650 (Washington, D.C.: U.S. Government Printing Office), p. 18.

Figure 1-5 PROJECTED CHANGES IN THE LABOR FORCE BY AGE GROUP, 1968-80

Problems Associated with Changing Attitudes and Values. The fact that organizations in the future will be staffed with a larger proportion of younger employees, who differ more from the preceding generation than has been the case before, will make it necessary for greater attention to be given to their needs and to the problems relating to their management. In one survey personnel managers listed several major problems and challenges confronting them with respect to young workers. These problems included drug and narcotic abuse, labor conflict created by young militants, and coping with the more permissive standards of conduct that many young workers expect. Problems of adjusting to the different attitudes and values possessed by many young workers and of reorienting supervisors to cope with these differences, as well as to bridge the gap between themselves and the younger workers, were also considered to be significant.[18]

Problems Associated with Leadership and Motivation. A labor force in which the majority of employees are under 35 will present a particular challenge in the area of leadership and motivation because such persons are likely to demand more than just pay from their jobs. Younger employees are likely to be more eager for work assignments that are interesting and that permit them to have more responsibility. They will want more opportunities to participate in management decisions affecting them. They also will have to be provided with advancement opportunities, thus creating pressures to provide more openings up the organizational ladder by encouraging older employees to retire at an earlier age than previously has been customary. If management is not able to serve the needs that the younger employees seek to satisfy through their work, they are likely to become alienated from the organization and create problems for it in the areas of discipline and union relations.

Meeting the Challenges to Personnel Management

While conditions in organizations have not always changed rapidly enough to satisfy many people, the social progress that has been achieved to date in these areas still is significant. Increasingly organizations, particularly those that are profit-making in nature, are recognizing that they must help in resolving the problems that confront society as a whole rather than concentrating their attention on internal problems as they have tended to do in the past. Only a relatively few years ago, for example, the employment process in most companies and other organizations was concerned largely with selecting those persons from available applicants who were considered capable of performing the available jobs with a minimum of training. Attention then was focused primarily upon serving the needs of the organization with little concern being given to the problems that the personnel policies and practices of the organization might create for society. Today, however, organizations increasingly are aware that they must provide opportunities for disadvantaged persons and others who comprise the unemployed ranks. The selection process is becoming one of attempting to find jobs for those in society who are culturally or physically disadvantaged rather than just concentrating on hiring those applicants who are considered to be best qualified as determined by the selection process.

Increasing Recognition of Employees' Psychological Needs. Greater recognition is being given by employers toward creating the type of organizational environment that will help to make work more satisfying.

---

[18] "The Personnel Department," *Personnel Policies Forum,* Survey No. 92 (Washington, D.C.: The Bureau of National Affairs, Inc., 1970), p. 13.

Employers are recognizing that organizations have a responsibility to contribute to the psychological as well as the economic and physical well-being of their employees. By so doing they hope to reduce the feeling of alienation that some people may develop toward their work and toward society, and to reduce the hostility and aggressive actions that may result from their antagonism toward their organization and the so-called establishment.

Growing Professionalism in Personnel Management. Efforts to cope with the many challenges that confront personnel management today are aided by the rising level of professionalism that is developing within the field. The growth of professionalism is evidenced by the greater sense of responsibility toward helping to cope with the problem of unemployment. It is evidenced also by the greater concern being shown for the effect such personnel practices as layoffs and retirements may have upon employees and upon the community. The demonstration of improved attitudes toward union relations and of a greater sensitivity to employees and to public opinion also is evidence of the sense of social responsibility that managers are developing.

Greater Emphasis on Research in Personnel Management. Another characteristic of this field's increasing professionalization is the growth in the emphasis that is being placed upon research and upon the development and exchange of the growing body of knowledge relating to personnel management. The need for higher levels of intelligence and education and other personal qualifications on the part of those who engage in personnel work also is becoming recognized more widely. Various personnel societies, furthermore, are assuming more active roles in contributing to the professional growth of those working in the field and to the development of ethical standards of conduct and performance. Among the societies which have helped to facilitate research and the exchange of information in the field are such professional organizations as the American Management Association, the American Psychological Association, the American Society for Personnel Administration, the American Society of Training Directors, The International Personnel Management Association, the Society for the Advancement of Management, the Academy of Management, and various local personnel organizations and government agencies. These organizations and agencies are contributing much to the development of personnel management as a profession and are helping to raise the level of competency and understanding, not only among personnel workers but also among managers and supervisors.

While experience and practice is essential for understanding human behavior and for managing people more effectively, the utilization of knowledge that has been accumulated on this subject can also prove to be very valuable. It is hoped therefore that the body of knowledge contained in this book that has been contributed by practitioners, researchers, and scholars will assist the reader to better understand this knowledge and its practical application in order to avoid many of the mistakes of the past and the pitfalls of the future.

Résumé

Since an organization must operate with and through people, its effectiveness will depend upon how efficiently these people perform individually and collectively. Efficient performance is essential to the success of all types of organizations because of the rising labor costs, the growth of the capital investment per worker, and the rapidly changing content of the jobs within the organization resulting from technological advancements. Such performance does not occur automatically, however, but rather is the result of good personnel management which requires that the personnel program be tailored to fit the needs of the type of organization that it is serving. It also must recognize differences in the specific needs and backgrounds of the employees who are to be managed.

In addition to serving the needs of the organization and its employees, personnel management also must recognize and serve those of society as a whole. Organizations must help to provide greater economic and social opportunities for the disadvantaged groups in society who previously have been denied them. In the management of their personnel, organizations must seek to make the work that employees perform both psychologically and economically rewarding. Organizations thus can contribute to the reduction of the hostile and even disruptive behavior that people exhibit in society by reducing those work-caused tensions and dissatisfactions that can lead to feelings of alienation toward their jobs and even toward society as a whole.

In spite of its importance, personnel management as a field of functional specialization is relatively new, with its beginnings dating back to the period just before World War I. The development of the personnel field has been aided significantly by the contributions of other disciplines, particularly the behavioral sciences. These disciplines also have contributed to improvements in the performance of the various processes of personnel management including those relating to selection, training, motivation, and communication. They also have enabled managers to gain a better understanding of human behavior and of how it affects and is affected by the organization in which people are employed.

The subject of personnel management is one of concern not only to the specialists in the personnel department but also to every manager within an organization who has responsibility for the work of others. The manager of a personnel department is responsible for managing only those within the department who are subordinate. However, this individual also assists in the administration and coordination of the personnel program and provides supervisors and managers in other departments with the service and assistance they may require to manage their subordinates more effectively. While the role of the personnel department in administering the personnel program of an organization will be recognized throughout the book, the major focus will be upon the responsibilities of managers and supervisors in the other departments for this program.

DISCUSSION QUESTIONS

1. What implications do the changes that are predicted in the composition of the work force over the next two decades have for personnel management?
2. What are the major changes that are occurring with respect to women in the labor force?
3. What contributions has scientific management rendered to the field of personnel?
4. How do the objectives of employee selection in many business organizations differ from those that existed a decade or more ago?
5. What are some of the problems that inflation creates for personnel management?
6. What effects, if any, does the advancement of computer technology have upon staffing requirements within an organization?
7. What are some of the problems confronting employers as a result of the entrance of proportionately larger numbers of younger employees into the work force?

SUGGESTED READINGS

Blum, Milton L., and James C. Naylor. *Industrial Psychology: Its Theoretical and Social Foundations*. New York: Harper and Row, 1968. Chapter 1.

Chamberlain, Neil W. *The Limits of Corporate Responsibility*. New York: Basic Books Inc., 1973.

Chruden, Herbert J., and Arthur W. Sherman, Jr. *Reading in Personnel Management,* 4th ed. Cincinnati: South-Western Publishing Co., 1976. Part 1.

Claude, George S., Jr. *The History of Management Thought,* 2d ed. Englewood Cliffs, N.J.: Prentice-Hall, Inc., 1972.

Davis, Keith, and Robert Blomstrom. *Business and Society: Environment and Responsibility*. New York: McGraw-Hill Book Company, 1975.

Ling, Cyril Curtis. *The Management of Personnel Relations, History and Origins*. Homewood, Illinois: Richard D. Irwin, Inc., 1966.

Merrill, Harwood F. *Classics in Management*. New York: American Management Association, 1960.

Peters, Lynn H. *Management and Society*. Belmont, California: Dickenson Publishing Company, Inc., 1968.

Ritzer, George, and Harrison M. Trice. *An Occupation in Conflict: A Study of the Personnel Manager*. Ithaca, New York: Cornell University, 1969.

Rush, Harold M. F. *Behavioral Science: Concepts and Management Applications,* Studies in Personnel Policy No. 216. New York: National Industrial Conference Board, Inc., 1969, pp. 1-8.

2

The Organization of Work and Jobs

In order for an optimal level of employee efficiency and satisfaction to be attained in any type of enterprise or institution, the work that is to be accomplished must be organized into jobs in such a way that it can be performed efficiently. The jobs thus created not only serve to establish the duties, responsibilities, and interpersonal relationships of the employees who are to perform each job but also provide a basis upon which their performance may be measured. Work, when organized and structured effectively into jobs, also provides the employees who are assigned to them with the means of understanding more clearly what is expected in the way of productivity and cooperation.

In recent years greater recognition has been given to human as well as technical considerations in determining how work and the job can be best organized. While efficiency is still a major objective, research indicates that it is more likely to be achieved if work is organized so as to take into consideration human characteristics, capabilities and differences, and the satisfactions that people may seek from their jobs.

The effective organization of each job should enable the employee to be aware of the duties, responsibilities, and authority that it entails. Information relating to these requirements thus must be compiled and communicated formally to employees so that they will be able to learn and understand these requirements fully. This job information can also help management to select and place persons in those jobs which they are best qualified to perform. It also can provide an objective basis upon which such decisions as those involving the placement, retention, promotion, and remuneration of employees may be made.

THE ROLE AND IMPORTANCE OF WORK

A wide variety of work activities must be performed in any organization if its objectives are to be achieved. These activities may range all the way from sweeping work areas, filing documents, assembling parts, or inventing new products to making vital managerial decisions affecting the survival of the organization. It is only through such activities that the organization can perform its functions and its employees can satisfy their various personal needs. Only through work activities, moreover, can the goods and services needed by society be produced and money required to purchase them be generated.

The Role of Work in the Organization

Even though it may be computerized, mechanized, or automated, there will always be work that can be performed more economically or more effectively by people than by machines. The reason in some instances may be due to the fact that the cost of the equipment required to replace employees exceeds the cost of employing people to perform the work. The $600,000 machine referred to in Figure 2-1, for example, might represent a rather expensive replacement for the employee if it could not be operated at capacity or if the machine were to become obsolete before its cost had been fully recovered. Also, in some instances people may be preferable to machines because they permit greater operating flexibility. It frequently is possible to reassign or retrain people to perform other work whereas it may be extremely expensive or even impossible to convert machines to do so. Furthermore, in spite of technological

"Look at it this way, Baxter. It took a $600,000 machine to replace you."

Source: Family Weekly, March 14, 1965. Reproduced with the permission of Brad Anderson.

Figure 2-1

advancements, there are certain activities that still can be performed more effectively by employees than by machines, just as there also are certain activities that machines can perform more efficiently. Normally it would be desirable, therefore, to use employees to do the work that involves those activities in which humans have an advantage over machines provided that it is not detrimental to their well-being. Information such as that presented in Figure 2-2 may be used in designing a particular human-machine system to determine the role of each.

The Role of Work for the Individual

Among the most important satisfactions that the majority of employees seek from their work are those gained from income and financial security that their jobs provide. Also gained from their work may be recognition, sense of achievement, opportunity to socialize with others, and other factors not related directly to the money they may earn. Because the degree of satisfaction that employees derive from their work may affect their motivation to work and in turn affect their productivity, considerable research and discussion in recent years have been devoted to the subject of job and work satisfaction. Much of this attention has been focused upon the jobs being performed by employees, how these jobs may be restructured, and how the working conditions relating to the jobs may be improved so as to increase job satisfaction.

Unfortunately, in spite of the research and experience relating to job satisfaction that has been accumulated, differences of opinion remain among leaders in business, government, labor, and the academic field regarding the causes of job dissatisfaction and the measures that can be taken to reduce it. Differences of opinion exist concerning the importance employees attach to job satisfaction in comparison with other returns derived from their work. Disagreement also exists concerning the extent to which employee dissatisfaction exists within the work forces and the extent to which it may be feasible or even possible to reduce this dissatisfaction through changes in the job structure and working conditions.

Individual Differences and Job Satisfaction. One of the greatest difficulties in coping with job dissatisfaction stems from the differences that exist among employees by virtue of differences in their abilities, backgrounds, and social conditioning which in turn affect their pattern of psychological needs and the specific returns they may seek from their jobs. As a result of these individual differences, "what would seem boring, repetitious, non-challenging work to one individual is a highly satisfying job to another."[1] Thus, there can be no single method for improving satisfaction on the job since improvement efforts must first identify the extent to which dissatisfaction may exist among employees and the specific causes for it. The methods used to overcome dissatisfaction therefore must be determined by the structure and working

[1] Richard D. Scott, "Job Enlargement—The Key to Increasing Job Satisfaction," *Personnel Journal*, Vol. 52, No. 4 (April, 1973), p. 314.

MAN VS. MACHINE	
MAN EXCELS IN	**MACHINES EXCEL IN**
Detection of certain forms of very low energy levels	Monitoring (both men and machines)
Sensitivity to an extremely wide variety of stimuli	Performing routine, repetitive, or very precise operations
Perceiving patterns and making generalizations about them	Responding very quickly to control signals
Detecting signals in high noise levels	Exerting great force, smoothly and with precision
Ability to store large amounts of information for long periods—and recalling relevant facts at appropriate moments	Storing and recalling large amounts of information in short time-periods
Ability to exercise judgment where events cannot be completely defined	Performing complex and rapid computation with high accuracy
Improvising and adopting flexible procedures	Sensitivity to stimuli beyond the range of human sensitivity (infrared, radio waves, etc.)
Ability to react to unexpected low-probability events	Doing many different things at one time
Applying originality in solving problems: i.e., alternate solutions	Deductive processes
Ability to profit from experience and alter course of action	Insensitivity to extraneous factors
Ability to perform fine manipulation, especially where misalignment appears unexpectedly	Ability to repeat operations very rapidly, continuously, and precisely the same way over a long period
Ability to continue to perform even when overloaded	Operating in environments which are hostile to man or beyond human tolerance
Ability to reason inductively	

Source: Wesley E. Woodson and Donald W. Conover, *Human Engineering Guide for Equipment Designers* (2d ed.; Berkeley: University of California Press, 1964). Reproduced with permission of The Regents of the University of California.

Figure 2-2

conditions of specific jobs and by the particular individual or individuals who perform the jobs.

Employee Reactions to Dissatisfaction. In spite of all the attention that is being devoted to the subject of dissatisfaction in the professional journals and public communication media, public opinion polls indicate that among the employees surveyed the proportion who expressed dissatisfaction with their work seldom exceeded 20 percent. The majority of employees, on the other hand, indicated that they were neither extremely satisfied nor dissatisfied with their jobs, but rather reacted on the positive side of neutrality, indicating they were ''fairly'' satisfied with their work.[2] The results of these opinion surveys, in the opinion of one author, would appear to be supported by the demands that employees make upon their employers through their union representatives at the bargaining tables. Thus, most of these demands continue to be concentrated on the ''bread and butter'' issues rather than on the ''quality'' of the work.[3] The author concludes:

> When hard choices have to be made between a monotonous job in a regimented environment which pays relatively well and which offers job security, and a poorer paying, less secure but more 'satisfying' job, most workers—particularly those with family commitments—are still not in a position to make a trade-off in favor of meeting their 'intrinsic' needs [*i.e.*, personal satisfactions].[4]

Employees for whom the disagreeable features of their jobs are offset by the money and security they receive or who have no alternative but to endure these features often ''play games'' to make the time pass more quickly and pleasantly. As someone observed:

> The middle-aged switchboard operator, when things are dead at night, cheerily responds to the caller, ''Marriott Inn,'' instead of identifying the motel chain she works for. ''Just for a lark,'' she explains bewilderedly. ''I really don't know what made me do it.'' The young gas-meter reader startles the young suburban housewife sunning out on the patio in her bikini, loose-bra'd, and sees more things than he would otherwise see. ''Just to make the day go faster.'' The autoworker from the Deep South will ''tease one guy because he's real short and his old lady left him.'' Why? ''Oh just to break the monotony. You want quittin' time so bad.'' The waitress who moves by the tables with the grace of a ballerina pretends she's forever on stage. ''I feel like Carmen. It's like a gypsy holding out a tambourine and they throw the coin.'' It helps her fight humiliation as well as arthritis.[5]

---

[2] Harry Wool, ''What's Wrong with Work in America?—A Review Essay,'' *Monthly Labor Review*, Vol. 96, No. 3 (March, 1973), p. 41.

[3] *Ibid.*, p. 42.

[4] *Ibid.*

[5] Studs Terkel, ''Work Without Meaning,'' *Business and Society Review/Innovation* (Spring, 1974), p. 17.

Alienation Toward Work. Some employees who fail to gain satisfaction from their work become alienated toward it and the organization in general. *Alienation* is a condition in which employees may have little if any feeling of identification with their work, with the organization, or with society. It is a condition that also may develop among certain groups of people, particularly those who feel they are being deprived of the opportunity to become involved in our social institutions, to influence the operation of these institutions, or to realize their own personal goals and aspirations. Alienation toward work may cause individuals to seek other employment and undoubtedly is one of the reasons for the high turnover among younger people during the years immediately following graduation. It is also one of the reasons why some college graduates may shun jobs at the professional level and become seasonal workers, drive cabs, work in restaurants, perform odd jobs, or become dropouts from society in general.

The Role of Work in Society

Work in our society provides not only a source of income for those employed but also the goods and services that are consumed by members of our society.

Growth in Unskilled Service Jobs. One recent problem is that the demand for employees is growing most rapidly in service jobs which tend to be shunned by persons seeking work because many of these jobs are regarded by them as being menial or degrading. The demand for unskilled hospital workers, such as orderlies and attendants, for example, has increased nearly 80 percent in the past decade; and that for refuse collectors has doubled. Many other lesser skilled jobs so essential to the functioning of a modern society, such as cleaning hotel rooms, stores, and offices, or working in restaurants, have been in equally increasing demand.[6] "In an effort to close the gap between supply and demand for such jobs, some organizations such as Texas Instruments have provided employees with greater opportunity and assistance for advancement out of these jobs."[7]

By upgrading the status of the jobs previously shunned through improvements in their titles and in the perquisites provided to the job holders, some organizations have been able to increase the quantity and quality of applicants for such jobs. Probably the most effective method of all, however, has been that of increasing the pay for such jobs. When the City of San Francisco announced that the pay for the job of street cleaner (which by city charter was tied to the local union wage scale for laborers) would rise to $17,000 per year, the employment office was overwhelmed with applications. Because the new salary was significantly higher than that paid many professional jobs requiring college degrees, numerous individuals with degrees including those in the teaching profession were among the applicants.

---

[6] Edmund Faltermayer, "Who Will Do the Dirty Work Tomorrow?" *Fortune* (January, 1974), p. 133.

[7] *Ibid.*, p. 136.

Underutilization of Employees. Society must be concerned not only with the problems of unemployment but also with underemployment. *Underemployment*, or *underutilization* as it is also termed, exists when a person is performing work that is below his or her capability level. Employees may be performing below their capability levels and thus be underutilized for a number of reasons. They may, for example, possess abilities that exceed the requirements of their jobs. However, even when job duties are commensurate with employees' abilities, the failure of management to organize their work or to permit them to carry out the authorities and responsibilities of their jobs may result in a waste of their talents.

Another exceedingly common cause for the underutilization of personnel is the failure of management to motivate them to utilize their abilities fully or to exert their maximum effort toward the achievement of organizational goals. Regardless of the reasons, such underutilization of personnel constitutes a waste of human talent and a resulting loss to society. This loss is a particularly acute one when underutilization is caused by long-standing prejudices that deny fully qualified individuals the opportunity for placement in jobs which they are fully qualified to perform. Fortunately social and legal pressures are forcing improvements to be made, even though slower than many desire, in initial employment and in advancement opportunities previously denied to minorities and women.

THE JOB AND ITS FUNCTIONS

Work in an organization must be divided into manageable units or tasks that can be performed by the employees who are assigned to them. The smallest organizational unit into which these tasks are grouped and structured is the *job*. As a work assignment it is separate and distinct from those of other jobs within the organization. For example, the job of keypunch operator would entail certain duties and responsibilities that would be distinct from those of a secretary or a file clerk within the same office. Employees who are placed in this job then should be able to identify clearly what tasks or activities they are expected to perform.

If the work load of a particular job is sufficiently heavy, more than one employee may be required to perform it. Separate positions each involving the duties and responsibilities of this job would then have to be created to which additional employees would be assigned. A *position*, therefore, constitutes the job or portion of it that is performed by an individual employee. The work load for a key punch operator in an EDP installation may require the services of six employees each of whom will occupy a separate position involving similar duties and responsibilities. Before an employee can be hired, moreover, a position involving a particular job must have been budgeted. The number of the positions that have been budgeted within the organizational structure determines the number of individuals who can be employed since each of them must occupy a separate position within the structure.

The Job and Management of Personnel

The job serves to define not only the activities of the organization that an employee is to perform but also the relationship of these activities to those being performed by other employees in the achievement of organizational objectives. It provides the means for dividing and assigning the authority and responsibility that must be exercised by the incumbent job holders. It also establishes the foundation for selecting and training employees, for evaluating their performance, and for determining their rate of pay. The job and its requirements are important to the management of personnel since the manner in which activities are organized can have a significant bearing upon the effectiveness with which the performance of these activities can be accomplished and controlled. The manner in which the activities within a job are organized can also be an important factor in the creation and solution of disciplinary problems and grievances.

The cause of job inefficiency at times can be due as much to the way in which the job is organized as it is to the caliber of the employee's performance. If the activities of a job are not organized properly, the confusion, interpersonal conflicts, and frustration that may result from this situation can cause the employee to become discontented and a problem to management.

Relationship of the Job to Role and Status

Certain patterns of action or behavior are expected from employees in their relationships with others in the organization. In sociological terms these patterns constitute what is referred to as their *roles* in the organization, and are determined in part by the jobs to which they are assigned. Other roles of employees involve off-the-job relationships such as those with their families, their churches, their social organizations, or other groups to which they may belong.

The job roles of employees help to determine their *statuses,* which are the ranks they occupy with respect to others within the organization. Each of their roles within an organization affects their statuses which in turn affects the roles they perform. The role of a supervisor, for example, generally carries more status than does the role of the individual who is being supervised. Supervisors may acquire status from their technical competency and favorable personal qualities, which in turn may enable them to perform their supervisory roles more effectively.

Roles Determined by the Job. The roles of employees on the job are determined formally by the duties and responsibilities which the job requires them to perform. These job requirements, for example, determine those persons to whom or from whom an employee is expected to give or receive directions or instructions and with whom that individual is expected to cooperate in performing his or her work.

The roles performed by employees also may be influenced by *role perception;* that is, their perception of how they are expected to act or how fellow employees may perceive that they should act in particular situations. Not infrequently employees may perceive their roles differently than others, including their boss. When such perceptions differ significantly, it may cause conflicts to arise between an employee and fellow employees. Cooperation and efficiency in an organization therefore require that supervisory personnel recognize the nature and importance of role and status in interpersonal relationships and their effects upon performance.

Status Derived from Jobs. The abilities that jobs require of individuals as well as the duties, the working conditions, and pay all help to determine their status on the job. The status in turn contributes significantly to their feeling of self-esteem. Whiting Williams, an early and respected leader in the personnel field, had the following observation many years ago after having spent an extended period living as a worker:

> . . . our hunger finds its chief and surest satisfaction in connection with our jobs, our work. I think I can claim rather varied contacts. To learn about people, I have associated with bums and with workers here and abroad, and I have sat with captains of industry in London, Paris, Berlin, Chicago, and New York. I give you my word, whether they were bums, board chairmen or in betweens, they were all just about equally less sure of themselves than they would *like* to be, all about equally as hungry to maintain "face," to have a word of approval.
>
> But here is the point. Whether they were at the bottom or the top of the ladder, every blessed one of them gave me as final, incontrovertible, proof of certificate: "This is my job; this is the kind of service I give my fellow men; this is the kind of equipment I make useful to my fellow citizens. On the basis of that I demand a certain amount of attention."[8]

Status Symbols. Tangible and visible expressions, which are commonly referred to as *status symbols,* can serve to call the attention of others to one's status. The location of an individual's desk or work place, the tools and equipment that are used, and the clothes that are worn may in some organizations symbolize status. At the executive level office location and furnishings, reserved parking space, and the like are typical status symbols that may provide executives a source of ego satisfaction. While status symbols are important, they cannot be considered a substitute for pay to the extent that Figure 2-3 would imply.

Upgrading Employee Status. In an effort to improve the status of their blue-collar workers and to provide them with a sense of equality with their white-collar counterparts, there is a trend by companies to eliminate the use of the term "workers" and to refer to all personnel as "employees." In many organizations this change has been accompanied by eliminating the hourly basis of pay computation for blue-collar personnel and by adopting the same salary

---

[8] From *Connecticut Industry* (May, 1951), as reprinted with permission in Herbert J. Chruden and Arthur W. Sherman, Jr., *Readings in Personnel Management* (4th ed.; Cincinnati: South-Western Publishing Co., Inc., 1976), Part 1.

system that is used for the white-collar employees, who traditionally have been paid on a weekly or monthly basis.

Another measure taken by companies to upgrade the status of their employees, even by those that still compute the pay of some personnel on an hourly basis, has been that of eliminating the use of the time clock. As a spokesman for one such company stated, "Taking out the time clocks was a sign we wanted to treat our employees like adults, not control them like children or mechanical devices."[9]

"No raise, Durkin, but effective the fifteenth of next month you may start calling me by my first name."

Source: The Saturday Evening Post. Reprinted by special permission of Chon Day.

Figure 2-3

Status Inconsistency and Status Anxiety. Since an employee's status is determined by many different factors, it is quite possible for some of these factors to be inconsistent with others. This situation is referred to as *status inconsistency* and may cause frustration and anxiety on the part of those who are the subject of the inconsistency. Employees, for example, are quick to resent the fact that someone in a job that is located on a lower level within the structure may be receiving higher pay or more privileges than they. Similarly, those individuals who have more status by virtue of their seniority, age, qualifications, or other factors may expect to receive preference with regard to work assignments and conditions of employment over other employees with less status. If these expected "privileges of rank" are ignored by supervisors

[9] James MacGregor, "The Honor System," *The Wall Street Journal,* May 22, 1970, p. 1.

when personnel decisions are made, it may generate resentment on the part of the individuals who possess greater status and cause them to become a problem. The employee's feelings of security and adjustment, thus, are likely to be more favorable if consistency exists with respect to the factors on which status is determined. Inconsistency, on the other hand, can contribute to *status anxiety* in which individuals experience feelings of discomfort in not knowing how they rank with respect to their colleagues.

INCREASING JOB SATISFACTION

The improvement of employee morale including satisfaction from their work has long been a goal of management. Initially, during the human relations era, attempts were made to develop better interpersonal relations, sometimes through the use of manipulative techniques, and various extrinsic rewards. Often such efforts did not result in any significant improvement in employee satisfaction, nor did any improvements so achieved necessarily lead to improvement in employee productivity. Furthermore, some of the manipulative techniques used by managers proved to be rather transparent and were thus resented by employees. While both management practitioners and theorists recognize that improvements in job satisfaction of employees may lead to improvements in production, they also recognize that dissatisfaction, particularly when it becomes severe, can lead to serious consequences both for the employer and for society in general.

Improving the Design of the Job

While the way in which jobs are designed or structured is not the only factor contributing to greater employee satisfaction and productivity, it is an important one and is a good place to begin in an improvement program. Traditionally jobs were designed to meet production and engineering rather than human requirements. Because assembly lines provided the most efficient means for mass producing goods, repetitive-type jobs were developed on these lines in which maximum productivity could be achieved in a minimum of learning time. Improvements in job design during and since the scientific management movement have been directed toward eliminating, rearranging, or combining the various motions and operations comprising a job so that it could be performed more easily and more rapidly. Job specialization or dilution resulting from such efforts frequently caused many jobs to be divided into two or more jobs, each having fewer duties.

Unfortunately efforts to gain efficiency through the use of work simplification or methods improvement techniques often have resulted in reduced satisfaction, thus offsetting any benefits that should have been derived from the engineering improvements. While an assembly line may constitute the most efficient layout from an engineering or production standpoint, it may leave much to be desired from a human relations standpoint. The higher rate of output that workers should be able to develop by performing repetitive-type operations is offset by the psychological restrictions resulting from the monotonous nature of the work. Individuals who perform repetitive work often have difficulty in gaining a sense of identification or meaning from their work. One author summarizes this situation as follows:

> The alienation of meaninglessness is further intensified by the workers' lack of a clear identification with a particular job. The division of labor is so extreme that most jobs are basically the same. In addition, because there are many lines operating at once, there are a number of men performing exactly the same tasks. One cannot, therefore, derive a sense of function as the left-front hubcap assembler. Fractionalized job assignments, cyclic rather than task-directed work rhythms, and the anonymous atmosphere of the large plants all dilute the sense of meaning, purpose, and function on the assembly line.[10]

Feelings of pressure and coercion that many workers develop on an assembly line as a result of mechanical pacing by the line also may act as a restriction on their productivity. The lack of opportunity for breaks in the job routine, or for social interaction with other workers, or for job advancement are other conditions often found on the assembly line that can make the work seem stifling to many workers. Such conditions may cause employees to conclude that they are wasting their lives in a skill-less and meaningless occupation.[11]

Job Enrichment. In recent years efforts to reduce employee dissatisfaction and to improve the quality of their working lives have been focused upon the "humanization" of work through *job enrichment*. This process includes adding duties, responsibilities, and authority to jobs through what is known as *job enlargement*. (Although the term *enrichment* has a broader connotation, it frequently is used synonomously with that of *enlargement*.) Job enrichment programs thus are concerned with designing jobs so that they will include a greater variety of work content; require a higher level of knowledge and skills; give employees more autonomy and responsibility for planning, directing, and controlling their jobs; and provide them with opportunity for personal growth and meaningful work experiences. In theory at least, job enrichment makes the performance of a job more rewarding and intrinsically satisfying and thereby motivates the employee to be more productive.[12] While it may not be possible to accomplish all of these objectives in the enrichment of a particular job, ideally the majority of these should be attained if job enrichment efforts are to be considered successful.

Examples of Job Enrichment at AT&T. The American Telephone and Telegraph Corporation, one of the early leaders in job enrichment, successfully provided such enrichment for employees engaged in the compilation of

---

[10] Robert Blauner, *Alienation and Freedom, The Factory Worker and His Industry* (Chicago: The University of Chicago Press, 1964), p. 108, as quoted in Charles R. Walker, *Technology, Industry, and Man, The Age of Acceleration* (New York: McGraw-Hill Book Company, 1968), p. 99.

[11] Charles R. Walker, *Technology, Industry, and Man, The Age of Acceleration* (New York: McGraw-Hill Book Company, 1968), pp. 97-101.

[12] William E. Reif and Ronald C. Tinnel, "A Diagnostic Approach to Job Enrichment," *M.S.U. Business Topics*, Vol. 21, No. 4 (Autumn, 1973), p. 29.

telephone books. Through job enlargement employees who originally worked on specific information pieces were given the responsibility for putting together all of the white pages of a book for a specific city. In another job, that of a keypunch operator, the duties were enlarged to include the responsibility for handling full units of work such as the payrolls for an entire department. The operators also were given the opportunity to schedule their own days and to maintain their own quantity and quality of performance.[13] In still another job, that of service representative, employees were given increased responsibilities and authority to make decisions, resulting in better customer service, greater job satisfaction, and greater productivity.[14]

The Volvo Company Job Enrichment Program. One job enrichment program to receive recognition internationally has been that initiated in the late sixties by the Volvo Company of Sweden. This program includes provisions for job rotation, job enlargement, teamwork, and the delegation of responsibility to work teams. In accordance with a schedule developed by their work groups, some employees may work on as many as five or six jobs during a workweek. This rotation is intended to provide them with both physical and psychological change and a greater understanding of their colleagues, as well as a greater feeling of teamwork.[15] The work teams, ranging from three to nine members, are intended to provide a tightly knit group with which employees can identify. Each team divides the work up among members, initiates control procedures, and elects its own representative to consult with supervisors. Pay is based upon total team results; and when a member is added, the group is paid a fee for training that person. Since the teams assume many of the supervisor's former responsibilities, the latter is freed to devote more time to planning and personal contact with colleagues.[16]

Limitations of Job Enrichment. In spite of the benefits to be achieved through job enrichment, it must not be considered as a panacea for overcoming production problems and employee discontent. Job enrichment programs, for example, are more likely to achieve success in some jobs and work situations than in others. Job enrichment, as Sirota states,

> . . . is not *the* solution to the "people" problems of industry, but rather one of many that needs to be applied with thought and care. Even more important, there ought to be good evidence that the ailment under treatment is really one for which job enrichment is the appropriate medication.[17]

It is *not* the solution, for example, to such problems as dissatisfaction with pay or fringe benefits, employment insecurity, technical incompetence, or such

---

[13] "Making a Job More Than a Job," *Business Week* (April 19, 1969), p. 88.

[14] J. Carroll Swart, "The Worth of Humanistic Management; Some Contemporary Examples," *Business Horizons,* Vol. 16, No. 3 (June, 1973), pp. 42-43.

[15] Charles H. Gibson, "Volvo Increases Productivity Through Job Enrichment," *California Management Review,* Vol. XV, No. 4 (Summer, 1973), p. 65.

[16] *Ibid.*

[17] David Sirota, "Is Job Enrichment Another Management Fad?" *The Conference Board Record,* Vol. X, No. 4 (April, 1973), p. 45.

roadblocks to productivity as poor tooling and materials or inadequate clerical or administrative support.[18]

Labor Leaders' Views on Job Enrichment. Some leaders in organized labor have expressed their suspicion and skepticism regarding the effectiveness of job enrichment and management's motives for its use. As the vice-president of one international union stated, "I have a sneaking suspicion that 'job enrichment' may be just another name for 'time and motion' study."[19] According to this leader, "If you want to enrich the job, enrich the pay check. The better the wage, the greater the job satisfaction. There is no better cure for the 'blue-collar blues'."[20] He concludes:

> All the studies tend to prove that worker dissatisfaction diminishes with age. That's because older workers have accrued more of the kinds of job enrichment that unions have fought for—better wages, shorter hours, vested pensions, a right to have a say in their working conditions, the right to be promoted on the basis of seniority and all the rest. That's the kind of job enrichment that unions believe in.[21]

The fact that many labor leaders are not enthusiastic about job enrichment should give management cause to proceed carefully with the initiation of any job enrichment programs. Most important, efforts at job enrichment should be based upon a thorough diagnosis of the total work situation and upon what the employees in the organization consider will enhance their satisfaction from their work.

Job Dilution

The opposite of job enrichment is *job dilution*, in which the number of activities performed by a job or the degree of skill and responsibility that it requires are reduced. As a result of job dilution, certain duties of a job are either eliminated or divided to form two or more jobs. In so doing it is possible to have the work of the original job performed by persons with lesser qualifications and/or training. By diluting the job of a machinist, for example, it would be possible to divide it into several jobs, each of which could be performed after a relatively short period of training on the job; whereas several years of apprenticeship normally are required in order for an individual to learn to become a machinist. Job dilution therefore can be used to overcome a recruitment problem that may exist for highly trained personnel who normally would perform the work and are in short supply. Not only is this situation true in the case of blue-collar workers but it is also true of engineering assignments in which engineering assistants can be trained to perform many duties previously handled by engineers, or of certain hospital jobs where medical

---

[18] *Ibid., op. cit.*, p. 43.

[19] William W. Winpisinger, "Job Satisfaction," *AFL-CIO American Federationist,* Vol. 80, No. 2 (February, 1973), p. 10.

[20] *Ibid.*, p. 9.

[21] *Ibid.*, p. 10.

technicians, nursing aides, and medical assistants can be given many of the tasks formerly performed by physicians and registered nurses.

Job dilution also may make possible the employment of disadvantaged persons whose skills and training are inadequate at the time of initial employment. Job dilution thus provides a means of creating special jobs in which certain individuals may be employed until they can be trained to meet the more demanding requirements of the full job or can be promoted into the next higher job in a career ladder.

Human Factors Engineering (Ergonomics)

Although it may be referred to as *human factors engineering, human engineering,* or *ergonomics,* the activities involved are "concerned with ways of designing machines, operations, and work environments so that they match human capacities and limitations."[22] Human factors engineering thus recognizes the fact that human mistakes can be reduced and productivity increased by designing machines so as to match the capacities and characteristics of those who are to operate them. Human factors engineering seeks to minimize the adverse effects upon the work that may be caused by carelessness, fallibility, and other human limitations and may result in defective products, damage to equipment, or, even worse, injury or death.

Human factors engineering recognizes that the equipment with which work is performed functions as a *system.* Although there are countless types of systems, such as the solar system, the free enterprise system, the nervous system, as well as various equipment systems, they all have one thing in common—namely, that they are composed of interrelated and interacting components. An equipment system therefore is composed of a group of components, of which at least some are units of equipment designed to work together for some common purpose. A soft-drink bottling plant has equipment systems commonly called bottling lines for filling, capping, inspecting, and conveying the filled and unfilled containers. An automobile engine, a printing press, or even a bicycle are equipment systems because they consist of parts that are designed to fit and work together to achieve some common purpose.[23]

Whenever people are required to operate, service, or monitor a machine, a human component is added to the equipment components, resulting in the creation of a *man-machine system.* Because of their complexity and their speed of operation, it is difficult for humans to react to many of the man-machine systems. Equipment components to be controlled by humans must be engineered to allow for the limitations in their ability to sense and to decide what actions are required from time to time to control the equipment. The design of jobs of a more complex nature thus can require the use of rather advanced human factors engineering.

---

[22] Alphonse Chapanis, *Man-Machine Engineering* (Belmont, California: Wadsworth Publishing Co., Inc., 1965), p. 8.

[23] *Ibid.,* pp. 13-14.

Variations in the Work Period

Some organizations have sought to make jobs more attractive by modifying the period that the employee is required to be on the job.

The Four-Day Week. One such modification to be widely adopted is the "compressed" workweek consisting of 4 days of 10 hours each, which is commonly referred to as the *four-day week*. The obvious result of the four-day week is to provide employees with an extra day each week to take care of personal matters or to engage in leisure activities. It also reduces by 20 percent the time and expense required to commute to work each week. Among the benefits organizations have hoped to achieve from the four-day week are improved productivity per man-hour, reduced start-up and shut-down time, reduced absenteeism and turnover, and improved worker morale.[24]

Disadvantages to Employees. One of the main disadvantages of the four-day workweek from the employees' standpoint is the increased fatigue created by the ten-hour day which requires some employees to spend part of the three-day weekend in recuperation. The necessity to leave home earlier and return later also can create problems when there are children to get off to school and both members of the family are employed or when the working hours do not fit public transportation schedules.

Labor Leaders' Reactions. Many labor leaders lack enthusiasm for the four-day week. After fighting for years to obtain an eight-hour day, they view the ten-hour day without overtime to be a step backwards.

Employers' Mixed Reactions. According to studies of the four-day week, employer reactions to it have been mixed. Some organizations have been very satisfied with the compressed week, whereas others have either changed back to the five-day week or consider the retention of the four-day week to be a mixed blessing. Gains achieved through improvements in productivity and reductions in absenteeism with the change to a four-day week in some instances were lost after the novelty of the new system had worn off.[25]

In spite of the unsatisfactory experiences with it, the fact that many organizations are quite satisfied with the four-day week would indicate that it can offer advantages if used in the right situations. Like job enrichment and other popular innovations, however, it must fit the needs and operating problems of a particular organization.

Flexi-Time. Another innovation that is proving popular, particularly in Europe, is called *flexi-time* which does not involve any change in the total

---

[24] Janice Niepert Hedges, "New Patterns for Working Time," *Monthly Labor Review* (February, 1973), p. 4.

[25] William M. Bulkeley, "Short Shift: For Some Companies the Four-day Week is a Four-day Headache," *The Wall Street Journal,* April 30, 1973, p. 1.

number of hours worked. Instead workers are permitted to set their own arrival and departure times, within certain limits.[26]

Extended Vacations or Leaves. Still another variation to the traditional work schedule is the *extended vacation.* The Steelworkers labor agreement, for example, provides 13 weeks of vacation to senior workers every five years. Extended leaves also are provided by such companies as the Xerox Corporation, which may give employees up to one year off with full pay if they engage in public service.[27]

JOB INFORMATION

Inevitably it is the employee who will determine to some extent how his or her job is to be performed and who will make the job what it is. However, some form of control must be provided which will help to insure that employees do not change their jobs too radically from the established structure. Controls can be provided by preparing a written statement of the duties and responsibilities of a job. A written statement of this type can serve to prevent a particular job from gradually being changed by the incumbent. It may also prevent differences of opinion from occurring between the incumbent and his or her supervisor over the nature of the duties that are to be performed by the former.

The written statement covering the duties and responsibilities of a job is commonly referred to as the *job description.* The personal qualifications that an individual must possess in order to carry out these duties and responsibilities are compiled into what is called the *job specification.* The job specification may be organized as a separate record or may be included as another part of the job description. The advantage of having a separate job specification is that the information contained in it is used for purposes other than those for which the information in the job description is used, such as for purposes of employee selection and wage determination.

The Job Description

Since there is no standard form for their development, job descriptions will vary from one organization to another. The job description for a personnel clerk, shown in Figure 2-4, illustrates the format, content, and writing style that may be followed. This description follows a rather typical format consisting of job identification, job summary, and job duties statements.

Job Identification Section. This section, by means of the job title and other identifying data, helps to distinguish a job from the others within the organization. The inclusion within the job title of such words as "senior,"

---

[26] Hedges, *op. cit.,* p. 3.

[27] "Thank God It's June: Unlikely As It Sounds, a 6-month 'Work Year' Is Called a Possibility," *The Wall Street Journal,* March 29, 1972, p. 16.

"junior," "trainee," "supervisor," "operator," or "clerk" can serve to indicate the duties and the skill level of the job.

Job Summary Section. This section, which is sometimes entitled "Statement of the Job," serves to provide a summary that should be sufficient to identify and differentiate the duties that are performed from those of other jobs.

Job Duties Section. The major duties and responsibilities of the job are covered by brief statements that indicate: (1) what the workers do, (2) how they do it, and (3) why they do it. The description of duties should also indicate the tools and equipment employed, the materials used, the procedures followed, and the degree of supervision received. An additional section of miscellaneous items may also be provided to indicate such things as the relationship of the job to other jobs with respect to transfer and promotion possibilities.

The Job Specification

The content and organization of a job specification, like that of the job description, will vary among companies. Generally the major requirements covered by a job specification include skill, effort, responsibility, and job conditions.

Skill. The education and experience needed to perform a job constitute the major requirements in this category. Educational requirements may be expressed in terms of the possession of a particular diploma, degree, or certificate, or the completion of some specific training program. Experience requirements usually set forth the minimum number of months or years of the type of previous work activities deemed essential for performing the job. The skill section of a job specification may also cover specific types of knowledge, as well as any special mental or manual skills, that the job holder is expected to possess in order to perform the job effectively.

Effort. The mental and physical demands of a job constitute the major portion of this requirement. Mental demands may include requirements for mental and visual concentration, as well as for enduring psychological stress. For example, the physical effort required may be expressed in terms of the amount of weight to be lifted and/or the amount of bending, stooping, walking, and other physical activities performed on the job.

Responsibility. Most jobs require the job holder to assume certain forms of responsibility for the care of equipment, materials, and other assets; for the quantity and quality of production and the control of costs; or for exercising initiative or making various types of decisions. In supervisory jobs a major responsibility is for the performance and safety of subordinates, which can be expressed in terms of numbers supervised and the importance of their activities.

Name of Company

JOB TITLE *Personnel Clerk* DEPARTMENT *Personnel*

NUMBER OF EMPLOYEES IN DEPARTMENT *15* NUMBER OF EMPLOYEES ON JOB *3*

DATE *February 10, 19--*

STATEMENT OF THE JOB

Under the supervision of the EMPLOYMENT MANAGER; interviews new workers in carrying out clerical routine of induction; performs miscellaneous clerical and stenographic work related to employment.

DUTIES OF THE JOB

1. Interviews new workers after they have been given induction information such as hours, working conditions, services, etc., to verify personnel information and prepare records; checks information on application, statement of availability, draft, citizenship, and the like; obtains necessary information for income tax withholding, and determines classification; prepares forms for hospitalization, group insurance, and bond deductions; assigns clock number, makes up time card and badge card.
2. Calls previous employer to get reference information while applicant is being interviewed; may check references by mail after employee is hired, and occasionally records information from Dun & Bradstreet or Retail Credit Association on personnel card.
3. Telephones employee's department or home after extended absence to determine when employee is expected to return, if at all; follows same procedure at end of leave of absence.
4. Handles stenographic work of EMPLOYMENT MANAGER.
5. Does miscellaneous clerical work; assigns clock numbers, and makes up time cards for employees transferred between departments; keeps record of equipment loaned to employees, such as micrometers, goggles, etc.; maintains current address file of employees in service; performs other clerical duties as assigned.
6. May substitute for RECEPTIONIST for short periods; give induction information to new employees in absence of PERSONNEL INDUCTION CLERK, escort new workers to departments; administer tests.

Figure 2-4 SAMPLE JOB DESCRIPTION

Job Conditions. Job conditions include the physical environment and surroundings that may affect the quality of the working life on the job. For example, the listing of any unpleasant condition, such as excessive heat, dust, odors, or noises that must be endured, should be included in this section of the job specification. Hazards affecting the health or safety of those performing the job are also included.

Considerations Affecting Job Specifications. In developing the specifications for a job, every effort should be made to insure that the requirements set forth actually are necessary. It is quite possible, for example, that certain specifications such as those relating to experience, education, or physical qualification might be based more upon opinion or tradition than upon fact.

Avoiding Overqualified Applicants. A high school education might be specified when the knowledge that is required to perform the job does not exceed that which could be acquired before reaching the eighth grade. If certain specifications established for a job are greater than those actually required to perform it, employees hired on the basis of these specifications may prove overqualified. If such employees cannot be advanced relatively soon into jobs where their qualifications can be fully utilized, a waste of human resources and quite probably an impairment of morale will be likely to result.

Avoiding Violations of the Civil Rights Act. Any requirements included in a job specification that are not necessary may constitute a violation of the Civil Rights Act of 1964. In the *Duke Power Case,* for example, the Supreme Court ruled that an employer must be able to show that screening standards, such as test scores or educational requirements used in hiring applicants, relate to the performance required on the job. The case left open, however, the use of screening devices that might take into account capability for future promotion.[28] As a result of the Duke Power Case, employers cannot require a high school or college diploma for a particular job merely because they believe they will "get better people" by instituting such requirements. Furthermore, employers must be prepared to demonstrate that any other hiring standards do not automatically screen out applicants whose speech, dress, and personal and work habits differ from those of the predominant group.[29]

Avoiding Sex Stereotyping in Job Titles. The federal government and many state governments have, where possible, made changes in some job titles to eliminate any reference to the sex of the persons who traditionally performed the job. Probably the most significant influence upon job titles has been that resulting from changes made in the Bureau of the Census. The principal change has been that of eliminating or substituting some other terms for the suffixes *man* or *men* in occupational titles. Thus, *firemen* are now classified as *firefighters*, railroad *switchmen* as *switch operators,* structural metal *craftsmen* as structural metal *workers*. *Busboys* are now *waiters' assistants,* and airline *stewardesses* have become *flight attendants*. Although these changes in occupational titles may not lead to any immediate change in the job titles used by private employers and by the general public, most sex stereotyping of job titles probably will be eliminated eventually.

Uses and Sources of Job Information

The value to be derived from job descriptions and specifications is determined to a large extent by the number of persons who make use of them

[28] Griggs *v.* Duke Power Company, U.S. Supreme Court, 1971, 3FEP Cases 175.

[29] Bureau of National Affairs Labor Relations Reporter, *Fair Employment Practice Manual* (Washington, D.C.: Bureau of National Affairs, Inc., December, 1973), p. 421:406.

and by the degree of use that is made of them. Even the job information that is prepared most carefully will be of little value if it remains stored in the personnel department files. The data pertaining to each job should be readily accessible to job holders and to their supervisors. This latter arrangement is of particular importance since employees are often hesitant to ask questions concerning their jobs for fear that such questions will be interpreted as an indication of their ignorance.

Common Uses of Job Information. In one study it was found that job information (see Table 2-1) was used primarily for job evaluation, recruitment and placement, and labor relations. Job information also was used in connection with personnel utilization (that is, in planning and organizing work and avoiding duplication of assignments) and personnel training.[30]

Table 2-1 MAJOR USES OF JOB ANALYSIS INFORMATION

	Programs for Salary-Rated Personnel	Programs for Hourly-Rated Personnel
Job Evaluation	98%	95%
Recruiting and Placing	95	92
Conducting Labor and Personnel Relations	83	79
Utilizing Personnel	72	67
Training	61	63

Source: Jean J. Jones, Jr., and Thomas A. DeCotiis, "Job Analysis: National Survey Findings," *Personnel Journal,* Vol. 48, No. 10 (October, 1969). Reproduced with permission.

While both the job description and the job specification are sources of job information, it is the job description that serves to inform and to remind employees about the details of their duties and provides them with a guide for improving performance and preparing for advancement. Job descriptions can constitute an important personnel tool for supervisors in helping them to orient and train employees, to reconcile employee grievances, and to support disciplinary actions.

Job specifications probably are utilized mostly in connection with the recruitment and selection of employees. Job specifications are particularly essential in a large organization where applicants for a wide variety of jobs must be screened by employment specialists who may not be familiar with the jobs. In the determination of differences in wage rates through the process of job evaluation, the data that are contained in the job specifications also can serve an important use.

Sources of Job Information. Traditionally job information has been gathered, analyzed, and compiled into job descriptions and specifications through the

[30] Jean J. Jones, Jr., and Thomas A. DeCotiis, "Job Analysis: National Survey Findings," *Personnel Journal,* Vol. 48, No. 10 (October, 1969), p. 806.

process known as *job analysis*. In larger organizations personnel specialists who may have the title of job analysts often are responsible for this process. Job information is obtained most frequently by means of questionnaires, interviews, personal observation, or a combination of these methods. When it has been compiled on a more formal and factual basis, the information can help to reduce, although not eliminate, the influence of personal preferences and biases in decisions relating to jobs.

In order to be of full value it is essential that job information be kept up-to-date. Unfortunately the information gained from job analysis usually is recorded in narrative form with the result that the updating of this information is neglected. The narrative form also has discouraged the computerization of job information and thereby reduced its utilization. Computerization of job information also has been deterred by the problems of economy and feasibility and by the competition for the limited financial resources available. In one study, only about 10 percent of the respondents using job analysis reported using computers for the processing, storage, and retrieval of job information.[31]

The Dictionary of Occupational Titles. An important source of job information is the *Dictionary of Occupational Titles,* which is commonly referred to as the DOT. It was compiled by the U.S. Employment Service of the Manpower Administration. Volume 1 of the third edition, published in 1965, contains definitions for 21,741 separate jobs which are known under 13,809 alternate titles, thereby making a total of 35,550 titles that are described in the *Dictionary*. Volume 2 of the DOT provides a classification system for grouping and identifying jobs.[32]

Job Description Information. The type of descriptions contained in the DOT is illustrated by the following description for a Production Lathe Operator job.

> **LATHE OPERATOR, PRODUCTION** (mach. shop) **604,885, automatic-lathe operator; production-lathe operator.** Tends one or more previously set-up lathes, such as turret lathes, bar-machines, and chucking machines, to perform one or series of repetitive operations, such as turning, boring, threading, or facing, of metal workpieces according to specifications on production basis. Lifts workpiece manually or with hoist, and places and secures it in holding fixture or in automatic feed mechanism. Starts machine and turns handwheels to feed tools to workpiece, and engages automatic feed. Observes machining cycle. Verifies conformance of machined work to specifications, using fixed gages, calipers, and micrometers. Changes worn tools, using wrenches. May move controls to adjust rotation speeds, feed rates, and depth of cut. May assist LATHE SET-UP MAN. May work on nonmetallic materials, such as plastics. May be required to have experience with particular materials or product, or with machine of particular size, type, or trade name.[33]

---

[31] *Ibid.*, pp. 807-808.

[32] U.S. Department of Labor, Manpower Administration, *Dictionary of Occupational Titles,* Vol. I, Definitions of Titles, Vol. II, Occupational Classification (3d ed.; Washington, D.C.: U.S. Government Printing Office, 1965). See also *Job Title Revisions to Eliminate Sex- and Age- Referent Language from the Dictionary of Occupational Titles,* Third Edition, published in 1975 by the U.S. Department of Labor, Manpower Administration.

[33] *Ibid.*, p. 413.

The DOT descriptions have helped to bring about a greater degree of uniformity in the job titles and descriptions that are used by employers in different sections of the nation. This fact has facilitated the exchange of statistical information about jobs as well as the movement of workers from sections of the country that may be experiencing widespread unemployment to those sections where employment opportunities are greater. The DOT numbers for jobs are also used in reporting personnel research, particularly as it applies to testing.

Occupational Category Information. The DOT system of code numbers permits jobs to be grouped into occupational classifications for use in vocational counseling and in the exchange of information pertaining to occupational employment. Each of the first three digits in the six-digit DOT job code number serves to classify the job into occupational categories and subcategories. The first digit of the three-digit job code indicates the occupational category: the second digit, the division within the category in which the job is classified; and the third digit, the group within the division into which the job is classified. The code number representing the first digit of the DOT code for each of the nine major job categories is as follows:[34]

0.
1. } Professional, technical, and managerial occupations.
2. Clerical and sales occupations.
3. Service occupations.
4. Farming, fishery, forestry, and related occupations.
5. Processing occupations.
6. Machine trades occupations.
7. Bench work occupations.
8. Structural work occupations.
9. Miscellaneous occupations.

A DOT job code number in which the first three digits are 201 would result in the job being classified into the following category, division, and group:[35]

Category Classification:

2 CLERICAL AND SALES OCCUPATIONS

This category includes occupations concerned with preparing, transcribing, transferring, systematizing, and preserving written communications and records; collecting accounts; distributing information; and influencing customers in favor of a commodity or service. Includes occupations closely identified with sales transactions even though they do not involve actual participation.

Division Classification:

20 STENOGRAPHY, TYPING, FILING, AND RELATED OCCUPATIONS

This division includes occupations concerned with making, classifying, and filing records, including written communications.

---

[34] U.S. Department of Labor, Manpower Administration, Vol. I, *op. cit.*, p. xviii.
[35] *Ibid.*

Group Classification:

201 SECRETARIES

This group includes occupations concerned with carrying out minor administrative and general office duties in addition to taking and transcribing dictation. Occupations concerned primarily with taking and transcribing dictation are included in Group 202.

Job Element Information. As a result of research that it has conducted, the U.S. Employment Service has concluded that every job requires the employee to function at varying levels of difficulty with respect to *data, people,* and *things.* These difficulty levels, which consist of eight different levels, are indicated by the fourth, fifth, and sixth digits of the DOT code as shown in Table 2-2.

Table 2-2 DIFFICULTY LEVELS OF THE DOT CODE

DATA (4th Digit)	PEOPLE (5th Digit)	THINGS (6th Digit)
0 Synthesizing	0 Monitoring	0 Setting-up
1 Coordinating	1 Negotiating	1 Precision Working
2 Analyzing	2 Instructing	2 Operating-Controlling
3 Compiling	3 Supervising	3 Driving-Operating
4 Computing	4 Diverting	4 Manipulating
5 Copying	5 Persuading	5 Tending
6 Comparing	6 Speaking-Signaling	6 Feeding-Offbearing
7 No Significant Relationship	7 Serving	7 Handling
8 No Significant Relationship	8 No Significant Relationship	8 No Significant Relationship

Source: U.S. Department of Labor, Manpower Administration, *Dictionary of Occupational Titles,* Vol. 1, Definitions of Titles (3d ed.; Washington, D.C.: U.S. Government Printing Office, 1965), p. xviii.

For example, if the digit covering *data* (4th digit) in the code were listed as 3, the difficulty level for this element would require the employee to be capable of compiling certain data in order to perform the job satisfactorily. The same situation would apply to each of the two remaining elements pertaining to *people* and *things* which are represented by the 5th and 6th digits respectively. Thus, if the last three digits of the DOT code for a job were 322, the minimal difficulty level for each of the elements of the job would be: 3—compiling (data), 2—instructing (people), and 2—operating-controlling (things).

Functional Job Analysis. The analysis of jobs on the basis of the elements of work that comprise these jobs represents an attempt to pinpoint more specifically the skills and abilities that employees must possess in order to perform them satisfactorily. Since the classifications of these elements by the DOT are of necessity rather broad, the specific elements comprising a particular job should be identified in greater detail through the analysis of the job. This type of job analysis, which is referred to as *functional job analysis* (FJA), offers significant possibilities for use in improving employee selection and placement. If the elements that comprise a job can be identified specifically and accurately, it is possible to develop tests through which individuals may be selected and placed with greater accuracy in those jobs for which they are best qualified. The elements that an employee must be capable of performing in a job can provide a basis for determining his or her training needs. The reassignment and retraining of personnel whose jobs have been eliminated can be made easier if there is job information available concerning the requirements of other jobs in which they might be placed. Furthermore, because the result of job element analysis can be adapted more readily to data processing systems, it may be compiled in data banks for use in connection with programs for the employment of disadvantaged as well as for other unemployed persons.

Résumé

Work is important in providing goods and services and a source of employment and income for members of society. When organized into jobs, work provides the means by which the goals of an organization may be achieved and the personal needs of its employees satisfied. The feelings of satisfaction and recognition that one derives from work will be influenced to a large extent by the demands of the job. The job, furthermore, can be a source of status and contribute to a sense of well-being both economically and psychologically. In organizing the work of the enterprise into jobs, it is important that each job be designed so as to permit the employee who is assigned to it to perform efficiently and to achieve a feeling of satisfaction and security from the job. It is essential, in this regard, that the duties, responsibilities, and performance requirements of each job be established formally so that each employee and each superior will understand clearly what is expected of them in the way of performance.

Today greater recognition is being given to human factors relating to job design, and the individual performing it is considered to be an integral part of a man-machine system. More effort is being given to making the job satisfying and rewarding for the employee. As a result of human factors engineering and job enrichment programs, human capabilities and needs are given more consideration by management in organizing work and in developing the job structure.

Accurate information pertaining to the duties of each job and the personnel requirements that they demand of the employee is essential to personnel management. It can be developed objectively through the process of job analysis and compiled formally into job descriptions and specifications. The information contained in these descriptions and specifications can prove to be of considerable value in connection with the selection, evaluation, and training of employees and in resolving grievance and disciplinary problems.

DISCUSSION QUESTIONS

1. In what way is job satisfaction on the part of employees affected by their individual differences?
2. What does the term "alienation" mean? How does it relate to job organization?
3. What is the nature of role and status and the relationships of each to the job and to each other?
4. How important is job enrichment to employees and to what extent is it desired by them?
5. Some managers have opposed the preparation of formal job descriptions on the grounds that such descriptions encourage employees to do only the work that is required by their job descriptions. What is your reaction to this statement?
6. As a project, prepare a description of the job at which you are currently working or have worked. Develop a specification listing the minimum qualifications that are necessary in order for one to perform this job. How do these job requirements compare with your qualifications?
7. What effects, if any, will the Duke Power Case have upon job specifications?

PROBLEM 2-1 THE "DIRTY" WORK

There are several million jobs in this country that might be described as mind-numbing or debilitating because of their monotonous nature. Furthermore, conditions under which such jobs must be performed are uncomfortable at best, and, at worst, life-threatening. Some of these jobs and the reaction of those performing them have been described in a *Wall Street Journal* article.[1]

One such job is that of a token seller in the New York Subway System which requires the employee to sit in a chair all day shuffling coins back and forth. In this job one employee reports that he is subjected to a continual stream of verbal abuse and is often the target of spit, cherry bombs, and holdups which, in turn, have given him nightmares and caused premature aging. The coin booth is in a dirty, noisy location and is unbearably hot in the summer and cold in the winter. Many of those performing this job would like to quit but are unable to find some other job or one that pays at least as much money.

Another "dirty" job is that of patrolman in the traffic tunnel under the East River which involves sitting in a cramped and poorly ventilated booth watching the cars whiz by. The purpose of the job is to use the phone when there is an emergency. In this job, one employee complained, there is no reward for doing the job well. Employees experience neither feelings of hope nor opportunity for advancement. Unlike various physically-demanding jobs, such as those tending a furnace in a foundry or stripping a hog carcass every 45 seconds in a slaughter house that involve some measure of skill or pride of workmanship, those of token seller or tunnel patrolman provide none. Furthermore, the complete lack of satisfaction, coupled with the monotony and poor working conditions in the latter jobs, make them even worse.

a. If it were possible to do so, should jobs of this type be eliminated through the use of electronic equipment?
b. What, if anything, might be done to improve jobs such as these?

[1] "The Dirty Work," *The Wall Street Journal,* July 22, 1971.

SUGGESTED READINGS

Chapanis, Alphonse. *Man-Machine Engineering*. Belmont, California: Wadsworth Publishing Co., Inc., 1965.

Foulkes, Fred K. *Creating More Meaningful Work*. New York: American Management Association, Inc., 1969.

McCormick, Ernest J. *Human Factors Engineering,* 3d ed. New York: McGraw-Hill Book Company, 1970.

Maher, John R. (ed.) *New Perspectives in Job Enrichment*. New York: Van Nostrand Reinhold Co., 1971.

Neff, Walter S. *Work and Human Behavior*. New York: Atherton Press, 1968.

U.S. Department of Labor, Manpower Administration. *Dictionary of Occupational Titles,* Volume I, *Definitions of Titles,* Volume II, *Occupational Classification,* Third edition. Washington, D.C.: U.S. Government Printing Office, 1965.

Walker, Charles R. *Technology, Industry, and Man, The Age of Acceleration*. New York: McGraw-Hill Book Company, 1968.

Zollitsch, Herbert G., and Adolph Langsner. *Wage and Salary Administration,* 2d ed. Cincinnati: South-Western Publishing Co., 1970. Chapters 11 and 12.

The Organization of Personnel

The preceding chapter discussed how work may be organized most effectively into jobs to achieve employee satisfaction and efficiency. Such achievement, however, also requires that a job be integrated closely with other jobs in the organization according to a planned structure. This structure serves not only to establish the duties, responsibilities, and authority of the people who are assigned to these jobs but also as the basis for planning, directing, coordinating, and controlling their work activities.

In more recent years the organization has come to be recognized as being more than a structure which is depicted by an organization chart or an organizational manual. According to the more modern theory, organizations are being recognized as systems in which people are working and interacting together in the pursuit of common goals. In this chapter, therefore, organization will be discussed from the standpoint of both the modern and the traditional theories. Particular attention will be given to the effects that people may have upon the functioning of the organization and the effects that the organization, in turn, may have upon them. The types of structures into which an organization may be formed and the effects of these structures upon the authority, responsibility, and behavior of the personnel comprising the organization will also be considered.

CONCEPTS OF ORGANIZATION

The word ''organization'' can present a semantic problem because of the different meanings that can be derived from it, depending upon who is using the term and the context in which it is being used. The term may be used to refer to any institution, such as a company, hospital, school, military unit, charitable foundation, or government agency, without distinguishing specifically its purpose, objectives, or ownership. It is in this context that the term is used most generally throughout the remainder of this book. The term organization may also be used to refer to the process by which a formal structure is established. In this context *organization* is defined as "the process of identifying and grouping the work to be performed, defining and delegating responsibility and authority, and establishing relationships for the purpose of enabling people to work most effectively in accomplishing objectives."[1]

Theories of Organization

Theories of organization and management have undergone substantial change as a result of research in behavioral science. Prior to the human relations movement, the classical or traditional theory of organization prevailed among management scholars and practitioners. It was upon this theory that military, government, business, and church organizations in earlier periods of history were based. With the advent of the human relations movement, however, the traditional theory was modified to accommodate the growing concern for the role of people in organizations. Such modifications gave rise to the neoclassical theory of organization. The influence of behavioral science and of the systems concept of management in turn provided the foundation for what is termed modern organization theory.

Classical or Traditional Theory. The *classical theory of organization* was primarily efficiency- and goal-oriented. Under this theory attention was focused upon developing a structure in which functional specialization and the division and coordination of work could be achieved. This structure was considered to be essential for establishing a hierarchy of authority and the channels through which this authority could be exercised, responsibility assigned, and performance controlled.

Assumption. Under the classical theory it was assumed that the organization of work was based upon a systematic and rational process that could be accomplished logically and impersonally without much regard to the problems and characteristics of the persons who were to perform it.[2] According to this assumption, efficiency could be achieved by securing the required type of performance and behavior from employees. The function of personnel management thus was considered to be largely one of placing the right employees in the right jobs and of training and motivating them to perform the duties of their jobs effectively.

---

[1] Louis A. Allen, *Management and Organization* (New York: McGraw-Hill Book Company, 1958), p. 57.

[2] Joel E. Ross, *Management by Information System* (Englewood Cliffs, New Jersey: Prentice-Hall, Inc., 1970), p. 56.

Weakness. The classical theory of organization has been criticized for being overly concerned with objectives, structure, principles, and controls, while neglecting the human dimensions of the organization. In other words, it has been criticized for being efficiency- rather than people-oriented. While there is some validity to this and other criticisms, it must be recognized that in terms of the knowledge that was available at the time the classical theory represented a significant breakthrough in the field of management. As a pioneering theory it provided an important foundation upon which the theories that followed have been expanded.

Neoclassical Theory. The Hawthorne Study and succeeding studies of human behavior helped to enlarge management's understanding of organizations and how they operate. Such understanding was embodied in the *neoclassical theory* which places greater emphasis upon humanizing the organization although this theory assumes somewhat erroneously that "a happy worker is a productive worker."

Strengths. While it did not discard the classical theory's concern for structure and for authority and controls, the neoclassical theory sought to relate these factors to the behavior and goals of the employees. The neoclassical theory thus encouraged management to recognize the role of the informal groups and the grapevine within their organizations and their effects upon employee behavior. It also helped to make managers more aware of the need for better formal communication, for more democratic styles of leadership, and for greater employee participation in decisions affecting their welfare.

Weaknesses. Although it contributed to improved management practices and helped to enlarge the foundation for modern organization theory, the neoclassical theory suffered from certain weaknesses. While it focused attention upon the human dimensions, namely individuals and groups, the neoclassical theory did not go far enough in recognizing certain other dimensions of organizations and their interaction and interrelationship. Some neoclassical theorists tended to overemphasize the human considerations to the neglect of formal objectives, authority, and controls within the organization. Furthermore, there were managers who were prone to overemphasize employee benefit and service programs and to concentrate upon trying to make the organization "one big happy family." Consequently, some of them discovered belatedly that it was quite possible to have a happy but relatively unproductive work force.

Modern Organization Theory. During the past decade a more comprehensive and sophisticated theory of organization has been evolving which is referred to as *modern organization theory*. Instead of viewing organization as being a mechanism through which people and their activities may be managed, modern theory conceives it as a dynamic system. Like the equipment systems and the man-machine systems that were discussed in the preceding chapter, the organization system is viewed as a group of interrelated and interacting components or parts that are held together in a dynamic state of equilibrium. It is this dynamic condition that gives particular meaning to the system concept of organization.

Strategic Components of the System Concept of Organization. As can be seen from Figure 3-1, the strategic parts or components that some theorists consider to comprise the organization system are: (1) the individual, (2) the formal organization structure, (3) the informal organization, (4) the role and status patterns, and (5) the physical setting.[3] Since modern organization theory is still in its frontier stages of development, further changes undoubtedly will be made with regard to the specific components that are considered to comprise the organization system.

Basic to the system is the *individual* component which includes attitudes, feelings, personality traits, motives, and other variables that help to determine the individual's behavior.

Included in the *formal organization* component are the formal structure, the hierarchy of authority, the communication channels, and the pattern of relationship that it provides together with its objectives, policies, procedures, and other management devices that help to formalize and to facilitate its operation.

The *informal organization* component includes the standards and behavioral patterns that are imposed upon its members by the work group (including those relating to informal leadership). The component also includes the informal systems for communication and the methods for short-cutting formal procedures.

The *role and status patterns* that comprise the fourth component are those that are created by both the informal and the formal organizations and by the backgrounds and behaviors of the individuals who comprise these organizations. These patterns, furthermore, are affected by the expectancies and perceptions of employees with respect to their own particular role and status and those of others. The office boy in Figure 3-2, for example, appears to perceive his role in the organization quite differently from his superiors.

As the term would imply, the *physical setting* component consists of such items as the tools, equipment, processes, and schedules by which the work is accomplished. It includes the physical demands, hazards, and surroundings of the job or, in short, all of the elements of the total physical work environment.

Relationships Among the Components. Since all of these components of an organization are interrelated and interacting, any changes that may occur in one of them will create changes in one or more of the other components. A change in the physical work setting resulting from the automation of certain production processes, for example, is likely to change the duties and responsibilities of some individuals as well as their respective roles and statuses. These changes may in turn affect the composition and relationships of the

[3] *Ibid.*, pp. 65-67.

members within the informal work groups. Furthermore, as a result of changes in production processes and in the duties and relationship of the jobs being performed, modifications also may be required in the formal organization structure. The interactions and relationships between the various components of the organization system thus are endless.

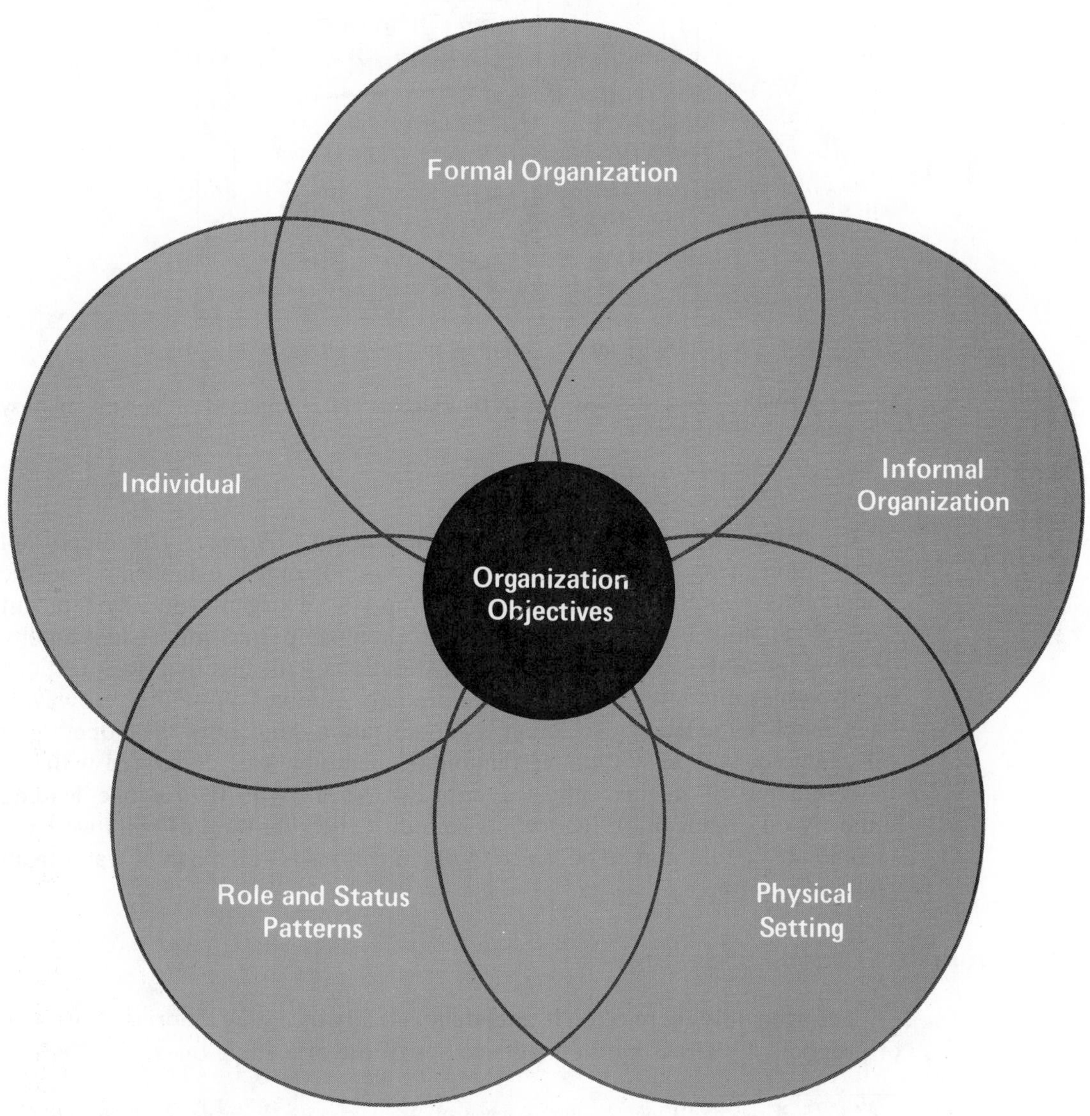

Figure 3-1 THE ORGANIZATION SYSTEM

"Boy, am I carrying a lot of people on my back!"

Source: STRICTLY BUSINESS cartoon by Dale McFeatters, reproduced through the courtesy of Publishers-Hall Syndicate.

Figure 3-2

Contribution of the Modern Organization Theory. The important contribution of modern organization theory is not that it establishes specific components which are considered to comprise an organization system but rather that it stresses the existence of interrelationships and interactions among these components. In so doing it focuses attention on the fact that organizations are dynamic, multidimensional, and extremely complex in nature. However, since much knowledge pertaining to organizations and how they operate is still required, our present understanding of them might be compared with our understanding of nuclear physics prior to World War II. As one leading authority on organization theory has stated, "The sum total of facts we have accumulated about human behavior in organizations is still a pail of water in an ocean of ignorance."[4]

Controversy on Organization Theories

Unfortunately there often is a tendency to advance new theories, concepts, or programs by stressing the inadequacies of the preceding ones.

[4] L. F. Urwich, "Papers in the Science of Administration," *Academy of Management Journal,* Vol. 13, No. 4 (December, 1970), p. 371. Quoting a statement by Simon from Harold Koontz (ed.), *Toward a Unified Theory of Management* (New York: McGraw-Hill Company, 1964). p. 80.

Some Criticisms of the Classical Theory. Modern theorists have not been reluctant to criticize the older theories of organization. Some of them have criticized the classical theory for placing too much stress upon tight controls, a very formal structure, tightly defined and definite policies and procedures, and what they feel is a nonhuman approach or lack of concern about differences between people.[5] Classical theory has been criticized as being derived from the military or church models of organization which are considered by some modern theorists to be inappropriate for contemporary enterprises. It has also been accused of supporting the concept that people do not enjoy working, of relying upon authority as the central and indispensable means of management control, and of viewing the employee as an inert instrument simply performing the assigned task.[6]

Rebuttal to Contemporary Criticisms. Some of the criticisms that have been leveled against the classical organization theory by behavioral scientists and modern organization theorists have in turn been challenged by contemporary scholars in the field of management. Koontz points out that a certain criticism of classical organization theory is the result of either a misstatement or misapplication by the critics of certain principles underlying this theory. He also believes that the criticism is due to the fact that the boundary lines of management (including organization) are not clearly defined, that other disciplines contributing to management have not been integrated fully with it, and that the terms used in the discussion of management are not clearly understood or interpreted uniformly.[7]

Urwick challenges some of the contemporary critics of organization theory, particularly with regard to their interpretation and use of the term "organization." He also points out that the bureaucratic rules and lack of humane leadership which might characterize the operation of certain institutions cannot be construed as a valid criticism of the concept of organizations per se.[8]

In spite of the preceding criticism and viewpoints concerning the various theories of organization, it should be recognized that each of these theories has contributed to the improvement of management practice. Certain concepts embodied in each of the earlier theories are still applicable and can contribute to better management if applied as intended. Unfortunately their failure to prove successful in practice can be as much the result of improper application as of invalid theory.

---

[5] Marvin D. Dunnette and Wayne K. Kirchner, *Psychology Applied to Industry* (New York: Appleton-Century-Crofts, 1965), p. 161.

[6] *Ibid.,* pp. 162-163.

[7] See Harold Koontz, "Management Theory Jungle," *Journal of the Academy of Management,* Vol. 4, No. 3 (December, 1961), pp. 182-183.

[8] Lyndall F. Urwick, "Have We Lost Our Way in the Jungle of Management Theory?" *Personnel,* Vol. 42, No. 3 (May-June, 1956), pp. 8-18.

THE FUNCTION OF THE ORGANIZATION

The fact that modern theory conceives organization to be more than a formal structure does not necessarily reduce the importance of this structure. The structure, for example, still serves to divide and group those activities into jobs that are to become the duties and responsibilities and authority of the persons in each job. The specific responsibility and authority of each person, furthermore, will be affected by the type of structure into which the jobs have been organized and by the locations and relationships of these jobs within this structure.

Nature of Responsibility

Responsibility is the obligation of subordinates to their superiors for performing the duties of their jobs. Responsibility for the management of an organization resides initially with its governing board which might be a board of directors, trustees, or commissioners. Ultimately, of course, it rests with the public who provides the consent and whose governments establish the legal framework under which all organizations exist and operate. The responsibility of managing an organization is assigned to a chief executive by the governing board. This executive, in turn, divides and assigns portions of this responsibility to subordinates, and so on downward through the various levels in the organization. Managers, regardless of their level, cannot escape the responsibility which is assigned to them even though they may reassign most of it to subordinates. Thus, although the chief executive may reassign the responsibility for the operation of the personnel program to the personnel manager, the chief executive is still the one who must answer directly to the board of directors for any difficulties that may arise in connection with the program. Since the major portion of a manager's responsibilities is carried out through subordinates, the success of that individual's performance is determined in a large measure by how effectively he or she can develop and motivate subordinates to assume those responsibilities that are assigned to them.

Nature of Authority

Authority in the management context constitutes a form of influence and a right to take action, and to direct and coordinate the actions of others in the achievement of an organization's goals. It is a right to use discretion that is inherent in the position an individual occupies rather than in that individual personally. As such, authority provides the basis for the assignment of responsibility within an organization and constitutes the force that binds the units of the organization together.[9] In an organization formal authority, like

[9] Harold Koontz and Cyril O'Donnell, *Principles of Management: An Analysis of Managerial Functions* (5th ed.; New York: McGraw-Hill Book Company, 1972), pp. 56-57.

responsibility, originates with the governing board and, of course, ultimately with society which has granted the organization the right to exist.

Through the process of delegation authority is passed downward within the organization and divided among subordinate personnel. Individuals can rightfully exercise only that authority which has been delegated to them and it is essential, therefore, that individuals be delegated authority equal to their assigned responsibilities. Conversely, they must be held responsible for exercising properly the authority that has been delegated to them.

It is only by developing subordinates and delegating to them the authority to make decisions that managers can multiply their contributions to the enterprise. The delegation of authority permits decisions to be made more rapidly by those who are in more direct contact with the problem. It also demonstrates confidence in subordinates and provides them with a greater feeling of recognition and a sense of participation.

Types of Authority

The authority that is exercised within an organization may be classified into three types: line, staff, and functional.

Line Authority. *Line authority* involves the right not only to direct subordinate personnel but also to take disciplinary action against them for violations of these orders or for other just causes. Line authority can be exercised only over subordinates in the chain of command and not horizontally over persons in other departments of the structure.

Staff Authority. In contrast to line authority, *staff authority* does not provide the right to exercise discretion or to take action. Instead it provides only the right to provide assistance, counsel, or service to others. Thus, the authority of a staff person is derived from the knowledge, expertise, and information that he or she possesses and involves only the right to obtain and disburse information relating to a particular field of expertise. Individuals whose jobs involve staff authority, therefore, must rely upon their power of persuasion and upon their reputation for competency and expertness in their field of specialization in order to have their advice and recommendations accepted. Staff authority typically is exercised by persons holding positions in staff departments in connection with their relations with individuals in other departments. It may also be exercised by persons in line positions when they are giving advice or assistance to persons in other departments who are not subordinate to them. Individuals occupying "assistant-to" positions usually exercise only staff authority since the person whom they are assisting exercises the line authority. In recent years, however, "assistant-to" positions have been eliminated in many organizations; the duties and responsibilities of these positions are being given to a committee or to some line position.[10]

---

[10] John Senger, "The Co-Manager Concept," *California Management Review,* Vol. XII, No. 3 (March, 1971), p. 80.

Functional Authority. What frequently is termed staff authority might be more correctly classified as *functional authority*. The distinction between functional and staff authority, however, is largely one of degree. Functional authority involves the right to issue orders that pertain to the performance of a particular function. It is not as binding as line authority since it does not carry the right to discipline others in order to enforce compliance.[11]

Whether or not the authority that a manager can exercise over another individual is line or functional in nature is determined by his or her relationship to that individual. Functional authority, thus, may be exercised only over individuals in other departments throughout the organizational structure, whereas line authority can be exercised only over subordinates within the chain of command. Personnel managers, for example, exercise functional authority over other managers, supervisors, and their subordinates with respect to the performance of personnel activities, but they exercise line authority only over subordinates within their own departments. Since it does entail the right to coordinate and enforce the policies and procedures governing the performance of a particular function, however, functional authority carries more power than staff authority.

Procedural Relationships

The relationships that probably are the most prevalent within an organization are those of a procedural or cooperative nature. Such relationships usually occur laterally within the organization between individuals performing their assigned duties. Procedural relationships are a potential source of confusion and conflict because their nature often is not well defined or understood by members of an enterprise and because neither party to such relationships is in a position of authority over the other. Thus, friction and resentment may result if either party to the relationship attempts to influence or to exercise initiative over the other. William F. Whyte, in one of his studies, for example, concluded that friction, tension, and accompanying emotional complications frequently were the result of one employee attempting to initiate action for another who considered himself to occupy an equal or higher status position.[12]

Since someone must exercise initiative in carrying out a particular procedure within the organization, it is inevitable that procedural or crosswise relationships may at times result in conflict rather than cooperation. One of the most important requirements for a smooth-functioning organization, therefore, is the development of procedures that will permit each member to understand better the nature of his or her relationships to others.

[11] Hall H. Logan, "Line and Staff: An Obsolete Concept?" *Personnel,* Vol. 43, No. 1 (January-February, 1966), pp. 28-29.

[12] William Foote Whyte, *Men At Work* (Homewood, Illinois: Richard D. Irwin, Inc., 1961), pp. 125-135.

ORGANIZATION STRUCTURES AND THEIR CHARACTERISTICS

Formal relationships among the various positions within an organization, as well as the authority, responsibilities, and activities connected with these positions, are determined by the formal structure that comprises the organization. The three basic types of organization structures as determined by the pattern of relationships are the functional, line, and line-and-staff structures.

Functional Type of Organization Structure

The *functional type* of structure, of which Frederick W. Taylor was one of the innovators, is intended to provide personnel with the opportunity to achieve maximum functional specialization. Each manager has authority over the personnel within all other departments with respect to their performance of the function for which he or she is responsible. For example, the personnel manager would have primary authority and responsibility for hiring, training, disciplining, and the handling of other functions relating to the management of personnel within all departments; the production manager would have authority and responsibility for the technical phases of production; and the quality control manager would have authority and responsibility for the maintenance of quality standards. Unfortunately in a functional structure the division of authority among several functional specialists requires employees to take orders from a number of bosses which leads to confusion and inadequate control. This type of structure in its pure form thus has little practical value.

Line Type of Organization Structure

The *line type* of organization structure, also called the *scalar structure*, is the oldest and simplest type of structure. It permits a clear line of authority to be maintained from the highest to the lowest level within the structure. Each member of the organization is held directly responsible to only one superior.

The line type of structure is best suited to the needs of the small business organization whose operations are generally divided into the functions of production, sales, and finance. The managers of the departments that are responsible for each of these functions, as indicated by Figure 3-3, have complete authority and responsibility over the activities and personnel of their departments. Each manager is also responsible for personnel management, quality control, purchasing, or any other functions which contribute indirectly to the performance of the department's primary function. Department managers in a line organization, therefore, must have broad and diversified qualifications because they must be able to cope with a variety of problems without assistance from functional specialists. As the activities of the line departments increase in number and complexity, the straight line type of structure becomes less satisfactory because managers cannot keep abreast of all of the fields that relate to the operation of their departments. Eventually individuals referred to as staff specialists, must be employed to assist the line managers with the performance of the more specialized functions. Additional positions may lead in turn to the formation of a staff department to coordinate the activities of employees in these positions, thereby creating a line-and-staff type of structure.

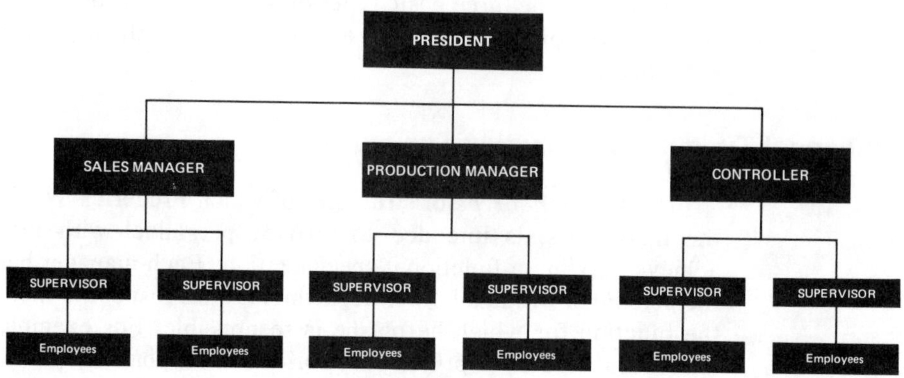

Figure 3-3 LINE TYPE OF ORGANIZATION STRUCTURE

Line-and-Staff Type of Organization Structure

The *line-and-staff type* of structure has characteristics of both the line and the functional structures. The line departments are those that are concerned directly with the accomplishment of the objectives of the enterprise. The addition of staff departments provides assistance in those more specialized areas in which line managers may require assistance. By utilizing staff assistance of this type, supervisors and managers are able to confine their attention to the primary work of their departments.

Figure 3-4 illustrates how a line-and-staff type of structure can be developed through the addition to Figure 3-3 of staff departments whose functional authority is indicated by the broken lines. The staff departments that have been created on this chart include, on the same level as the line departments, those of engineering, personnel, and purchasing.

Conflicts Within Line-and-Staff Organizations

Despite their widespread usage, certain conflicts may arise within line-and-staff organizations. Many of these conflicts result from the failure of individuals to understand fully the role of functional authority, or to exercise it properly, and the failure to utilize the assistance of staff personnel effectively within the organization. Conflicts also may arise from differences in the background that exist between line personnel and staff personnel which can create a basis for misunderstandings and personality clashes between the two groups.

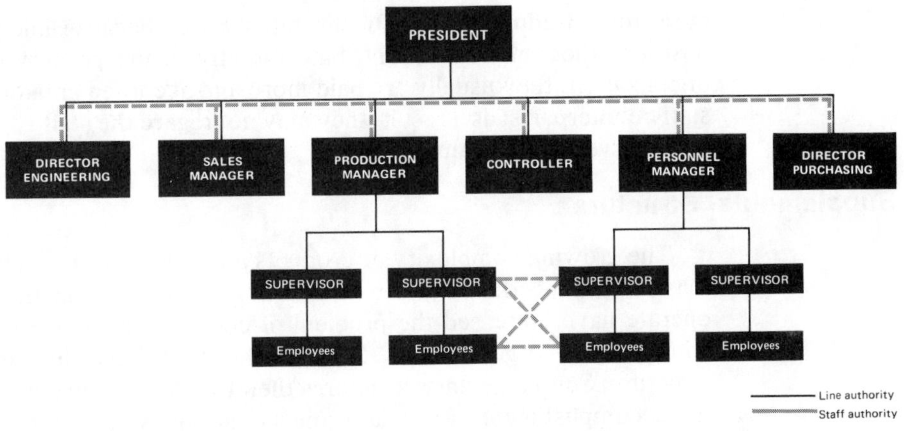

Note: For simplification the structures for only two departments are given.

Figure 3-4 LINE-AND-STAFF TYPE OF ORGANIZATION STRUCTURE

Conflicts Created by the Nature of Staff Authority. In a line-and-staff organization the supervisors may believe that their authority is being eroded by the functional authority of staff departments, such as personnel, and by the more formal personnel policies, procedures, rules, and regulations relating to this function. Attempts by staff specialists to force line managers and supervisors to accept staff assistance or to change certain personnel practices can reinforce this belief.

On the other hand, whenever line supervisors are unable or unwilling to cope with certain problems of a particular functional area such as personnel, the staff specialists may be forced to assume certain duties of the supervisor relating to the function. The personnel staff in some organizations, for example, may at times be required to assume a direct role in conducting training programs, handling disciplinary problems, or in taking care of other personnel functions that are the primary responsibility of the line but which are being neglected by them. Whenever a staff department assumes the responsibilities that should be borne by the line departments, however, the authority of the line manager may be weakened in the process. Therefore, staff personnel should attempt through educational and persuasive means rather than pressure tactics to get their advice and assistance accepted by the line departments. They must be capable of gaining the respect and confidence of the line personnel by demonstrating the ability to serve the latter's needs rather than pointing out their errors and deficiencies.

Conflicts Created by Background Differences. Differences in background between executives in line positions and those in staff positions may, at times, create disharmony. Many line supervisors have risen to their positions as a result of practical operative experience rather than as the result of formal education. Thus, they may tend to be somewhat apprehensive or resentful toward staff personnel who frequently are younger and possess significantly more formal education.[13] On the other hand, because line personnel are in positions that relate and contribute directly to the primary objectives of the organization, they usually are paid more and accorded greater status than their staff counterparts; as a result, they may not regard the staff advice or assistance to be of very great value.

Supplemental Structures

The growing complexity of products and services, the technology by which they are produced, and the environment in which organizations are required to operate have increased the problem of coordinating and controlling activities within these organizations through the traditional line-and-staff type of structure. Supplementary structures therefore have been developed to facilitate the accomplishment of special projects and tasks or to cope with a particular problem or crisis. These supplemental structures, which are discussed below, serve to cut across the vertical lines of authority and communication within an organization. In doing so they help to eliminate "red tape" and permit better coordination of a particular project or activity by facilitating communication and procedural relations horizontally within the structure.

Project or Task Force Organization. *Project* (or *task force* or *program*) *organizations* generally are developed to accomplish some specific goal, after which they are disbanded. Not infrequently this structure is created because of some crisis or necessity that may require results to be accomplished under pressure of time limitations. Membership in a project organization, or at least the nucleus of this membership, usually is drawn from the regular departments of the organization with additional personnel being employed from the outside as needed. The fact that the project is operated independently of the regular organization under its own leadership can help to stimulate a greater sense of unity, purpose, and achievement among its members. This unity in turn can contribute to a higher level of morale and teamwork than otherwise might be achieved in a regular department. Project assignments can also serve to broaden the qualifications of the members.

A potential weakness of the project organization is that the efficiency of regular departments may suffer, temporarily at least, through the loss of personnel to the project organization. Also, the problem of finding a place for members of the project upon their return may arise if their department has adjusted to operating without them. Furthermore, if transfers between their regular job and project team assignments occur too frequently, the resulting instability could adversely affect morale within the organization.

Matrix Organizations. The *matrix organizations* may be thought of as an organizational overlay in which a series of horizontal relationships are superimposed upon the hierarchical structure of the traditional organization.[14]

---

[13] Melville Dalton, "Changing Staff-Line Relationships," *Personnel Administration,* Vol. 29, No. 2 (March-April, 1966), p. 3.

[14] Ray Gullet, "Personnel Management in the Project Organization," *Personnel Administration and Public Personnel Review,* Vol. 1, No. 2 (September-October, 1972), p. 17.

Figure 3-5 provides an example of this type of organization in an aerospace company. Each project listed on the left side of the chart is coordinated by a project manager with the assistance of a staff. The actual work on a project is performed by the personnel in the departments listed at the top of the chart. For this reason the managers of the projects occupy a critical role because their authority over the work being performed in each of the departments is limited, while their responsibility for the successful completion of the project is very great. Because of this fact, project managers must rely heavily upon their personal leadership skills and upon their powers of persuasion.

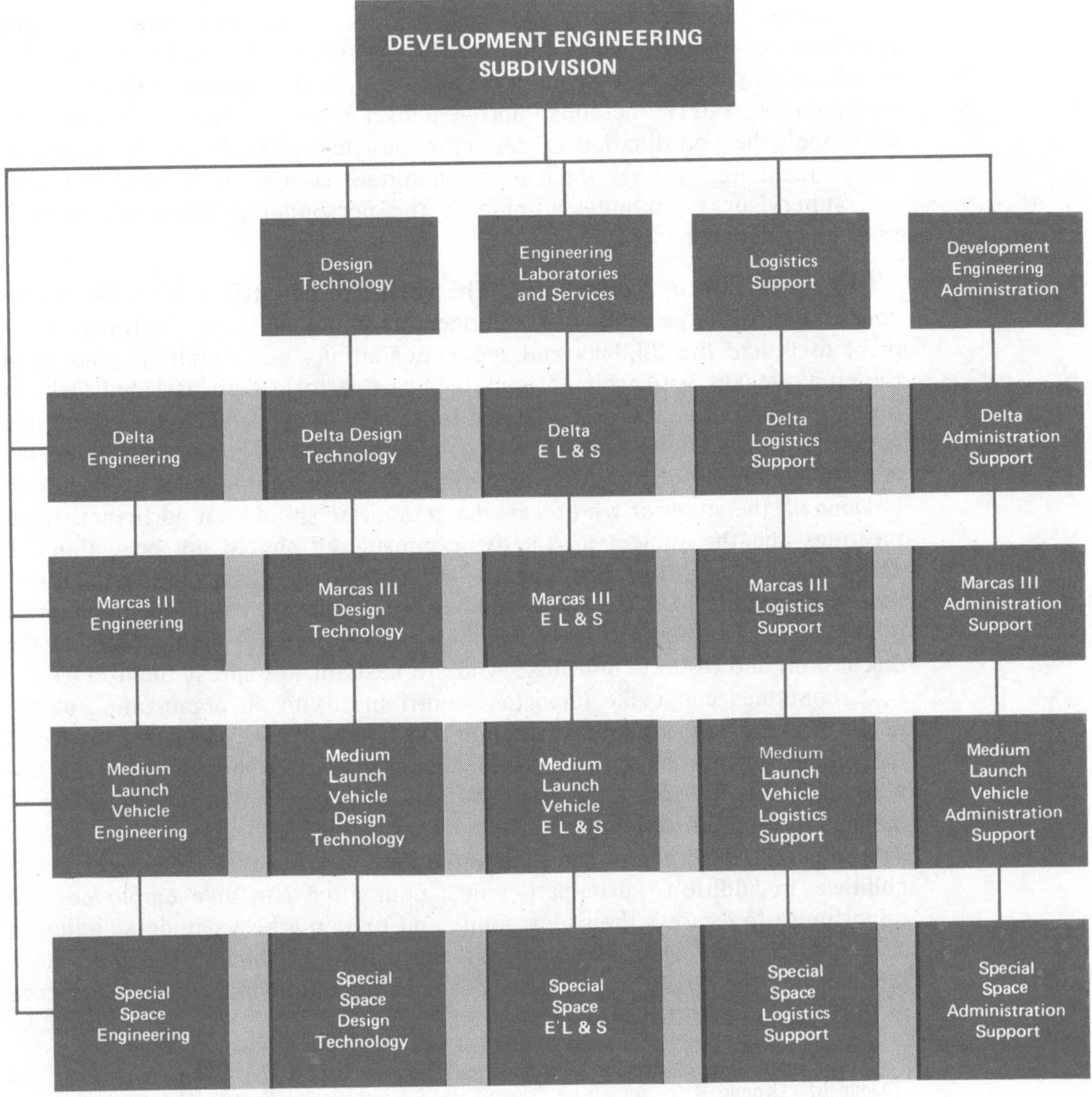

Figure 3-5 A MATRIX ORGANIZATION

Committees. A supplement to the regular structure that is found in all sizes and types of organizations is the *committee*. It may be utilized for many different purposes such as to facilitate group communication, to secure group interaction, or to deal with specific problems. It may also be utilized to plan, to coordinate, or to control the performance of various functions within the organization.[15]

The use of committees in the administration of the personnel program is quite widespread, for management must be knowledgeable as to employee reactions to the program and must secure employee support for the program. Committees in the personnel field may be used to appraise employee suggestions, to resolve grievances, to evaluate jobs and employee performance, and to select candidates for promotions. Committees can also enable employees to participate in the administration of programs in areas such as recreation, safety, methods improvement, and cost reduction. In managing personnel, the coordination of personnel policies, procedures, and practices can be facilitated through the use of committees composed of those managers and supervisors who must administer the personnel program within their respective departments.

Effective Use of Committees. The values to be derived from the use of committees to a large extent are contingent upon the willingness of top management to utilize the findings and recommendations of committees and upon the effectiveness with which committees can perform their assigned task. In forming a committee it is essential that those persons assigned to the committee have the qualifications necessary to discuss and to act intelligently upon the task for which the committee was created. In a true committee, according to O'Donnell, the superior who forms the committee should not participate in its meetings and the subject matter to be considered should not be within the assigned duties of any of its members.[16] The presiding officer of the committee, moreover, should have the ability to keep the discussion within the boundaries of the agenda, to control those members who otherwise might dominate the discussion, and to draw out those who are hesitant to express themselves.

Committees can make important contributions to an organization as the result of enhancing the job satisfaction and improving the job performance of individuals on the committee. Working as a committee member provides the individual with a sense of participation in the organization and a feeling of having contributed to the organization. A committee assignment can also give subordinates the feeling that their superiors respect their intelligence and abilities. In addition, participation in a committee can give employees the opportunity to express their viewpoints and to gain a better understanding of the viewpoints of their associates; it can also help them to become more familiar with the operating problems of the organization and to gain experience in the decision-making process.

---

[15] An interesting discussion of committees is provided in the following article: Cyril O'Donnell, "Ground Rules for Using Committees," *Management Review* (October, 1961), pp. 63-67.

[16] *Ibid.*, pp. 63-67.

Limitations of Committees. While committees can serve many useful purposes within an organization, they do not always constitute the most productive approach to decision making. In determining whether or not to utilize a committee, therefore, it is important to consider whether or not a group decision is superior to one that might be made by a capable individual. Committee consensus may require certain compromises which weaken the decision. Furthermore, unless the members have the required qualifications, the information, and the interest necessary for deliberating on a problem, committee meetings may waste time which the committee members could better utilize in performing their regular job assignments.

One of the unfortunate trends in many organizations has been the formation of committees of questionable need which, once established, have continued to exist. Some organizations have attempted to reduce the drain of committee work upon executive time by providing certain controls to govern the formation and continuation of committees.

HUMAN BEHAVIOR IN ORGANIZATIONS

It was revealed earlier in this chapter that students and practitioners of management are becoming increasingly aware of the effects that people and the informal groups of which they are members may have upon the formal organization. As a result of this awareness, greater recognition is being given to human behavior in the organization and how it influences and is influenced by the formal structure and other components of the organization system.

Influence of Size and Shape of Structure upon Behavior

The growth of an organization can exert a significant influence upon human behavior. As the organization increases in size, additional levels of management usually are created in order that the span of management of each manager and supervisor may be kept within satisfactory limits. Additional levels cause the employee to become further removed from top management, and lines of communication and supervision become lengthened. Managers at the top have greater difficulty in recognizing and understanding the feelings of employees at the lower levels. Employees under these conditions may have greater difficulty in identifying themselves with the goals and activities of the organization and consequently are likely to feel that they have become forgotten as individuals.

Organization structures with a number of levels of management are sometimes referred to as *tall* structures in contrast to the *flat* structures which have relatively few levels. Some large companies have made a concerted effort to flatten the structure by eliminating some levels of management. Figure 3-6 illustrates how some of the levels in the structure in the top chart can be eliminated to create the flatter structure in the bottom chart.

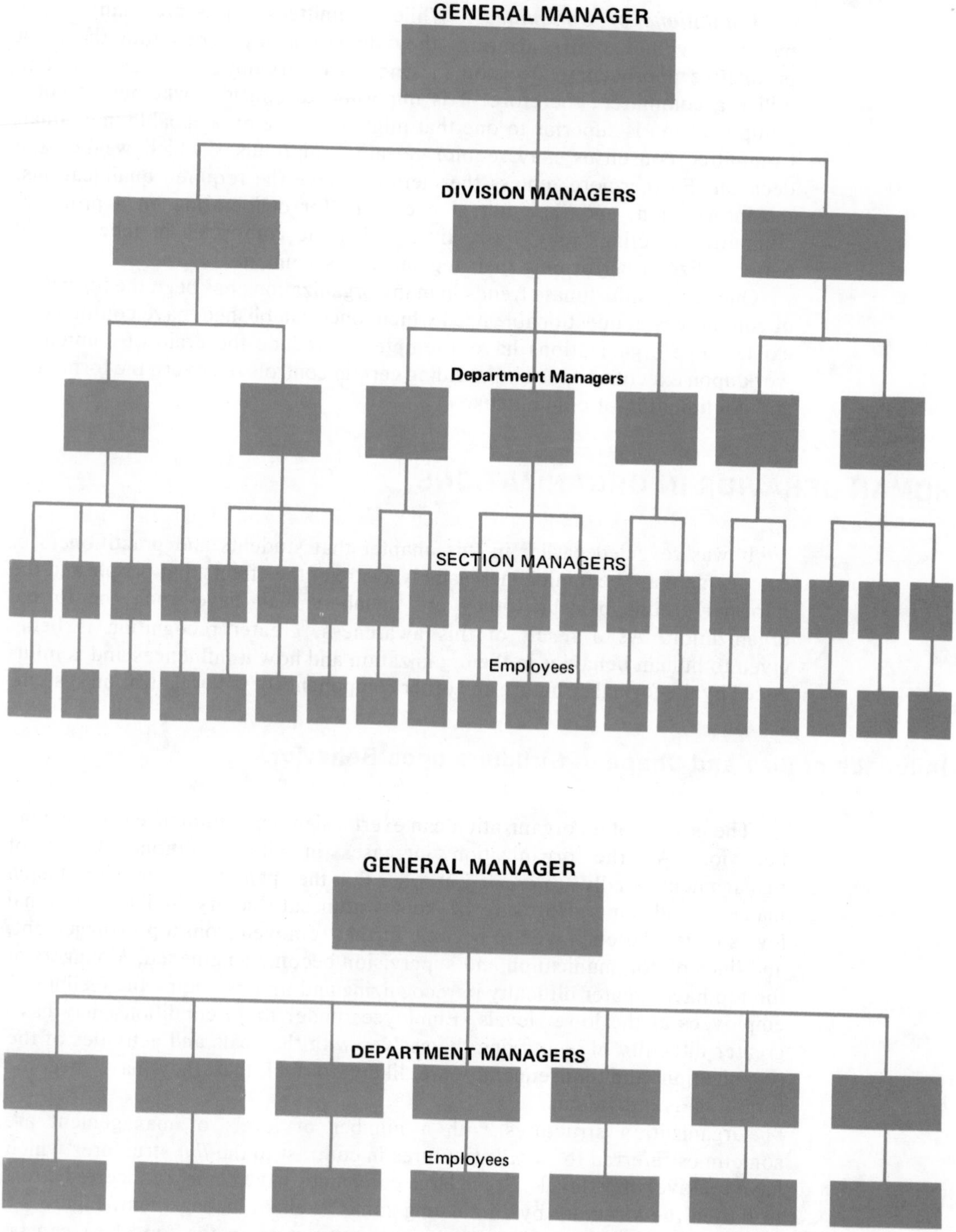

GENERAL MANAGER
DIVISION MANAGERS
Department Managers
SECTION MANAGERS
Employees
GENERAL MANAGER
DEPARTMENT MANAGERS
Employees

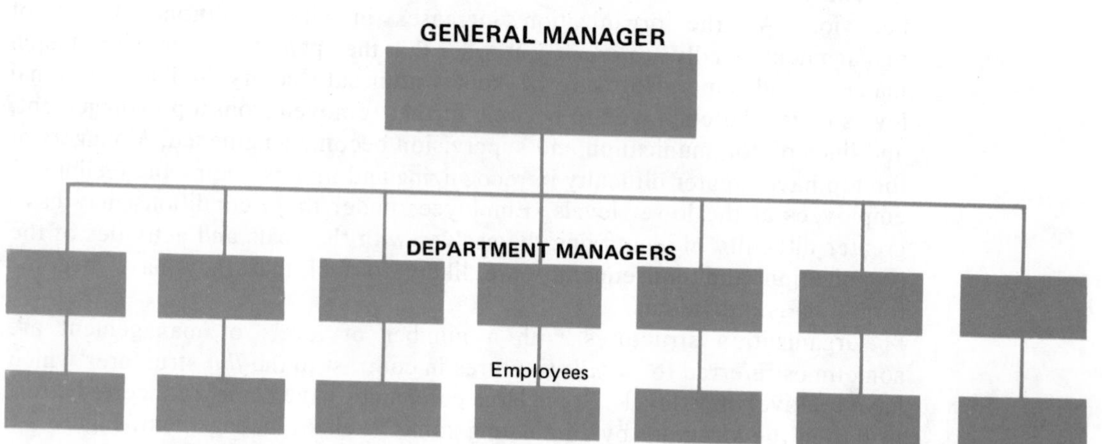

Figure 3-6 "TALL" AND "FLAT" ORGANIZATION STRUCTURES

The elimination of some of the levels of management forces the span of management of each manager to be increased and authority to be decentralized. The authority to make decisions must be delegated downward as far as possible within the organization. Departments and other units within the structure are afforded greater autonomy, with the result that personnel at each level are given greater responsibility as well as opportunity for self-development and for realizing their potential.[17]

Influence of the Informal Organization

Research in the behavioral sciences has done much to make management aware of the important role played by the informal organization. The term *informal organization* was first used by the Mayo Group during the well-known Hawthorne Study at the Western Electric Company. It refers to the network of personal and social relations not established or required by formal authority but arising spontaneously as people associate with one another.[18] The informal organization or group within a company helps to satisfy the needs of employees for social interaction and for group identification. Contacts among individuals are stimulated by commonality of age, social background, education, religion, marital status, or other factors. Common interests, objectives, fears, or opposition to management also can contribute to the formation of informal organizations.

Nature of Its Influence on Its Members. Informal groups tend to develop certain sentiments, values, and folkways to which the members are under pressure to conform if they are to remain in good standing within the group. The informal organization also may develop certain standards of conduct or performance that its members are expected to observe, to either the benefit or detriment of management's expectations. It is not uncommon for informal limits of output or "bogeys" to be adopted by the organization to protect the slower worker and to insure a constant backlog of work which is sufficient to guarantee the continued employment of the members. Attempts of superiors to counteract restrictions and resistances of the informal organizations are likely to be frustrated, for the members usually are more anxious to please the members of their group than their superior; and rejection by the group sometimes can be more unpleasant for members than disciplinary action by a superior.

Providing an Informal Communication System. Aside from the influence that it can exert upon its members, the informal organization can provide a system of *informal communication* that may function much more effectively than the formal one. The informal communication system, or *grapevine,* is

[17] For a study covering this subject, see Lyman W. Porter and Edward E. Lawler, III, "The Effect of 'Tall' versus 'Flat' Organization Structures on Managerial Satisfaction," *Personnel Psychology* (Summer, 1964), pp. 135-148.

[18] Keith Davis, *Human Behavior at Work: Human Relations and Organizational Behavior* (4th ed.; New York: McGraw-Hill Book Company, 1972), p. 83.

strengthened considerably by the failure of formal channels to function properly. If management does not provide its employees with the information and the answers that they seek to obtain, the employees are likely to provide their own answers which may be far from correct.

Developing Potential Leaders. The informal organization also provides an opportunity for persons with potential leadership abilities to make use of their talents. The *informal leader* may serve in the roles of disciplinarian, spokesperson, arbitrator, or counselor for group members. It may be possible for more than one leader to emerge within an informal group, depending on whether group members at the moment are seeking to obstruct management action, are reacting to job boredom, or are soliciting favor and recognition from management.

If utilized properly, management can benefit from the presence of an informal organization and the leadership talent that it helps to develop. The use of informal leaders in some instances can permit management to gauge group reaction or to gain the support of the group for management goals. In other cases, informal leaders can be trained for supervisory positions. These leaders can be utilized to provide instruction and assistance to other employees and to aid in the orientation of new employees to the work situation. However, management must recognize that some individuals may falsely convey the impression that they are group leaders. They may have group support only because they oppose management practices and not because they possess any real leadership qualities.

Coping with the Informal Organization. Regardless of whether they prove to be beneficial or detrimental, informal organizations exist in every organization. It is well for management to attempt to recognize these groups and to develop them into a force that will be beneficial rather than harmful to the formal organization. Since informal group activities can serve to relieve the monotony of certain routine production work by facilitating social interaction and since these groups can help satisfy the need of employees for security and belongingness, management may at times find it desirable to create or strengthen these groups. The strengthening of informal groups may be achieved by modifying formal organizational relationships, by adjusting work procedures or layout, and by staffing the work groups with individuals who have a certain commonality of interest or background. Conversely, when the actions of a work group become detrimental to production goals, it may become desirable to weaken the group by making changes in its membership or by changing the formal relationships or work places of certain members.

The Power Structure

Closely related to the informal organization is the *power structure* within an organization which is determined by the pattern of relationships which reflect the influence or power that some members are able to exert over others within the organization.

Formal and Informal Sources of Power. Since the formal authority that individuals derive from their jobs provides them with an official source of power, the power structure in an organization usually will correspond, in part at least, with the formal structure. The extent of this coincidence, however, will depend upon the informal sources of power that some members may be able to develop to augment their legitimate power. Informal sources may include those that are derived from personal expertise and informal leadership skills that enable individuals to develop the loyalty and the following of others. Informal power may also be derived from holding a position in which it is possible to play organizational politics by being able to dispense certain favors or rewards to other people or to withhold these gratuities from them. Membership on a promotion committee, for example, may enable an individual to help those persons who have rendered favors to him. A job that provides services upon which others depend in order to perform their own jobs efficiently also can be a source of power. A person in a staff position such as that of a purchasing agent, for example, may derive certain power from the fact that he or she can expedite or delay the procurement of items that other members of the organization may urgently require. The "political pull" that an employee may possess by virtue of being a relative, lodge brother, or personal friend and confidant of other persons who are in positions of formal authority can be another source of power.

Other Tactics for Gaining Power. While hard work, perseverance, and other Algerish type qualities are not to be discredited, there are also other bases for gaining advancement and power within an organization that may not always be recognized or admitted readily. In one study conducted by Dale Tarnowieski, for example, 82 percent of the respondents to a survey of nearly 3,000 U.S. businesspeople indicated that "pleasing the boss" is the critical factor in determining "promotability" in today's organization. An even larger proportion (88 percent) indicated that a dynamic personality and the ability to sell oneself and one's ideas are more the attributes to upward mobility than a reputation for honesty or an adherence to principles.[19]

Whether or not one may agree with the majority views expressed in the study, the fact remains that politics and power tactics are a part of life in all organizations—in government and elsewhere as well as in business. Rather than ignore this fact, Auren Uris suggests that the power structure within an organization be analyzed by its members to find out what is going on inside. This analysis might seek to determine "Who are the 'big guns'? Who are the 'little guns'? Who's on top? And who will be on top tomorrow?"[20]

A Graphical Illustration of Informal Patterns of Power. McMurry has constructed a circular or beehive chart shown in Figure 3-7 which illustrates how the power structure and informal patterns of relationships might exist in a

---

[19] Peter Chew, "Backstabbing Inc.: Toadies Flourish, Talent Wilts Amid Office Politics," *The National Observer* (January 26, 1974).

[20] *Ibid.*

company. The location and relationship of the positions shown on this chart of an informal organization differ considerably from those that would appear on a chart representing the conventional organizational structure. This informal organizational chart of a company which reveals the actual power within it indicates that the chief executive of the company really is the secretary-treasurer. (This is because of the large stockholdings of his family.)

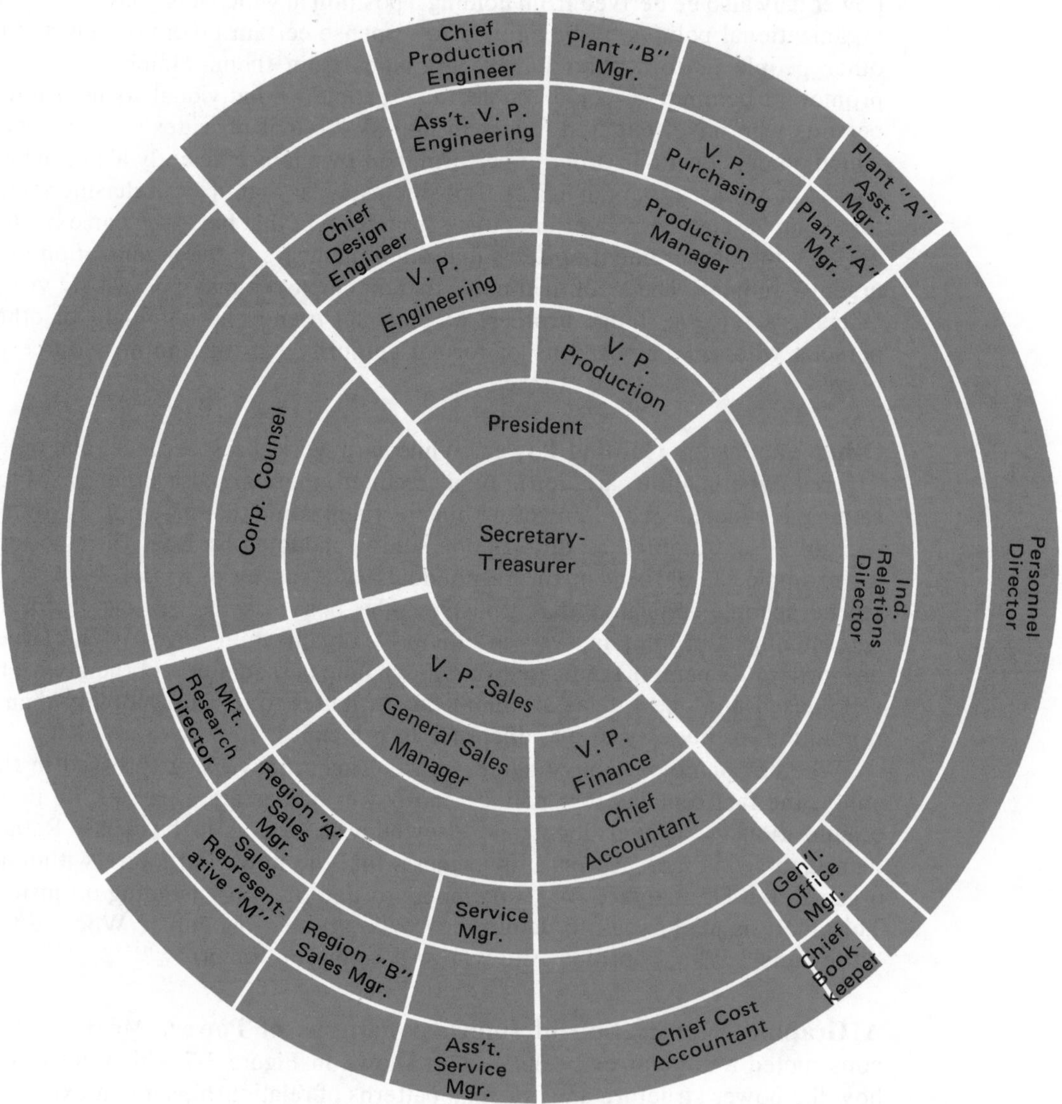

Source: Robert N. McMurry, *McMurry's Management Clinic* (New York: Simon and Schuster, Inc., 1960), p. 13. Reproduced with permission.

Figure 3-7 CIRCULAR INFORMAL ORGANIZATION CHART

The president, while undoubtedly at the top on the chart of the formal organization, actually takes orders from the secretary-treasurer. The vice-presidents, likewise, are not in one ring next to the president but are at varying distances from the center of the chart, representing different degrees of closeness to the chief executive.

Such a chart made on the basis of the informal organization reveals which communication routes are actually functioning. Notice that the vice-president in charge of finance does not communicate directly with the secretary-treasurer but goes through the vice-president in charge of sales. The status of the personnel director in this informal organization is somewhat alarming. His role is apparently nothing more than that of a record keeper since the individual is not in communication with anyone (as revealed by the blank circle between this position and that of the industrial relations director), and is quite remote from the key executives in the hub of the circle.

McMurry recommends that such a chart be prepared in every company in order that interpersonal relationships may be viewed realistically and adjustments made in the formal organization, where desirable, to facilitate communication and the achievement of the organizational objectives.[21]

Bureaucracy in Organizations

Although bureaucracy has been associated more with government organizations, it can also exist in a corporate, church, labor, or any other type of organization. As interpreted originally by Max Weber, bureaucracy was an administrative tool to be used in facilitating the achievement of organizational goals. More recently, however, *bureaucracy* has been studied as an instrument of power and influence that affects the formal and informal structures of an organization.

Characteristics of Bureaucracy. In the management of people, bureaucracy encourages personnel decisions to be made on a rational and consistent basis. It thus seeks to avoid the influence of nepotism, personal judgment, prejudices, and the "cult of personality" or other subjective influences that affect an employee's welfare. According to one author, bureaucracy exhibits the following characteristics:[22]

1. A division of labor based on functional specialization.
2. A well-defined hierarchy of authority.
3. A system of rules covering the rights and duties of employees.
4. A system of procedures for dealing with work situations.
5. Impersonality of interpersonal relations.
6. Promotion and selection based on technical competence.

---

[21] Robert N. McMurry, *McMurry's Management Clinic* (New York: Simon and Schuster, Inc., 1960), pp. 12-14.

[22] Warren G. Bennis, *Changing Organizations* (New York: McGraw-Hill Book Company, 1966), p. 5.

Criticisms of Bureaucracy. From a behavioral standpoint one of the major criticisms of bureaucracy is that it treats employees impersonally on the basis of established policies, procedures, and rules. While it represents an improvement over the inconsistent and arbitrary treatment of earlier eras, bureaucracy is incompatible with a more humanistic approach that many behavioral scientists conceive to be the trend of the future. The decline of bureaucracy therefore has been predicted on the basis of its inability to adapt to rapidly occurring changes within our environment.[23] Since bureaucracy is a very basic and mechanized instrument and well entrenched in most large organizations, any current forecasts of its impending demise may prove to be somewhat premature.

Résumé

One of the major functions of an organization is to provide the structure that is necessary in order for the work within it to be performed and controlled and its objectives achieved efficiently. Recent theories of organization, however, give more recognition to the human aspects of organization and to the influence that the roles and status patterns of people acting individually and in informal work groups can have upon the functioning of an organization. Modern organization theory views the formal structure as being only one of several interacting and interrelated components which comprise the organization system.

The structure, nevertheless, is still an important part of this system. The most common structures into which activities and personnel may be organized are the line and the line-and-staff types of structures. In the line type of organization, the functions that pertain to the management of personnel are performed exclusively by department supervisors. Through the development of a line-and-staff type of structure, it is possible to establish a personnel department to provide these supervisors with assistance in the handling of personnel functions. In order for line-and-staff departments in this type of structure to function as intended, the role of each department with respect to personnel management must be clearly established and understood by the members of the departments.

In addition to the basic structure, various supplemental ones also may be established to pursue specific and often short-term objectives. These supplemental structures, which often are well suited for the solution of complex problems of modern technology, may include project organizations, matrix organizations, and committee organizations.

Recent research in behavioral science has focused attention on the interrelationships between organization and human behavior. The size and shape of the structure and the extent to which authority is centralized are being recognized as having a significant effect upon the individuals within the organization and upon their feelings of conflict, pressure, and frustration. The influence that the informal organization, the power structure, and bureaucracy

[23] *Ibid.*, p. 10.

within an organization can have upon human behavior also has become the subject of growing attention. An awareness of the conditions may help to make organizations of the future, therefore, to be more humanistically oriented and to place more emphasis upon the creation of a favorable organization climate that will enable people to work together in greater harmony and efficiency.

DISCUSSION QUESTIONS

1. How does modern organization theory differ from the classical theory?
2. What are the principal criticisms of the classical theory of organization, and to what extent, if any, do you consider them to be valid?
3. How does the responsibility of a project manager in a matrix organization compare with the authority that is delegated to that individual?
4. To what extent, if any, should the authority for recommending employees for promotions to supervisory levels be delegated to a management committee? If such a committee is established, to what extent should its recommendations be followed?
5. Why do some individuals who have established themselves as the informal leaders of their groups fail to become effective formal leaders when assigned to supervisory positions?
6. What did the majority of the businesspeople responding to the study cited in this chapter on page 71 consider to be the key to advancement within an organization? To what extent do you agree or disagree with their expressed views?
7. What is the basis for the power structure within an organization, and what possible effects may it have upon its operation?
8. To what extent, if any, is bureaucracy beneficial and/or detrimental to good personnel management?

PROBLEM 3-1 CONSOLIDATION JITTERS

The Arbuckle Energy Corporation was the holding company for the Metropolitan and the Suburban utility companies which served adjoining areas in a western state. Although Metropolitan employed approximately 5,000 persons and Suburban only about 1,500, their organization structures were similar with the result that certain functions being performed by each company were duplicated. Consequently, in an effort to reduce costs the management of Arbuckle decided to consolidate the two companies into a single company. For nearly a year, planning for the consolidation proceeded secretly as members of top management with the assistance of outside consultants met to consider various organization structures as well as policies and procedures governing the actual consolidation process. As it became necessary to broaden and implement the planning operation, task forces were established involving additional personnel.

As might be expected, news of the impending consolidation began to leak out and then spread rapidly through the grapevine. Suddenly the only conversation in the cafeterias or the lounges of the two companies was that concerning the reorganization and how various individuals might be affected by it. Since the positions from executive vice-president to manager of the data processing, and so on down the structure, existed in each company, speculation soon turned to the question of which of the position holders in each of the companies would end up on top. Employees began to wonder whether their boss would stay or be replaced by one from the other company. Anxiety began to increase as managers in each company maneuvered to gain power, to impress the superior who might control their destinies, or to undercut the position of a rival. In the task force meetings, for example, hostilities between rivals often came to the surface and not infrequently were directed toward the subordinates of the rivals with whom they were competing for a coveted position. During the planning period employee morale and productivity suffered greatly. Finally, however, the names of those who were to retain their existing positions as well as those who were to be reassigned to other positions were announced. Although there was a reduction in rank and status for many of the management personnel, none, in accordance with company policy communicated well in advance, suffered either a loss of employment or a reduction in pay.

a. What is your reaction to the methods by which the consolidation was accomplished?
b. Would the fact that the companies were utilities rather than, say, aerospace companies, have had any effect upon the reaction of their management personnel to the consolidation?
c. Would it have been better to have made the consolidation gradually over a period of years, a division or function at a time?

SUGGESTED READINGS

Bennis, Warren G. *Changing Organizations*. New York: McGraw-Hill Book Company, 1966.

Chruden, Herbert J., and Arthur W. Sherman, Jr. *Readings in Personnel Management*, 4th ed. Cincinnati: South-Western Publishing Co., 1976. Part 2.

Dale, Ernest. *Management: Theory and Practice*. Third edition. New York: McGraw-Hill Book Company, 1973. Chapters 8-12.

Kelly, Joe. *Organizational Behavior*. Homewood, Illinois: Richard D. Irwin, Inc., and The Dorsey Press, 1969.

Koontz, Harold, and Cyril O'Donnell. *Principles of Management*, 5th ed. New York: McGraw-Hill Book Company, 1972. Chapters 3, 18-20.

Levinson, Harry. *Organizational Diagnosis*. Cambridge, Mass.: Harvard University Press, 1972.

Stewart, Rosemary. *The Reality of Organizations*. Garden City, N.Y.: Doubleday & Company, Inc., 1972.

Tausky, Curt. *Work Organizations*. Itasca, Illinois: F. E. Peacock Publishers, Inc., 1970.

The Program for Personnel Management

By simple definition management involves accomplishing results with and through people in an organization. To accomplish results, however, managers must engage in the processes of management which consist of planning, organizing, staffing, directing, and controlling the activities of these people. Essential for effective planning, which is the most basic of these processes, is the development of programs to govern the performance of these activities within an organization. Management programs might be compared to the navigational charts used by the mariner to determine the course his ship must follow to reach its final destination or objective. Personnel management programs serve as a source of guidance for resolving problems and making decisions pertaining to employee relations within the organization. Such guidance serves to govern personnel actions and decisions involving selection, training, performance evaluation, remuneration, and other personnel functions. By doing so, programs contribute to the productivity of employees and to the consistent and equitable treatment of them.

THE NATURE OF THE MANAGEMENT SYSTEM

Within the past two decades there has developed what is known as the *systems concept* of management. This concept recognizes management to be dynamic in nature and comprised of interacting and interrelated components which were referred to as management processes in the preceding paragraph. Aided by the development of more sophisticated electronic computers and mathematical tools for processing and analyzing the vast amounts of information upon which decisions must be based, the systems concept of management has made it possible to cope more effectively with the growing complexities of decision making.

Processes of the Management System

The processes of planning, organizing, staffing, directing, and controlling constitute the components of the management systems in which all managers from the chief executive down to the first-line supervisor must engage in the performance of their jobs. While managers at the higher levels within an organization normally devote proportionately more time to planning and organizing and their colleagues at the lower levels devote proportionately more time to directing and controlling, every individual who acts in a managerial capacity must perform, at least to some degree, each of these processes of management, often simultaneously. For example, a manager may be planning and organizing various work activities while also directing and controlling them. How effectively any one of these processes is accomplished, therefore, will affect how all the other processes are accomplished.

Planning. Probably the most important management process is planning, which involves forecasting, anticipating, and preparing to meet those conditions that may affect the enterprise and its operations. More important, it is the process of attempting to make those conditions occur that are favorable to the enterprise. Planning involves determining the objectives that are to be achieved and the processes that must be performed to insure their achievement. Essentially it is a process of *decision making*, which consists of determining and evaluating the alternative courses of action that may be taken and of selecting the course that is considered to be the most feasible. Although planning is concerned primarily with the future, it requires the use of data from the past as the basis for projecting future trends and events. The development of computers and more advanced mathematical (or operations research) techniques for studying the many variable forces affecting a decision have made possible significant improvements in forecasting and planning.

Advantages of Effective Personnel Planning. Plans that are formulated carefully and understood fully can serve as a foundation for organizing and coordinating the activities of employees and for clarifying their interpersonal relationships. Such plans also can make employees more aware of what to expect from management and what management expects of them. Plans thus help to provide employees with a basis for engaging in a greater degree of self-direction by setting forth certain standards or criteria against which they can measure the results of their endeavors.

Effective planning also contributes to the development of a more favorable human relations climate. As the result of careful personnel planning, employees are more likely to be placed in those jobs where they can render the greatest contributions and gain the most satisfaction from their work. Effective planning makes possible the more orderly flow, distribution, and assignment of work and thus results in more efficient performance by employees and in the achievement of greater work satisfaction by them. It also enables many personnel problems that might otherwise develop into major grievances or disciplinary issues to be avoided, or at least minimized.

Personnel Planning in the Future. Personnel planning probably will become even more important in the years that lie ahead. Continuing advancement in science and technology, coupled with the increased use of automation and data processing, will cause continual change in the number and qualifications of personnel required within an enterprise. By using forecasting techniques these changes can be anticipated and planned for so that a minimum of adjustment of physical and human resources will be required. Planning for such changes may cover the training or retraining of employees and their placement in jobs where their services can be utilized.

Organizing. Since the organizing process was covered and defined in the preceding chapter, it will be discussed only briefly at this point. Organizing entails the building of a structure within which the functions to be performed may be divided and assigned to the appropriate departments, divisions, jobs, and positions. Organizing also involves defining the duties, authority, responsibilities, and relationships of each of the units. The effectiveness with which the work can be organized and assigned to the individuals who are the most qualified, as noted earlier, will help to determine the efficiency with which they are able to do their work and the satisfaction they derive from it.

Staffing. The procurement and development of the human resources to perform each job within the organization is the role of the staffing process. This process is interrelated closely with planning because personnel needs must be anticipated sufficiently in advance to enable qualified individuals to be available for job openings as they occur. While every manager is involved with staffing, it is the personnel department's responsibility to coordinate staffing policies and the various personnel activities associated with the staffing process. These latter activities include employee recruitment, selection, personnel development and evaluation, as well as those activities pertaining to job assignment changes and terminations. Usually, however, members of the personnel department do not make the final staffing decisions since this is a responsibility of managers in the departments affected by these decisions.

Directing. The process of directing consists of overseeing and supervising the activities and personnel within the enterprise. It provides the guidance for translating organizational plans into action and for insuring that established organizational relationships are observed. Directing includes training, motivating, counseling, and disciplining employees for the purpose of gaining their maximum contributions.

The direction of personnel can be facilitated if their duties, responsibilities, and organizational relationships have been properly planned, organized, and communicated to them. Since contemporary theory holds that most employees want to do a good job if conditions will permit them to do so, it follows that such individuals should be given as much freedom as possible to engage in self-direction. By affording them a greater opportunity for independence and self-direction, managers can contribute to the motivation of their subordinates. However, the degree of freedom a manager is able to provide subordinates will, in a large measure, be determined by how well their work has been planned and organized and by the controls that have been developed to insure that their assigned responsibilities are carried out effectively.

Controlling. Controlling is the process of reviewing and measuring performance in order to insure that organizational plans and objectives are achieved. Controls provide managers with a basis for detecting and correcting deviations from these plans, for correcting errors in the plans, and for improving the plans. Within an enterprise controls provide a source of valuable information to aid managers in making decisions and to provide a means for evaluating performance and delegating authority. Controls in the form of performance standards are especially helpful in making individuals more aware of the results of their performance and in providing them with a source of motivation for improvement.

Interrelationship with Other Systems

Since the management system is interrelated with the organizational system, the success with which the latter system is able to achieve its objectives is dependent in no small measure upon the effectiveness of the management system; conversely, the management system requires an effective organization system.

Information System. A closely interrelated component of the management and organization systems, as can be seen from Figure 4-1, is the information system that functions as the nervous system of the organization. The *information system* has been defined as:

> . . . a network of component parts developed to provide a flow of information to decision makers. It is composed of procedures, equipment, information methods to compile and evaluate information, the people who use the information, and information management.[1]

This system provides the information required for planning, for translating plans into actions, and for providing the feedback necessary for control.[2] Such control is particularly essential as a means of detecting how well plans are being achieved, what improvements may be required in their administration, or what future changes may be required in the plans themselves to accommodate internal and external changes affecting the organization.

---

[1] Joel E. Ross, *Management by Information System* (Englewood Cliffs, New Jersey: Prentice-Hall, Inc., 1970), p. 106.

[2] *Ibid.*, pp. 100-102.

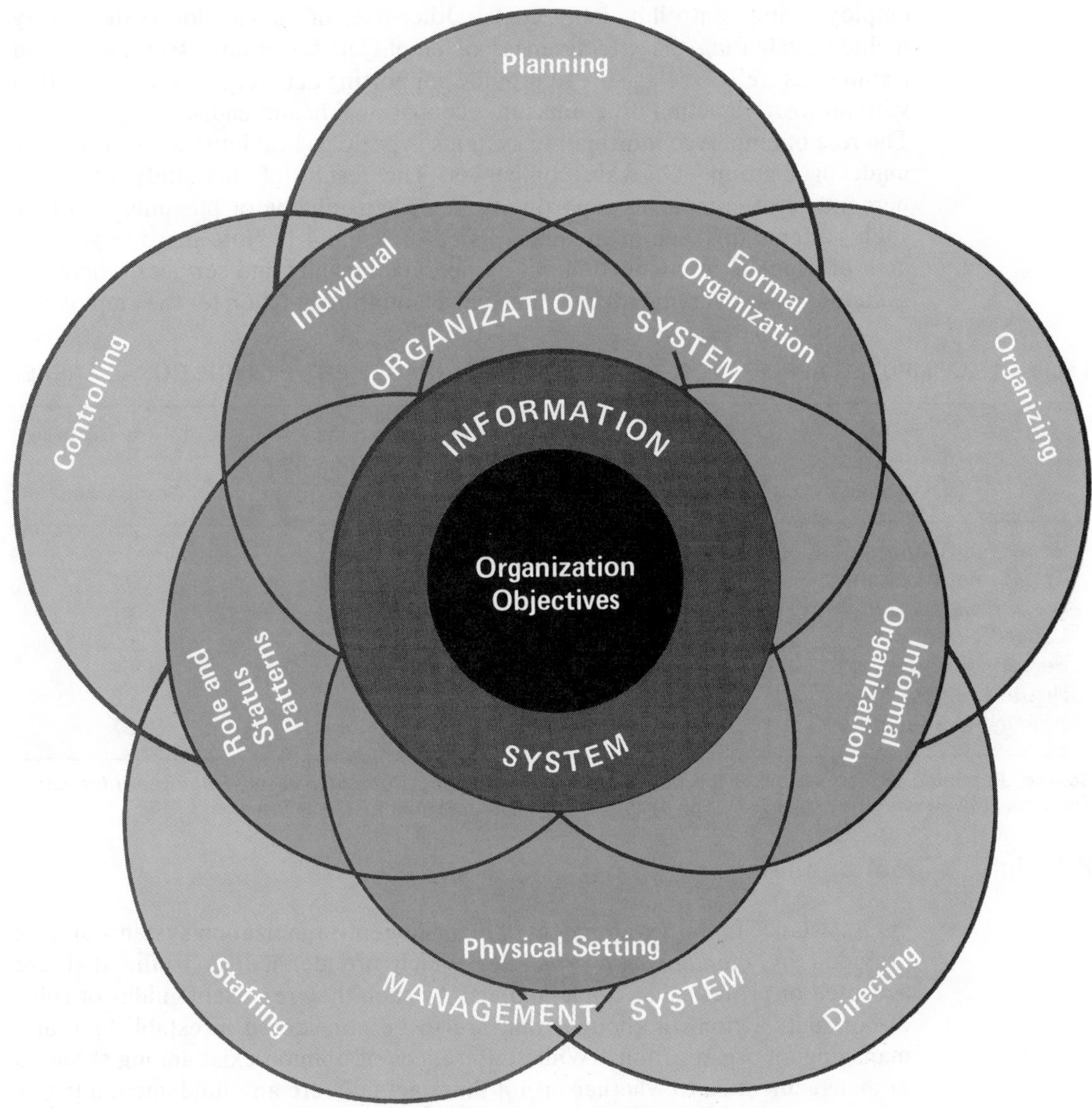

Figure 4-1 THE MANAGEMENT-ORGANIZATION-INFORMATION SYSTEM

Uses of Information Systems. Management information systems have been aided by computers that permit the storage and the rapid retrieval and analysis of data for decision-making purposes. In the management of personnel, employee information systems are essential for making personnel decisions and taking required actions. These systems, for example, can provide data upon which staffing decisions may be based. In the area of remuneration, these data can be invaluable both in terms of providing equitable treatment for each employee and controlling labor costs. Other uses of information systems may include evaluating the effectiveness of employee selection, assessment, and training, as well as being able to provide supporting data required in connection with affirmative action programs and occupational health and safety programs. The role of employee information systems is perhaps best illustrated by a study made of a group of private companies. The results of this study show the percentage of companies reporting to be either utilizing or planning to utilize such systems for each of the areas listed in Table 4-1. Note that the greatest area of usage is in connection with employee benefits and services where the systems serve a very important financial accounting function for the employer.

Table 4-1 COMPUTER APPLICATION TO PERSONNEL MANAGEMENT BY FUNCTIONAL AREAS

Area of Application	No. of Companies with or Planning Computer Applications	Total Percentage of Companies
Employee Services	307	75
Employment & Staffing	296	73
Wage & Salary Administration	274	67
Labor Relations	271	66
Personnel Research	222	54
Health & Safety	189	46
Training & Education	150	37

Source: Reprinted by permission of the publisher from *Developing Computer-Based Employee Information Systems,* AMA Research Study #99 © 1969 by the American Management Association, Inc., p. 13.

Principles of Management

Assistance in the development of management-organization systems may be provided by *management principles* which are defined as truths that are accepted or professed as fundamentals. As such they represent guides or rules of conduct, action, or thought that are to be considered in establishing and managing an organization.[3] While differences of opinion exist among students of management as to whether or not there actually are any fundamental truths or principles that have universal application in management, there are certain guidelines that, if applied in appropriate situations, can contribute to more effective organization and management. Even though they may not be regarded as principles by some students of management, the following are at least worthy of consideration.

Principle of Division of Work. The primary purpose for organizing work is to divide it into units that can be performed more effectively by those to whom it is assigned. The division of work, therefore, should be accomplished in such a

[3] M. Valliant Higginson, *Management Policies 1, Their Development as Corporate Guides,* AMA Research Study 76 (New York: American Management Association, 1966), p. 16.

way as to facilitate its performance and the achievement of the objectives of the enterprise.

Principle of Responsibility. Individuals cannot escape the responsibilities that have been assigned to them merely by passing these on to subordinates. It remains their obligation to see that subordinates observe their responsibilities.

Principle of Parity of Authority and Responsibility. The authority that is delegated to an individual should be equal to that person's responsibility and not more or less than it.

Principle of Unity of Objective. According to this principle, the objectives of each department and other units within the organizational structure should be integrated with and contribute to the achievement of the objectives for the organization as a whole.

Principle of Organizational Balance. This principle requires that the relative size and budget of each department be consistent with the contributions to the organization that is desired from the department.

Principle of Span of Management. There are limits to the number of people that can be directly supervised by a manager. It usually is possible for the span of management (or span of control as it also is called) to be greater for managers at the lower organizational levels than for those at the upper levels. Span of management, thus, cannot be translated into any "magic" numbers but, rather, is contingent upon such factors as the nature of the activities being supervised, the number and frequency of the supervisor's contacts with others, the training and capacity of the supervisor and subordinates, and the extent to which the supervisor is able to delegate authority.

Principle of Delegation. Managers can increase their span of management by delegating more of their authority to subordinates. While the delegation of authority is essential to the growth of an organization and the capacities of its members, it cannot be accomplished merely by recognizing the need for it. Effective delegation requires that managers plan and organize their work to determine what decisions to delegate. It also requires the training of subordinates to assume authority and the establishment of controls to insure that the delegated authority is being exercised properly by subordinates.

Principle of Unity of Command. The exercise of authority requires that subordinates report directly to only one boss. An unbroken line of authority should exist through the intermediate levels of management from the chief executive to the operative employees. Directions and other communications should be transmitted to subordinates and control exercised over them through these channels.

Principles of Flexibility and Stability. Changes that take place within an organization should be planned and directed toward the achievement of established objectives and should not be influenced unduly by short-term conditions. An organization should be capable of coping with such problems as those resulting from sharp changes in business activity or the loss of personnel.

The principle of stability can be implemented by developing versatile qualifications among subordinates, by decentralizing authority, and by effecting long-range planning and variable budgets that permit changing conditions to be met with a minimum of adjustment by the organization.

THE NATURE OF THE PERSONNEL PROGRAM

An important outcome of planning is the development of programs governing the performance of the various activities in which the organization is to be engaged. These programs constitute the overall plans that define formally the objectives, policies, procedures, and budgets governing the performance of the various functions to which they apply. Personnel programs in turn provide guidance for the various decisions and actions that are taken in the management of personnel. Within the personnel program more specific programs must be developed covering those functions that the personnel management serves to coordinate and control. For example, if the organization is of sufficient size, these programs may cover such functions as recruitment, selection, training, wage and salary administration, and fringe benefits.

Objectives

Objectives represent the results or goals toward which the efforts of the organization are directed. They are established as the first step of the planning process and apply to some period of time in the future. Long-term objectives are required to be rather broad with the result that they may need to be translated into more specific terms for shorter periods if they are to be of realistic value. Objectives for shorter periods usually are expressed in quantitative terms such as dollars or other numerical measures.

Social Objectives of an Organization. Regardless of whether or not an organization exists to earn a profit, its objectives should be concerned with serving the public welfare. One of the nation's outstanding business leaders once expressed this concept very effectively as follows:

> The primary goal of any industry to be successful continuously must be to make a better and better product to be sold to more and more people at a lower and lower price. Profit, therefore, will and must be a by-product of services only.[4]

While the statement by Johnson and Johnson in Figure 4-2 is more a credo than an objective, it also reflects the concern that even profit-making organizations must have for the welfare of society. These social objectives may include

[4] James F. Lincoln, *Incentive Management* (Cleveland, Ohio: The Lincoln Electric Company, 1951), p. 14.

Our Credo

WE BELIEVE THAT OUR FIRST RESPONSIBILITY IS TO THE DOCTORS, NURSES, HOSPITALS,
MOTHERS, AND ALL OTHERS WHO USE OUR PRODUCTS.
OUR PRODUCTS MUST ALWAYS BE OF THE HIGHEST QUALITY.
WE MUST CONSTANTLY STRIVE TO REDUCE THE COST OF THESE PRODUCTS.
OUR ORDERS MUST BE PROMPTLY AND ACCURATELY FILLED.
OUR DEALERS MUST MAKE A FAIR PROFIT.

OUR SECOND RESPONSIBILITY IS TO THOSE WHO WORK WITH US—
THE MEN AND WOMEN IN OUR PLANTS AND OFFICES.
THEY MUST HAVE A SENSE OF SECURITY IN THEIR JOBS.
WAGES MUST BE FAIR AND ADEQUATE,
MANAGEMENT JUST, HOURS REASONABLE, AND WORKING CONDITIONS CLEAN AND ORDERLY.
EMPLOYEES SHOULD HAVE AN ORGANIZED SYSTEM FOR SUGGESTIONS AND COMPLAINTS.
SUPERVISORS AND DEPARTMENT HEADS MUST BE QUALIFIED AND FAIR MINDED.
THERE MUST BE OPPORTUNITY FOR ADVANCEMENT — FOR THOSE QUALIFIED
AND EACH PERSON MUST BE CONSIDERED AN INDIVIDUAL
STANDING ON HIS OWN DIGNITY AND MERIT

OUR THIRD RESPONSIBILITY IS TO OUR MANAGEMENT.
OUR EXECUTIVES MUST BE PERSONS OF TALENT, EDUCATION, EXPERIENCE AND ABILITY.
THEY MUST BE PERSONS OF COMMON SENSE AND FULL UNDERSTANDING.

OUR FOURTH RESPONSIBILITY IS TO THE COMMUNITIES IN WHICH WE LIVE.
WE MUST BE A GOOD CITIZEN — SUPPORT GOOD WORKS AND CHARITY,
AND BEAR OUR FAIR SHARE OF TAXES.
WE MUST MAINTAIN IN GOOD ORDER THE PROPERTY WE ARE PRIVILEGED TO USE.
WE MUST PARTICIPATE IN PROMOTION OF CIVIC IMPROVEMENT,
HEALTH, EDUCATION AND GOOD GOVERNMENT,
AND ACQUAINT THE COMMUNITY WITH OUR ACTIVITIES.

OUR FIFTH AND LAST RESPONSIBILITY IS TO OUR STOCKHOLDERS.
BUSINESS MUST MAKE A SOUND PROFIT.
RESERVES MUST BE CREATED, RESEARCH MUST BE CARRIED ON,
ADVENTUROUS PROGRAMS DEVELOPED, AND MISTAKES PAID FOR.
ADVERSE TIMES MUST BE PROVIDED FOR, ADEQUATE TAXES PAID, NEW MACHINES PURCHASED,
NEW PLANTS BUILT, NEW PRODUCTS LAUNCHED, AND NEW SALES PLANS DEVELOPED.
WE MUST EXPERIMENT WITH NEW IDEAS.
WHEN THESE THINGS HAVE BEEN DONE THE STOCKHOLDER SHOULD RECEIVE A FAIR RETURN.
WE ARE DETERMINED WITH THE HELP OF GOD'S GRACE,
TO FULFILL THESE OBLIGATIONS TO THE BEST OF OUR ABILITY.

Johnson & Johnson

Reproduced by permission of Johnson & Johnson.

Figure 4-2

paying wages that support adequate living standards, providing a safe and healthy work environment, producing useful goods or services, observing ethical business practices, contributing to the environment and welfare of the community, and other objectives of a similar nature. It must be recognized, however, that every private enterprise must earn a profit over the long run if it is to continue to operate and provide a source of employment for its personnel—which is a major social objective.

Objectives of Specific Personnel Functions. The statement of objectives for the personnel program as a whole generally is augmented by more detailed statements covering the objectives of specific personnel functions. The objectives of the safety program, for example, may be directed toward reducing the number of accidents during a future period. The objective of the suggestion program may be to increase the number of suggestions being submitted and/or the savings being derived from them. A specific reduction in the employee turnover or in absenteeism or an improvement in employee attitudes as expressed in opinion surveys, furthermore, may constitute the objectives for employee selection, training, or supervisory development programs. Improvements in the number and the qualifications of individuals applying for work would be a logical objective of employee recruitment and selection programs. These and other personnel objectives thus serve to guide and to coordinate the activities of the various divisions comprising the personnel department.

Policies

Closely related to an organization's objectives are its policies which serve to guide the actions that are required to achieve these objectives. Policies thus provide the means for carrying out the management processes and as such are an aid to decision making. Like objectives, they may be idealistic or realistic; general or specific; flexible or inflexible; qualitative or quantitative; broad or narrow in scope.[5] However, while objectives determine *what* is to be done, policies explain *how* it is to be done. They also differ from objectives in that they are effective when formulated and exist until they are revised or terminated. Objectives on the other hand are achievable at some period in the future rather than at the time when they are formulated.[6]

Need for Policies. Carefully developed policies are vital to the management of personnel because each person is sensitive to any differences in the treatment, no matter how slight, that he or she may receive as compared with other persons. One thing that will impair employee efficiency and morale most quickly is for the boss to display favoritism when making decisions, such as those relating to promotions, vacations, schedules, wage increases, assignment of overtime, or infractions of rules. A statement of personnel policy, such as the one contained in Figure 4-3, can serve to reassure employees that they

[5] Higginson, *op. cit.*, pp. 21-22.
[6] *Ibid.*

Personnel Administration Policies

OF THE CHASE MANHATTAN BANK, N. A.

The personnel policies of The Chase Manhattan Bank are based upon the belief that the success of the Bank and its usefulness to the Country are primarily dependent on its personnel and that the development of the greatest potential for each employee is not only good for the employee, but of maximum advantage to the Bank.

It is the policy of The Chase Manhattan Bank, therefore, to give its employees training and opportunity so that they can have the satisfactions and happiness that come from good surroundings, good rewards and the consciousness of work well done.

TO ACHIEVE THESE ENDS IT IS THE POLICY OF THE BANK:

To employ individuals solely on the basis of qualifications.

To recognize each person as an individual throughout his or her entire period of association with the Bank.

To implement continually positive affirmative action that will ensure that equal opportunity is afforded to all qualified staff members and to applicants for employment regardless of race, creed, color, national origin, sex, age, or physical handicap.

To review periodically the performance of all members of the staff and to keep them informed concerning their status; to provide continuous guidance to help staff members to progress.

To promote from within on a bank-wide basis individuals qualified to fill vacancies in more advanced positions.

To maintain salary scales which compare favorably with those paid for similar work by the better-paying companies in our employment markets; to administer individual salaries in a manner which recognizes the relative importance of each position and rewards meritorious performance.

To maintain a generous and comprehensive benefits program having in mind that financial security and personal welfare are of great value to members of the staff, their dependents, and to the Bank.

To provide an attractive and efficient environment by maintaining good physical working conditions and by fostering harmonious relations among staff members.

To regard planned training, education, and staff development activities as an investment for the mutual benefit of individuals and the Bank.

To communicate freely to all members of the staff and to encourage communication from them and among them.

To encourage members of the staff to participate in activities relating to national defense, civic affairs, and community welfare projects.

To be guided by the Golden Rule in all dealings with the staff.

Source: The Chase Manhattan Bank. Reproduced with permission.

Figure 4-3 EXAMPLE OF A PERSONNEL POLICY STATEMENT

will be treated fairly and objectively and enable them to know what to expect of their employer. Decisions can be made more rapidly and more consistently if policies relating to these subjects have been formulated. Personnel policies permit employees to enjoy a greater sense of security by enabling them to know what treatment to expect. Managers and supervisors also can act with a greater degree of confidence in resolving problems since they have a more objective basis upon which to make and to defend their decisions.

Policy Formulation. Since personnel policies affect the entire organization, it is essential that these policies receive the approval and support of top management. Top management, however, should rely heavily upon the experience of its managers and supervisors and upon the professional competency of its personnel staff to help formulate and enforce those policies that it may approve. In the formulation of personnel policies, the personnel manager and the staff have the responsibility for exercising leadership to insure that these policies are desirable in terms of current research and practice. They also ascertain that such policies are compatible with current economic conditions, collective bargaining trends, and federal, state, and local laws.

The personnel department's training and communication programs can be used to familiarize managers, supervisors, and operative personnel with the personnel policies and thereby aid in achieving a uniform understanding and interpretation of these policies. As a result of such efforts, managers and supervisors are more likely to view policies as a source of help rather than as an infringement upon their freedom of action. Cooperation in the administration of personnel policies can be enhanced considerably if the personnel staff is able and willing at all times to assist supervisors and managers with the interpretation and enforcement of personnel policies.

Policy Statements. In order that they may be made more authoritative, it is desirable that policies be formalized into written statements. Such statements permit policies to be communicated more rapidly and accurately to each individual within the organization. Written policies also can serve as invaluable aids in orienting and training new personnel, in administering disciplinary action, and in resolving grievance issues with individuals and with unions. When distributed to employees, these statements can provide answers to many questions that might otherwise have to be referred to supervisors. The statements also should provide the reasons for the policy's existence as a means of contributing to its effectiveness.

Administration of Policies. Since policies should aid rather than hinder decision making, they must not be permitted to impair freedom of action or to discourage the use of initiative by managers in searching for better courses of action. Furthermore, policies must never serve as an excuse for not taking action or for not approving a request; rather, they should serve as a guide for determining how to grant a request and how to satisfy employee desires. Personnel policies, like the objectives that they should help to achieve, must be dynamic in nature and change in accordance with the conditions affecting them.

It was once the policy of most airlines, for example, to employ only registered nurses as flight attendants in order to provide maximum care for passengers. As a shortage of nurses developed, this selection policy had to be changed in order to maintain a sufficient supply of flight attendants.

Coordinating Various Policies of the Organization. Personnel policies must be integrated closely with policies relating to other functional areas. The policy of providing stabilized employment, for example, could not be accomplished without considering policies pertaining to sales, production, and inventory control. A policy of expanding manufacturing operations into foreign countries, on the other hand, might necessitate the review and change of certain personnel policies, such as those relating to employee selection, training, transfer, and remuneration.

Allowing for Some Flexibility. Fair and consistent treatment of employees does not mean that they must receive identical treatment. Some degree of flexibility in administering policy must be permitted in order to allow for the particular conditions or circumstances surrounding the problem that is the subject of decision. An employee who previously had established a good work record and had demonstrated a cooperative attitude, for example, probably would not be disciplined as severely for violating a work rule as would another employee with a poor personnel record. Policies, therefore, should merely provide the tolerance limits within which some range of discretion can be permitted. A certain degree of flexibility in the administration of disciplinary action, for example, need not be inconsistent with the fair treatment of employees provided that they understand the basis upon which variations are made and to be expected.

Procedures

Procedures serve to implement policies by indicating the chronological sequence of steps to be followed in carrying out the policies. Procedures relating to employee selection, for example, might provide that individuals first be required to complete an application blank and be interviewed by a personnel office representative after which they would complete other prescribed steps. Grievances, promotions, transfers, or wage adjustments likewise must be administered according to established procedures in order to prevent oversights from occurring that might be detrimental to the best interests of either the employee or the organization. As an example, the failure to give written warning of a violation to the employee, as a step in the disciplinary procedure, might prevent the organization from discharging the employee for a second violation since no formal record of the first violation exists.

In spite of their importance to the program, personnel procedures like policies must be treated as means to an end and not as ends in themselves or as excuses for failure to take needed action. It is not uncommon in many organizations to hear complaints about excessive "red tape," inflexibility, and impersonality in making personnel decisions, all of which are characteristics of a bureaucracy. Unfortunately, when procedures become too detailed or numerous, they may impair rather than contribute to the interests of the organization and its employees. In order that this hazard may be avoided, procedures need to be reviewed periodically and modified to meet changes in the conditions that may affect them.[7]

Budgets

Statements relating to objectives, policies, procedures, or to a program as a whole can be meaningful only if they are supported financially through the budget. A *budget* constitutes both a financial plan as well as a control for the expenditure of funds necessary to support the program. As such, it provides one of the best indicators of management's real attitude toward the program.

Thus, while an organization's selection policy may be to hire only fully qualified applicants to fill vacancies, its ability to observe this policy will be contingent upon the expenditure of sufficient funds to permit applicants to be screened carefully. Similarly, a policy of paying a "fair wage" can be realized only if the organization is willing to establish a sound wage structure and provide in the budget funds that are necessary to support it. In order to gain adequate funds for the personnel budget, however, the personnel staff must be able to convince top management, as well as managers of other departments who are competing for a share of available funds, that the personnel program is producing results.

DEVELOPING AND ADMINISTERING THE PERSONNEL PROGRAM

It is essential for any program to be tailored to the specific needs and objectives of the particular organization that it is to serve. Thus, a personnel program that serves the needs of one organization most effectively might not do so for some other one. The functions being performed by the organization, its size, geographic location, the number and qualifications of its employees and whether or not they are unionized, as well as the various economic, political, and legal constraints that are placed upon its operation are among the factors that will determine the needs of its program.

Gaining Support for the Personnel Program

The cooperation of department managers and supervisors is essential to the success of the personnel program since it is they who must interpret and follow the policies and procedures of the program and make them work. They are the individuals who are directly responsible for translating the program into action.

---

[7] See *Personnel Procedure Manuals,* Studies in Personnel Policy, No. 180 (New York: National Industrial Conference Board, 1961). Also consult the labor services of the Bureau of National Affairs, Prentice-Hall, Inc., and the Commerce Clearing House for sample statements of personnel policy and procedure and their interpretation.

Top Management's Support. Support for the personnel program by top management is particularly essential to its success. Since individuals at the higher levels of management are interested in reducing costs and increasing efficiency, their support for the program may be contingent upon the contributions that they feel the program may offer in this regard. If the personnel staff are able to provide tangible evidence of the personnel program's contributions, their task of gaining top management's support will be made much easier.

Support by Middle- and Lower-Level Management. In order for the middle and lower levels of management to support the program, they must be convinced that the personnel program is helping them to manage their personnel more effectively and to achieve higher productivity from them. Educational and communication efforts by the personnel department which can help to make managers more aware of benefits and assistance that the program offers them will contribute to the enlistment of their suport. Staff specialists, through the help they are able to provide, must also be able to demonstrate the professional competency necessary to gain the respect of these managers. Support for the personnel program, or any other program for that matter, also will be encouraged if those who are subject to its provisions are given the opportunity to participate in its development, to voice their complaints, and to suggest ways for improving it.

Organization and Status of the Personnel Department

The structure of an organization and the nature of the personnel program that it is to serve are important factors in determining the structure of the personnel department. Figure 4-4 illustrates some of the divisions into which a personnel department may be organized and the functions that each division normally would perform.[8]

Management's Influence. The importance management attaches to the personnel program will help to determine the department's organization and the status accorded to it. One study of personnel departments, for example, revealed that in 26 percent of the larger companies the head of the department had the title of vice-president.[9] This percentage represented a slight increase over that reported in a survey six years earlier.[10]

In another study, however, it was found that the influence of the personnel executive in some companies tended to decrease as the importance of personnel relations increased.[11] In these companies it would appear that top

[8] See Bureau of National Affairs, Inc., *The Personnel Department,* Personnel Policies Forum Survey No. 73, 1964.

[9] Bureau of National Affairs, Inc., *The Personnel Department,* Personnel Policies Forum Survey No. 92, 1970.

[10] Personnel Policies Forum Survey No. 73, *loc. cit.,* p. 4.

[11] Dalton E. McFarland, *Cooperation and Conflict in Personnel Administration* (New York: American Foundation for Management Research, 1962), p. 11.

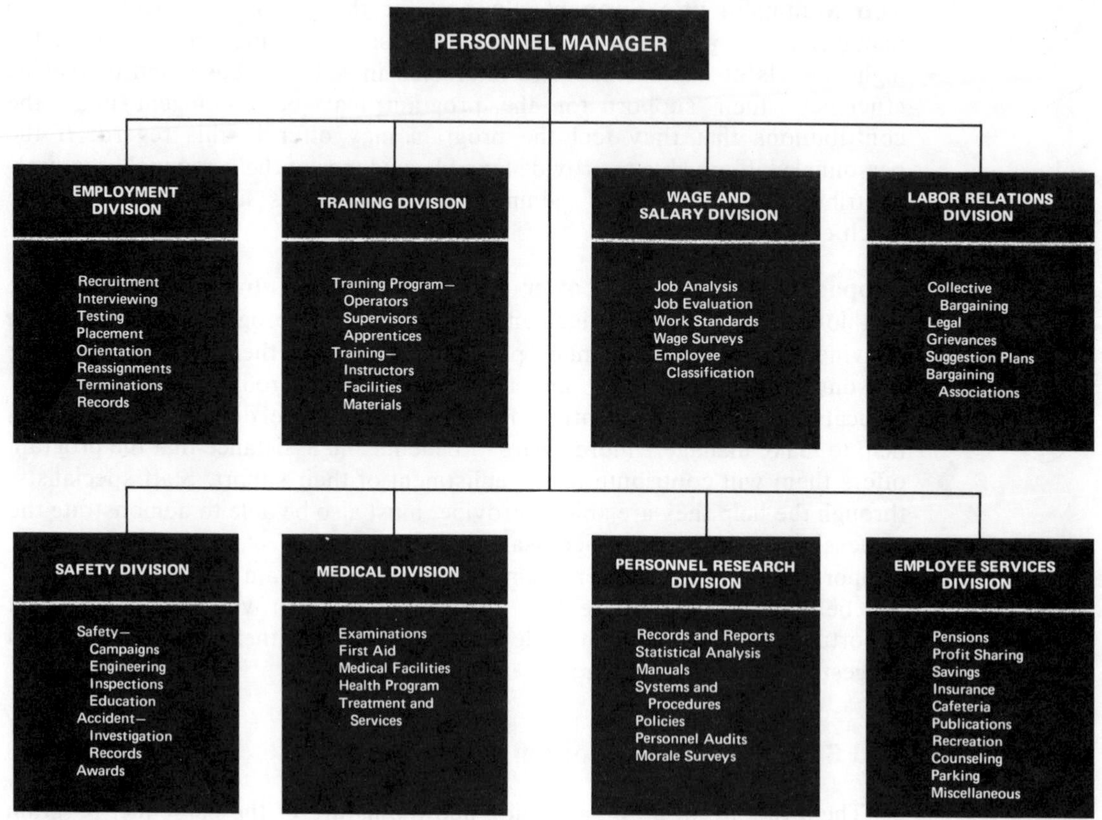

Figure 4-4 PERSONNEL DEPARTMENT ORGANIZATION

management has been prone to become involved directly in the performance of certain personnel functions, particularly collective bargaining.

Increasing Employment of Personnel Workers. The increasing number of individuals who are being employed in personnel work also is evidence of the growing role and status of personnel management in organizations. For example, in 1972 approximately 235,000 persons, three fourths of whom were men, were employed as personnel workers. This number represents an increase of 25,000 persons or nearly 11 percent over the number of personnel workers reported to have been employed in 1968.[12] More than half of these persons are employed by private companies; most of the remaining ones are employed by federal, state, and local governments. There is also a small group of personnel workers who are self-employed as management consultants and as employee and labor relations specialists.

[12] U.S. Department of Labor, Bureau of Labor Statistics, *Occupational Outlook Handbook,* 1974-1975 edition, Bulletin 1785 (Washington, D.C.: U.S. Government Printing Office, 1974), p. 146, and 1970-1971 edition, Bulletin 1650, 1970, p. 36.

Growing Importance of Personnel Functions. The growth in importance of personnel management can be attributed to the increased involvement of this function in planning and decision making relating to the human resources of the organization. To a considerable degree this involvement is due to the data banks developed by personnel departments that provide personnel managers with a source of information for organization planning and decisions affecting all facets of the organization. In the future the personnel department is likely to become more involved with organizational planning and analysis rather than confining its activities exclusively to the traditional personnel function.[13] Furthermore, there appears to be a growing recognition of the increased need for professional attitudes and strong personalities within the personnel department in order for the department to perform the vital role that it should within an organization. As one personnel executive expressed it, "We should shed the old 'office manager' cloak and assume the proper position of being key staff members."[14]

Maintaining the Personnel Program

A personnel program must be reviewed periodically to determine if its objectives are being satisfactorily realized and if each of the existing personnel policies or procedures is still required. Reviewing the program regularly may also help to reveal whether or not any of its functions is receiving too much emphasis, is being neglected, or is not contributing adequately to the program. An examination of the training programs, for example, might disclose that the training function is being neglected by some departments. Similarly, a study of the results being achieved from psychological tests might indicate that changes in the selection program should be made.

Making Necessary Changes. A dynamic program should permit changes to be made in the objectives, policies, procedures, and budgets of the program whenever they are necessitated by changing conditions. A shortage of engineers, for example, forced some companies in the past to modify their selection policies by hiring technicians without college degrees for certain duties that engineering graduates were once hired to perform. In other instances, the automation of production processes has made it necessary for some companies to provide more retraining activities and to modify their retirement policies to permit an earlier retirement of those workers displaced by machines.

Preserving a Balance. In maintaining the program it is important for management to recognize the need for preserving a balance within the program. There is often a temptation for management to become overly occupied with certain problem areas of personnel management to the neglect of other areas.

---

[13] See Charles J. Coleman, "Personnel: The Changing Function," *Public Personnel Management,* Vol. 2, No. 3 (May-June, 1973), pp. 186-193, as reprinted in Herbert J. Chruden and Arthur W. Sherman, Jr., *Readings in Personnel Management* (4th ed.; South-Western Publishing Co., 1976), pp. 34-46.

[14] Personnel Policies Forum Survey No. 92, *op. cit.,* p. 15.

The excessive time consumed in handling grievance, disciplinary, and labor relations problems, for example, could otherwise be devoted to such other functions as training or communication. Certain areas of a personnel program, furthermore, may receive disproportionate attention because of the interest and publicity that has been given to these areas by the professional literature or at professional meetings.

Establishing Suitable Controls. If the personnel program is to be maintained in accordance with the aims mentioned in the preceding paragraphs, suitable controls must be developed to insure this achievement. The personnel budget offers one of the most effective forms of control by establishing the financial limits within which the program must operate. Statistical records of employee turnover, absenteeism, accidents, grievances, and disciplinary action, as well as performance ratings and production records, provide some of the other sources of control information that may be utilized in the administration of the personnel program. Information can be gained through these sources by means of periodic audits or appraisals. Considerable information also can be obtained through personal observation. While the latter source of information may be subject to certain limitations, the intuitive judgments of experienced staff specialists can be most useful as a basis for developing more objective surveys and audits of the personnel process.

Résumé

Closely interrelated and interacting with the organization system is the management system. It is composed of the planning, organizing, staffing, directing, and controlling processes, all of which are dynamic in nature. Linking these processes together is the management information system that functions as the nervous system by coordinating and guiding the performance of these activities toward established objectives.

Organizational guidance is furnished by means of programs established to facilitate decision making. Such programs provide the objectives, policies, procedures, and budgets that are necessary in order that the function for which they are developed may be coordinated and performed. In the management of an organization, it is the personnel program that enables decisions and actions involving employees to be carried out consistently and rationally.

A formal personnel program consisting of the written statements covering its objectives, policies, procedures, and other elements also enables employees to understand better what is expected of them and to anticipate decisions and actions affecting them. While these statements afford evidence of a personnel program's worth, the best measure is determined by the personnel practices that the program generates and by how effectively it serves the needs of the organization.

DISCUSSION QUESTIONS

1. What interrelationships, if any, are there between the planning and the controlling processes of management?
2. How does a personnel policy differ from a personnel objective? From a personnel procedure?
3. Would identical treatment of employees necessarily insure equitable treatment of them? Discuss.
4. Because of the presence of combustible materials, smoking is forbidden in the shipping department of a large company. Although notice of this fact is stated in the employee's handbook and is posted on signs throughout the departmental areas, the regulation was not enforced until the company was required by fire insurance inspectors to do so. As a result of this development, notice was issued that any future violations would result in a three-day layoff without pay for the first offense and a discharge for a second offense.
   a. Comment on the reactions and problems that this approach might create.
   b. What other approach, if any, might prove to be more desirable?
5. In spite of the efforts of the personnel manager to correct the situation, the manager and supervisors in the manufacturing department persist in the violation of certain personnel policies within their department. What action can and should the personnel manager take to correct this situation, and what human relations problems may be encountered?
6. What are some of the changes that are occurring in the role and status of the personnel department?

PROBLEM 4-1 A POLICY ON LEAVES OF ABSENCE

On September 10th Dr. Will Rudnik, assistant superintendent for personnel of the Garden Valley School District, received a request from Mrs. Beatrice Boggs for a leave of absence without pay during the coming month. Mrs. Boggs stated on the request form that the leave was necessary in order to accompany her husband on a business trip to Bermuda in October. Mrs. Boggs indicated further that she and her husband Elmer had been forced to cancel their scheduled vacation in August because of a heart attack suffered by Harry Marx, owner of the appliance store where Elmer was sales manager. Since Harry was under his doctor's orders not to travel, he had agreed to pay Elmer's expenses to represent the store at the fall sales conference in Bermuda conducted by his appliance supplier. Elmer planned to extend the trip to include a visit to the appliance manufacturer's plant and a two-week vacation in the Caribbean.

Dr. Rudnick's first action was to refer to the district personnel manual and to the following section in it pertaining to leave requests:

> Section 4 (d) *The Special Leave*—The district may grant special short-term leaves under certain conditions. This type of leave shall be of reasonably short duration and one that would not work a serious hardship on the children involved. The superintendent may exercise judgment in his recommendation of this type of leave. This shall be a leave without pay.

After studying the policy statement, Dr. Rudnick wrote a letter to Mrs. Boggs in which he denied her request on the grounds that it would impair the instructional continuity of the children in her class and thus not be in the district's best interest. He expressed his confidence that Mrs. Boggs was as dedicated to her job as her husband was to his job. He concluded his letter by saying that he hoped they might be able to arrange a substitute vacation together during either her vacation at Christmas or next summer.

Upon receiving the letter Mrs. Boggs appealed to the district superintendent who upheld Dr. Rudnick's decision. Being a very determined woman, Mrs. Boggs requested and received a hearing before the school board at its next meeting. After listening to her at length, the majority of the board members present voted to grant her request for leave.

a. What are some of the possible implications of the board's action from the standpoint of personnel policy and sound management practice?
b. Would you have granted the request if you had been Dr. Rudnick? Explain.

SUGGESTED READINGS

Barnard, Chester I. *The Functions of the Executive*. Cambridge: Harvard University Press, 1954.

Benge, Eugene J. *How to Manage for Tomorrow*. New York: Dow Jones-Irwin, 1975.

Chruden, Herbert J., and Arthur W. Sherman, Jr. *Readings in Personnel Management*, 4th ed. Cincinnati: South-Western Publishing Co., 1976. Part 2.

Dale, Ernest. *Management: Theory and Practice,* 3d ed. New York: McGraw-Hill Book Company, 1973. Chapters 13-18.

Drucker, Peter F. *Management: Tasks, Responsibilities, and Practices*. New York: Harper and Row, 1974.

Higginson, M. Valliant. *Management Policies I: Their Development as Corporate Guides*. AMA Research Study 76. New York: American Management Association, 1966.

———. *Management Policies II: Sourcebook of Statements*. AMA Research Study 78. New York: American Management Association, 1968.

Holden, Paul E., *et. al. Top Management*. New York: McGraw-Hill Book Company, 1968.

Koontz, Harold, and Cyril O'Donnell. *Principles of Management,* 5th ed. New York: McGraw-Hill Book Company, 1972.

McConkey, Dale D. *Updating the Management Process*. New York: American Management Association, 1971.

McFarland, Dalton E. *Company Officers Assess the Personnel Function*. New York: American Management Association, 1967.

Morrison, Edward J. *Developing Computer-Based Employee Information Systems*. AMA Research Study 99. New York: American Management Association, 1969.

Odiorne, George S. *Management Decisions by Objectives*. Englewood Cliffs, N.J.: Prentice-Hall, Inc., 1969.

Ross, Joel E. *Management by Information System*. Englewood Cliffs, New Jersey: Prentice-Hall, Inc., 1970.

Sisk, Henry L. *Management and Organization,* 2d ed. Cincinnati: South-Western Publishing Co., 1973. Parts II and III.

Townsend, Robert. *Up the Organization*. New York: Alfred A. Knopf, 1970.

Staffing the Organization

Personnel Recruitment

The staffing of an organization involves the process of analyzing present and future needs for human resources and of obtaining personnel to meet these needs. Effective staffing, furthermore, includes the developing and maintaining of adequate sources of human resources from which applicants may be recruited and selected. As a result of the Civil Rights Movement and government legislation, recruitment no longer can be considered as being solely a process of locating those applicants most qualified for the job. Neither can it involve any policies or practices that may serve to discriminate against women and members of minority groups who previously might not have been considered for employment. Instead, recruitment must include positive efforts to seek out *qualifiable applicants* from these groups and to help them to qualify for employment through special training programs and, if necessary, through the redesign of certain jobs at the entrance level.

ANTICIPATING PERSONNEL REQUIREMENTS

Since considerable lead time may be required to recruit, select, and develop employees for many of the jobs within an organization, it is essential that job vacancies be anticipated as far as possible in advance. Similarly, when positions are to be eliminated, this fact should become known sufficiently in advance to permit the employees affected to be retrained and reassigned, if possible, to other positions in order that an efficient and stable work force can be maintained. Formal planning is also required in the development of programs for affirmative action that may comply satisfactorily with existing laws and the executive orders relating to these laws.

The anticipation of changes in personnel needs for specific jobs is a part of effective human resources planning. In a private company such planning also requires effective sales, inventory, and production planning, for it is the demand for a company's products or services that determines the number and qualifications of the personnel to be employed by it. In government and other nonprofit organizations, personnel requirements are determined by the volume of services or other work that the organization is expected to provide the public, and by what the public is willing to pay for the services.

Personnel Planning in Private Companies

Since a company's work load and personnel requirements are determined by its sales, adequate planning with respect to this function will enable it to anticipate the customer demand and to achieve a more stable rate of production. Effective sales planning, for example, can make it possible for a company to influence the demand for its products by designing and promoting them on the basis of research which indicates what the customer wants.

The pressure of unions for stabilized employment and the desire of management to reduce the high cost of employee turnover have caused many companies to stress sales planning in an effort to minimize fluctuations in the work force. Efforts to stabilize sales are particularly essential for companies that are affected by seasonal and cyclical fluctuations. Changes resulting from cyclical fluctuations in business activities are more difficult to anticipate and to counteract than are those of a seasonal nature. Through the use of forecasting techniques, a company may be able to discover cyclical trends affecting product sales and organizational growth and to project these trends into the future as a means of predicting its own business activity.

The production rate of a company is generally determined by the customer orders that are on hand or are anticipated, with proper allowances being made for desired increases or decreases in inventory. Generally, overall production schedules are developed for a season or for some other suitable period of time and subsequently for monthly and weekly periods. While certain adjustments in long-term production plans are inevitable, their development is essential to good personnel planning.

Temporary fluctuations in the rate of production need not make necessary any changes in the size of the regular work force. Adjustments to temporary increases in the work load can be accomplished through the use of overtime, by subcontracting some of the work, by hiring temporary help, or by utilizing the services of companies that supply temporary personnel. Conversely, temporary decreases can be accommodated by shortening the workweek, encouraging the use of accumulated vacation time, or by assigning some employees to maintenance work or other projects that have been deferred for this purpose.

Personnel Planning in Public Organizations

The need for effective *personnel planning* is by no means limited to private enterprises. Government agencies, educational institutions, hospitals, and other public enterprises also must operate efficiently within established budgets even though they are not profit-making in nature. Many of these public enterprises also experience long-term as well as short-term changes and fluctuations in the demand for their services. Changes and shifts in population, international tensions and conflicts, political pressures, and fluctuations in the business cycle may have an effect upon the services that a public agency or institution may be required to provide or upon the budget on which it must operate. These factors may also affect the number and types of positions that must be staffed for any particular period. Therefore, if possible, they must be anticipated as a part of the organization's personnel planning program.

Determining Staffing Requirements

The personnel requirements of an organization which are determined by the volume of work being performed by it must be translated into specific job and position allocations. In determining these allocations, adjustments must be made for the degree of competency that is possessed by the personnel who staff these positions. Adjustments must also be made for losses in productivity resulting from absenteeism, vacations, turnover, training assignments, and other factors affecting employee efficiency.

Authority to staff positions is limited by departmental payroll budgets which specify the positions to be filled and the wages to be paid each position. In evaluating their personnel needs, managers and supervisors often tend to believe that their departments are understaffed with the result that they may sometimes seek more personnel than their departments require. The use of cost control procedures to indicate the efficiency with which a department is being managed, however, can help to discourage this practice. If managers are placed under pressure to improve efficiency, they will have greater incentive to reduce costs by eliminating unnecessary personnel within their departments.

RECRUITMENT SOURCES OF QUALIFIED PERSONNEL

An individual who is placed in a particular opening may be one who is selected from another position within the organization, or one who is recruited from the outside. The recruitment of personnel thus requires the canvassing of all possible sources of candidates, both external and internal, for the purpose of encouraging individuals who are qualified or who can be made qualified for present or future job openings. Because of the wide variety of qualifications that may be required and possessed by persons available to perform the different jobs in many organizations, it may be necessary to consider several sources of applicants, depending upon the particular job to be staffed and the conditions of the labor market.

Internal Sources

Employers should neither neglect nor rely too heavily upon *internal sources* of personnel to fill openings above the starting level. Unfortunately, because they are better acquainted with the weaknesses and deficiencies of their own employees, employers may consider outside applicants—whose weaknesses are not known—to be better qualified than actually is the case. On the other hand, if employers ignore outside sources to fill openings above the starting level, this practice may serve to shelter employees from the competition of "outsiders" who may be more qualified.

Pros and Cons of Internal Sources. The use of internal sources, if it serves to prevent layoffs or to create promotion opportunities for employees, can be beneficial to morale and can enable an organization to realize a return from the training investment it has in its employees. Internal sources may prove unsatisfactory, however, if those individuals available within the organization do not have and cannot develop the qualifications needed for a particular vacancy. Furthermore, experienced personnel hired from the outside can help to reduce inbreeding within an organization by bringing to it new ideas, knowledge, and enthusiasm.

Values of Computerized Data Banks. Computerized information systems have made possible the creation of *data banks* containing the complete record of the qualifications of each employee. With these computerized records an organization can screen its entire force of personnel in a matter of minutes to locate candidates who have the qualifications required to fill a specific opening. These data also can be used to prepare reports pertaining to personnel statistics, labor costs, absenteeism, and employee turnover by job classes, department, or for the organization as a whole. Since the value of the data is contingent upon their currentness, the information system must include provisions for recording changes in employee qualifications as they occur.

Computerized data pertaining to the work force and to the qualifications of each employee can benefit personnel planning and recruitment efforts. These data, for example, can be used to predict the career paths of personnel in organizations and to anticipate the openings and staff requirements resulting from them and from attrition. Information systems may help management to determine where and when to expand or to modify recruitment efforts as well as the types of people that it should seek to recruit.[1] Data banks can also serve to improve recruitment efforts by providing data on the employees who have been recruited, the sources from which they were recruited, and the factors contributing to their recruitment. They can also help an organization to evaluate and improve its efforts to recruit minorities and women, as well as to confirm its record of performance in this area. Data pertaining to applicants who were not hired and the reasons why they were not hired, as well as

[1] Robert D. Smith, "Information Systems for More Effective Use of Executive Resources," *Personnel Journal,* Vol. 48, No. 6 (June, 1969), p. 455.

follow-up records on the performance of those who were employed, also can be used to develop better recruitment and selection programs.

External Sources

Personnel may be recruited from various *external sources*. Some of these sources may be used for filling a variety of different jobs. Others may be used only for certain types of jobs such as those for executive, professional, technical, clerical, and blue-collar personnel. The specific sources utilized by the employer will depend upon such factors as the size of the organization, its resources, and economic conditions.

Advertising. For many employers advertisements may be the only source that is used when seeking to staff position vacancies. Radio, television, posters, magazines, and newspapers may be utilized as advertising media in attempting to reach interested applicants that might not otherwise be contacted. Advertising can have the advantage of permitting a large audience to be reached and of providing another possible source of applicants. If the advertisement is placed in a professional or trade publication that reaches a selected and desired group of readers, it is more likely to produce favorable results than if placed in a publication with mass circulation. For example, advertisements directed toward business and professional readers might be placed in *The Wall Street Journal*.

The effectiveness of advertising as a recruitment tool is dependent, among other things, upon the nature of the appeal that it makes to the reader. While cleverness and exaggerated claims may sell household products, they are less likely to influence intelligent applicants in making job decisions that can affect their future careers, particularly if the job requires a reasonable degree of formal education. Similarly, the "blind type" ad or the ad that misrepresents or conceals the true nature of the job will attract only the more gullible applicants who, when the true facts about its duties are discovered, may become resentful and reject the job.

The principal limitation of advertising, aside from the cost, is the unpredictable nature of its results. In some instances an advertisement may fail to attract any significant response, as apparently was the situation in Figure 5-1 on page 103. In other instances it may cause an employer to be overburdened with applicants, many of whom are marginal but who respond in hopes that there may be a remote possibility that they will be considered.

Educational Institutions. During the past decade, many students attended colleges and universities primarily for the sake of gaining a liberal education and learning more about society and about themselves. Today, however, students are more concerned with preparing themselves to earn a living in professional and vocational fields than for a life of "genteel poverty." Unfortunately the supply of graduates in many fields now exceeds the demand for their services. As a result, the levels at which many entrance job

"He has one big qualification for the job – he's the only man who answered our ad!"

Source: STRICTLY BUSINESS cartoon by Dale McFeatters, reproduced through the courtesy of Publishers-Hall Syndicate.

Figure 5-1

opportunities occur are below those which existed during the past decade.[2] Because of this situation, the role of college placement services in helping graduates to obtain jobs has increased.

In spite of the difficulty that some college graduates may have in obtaining employment, a college degree is helpful since unemployment among college graduates is considerably lower than it is for those who are not. The college degree, however, has ceased to provide any guarantee of employment.[3]

The College Placement Council is undertaking a placement assistance program for employers and for college graduates and alumni to provide an information retrieval system that is operated nationally. This system which is known as the *Graduate Résumé Accumulation and Distribution* (GRAD) *Program* is designed to store on magnetic tape the personal placement files of graduates seeking employment. These files are made available to employers who are seeking applicants with the particular set of qualifications that are needed for a job opening. College graduates using the system have the advantage of being considered by an unlimited number of employers at no cost.

Employment Agencies. It may be advantageous at times for employers to utilize the assistance of employment agencies in recruiting applicants. These agencies differ considerably in terms of their policies, services, costs, and the type of applicants that can be obtained through them. Some agencies are

[2] "The Job Gap for College Graduates in the 70s," *Business Week* (September 23, 1972), p. 48.
[3] *Ibid.*

publicly supported or are operated on a nonprofit basis, while others operate as profit-making enterprises and charge a fee to the applicant and/or the employer. Employment agencies may supply applicants representing a variety of occupational areas, or they may provide applicants for only certain professional, technical, office, or domestic jobs. When seeking the assistance of an employment agency, it is advisable for an organization to utilize those agencies that can provide the services and applicants at a cost which it can afford to pay. Three types of employment agencies that will be discussed in terms of their objectives and areas of service are public employment agencies, private employment agencies, and executive recruiting firms.

Public Employment Agencies. Public employment offices are maintained in most of the larger communities throughout the nation, and part-time offices are located in many of the smaller ones. These offices are administered by the state in which they are located, but they are subject to certain general controls by the United States Employment Service (USES) since states receive financial support from federal tax rebates.

In order to be eligible to collect unemployment insurance benefits, individuals are required to register for work with their state employment services and to be willing to accept any suitable employment that is offered to them. This requirement serves to identify those persons who are unemployed and who may be referred to employers who are seeking employees. Since public employment agencies are administered by state governments, the type and quality of services that they provide tend to vary. In addition to supplying job applicants, the services of some state agencies may include assisting employers in performing employment testing, job analysis and evaluation, community wage surveys, and other personnel functions. By cooperating and exchanging job-market information, the state agencies have been able to help employers in those regions where there is a shortage or an oversupply of qualified employees.

The USES is now developing a nationwide computerized job bank to which all state employment offices eventually will be connected. In those offices that have a local job bank, a computer print-out similar to the one in Figure 5-2 and known as a *job book* can be provided which contains a list of the job openings for the day. The bank makes it possible for employment interviewers to have a list of all job openings for which the job applicants they are counseling may qualify. Although the job book expands the information available about the job openings and facilitates matching of applicants with openings, some employers have complained that it impersonalizes their relations with the employment service. Whereas they formally dealt directly with those employment interviewers who were familiar with their job requirements and employment preferences, they now must deal with a computer. Many of these employers still believe that a good interviewer is more reliable and more capable of making "feasibility matches" than the job bank.[4]

---

[4] "Job Bank in a Computer Pays Off and Branches Out," *Business Week* (July 5, 1969), pp. 70-71.

```
RM– 1                               P–  0                        REF– 3        OPN– 1     STS–       CD–       CLS–RL/DATE–             9
                                        WK/WK–FULL PAY–       2.25-3.00/PER HR              NURSE LIC PRAC                      079.378026    048623
079.378 048623 08/24/70 CT-A            **CALL FIRST       HRS/WK–40 PAY PD–BI-WEEK      HRS 7AM-3PM MUST OWN TRANS WILL GIVE MEDICINES AND SUPER-
NURSE LIC PRAC                          DURATION–PERM    TST/RQ–N/A  TST/BY–N/A           VISE NURSING PERSONNEL
KIND CARE NURSING            LOC-0130   JOB REQUIRES–EDUC–13 MTH/EXP–12 AGE–18-99
2100 PLEASANT LANE           S/D-4339   PHY/DMD–   WK/COND–    MAR/SIN.
ANYTOWN, US 09241            SIC-8092
490-625-4980  119
MRS GRAHAM                   SPCL
-----------------------------------------------------------------------------------------------------------------------------------
RM– 0                               P–  0                        REF– 4        OPN– 1     STS–       CD–       CLS–RL/DATE–             8
                                        WK/WK–FULL PAY–       3.00– 4.00/PER HR             ACCOUNTANT                          160.188010    048713
160.188  048713  08/26/70 CT-A                             HRS/WK–40 PAY PD–WEEKLY       8 TO 5PM MON THRU FRIDAY MAINTAIN RECORDS OF ASSETS AND
ACCOUNTANT                              DURATION–PERM    TST/RQ–N/A  TST/BY–N/A           LIABILITIES AND FINANCIAL TRANSACTIONS PREFER EXP IN ACCOUNT-
BUTLER RUBBER CO             LOC-0110   JOB REQUIRES–EDUC–13 MTH/EXP  AGE–21-99          ING WILL ACCEPT TRAINEE WHO HAS 2 OR MORE YEARS IN COLLEGE
MILLER CREEK ROAD            S/D-2625   PHY/DMD–   WK/COND–    MAR/SIN.                   ACCT. COURSES
ANYTOWN, US  09241           SIC-3069
490-713-5068  051                                WILL ACCEPT–TRAINEE.
MR JAMES PARSONS             SPCL
-----------------------------------------------------------------------------------------------------------------------------------
RM– 0                               P–  0                        REF– 6        OPN– 3     STS–       CD–       CLS–RL/DATE–             5
                                        WK/WK–FULL PAY–      76.00-99.00/WEEKLY             CLERK TYPIST                        209.388022    049000
209-388  049000  08/31/70 CT-A          **CALL FIRST       HRS/WK–40 PAY PD–BI-WEEK      WORK 8 TO 445 5 DAYS TYPE 40 WPM ACCURATE
CLERK TYPIST                            DURATION–PERM    TST/RQ–N/A  TST/BY–N/A           VARIED DUTIES ONE TO WORK 9 TO 3PM 5 DAY WILL
CITY  LIFE INSURANCE         LOC 0130   JOB REQUIRES–EDUC–12 MTH/EXP–36 AGE–18-99         TRAIN TO RELIEVE ON PBX
CITY LIFE BLDG               S/D-1518   PHY/DMD–   WK/COND–    MAR/SIN.
ANYTOWN, US  09241           SIC-6312
490-621-3114  119                                WILL ACCEPT–TRAINEE
MRS COHEN                    M/M SPCL
-----------------------------------------------------------------------------------------------------------------------------------
RM– 0                               P–  0                        REF– 3        OPN– 1     STS–       CD–       CLS–RL/DATE              7
                                        WK/WK–FULL PAY–       1.70 –      /PER HR           SALESPERSON GENERAL                 289.458014    0488.19
289.458  048819  08/27/70 CT-A                             HRS/WK–40 PAY PD–WEEKLY       HOURS VARY 5 DAYS WORK SAT SELLING HOUSEWARES COOKWARES
SALESPERSON GENERAL                     DURATION–PERM                                     SMALL APPLIANCES PREFER MATURE PERSON WITH SALES EXPER
ANYTOWN DEPARTMENT STORE     LOC-0130   JOB REQUIRES–EDUC–10 MTH/EXP–24 AGE–18-99
FIFTH AND MAIN               S/D-3188   PHY/DMD–   WK/COND–    MAR/SIN.
ANYTOWN, US  09241           SIC-5311
490-621-9382  119
MISS PERKINS                 M/M SPCL
-----------------------------------------------------------------------------------------------------------------------------------
RM– 14                              P–  0                        REF– 25       OPN– 15    STS–       CD–       CLS–RL/DATE–             4
                                        WK/WK–FULL PAY–       1.60-2.30/PR HR               WATCH ASSEMBLER                     715.381010    046249
715.381  046249  09/01/70 CT-A                             HRS/WK–40 PAY PD–WEEKLY          ASSEMBLES COMPLETE WATCH MOVEMENTS USE TWEEZERS AND OTHER
WATCH ASSEMBLER                         DURATION PERM    TST/RQ–SATB  TST/BY–E.S          HAND TOOLS WORK UNDER MAGNIFYING LAMP INSPECT MOVEMENT OF
RIGHT TIME CORP              LOC-0130   JOB REQUIRES–EDUC–08  MTH/EXP–  AGE–18-99         PARTS REPLACE DEFECTIVE PARTS CLEAN ADJUST AND OIL MUST
FOURTH AND CARSON            S/D-2443   PHY/DMD–   .WK/COND–    US/CIT.                   HAVE GOOD FINGER DEXTERITY 20/20 VISION RIGHT HANDER CHILD
ANYTOWN, US 09241            SIC-3871   PHYSICAL                                          CARE ARRANGED
490-189-3006  119                                WILL ACCEPT–TRAINEE. HANDICAP
MR MILLER                    M/M        BENEFITS–INS. HOSP. SCKLV. VAC.
```

Source: "The Job Bank: Using a Computer to Bring People and Jobs Together" (Washington, D.C.: U.S. Department of Labor, Manpower Administration, 1971).

Figure 5-2 AN EXAMPLE OF A JOB BANK PRINTOUT

Private Employment Agencies. Because they charge fees, private agencies may provide more specialized employment services than public agencies and often cater to a particular class of clientele. Whether the employer or the applicant is charged the fee depends upon which party is receiving the primary benefit. In addition to job referrals, services to the applicant may include vocational counseling and guidance or assistance in preparing personal résumés. Services to employers may include the advertising of vacancies so that the employer's identity is not revealed and the conducting of initial interviews. Having an employment agency advertise vacancies may be desirable if employers wish to consider persons outside of their own organizations without the knowledge of their employees or if they wish to avoid interviewing a large number of applicants who might respond to an advertisement.

Temporary help services are another source of personnel. The use of temporary employees during peak periods has the advantage of reducing layoffs during slow periods which would lead to an increase in the unemployment insurance rates. Since temporary employees are carried on the payroll of the temporary help service, employers are spared the clerical, payroll accounting, and fringe benefit costs that they otherwise would encounter. Because of the advantages they can offer an employer, temporary help services have grown rapidly during the past decade; and some are now international in their operations.

Executive Recruiting Firms. The need for persons with proven managerial ability and experience has encouraged the growth of firms which specialize in the recruitment of management personnel. The fee for their services, which usually amounts to 25 percent of the salary the recruited executive is to receive for the first year, provides an incentive for them to investigate and appraise very thoroughly those persons whom they recommend. By means of personal inquiries, personal contacts, and selective advertising, firms that specialize in executive recruitment attempt to locate qualified executive prospects who are interested in changing their employment and improving their salaries. Qualified executives whose capabilities exceed the challenge or promotion opportunities of their present jobs are also among the individuals that these firms seek to locate and refer to their clients. Some recruitment firms have developed personal data files covering several thousand executives in this category; through the use of computers, such files can be screened rapidly to locate possible candidates for a particular management opening.

Employee Referrals. Employees may be encouraged to help locate qualified applicants. High morale can make employees boosters of their organization and can contribute indirectly to the recruitment of needed applicants. If an employee knows an applicant and believes he or she would do a creditable job for the employer and if the applicant is a person with whom the employee is willing to work and associate, the employee has a definite incentive to recommend that individual. In recommending applicants, employees, in a sense, place their own reputations at stake; consequently, they are more likely to do everything possible to help those they have recommended to succeed. However, even though employees may exercise caution in making recommendations, they can make mistakes or can be influenced by personal friendship. In utilizing employee recommendations as a means of filling vacancies, management must be alert to the potential danger of building up cliques composed of employees from the same school, church, club, or some other group.

Unsolicited Applications. Most employers receive inquiries about employment opportunities from individuals representing a variety of backgrounds and qualifications. Applications from persons who appear to be well qualified but who cannot be hired immediately should be kept on file as a source of employees for future vacancies. It should be recognized, however, that such applicant files can become outdated very rapidly.

Although this source may not yield a very high percentage of acceptable candidates, it should not be ignored. The fact that the applicants had taken the initiative to apply for employment may indicate that they have a definite interest in the organization and a desire to work for it. To maintain good public relations, every person who applies for work should be treated with courtesy and consideration whether or not the application has been directly solicited.

Professional Organizations. Many professional organizations and societies operate a placement service for the benefit of members and employers. These societies may carry advertisements or lists of job openings and of applicants who are seeking positions in the journals that they publish.

The regional and national meetings of technical and professional societies have tended to attract increasing numbers of recruiters, sometimes to the consternation of the sponsoring organizations. This consternation has resulted from the fact that the lobbies and rooms where the recruiters have established their headquarters have often attracted a greater delegate interest than many of the conference sessions. Unfortunately such conditions may discourage some companies from sending representatives to the meetings for fear that certain of their personnel may be recruited away by some other firm.

Labor Unions. Labor unions are a principal source of applicants, particularly for blue-collar jobs. In some industries the unions traditionally have been able to maintain control over most of the supply of a particular type of labor through their apprenticeship programs and through their labor agreements with employers.

In the maritime, printing, and construction industries unions furnish a labor pool from which they can dispatch personnel through their hiring halls to meet the short-term needs of employers. In doing this the unions provide a very useful economic service. The Landrum-Griffin Act, furthermore, permits employers in the construction industry to sign labor agreements with unions to provide for the workers who may be needed even before work at a construction site has begun.

Underdeveloped Sources of Personnel

Several sources of potential employees within our society have never been utilized fully. These sources include culturally disadvantaged individuals, women, and handicapped persons. Because of prejudices toward applicants from these groups, many organizations have deprived themselves of potential employees who have the talents and qualifications to render a worthwhile contribution. Society also has shared in the loss resulting from this waste of human resources.

Fortunately there is a trend for more organizations to utilize the services of individuals from those groups which previously were rejected for many jobs. This trend has resulted not only from a reduction in prejudices on the part of many employers but also from the growing recognition by many of them that these prejudices serve to deprive them of needed human talent. Undoubtedly the most significant factor contributing to greater positive effort to employ minorities and women, however, has been the government pressures to install affirmative action programs in compliance with the Civil Rights Act of 1964 and subsequent supplementary legislation and executive orders.

Culturally Disadvantaged. In years past the primary objective of recruitment programs was to make contact with those applicants who were considered to be the most qualified for a job opening and to encourage them to seek employment with the organization. Because of their lack of education or job skills, or because they had a background record that was considered unsatisfactory, disadvantaged members of society previously have had little chance of being selected for employment, much less of being sought for it. During the past decade, however, recruitment practices with respect to members of the disadvantaged, or hard-core groups, have undergone a substantial change. As a result, employers are actively seeking to create job opportunities and to recruit them. Because the problems of recruiting the disadvantaged differ from those encountered with other groups, employers have been forced to adjust their recruitment programs to the realities of hard-core life, such as are described in Figure 5-3.

Factors to Consider in Recruiting the Hard-Core. Some employers seeking to provide jobs for the disadvantaged have been surprised and sometimes embittered to learn that their efforts are viewed by hard-core members with suspicion, skepticism, and even hostility. As one black employee is quoted:

> If Whitey thinks it's enough to get me in a job, to get me to work everyday, I've got news—it's not enough. If I'm not accomplishing anything, if I'm not getting anywhere, it's the same as welfare. Unless 'the man' can make me feel I'm doing something, that I'm part of something real, he can forget his job.[5]

[5] "Effectively Employing the Hard-Core," The National Association of Manufacturers, New York, 1968, p. 15.

REALITIES OF HARD-CORE LIFE

The undereducated, unskilled, chronically unemployed poor person tends to live in a different world from the one we inhabit. And the impact of his world colors all of his actions and reactions when he comes into contact with the industrial world. This fact is stressed because any attempt to understand the behavior of disadvantaged persons coming into our plants is contingent upon the ability to step out of our own frame of reference and grasp the impact that living in poverty has on individuals.

Most of us find it difficult to appreciate the extent to which the minority group person living in a white man's world suffers damage to his self-respect, dignity, and sense of manhood. Without spelling out how this damage comes about, it is important to bear in mind that the toughness, the surliness, the indifference of some disadvantaged persons is a mask that is worn for protection. Underneath that mask there is often hurt and anger.

Source: "Effectively Employing the Hard-Core," The National Association of Manufacturers, New York, 1968, p. 3. Reprinted with permission.

Professing to be an "equal opportunity employer" through statements of this fact in an employment advertisement, unless it is backed up with deeds, is not likely to impress hard-core members.[6] Minority groups must be convinced that an employer will in fact provide them with the opportunity to demonstrate their ability and enable them to be advanced on this basis. Conversely, they do not want tokenism in which the employer is merely trying to alleviate external pressures to employ a certain quota of hard-core applicants. Neither do the disadvantaged want to be the subject of a publicity campaign or to be exhibited in some well-exposed location in the building as an example of the employer's contribution to solving minority group problems. What they do want is to be absorbed into the organization and treated like any other employee.

Where to Reach the Hard-Core. Because they live in a different cultural world, reliance upon the traditional sources of applicants may not prove to be very effective in reaching the hard-core. In his study of the unemployed, Jacobs found that hard-core members relied heavily upon the grapevine in locating job

[6] Ulric Haynes, Jr., "Equal Job Opportunity—The Credibility Gap," *Harvard Business Review,* Vol. 46, No. 3 (May-June, 1968), pp. 113-120.

openings, even more than upon the public employment service, because the latter existed outside their world.[7] Public employment agencies, however, are attempting to reach the jobless where they live by bringing job banks into their communities; sometimes, as Figure 5-4 illustrates, by establishing mobile employment offices. Contacts made through community action agencies, settlement houses, or other agencies within their community also can be a fairly good way of reaching the hard-core members.[8]

Source: "The Job Bank: Using a Computer to Bring People and Jobs Together" (Washington, D.C.: U.S. Department of Labor, Manpower Administration, 1971).

Figure 5-4 AN EXAMPLE OF A MOBILE EMPLOYMENT OFFICE

Women. The difficulties encountered by women in obtaining employment have not been as great as those encountered by minorities. Nevertheless, women have had difficulty in obtaining jobs other than those traditionally performed by them, such as secretarial work. Perhaps their greatest problem has been that of achieving advancement into managerial positions, particularly above the level of first-line supervisor. As the Presidential Task Force on Women's Rights and Responsibilities reported: "Social attitudes are slow to change. So widespread and pervasive are discriminatory practices against women that they have come to be regarded, more often, as normal."[9]

---

[7] Paul Jacobs, "Unemployment as a Way of Life," as published in *Employment Policy and the Labor Market,* Arthur M. Ross, editor (Berkeley, Calif.: University of California Press, 1965), p. 396.

[8] "Effectively Employing the Hard-Core," *op. cit.,* p. 4.

[9] "Women at Work," *The Morgan Guaranty Survey* (New York: Morgan Guaranty Trust Company, November, 1970).

Stereotyped Attitudes Toward Women. Some of the discrimination against women in employment has been the result of stereotyped thinking on the part of management, which has been and remains almost entirely male in composition. Among the more common stereotypes about women are the following:

1. Women work merely to supplement the family income.
2. Women do not want to be managers because it would involve an extra work load which would intrude upon family obligations.
3. Women are unable to meet certain work demands for emotional toughness and stability because of their physiological makeup. They tend to take things personally, to respond to anger and frustration by crying, and to be insufficiently "hard-nosed" to make unpleasant decisions.

These and other stereotypes, as Loring and Wells and other researchers on the subject reveal quite conclusively, are not supported by fact.[10]

Improving Women's Employment Opportunities. Eliminating the stereotypes that have impeded the placement of women in higher-paying and higher-level jobs can provide an important step toward more equitable employment conditions for women. However, other positive measures on the part of top management are also essential. To achieve effective results, as well as to comply with government regulations, top management should take the leadership and participate in affirmative action programs designed to correct any previous discriminatory employment practices against women. The review of personnel policies and job requirements and the modification of recruitment, selection, and training programs with the objective of not only hiring but also advancing women to positions of greater opportunity are important parts of any affirmative action endeavor.[11]

Handicapped Persons. There are many applicants whose performance capabilities have been reduced by physical disabilities, mental illness, mental retardation, or old age. In certain jobs, however, some of which may have to be specially created, these individuals can perform quite effectively. When placed in jobs where their handicaps are not an impediment to performance and where their skills can be utilized, such individuals can make a valuable contribution. Because employment opportunities for them are limited, absenteeism and turnover among handicapped persons often are much less than for the organization as a whole. Since there are many private and public agencies seeking to find employment and rehabilitation for members of different handicapped groups, such individuals can be contacted readily. The main problem in their employment, therefore, is one of helping them to adjust to their

---

[10] Rosalind Loring and Theodora Wells, *Breakthrough: Women into Management* (New York: Van Nostrand Reinhold Company, 1972). See also Joan E. Crowley, Teresa E. Levitin, and Robert P. Quinn, "Seven Deadly Half-Truths About Women," *Psychology Today* (March, 1973), pp. 94-95.

[11] M. Barbara Boyle, "Equal Opportunity for Women Is Smart Business," *Harvard Business Review*, Vol. 51, No. 3 (May-June, 1973), pp. 88-95. As reprinted in Herbert J. Chruden and Arthur W. Sherman, Jr., *Readings in Personnel Management* (4th ed.; Cincinnati: South-Western Publishing Co., 1976), pp. 57-74.

work without appearing to be overly solicitous toward them or focusing attention on their handicaps.

Individuals with criminal records have even greater employment problems than the physically and mentally handicapped. Persons who have "served time" find many employers reluctant to hire them or unable to do so in certain jobs because of bonding requirements or restrictions involving defense work. Recognizing that ex-convicts must have an opportunity to earn a livelihood if they are not to return to their former ways, certain organizations and government agencies are now seeking to assist them in obtaining jobs where their past will not be a handicap or become known to fellow employees.

Affirmative Action Under the Civil Rights Act

Although definite progress has been made in reducing past discrimination barriers to the employment of women and minorities, many members of these groups believe that this progress has not been rapid enough and that discriminatory practices still persist. On the other hand, critics of affirmative action efforts by the federal government allege that the goals and timetables required of employers as a part of their affirmative action programs for increasing the proportion of minorities and women being employed within the organization and improving their advancement opportunites constitute a quota system in disguise.[12] The critics contend that such a system, in the name of nondiscrimination, precipitates discrimination of a reverse nature against members of "the majority" and thus constitutes an injustice against those who are not responsible personally for the unfair treatment of certain groups in past years.[13] Furthermore, the critics hold that enforcement measures taken by the government against employers who have not met affirmative action goals are alien to traditional concepts of due process. Such concepts normally would require the government to prove that affirmative action goals were not met because the employer acted in "bad faith."[14]

While affirmative action practices in the future eventually will be tempered to insure employers greater due process and to provide the "majority" as well as minorities the right to equitable treatment, pressure undoubtedly will continue to be maintained upon employers to provide greater opportunities for women and minorities than they have been accorded in the past. It is through continued pressure that progressive social change will be more likely to occur in the future.

STAFFING POLICIES

It is as much to the employer's benefit to have qualified and qualifiable applicants seek employment as it is to the applicants' benefit to be considered

---

[12] Thomas H. Patten, Jr., "Personnel Management in the 1970s: The End of Laissez-Faire," *Human Resource Management,* Vol. 12, No. 3 (Fall, 1973), p. 10.

[13] Daniel Seligman, "How 'Equal Opportunity' Turned into Employment Quotas," *Fortune* (March, 1973), p. 168.

[14] *Ibid.*

for employment. The employer's staffing policies and procedures therefore should insure that all applicants receive fair and considerate treatment.

Public Relations and Recruitment

An organization's recruitment and public relations programs are closely interrelated since its ability to attract qualified applicants is affected by its public image. The pride that employees feel toward their organization and the favorable comments that they make about it in public contribute to its recruitment efforts. Thus, factors which have an impact on the recruitment function are operating continually even though an organization may be unaware of them.

Many individuals may experience their only contact with an organization in connection with their application for employment and may develop a lasting impression of it from this contact. It is important, therefore, that representatives of the personnel department, as well as those from other departments who may have contacts with job applicants, make every effort to generate goodwill through these contacts. An organization can do much to preserve goodwill by providing courteous treatment to all applicants and by advising those who are being considered for a position promptly and tactfully when the position has been filled. An organization's reputation will also be aided if the employment conditions that an employee must experience are accurately and completely described, even though these conditions may be such as to discourage some applicants from accepting employment.

Special Recruitment Problems

For many organizations it is also desirable to establish specific staffing policies and procedures governing jobs for which there is a scarcity of human talent or which present special problems of recruitment and selection. The special recruitment problems that are discussed in the remainder of this chapter relate to the employment of scientific and technical personnel, personnel for overseas assignments, and moonlighters.

Recruiting Scientific and Technical Personnel. The limited supply of applicants who possess specific scientific and technical skills has made the recruitment of these applicants increasingly difficult. Even with cutbacks in the aerospace industry and in government supported research, the demand for personnel in certain professional areas is likely to remain acute. By recognizing that the ultimate solution to the problem is one of substantially increasing the available supply, many organizations are attempting to utilize recruiting brochures, part-time employment, and plant visitations as a means of acquainting high school and college students with the opportunities available in the scientific and technical fields. Some of them also are attempting through films, exhibits, and other educational aids to develop a greater interest among students at the high school and even lower grade levels in scientific and technical careers. Scholarships sponsored by government and private organizations also are becoming increasingly common.

Aside from the problems relating to the scarcity of the supply, the recruitment of scientific personnel also involves the problem of motivating these individuals to join an organization since the things that they look for in a job may be different from those sought by other groups of applicants. Besides increasing the available supply of scientific and technical personnel and obtaining a proportionate share of them, many organizations can do a more effective job of utilizing those that they already employ. There has been a definite trend in recent years for organizations to assign many of the more routine duties of technical personnel to qualified assistants. This practice has permitted the technical personnel to confine themselves to duties commensurate with their education to the benefit of both the efficiency of the organization and the morale of those affected.

Recruiting for Overseas Assignments. In the past some American companies with subsidiaries in foreign countries have been criticized by the native personnel for sending over some individuals whom they did not consider to be fully qualified for management assignments. Since Americans generally are paid higher salaries than the native personnel, it is particularly important that they demonstrate to the native personnel the fact that they deserve the extra differential.[15]

Personality Factors to be Considered. The selection of persons for these jobs presents a problem since an individual who may be an excellent employee within the United States may prove to be highly unsatisfactory in a job overseas. One of the reasons for this is that the employees must face many adjustment problems including those relating to language barriers and cultural differences. Furthermore, since they are operating far removed from the headquarters staff, they must assume greater responsibilities than those encountered in a comparable level job in the United States.[16] Individuals chosen to work overseas, therefore, must be carefully screened in terms of their emotional stability and ability to adjust to the requirements of different cultures and living standards and their ability to make decisions. Since the loss that can result from the choice of wrong persons for overseas assignments can be extremely high, it is important that special care be given to their selection. A personality evaluation and the careful analysis of work histories for evidences of emotional problems may be well worth the extra expense and effort that they involve.

Orientation for Employees' Spouses. If employees are taking their families overseas, it may be well for the employer also to consider the personality of their spouses so as to be certain they will be able to adjust to the "cultural shock" that people encounter when they discover that many of their customary responses and behavioral patterns are not appropriate to the local culture. Wives in particular often have more problems since they are the ones who must

[15] Herbert J. Chruden and Arthur W. Sherman, Jr., *Personnel Practices of American Companies in Europe* (New York: American Management Association, 1972), p. 49.
[16] *Ibid.*, p. 54.

shop and manage the household in an economy and a society that may be quite different from the one at home. Because many companies are aware of the significant contributions that a wife can make to her husband's career overseas, or vice versa, many organizations are providing orientation and training programs to help prepare spouses for the foreign assignment.[17]

In general, employees and their families who adjust best to foreign jobs are more likely to be those who have a genuine interest in learning about the people, customs, traditions, history, and language of the country in which they are placed. For them a foreign assignment represents an educational opportunity rather than just a means of building a financial nest egg or of attempting to escape from those problems which they have not been able to solve at home. The citizens of foreign countries, furthermore, are particularly critical of those Americans who tend to isolate themselves by living in "Little Americas" and making little effort to mix with the local population or to try to learn the local language.[18]

Policies Toward Hiring Moonlighters. For a variety of reasons, such as the desire to use profitably the hours left over from a shorter workweek, many employees moonlight by holding down a second job. While some organizations are hesitant to employ *moonlighters* and discourage their employees from holding a second job, most employers do not have an official policy either sanctioning or forbidding it.[19] According to a Department of Labor Survey, about 5.2 percent of all employed persons are moonlighters.[20] Some organizations, particularly those in the retailing and service fields, use moonlighters as temporary personnel to meet weekend and evening personnel requirements. As efforts to achieve a shorter workweek are realized, there is every reason to believe that the number of persons seeking a second job will increase even more.

Résumé

If an organization is to operate efficiently, each position within the structure must be staffed by the person who is best qualified to perform it. Since lead time may be required in order to recruit and train personnel who will be qualified, it is necessary to anticipate personnel needs in advance of their occurrence. The satisfactory anticipation of personnel needs and of the factors affecting these needs will help to prevent a surplus or a shortage of personnel from developing within an organization. It also will permit a more careful selection of new personnel and the location of new positions for those persons whose jobs are being eliminated by changes in organization or work load.

In order to obtain qualified personnel for each job, it is also necessary for an employer to search actively for such personnel from a variety of sources both

[17] "That Glittering Overseas Investment, the Executive's Lady," *Fortune* (June, 1966), pp. 132-139.

[18] Chruden and Sherman, *op. cit.*, p. 6.

[19] Vera C. Perrella, "Multiple Job Holders in May, 1969," *Special Labor Force Report 123* (Washington, D.C.: U.S. Department of Labor), p. 63.

[20] *Ibid.*, p. 57.

within and outside of the organization. The sources that may prove to be the most productive are likely to vary according to the type of job to be filled and the condition of the labor market. Regardless of which sources of applicants are utilized, consideration must be given to the effect that staffing policies will have upon the attitude of its employees and of the general public, as well as upon the fulfillment of an organization's responsibility to society. During the past decade greater attention has been directed toward the active recruitment of minorities and women and toward the elimination of prejudices that have barred them from equal opportunities. These drives have sought to create opportunities within the organization for members of these groups and to locate and encourage these members to seek employment. The employment image of the organization in the community and the desire of employees, supervisors, and managers to assist in providing employment opportunities that are truly equal thus are recognized as essential to the success of a recruitment program.

DISCUSSION QUESTIONS

1. What are the comparative advantages and disadvantages of filling openings from internal sources?
2. An employment agency seeking to recruit salespeople for an insurance company advertised for applicants in the local newspaper. The position was described as a "management trainee" job with an insurance company. The advertisement did not list the name of either the employment agency or the insurance company but only the telephone number of the agency. What are the possible reasons for this practice? What would be your reaction upon reading the ad? Upon learning all the facts about the job?
3. What are some of the possible strengths and limitations of a national placement file of job applicants such as that provided by the GRAD program?
4. How do the problems of equal opportunity for women differ from those for the culturally disadvantaged?
5. What causes the development of stereotypes about certain groups such as women?
6. What are some of the criticisms made of the federal government's efforts to provide equal opportunity for persons in our society? Do you agree or disagree with these criticisms?

PROBLEM 5-1 PERSONAL RÉSUMÉ

JOHN M. WILLIAMS, JR.
135 Sutter Drive
Sacramento, CA 95815

Telephone: 916-487-4644

Marital Status: Single
Age: 28
Height: 6′1″
Weight: 160 pounds

Draft Status: 5A—Honorable Discharge, September, 1972, Staff Sergeant USAF

JOB OBJECTIVE

To begin work in the technical department of a company dealing with electronics with the purpose of qualifying eventually for full management responsibilities. No geographic limitations.

EDUCATION

California State University, Sacramento

Class: June, 1974
Degree: B.S.
Major: Industrial Management
Minor: Speech

HONORS

Dean's List, Beta Gamma Sigma National Honor Society in Business Administration, Blue Key National Honor Fraternity, Associated Students Service and Leadership Award, National Transportation Association Scholarship Award.

ACTIVITIES

Station Manager and Head Engineer of college radio station KERS-FM, member of the Society for the Advancement of Management, Vice-President of the Young Republicans.

EXPERIENCE

United States Air Force, Electronics-Communications, 6/64 to 9/72. *Duties and responsibilities:* NCOIC Electronic Equipment Depot Overhaul and Fabrication Shop (supervised 8 men in the overhaul and building of weather and ionospheric research equipment), Shift Chief Long-Haul Transmitter Site (supervised 3 men in operation of 52 transmitters and 2 microwave systems), Team Chief Group Electronics Engineering Installation Agency (supervised 3 men on installing weather and communications equipment), Tech-Writer (wrote detailed maintenance procedures for electronic equipment manuals), Instructor in Electronic Fundamentals (continuous 3-month classes of 10 men each).

Special Qualifications: Federal Communications Commission First Class Radio Telephone License. Top Secret Clearance for Defense Work.

Summer and Part-Time: Manager, Campus Apartments; Disc Jockey for KXOA and KXRQ; Laboratory Assistant for Radio-TV Speech Department, Stage Technician.

PERSONAL BACKGROUND AND INTERESTS

Attented public elementary and high school in Crisfield, Maryland. Traveled while in Air Force through United States, Caribbean, Europe, Middle East, South Pacific, and Australia. Interested in water skiing, scuba diving, jazz, and building hi-fi equipment.

REFERENCES

References available upon request at Placement Planning Center, California State University, Sacramento.

a. Comment on what you consider to be the strengths and weaknesses of this résumé in terms of organization and content.
b. If you were an employer, which of the data about Williams might impress you the most? the least?
c. Would you hire this man for a management trainee position?

SUGGESTED READINGS

Bird, Caroline. *Born Female*. New York: Pocket Books, 1969.

Chruden, Herbert J., and Arthur W. Sherman, Jr. *Readings in Personnel Management*, 4th ed. Cincinnati: South-Western Publishing Co., 1976. Part 2.

Cook, Alice H. *The Working Mother*. Ithaca, New York: New York State School of Industrial and Labor Relations, Cornell University, 1975.

Cross, Frank. *Recruitment Advertising*. New York: American Management Association, 1968.

Doeringer, Peter B. (ed.). *Programs to Employ the Disadvantaged*. Englewood Cliffs, N.J.: Prentice-Hall, Inc., 1969.

Hawk, Roger H. *The Recruitment Function*. New York: American Management Association, 1967.

Jaquish, Michael P. *Recruiting*. New York: John Wiley & Sons, Inc., 1968.

Johnson, Lawrence A. *Employing the Hard-Core Unemployed*. AMA Research Study 98. New York: American Management Association, 1969.

Patten, Thomas H., Jr. *Manpower Planning and the Development of Human Resources*. New York: Wiley, 1971.

Selection

Personnel selection is the process of determining from among the applicants for employment which ones best fit the manpower requirements and should be offered positions in the organization. In some cases these applicants may be evaluated for a specific job opening in which they may be interested. Many times, however, because of the continuing needs for new personnel, applicants may be evaluated against the requirements of a number of different jobs that are open or that may be open in the future. By engaging in a continuous recruiting and selection process for both present and future job openings, an organization should be in a better position to locate and employ the type of talent that best meets its requirements.

Employers are giving greater attention to the selection process because they recognize that it is the starting place for building quality into their organizations. Individuals who are carefully screened against established specifications are most likely to learn their job tasks more readily, to become better producers, and to become better adjusted to their employment situation than are those persons who are hired on an informal basis. As a result of careful selection, both the individual and the organization benefit. There is an additional incentive for management to have sound selection policies and procedures where the job tenure of employees is protected by the union or civil service. If poorly qualified applicants are hired and permitted to remain on the job, it becomes increasingly difficult for management to discharge them the longer they remain on the job.

The selection program typically is the responsibility of the personnel department. An employment division usually is established within the larger departments to carry out the many functions that this program may entail. Since managerial and supervisory personnel in all of the other departments of an organization are also given an important role in the selection process, it is essential that they understand the objectives and policies relating to selection and that they are oriented in and motivated to use the most scientific approaches to evaluating applicants that will be discussed in this and the chapter that follows.

MATCHING PEOPLE AND JOBS

The selection of personnel for an organization is a complex process involving the matching of the abilities, aptitudes, interests, and personalities of applicants against the specifications of the job. Personnel responsible for selection should have as much information as possible about the applicants and the jobs, as well as a policy to guide them. Policy statements relating to selection help to insure that this function will be carried out in a manner that is consistent with other aspects of the personnel program and the expectations and requirements of society. The decision to hire or to reject an applicant represents one of the most important decisions that are made within an organization. To increase the likelihood of hiring a person who will be able to get along harmoniously with the supervisor and members of the work group, managerial and supervisory personnel usually make the final selection after the personnel department has determined through analysis of various types of information that the applicant meets the basic qualifications.

Information Needed for Selection

Those individuals in an organization who are responsible for making the selection decision should have adequate information upon which to make such decisions. Information about the jobs to be filled, the ratio of job or position openings to the number of applicants, and as much information as possible about the applicants themselves are essential. Since the information that is given to them may not always be complete and accurate, it is their responsibility to seek out further information from available sources.

Job Specifications. Ordinarily the managers and supervisors are well acquainted with the job requirements pertaining to skill, physical demands, personality, and other factors in their respective departments. It is desirable that interviewers and other members of the personnel department who participate in selection maintain a close liaison with the various departments in the organization in order to become thoroughly familiar with the jobs for which they are to make selections. In large organizations it may be possible for interviewers to be made responsible for a particular class of jobs and thereby become more knowledgeable about those jobs.

Selectivity in Hiring. The extent to which selectivity can be achieved will depend upon the number of qualified applicants who are available for consideration. If the number of applicants is small, either because of a short labor supply or ineffective recruiting efforts, the degree of selectivity will be reduced. Selectivity is typically expressed in terms of a *selection ratio* which is the ratio of the number of applicants to be selected to the total number of applicants available. A ratio of .10, for example, means that 10 percent of the applicants will be selected; a ratio of .90 means that 90 percent of the applicants will be selected. If this ratio is small, only the most promising applicants normally would be hired. When the ratio is high, very little selectivity is possible since even those applicants of mediocre ability will have to be hired if the vacancies are to be filled.

Information About Applicants. Employers basically desire as much information as possible about what an applicant *can do* and *will do*. The *can do* factors include knowledge and skills as well as aptitude or potential for acquiring new knowledge and skills. The *will do* factors include motivation, interests, and other personality characteristics. In order to determine what an individual can do and will do, it is essential to obtain information about applicants that is sufficiently reliable and valid.

Reliable Information. *Reliability* refers to the extent to which interviews, tests, and other selection tools are consistent in the information that they provide. Unless interviewers judge the capabilities of applicants to be the same today as they did yesterday, their judgments are unreliable. Likewise, a psychological test that gives widely different scores when it is administered to an individual a few days apart is just as worthless as a scale in a supermarket that gives a different reading each time the same object is placed upon it. Both measures are unreliable.

Valid Information. In addition to having reliable information pertaining to a person's suitability for a job, it is also essential to have information that is valid. *Validity* refers to the degree to which the information is predictive of an applicant's success or failure on a particular job. Determining the degree of validity requires that the information obtained from interviews, tests, and other selection methods be related to the actual job performance of employees, commonly referred to as the *criterion*. The criterion may be production records, supervisory ratings, and other measures of success that are appropriate to each type of job. In a sales job, for example, it is common to use dollar sales figures. In production jobs quantity and quality of output may provide the best criterion of job success. While validity is ordinarily computed by using correlational methods and other approaches that will be discussed in the next chapter, Figure 6-1 illustrates the difference between valid and invalid tests in predicting success in the criterion. It will be noted that in the valid test individuals with the same test score achieve similar criterion ratings, whereas in the invalid test individuals with the same test score receive a variety of criterion ratings. The test or interview that is reasonably valid has predictive value; the one that is invalid gives misleading information about the probable success of applicants if it is used. The validity of each one of the methods and of the information obtained about applicants should be determined in order that the extent of its contribution to the selection process is known.

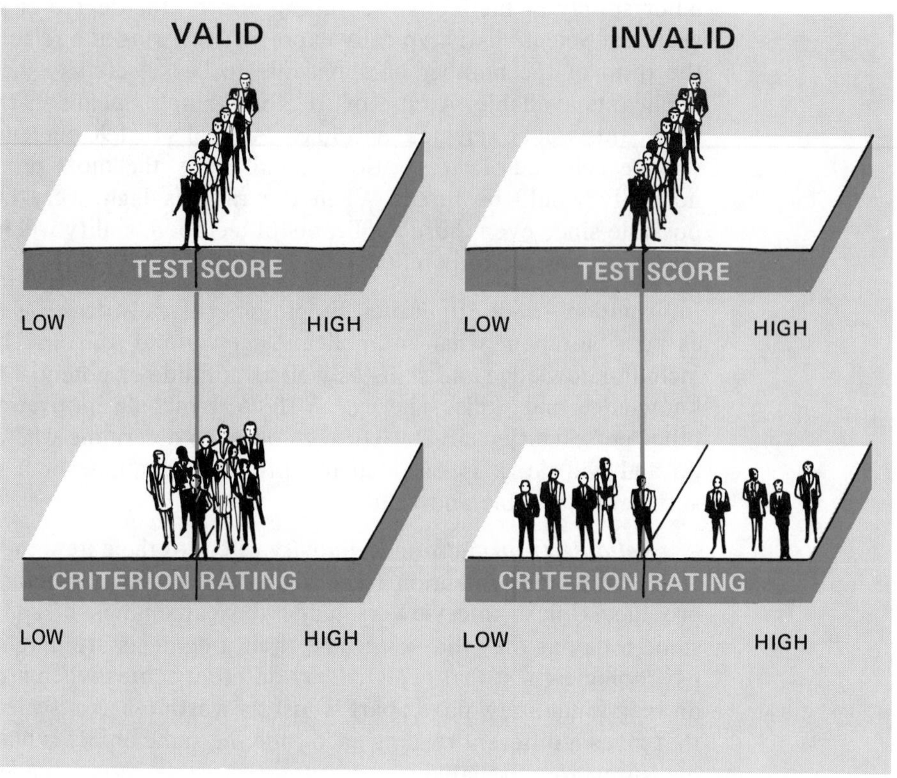

Figure 6-1 VALID AND INVALID TESTS

Importance of Policies

The primary objective of employee selection is to choose those individuals who are most likely to perform their jobs with maximum effectiveness and to remain with the organization. In order to achieve this objective, it is necessary to have policy statements as guides. The policy statement may cover a wide variety of matters considered to be important in making policy decisions. It is typical, for example, to have policy statements concerning the extent to which present or former employees and relatives of employees should be given priority over other applicants for jobs. In recent years greater attention has been given to the social significance of recruiting and selection policies. Policies that are concerned with the ethics of recruiting and selection, fair and equal employment practices, the utilization of handicapped persons, and the employment of persons with histories of mental illness or imprisonment are more prevalent.

Ethical Considerations. The selection process involves procedures that should be examined from an ethical standpoint. Application blanks, for example, frequently ask for information that may be construed as an invasion of privacy. The same is true of certain tests, particularly personality inventories, that require the examinee to reveal opinions and feelings about intimate areas of his or her life. Many organizations have found it desirable to have specific policy statements concerning the solicitation and use of information that may be considered as intimate and revealing. The type of information that is to be recorded and the identity of those in the organization who are to be permitted access to such records should be delineated clearly. Other sources of information used in selection, such as that gained by means of the polygraph (lie dector), peepholes, see-through mirrors, hidden cameras, and microphones, have come under severe attack because they tend to invade the applicant's privacy. Their use is not only considered unethical but legislation restricting or outlawing their use has been passed in several states.[1] Finally, the ethical handling of personnel matters requires that confidentiality be demanded of all individuals who have access to private information and that the security of personnel files be strictly enforced.[2]

Fair and Equal Employment Practices. Prior to the passage of the Civil Rights Act of 1964, employers, unless restricted by a federal executive order in the case of government contracts or state fair employment practice laws, were free to establish their own policies with regard to whom they should hire.

Civil Rights Act of 1964. Title VII of this act[3] expressly prohibits discrimination in employment on the basis of race, color, religion, sex, or national origin. It also created an Equal Employment Opportunity Commission (EEOC) to assist in implementing its provisions. An amendment to the act, known as the Tower Amendment to Title VII, expressly permitted the use of professionally developed ability tests, but there were numerous questions concerning the appropriateness of specific testing procedures for personnel decisions. Public policy was shaped by the guidelines for the use of tests and other selection devices drawn up by the Office of Federal Contract Compliance (OFCC), the EEOC, and the Supreme Court ruling in the case of Griggs *vs.* Duke Power Company.[4] The Griggs case is particularly important because of the ruling that selection tests and other types of information used in selection must be job related.

Equal Employment Opportunity Act of 1972. In 1972 the Civil Rights Act was amended by the Equal Employment Opportunity Act.[5] The amendment changed Title VII to cover all private employers of 15 or more persons, all public and private educational institutions, state and local governments, public

---

[1] "Unions Act in Threats to Privacy," *Business Week* (March 13, 1965), pp. 87-88. See also Philip Ash, "Selection Techniques and the Law: Discrimination in Hiring and Placement," *Personnel*, Vol. 44, No. 6 (November-December, 1967), pp. 8-17.

[2] For detailed instructions on security of personnel offices, see Ed San Luis, *Office and Office Building Security* (New York: Security World Publishing Company, 1973).

[3] 78 Stat 265; 42 USC 2000e *et seq.*

[4] A detailed historical account may be found in Cameron Fincher, "Personnel Testing and Public Policy," *American Psychologist*, Vol. 28, No. 6 (June, 1973), pp. 489-497.

[5] Public Law 92-261.

and private employment agencies, labor unions, and joint labor-management committees for apprenticeship and training. The Equal Employment Opportunity Act also strengthened the enforcement powers of the EEOC and gave the EEOC power to go directly to court to enforce the law. Regional litigation centers were established with substantial legal staff to provide more rapid and effective court action.

Other Antidiscriminatory Laws and Regulations. While the Civil Rights Act and the Equal Employment Opportunity Act are the primary laws established to fight discrimination in employment, other laws and regulations form the basis for personnel policy. The federal Age Discrimination in Employment Act of 1967 [6] prohibits employers of 25 or more persons from discriminating against persons 40-65 in any area of employment because of age. Executive Order 11246 (as amended by E.O. 11375) requires affirmative action programs by all federal contractors and subcontractors. Title VI of the Civil Rights Act of 1964 prohibits discrimination in all programs or activities which receive federal financial aid such as in apprenticeship, training, and work-study programs. Other laws and regulations that relate to discrimination are those of state and local governments, the NLRB, and the Equal Pay Act of 1963, which will be discussed in Chapter 19.

The laws, orders, and regulations cited above have been a major influence in determining selection and hiring policies and procedures. What some organizations were doing out of choice has become a requirement for the majority. Most individuals recognize the need for equal opportunity laws and the enforcement of them. One should be aware, however, that their enforcement has resulted in instances of reverse discrimination which can have the effect of denying minority-group members the satisfaction of knowing that they have made it on their own.[7]

Policies Concerning Handicapped Persons. As a result of the success that has been experienced in the employment of handicapped persons, the slogan, "Hire the handicapped—It's good business," has become a standard employment policy for many organizations. This slogan does not suggest that handicapped persons can be placed in any job without giving careful consideration to their disabilities, but rather that it is good business to hire qualified persons who can work safely and productively. Members of the personnel staff should be trained in the assessment of individual variations in types and degrees of limitations and be aware of how these restrictions are related to different jobs in the organization.

In addition to supplements to the *Dictionary of Occupational Titles*[8] that give physical demands for all jobs defined in the *DOT*, the United States

---

[6] PL 90-202; 81 Stat 602.

[7] Daniel Seligman, "How 'Equal Opportunity' Turned into Employment Quotas," *Fortune*, Vol. 87, No. 3 (March, 1973), pp. 160-168.

[8] United States Department of Labor, *A Supplement to the Dictionary of Occupational Titles (Third edition)—Selected Characteristics of Occupations (Physical Demands, Working Conditions, Training Time)*, 1966, and *Supplement 2 to the Dictionary of Occupational Titles (Selected Characteristics of Occupations by Worker Traits and Physical Strength)*, 1968 (Washington, D.C.: Superintendent of Documents).

Department of Labor has prepared a series of *Interviewing Guides for Specific Disabilities*[9] that may be used when considering applicants with certain types of disabilities. Interviewing guides are available covering applicants with epilepsy, heart disease, diabetes, orthopedic disabilities, and other impairments. These guides as well as other sources of information can assist an organization in utilizing the talents of disabled persons effectively and safely. In many cases the restructuring of jobs or the use of special equipment permits them to qualify for employment.

Policies for Other Groups. In an effort to assume a greater responsibility for alleviating some of society's problems, many organizations have established policies relating to the employment of individuals who have been released from mental hospitals and prisons. These individuals typically need assistance of many types but probably none is more important to them as help in getting a job. Policies concerning the hiring of individuals with such backgrounds can be established and administered effectively. The implementation of policies requires that each applicant's background be assessed in the light of what the person can do rather than what he or she has done. With former mental patients the advice and assistance of available medical personnel in evaluating their probable job success and adjustment should be sought if it is not offered. Many of them are able to do an effective job and should be given an opportunity to be productive.

For people with criminal records, a number of the courts, state legislatures, and government agencies are insisting that employers disregard criminal records unless they are clearly relevant to the job. One individual who has been frustrated by barriers to obtaining employment is Melvin Rivers, a director of the Fortune Society, an organization of ex-convicts.

> As a teen-ager, Mr. Rivers was convicted of assault and robbery. "When I got out, the one thing I wanted to do was to go straight, get a job and settle down," he recalls. But that was far from easy to do.
>
> Mr. Rivers found construction work closed off because, with a record, he couldn't get into the union. He could no longer sing with a group as he used to do because he couldn't get a cabaret license to sing anywhere that alcoholic beverages were sold. Most ironically, he couldn't even get a license to practice the one trade he had learned in prison, barbering.
>
> At last, by lying about his past, he got a job scrubbing pots in a hospital. Five weeks later the truth was discovered. He was fired.[10]

The barriers like these that Mr. Rivers encountered are believed to be responsible for one out of three ex-convicts returning to a life of crime.

---

[9] Published by the United States Department of Labor and available from the Superintendent of Documents.

[10] Richard A. Shaffer, "Erasing the Past—Effort Grows to Assist Job Hunters Haunted by Criminal Records," *The Wall Street Journal,* November 13, 1973. See also George H. Ebbs and Bert C. Shlensky, "Want To Cut Crime Costs? Hire The Ex-Offender," *The Personnel Administrator,* Vol. 19, No. 2 (March-April, 1974), pp. 15-19, as reprinted in Herbert J. Chruden and Arthur W. Sherman, Jr., *Readings in Personnel Management* (4th ed.; Cincinnati: South-Western Publishing Co., 1976), pp. 149-158.

THE SELECTION PROCESS

The selection process is initiated when vacancies occur in an organization as the result of such personnel actions as transfers, promotions, and separations or by an increased authorization of personnel. The vacancies may be filled either by employees in the organization through transfer or promotion, by those who are on a waiting list, or by new applicants. The steps that are typically found in the selection process are shown in Figure 6-2. The number of steps in the selection process and their sequence vary not only with the organization but also with the type and level of job to be filled, the cost of administering the particular function at each step, and the effectiveness of a step in eliminating unqualified candidates. In the discussion that follows, the selection forms and procedures that are commonly used as a basis for obtaining information about an applicant will be examined.

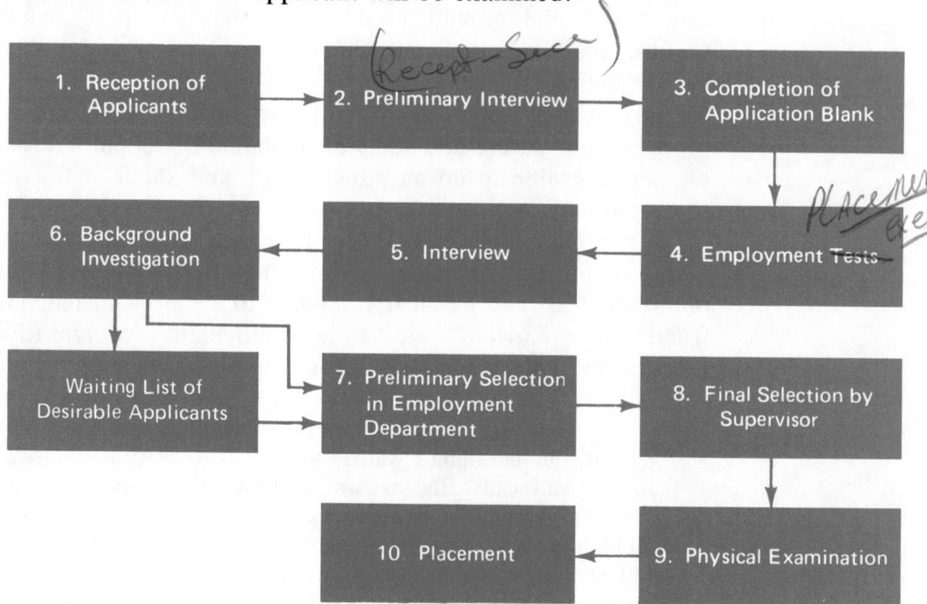

Note: An applicant may be rejected after any step in the process.

Figure 6-2 STEPS IN THE SELECTION PROCESS

Interviews

The applicant may be interviewed by one person or by several, depending primarily upon the importance of the job. The interview serves many purposes and thus may be used at different stages in the selection process. The preliminary interview is often used to screen out those who are obviously unqualified, and it may be conducted on the basis of a preliminary questionnaire that the applicant has completed in the waiting room. Throughout the selection process the interview may be used to verify and clarify application blank data, to obtain further information about what an individual can do and will do, and to provide information about available jobs and the values of being affiliated with the organization. Since the interview plays a major role in personnel selection, it will be examined more thoroughly later in this chapter.

Completion of Application Blanks

Most organizations require *application forms* to be completed because they provide a fairly quick and systematic approach to obtaining a variety of information about the applicant. Such information as educational background, work history, and character references can usually be recorded more efficiently by applicants if they are able to read and write with any degree of facility. Even the best-educated applicants rebel at times, however, because in many companies the application forms have grown with successive generations of personnel managers until they have reached unwieldy proportions. It is essential that forms be reviewed periodically for the purpose of eliminating items that are no longer essential or that may be illegal.

The Equal Employment Opportunity Commission (EEOC) and the courts have found that many questions commonly asked on application forms and in interviews disproportionately reject minorities and females and often are not job related. Employers are warned that questions which inquire into a factor that *might* be considered in a manner which *might* violate Title VII should be avoided or carefully revised to assure that their use is job related and nondiscriminatory in effect. For example, questions that are asked *before hiring* about sex, age, race, national origin, religion, education, arrest and conviction records, marital status, or credit ratings may lead to charges of unlawful discrimination.[11] With the strengthening of the EEOC enforcement policy, the federal laws relating to discrimination have been in the spotlight. One should be aware, however, of state and local laws that may impose additional restrictive provisions.

Employment Tests

For the past half century tests have been part of the selection process of many organizations. The extent to which they are used and the importance that is attached to them vary considerably, depending upon the jobs and the employer. One of the major advantages of tests is their objectivity, especially when compared to the interview. The assessment of what an individual *can do,* for example, often can be done more effectively through ability tests that are constructed or selected for the specific job than through an interview that is unstandardized and incomplete in its coverage of the skills or information required for satisfactory job performance and in which the interviewer's biases

[11] U.S. Equal Employment Opportunity Commission, *Affirmative Action and Equal Opportunity—A Guidebook for Employers,* Vol. II (Washington, D.C.: Equal Employment Opportunity Commission, 1973), pp. 40-44.

may result in overlooking important and relevant information. The tests, however, must first be used under "tryout" conditions and chosen on the basis of their ability to predict success in the job.

Background Investigations

If the interviewer is satisfied that the applicant is potentially suitable, previous employment and other information provided in the application form and in the interview may be investigated. Obviously all information cannot be checked; it may be well to verify those items that are known to be most significant in determining one's acceptability for the job. Some of the approaches that are used in conducting background investigations will be considered in the next chapter.

Preliminary and Final Selection

After the information about the applicants has been obtained from the various sources that have been described, the employment department (or division of the personnel department) usually makes the preliminary selection of those applicants who appear to be most promising. One or more of these applicants are then referred to the requisitioning department for interview and final selection, usually by the supervisor. The number of applicants to be considered at this level will depend upon how many individuals are found to be qualified by the personnel department.

In government agencies—federal, state, and local—the selection of individuals to fill job openings is made from lists or registers of eligible candidates. These lists contain the names of all who meet the required qualifications and who have received the passing grade on the examinations. Ordinarily three or more names of individuals at the top of the register are submitted to the requisitioning official. This arrangement provides some latitude in making a selection and at the same time preserves the merit system.

Physical Examination

The physical examination often is one of the final steps in the selection process because it can be costly and because it should be given immediately prior to hiring. If an organization has its own medical staff and laboratory facilities, the physical examination or parts of it, such as visual or auditory tests, may come earlier.

Extent of Use. A preemployment physical is required in a large percentage of organizations. It may be noted from the data shown in italics in Table 6-1 that the percentage varies, ranging from a low of 30 percent for the wholesale trade industry to a high of 95 percent for gas and electric utility companies. The data cited in Table 6-1 also indicate that United States companies' policies and practices vary with regard to preemployment physicals. In several European

Table 6-1 COMPANY SPONSORED MEDICAL EXAMINATIONS

Industry	Number of Companies	Percentage Requiring Preemployment Examination	Percentage Requiring* Periodic Examination During Employment	Percentage Requiring* Examinations When Returning After Illness
Manufacturing Companies	426	*85*	30	*Data not given*
Insurance	129	*70*	16	29
Banks	158	*50*	9	11
Gas & Electric Utilities	92	*95*	10	43
Retail Trade	100	*42*	10	37
Wholesale Trade	50	*30*	4	8

Source: National Industrial Conference Board, *Personnel Practices in Factory and Office: Manufacturing, 1964; Office Personnel Practices: Nonmanufacturing, 1965.* Reproduced with permission.
* For one or more categories of personnel. These examinations are usually not required for all personnel.

countries, however, preemployment physicals are required by law. In The Netherlands, Belgium, and France they are mandatory. In France a company physician not only can determine whether or not an applicant is physically fit for a particular job but also has the authority to halt any work activities that are believed to endanger the health of the workers.[12]

Objectives. The preemployment physical examination has three primary objectives: (1) to assure the applicant's fitness for work in the organization, (2) to assure the applicant's fitness for a particular job, and (3) to provide a base line against which subsequent physical examinations may be compared and interpreted. The last objective is particularly important in determinations of work-caused disabilities under workmen's compensation laws. The preemployment physical should provide a detailed medical and occupational history with special reference to previous hazardous exposures, particularly those whose effects may be cumulative such as noise, lead, and ionizing radiation. For jobs involving unusual physical demands, the applicant's muscular development, flexibility and agility, range of motion, and cardiac and respiratory functions should be determined. The preemployment physical is particularly valuable in the placement of handicapped persons.[13] Finally, in recent years employers have been confronted with the pressing problem of drug abuse and what to do about it. The preemployment physical with its laboratory analyses provides an opportunity to detect those applicants who are on drugs.[14]

---

[12] Herbert J. Chruden and Arthur W. Sherman, Jr., *Personnel Practices of American Companies in Europe* (New York: American Management Association, 1972), p. 35.

[13] May R. Mayers, *Occupational Health* (Baltimore: The Williams and Wilkins Co., 1969), Chapter 37.

[14] Alvin Keltz, "Preemployment Drug Screening," *The Personnel Administrator,* Vol. 17, No. 4 (July-August, 1972), pp. 15-18.

Placement

The applicant who passes all of the foregoing steps in the selection process is then assigned to a position in a department where the manager or supervisor has accepted the individual. At this point orientation and training on the job will begin. In order that the supervisor may do an effective job of orienting and training the new employee, the supervisor should have access to pertinent parts of the file that was developing during the selection process. Too frequently members of the personnel staff assume that supervisors in other departments are incapable of using the information with discretion, thus defeating the purposes for which the files are maintained.

THE EMPLOYMENT INTERVIEW

The interview traditionally has had an important role in the process of selecting personnel. Various surveys indicate, for example, that about 99.5 percent of employers use the interview as a basis for obtaining information from applicants and for communicating information about the nature of available jobs and the organization. Unlike some of the steps in the selection process that involve the services of professionally-trained personnel or fairly standardized procedures, interviews tend to be conducted by individuals with different orientations and competencies who use a variety of methods.

Interviewing Methods

Employment or selection interviews are classified primarily according to the methods or approaches that are used to obtain information and to elicit attitudes and feelings from an applicant. These methods differ from one another in various ways. The most significant difference is with respect to the amount of *structure* or control that is exercised by the interviewer as a particular method is used. In the highly structured type of interview, the interviewer determines the course that the interview will follow as each question is asked, whereas in a less structured interview the applicant plays a larger role in determining the way in which the discussion will go.

Nondirective Interview. In the *nondirective interview* the interviewer carefully refrains from influencing the applicant's remarks. The applicant is allowed the maximum amount of freedom in determining the course of the discussion. This is achieved by the interviewer asking broad, general questions, such as "Tell me more about your experiences in your last job," and by permitting the applicant to talk freely with a minimum of interruption. Brief interviewer responses, as, for example, "What happened then?" or "What were the circumstances?" are used to keep the applicant talking about the subject. In general, the nondirective approach is characterized by such interviewer behavior as listening carefully, not arguing, using questions sparingly, not interrupting or changing the subject abruptly, phrasing responses briefly, and allowing pauses in the conversation. This latter technique is the most difficult for the beginning interviewer to master, perhaps because our everyday conversational folkways dictate that someone should be talking if two or more persons are gathered together.

The greater freedom afforded to the applicant in the nondirective interview provides an opportunity to discuss at length any points that he or she would like to talk about. This may be particularly valuable in bringing to the interviewer's attention any information, attitudes, or feelings that are often concealed by more rapid questioning of the applicant. On the other hand, the interviewer should not come to a nondirective interview without some objectives to be achieved.

Depth Interview. The *depth interview* goes a step beyond the nondirective interview by providing additional structure in the form of questions that cover different areas of the applicant's life that are related to employment. A *Depth Interview Pattern* form developed by Martin M. Bruce provides 37 questions covering work, education, social relationships, economics, and personality to be responded to by the applicant. These questions, a few of which have been reproduced in Figure 6-3, are designed so as to permit the applicant to respond fully to them. The applicant is encouraged to answer each question in depth enough so as to permit the interviewer to obtain sufficient information to make an evaluation. The *Depth Interview Pattern* form provides an evaluation sheet to guide the interviewer in evaluating the six major areas covered by the interview.

Would you tell me about your work history; how you got the jobs, the kinds of work you did and your reasons for leaving?

What is most important to you in a job? What do you care least about in a job?

What experience during your school days stood out as meaning the most to you?

What do you believe to be your strong points as a person?

What position do you want to hold ten years from now?

Why should we hire you?

Source: Depth Interview Pattern by Martin M. Bruce. Copyright 1956, Judd-Safian Associates, New York. Reproduced with permission.

Figure 6-3 SOME QUESTIONS FROM THE DEPTH INTERVIEW PATTERN

Patterned Interview. The most highly structured type of interview is the *patterned interview* which adheres closely to a highly detailed set of questions on specially prepared forms such as the one shown in Figure 6-4. The questions in black ink are to be asked of the applicant during the course of the interview. The questions in color beneath the line are not asked of the applicant but rather are designed to help the interviewer to obtain complete information, to interpret its significance, and to become aware of inconsistencies. The interpretations are later recorded on a summary sheet that is completed on the basis of information obtained from the interview and from the application form, tests, telephone checks, and sources of information about the applicant. A summary sheet is used for rating the applicant on "can do" and "will do" factors and for summarizing the ratings into an overall rating. Studies made in organizations using the patterned interview have shown that it is a method that produces moderate-to-highly-valid results.[15] The training required for this type of interviewing, as well as the standardized procedure, probably contributes to its reported success.

Special Interview Methods. Most employment interviews will follow one of the approaches that have been described. There are other approaches, however, that are utilized for special purposes. The *group interview* (also called a group oral-performance test) is a popular approach in the selection of executive trainees. When the group interview approach is used, a half dozen or so candidates assemble for a group discussion. Seated to the side or behind the group will be company executives who observe and evaluate the candidates as they engage in a round-table discussion with or without a leader. Revlon, Inc., reports that this method not only saves top executives' time but seems to result in better selection decisions.[16] While the group interview is generally used along with other selection techniques, it has been found to facilitate observations of such factors as initiative, aggressiveness, poise, adaptability to new situations, tact, ability to get along with people, and similar qualities.

One type of interview, commonly used by government agencies including the military services, involves having a panel of interviews or observers who sit as a "board" and question and observe a single candidate in what is called a *board interview*. Another type that was developed during World War II as a technique for selecting military espionage personnel places the candidate under considerable pressure and hence is known as the *stress interview*. It usually involves rapid firing of questions by several interviewers who appear unfriendly. While it would seem to be a useful approach in selecting individuals for jobs where resistance to stress is important, validation data on its effectiveness are lacking.

---

[15] Roger M. Bellows and M. Frances Estep, *Employment Psychology: The Interview* (New York: Rinehart & Company, Inc., 1954); and Robert N. McMurry, *Tested Techniques of Personnel Selection* (Revised ed.; Chicago: The Dartnell Corporation, 1966).

[16] Jules Z. Willing, "The Round-Table Interview—A Method of Selecting Trainees," *Personnel*, Vol. 39, No. 21 (March-April, 1962), pp. 26-32.

PATTERNED INTERVIEW FORM

SUMMARY	
S U M M A R Y	Rating: [1] [2] [3] [4] Interviewer ______ Date ______ Comments (List both favorable and unfavorable points) ______ In making final rating, be sure to consider not only the man's ability and experience but also his stability, industry, perseverance, ability to get along with others, loyalty, self-reliance, and leadership. Is he mature and realistic? Is he well motivated for this work? Are his living standards, finances, his domestic situation, and the family influence favorable to this work? Does he have sufficient health and physical reserve? ______ ______ Position Considered for ______

Name ______ Telephone Number ______ Is it your phone? ______

Present Address ______ City ______ State ______
Will this location affect his attendance? Is this a desirable neighborhood? Does it appear consistent with income?

Date of your birth ______ Age ______ Have you served in the Armed Services of the United States? ☐ Yes ☐
In some States, legislation forbids discrimination because of age.

(If yes) What were the dates? ______19 ___ to ______19 ___ If rejected or exempted, what were the reasons? ______
Discuss military service as a job in chronological order with other jobs. Will this affect his performance on our job?

Why are you applying for this position? ______
Are his underlying reasons practical? Does he have a definite goal?

Are you employed now? ☐ Yes ☐ No; (If yes) how soon available? ______
What are relationships with present employer?

WORK HISTORY: LAST OR PRESENT POSITION Dates from ______19 ___ to ______19 ___
If out of work—how long?

Company ______ Division ______ Address ______
Does this check with application?

How did you get this job? ______
Did he show self-reliance in getting this job? Stability of interests? Perseverance?

Nature of work at start ______ Earnings at start ______
Did this work require energy and industry? Close attention? Cooperation?

How did the job change? ______ Earnings at leaving ______
Was progress made? Any indications of strong motivation? Is this in line with what he can earn here?

What were your duties and responsibilities at time of leaving? ______
Did he accept them? Indications of industry? Self-reliance? Perseverance? Leadership?

Superior ______ Title ______ How was he to work with? ______
Was this close supervision? Are there indications of loyalty? Hostility?

What did you especially like about the position? ______
Has he been happy and content in his work? Indications of loyalty, ability to get along with others?

What did you especially dislike? ______
Did he get along well with people? Is he inclined to be critical? Were his dislikes justified?

How much time have you lost from work? ______ Reasons ______
Is he regular in attendance on the job? Are there other interests?

Reasons for leaving ______ Why right then? ______
Are his reasons for leaving reasonable and consistent? Do they check with records?

Part-time jobs during this employment ______
Does this indicate industry? Ambition? Lack of loyalty? Lack of interest in duties of position?

NEXT TO LAST POSITION Dates from ______19 ___ to ______19 ___
Any time between this and last job?

Company ______ Division ______ Address ______
Does this check with application?

How did you get this job? ______
Did he show self-reliance in getting this job? Stability of interests? Perseverance?

Nature of work at start ______ Earnings at start ______
Did this work require energy and industry? Close attention? Cooperation?

How did the job change? ______ Earnings at leaving ______
Was progress made? Any indications of strong motivation? Is this in line with what he can earn here?

What were your duties and responsibilities at time of leaving? ______
Did he accept them? Indications of industry? Self-reliance? Perseverance? Leadership?

Superior ______ Title ______ How was he to work with? ______
Was this close supervision? Are there indications of loyalty? Hostility?

Source: Published by the Dartnell Corporation, Chicago. Reproduced with permission.

Figure 6-4 McMURRY PATTERNED INTERVIEW FORM (page 1 only)

Research on the Employment Interview

The employment interview has been popular not only as a tool in selection but also as a subject of criticism over the years because it has often been used to the exclusion of other procedures, such as psychological tests that have been researched and validated far more thoroughly. The unquestioned acceptance of the employment interview as a basis for obtaining information and making judgments about applicants still continues in spite of the fact that as early as 1915 articles that cited limitations of the typical employment interview were appearing in the literature.[17]

In the last half century hundreds of articles and scores of books have been written about the interview, but unfortunately most of them have been of the "how to do it" type, based primarily upon opinion. Reviews of the literature show that only a small proportion of the articles are concerned with actual experiments to determine which methods are the most reliable and valid. However, when one looks at some of the more current research findings that have accumulated, it is apparent that more is known about the subject than most interviewers take the opportunity to utilize.[18] The more significant findings will be discussed here according to major factors that determine the effectiveness of employment interviews.

Reliability of the Interview. The reliability or consistency with which information obtained from the interview is evaluated is the first consideration in determining its usefulness. Reliability involves two types: intrarater reliability and interrater reliability. According to Mayfield *intrarater reliability,* i.e., an interviewer reinterviewing the same interviewee or listening to a tape of the original interview, exists when the interviewer tends to arrive at approximately the same evaluation as he or she did originally. *Interrater reliability* takes place when two or more interviewers evaluate the same applicant similarly. The extent of their agreement about the applicant's qualifications is largely a function of the type of interview. Structured interviews, in general, provide a higher interrater reliability than do unstructured interviews.[19]

Validity of the Interview. The validity of the interview is concerned with the extent to which it yields information that is predictive of applicant success or failure on the job. Several studies cited by Mayfield have shown that

[17] Walter Dill Scott, "The Scientific Selection of Salesmen," *Advertising and Selling,* Vol. 25 (1915), pp. 5-6 and 94-96.

[18] E. C. Mayfield, "The Selection Interview—A Reevaluation of Published Research," *Personnel Psychology,* Vol. 17, No. 3 (Autumn, 1964), pp. 239-260; Lynn Ulrich and Don Trumbo, "The Selection Interview Since 1949," *Psychological Bulletin,* Vol. 63, No. 2 (February, 1965), pp. 100-116; Orman R. Wright, Jr., "Summary of Research on the Selection Interview Since 1964," *Personnel Psychology,* Vol. 22, No. 4 (Winter, 1969), pp. 391-414; Robert E. Carlson, Paul W. Thayer, Eugene C. Mayfield, and Donald A. Peterson, "Improvements in the Selection Interview," *Personnel Journal,* Vol. 50, No. 4 (April, 1971), pp. 268-275 and 317.

[19] Donald P. Schwab and Herbert G. Heneman, "Relationship Between Interview Structure and Interinterviewer Reliability in an Employment Situation," *Journal of Applied Psychology,* Vol. 53, No. 3 (June, 1969), pp. 214-217.

predictions based on the interview and the test scores are generally no more (and frequently less) accurate than those based solely on the test scores. It should be noted, however, that where more than one interviewer is involved the interview does contribute to the prediction of job success. As noted earlier, the McMurry patterned interview has been found to be reasonably valid as a method. This validity is likely to be the result of its high degree of structure and its requirement for interviewer training.

Accuracy of Information Obtained. Another important consideration with respect to the interview is the accuracy of the information that is obtained. Such accuracy is particularly essential if the interview is being used primarily to gather information that might otherwise be obtained by other methods.

Several studies have been conducted to evaluate the accuracy of interview data. In one study high agreement was found between the information provided by job applicants about their wages, duration of employment, and job duties and that provided by previous employers.[20] Other studies report somewhat different findings, especially where the interviewees were asked to supply information about themselves that had what they perceived to be socially undesirable connotations. Errors in reporting information tended to be in the direction of applicants providing the type of information that they considered to be more socially acceptable.[21] In a subsequent study, statements about work history that had been provided in a special interview were verified against records of their employers for at least five years preceding the interview. It was found that on only 3 of the 11 work history items studied did the proportion of valid information exceed 70 percent. On four items, 40 percent or more of the interview information was invalid. It was also found that information for the interviewee's present job was no more valid than for past (or earlier) jobs, thereby indicating that poor memory was not the only factor operating to cause a discrepancy.[22] It appears from these and other studies that the degree of accuracy of information is determined by the applicant's perception of what responses would be more desirable in terms of social acceptability.

Decision Making by Interviewers. Research in recent years has focused on the interview as a decision-making process. A series of studies undertaken at McGill University has had the objective of determining how interviewers arrived at their evaluations of the applicant. Webster and five of his colleagues report seven principal findings from their studies covering a nine-year period:

1. Interviewers develop a stereotype of a good candidate and seek to match men and stereotypes. Personnel officers who differed considerably in training and experience were found to be looking for the same characteristics in interviewees.

---

[20] E. Keating, D. G. Paterson, and C. H. Stone, "Validity of Work Histories Obtained by Interview," *Journal of Applied Psychology,* Vol. 34, No. 1 (February, 1950), pp. 6-11.

[21] D. J. Weiss and R. V. Dawis, "An Objective Validation of Factual Interview Data," *Journal of Applied Psychology,* Vol. 44, No. 6 (December, 1960), pp. 381-385.

[22] David J. Weiss, René V. Dawis, George W. England, and Lloyd H. Lofquist, *Validity of Work Histories Obtained by Interview,* Minnesota Studies in Vocational Rehabilitation: XII (Minneapolis: Industrial Relations Center, University of Minnesota, 1961).

2. A bias is established early in the interview, and this tends to be followed either by a favorable or by an unfavorable decision.
3. Interviews are more influenced by unfavorable than by favorable information. While the interviewer has a stereotype of a "good" applicant, he is more influenced by clear and definite unfavorable information than by good qualities when faced with the necessity of reaching a decision. He is not prepared to take a chance.
4. Interviewers seek information to support or refute hypotheses and, when satisfied, they turn their attention elsewhere. Interviewers seek to confirm early impressions by altering the emphasis they place on parts of information made available.
5. Empathy relationships are specific to individual interviewers. Some interviewers "place themselves in the shoes" of applicants in order to try to understand the applicant's motives.
6. Feeding information piece by piece to one who is making a judgment affects his decision. When he is given all information simultaneously, his judgment is both different and better than when information is fed to him piece by piece.
7. Experienced interviewers rank applicants in the same order although they differ in the proportion that they will accept. A high degree of consistency as to the percentage of applicants accepted by the individual judge was found. A tendency for more experienced interviewers to be more selective than less experienced ones was also found.[23]

Other researchers are also devoting more attention to the decision-making process as it occurs in the selection interview. A series of studies pertaining to the selection interview in a life insurance agency provides information much of which confirms the findings from the McGill studies.[24]

Selection and Training of Interviewers

Considerable care should be given to the selection of employment interviewers. While the specific qualifications will vary, there are some qualities that should characterize the individuals who are selected for the job of interviewing. The most fundamental quality should be humility because it motivates the interviewers to avoid hasty judgments, to improve their skills, to

[23] Edward C. Webster, *Decision Making in the Employment Interview* (Montreal: McGill University, Industrial Relations Center, 1964), pp. 85-91.

[24] Robert E. Carlson, "Selection Interview Decisions: The Effect of Interviewer Experience, Relative Quota Situation, and Applicant Sample on Interviewer Decisions," *Personnel Psychology,* Vol. 20, No. 3 (Autumn, 1967), pp. 259-280; Robert E. Carlson, "Employment Decisions: Effect of Mode of Applicant Presentation on Some Outcome Measures," *Personnel Psychology,* Vol. 21, No. 2 (Summer, 1968), pp. 193-207; Robert E. Carlson, "Relative Influence of a Photograph vs. Factual Written Information on an Interviewer's Employment Decision," *Personnel Psychology,* Vol. 22, No. 1 (Spring, 1969), pp. 45-56. For similar research in other settings, see Thomas D. Hollman, "Employment Interviewers' Errors in Processing Positive and Negative Information," *Journal of Applied Psychology,* Vol. 56, No. 2 (April, 1972), pp. 130-134; Enzo Valenzi and I. R. Andrews, "Individual Differences in the Decision Process of Employment Interviewers," *Journal of Applied Psychology,* Vol. 58, No. 1 (August, 1973), pp. 49-53; and Manuel London and Milton D. Hakel, "Effects of Applicant Stereotypes, Order, and Information on Interview Impressions," *Journal of Applied Psychology,* Vol. 59, No. 2 (April, 1974), pp. 157-162.

obtain the evaluations of others, and to rely on other selection devices. Other specific qualities that are desirable for interviewers are: ability to think objectively, critically, and systematically; experience in associating with people who have a variety of backgrounds; recent extensive experience with people similar in age and occupation to those being interviewed; association of experience with people in particular occupational groups; freedom from overtalkativeness, extreme opinions, and biases; maturity and poise.[25]

A training program should be provided on a continuous basis for employment interviewers and at least periodically for managers and supervisors in other departments.[26] Many organizations, however, fail to provide any special training even for their full-time interviewers. A training program should include a review of the research on interviewing and other aspects of selection, as well as provide for experience in conducting interviews either through role playing or by recording actual interviews preferably on video tapes that may then be evaluated and discussed.[27] Since interviewers differ in personality and the interview methods described previously require different approaches, some variation in technique may be expected. There are, however, some ground rules for employment interviews that are commonly accepted and supported by research evidence. Their apparent simplicity should not lead one to underestimate their importance.

Preparing for the Interview. Even the most highly trained and experienced interviewer should prepare for this activity. The preparation typically includes an examination of the purpose of the interview and the outlining of areas and specific questions to be covered. A review of the application form, test scores, information from reference checks, and other pertinent data is essential. Preparation desirably extends to the interview climate to insure that the setting is private and as free from distractions as possible.

Establishing and Maintaining Rapport. The first step in an interview is to establish friendly and cordial relationships with the interviewee. The interviewer achieves this condition, referred to as *rapport*, by greeting the applicant pleasantly, by displaying sincere interest in the applicant, and by listening carefully to what the applicant is saying as well as what the applicant is trying to say. Follow-up questions that begin with *why, what, when, where,* and *how* may be used appropriately to elicit more complete information. The interviewer must also be careful to phrase questions so that any biases are not so apparent as to influence the applicant's responses.

Giving Information. One of the distinctive features of the interview is the opportunity that it provides for giving information to the applicant. Some years ago Bingham pointed out that there are four duties of the employment interviewer that will never be delegated to a computer:

---

[25] Milton M. Mandell, *The Selection Process* (New York: American Management Association, 1964), pp. 187-192.

[26] Louis A. Ordini, Jr., "Why Interview?" *Personnel Journal,* Vol. 47, No. 6 (June, 1968), pp. 430-432.

[27] See selection on ethical considerations on page 122.

(1) He must answer fully and frankly the applicant's questions about your business, the job, and the working conditions. Who has invented a regression equation which will do that? (2) He must convince the man he is interviewing that yours is a good firm to work for since it furnishes such and such opportunities for growth and advancement (if it does). In other words, he must be skillful in selling your firm to the applicant. (3) He must steer the applicant toward a job for which he is better suited, if there is one somewhere, lest he discover that job and shift to it only after you have spent a few hundred dollars in training him. (4) Finally, the interviewer should leave the prospect, in any case, with the feeling that he has made a personal friend.[28]

Making Observations and Inferences. In addition to providing an opportunity to obtain information from the applicant, the interview also provides a setting in which the applicant's personal characteristics such as neatness, fluency of speech, correctness of grammar and pronunciation, mannerisms, poise, and other characteristics may be observed.

Personal Biases. In the typical interview, which is likely to be of short duration, judgments are made on the basis of a very small sample of an individual's behavior. Furthermore, since most applicants "dress up" for the occasion and usually go out of their way to make a good impression, the opinions that untrained interviewers form are likely to rest on shaky grounds. Their opinions of applicants may be influenced by their biases and prejudices which they are unlikely to recognize. One typical bias is the tendency to consider strangers who have interests, experiences, and backgrounds similar to their own as being more acceptable than those who differ from them. This type of bias is illustrated in exaggerated form in Figure 6-5.

The Halo Error. Another problem in interviewing is the *halo error*. This refers to the tendency to judge an individual favorably in many areas on the basis of one strong point. The interviewer who places a high value on personal neatness may judge the applicant who is neat to have many other favorable qualities that he or she may or may not possess, such as those pertaining to intelligence, honesty, and judgment. The halo error can also work in the opposite direction, in which case the above interviewer would probably assume that an unkempt individual is stupid and dishonest.

Influence of Physiognomy. The fact that some individuals happen to resemble each other can constitute a hazard for interviewers. A job applicant who has facial characteristics similar to those of a friend may result in the interviewer's ascribing the same characteristics to this new person. Thus, while an interviewer may recognize physiognomy as being a pseudo-scientific approach to personality assessment, it is easy to fall into the trap of using it. A study conducted by Waterworth revealed that even trained interviewers, who were aware of the fallacy of judging character and personality on the basis of

[28] Walter Van Dyke Bingham, "Today and Yesterday," *Personnel Psychology,* Vol. 2, No. 2 (Summer, 1949), pp. 272-274.

"You're exactly the kind of man we need around here."

Source: Dun's Review and Modern Industry, March, 1957. Reproduced with permission.

Figure 6-5 AN EXAGGERATED FORM OF INTERVIEWER BIAS

facial features, fell into the trap of making such judgments under experimental conditions that provided a "Can't tell from the picture" as one type of response.[29] One might assume, therefore, that interviewers and others engaged in personnel selection may, either consciously or unconsciously, be using methods that should be examined more closely.

Separating Facts from Inferences. On the basis of information and observations, the interviewer makes inferences or interpretations about the individual's behavior. A useful form developed by Moyer of the New York Bell Telephone Company requires the interviewer to record "findings" in one column and "interpretations" of these findings in another column. This is particularly desirable since most interviewers, subject to human error, are likely to combine facts and interpretations together and assume that both are facts. For example, the interviewer might record the fact that a male applicant "sings in church choir." From this fact the interviewer might infer or conclude that the applicant's "Conduct is wholesome." While this may be a reasonably sound inference, it is still an inference and not a fact. One could also infer from the same fact that the applicant has a desire to make himself heard in the community or that he has a girl friend who sings in the choir.

Nervous behavior on the part of the applicant during the interview may be viewed by the interviewer as an indication of emotional maladjustment and, as the result of this impression, the interviewer may give the applicant a low

[29] William H. Waterworth, "Analysis of Physiognomic Stereotypes Held by Professional Interviewers" (Master's thesis, California State University, Sacramento, 1960).

rating. Actually, this is a very natural reaction and may be an indication of the applicant's intense desire to obtain employment with that particular organization.

Since employment interviewing involves making inferences about an individual's probable success on the job, it is essential that interviewers be required to examine the process by which they make inferences. This can be accomplished through the training program where participants are given an opportunity to compare their inferences. The training program should also provide participants with checklists that they can use in evaluating their interviews. However, effective interviewers will not stop with selection and placement on a job. They will keep a file on turnover and periodically review their "batting averages."

THE EMPLOYMENT DECISION

While all of the steps in the selection process are important, the one that is most critical is the decision to accept or reject the applicant for employment. The applicant may be accepted for a job other than the one for which application was originally made since the purpose of the selection program is to consider the total needs of the organization and to match people and jobs as effectively as possible. Because of the cost of placing new employees on the payroll, the shortening of the probationary period in many industries, and other factors such as those related to employee satisfaction and adjustment, it is essential that the final decision be as sound as possible.

Factors in Decision Making

In making decisions one of the major questions that arises is, how much weight should be given to the facts about the applicants? For example, should test scores be given a priority over interviewer judgments? The desirable procedure is for the organization to determine what information has high predictive value and to decide how this information can be obtained most effectively. It may be found that the verified work history and the judgments of the requisitioning department are the most valid indicators for some jobs, whereas for others test scores and evaluations made by former teachers are best.

Reaching a Decision

Once all of the information about an applicant has been assembled by the personnel department, there has to be some method for summarizing it. It is common to find organizations that use summary forms and checklists in order to determine that all of the pertinent information has been included in the evaluation of the applicant. Some organizations use mathematical models for decision making. These involve statistical procedures for combining data such as interviewer ratings, test scores, and other information that can be reduced to numerical terms.[30] Properly developed statistical approaches to decision making that use validated information have been shown to be superior to methods involving personal judgment of experts.[31]

The availability of computers for use in personnel work has made it possible for organizations to improve the decision-making process in personnel selection. It is particularly valuable in validating selection decisions made by other methods involving personal judgment.[32] It is now possible with computers to use the method known as *multiple discriminate function*—a statistical approach which predicts the probability of membership in alternative groups rather than placing individuals at a point along some continuum. It answers the question, "What group is this person most like?" By matching applicant characteristics against the detailed specifications for many jobs, an organization can help to insure that it is not overlooking qualified persons.

Whatever method is used in arriving at a selection decision, it should involve more than weeding out potential misfits. Any strengths that may compensate for weaknesses should be considered. It has been suggested that every personnel department should question its approach in order to determine if it is hiring mediocre people free from any "weaknesses" or whether it focuses its attention on hiring people with strengths and potentialities.[33] Care should be exercised, however, in avoiding the establishment of unrealistic hiring standards which cause talented personnel to become dissatisfied and leave their jobs[34] or which may lead to charges of discrimination.

Notifying Applicants of Decision

It is usually the responsibility of the personnel department to administer the final phases of the selection process that involve notifying applicants of the decision and making job offers to those who have been accepted by the organization. The job offer will confirm the details of the job, working arrangements, wages, and other information that has already been provided in interviews and will specify a time limit in which the applicant must reach a decision. There will be some individuals who are rejected and must, therefore, be advised of it. While the general principle to be followed in rejections is to be as honest as possible with the applicant, it is necessary to maintain confidences and to minimize the possibility of creating more problems by the rejection.

---

[30] Lawrence J. Clarke, "Decision Models for Personnel Selection and Assignment," *Personnel Administration*, Vol. 32, No. 2 (March-April, 1969), pp. 48-56.

[31] P. E. Meehl, *Clinical v. Statistical Prediction* (Minneapolis: University of Minnesota Press, 1954); and J. Sawyer, "Measurement *and* Prediction, Clinical *and* Statistical," *Psychological Bulletin*, Vol. 66, No. 3 (September, 1966), pp. 178-200.

[32] Thomas P. Ference, "Can Personnel Selection Be Computerized?" *Personnel*, Vol. 45, No. 6 (November-December, 1968), pp. 50-55.

[33] Glenn A. Bassett, "The Screening Process: Selection or Rejection?" *Personnel*, Vol. 39, No. 4 (July-August, 1962), pp. 31-37.

[34] Harold Mayfield, "Employee Selection—Don't Overshoot the Mark," *Supervisory Management*, Vol. 9, No. 7 (July, 1964), pp. 9-12.

Evaluating the Selection Program

The function of selecting employees is one of the most important aspects of the personnel program and, therefore, deserves more attention than is frequently given to it. Through analysis of information obtained from such sources as performance records, supervisory evaluations, and exit interviews, it is possible to realize the sources of errors in selection and to make corrections and improvements. Keeping the staff research-oriented in the midst of filling personnel requisitions is not an easy task, but it is a necessary task if selection is to be successful and is to meet the objectives set for it.

Résumé

The process of selection involves obtaining as much information as possible about an applicant for the purpose of making a sound employment decision. While there is a practical limit to the amount of time and money that can be spent for this purpose, the collection of pertinent data covering many different facets of the individual can generally be profitable to the organization as well as to the individual. While the personnel department has a major role in the selection process, the success of the program also depends upon the efforts of the managers in the other departments who have an important role to play in the final evaluation of the applicants that have been initially screened. Since managers who are involved in the final decisions about employees may overlook the need and the opportunity to approach this task scientifically, the personnel staff should not only set a good example by its application of the most reliable and valid methods but should also endeavor to provide assistance and guidance to others who participate in the important process of selecting personnel.

Because of the complex nature of the interpersonal relationship that characterizes the interview, those who conduct interviews should receive special training and their performance in this role should be evaluated continually.

In the cooperative process of selection, care must be taken to assess applicants on the basis of the qualities that are essential to the job. While it is usually easier to determine what a person can do, some judgment must be arrived at concerning what an individual will do if he or she is given the opportunity. It was noted that tests provide one of the most objective approaches to assessing ability and aptitude, whereas interviews and evidences from past experience may give insights that permit making some evaluation of what an individual will do. In the final process of arriving at a decision, however, all available information should be assembled and weighted in the light of its known validity in order that the selection process may contribute maximally to the total personnel program.

DISCUSSION QUESTIONS

1. In selecting personnel for the following jobs, what procedures would give the best measures of what an applicant *can do*? Of what an applicant *will do*?
   a. Supervisor of an office force.
   b. Lathe operator.
   c. Research chemist in an oil company.
2. It was mentioned in this chapter that the Civil Rights Act of 1964 prohibited discrimination in employment because of sex.
   a. What are some of the problems that may arise from men working in jobs that were typically considered as women's jobs and women working in so-called jobs for men? Cite some specific examples.
   b. Do you view these problems as serious or insolvable?
3. The burden of proof is placed on employers to show that their selection procedures have not resulted in unlawful discrimination against a particular group, i.e., women, minorities, or older persons.
   a. What items have you seen recently in newspapers and magazines about organizations that have been charged with discrimination?
   b. What steps should an employer take to avoid such charges?
   c. What types of records should be kept to refute such charges?
4. In recent years an increasing number of employers have instituted programs for hiring the handicapped. Why it it necessary to have a special program for such individuals?
5. Many interviewers attempt to achieve rapport by starting an interview with "small talk" about the day's baseball game or some other topic to put an individual at ease.
   a. How do you feel about this approach?
   b. Is there a better approach?
6. In an advertisement for a personnel department interviewer, one company included the following statement: "Qualifications such as liking to work with people, knowing people, and good judge of people are not wanted."
   a. Why were these restrictions included?
   b. What was the company probably looking for in its applicants for this position?

PROBLEM 6-1 JUST ONE MORE CHANCE

Martinson's Department Store has been serving the community for over 100 years. It is recognized as the leading store of its type and its image is one of quality and service. Because of these characteristics and its sponsorship and support of many community projects, the store has created an excellent image among the residents. As the community has grown, so has Martinson's. It now has five stores with over 1,500 employees. While it is not stated policy, Martinson's will not employ anyone who has a conviction record other than for a minor traffic violation.

Richard Wright, age 26, made application for employment as a sales clerk at Martinson's. During the employment interview he was asked if he had ever been convicted for other than a minor traffic violation. His response was "no." Since he appeared to meet all qualifications, Wright was hired as a part-time sales clerk pending a vacancy for full-time work. When he was given a form to be completed for the bonding company, Wright asked the personnel representative if he should include a shoplifting incident that occurred when he was 11 years old and had since been expunged from the police records. He was advised to put it down. As soon as the form reached the security office at Martinson's, the personnel department was advised that Wright's services would have to be terminated.

Wright had been called in to work three different times before this order was received from security. The manager of the department where he was assigned to fill in said that he was one of the best clerks they had working for them. Security, however, had the final word and Wright would have to go in spite of attempts made by the personnel representative to convince them that his man deserved another chance.

a. With whom do you agree—the personnel representative or the security department? Why?
b. Is the store living up to the image that it has in the community?

SUGGESTED READINGS

Banaka, William H. *Training in Depth Interviewing*. New York: Harper & Row, Publishers, 1971.

Bass, Bernard M. and Gerald V. Barrett. *Man, Work, and Organizations*. Boston: Allyn and Bacon, Inc., 1972. Chapter 11.

Bellows, Roger M., and M. Frances Estep. *Employment Psychology: The Interview*. New York: Holt, Rinehart and Winston, Inc., 1954.

Bingham W. V., B. V. Moore, and John W. Gustad. *How to Interview*, Fourth edition. New York: Harper & Brothers, 1959.

Chruden, Herbert J., and Arthur W. Sherman, Jr. *Readings in Personnel Management*, 4th ed. Cincinnati: South-Western Publishing Co., 1976. Part 2.

Dunnette, Marvin. *Personnel Selection and Placement*. Belmont, California: Wadsworth Publishing Company, 1966.

Lipsett, Laurence, Frank P. Rodgers, and Harold M. Kentner. *Personnel Selection and Recruitment*. Boston: Allyn and Bacon, Inc., 1964.

Lopez, Felix M., Jr. *Personnel Interviewing, Theory and Practice*. New York: McGraw-Hill Book Company, 1965.

McCormick, Ernest J. and Joseph Tiffin. *Industrial Psychology*, 6th ed. Englewood Cliffs, N.J.: Prentice-Hall, Inc., 1974. Chapter 4.

McMurry, Robert N. *Tested Techniques of Personnel Selection*, Revised edition. Chicago: The Dartnell Corporation, 1966.

Mandell, Milton M. *The Selection Process: Choosing the Right Man for the Job*. New York: American Management Association, 1964.

Peskin, Dean B. *Human Behavior and Employment*. New York: American Management Association, 1971.

Stahl, O. Glenn. *Public Personnel Administration*, 6th ed. New York: Harper & Row, Publishers, 1971. Part III.

Webster, Edward C. *Decision Making in the Employment Interview*. Montreal: McGill University, Industrial Relations Center, 1964.

Wesley, Kenneth N. and Gary A. Yukl. *Organizational Behavior and Industrial Psychology* (*Readings with Commentary*). New York: Oxford University Press, 1975. Part 6.

Personnel Assessment

In the preceding chapter the objectives of personnel selection and the contributions of the various steps of the selection process to the achievement of these objectives were examined. Considerable attention was given to the interview as one of the major tools for assessing the qualifications of applicants. Other important methods of personnel assessment, such as psychological testing, evaluation of application form data, and background investigations, will be covered in detail in this chapter.

Although tests are used for a variety of purposes, their primary use in personnel management is to obtain information about an applicant's abilities, aptitudes, and personality that will help to predict his or her probable success on the job. Unlike the interview, tests are objective and unbiased when used properly. Unfortunately, however, tests frequently tend to be used improperly or without regard to their general or specific limitations. In recent years attention increasingly has been given to the ethical implications of using tests, especially in the assessment of job applicants. Federal and state legislation has a profound influence on the use of tests in assessing job applicants as well as employees under consideration for promotion. While psychologists have always emphasized that employers should give careful attention to determining the predictive value of tests, it is only recently that the full force of the law made this a necessity.

Psychological tests, like interviews, can only provide some of the information that is needed for making a full-scale assessment of a job applicant. Information supplied on the application form is not only useful as a basis for the interview but may be treated much like data from psychological tests. Methods have been developed for scoring the personal data that are furnished on an application form, thereby providing a more objective basis of assessment.

Through background investigations the information supplied by the applicant may be verified and additional information obtained. In the discussion that follows, all of the above sources of information will be examined. The major emphasis, however, will be upon psychological testing.

PSYCHOLOGICAL TESTING

Since World War I when about two million recruits were examined by means of the *Army Alpha Test* of mental ability, tests of all types have been used in personnel selection and classification in many different types of organizations. Tests have continued to have an important role in all branches of the defense establishment and have been used traditionally in civil service programs at federal, state, and local levels of government where hiring on the basis of merit is required by law.

Testing in Business Firms

Tests have also played an important part in business organizations. It is interesting to note that in a 1963 survey, nine out of ten companies were using tests. However, in a recent survey only about three out of five reported that they use personnel tests—a considerable decrease in test usage.[1] These findings are supported by another study in which the reduction in the number of companies using tests is stated to be a direct consequence of the Griggs *vs.* Duke Power ruling.[2] Of the companies using tests, 94 percent use them for the preemployment testing of office personnel such as typists, clerks, and secretaries. The tests are also used for other groups with the following frequencies: supervisors, 48 percent; managers, 43 percent; plant personnel, 43 percent; salespersons, 32 percent; and others, including technical and professional personnel, 31 percent.[3]

Benefits from Testing

In organizations where tests are used properly, both tangible and intangible benefits have been realized. Some of the tangible benefits obtained from the use of tests in the selection of personnel include reduced training costs, fewer accidents, and less turnover. Intangible benefits such as improved worker adjustment, increased job satisfaction, and better group morale have likewise been obtained through the attraction of better applicants and the "weeding out" of those who do not meet the job requirements. The use of tests in selecting employees to be advanced to higher positions is not only desirable from the standpoint of placing the best talent in these positions but also has

---

[1] *Labor Policy and Practice—Personnel Management* (Washington, D.C.: The Bureau of National Affairs, Inc., 1964), par. 201:241-248.

[2] Donald J. Petersen, "The Impact of Duke Power on Testing," *Personnel, Vol. 51, No. 2 (March-April, 1974)*, pp. 30-37.

[3] *Labor Policy and Practice, op. cit.*

generally had a salutary effect on employees who realize that ability is given a higher priority than personal favoritism.

Criticisms of Testing

It should be recognized, however, that tests and testing programs have come under closer scrutiny in recent years. Leaders of unions have traditionally raised questions about the fairness of tests.[4] Members of minority groups have also found themselves discriminated against by tests. Others have criticized them on the ground that they are an invasion of privacy. Where criticism is justified, it is usually not because of inadequacies in the tests themselves but in the manner in which they are used or misused. Employees should have a complete understanding of the nature of psychological testing as well as the types of tests that are available and the procedures for using them in accordance with scientific, ethical, and legal proscriptions.

Nature of Psychological Tests

A *psychological test* is an objective and standardized measure of a sample of behavior. It is used to measure such human characteristics as abilities, aptitudes, interests, and personality in quantitative terms. Through the use of tests, it is possible to determine "how much" of a given characteristic an individual possesses in relation to others with whom comparisons are made.

Tests are constructed so that when large numbers of individuals are tested with a test that is of the appropriate difficulty level for the group being tested and when the individuals are selected at random, the distribution of scores will follow the normal probability curve as graphically illustrated in Figure 7-1.

Tests should be constructed so that scores will follow the pattern shown in Figure 7-1. This type of pattern does not occur if the test is too easy or too difficult for the group being tested or if individuals have been selected on some basis that would influence their test performance.

Reliability and Validity of Tests. A psychological test can only sample the total aspect of behavior that it is designed to measure. The proper sampling of behavior, whether it be verbal, manipulative, or some other type of behavior, is the responsibility of the test author. It is also the responsibility of the test author to develop the test in such a manner that it meets accepted standards of reliability, i.e., measures with a high degree of consistency (see page 134 in Chapter 6).[5] Reliability is a function in part of the length of the test as well as

[4] Rodney F. Rhoads and Frank J. Landy, "Measurement of Attitudes of Industrial Work Groups Toward Psychology and Testing," *Journal of Applied Psychology*, Vol. 58, No. 2 (October, 1973), pp. 197-201.

[5] Standards that psychological tests and testing programs should meet are described in *Standards for Educational and Psychological Tests* (Washington, D.C.: American Psychological Association, Inc., 1974).

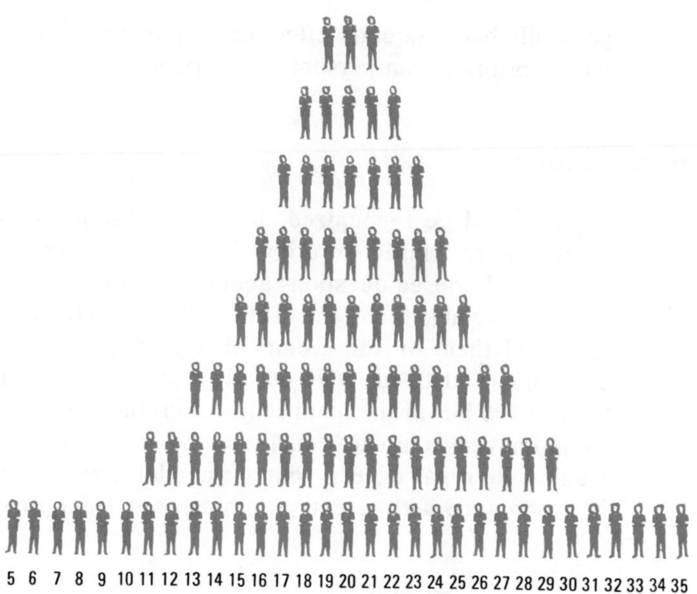

When large numbers of individuals are tested, the scores will distribute themselves in the pattern shown above if the test is of appropriate difficulty level for the group being tested and the individuals are selected at random rather than according to ability, experience, or other factors that would influence their test performance.

Source: Drawing adapted from the Esso Scale for Performance Report. Reproduced with permission of Exxon Corp.

Figure 7-1 THE NORMAL PROBABILITY CURVE

the sample of items included. The reliability of a test is ordinarily discussed in the examiner's manual which accompanies the standardized test. While a test or other measuring device must be reliable in order to be of value, high reliability offers no assurance that the test is valid with respect to the purpose for which it is used. It is the responsibility of the personnel staff to determine the validity of any test, i.e., the extent to which it predicts success in a particular job, before it is adopted for regular use. The procedures that are used in validating tests will be discussed later.

Other Requirements for Tests. While reliability and validity represent the fundamental requirements for psychological tests, there are other requirements to be considered. These include:

1. *Cost.* There is little relation between the cost of tests and their quality, so that even a limited budget permits the use of well-constructed tests.
2. *Time.* Short tests are preferred, other things being equal. Too long a testing period bores the subject and makes him uncooperative.
3. *"Face" validity.* The cooperation of the subject is likely to be greater if the test appears to be related to the purpose for which the individual is being tested. However, "face" validity is not a substitute for empirical validity.

4. *Ease of administration and scoring.* Tests requiring the services of expert testers and scorers may not be feasible.[6]

Classification of Tests

Tests may be classified in different ways. Most tests are *group tests,* which allow for testing many individuals at one time. These are in contrast to *individual tests,* which require one examiner for each person being tested. Another classification is by the manner in which the individual responds to the test items. *Paper-and-pencil tests* require the subject to respond by writing or marking answers on a booklet or answer sheet, whereas *performance* or *instrumental tests* require the examinee to manipulate objects or equipment. The *Stromberg Dexterity Test* shown in Figure 7-2 is an example of this latter type. In *oral tests* the examiner asks questions, and the subject responds orally to the question. Paper-and-pencil tests are the most commonly used since they can be administered easily to groups as well as to individuals, and the expense of testing is considerably less than for the other types of tests.

Major Standardized Tests. In addition to the classifications mentioned above, there is a more fundamental breakdown of tests according to the characteristics that are measured. Figure 7-3 includes major categories of tests together with

Reproduced with permission of The Psychological Corporation.

Figure 7-2 STROMBERG DEXTERITY TEST

[6] Lee J. Cronbach, *Essentials of Psychological Testing* (3d ed.; New York: Harper and Row, 1970), pp. 182-193.

NAME OF TEST	EXAMPLE OF JOBS FOR WHICH USED
INTELLIGENCE	
Wonderlic Personnel Test Adaptability Test Wesman Personnel Classification Test	Clerical, factory, maintenance, and sales jobs
Concept Mastery Test	Managerial or executive job candidates
General Aptitude Test Battery Nonreading Aptitude Test Battery	United States Employment Service programs
Employee Aptitude Survey	All types of jobs from executive to unskilled
Flanagan Industrial Kit	Wide variety of jobs—battery includes 18 short tests covering 18 different job elements
DEXTERITY	
Stromberg Dexterity Test	Foundry moulders, punch press operators, assemblers
Purdue Pegboard	Radio tube mounters, production jobs
O'Connor Finger and Tweezer Dexterity Tests	Instrument assembly
CLERICAL APTITUDE	
Minnesota Clerical Test	Office jobs
SRA Typing Skills	Typists
The Short Employment Tests	Office jobs
MECHANICAL APTITUDE	
Test of Mechanical Comprehension	Variety of engineering and mechanical jobs
Revised Minnesota Paper Form Board Test	Mechanical shop work, drafting, design
PERSONALITY	
Gordon Personal Profile and Inventory	Office workers, computer programmers, others
Edwards Personal Preference Schedule	Salespersons, supervisors
Guilford-Zimmerman Temperament Survey	Insurance salespersons, office workers
Thematic Apperception Test	Executives
California Personality Inventory	Managers and supervisors
CREATIVITY AND JUDGMENT	
AC Test of Creative Ability	Engineers
Owens Creativity Test for Machine Design	Engineers
Watson-Glaser Critical Thinking Appraisal	Executives
SUPERVISORY AND MANAGERIAL ABILITIES	
How Supervise? Supervisory Practices Test Management Aptitude Inventory Leadership Opinion Questionnaire	Managerial and supervisory jobs
INTEREST	
Strong Vocational Interest Blank	Administrative and sales jobs
Minnesota Vocational Interest Inventory	Various skilled jobs

Figure 7-3 SOME COMMERCIALLY AVAILABLE STANDARDIZED TESTS COMMONLY USED IN PERSONNEL TESTING

some representative tests of each category and examples of jobs for which they are used.[7]

Intelligence Tests. The test most commonly used is the *intelligence* or *general mental ability test* that has been found useful in predicting success in a variety of occupations, but especially those requiring verbal and numerical skills. There are many different types of intelligence tests available. Some of these are particularly suited for selecting clerical and supervisory personnel; others are designed for testing applicants for factory and maintenance jobs.

Multiaptitude Tests. Tests designed to measure many *aptitudes*, i.e., the potential or capacity to learn, are called *multiaptitude tests*. The *General Aptitude Test Battery* (GATB) developed by the United States Department of Labor measures nine different aptitude areas as follows: intelligence, verbal aptitude, numerical aptitude, spatial aptitude, form perception, clerical perception, motor coordination, finger dexterity, and manual dexterity. Since 1947 the federal government has had a large research program in which the *GATB* has been validated against job performance in a wide variety of jobs ranging from professional to unskilled. The information that has been gained through these research efforts has been organized in Occupational Aptitude Patterns (OAP) that list occupations according to aptitude scores required for minimally successful performance. The OAPs are used primarily by employment service counselors in their efforts to place individuals in jobs.[8]

In 1971 the *Nonreading Aptitude Test Battery* (NATB) was made available for use in local offices with disadvantaged persons whose limitations are too great to permit the GATB to give a fair assessment of their abilities. Instructions and questions for all tests are read aloud by the test administrators.[9]

Dexterity Tests. The GATB, like other multiaptitude test batteries, includes *dexterity tests*. Other dexterity tests which are not part of any battery that may be used in selecting applicants for jobs are those involving the assembling of small electrical parts, watch and instrument making, and similar operations that require good hand, finger, or tweezer dexterity.

---

[7] Publishers of tests have rigid standards in order to insure that users will be qualified to administer, score, and interpret the test that they are using. The Psychological Corporation, for example, specifies three levels of tests in its catalog:

Level a—Those commonly used for employment purposes. Company purchase orders are filled promptly.

*Level b—Available to firms having a staff member who has completed an advance-level course in testing in a university, or its equivalent in training under the direction of a qualified superior or consultant.

*Level c—Available to firms only for use under the supervision of qualified psychologists, i.e. members of the American Psychological Association or persons with at least a Master's degree in psychology and appropriate training in the field of personnel testing. The qualified person may be either a staff member or a consultant.

*A registration form must be completed by individuals and organizations desiring to use Level b and Level c tests.

[8] Stephen E. Bennis, "Occupational Validity of the General Aptitude Test Battery," *Journal of Applied Psychology,* Vol. 52, No. 3 (June, 1968), pp. 240-244.

[9] Patricia Marshall, "Tests Without Reading," *Manpower* (May, 1971), pp. 7-12.

Clerical Aptitude Tests. Tests of *clerical aptitude* are among the earliest employment tests devised and are still widely used. Clerical tests typically measure verbal and numerical aptitudes as well as perceptual speed. Tests that measure learned skills, such as spelling and typing, are also commonly used.

Mechanical Aptitude Tests. *Mechanical aptitude tests* may measure a variety of functions. The principle functions measured are: mechanical comprehension, i.e., the ability to understand mechanical operations such as those involving gears, pulleys, etc.; and spatial relationships, i.e., the ability to visualize and manipulate objects in space.

Personality Tests. Usually of the questionnaire or inventory type, *personality tests* are designed to measure such characteristics as emotional adjustment, perseverance, self-confidence, and many other "traits."

Creativity and Judgment Tests. In recent years there has been considerable interest in measuring creativity. As yet, most of the *tests of creativity* are in the experimental stage, except for some that have been designed for specific jobs—especially in the engineering fields.

Supervisory and Managerial Abilities Tests. The *tests for supervisory and managerial abilities* are primarily designed to measure attitudes and perceptions of practices that people use in supervising others. These tests are especially useful in training programs to give leaders and potential leaders a greater awareness of the important factors in human relations.

Interest Inventories. Tests that measure the relative strength of one's interests for certain occupations or that compare one's interests with those of people in various occupational areas, known as *interest inventories,* are used occasionally for selection purposes. Their more important use, however, is in vocational counseling.

Job Knowledge Tests. Government agencies, the military services, and licensing boards have developed their own tests that are used in place of or together with those that are commercially available, especially those that measure job knowledge. These *job knowledge tests* are a type of achievement test designed to measure a person's level of understanding about a particular job. Most civil service examinations of this type are used to determine whether an applicant possesses the information and understanding that will permit placement in a job without further training.[10] A large number of tests is required to cover all jobs but the number can be reduced by isolating job elements (see page 47, Chapter 2) and building tests to cover the job elements. For example, if the element "operating bookkeeping equipment" appears in several jobs, one test to measure that element could be used for all of these

---

[10] It is interesting to note that the origins of the system go back to 2200 B.C. when the Chinese emperor examined officials every 3 years to determine their fitness for continuing in office. In 1115 B.C. candidates for government posts were examined for their proficiency in music, archery, horsemanship, writing, arithmetic, and the rites and ceremonies of public and private life. (See Philip H. DuBois in Suggested Readings at the end of the chapter.)

jobs. Civil service test development agencies usually maintain test banks of multiple choice items organized by job elements so that tests for various jobs may be assembled from items in the bank that have met the technical requirements and are known to be relevant.

Job knowledge tests have not been used to any extent in industry although many organizations could probably benefit from their use. Job knowledge tests that are used in promoting as well as hiring individuals in government agencies probably could find applications in business and industry in helping to insure that individuals have the requisite knowledge for handling the demands of a higher-level job. Such tests may also be used to measure the effectiveness of training programs—a subject to be considered in the next chapter.

THE SCIENTIFIC USE OF TESTS

Most organizations have been confronted with the problem of determining how much emphasis to place upon the use of tests in the personnel selection program. The problem cannot be easily solved by examining a few of the tests that have been listed because any value to be derived from tests is largely dependent upon the manner in which they are used. The extent to which they are used as a basis for employee selection, promotion, or supervisory and managerial selection must be based upon research that has determined their contribution to the program. This type of research requires the *validation process* to be accomplished in which the scores on tests are related to job performance in order to determine how effective the tests are as predictors of job performance.

Once the tests are validated, the next step is to determine how they will be used in the selection process with maximum effectiveness. This step requires not only that all of the objective data pertaining to the value of the tests be evaluated but also that legal and ethical aspects of testing be considered. Since a testing program requires special research and analysis, it should not be undertaken without the assistance of a person who is trained to develop it. If one is not available within the organization, a professional consultant should be hired for the purpose. As a result of the Griggs *vs*. Duke Power case ruling, there has not only been a radical change in the percentage of firms validating all of their tests but also a trend toward using more outside psychological consultants as test validators, especially among medium-sized firms that do not have in-house psychologists.[11]

The Validation Process

The importance of validity has been stressed in this and the preceding chapter. It should be emphasized again, however, that unless the validity of a test is known it should not be used. Violation of this principle is contrary not only to sound personnel practices but also to ethical and legal considerations which will be discussed later. Validation of tests in personnel selection will

[11] Peterson, *op. cit.*

typically follow a pattern that has become a traditional model or experimental design. It contains six steps which are discussed in the following paragraphs.

Step 1. Examination of the Job. This step consists of using information from job analyses and job specifications, as described in Chapter 2. It should provide answers to such questions as: What, specifically, is required of persons in this job? Are they required to work rapidly with numbers, read drawings accurately, take shorthand, or assemble electronic devices with precision? A study of what is required of the individual, including careful observation of several persons holding that job, will give clues as to the basic aptitudes and abilities that are essential for successful job performance.

Step 2. Selection of Criterion and Test. This step involves two parts: (1) choosing a *criterion,* i.e., an indicator which measures the extent of how "good" or successful an employee is considered to be, and (2) selecting a test. Through discussion and investigation of job performance, usually it is possible to arrive at some definition of job success. Some of the factors that may be used singly or combined as criteria of job success are production (quantity or quality), job tenure, accidents, commissions, and performance ratings. Each job for which tests are to be used should have definitely established standards based on criteria that are reliable (consistent), acceptable to line personnel, relevant to the job, and as objective as possible. The selection of the test to be validated will be based upon the job specifications plus insights obtained from observations of people at work and any other approaches that will reveal the abilities, aptitudes, interests, and personality characteristics required for the job. Actually several possible tests in each of these categories should be selected for tryout or validation. Most of the tests are likely to be available commercially but special tests may be constructed if necessary. Many organizations develop their own tests not only to obtain higher validities but to insure that applicants have not had test-taking experience with any of the tests that they administer.

Step 3. Measurement of Performance. Once the tests and the criterion have been determined, the test is then administered to a group of employees and criterion data are obtained. The criterion data, usually expressed in terms of a score combining supervisory ratings, production figures of employees, or other criteria, may be obtained immediately or at a later time. When criterion data are obtained immediately, the process is referred to as the *concurrent* or *present employee method of validation.* A better approach involves the *predictive validation method* in which individuals are tested at the time of making application; and criterion scores, performance ratings, etc., are obtained later.[12] This latter approach, however, requires waiting for criterion data. In either approach supervisors must not be aware of the test scores of those persons whose performance they are to evaluate. Otherwise they may judge

[12] George K. Bennett, "Factors Affecting the Values of Validation Studies," *Personnel Psychology,* Vol. 22, No. 3 (Autumn, 1969), pp. 265-268.

performance with the individual's test scores in mind, thus creating *criterion contamination*.

Step 4. Relating Test Scores to Criterion. This step involves determining whether or not a significant and meaningful relationship exists between the employees' scores on the test and the criterion. It typically involves a correlational technique in which data may be plotted on a scatterplot similar to the one shown in Figure 7-5 on page 158. The higher the validity coefficient is, the less error there will be in predicting criterion scores from test scores.[13]

Step 5. Making Decisions About the Test. Making the final decision as to whether or not to use the test depends upon many factors, primarily the magnitude of the validity coefficient and the extent to which it overlaps with what other tests measure. Those tests that overlap too much with other tests in what they measure usually are rejected. The remaining tests that are found to predict the criterion reasonably well and are fairly independent of each other are combined into a test battery.

Step 6. Cross-Validation. Before any test battery is put to use in a selection system, it should be subjected to *cross-validation*. Cross-validation means that the battery is administered to a totally new sample, expected criterion levels are determined for each person, and expected performance is correlated with actual performance. Cross-validation studies should be continued even after a battery has been put into operational use. Applicants, jobs, and employment conditions are constantly changing with the result that the validity of a test or any other assessment procedure will change over a period of time.

Synthetic Validity—A Newer Approach. A recent departure from the traditional validation design described above is known as *synthetic validity*. It involves inferring the validity of a battery of tests from predetermined validities of individual tests in the battery for specific components or elements of the total job. An important difference between synthetic validity and the traditional validity approaches is the attempt to predict success on parts of the job instead of for the total job. The idea of synthetic validity was first used in small businesses; but trends toward job enrichment, technical employment, and service occupations and away from large numbers of workers performing identical functions make the need for synthetic validity greater.[14]

Operational Use of Tests

Once the experimental phase has been completed and a battery with a known validity has been assembled, it is then ready to be administered to job applicants. Because of the important use to be made of the scores and because the operational use of the test must conform to the same rigid standards as the

[13] Formulas for various correlational methods may be found in most statistics books as well as in the books on psychological testing listed at the end of this chapter.

[14] Robert M. Guion, *Personnel Testing* (New York: McGraw-Hill Book Company, 1965), pp. 169-174.

experimental phase, it should not be assumed that less diligence and caution are needed at this point in the program.

Administration. Any factors that might influence the examinee's performance on the tests must be given careful consideration. The physical conditions of the test room, such as lighting, ventilation, and freedom from noise, should be carefully checked. The examiner should insure that examinees are properly motivated, understand the instructions, and are doing their best. Those who are fearful of the testing procedure should be reassured. The examiner should also review the procedure for administration and scoring and be prepared to give full attention to the testing session. Unfortunately test administration is often delegated to someone who views it as an unwanted and annoying interruption. Such an individual can contribute to the unreliability of the test and possibly even cause legal action to be taken by examinees.[15]

Interpretation of Scores. The basic principle underlying all psychological testing is that individuals differ in degree with respect to their abilities, interests, personalities, aptitudes, and achievements. To the extent that these characteristics can be defined and measured, it is possible to compare individuals. The number of answers that agree with the scoring key is commonly referred to as the *raw score*. For example, if a test has 100 items and the individual answers 65 of these items correctly, the raw score is 65. But what does it mean? Without some basis for comparison, it is impossible to attach any meaning to the score, for it tells nothing about the individual's standing in relation to others who have taken the test. If the average (mean) score for a group of persons tested with this test is 60, however, it is then known that the score of 65 is slightly above average. Ordinarily it is desirable to state scores in more specific terms in order that careful evaluations may be made.

When large numbers of individuals have been tested, the distribution of raw scores provides the basis for converting the raw scores into *percentile* equivalents as shown in Figure 7-4. It will be noted from this figure that a person scoring at the 50th percentile has exceeded the scores of half of those tested. Similarly, a person scoring at the 84th percentile on a given test has 84 percent of the individuals scoring below her or him.[16]

Establishing Cutoff Scores. While the conversion of raw scores to percentile scores introduces a basis for comparing individuals who were tested, it does not indicate the point in the distribution above which a person should be carefully considered and below which the person should probably be rejected. The score that an applicant must achieve before being selected is referred to as the *cutoff*

[15] William C. Byham and Stephen Temlock, "Operational Validity—A New Concept in Personnel Testing," *Personnel Journal,* Vol. 51, No. 9 (September, 1972), pp. 639-647.

[16] While percentile scores are easily computed and readily understood, they are somewhat limited in their application in testing for personnel selection purposes. *Standard scores* which are computed on the basis of the mean and the standard deviation of the distribution are normally used. An explanation of these scores may be found in most of the books on testing listed at the end of this chapter.

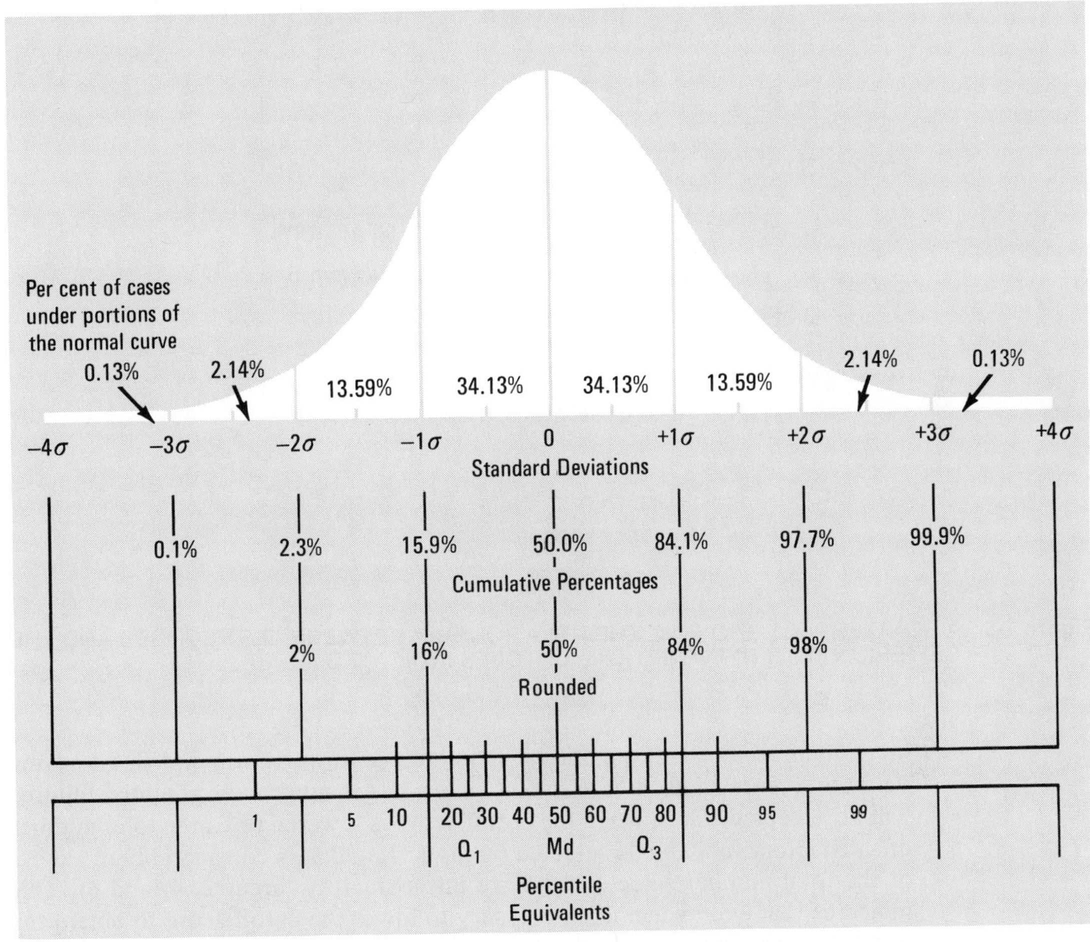

Source: Adapted from *Test Service Bulletin* No. 48, The Psychological Corporation (January, 1955), page 6.

Figure 7-4 NORMAL PROBABILITY CURVE SHOWING PERCENTILE EQUIVALENTS

or *critical score*. This score is seldom constant since the number of applicants in relation to the number of job vacancies varies. Depending upon the labor supply, it may be necessary to lower or raise the critical score.

The effects of raising and lowering the critical score are illustrated in Figure 7-5. Each dot in the center of the figure represents the relationship between the test score and the criterion of success for one individual. In this instance the test has a fairly high validity as represented by the elliptical pattern of the dots. It will be noted that the individuals scoring high on the test are concentrated in the satisfactory category on job success, whereas the low scoring individuals are concentrated in the unsatisfactory category on job success.

If the cutoff score is set as A, only the individuals represented by areas 1 and 2 will be accepted, and nearly all of them will be successful. If more

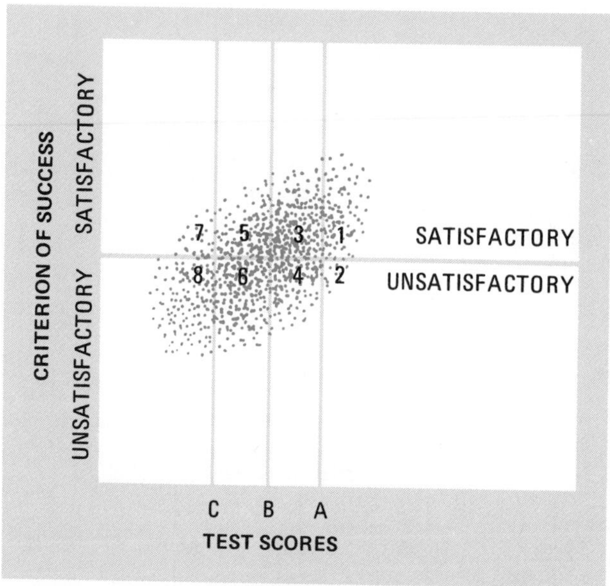

Figure 7-5 A SCATTERPLOT SHOWING THE RELATIONSHIP BETWEEN TEST SCORES AND THE CRITERION WITH HYPOTHETICAL CUTOFFS INDICATED

individuals are needed, the critical score may be lowered to point B. Lowering the cutoff score in each case means that a larger number of potential failures will be accepted. Even when the cutoff score is lowered to C, the total number of satisfactory individuals selected (areas 1, 3, and 5) is considerably in excess of the total number selected who are unsatisfactory (areas 2, 4, and 6). This indicates that even when it is necessary to lower the cutoff score to obtain the number of persons needed, the use of tests will result in the rejection of those applicants who are most likely to fail. In other words, *the test serves to maximize the selection of probable successes and to minimize the selection of probable failures.*

Contributions of Testing

"Just what do tests contribute to a selection program?" is a question that is often asked of personnel managers who are frequently called upon to defend the use of tests to their superiors, union representatives, applicants, the EEOC, and state fair employment practices commissions. Answers to this question are acceptable only if they are based upon validation data pertaining to the tests. Although validation data may be presented in the form of correlation coefficients, it is more likely to be understood by the layman if it is presented in the form of an expectancy chart. An *expectancy chart* shows the relationship between the scores achieved on a selection test and performance on the job, as illustrated in Figure 7-6.

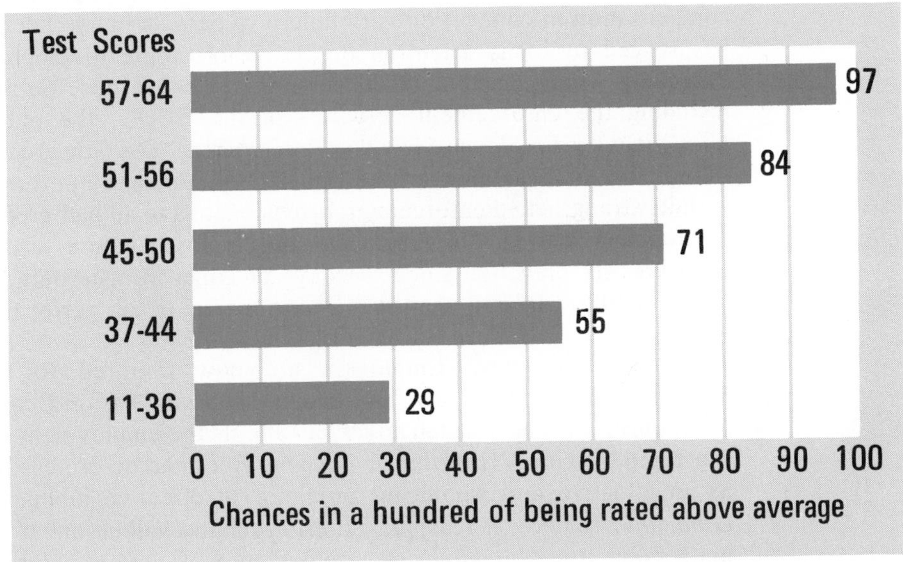

Source: Ernest J. McCormick and Joseph Tiffin, *Industrial Psychology* (6th ed.; Englewood Cliffs, New Jersey: Prentice-Hall, Inc., 1974), p. 105. Reproduced with permission.

Figure 7-6 EXPECTANCY CHART SHOWING THE RELATION BETWEEN SCORES MADE ON THE MINNESOTA PAPER FORM BOARD AND RATED SUCCESS OF JUNIOR DRAFTSMEN IN A STEEL COMPANY

By referring to the chart one can estimate the probabilities of job success for an applicant who has attained a given score on the test. In this illustration supervisory ratings serve as the criterion of job success. Assuming that this criterion is the best one for evaluating success in this job, the expectancy chart shows the probable success of individuals who score in different ranges on the test. If it is possible to restrict hiring to those individuals who attain high scores, the probabilities of ultimately having superior employees may be increased considerably.

LEGAL AND ETHICAL CONSIDERATIONS

It is important that management give full attention to the legal and ethical aspects of testing. While the legal and ethical considerations concerning tests are consistent with the scientific approach, they are given special emphasis because of the major problems and criticisms that have arisen in connection with the use of tests.

Tests and Discrimination

There have been many charges that employment tests may have been used, inadvertently or deliberately, as instruments of racial discrimination. The now-famous Motorola case,[17] in which a black applicant was awarded compensation in connection with failure to pass an employment aptitude test, has served to focus attention on the whole topic of employment testing, especially where disadvantaged persons are concerned. Subsequent events, including the enforcement activities of the EEOC, the publication of the *Guidelines on Employee Selection Procedures,*[18] the Griggs-Duke Power case ruling, and the enactment of the Equal Employment Opportunity Act of 1972 with its strengthened enforcement provisions, have all had profound effects on employment testing. No longer can an employer ignore what psychologists have literally preached since the days of Hugo Münsterberg,[19] namely, that tests must be validated against *relevant* criteria of job performance.

EEOC's Guidelines. Employers are now required to meet minimum standards for validation as prescribed in the *Guidelines on Employee Selection Procedures*. Any test which adversely affects the employment status of groups protected by Title VII of the Civil Rights Act must be professionally validated as an effective and significant predictor of effective job performance. The *Guidelines* require, if feasible, criterion-related validation. If such a study is not feasible, the *Guidelines* require evidence of *content validity* (i.e., that the test is an actual sample of the work to be done) or *construct validity* (i.e., that the test or other standard measures some characteristic needed for the particular job). In any case, validity should be studied for each minority and sex group separately (if feasible) because the same test scores or test performance may not predict the same level of job performance for various groups. Validity studies prescribed by the *Guidelines* must be conducted by professionally trained psychologists, and all records must be kept for documentation. Finally the *Guidelines* require that the employer identify, analyze, and monitor every step of the selection and assignment process including all procedures for initial hiring, transferring, promotion, training, and any employment opportunity to discover if any steps have adverse impact on groups protected by Title VII.[20]

Possible Discriminatory Factors. There are many factors that may contribute to a test or test battery being declared discriminatory. Even though there is

---

[17] "Hiring Tests Wait for the Score: Myart *vs.* Motorola," *Business Week* (February 13, 1965).

[18] Equal Employment Opportunity Commission, *Guidelines on Employee Selection Procedures,* Title 29, Chapter XIV, Part 1607 of the Code of Federal Regulations. Published in the *Federal Register,* Vol. 35, No. 149 (August 1, 1970), pp. 12333-12336. The *Guidelines* are reprinted in Herbert J. Chruden and Arthur W. Sherman, Jr., *Practical Study Experiences in Personnel Management* (5th ed.; Cincinnati: South-Western Publishing Co., 1976), Chapter 7. Guidelines that are coordinated with those of the EEOC have also been published by the Office of Federal Contract Compliance and may be found in the *Federal Register,* Vol. 36, No. 77 (April 21, 1971), pp. 7532-7535.

[19] Hugo Münsterberg, *Psychology and Industrial Efficiency* (Boston: Houghton Mifflin Company, 1913).

[20] The student who desires to pursue this topic more thoroughly may wish to consult the following articles: Lawrence Plotin, "Coal Handling, Steamfitting, Psychology, and Law," *American Psychologist,* Vol. 27, No. 3 (March, 1972), pp. 202-204; Cameron Fincher, "Personnel Testing and Public Policy," *American Psychologist,* Vol. 28, No. 6 (June, 1973), pp. 489-497; and David C. McClelland, "Testing for Competence Rather Than for Intelligence," *American Psychologist,* Vol. 28, No. 1 (January, 1973), pp. 1-14.

no intent to discriminate, it should be recognized that disadvantaged persons, as a group, score lower on aptitude tests as a result of cultural deprivation. The nature of tests and the way in which they are used also contribute to poorer performance by this group.[21]

Test Anxiety. Disadvantaged persons may score poorly on tests partly because of anxiety resulting from their lack of familiarity with the testing situation as well as the fact that tests are administered by persons representing more advantaged backgrounds. Poor testing conditions in terms of space, lighting, and freedom from noise also can contribute to anxiety and should be avoided. In the case of disadvantaged persons, it is particularly desirable that opportunities for retesting be provided. Some organizations use the *Test Orientation Procedure*[22] designed to familiarize applicants with different types of tests and to provide practice on them before administering their regular tests.

Unfairness of Test Content. Many paper-and-pencil tests emphasize concepts and information to which disadvantaged persons may never have been exposed. If paper-and-pencil tests are used, the vocabulary required for them should be appropriate to the level of the applicant. The use of shorter sentences, the elimination of unnecessary verbiage in the tests, and the development of more simplified instructions for them are other improvements that have been introduced into at least one civil service testing program.[23]

For many jobs it is better to use oral trade tests and work sample tests. *Oral trade tests* consist of questions concerning tools, methods, techniques, and procedures in the skilled and apprenticeship trades. *Work sample tests* require the applicant to perform a standard sample of work. About 1,350 local offices of the United States Employment Service are equipped to help employers develop a battery of such tests tailor-made to the requirements of various jobs.[24]

Lack of Validity for the Disadvantaged. Because tests may be valid for some groups of applicants but not for others, their validity should be determined not only on the total group but on the various subgroups. It is possible, for example, that a test would be a valid selection device for whites but not for blacks. In such cases the tests should not be used for blacks, but some other information that is a valid predictor of their success should be used.[25] The possible use of alternative sources of information about applicants should not be overlooked.

---

[21] APA Task Force on Employment Testing of Minority Groups, "Job Testing and the Disadvantaged," *American Psychologist,* Vol. 24, No. 7 (July, 1969), pp. 637-650.

[22] Published by The Psychological Corporation, 304 East 45th Street, New York, NY 10017.

[23] Vernon R. Taylor, "Cultural Bias in Testing: An Action Program," *Public Personnel Review,* Vol. 29, No. 3 (July, 1968), pp. 168-179.

[24] *Personnel Management—Policies and Procedures, op. cit.,* par. 201-243.

[25] The reader who is interested in the technical details of this issue should consult "The Industrial Psychologist: Selection and Equal Employment Opportunity (A Symposium)," *Personnel Psychology,* Vol. 19, No. 1 (Spring, 1966), pp. 1-39; and Richard S. Barrett, "Gray Areas in Black and White Testing," *Havard Business Review,* Vol. 46, No. 1 (January-February, 1968), pp. 92-95.

Invasion of Privacy

The criticisms of testing in recent years have not been confined to the issue of disadvantaged persons. Personality testing has been criticized on the basis of invasion of privacy and failure to demonstrate that the personality tests meet the requirements for reliability and validity. Questions on tests (as well as on application forms and in interviews) pertaining to personal habits, attitudes about sex, etc., when not related to job requirements are considered to constitute an unwarranted invasion of the applicant's rights to privacy. During Congressional hearings concerning the use of tests in government agencies, however, it was argued that individual rights were not being violated because an applicant or employee consented to take them. Even so, the validity of this argument was questioned on the basis that individuals can hardly be said to consent voluntarily when they know that they will probably not be hired if they do not submit to testing. Furthermore, consent is meaningless unless the examinees understand what such consent entails. The same reasoning could also be applied to personality testing for industrial and other nongovernmental jobs.[26] In view of the special knowledge and understanding required in using personality tests, it is recommended that they be used only upon the advice of professional test consultants and that the fundamental question be asked: "What is the test's relevance to job success?" [27]

OTHER METHODS OF PERSONNEL ASSESSMENT

One of the major contributions that testing can make to a personnel program is to provide information about individuals that is more reliable and more valid than that usually obtained from other methods. It is possible, however, to improve other approaches to personnel assessment so that the results that they achieve can approach the degree of objectivity reached by tests. Application forms have been made to produce more objective results by handling them much like tests, and improvements in methods for conducting background investigations have resulted in increased reliability and validity of information obtained about applicants.

Scoring Application Forms

The scoring of application forms requires that the items on the form that are valid predictors of job success be identified and that weights be established for different responses to these items. By totaling the scores for each item, it is possible to obtain a composite score on the application blank as a whole for each applicant. This approach has been used successfully since 1919 by the Phoenix Mutual Life Insurance Company to select insurance salespersons.

---

[26] John H. Kirkwood, "Selection Techniques and the Law: To Test or Not To Test," *Personnel,* Vol. 44, No. 6 (November-December, 1967), pp. 18-26.

[27] Christopher Orpen, "The 'Correct' Use of Personality Tests: A View from Industrial Psychology," *Public Personnel Management,* Vol. 3, No. 3 (May-June, 1974), pp. 228-229.

One company employing approximately 1,500 chemists and engineers used this approach to personnel prediction when it found that the interview did nothing more than weed out obvious misfits. A systematic evaluation was made of background information provided on the original application blanks of chemists and engineers hired over the past five years. The information for high-performance employees was then compared to that for all others (including some who had been encouraged to leave). As a group, the high-performance men were found to differ significantly from the others on a number of application blank items, such as amount and type of extracurricular activities in college, previous experience, and honor society memberships. Weights were then assigned to the various items based upon the magnitude of the differences between the high-performers and all others, and the original application forms of 239 employees were scored accordingly. It will be noted in Figure 7-7 that the high-performance employees in the group studied scored considerably higher than the others on the application blank. Similar results were obtained on another group, thus confirming the original findings.[28] An organization that has collected such information can construct a template or scoring key for use in scoring the application blanks of new applicants. It should be recognized, however, that the specific weights assigned to the application form items must be kept confidential and new analyses of the weighting must be made periodically.

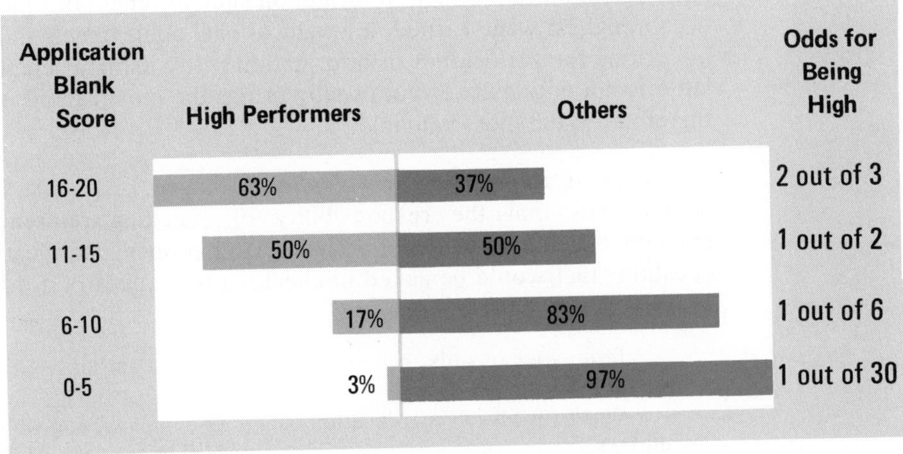

Source: J. R. Hinrichs, "Technical Selection: How to Improve Your Batting Average," *Personnel,* Vol. 37, No. 2 (March-April, 1960), p. 59. Reproduced with permission of the American Management Association.

Figure 7-7 APPLICATION BLANK SCORES FOR 239 TECHNICAL PERSONS

[28] J. R. Hinrichs, "Technical Selection: How to Improve Your Batting Average," *Personnel,* Vol. 37, No. 2 (March-April, 1960), pp. 56-60. The cross-validation process described on page 155 is particularly important where weighted application blanks (or biographical information blanks) are used.

The use of the *weighted application blank* is by no means restricted to professional and managerial jobs. It also has been used successfully with unskilled employees. For example, in one study of unskilled female workers in a small canning factory, it was found that those who lived close to the plant and had a fair amount of family responsibility were more likely to become long-term employees.[29]

In order to conform to the EEOC *Guidelines*, most of the companies using this approach have competent researchers on their staffs who are able to develop special procedures for insuring that minority-group applicants are not unfairly penalized by this selection device.[30]

Background Investigations

Since most job applicants are eager to obtain employment, it follows naturally that many of them will distort information pertaining to their abilities or experiences; and some will give completely false information in order to attain their objective. These tendencies require the employer to use every reasonable method available to verify the information that is supplied by the applicant and by others.

Traditional Sources of Verification. Former employers, teachers, credit bureaus, and individuals named as character references are usually contacted for verification of pertinent information such as length of time on the job, type of job, highest wage earned, and educational achievements. This can be done by writing for verification of information or by using a telephone check. The latter is not only quicker but usually brings the most candid type of reply and, therefore, is the most valuable.

Checking References by Telephone. Magee, of Helene Curtis Industries, recommends that the responsibility of checking references fall on the employment interviewer, not a clerk. After proper identification, some of the questions that would be asked in checking references of a male applicant, for example, over the telephone are:

> From your records, can you tell me when he started with your firm and when he left the company?
>
> What was his job classification with your company, and what were his job duties?
>
> How would you rate his job performance in terms of work volume and work quality?
>
> Did he receive any promotions or demotions while with you?

---

[29] Richard D. Scott and Richard W. Johnson, "Use of the Weighted Application Blank in Selecting Unskilled Employees," *Journal of Applied Psychology*, Vol. 51, No. 5 (October, 1967), pp. 393-395. For another study showing some of the biographical information items and expectancy tables, see William D. Buel, "An Alternative to Testing," *Personnel Journal*, Vol. 51, No. 5 (May, 1972), pp. 336-341.

[30] William C. Byham and Morton Edward Spitzer, *The Law and Personnel Testing* (New York: American Management Association, 1971), pp. 98-99.

As his supervisor, what did you find was the most effective way to motivate him?[31]

The above questions are designed primarily to establish the fact that the individual was employed and, if so, the type of job that he held and evidence of the caliber of his performance. For the most part these questions solicit fairly objective types of information. To go beyond these types of questions by requesting ratings or evaluations of the applicant's performance or personality and character traits probably would not yield significant information, especially if it is requested in writing. Many organizations are reluctant to put into writing an evaluation of a former employee's work record. One reason for this trend is that several firms have been sued by former employees who discovered that they had been given poor recommendations.[32] United States companies with operations in Europe, furthermore, have found that they are prohibited by law in Belgium and France and by court decision in West Germany from making unfavorable statements about former employees.[33]

Requiring Signed Requests for References. It is generally advisable to ask the applicant to fill out forms requesting the information. Most colleges require a signed request before they will send a former student's transcript, and many companies refuse to supply information without a signed statement from a former employee. The use of consumer credit reports as a basis for establishing an applicant's eligibility for employment has become more restrictive for employers. Under the federal Fair Credit Reporting Act,[34] effective in 1971, the employer must advise applicants if such reports will be requested; and if the applicant is rejected on the basis of the report, the applicant must be so advised of that fact and provided with the name and address of the reporting agency.

Unfortunately there has been very little published research on the use of reference ratings. However, in one study it was found that when they were used to predict the performance of public school teachers, they had a low level of validity.[35]

Verification by Lie Detector. In addition to the traditional methods of verifying an applicant's statements, some organizations are now using the *polygraph* (lie detector). The device is attached to the applicant's hand and/or arm, depending on the type of equipment, and involuntary physiological responses are recorded as the individual answers questions about his or her former employment record, subversive activity, prior arrests, and other areas believed to be important.

---

[31] Richard H. Magee, "Reference Checking—Objectives and Techniques," *Personnel Journal,* Vol. 43, No. 10 (November, 1964), pp. 551-555.

[32] E. C. Stephens, "Polygraph Preemployment Screening," *North Texas State University Business Studies,* Vol. 8, No. 1 (Spring, 1969), pp. 30-34.

[33] Herbert J. Chruden and Arthur W. Sherman, Jr., *Personnel Practices of American Companies in Europe* (New York: American Management Association, 1972), pp. 32-33.

[34] PL 91-508; 84 STAT 1128.

[35] Rufus C. Browning, "Validity of Reference Ratings from Previous Employers," *Personnel Psychology,* Vol. 21, No. 3 (Autumn, 1968), pp. 389-393.

While effective results have been obtained by this approach, the use of the polygraph raises many questions. Are the polygraph operators adequately trained for the work? Since they are probing and revealing a person's innermost secrets, can they be trusted to use the information wisely and honestly? Should they advise the police if they uncover information about a person that represents illegal behavior? These and other questions have been raised by many thoughtful individuals who are concerned about the rights of individuals in a free society.

Extent of Legal Use of the Polygraph. At the present time some states have passed laws limiting the use of the polygraph. On the other hand, there are states that have polygraph licensing laws designed to regulate the professional standards of practicing polygraph examiners. Still other states have no requirements that a polygraph operator possess any formal training, even grammar school, let alone any specialized training in the operation and interpretation of this sophisticated instrument.[36] It is likely that more states will enact legislation either to restrict its usage or to license qualified examiners.

Pros and Cons of the Polygraph. The main arguments for antipolygraph legislation proposed by the layperson are concerned with invasion of privacy, self-incrimination, and violation of human dignity. Psychology experts in this area also warn that a high proportion of those who "fail" the lie detector test in preemployment screening situations will be *false-positives,* i.e., will actually be innocent but rejected by the test. In certain occupations, such as police work, its use may be warranted. Similarly, in criminal investigations polygraphic interrogation can serve a useful purpose. The fundamental difference, however, is that although one cannot send a person to prison for flunking a lie detector test, there are no constitutional guarantees which prevent that person from being deprived of a job for the same reason.[37] Before attempting to use the polygraph, therefore, it would be well for an employer to investigate all of the ramifications of its use in a particular setting.

Questionable Approaches to Assessment

At this point it should hardly be necessary to warn against using methods in personnel selection that have not been validated scientifically, but occasionally one finds trained and experienced personnel managers who rely to some degree upon astrology, handwriting analysis (graphology), facial characteristics (physiognomy), and other approaches to personality assessment that are of questionable value. There appears to be a renewed interest in astrology, and it is likely that some personnel managers will be tempted to rely to some extent on the stars in making decisions. Handwriting analysis has also been receiving

[36] Bruce Gunn, "The Polygraph and Personnel," *Personnel Administration,* Vol. 33, No. 3 (May-June, 1970), pp. 32-37.

[37] David T. Lykken, "Psychology and the Lie Detector Industry," *American Psychologist,* Vol. 29, No. 10 (October, 1974), pp. 725-739.

increased attention and a considerable amount of research has been conducted to determine its validity as a selection tool, with disappointing results in most instances.[38] Handwriting analysis has been popular in European countries, particularly Germany, where psychologists as well as employers tend to have more faith in its value than is revealed by scientific study.[39] The use of physiognomy is a trap into which anyone can fall; in fact, there was a period in the United States from about 1915-1925 when some professional physiognomists were promoting it as a scientific approach to personnel selection. Dr. Katharine Blackford, a physician, wrote several books and articles in which she explains how to read faces; and in 1953 *Fortune* published a serious and sympathetic account of a personnel selection system based on facial characteristics.[40] There will always be those who are overly eager to promote a new system but who lack the understanding, ability, and motivation to subject it to scientific scrutiny.

EVALUATION OF ASSESSMENT METHODS

All of the methods used to assess the qualifications of job applicants that have been discussed in this and the preceding chapter require continuous review and evaluation. Too often when an expert is employed to establish some program, such as a testing or other type of program, it is assumed that the program will have lasting effectiveness. As noted earlier, a test or test battery that is performing effectively at one time may not be as effective a few months later. A continuous check of the validity of the tests is essential if the testing program is going to serve its purpose.

In evaluating the success of a testing program, it is essential to think in terms of averages rather than specific cases. It is easy to point to the exceptional case and say, "There's a man who scored at the top on our test battery, but look at his poor job performance." It is just as true in testing as in other areas that exceptions occur, but they do not necessarily prove anything. The real value of a testing program lies in such benefits as the increase in average production, decrease in average absenteeism and turnover, decrease in average number of accidents, and other criteria that can be applied to a number of persons.

While it is sometimes difficult to show outstanding results from a testing program, even minor changes in such benefits can represent a sizeable savings to the organization. By maintaining adequate records on personnel who are hired, it is possible to calculate the savings resulting from testing and other methods used to assess the qualifications of applicants.

---

[38] For a list of references of such studies, see S. M. Zdep and H. B. Weaver, "The Graphoanalytic Approach to Selecting Life Insurance Salesmen," *Journal of Applied Psychology*, Vol. 51, No. 3 (June, 1967), pp. 295-299.

[39] Chruden and Sherman, *op. cit.*, pp. 31-32.

[40] Katharine Blackford and A. Newcomb, *The Job, the Man, the Boss* (Garden City, New York: Doubleday, 1919); P. Stryker, "Is There an Executive Face?" *Fortune*, Vol. 48, No. 5 (November, 1953), pp. 145-147, 162-168.

7

Résumé

For the past half century psychological tests have had an important role in personnel selection and placement in government, business, and other types of organizations. In recent years, however, tests and testing programs have come under closer scrutiny because of questions that various groups have raised about their use. While the experts have always emphasized the importance of validating tests prior to their operational use, the validation process has become even more important. Validation basically involves "testing the test" in order to determine its power to predict job success. Measures of job success that are combined into a composite criterion will vary from job to job. It is the responsibility of management to define what constitutes job success in order that the tests most likely to predict it may be tried out in validation process. On the basis of tryout data, those tests that have the highest degree of validity and the least amount of overlap with other tests are finally selected for use with job applicants.

Administration of tests to job applicants requires as much diligence and caution as the validation process in order that applicants may be properly motivated for taking the tests and that tests are scored and interpreted properly. While tests provide an objective basis upon which to make decisions and are frequently more valid than other methods that may be used, a test is never a perfect predictor of job success. It serves, however, to maximize the selection of probable successes and to minimize the selection of probable failures. In using tests in a selection program, there are ethical and legal considerations that require careful attention. Ability and aptitude tests may prove to discriminate unfairly among certain groups, and personality tests may be viewed as invading the privacy of applicants.

Some of the methods of assessment, other than testing, were also considered. The objective scoring of data supplied on the application form and the use of background investigations were found to be valuable sources of information about applicants. Finally, in any assessment program provision should be made for evaluating its effectiveness, and assessment methods that have not been scientifically validated should not be used until more is known about them.

DISCUSSION QUESTIONS

1. What do you see as some of the problems in selecting specific criteria (production, sales, errors, etc.) by which to evaluate job performance? Does this mean that little or no attention should be given to criteria in the management of personnel?
2. Recall some of the situations in which you were a member of a group being administered psychological tests. What do you recall about the administrators and their skill in giving the tests? What were your own feelings during the test period? How can you utilize these experiences if you are called upon to administer tests?
3. It was mentioned in this chapter that disadvantaged persons often obtain low scores on employment tests.
   a. What is meant by a disadvantaged person?
   b. What causes many of them to obtain low scores on tests?

c. Are there any characteristics of a paper-and-pencil test that may discriminate unfairly against a disadvantaged person?

d. What can be done to overcome this problem immediately? in the future?

4. The vice-president of the company of which you are personnel manager calls you into his office and asks you to explain why a person who scored high on the test battery turned out to be a failure in the company after six months on the job. What would you tell him?

5. The Supreme Court ruling in the Griggs *vs.* Duke Power case is explicit in the requirement that "tests must measure the person for the job and not the person in the abstract."

   a. In your own words explain what is meant by the statement.

   b. What effect does this statement have on the types of tests and the manner in which tests are to be used?

   c. Would it preclude administering tests for the purpose of assessing an applicant's potential for a higher-level position at some future time?

6. A battery of tests was administered to a group of employees who had been told that the tests were for experimental purposes only and that their scores would not be recorded on their personnel records. At a later date, after the tests had been proved to be valid, the personnel manager ordered that the scores be entered on the employees' records. What is your opinion of the personnel manager's decision?

7. As a well-known and highly respected accountant, you are asked by the Civil Service Commission of your state to serve as a subject matter specialist in developing a test to be used in qualifying persons for accounting positions with state agencies. What contributions would you be able to make?

8. The scoring of application forms dates back as far as 1919, yet there are many organizations that do not use this procedure. What are possible explanations for the failure to use it?

PROBLEM 7-1 TO TEST OR NOT TO TEST

After many hearings and considerable debate, the supervisors of Jackson County decided that the county would assume the function of trash collection. The private company that had been servicing the county agreed to sell the business and to turn its personnel and equipment over to the county for it to manage and operate.

Since county employees are under civil service and are required to qualify on an intelligence test and a job knowledge test, the personnel who transferred from the private company to the county payroll were likewise required to qualify on the tests. The test battery developed for them consisted of the standard intelligence test and a multiple-choice job knowledge test specifically constructed to cover various aspects of the trash collector's job.

Subsequently several men who had been with the trash collection company for many years and apparently were performing well on their jobs were advised that they had failed the tests and would therefore not qualify for employment with the county. These men immediately filed a complaint with the county supervisors. The supervisors are now investigating the situation.

a. When an employer takes over the personnel from another organization, should he make them meet the same selection standards that he has established for his own employees?

b. Comment on the probable validity of tests for employees in this job classification.

SUGGESTED READINGS

Adkins, Dorothy C. *Test Construction,* 2d ed. Columbus, Ohio: Charles E. Merrill Books, Inc., 1974.

Albright, Lewis E., J. R. Glennon, and Wallace J. Smith. *The Use of Psychological Tests in Industry*. Cleveland: Howard Allen, Inc., 1963.

Anastasi, Anne. *Psychological Testing,* 3d ed. New York: The Macmillan Company, 1968.

Buros, O. K. *Seventh Mental Measurements Yearbook*. Highland Park, New Jersey: The Gryphon Press, 1972.

———. *Tests in Print, II*. Highland Park, New Jersey: The Gryphon Press, 1974.

Byham, William C. and Morton Edward Spitzer. *The Law and Personnel Testing*. New York: American Management Association, 1971.

Chruden, Herbert J., and Arthur W. Sherman, Jr., *Readings in Personnel Management,* Fourth edition. Cincinnati: South-Western Publishing Co., 1976. Part 2.

Cronbach, Lee J. *Essentials of Psychological Testing,* 3d ed. New York: Harper & Brothers, 1970.

DuBois, Philip H. *A History of Psychological Testing*. Boston: Allyn and Bacon, Inc., 1970. Chapter 1.

Ghiselli, Edwin E. *The Validity of Occupational Aptitude Tests*. New York: John Wiley & Sons, Inc., 1966.

Guion, Robert M. *Personnel Testing*. New York: McGraw-Hill Book Company, 1965.

Kirkpatrick, James J., Robert B. Ewen, Richard S. Barrett, and Raymond A. Katzell. *Testing and Fair Employment*. New York: New York University Press, 1968.

Lawshe, C. H., and Michael J. Balma. *Principles of Personnel Testing,* 2d ed. New York: McGraw-Hill Book Company, 1966.

McCormick, Ernest J., and Joseph Tiffin. *Industrial Psychology,* 6th ed. Englewood Cliffs, New Jersey: Prentice-Hall, Inc., 1974. Chapters 2, 5, 6, 7, and 8.

Miller, Robert B. *Tests and the Selection Process*. Chicago: Science Research Associates, 1966.

PART THREE

Maximizing Employee Potential

8

Employee Development

The functions of recruiting and selecting employees represent only the initial stages in the building of an efficient and stable work force. Employees also require continuous development if their potential is to be utilized effectively. The development of employees, in fact, should be viewed as beginning with their orientation and continuing throughout their employment with the organization.

Employee development programs typically include a wide variety of activities that are concerned with informing employees of company policies and procedures, training them in job skills, motivating and evaluating performance, and providing counseling as it is needed. The primary purpose of these activities is to develop employees who will contribute more effectively to the goals of the organization and who will gain a greater sense of satisfaction and adjustment from their work. Development, therefore, is a process to assist employees in attaining a level of performance and a quality of personal and social behavior that meets their needs and those of the organization.

Employee development has become increasingly vital to the success of modern organizations because rapid changes in technology require that employees possess the knowledge and skills necessary to cope with the new processes and production techniques being introduced. The growth of organizations into large, complex operations whose structures are continually changing also requires that many employees be prepared for new assignments. These objectives may be achieved through the various development programs found in most organizations. Among the types of developmental activities discussed elsewhere are management development (Chapter 9), performance evaluation (Chapter 10), and the development of supervisory personnel (Chapter 15). In this chapter the emphasis will be on such functions as orientation of employees, the designing of training programs, learning theory and its application to job training, and the evaluation of job training programs.

ORIENTATION

A formal *orientation program* should provide the new employee with an understanding of how job performance contributes to the success of the organization and how the services or products of the organization contribute to society. Although it is likely that employees already have knowledge and opinions about the organization and have awareness of the importance of the job, it is essential that they be furnished information that will enable them to find places in the organization. While the methods used to achieve these objectives may vary, it is essential that there be careful planning in order that new employees are provided with essential information.

Although the type of information that employees will need will vary with the job, it is customary to provide information about those matters that are of immediate concern to them, such as working hours, pay, and parking facilities. The employer, at this point, is also concerned that the new employees have a clear understanding of safety rules, security requirements in defense projects, and any other important matters of which they must be advised immediately so as to minimize the possibility of accidents and errors, and subsequent undesirable consequences. Later, attention may be devoted to informing employees about those areas that have a lower priority and/or that require more time for presentation and comprehension.

For All Employees—New and Present

Since an organization must be dynamic in order to meet the ever-changing conditions affecting its operations, policies and procedures and the structure and content of jobs must change with it. Unless present employees are kept up-to-date on these changes, they may find themselves unaware of activities about which new employees are currently being advised. While the discussion that follows focuses primarily upon the needs of the new employees and how these may be met through an initial orientation program, the fact that all employees need to be kept oriented to conditions that are ever changing should not be overlooked. No employee likes to be advised about the new policies in the department by outsiders.

A Cooperative Endeavor

The orientation program cannot be carried on effectively by either the personnel staff or the supervisors acting independently. For a well-integrated program that is carried out enthusiastically, cooperation between line and staff personnel is essential.

The personnel department is ordinarily responsible for coordinating orientation activities in the organization and for providing information concerning conditions of employment, pay and benefits, and other areas that are not directly under the supervisor's direction. The supervisor has the most important role in the orientation program. The new employee is primarily concerned with the "boss" and will be likely to give closest attention to what he or she says and does. It is essential, therefore, that the supervisor allow sufficient time for discussing the job on the employee's first day at work as well as for establishing a cordial relationship that will facilitate communication and learning. Prior to introducing the new person to the other members of the work group, it is also desirable for the supervisor to inform members of the group that a new employee is being added. Similarly, where there are proposed changes, such as the introduction of minority groups or transfers of large numbers of employees, it is usually desirable to discuss them with present employees on a basis that will facilitate acceptance of the change.

Orientation Requires a Plan

Those who plan orientation programs frequently expect the new employee to assimilate readily all types of detailed and assorted facts about the company, such as work rules, safety practices, executive biographies, and any other areas believed to be important. While the new employee should know these things eventually, it should be recognized that more learning may be effected if some things are covered over a period of time and in a series of meetings.

Use of a Checklist. To avoid overlooking items that are important to employees, many organizations devise checklists for use by those responsible for conducting some phase of orientation. A checklist developed by the General Electric Company (Figure 8-1) for use by supervisors insures that there will be no confusion as to whether or not a supervisor is expected to cover a particular item.

It has also been found that the use of a supervisor's checklist in the initial orientation of new employees compels a supervisor to pay more attention to each new employee at a time when personal attentiveness is critical to building a long-term relationship. The use of a checklist may also serve to reduce turnover by making it more likely that the new employee will receive information at the outset that provides a more realistic view of the job and working conditions.[1]

Reduction of Employee Anxiety. The planning of an orientation program should take into account findings from a study conducted at Texas Instruments which showed that for most new employees (1) the first few days on the job are anxious and uncertain ones, (2) new employee initiation practices by peers intensify anxiety, and (3) such anxiety interferes with the orientation and training process. To overcome these problems an experimental group of new employees had no contact with their peer work group but had unlimited

---

[1] Richard Scott, "Job Expectancy—An Important Factor in Labor Turnover," *Personnel Journal,* Vol. 51, No. 5 (May, 1972), pp. 360-363.

CHECKLIST FOR HELPING THE NEW EMPLOYEE GET STARTED

When Employee First Reports:

- [ ] Welcome to Company and job.
- [ ] Show locker or coat rack and wash room.
- [ ] Acquaint employee with cafeteria and other lunch facilities.
- [ ] Review security regulations including badge system.
- [ ] Show work place.
- [ ] Review rate, hours, use of time card.
- [ ] Briefly describe group's work.
- [ ] Introduce to fellow workers.
- [ ] Start employee on job, remembering the four steps of instruction.
  1. Prepare the worker.
  2. Present the operation.
  3. Try out his performance.
  4. Follow up.
- [ ] Briefly cover main safety rules and use of safety equipment.
- [ ] Remind employee to come to you for information and assistance.

Later During First Day:

- [ ] Review pay procedure.
- [ ] Discuss parking, car-pools.
- [ ] Explain dispensary facilities.
- [ ] Review safety rules.
- [ ] Briefly tell about work of department and how employee's job ties in.
- [ ] Shortly before quitting time, check with employee on progress and any questions.

During First Two Weeks:

- [ ] Review Benefit Plans*
  - Insurance and M. B. A.
  - Stock Bonus
  - Pension
  - Relief and Loan
  - Suggestion System
- [ ] Review items in "Your Guide to the River Works."
- [ ] Check on safety habits.
- [ ] Continue to follow up on progress and performance.

*Plans for which employee signed applications in Employment Office are underlined.

Source: General Electric booklet, "Orientating the New Employee." Reproduced with permission.

Figure 8-1 SUPERVISOR'S CHECKLIST

opportunities to talk with each other and with company personnel who make informal orientation presentations. It was considered a one-day, anxiety-reduced session. Compared with a control group that did not receive this session, training time, training costs, absenteeism and tardiness, and waste and rejects were lowered remarkably, saving $35,000. Improvement in job performance of the experimental group as compared with the control group (see Figure 8-2) represented an additional savings of over $50,000.[2] It would appear that time spent at the beginning of an orientation period to reduce the anxiety level of the new employees will result in greater productivity and reduced personnel costs.

TRAINING PROGRAMS

The need to orient employees and to provide job information and training has been well recognized by managers and supervisors who are alert to the role that people play in the attainment of the organization's objectives. Through training activities old talents may be updated and new ones developed. The

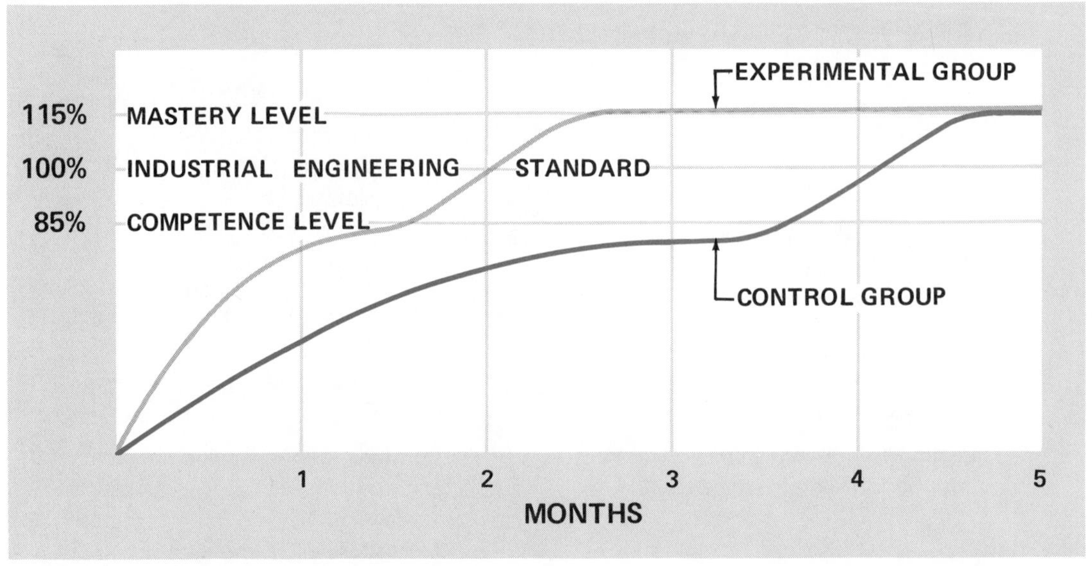

Source: Earl R. Gomersall and M. Scott Myers, "Breakthrough in On-the-Job Training," *Harvard Business Review*, Vol. 44, No. 4 (July-August, 1966), pp. 62-72. Reproduced with permission.

Figure 8-2 ANXIETY-REDUCING ORIENTATION PERIOD RESULTS IN HIGHER JOB COMPETENCY

---

[2] Earl R. Gomersall and M. Scott Myers, "Breakthrough in On-the-Job Training," *Harvard Business Review,* Vol. 44, No. 4 (July-August, 1966), pp. 62-72; and Otis Lipstreu, "A Systems Approach to Orientation," *Personnel Administration,* Vol. 32, No. 2 (March-April, 1969), pp. 41-47.

impact of automation, however, has made training even more important for the reasons that (1) some jobs will be enlarged, thereby requiring additional skills and knowledge; (2) others will require a narrower range of skills; and (3) many jobs will be replaced entirely by jobs newly created.[3] These situations require that supervisory personnel and representatives of the personnel department work together in preparing employees for changes in jobs through training activities.

In the larger organization the personnel department may provide managers and supervisors with considerable assistance in conducting training activities, including the organization of formal training classes, the selection and training of instructors, the procurement of training equipment and other aids, and the establishment of liaison with educational institutions and government agencies. Frequently, in the larger organization these activities are handled by a separate training division within the personnel department. In the smaller organization, however, most of the training tasks fall upon the managers and supervisors of the departments where employees work.

Assessing Training Needs and Priorities

Managers and personnel staff members should be alert to indications of employee training needs. If production records indicate, for example, that workers are not achieving production standards, additional training may be required. Similarly, an excessive number of rejects or a waste of material may be caused by inadequate training. An increase in the number of accidents also may be an indication that employees need refresher training in the use of safety devices and in safe working procedures.

A Systematic, Threefold Approach. In order to approach training needs more systematically, McGehee and Thayer suggest a threefold approach to thinking about the training requirements of an organization or a component of an organization. It consists of (1) determining where within the organization training emphasis can and should be placed; (2) determining what the content of training programs should be based upon a study of the tasks or duties involved; and (3) determining what skills, knowledge, or attitudes an *individual* employee must develop if he or she is to perform the assigned tasks or job duties effectively.[4]

Indexes that may be used to determine where training emphasis should be placed within the organization include direct and indirect labor costs, quality of goods or services, and employee morale. Indexes that also may be used to determine the content of training programs include data obtained from observing employees at work, such as is done in making a job analysis. Units produced, cost of producing units, absenteeism, tardiness, and accidents

[3] William McGehee and Paul W. Thayer, *Training in Business and Industry* (New York: John Wiley & Sons, Inc., 1961), pp. 10-11.

[4] *Ibid*. p. 25.

constitute still other determinants of individual training needs. For scientific and technical jobs where obsolescence of an employee's education may hinder individual and organizational progress, an analysis may focus on personal factors such as how long ago an individual received his or her last degree. Such information may give a hint or clue to those individuals who are more susceptible to obsolescence. However, further investigation must be carried on to determine those whose ability to perform is actually obsolete.[5]

Cost and Feasibility Factor. After conducting these various analyses, decisions must be made about the relative seriousness and the relative costs of discrepancies between expected and actual employee performance. It may be decided that the benefits derived from a training program for certain jobs would not be offset by the costs. For some jobs in an organization, improved selection procedures may be cheaper and more effective than a training program. The various analyses, however, should yield a listing of training need priorities based on cost and feasibility factors which will be the basis for developing training programs for the different task requirements in the organization. Since research has shown that not all employees respond to the same method of training, consideration should be given to such factors as which employees are likely to benefit from training and what methods should be used when developing a program.

A Positive Approach, But Not a Cure-all. While training represents a positive approach to the improvement of performance, it cannot provide the solution to all such problems. For example, if production is dropping because workers are disgruntled and resentful over working conditions, providing additional training for them will not be likely to increase production. It may, in fact, cause further resentment among employees because management may appear to them to be indifferent to the basis for their original feelings. The cause of each personnel problem, therefore, must be accurately determined and the most appropriate action taken.

Duties or Task Analysis

Designing a specific training program requires that particular attention be given to duties or *task analysis*—determining what should be the content of training in terms of what an employee must do to perform the job responsibilities in an effective way.

Steps in Task Analysis. The first step in the task analysis is listing all the tasks or duties that are included in the job. The second step is to list the steps involved in each of the duties on the list in terms of what the person *does* when performing the step, rather than in terms of what must be known. Figure 8-3 illustrates the task-detailing procedure for taking an X-ray of the chest. In addition to the steps in performing the task, the type of performance and the learning difficulty level are indicated.

[5] Richard Morano, "Determining Organizational Training Needs," *Personnel Psychology*, Vol. 26, No. 4 (Winter, 1973), pp. 479-487.

VOCATION: X-RAY TECHNICIAN

Task: Take an X-ray of the chest

No.	Steps in Performing the Task	Type of Performance	Learning Difficulty
1.	Patient is asked to prepare for the X-ray by removing excess clothing.	Speech	Easy
2.	Correctly position the patient, giving special instructions.	Manipulation, speech	Moderately difficult
3.	Position and check the proper distance of the tube with respect to the patient.	Discrimination	Moderately difficult
4.	Turn on the X-ray equipment and adjust machine.	Recall	Easy
5.	Insert the X-ray film and identification marker into the proper holder.	Manipulation	Easy
6.	Expose film and release patient from examining room.	Manipulation	Moderately difficult
7.	Process film.	Manipulation	Difficult
8.	Check film for specified positioning or developing errors.	Discrimination	Very difficult
9.	Release patient if film is acceptable to the radiologist.	Recall	√
10.	Clean examining table and film areas.	Manipulation	√

Source: Robert F. Mager and Kenneth M. Beach, Jr., *Developing Vocational Instruction* (Belmont, California: Fearon Publishers/Lear Siegler, Inc., 1967), p. 22. Reproduced with permission.

Figure 8-3 TASK DETAILING SHEET

Types of Performance. Analyses of a wide variety of jobs by Gagné reveal that there are eight different kinds of performance. Mager and Beach, for purposes of simplification, have modified Gagné's eight categories into five types of performance which are:

1. *Discrimination*—being able to tell the difference between two or more things. To tell when a proper job has been done, to tell when a task needs to be done, or to see the difference between what is correct and what is incorrect involves discrimination. For example: An industrial inspector determines that a product does not conform to specified standards.
2. *Problem-solving*—the process of finding solutions to problems. Problem-solving is taught by showing the employee relationships between symptoms and possible causes. For example: A TV repairman trainee is taught the meaning of different symptoms of malfunctioning and encouraged to seek the source of the trouble.
3. *Recall*—knowing what to do, what to use, and the order or sequence in which to perform a task are examples of the mental performance known as recall. For example: The highly skilled worker remembers what to do and how to do it when a problem has been identified.
4. *Manipulation*—the ability to use tools or devices to accomplish a given task. An individual may know what to do but lack the ability to do it. For example: One can learn the steps in flying an airplane from a book, but actual practice in manipulating the controls is essential to becoming a skilled pilot.
5. *Speech*—for many jobs speech is merely a form of communicating knowledge. In some tasks, however, speech is an essential feature of desired performance as, for example, in the announcer, actor, salesperson, telephone operator, waitress, etc.

If the type of performance that is primarily associated with each of the steps is determined, one is in a good position to select the content, methods, and materials for training employees in each step of a task sequence. Since a task may consist of more than one type of performance, however, the important thing is to identify the principal type of performance associated with each step. With the principal type of performance identified, the selection of content and instructional procedures is facilitated.[6]

Content of Training Programs

One of the major types of training is commonly referred to as *job training*. The primary purpose of job training at the beginning of an individual's employment is to bring his or her knowledge and skills up to a satisfactory level. As the individual continues on the job, training may be used to provide additional information and opportunities to acquire new skills. As a result of the training, the employee may then be more effective in the present job and may qualify for jobs at a higher level.

[6] Robert F. Mager and Kenneth M. Beach, Jr., *Developing Vocational Instruction* (Belmont, California: Fearon Publishers/Lear Siegler, Inc., 1967), pp. 44-51.

The invention and installation of new equipment, much of which is highly automated, have resulted in many employees having skills that are no longer required by their employer or by any other potential employer. In order for these occupationally dislocated persons to remain on the payroll or to obtain employment elsewhere, it is necessary for them to learn new skills through some type of retraining.

The fact that there are over 21,000 jobs in the United States involving many different tasks and performance requirements indicates that training programs in a single organization may cover a wide range of content reflecting the particular demands of the jobs established within it. In addition to providing training for specific jobs, most organizations have training programs for supervisory and managerial personnel that focus on human relationships, communication, personal development, and similar topics. Training programs may also include broader educational programs which frequently involve such subject matter areas as economics, psychology, statistics, or computer science. Many employers provide opportunities for those employees who need more basic education to learn the fundamental skills of reading, writing, and arithmetic.[7]

Recognition of the need for courses covering specific areas is illustrated in a major way in a study of United States subsidiaries in Europe where emphasis is placed on training sales and service personnel. This emphasis is understandable because of the growing competition that American subsidiaries in Europe are encountering from both native European and Japanese competitors. Most participating companies have well organized training programs for their sales and service personnel. American pharmaceutical and data processing equipment companies in particular have established sales training programs in Europe that compare very favorably with those found in the United States. Most of these programs consist of concentrated courses of two to four weeks' duration coupled with refresher courses for experienced salespersons. Cyanamid G.m.b.H. in Germany, for example, employs a full-time sales trainer and makes extensive use of closed-circuit television and tapes to permit participants to observe a playback of their sales presentations.[8]

Need for Clearly Stated Objectives

Regardless of the purposes for which training programs or courses are developed, it is essential that the desired outcomes be stated formally in what are referred to as *training objectives*. Generally these objectives involve the acquisition of skills or knowledge or the changing of attitudes. While objectives may be stated in many different ways, the performance-centered objective is utilized widely because it lends itself best to objective evaluation of results. For example, the stated objective for one training program is, "The trainee will be able to operate a keypunch at the rate of 40 WPM with less than 1 percent error

[7] Don Frederick, Jr., "Company Courses Teach Workers Reading, Basic Skills," *The National Observer*, November 4, 1972, p. 18.

[8] Herbert J. Chruden and Arthur W. Sherman, Jr., *Personnel Practices of American Companies in Europe* (New York: American Management Association, 1972), pp. 37-40.

for a period of 10 minutes.'' Performance-centered objectives typically include precise terms such as *to calculate, to repair, to adjust, to construct, to assemble, to classify, etc.* With clearly stated objectives that describe the desired changes of behavior, the instructors can do a better job of instructing and the trainees can do a better job of learning.[9]

Training Methods

Several different methods by which the objectives of the training program may be met are available. In the larger organization all of the methods to be described will probably be used at one time or another. Some methods, however, appear to be used more frequently than others. Data from a survey study of training methods in 63 manufacturing firms and 49 nonmanufacturing firms in the Minneapolis-St. Paul area indicate that the most frequently used training methods are: job instruction training, conference or discussion, apprenticeship training, job rotation, coaching, and lecture.[10] The use of a particular method, however, should be determined by the objectives of the particular training course, the abilities and potentialities of the trainer and of the individuals to be trained, the probable number of trainees, their job level, and such factors as the time and expense involved.

On-the-Job Training. Also called job instruction training, *on-the-job training* is the most commonly used method in the training of employees. It is conducted by the supervisor or by a senior employee who is responsible for instructing employees. It has the advantage of providing firsthand experience under normal working conditions. There is a potential disadvantage in this method, however, if the supervisor emphasizes production rather than learning to perform the job in the safest and most efficient manner. Still, by allowing sufficient time for job training and by correcting the trainee's mistakes as they occur, the supervisor can also use this as an opportunity to build a good relationship with the employee.

Conference or Discussion. A method of individualized instruction frequently used with clerical, professional, scientific, and supervisory personnel where the training involves primarily the communication of ideas, procedures, and standards is the *conference* or *discussion* method. Those individuals who have the general educational background and whatever specific skills are required, such as typing, shorthand, and office equipment operation, may then be provided with specific job instructions by this method. This method allows for considerable flexibility in the amount of employee participation that is encouraged or permitted. With professional and scientific personnel a high degree of employee participation is usually allowed.

---

[9] William R. Tracey, *Designing Training and Development Systems* (New York: American Management Association, 1971), pp. 76-105.

[10] Stuart B. Utgaard and René V. Dawis, ''The Most Frequently-Used Training Techniques,'' *Training and Development Journal*, Vol. 24, No. 2 (February, 1970), pp. 40-43.

Apprenticeship Training. A system of training in which the young worker entering industry is given thorough instruction and experience, both on and off the job, in the practical and theoretical aspects of the work in a skilled trade is known as *apprenticeship training*. Apprenticeship programs are based on voluntary cooperation between management and labor, industry and government, and the company and the school system. Although apprenticeship wages are less than those of fully qualified workers, this method does provide training with pay for individuals who are interested in qualifying for the types of jobs, such as those listed in Table 8-1, where this method of training has traditionally been used.

Table 8-1 SOME OF THE APPRENTICEABLE JOBS IN THE UNITED STATES

Job	No. of Years of Training	Job	No. of Years of Training
Airplane Mechanic	3-4	Machinist	4
Automotive Body Repairer	3-4	Millwright	4
Baker	3	Painter-Decorator	2-3
Barber	2	Photoengraver	5-6
Bricklayer	3	Plasterer	3-4
Candy Maker	3-4	Printer	4
Carpenter	4	Roofer	2-3
Cook	3	Sheetmetal Worker	3-4
Electrical Worker	4-5	Stonemason	3
Engraver	4-5	Tile Setter	3
Foundry Worker	2-4	Upholsterer	3-4
Ironworker	2-4	Wire Weaver	3-4

On the whole, apprenticeship training in Europe is superior to that in the United States. One of the reasons is that in Europe the dual-track system of education directs into vocational training a large proportion of the population who, in the United States, would feel under social pressure to take the academic route through high school and even college. Another possible reason for the strength of European apprenticeship training is that it is a part of the national educational system and not subject to control by unions which otherwise might use it to restrict entrance into the trade.[11]

Classroom Training Methods. *Classroom training* provides for handling the maximum number of trainees with a minimum number of instructors. It lends itself particularly to instruction in areas where information and instructions can be imparted by lectures, demonstrations, films, and other types of audiovisual materials. If the size of the group is small, as is frequently the case in supervisory and executive development programs, instructional methods of a participative nature may also be used, such as role playing, sensitivity training, and discussion of cases (see Chapter 9).

[11] Chruden and Sherman, *op. cit.*, pp. 40-41.

A special type of classroom facility is used in *vestibule training*. Trainees are given instruction on the operation of equipment which is like the equipment they will use when assigned to operating departments. Advantages of vestibule training are that training activities can be conducted without interrupting the flow of work in operating departments, and the emphasis is definitely on instruction rather than production. Furthermore, under controlled training conditions it is possible to evaluate the progress of the trainee more accurately than where on-the-job training is used. In a survey of 124 companies participating in programs for the disadvantaged, vestibule training is reported as being the most successful of the training methods used in terms of overall on-the-job performance.[12]

Programmed Instruction. Since the late 1950s organizations have been making increasing use of *programmed instruction* in employee and executive development to the point that most training directors have some familiarity with this form of instruction. While some of the programmed materials use a book or manual format, teaching machines offer a more dramatic means of presenting programmed subject matter. A program represents an attempt to break down subject matter content into highly organized, logical sequences which demand continuous responding on the part of the trainee. After being presented a small segment of information, the trainee is required to answer a question either by writing an answer in a response frame or by pushing a button on a machine. Equipment calling for the latter type of response is illustrated in Figure 8-4. If the response is correct, the trainee is advised of that fact and is presented with the next step (frame) in the material. If the response is incorrect, further explanatory information is given and the trainee is then told to "try again."

Programmed instruction has the advantage of recognizing individual differences in aptitude since each trainee learns at his or her own pace, and surveys have shown that trainees come away from this training experience with a higher disposition toward action and application. The major disadvantage is the cost in preparing special programs; but if sufficient numbers of personnel are to be trained, this cost can be readily absorbed.

While the first teaching machine was invented in 1922, the recent publicity given to this method may result in an uncritical attitude toward the device that some persons classify as a gadget. Certainly, the teaching machine is not a gadget if used to meet well-defined objectives through a professionally developed program.[13] A critical analysis of 32 evaluation studies of the programmed instruction method concludes that (1) this method reduces training time to a significant amount, the average saving time being one third; (2) such materials do not usually improve performance on measures of immediate

[12] William H. Holley, Jr., "Evaluation of Programs to Facilitate Effective Performance of the Disadvantaged Worker," *Training and Development Journal,* Vol. 27, No. 2 (February, 1973), pp. 18-21.

[13] One expert has written a provocative book about the need for clear statements of objectives of training programs—with or without teaching machines. See Robert F. Mager, *Preparing Objectives for Programmed Instruction* (San Francisco: Fearon Publishers, 1961).

Source: The AutoTutor Mark II of United States Industries—Educational Science Division. Reproduced with permission of USI.

Figure 8-4 A TEACHING MACHINE

learning and retention; and (3) the application of programmed methods in industry has had slightly more positive results than when applied in academic settings.[14]

Computer-Assisted Instruction. *Computer-assisted instruction* (CAI) is a sophisticated descendant of programmed instruction. The memory and storage capabilities of computers make it possible to provide drill and practice, problem solving, simulation, gaming forms of instruction, and certain very sophisticated forms of individualized tutorial instruction. Some specialists predict that, while to date CAI has been used primarily in educational institutions, it has considerable promise for industry, particularly where the costs can be spread over many trainees.[15]

Simulators and Other Training Devices. For some jobs it is either impractical or unwise to train the worker on the equipment that is used on the job. An obvious example is found in the training of personnel to operate

[14] Allan N. Nash, Jan P. Muczyk, and Frank L. Vettori, "The Relative Practical Effectiveness of Programmed Instruction," *Personnel Psychology,* Vol. 24, No. 3 (Autumn, 1971), pp. 397-418.

[15] Ernest J. McCormick and Joseph Tiffin, *Industrial Psychology* (6th ed.; Englewood Cliffs, New Jersey: Prentice-Hall, Inc., 1974), p. 268.

commercial or military aircraft and aircraft equipment. By using simulators in classroom situations, personnel may be given training and experience on airborne equipment under safe conditions. The design of *simulators* emphasizes realism in equipment and its operation so that the trainee learns how to perform the tasks in a setting as close to the real thing as is possible. Training devices are also used in teaching job skills and procedures of an industrial nature. An interesting trainee device known as Videosonics is being used to give employees step-by-step job procedures at their work benches. The device, which looks like a portable TV set, uses magnetic tape that is synchronized with 35 mm color slides. The slides together with the instructor's voice have been used successfully in describing and illustrating steps in the manufacture and assembly of electronic component parts. Even after an employee has mastered an assembly operation, this device can be used to check on a particular phase of the work about which there may be some doubt or questions.

Closed-circuit television and video tape recording equipment have become popular as training devices. Closed-circuit television allows an instructional program to be transmitted to many locations simultaneously. The use of video tape permits on-the-spot recording and immediate playback which are valuable for any type of instructional program. In personnel work video taping of employment and performance evaluation interviews provides the basic data for training personnel in interviewing methods. The potential value of video tape equipment for use in training programs is unlimited.

Education-Employer Cooperation in Training. Training programs which combine practical on-the-job experience with formal classes are called *cooperative training*. The term "cooperative training" is used in connection with high school and college level programs which incorporate part-time work experiences. At the high school level such programs enroll students preparing for clerical, retailing, and manual jobs; students in college programs are preparing for technical and executive jobs. The company that participates in providing practical experience to students obtains a source of part-time workers and is also provided with an excellent opportunity to evaluate them for possible full-time employment upon their graduation.

Supplementary training provided by high schools, colleges, and universities has become increasingly popular. With the explosive growth of new knowledge making its influence felt at nearly every level of the work force, an ever-increasing number of organizations are using tuition-aid plans to encourage more of their employees to study courses at school that will improve their productivity on the job. A study of the tuition-aid plans of 200 companies reveals that 168 of the work plans are open to all full-time employees; the remainder are restricted to salaried, nonunion, managerial, or professional personnel. Although the entire cost of tuition is met by 71 companies, payments generally average about 80 percent. In 155 of the companies studied, the median rate of employee tuition-aid participation is 4.4 percent.

All but 13 companies express a desire to have more employees participate in the program.[16]

Government-Sponsored Training Programs

Many organizations as well as individuals have benefited from the various manpower training programs developed by the federal government since the enactment of the Manpower Development and Training Act (MDTA) of 1962. The emphasis has been on providing underemployed persons with the opportunity to upgrade their skills and to equip the unemployed with new skills required by a changing job market. Special efforts have been made in the various programs to assist such occupationally disadvantaged groups as minority races, handicapped workers, public assistance recipients, and unemployment insurance claimants.

After a decade of numerous manpower development programs operated by the Department of Labor, the Comprehensive Employment and Training Act of 1973 was passed. The new law eliminates the numerous categorical programs and provides for decentralization. About 80 percent of the funds will be distributed to state and local governments who are authorized to sponsor manpower programs under Title I. Funds may be used for a wide variety of purposes including recruitment, testing, and supportive services; but the act clearly emphasizes training.

Government-sponsored training programs have involved tens of thousands of individuals in all types of training situations—on the job, classroom, vestibule—and they have undoubtedly contributed to the employability of many individuals and to the productivity of the hiring organizations. Many organizations participating in such programs, however, fail to recognize that for some individuals, such as the hard-core unemployed, a carefully planned induction and orientation program is essential to facilitate the transition from the ghetto culture to an industrial culture.[17]

PSYCHOLOGICAL PRINCIPLES OF LEARNING

The success of a job training program depends upon more than the identification of training needs and the preparation of the program. If the trainee has not learned, it is probably because some important principle of learning has been overlooked. Because the success or failure of a training program is frequently related to this simple fact, those who are concerned with developing instructional programs should recognize that attention must be given to the basic psychological principles of learning. The application of these principles, which are equally relevant to school classrooms and to company training programs, represents the major approach to making training effective.

---

[16] Roger O'Meara, *Combating Knowledge Obsolescence—II, Employee Tuition-Aid Plans, Studies in Personnel Policy,* No. 221 (New York: National Industrial Conference Board, 1970).

[17] Ross Stagner, "A Psychological Perspective on Manpower Programs," *Manpower,* Vol. 1, No. 2 (February-March, 1969), pp. 19-21.

The different methods or techniques used in training personnel that were described in the preceding section vary in the extent to which they utilize the principles of learning. Table 8-2 from Bass and Vaughn presents this information in summary form.

Table 8-2 EXTENT TO WHICH TRAINING TECHNIQUES UTILIZE CERTAIN PRINCIPLES OF LEARNING

	Motivation: Active Participation of Learner	Reinforcement: Feedback of Knowledge of Results	Stimulus: Meaningful Organization of Materials	Responses: Practice and Repetition	Stimulus-Response Conditions Most Favorable for Transfer
On-the-Job Techniques					
Job-Instruction Training	Yes	Sometimes	Yes	Yes	Yes
Apprentice Training	Yes	Sometimes	?	Sometimes	Yes
Internships and Assistantships	Yes	Sometimes	?	Sometimes	Yes
Job Rotation	Yes	No	?	Sometimes	Yes
Junior Board	Yes	Sometimes	Sometimes	Sometimes	Yes
Coaching	Yes	Yes	Sometimes	Sometimes	Yes
Off-the-Job Techniques					
Vestibule	Yes	Sometimes	Yes	Yes	Sometimes
Lecture	No	No	Yes	No	No
Special Study	Yes	No	Yes	?	No
Films	No	No	Yes	No	No
Television	No	No	Yes	No	No
Conference or Discussion	Yes	Sometimes	Sometimes	Sometimes	No
Case Study	Yes	Sometimes	Sometimes	Sometimes	Sometimes
Role Playing	Yes	Sometimes	No	Sometimes	Sometimes
Simulation	Yes	Sometimes	Sometimes	Sometimes	Sometimes
Programmed Instruction	Yes	Yes	Yes	Yes	No
Laboratory Training	Yes	Yes	No	Yes	Sometimes
Programmed Group Exercises	Yes	Yes	Yes	Sometimes	Sometimes

Source: Bernard M. Bass and James A. Vaughn, *Training in Industry: The Management of Learning,* © 1966 by Wadsworth Publishing Company, Inc., Belmont, California 94002. Reprinted by permission of the publisher, Brooks/Cole Publishing Company.

Motivation

One of the fundamental conditions for learning is that the trainee be properly motivated. That is, for optimum learning the trainee must recognize the need for acquiring new information or for having new skills; and a desire to learn as training progresses must be maintained. While people at work are motivated by certain common needs, they differ from one another in the relative importance of these needs at any given time. The needs for recognition, for safety, and for self realization are among some of these needs that can be satisfied through training activities. Trainers should be alert to individual needs in the training situation and use them as a basis for motivating employees. Performance standards should be set so that an individual is not frustrated by the trainer who requires too much or too little. It is often desirable to group individuals according to their capacity to learn as determined by scores from intelligence and aptitude tests or to provide a different or extended type of instruction for those who need it.

Knowledge of Results

As an employee's training progresses, motivation may be maintained and even increased by providing *knowledge of progress*. Progress, as determined by tests and other records, may be plotted on a chart, commonly referred to as a learning curve. A learning curve for a group of employees is shown in Figure 8-5. Note that the curve expresses the relationship between time (in days and weeks) and units of production.

In many learning situations there are times when progress does not occur. Such periods of no return show up on the curve as a fairly straight horizontal line, which is called a *plateau*. A plateau may be the result of ineffective methods of work, or it may come because of reduced motivation. Proper guidance by the instructor may reveal the cause of a plateau and may enable the instructor to assist the trainee by such means as suggestions for new work procedures or aid in establishing new incentives.

While knowledge of results provides a strong incentive at all stages in learning, it is especially needed after the initial enthusiasm of the learning situation has diminished. It is important, therefore, that employees be advised of their progress during all of the phases of training and, preferably, throughout their careers with the organization.

Principle of Reinforcement

Closely related to knowledge of results is the principle of reinforcement. *Reinforcement* is anything which strengthens the response. It may be in the form of approval from the trainer or the feeling of accomplishment that follows the performance; or it may take the forms such as confirmation by a teaching machine that the trainee's response was correct. Regardless of the type of reinforcement, it is generally most effective if it occurs immediately after a task has been performed.

Behavior Modification

In recent years some industrial organizations have utilized *behavior modification,* a technique that operates on the principle that behavior that is rewarded—positively reinforced—will be exhibited more frequently in the

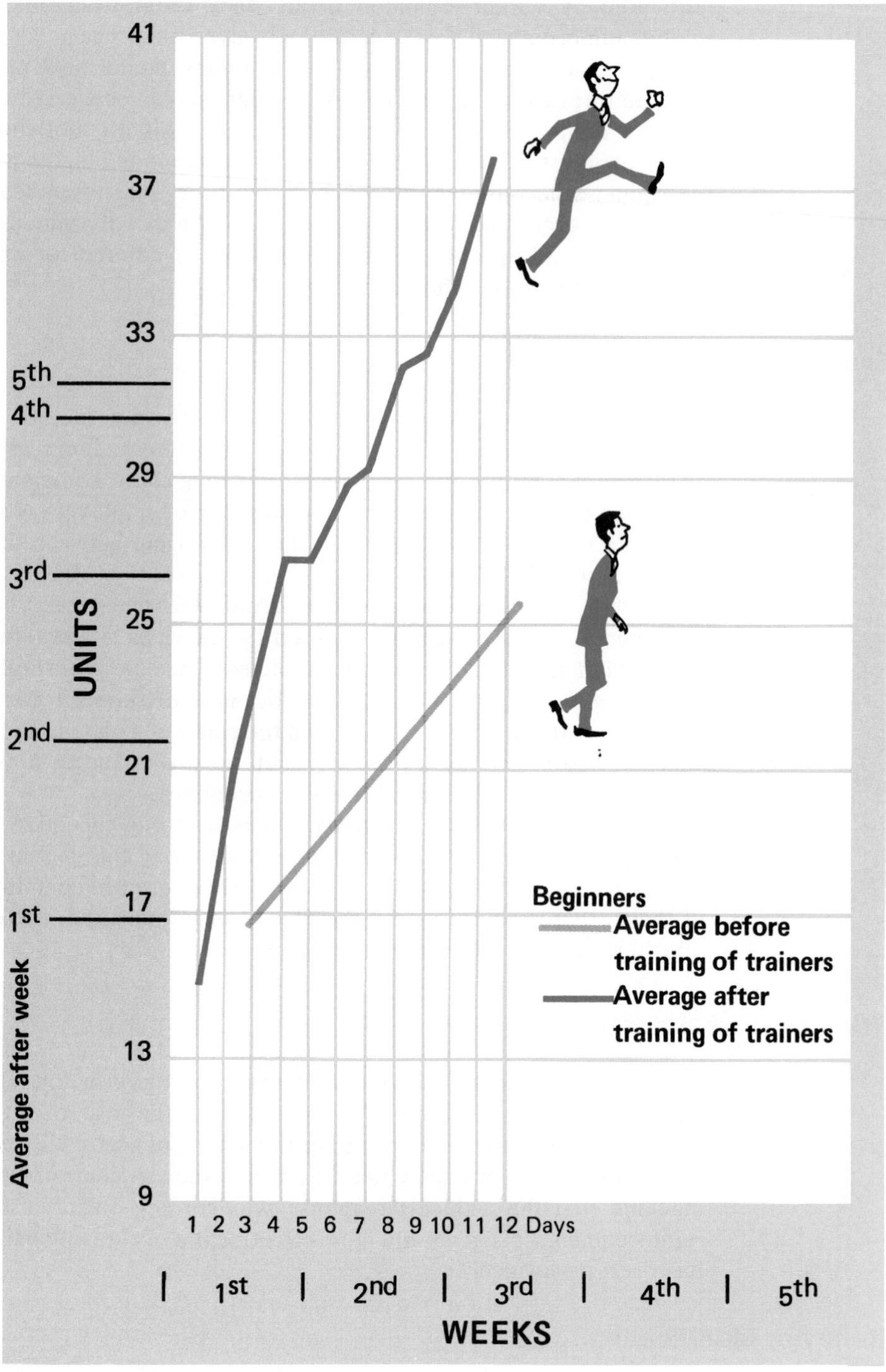

Reproduced with permission of Alex Bavelas.

Figure 8-5 LEARNING CURVES OF EMPLOYEES

future, whereas behavior that is penalized or unrewarded will decrease in frequency. Elaborate systems may be used for training employees that provide for changing the amount and frequency of reinforcement as specific job behaviors appear. Positive reinforcement may be anything that increases the likelihood of the response being repeated, and in the job situation it usually involves money or verbal praise from the supervisor. It is interesting to note that research has shown that for the behavior to continue after it is established it should be reinforced only periodically or intermittently. Intermittent reinforcement is at the heart of all gambling since not knowing when the next reinforcement will come is a powerful motivator to continue gambling. Emery Air Freight Corporation has used the behavior modification principles set forth by B. F. Skinner in scientific and popular publications throughout its organization. The executives report improved profits as well as greater contentment on the part of the employees.[18]

Meaningful Organization of Materials

Another principle of learning is that the material to be learned should be organized in as meaningful a manner as possible. The material should be arranged so that each successive experience builds upon preceding ones and that the trainee is able to integrate the experiences into a usable pattern of knowledge and skills. The presence of gaps, uncertainties, and contradictions frequently results in loss of interest by the trainees and often in failure to learn what is required for effective job performance.

Practice and Repetition

It is those things we do daily that become a part of our repertoire of skills. Trainees should be given frequent opportunity to practice their job tasks in the manner that they will ultimately be expected to perform them. The individual who is being taught to operate a machine should have an opportunity to practice on it, and, similarly, the supervisor who is being taught "how to train" should have supervised practice in training. Supervision while practicing is important because "practice makes perfect" only when the trainee is performing correctly. The incorrect responses can be learned just as easily as the correct ones.

Participation facilitates the acquisition of learning even when it involves only oral material, as, for example, reciting what one has just read either to another person or to oneself. One method of study emphasizes reciting to oneself the main points covered in what was read. This method recognizes the fact that the reader's time is utilized more efficiently in reciting than in spending more time rereading the material.[19]

---

[18] "New Tool: Reinforcement for Good Work," *Psychology Today,* Vol. 5, No. 11 (April, 1972), pp. 68-69.

[19] The reader who desires to improve reading and study skills will find the cited study method very effective. It is discussed in F. P. Robinson, *Effective Study* (4th ed.; New York: Harper & Brothers, 1970) and in *Effective Reading* (New York: Harper & Brothers, 1962).

Transfer of Training

Unless what is learned in the training situation is applicable to what is required on the job, the training effort has been of little value. The ultimate effectiveness of learning, therefore, is to be found in the answer to the question, "To what extent does what is learned *transfer* to the new situation?" While there is still much to be learned about transfer of training, there are two theories that have a reasonable amount of empirical support.

Identical Elements Theory. The *identical elements theory* states that transfer (learning in one situation enhances performance in a new situation) will occur only if identical elements are present in the old and new situations. Thus, the more closely the learning situation resembles the job situation, the higher the degree of transfer that can be expected. On the other hand, if the stimuli in two situations are similar but the responses they require are different, negative transfer will occur; i.e., learning in the first situation inhibits performance in the new situation. Thus, if the responses learned in training are contrary to those required on the job, such training may interfere with a trainee's work performance.

Transfer Through Principles Theory. The *transfer through principles theory* states that the learner need not be aware of the presence of specific identical elements in the two stimulus situations, but that positive transfer results when the learner applies those principles learned in past specific situations. The primary focus in applying this theory is in creating circumstances that best help trainees to learn appropriate principles and shape their perceptions for sensitive discrimination of their environment.[20]

Distributed Learning

Another factor that determines the effectiveness of training is the amount of time given to practice in one session. Should trainees be given training in five 2-hour periods or in ten 1-hour periods? While there are operating problems to be considered in answering this question, it has been found in most cases that spacing out the training will result in more rapid learning and more permanent retention. Since the most efficient distribution will vary according to the type and complexity of the task to be learned, it is desirable to make reference to the rapidly growing body of research in this area when an answer is required for a specific training situation.[21]

Whole vs. Part Learning

Most jobs and tasks can be broken down into parts that lend themselves to further analysis. The analysis of the most effective manner for completing each

---

[20] Bernard M. Bass and James A. Vaughn, *Training in Industry: The Management of Learning*, (Belmont, California: Wadsworth Publishing Company, 1966), pp. 38-40.

[21] *The Journal of Applied Psychology* is an excellent source of research studies of this type. Its articles are indexed in *Psychological Abstracts*.

part then provides a basis for giving specific instruction. Typing, for example, is made up of several skills that are part of the total process. The typist starts by learning the proper use of each finger; eventually, with practice, the individual finger movements become integrated into a total pattern. Practice by moving individual fingers is an example of part learning. In determining whether part learning or whole learning is the most efficient approach, it is necessary to consider the nature of the task to be learned. If it can be broken down successfully for part learning, it probably should be broken down in order to facilitate learning; otherwise, it probably should be taught as a unit.

Train the Trainers

Research indicates that when instructors are given training the trainees will show much greater progress than when the instructors are not given such training. In one study approximately eight hours of special training by the discussion method were given to trainers who taught the operation of a stitching machine.[22] The effects of the training are shown in Figure 8-5 on page 190 which was also used to illustrate the nature of learning curves. Note that the rate of learning a stitching operation was distinctly more rapid after the company trainers received the special instruction in teaching methods.

The *Training Within Industry* (TWI) program of World War II emphasized the importance of training instructors in industry by means of the *Job Instruction Training* (JIT) program. The basic ideas of the JIT Program were summarized on a reminder card which emphasized the following steps:

How to Get Ready to Instruct

1. Have a time table.
2. Break down the job.
3. Have everything ready.
4. Have the work place properly arranged.

How to Instruct

1. Prepare the worker.
2. Present the operation.
3. Try out performance.
4. Follow up.

This program, which was taught throughout the United States along with the other TWI courses in job methods, job relations, and program development training plans, undoubtedly provided the major stimulation for improved company training programs. Over 1,750,000 individuals received instruction under the TWI Program with the result that its effect has been felt in most companies.

EVALUATION OF TRAINING PROGRAMS

Training, like any other function of personnel management, should be evaluated to determine its effectiveness. The existence of a training staff and an

[22] This study was conducted by Alex Bavelas.

array of courses and other training experiences for employees does not insure that learning is taking place. It is the responsibility of the training director to determine not only the needs for training but to have proof that the needs are being met through the program. Unfortunately, information concerning the achievement of goals and the most effective methods of reaching them are obtained in only a few instances, and then by research approaches that are often inadequate.

While an examination of various research approaches is beyond the scope of this book, there are certain basic principles that should be mentioned. In the first place, it is essential that experimental controls be employed in evaluation research. Not only should trainees be tested before and after receiving training, but the same tests or evaluations should be made of individuals in a control group which has not received the training and whose members are matched with the trainees on the basis of relevant variables such as intelligence, experience, and level of job.

Some of the criteria that are used in evaluating the effectiveness of training are: increased productivity, total sales, decreased costs and waste, and similar evidence of improved performance. If a course were designed to change the behavior of supervisors, the evaluation should be in terms of supervisory behavior, not knowledge. Measures used to evaluate training, such as production records, supervisory ratings, cost records, accidents, etc., should be sufficiently reliable or consistent to serve as dependable indicators. They should also be free from bias, if possible. Just because Roger Smith attended a particular training course does not insure that Roger actually benefited from the course in terms of the company objectives. His job performance, after training, should be observed and comparisons made with his performance before training on whatever measurable characteristics are considered pertinent.

The training department can make itself a major factor in achieving organizational effectiveness if it can design and implement programs which insure that employee development programs conform to the need for organizational growth and effectiveness. Training directors have handicapped themselves by not being able to prove their effectiveness objectively. Quite often the training director's clout within the organization has depended upon the good will of top management.[23]

Résumé

Because of rapid changes in technology and the growth of organizations into large, complex operations, orientation and training programs are vital to an organization's success. Beginning with the orientation program, employees should be made to feel that their contributions are important and appropriate steps should be taken to assess their needs for information and skills. In designing training programs, particular attention should be given to task

[23] Joseph Wolfe, "Evaluating the Training Effort," *Training and Development Journal*, Vol. 27, No. 5 (May, 1973), pp. 20-27.

analysis so that the content, methods, and materials selected will facilitate the learning process. From the wide variety of training methods that are available, those methods that best meet the training objectives and that utilize as many of the principles of learning as possible should be used.

In recent years manpower development programs sponsored by the federal government have played an important part in helping many individuals, especially the disadvantaged, to develop their skills and potentials so as to contribute to their own welfare as well as that of the nation. With employers having a greater participative role in such programs, there is greater need for flexibility and adaptability on their part in order that the interests of the individual employees, the organization, and society may be served.

While the personnel in each department should have an important part in the planning and carrying out of their programs, the training division should not wait until the other departments make their problems known. It should, like an educational institution, be looking ahead and anticipating the role that it can play in providing a service. In some instances the training division will be concerned with problems in teaching simple motor skills. At other times it will have the task of planning for the development of attitudes toward intricate social issues. Regardless of the area, training and development must be backed up by careful research. While new methods must always be considered and explored, the focus should be on the objectives to be attained through training. Whether or not the objectives are being met can best be determined by proper attention to evaluation.

DISCUSSION QUESTIONS

1. The new employee is likely to be anxious the first few days on the job.
   a. What are some possible causes of such anxiety?
   b. How may the anxiety be reduced?
2. A training manual was developed for training employees in the U.S. Employment Service and other agencies in how to use the Third Edition of the *Dictionary of Occupational Titles* (1965). The manual uses one of the programmed instruction techniques in which the blanks are filled in after reading a statement in the manual and often after consulting the DOT.
   a. What advantages is this method likely to have over a lecture on the same material? Over programmed instruction by a teaching machine?
   b. Why don't more employers use a similar approach in providing information to employees on how to perform their job tasks?
   c. How would you evaluate a training program in which programmed instructional methods were used?
3. The production manager of a company blames the high rate of production waste on poor training. Would this necessarily be the cause? What factors other than training may be at fault?
4. Some companies use a sponsor or "buddy" system to aid employees in their initial on-the-job adjustment. Experienced employees are given the assignment in addition to their regular duties.
   a. What advantages are there in such an approach? What disadvantages?
   b. If you were given the assignment, what are the most important things you would feel you should do?
5. What conditions make it necessary to have special manpower development and training programs for the occupationally disadvantaged? What benefits may be derived from such programs?
6. In Table 8-2 films and television are indicated as utilizing only one of the principles of learning. Should this be interpreted to mean that films and television should not be used as training techniques?

PROBLEM 8-1 AUDITING THE AUDITORS

A state auditing agency with its headquarters in the capital city and two field offices in other cities found it necessary to recall auditors from its field offices to its headquarters to work on a special study of high priority. All of these auditors had been in the state service for many years and had been promoted regularly on the basis of supervisory recommendations. After these individuals had worked on the special study for a few weeks, however, it became apparent to the head of the state auditing agency that the quality of their performance was far below that of those headquarters personnel who possessed the same job classification. Consequently, he decided to close the field offices and move their personnel to the headquarters office. Further evaluation of the personnel formerly in the field offices resulted in some demotions and in the resignation of others slated for demotion. Those who were retrained were given intensive training and coaching and brought up to the performance standards expected of persons with their classifications.

a. What weaknesses, if any, in the agency's personnel management program are indicated by this incident?
b. What can an organization do to achieve uniform qualifications among employees performing the same job but in different departments and locations? Is such standardization desirable?

SUGGESTED READINGS

Belasco, James A., and Harrison M. Trice. *The Assessment of Change in Training and Therapy*. New York: McGraw-Hill Book Company, 1969.

Bienvenu, Bernard J. *New Priorities in Training*. New York: American Management Association, 1969.

Bond, Nicholas A. "Auditing Change: The Technology of Measuring Change," in Marvin D. Dunnette, *Work and Nonwork in the Year 2001*. Monterey, California: Brooks/Cole Publishing Company, 1973.

Broadwell, Martin M. *The Supervisor and On-the-Job Training*. Reading, Massachusetts: Addison-Wesley Publishing Co., 1969.

Chruden, Herbert J., and Arthur W. Sherman, Jr. *Readings in Personnel Management*, 4th ed. Cincinnati: South-Western Publishing Company, Inc., 1976. Part 3.

Craig, Robert L., and Lester R. Bittel (eds.). *Training and Development Handbook*. New York: McGraw-Hill Book Company, 1967.

Goldstein, Irwin L. *Training: Program Development and Evaluation*. Monterey, California: Brooks/Cole Publishing Company, 1974.

Lovin, Bill C. and Emery Reber Casstevens. *Coaching, Learning, and Action*. New York: American Management Association, 1971.

Mager, Robert F., and Kenneth M. Beach, Jr. *Developing Vocational Instruction*. Belmont, California: Fearon Publishers/Lear Siegler, Inc., 1967.

Saint, Avice. *Learning at Work*. Chicago: Nelson-Hall Company, 1974.

Somers, Gerald G. (ed.). *Retraining the Unemployed*. Madison, Wisconsin: The University of Wisconsin Press, 1968.

Stokes, Paul M. *Total Job Training*. New York: American Management Association, 1966.

Tracey, William R. *Designing Training and Development Systems*. New York: American Management Association, 1971.

Management Development

Organizations today must have competent managers in order to cope with the many complex problems affecting their operations. Furthermore, in most organizations it is recognized that such competency is acquired not only by formal education but also through experience gained in decision making and in exercising other managerial skills on the job. Consequently, greater attention is being placed upon formal programs as a means of developing present and future managers to realize their potential to a maximum within the organization.

Because of its recognized importance, few areas of personnel management have been the subject of more research and articles than management development. In spite of this fact, much is still to be learned about the management processes in order to understand more precisely the talent that is required of a good manager and how this talent can be detected, developed, and measured more effectively. As new knowledge on the subject is being acquired through research and experience, some of the earlier concepts and techniques pertaining to management development are changing and can be expected to continue to do so in the future. The purpose of this chapter, therefore, will be to discuss some of the problems in management development as well as some of the trends in the methods being used to achieve such development.

THE NATURE OF MANAGEMENT DEVELOPMENT

Development programs for managers tend to be more long-range in nature than those for employees below the management level. Rather than seeking to develop specific skills to perform a certain job more effectively, management programs provide for development in the broader sense to include attitudes, abilities, perceptions, and personality traits, as well as the knowledge and skills that are considered essential to the performance of present and future management assignments. While management development is concerned with future staffing needs, this concern is not at the neglect of improving performance and satisfaction on the part of personnel in their current assignments. Management development programs, therefore, assume that managers, regardless of how well they are performing, should be encouraged to improve their performance and avoid professional obsolescence.

Evolution of Management Development

Prior to the existence of formal programs, managers in most organizations were expected to assume the responsibility for meeting their needs for personal development. Management skills and abilities were to be acquired by working on the job and through whatever other learning experiences individuals might encounter. Furthermore, managers were expected to be able to move upward within an organization as a result of demonstrating their abilities on the job. Unfortunately, under such an informal system, capable individuals were not always able to receive the type of development opportunities or the type of exposures at work required to attract the attention of those superiors who were in a position to help their advancement. Many persons with significant management potential, therefore, often were overlooked and found themselves in dead-end assignments.

The need for management development began to be recognized during World War II when the war industries, because of rapid expansion and the loss of managers to the armed services, were faced with severe shortages of seasoned executive talent. The initial emphasis, therefore, was primarily upon the development of personnel for managerial positions where shortages of qualified personnel for such positions were not acute. Following World War II, business organizations in particular were confronted with the problem that the personnel in management positions who had grown older had not developed qualified replacements for their positions. In addition, many of the individuals who were in management positions were incapable of coping with the many problems of organizational expansion, technological progress, and renewed competition that was arising during the postwar era. As a result of such conditions, some companies initiated "crash programs" to recruit and to accelerate the training and seasoning of promising junior managers for rapid advancement. In order to increase the supply and continuity of young management talent, emphasis in these programs was placed upon providing courses and special work experiences in an effort to shorten the years of practical experience considered to be required for becoming a competent manager. As the need for crash programs declined, however, management development programs became subject to more critical appraisal. Management development increasingly began to be recognized as something that was needed by all managers and not just by an elite group of management trainees. Instead of providing trainees with a prolonged period of special courses and work experiences and recognizing them as a separate group, furthermore, many companies began to assign their newly-hired management trainees to regular production jobs in which they were expected first to prove themselves.

Current Emphasis in Management Development

The rapidly occurring technological and environmental changes confronting most organizations have created a distinct occupational hazard for managers to avoid. This is the hazard of *professional obsolescence* resulting from their failure to engage in continual reeducation and renewal efforts. While there is no way of determining the number of times managers will have to reeducate themselves during their careers, two or three times would be a safe estimate. Thus, according to Levinson, it is not uncommon for jobs today to outgrow their job holders. He recommends that organizations observe the "total push"[1] concept by maintaining pressure upon managers to continue their self-development and thereby avoid professional obsolescence.[2]

Greater attention in management development is being focused upon individual redevelopment and upon the development needs of all management personnel rather than just those at the trainee and lower levels. There also is a trend to place more emphasis upon organization development as a means of furthering individual and team growth.[3] Organization development which is discussed in Chapter 15 is concerned with the environment and culture of the organization, with locating and solving organizational problems, and with making the changes necessary to achieve this growth. These management-organization development programs, furthermore, are tending to be treated as a subsystem closely integrated and interrelated with manpower planning, management assessment, performance appraisal, and human resource accounting systems that comprise the total personnel management system.[4]

Problems Relating to Management Development

In spite of the experience gained from development programs over the past two decades, there still are problems to be resolved. Although most major U.S. corporations have development programs, according to one study relatively few of them are doing a really outstanding job in this area and ironically these are the corporations that lose the most managers to other corporations.[5]

---

[1] The "total push" concept which originated in connection with the treatment of mental patients advocates returning the patients to an active role in society with out-patient treatment rather than permitting them to remain in a hospital and become more helpless.

[2] Harry Levinson, "Is There An Obsolescent Executive in Your Company—or in Your Chair?" *Think,* Vol. 34, No. 11 (January-February, 1968), p. 30.

[3] Michael E. Spautz, "A Survey of the Effectiveness of Management Development Programs." Mimeographed publication sponsored by the U.S. Civil Service Commission, San Francisco Region (1970), pp. 73-74.

[4] *Ibid.*

[5] John C. Perham, "The Companies That Build Executive Talent," *Dun's*, Vol. 101, No. 5 (May, 1973), p. 51.

Problems Relating to Mobility. One of the reasons why companies with outstanding development programs, such as IT&T, IBM, and Xerox, lose many managers is because the reputation of their development program enables them to recruit many of the most capable graduates. As a result of successful recruitment, these companies are able to develop management talent in such numbers that many of these personnel become impatient and go elsewhere to accelerate their career advancement. Such conditions encourage as well as facilitate mobility and give rise to a nomadic type of *journeyman executive*.[6]

For many such individuals mobility has become a way of life, with change itself becoming an important value; and Jennings has coined the term *mobicentric* to identify them.[7] As a result of his research, Jennings concluded that there has been a high degree of movement and a close relationship between mobility and success among top management personnel in many corporate organizations. The increasing mobility of managers has reduced the accuracy of long-term career and replacement planning in those organizations where managers are unwilling to wait patiently for advancement in their jobs. The increased mobility of managers to some extent, however, has also been the result of a change in the philosophy on the part of employers who are less prone to regard the employment of managers as a life-time contract. Accordingly, they exhibit less and less reluctance to terminate the services of non-union personnel, from president to trainee, for any reason or for no reason.[8]

Problems with the Young Manager. Since college graduates who now are being recruited for the executive ranks are particularly mobile, many of them have little sympathy for the virtues of patience and endurance that many large bureaucratic organizations tend to expect of them. Instead, young managers today seek meaningful training assignments that are interesting and that involve challenge, responsibility, and a "piece of the action." They also have greater concern for the contribution that their work in the organization will render to society. What these young people seek in a development program is the opportunity to sustain or even accelerate the pace of their former academic experiences. As described by Stessin,

> "What they don't want is a classroom atmosphere and to be lectured to by superiors. Neither do they want 'Mickey Mouse' assignments, paper shuffling, busy work, or meaningless warmed-over subjects for studies and surveys that had been exhausted by their predecessors."[9]

Unfortunately those management experiences the younger managers frequently encounter often impress them as being rudimentary, boring, and composed of too many "make-work" activities. If management development programs are to accomplish their intended purpose, they must provide learning

---

[6] Patrick Kimball, "The Journeyman Executive: The Demise of the Lifetime Contract," *Business Horizons,* Vol. 16, No. 2 (April, 1973), p. 50.

[7] Eugene Jennings, "Mobicentric Man," *Psychology Today,* Vol. 4, No. 2 (July, 1970), pp. 34-36, 70-72.

[8] *Ibid.,* p. 49.

[9] Laurence Stessin, "Developing Young Managers: Immediacy Sets the Tone," *Personnel,* Vol. 48, No. 6 (November-December, 1971), pp. 32-33.

experiences that are sufficiently interesting and challenging to induce the younger and more ambitious participants to remain with the organization. One of the ways in which some organizations are encouraging young managers with high potential to remain is by providing a "fast-track" program that enables these individuals to advance more rapidly than those with less potential. One survey, however, revealed that although 31 percent of the responding corporations had such programs, less than one percent of their management, professional, and technical personnel were covered by them. Thus, it would appear that to be effective a "fast-track" program must be utilized only on a limited basis and under proper conditions.[10]

THE MANAGEMENT DEVELOPMENT PROGRAM

In every organization managers have the opportunity to become more knowledgeable and more proficient in their assignments by reading, taking courses, attending meetings, and most important of all, through the process of trial and error in performing their jobs. If a formal development program exists, however, there is a greater possibility that these development opportunities will be more purposeful and receive better coordination and direction toward the objectives of both the individual and the organization. A formal program normally should provide for:

1. An analysis of the organization structure and objectives.
2. An inventory of management requirements and resources.
3. A determination of individual development needs.
4. An appraisal of individual progress.
5. A means for program evaluation.

Analysis of the Organization Structure and Objectives

The first step in the establishment of a management development program should be a review of the organization's objectives and its structure in order that subsequent development efforts may proceed in the right direction. The organization structure should be studied carefully for the purpose of correcting any unsatisfactory organizational conditions affecting its operation. These conditions might include unassigned or overlapping authority and responsibility, inappropriate division of duties, improper span of control, or the absence of clearly defined channels of authority. Thus, an important by-product of a management development program can be the development of objectives and structures that are more suited to the needs of the organization.

Inventory of Management Requirements and Resources

The inventory of manager requirements should serve to identify the management jobs within the organization that must be staffed at present and/or

[10] James Walker, "Tracking Corporate Tigers in the Seventies," *Human Resources Management,* Vol. 11, No. 4 (Winter, 1972), pp. 18-24.

in the future. Records containing information about each position, such as code number, title, department, physical location, name of incumbent, date for incumbent's replacement, and names of potential replacements, are usually desirable in order to identify the jobs in which and for which executives must be developed. These records can be included as a part of a computerized personnel information system and can also be depicted graphically by means of charts similar to the executive replacement schedule illustrated in Figure 9-1. This particular schedule identifies each management position, when it is likely to become vacant, and the individuals being groomed as possible replacements for the manager currently in the position.

Uses of the Inventory. As managers accumulate experience, an inventory of their management potential can be developed which can serve several purposes. First, it can help to direct attention to the developmental needs of employees in terms of their current job assignments and those into which they may be promoted. Second, the inventory can help management to anticipate vacancies resulting from expansion, retirements, or promotions sufficiently in advance to permit qualified replacements to be developed and, if necessary, recruited for these vacancies. Third, it can enable an organization to be prepared to staff vacancies that may result unexpectedly from death or resignation. Finally, the inventory can contribute to better morale among management trainees and other personnel who are attempting to qualify themselves for eventual promotion into executive positions by helping to reassure them that management has been observing and keeping a record of their progress.

Identifying Talent Below the Managerial Level. Every management development program should include provisions for recruiting personnel with management potential from supervisory and lower levels. The practice of screening the lower levels of the organization for management talent may help not only to identify executive talent but also to encourage the future development of this talent. While many personnel below the managerial level may have no desire to put forth the required effort to become managers, most of them will regard their employment more favorably if they know that the opportunity for advancement does exist if they wish to take advantage of it. Management potential among personnel at the supervisory level and below can be difficult to assess; such personnel generally have less employment history and have had fewer opportunities to exhibit their potential at work. In order to identify management potential among personnel at the supervisory level and below as early as possible, some organizations have established assessment centers of the type pioneered by the American Telephone and Telegraph Company. Possible candidates for management are brought into an assessment center for a few days of intensive evaluation the nature of which will be discussed in the next chapter.

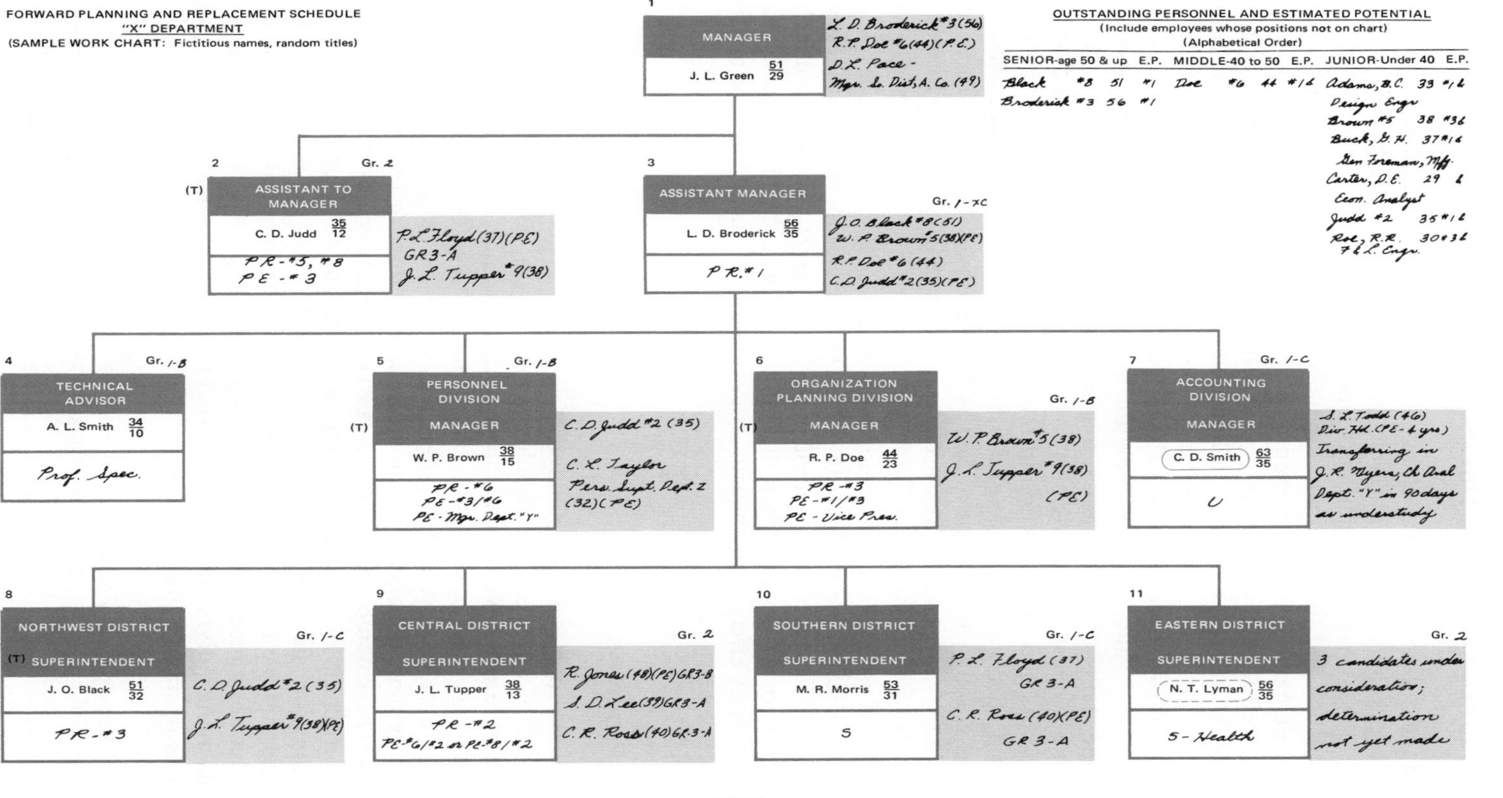

Reproduced with the permission of the Standard Oil Company of California.

Figure 9-1 AN EXECUTIVE REPLACEMENT SCHEDULE

Determination of Individual Development Needs

Because the requirements of each managerial job and the qualifications and potential of every individual are different, no two managers will have identical development needs. A management development program in effect, therefore, serves to establish and to coordinate the individual development programs in terms of the demands of their present jobs and their ability to meet these demands, as well as higher ones into which they may have the potential to advance. Individual programs for self-improvement should provide for those developmental experiences that will enable persons to realize their particular potential by improving themselves with respect to their knowledge, skills, or personality traits. Thus, for one individual, self-development may involve developing the ability to write reports, to give talks, or to lead conferences; for another, it may consist of learning how to understand oneself better and one's reaction to others and their reaction in return. It also may involve improving the leadership, decision making, and other skills that the manager should possess. The granting of sabbatical leaves to executives for the purpose of enabling them to study, conduct research, teach, or to engage in other forms of self-renewal also is becoming more prevalent.[11]

Figure 9-2 illustrates how development needs are determined by one company and indicates the methods by which the development of managers is accomplished. Each of these methods of development, however, merely provides the opportunities by which the individuals may improve themselves. In the final analysis effective management development must consist primarily in guided self-development.

Appraisal of Individual Progress

The periodic appraisal or evaluation of each individual's progress is a very important part of an executive development program. Such evaluation can serve to measure the development progress and provide a basis for making those adjustments that appear advisable, and to overcome deficiencies in progress that may be revealed. Conferences covering these evaluations are essential for helping managers to plan a course of action for overcoming their weaknesses. These conferences also can serve to reconcile any disagreements that the subordinates may have regarding the ratings or comments that appear on their evaluation sheets or any misconceptions they may have regarding the opportunities and the requirements governing their promotions. If conducted effectively, performance evaluation can contribute to a more open and candid interaction among individuals on the different levels within an organization and, in turn, to its operating effectiveness.[12]

---

[11] "Letting the Boss Take a Sabbatical," *Business Week* (April 8, 1972), pp. 41-42.

[12] Varian A. Knisely, "The Science of Telling Executives How They're Doing," *Fortune*, Vol. 84, No. 1 (January, 1974), pp. 102-106, as reprinted in Herbert J. Chruden and Arthur W. Sherman, Jr., *Readings in Personnel Management* (4th ed.; Cincinnati: South-Western Publishing Co., 1976), pp. 173-185.

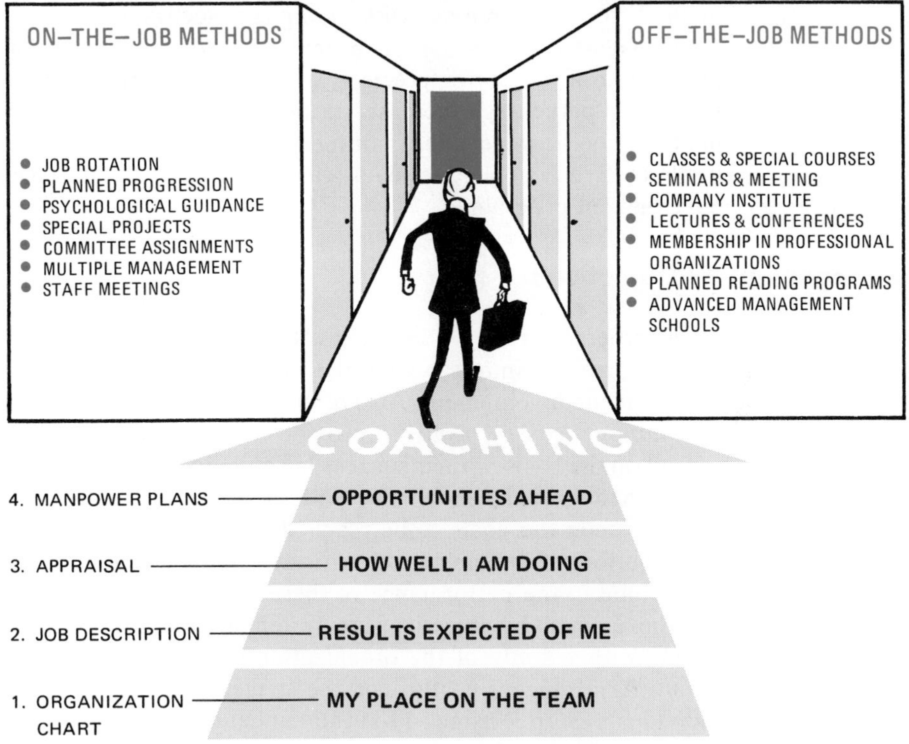

Source: Sylvania's Plan for Management Development, prepared by Sylvania Electric Products, Inc. Reproduced with permission.

Figure 9-2 A COMPANY'S DEVELOPMENT PROGRAM

Evaluation of the Program

It is desirable that a management development program be evaluated periodically to determine if it is meeting the development needs of the organization and of its managers. This evaluation should include a reexamination of the program's objectives in order to determine whether or not any changes in these objectives are considered necessary. The solicitation of information through the use of questionnaires and by means of counseling sessions with participants can provide one source of information relating to changes in the program that may have become necessary. The effectiveness of the development program also should be reflected in the performance records of each department and of the organization as a whole. An analysis of these records and of the performance ratings of the managers thus can provide some basis for determining what improvements may be needed in the development program. Records relating to costs, output, production quality, and other achievements are typical of those which can indicate whether or not the development program is producing favorable results.

Unfortunately the evaluation of a management development program must be based upon information that often is subjective in nature. Actually, no method for determining with complete accuracy the effectiveness of a development program has been devised to date. Neither has any way been discovered of measuring precisely a program's contribution in terms of dollar savings or percentage increases in operating efficiency. The absence of such precise data, however, does not mean that attempts to evaluate a program are useless. Even subjective data can contribute to the improvement of a development program.

Management by Objectives

A program widely adopted today is *management by objectives* (MBO) which combines into a system the evaluation and development processes of management development. Also referred to as *planned performance evaluation* and *management by results,* it provides for the performance of managers to be judged on the basis of their success in achieving those objectives that they have established through consultation with their superiors. Under MBO, emphasis is focused upon the goals to be reached rather than upon the various activities being performed by the managers or upon the traits that he or she may or may not exhibit in the performance of these activities.

Management by objectives is a system involving a cycle (see Figure 9-3) that begins with a study of the organization's common goals and returns to that point. A significant feature of the cycle is the establishment of goals by individuals (Step 3) using a broad statement of responsibilities prepared by their superiors. The goals or targets are accompanied by a detailed account of the actions they propose to take in order to reach them. This document is then discussed with the superior and modified until both are satisfied with it (Step 4). Progress that the subordinate is making toward the goal is then assessed as objective data are made available (Step 5). At the conclusion of a period of time (usually 6 months), the subordinates make their own appraisals of what they have accomplished relative to the targets they had set earlier substantiating it with factual data wherever possible. The "interview" is an examination by superior and subordinate together of the subordinate's self-appraisal (Step 6).

Requirements of the MBO System. Management by objectives requires that individual executive responsibilities be defined in terms of the objectives of the total organization. It enables managers to plan and measure their own performance, as well as that of their subordinates, in terms of concrete results. The expected results must be consistent with the controllable areas of responsibility for the individual manager; e.g., profit, cost of product made, cost of unit of service delivered, etc. Odiorne emphasizes that the success of MBO depends heavily upon three points of emphasis:

1. MBO is a system of managing, not an addition to the manager's job.
2. The managers who adopt MBO as a system of managing must plan to drop some of their more time-consuming vocational hobbies, i.e., they must delegate.

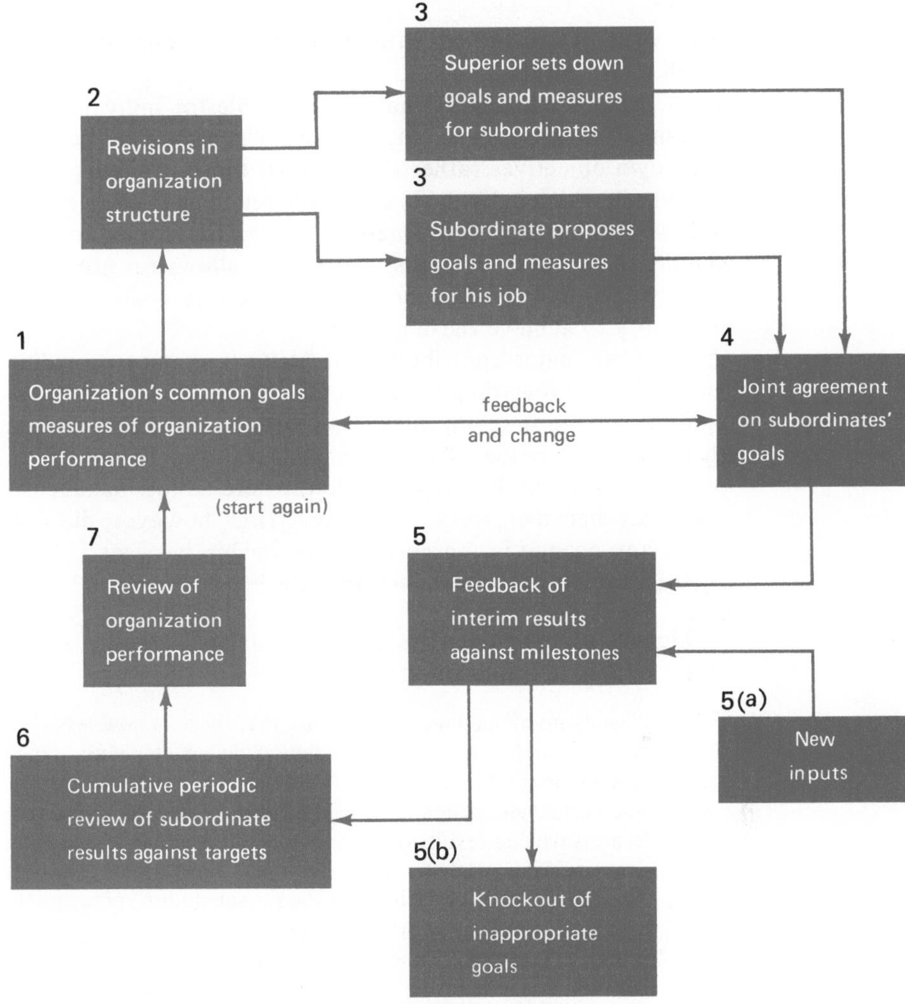

Source: George S. Odiorne, ***Management by Objectives*** (New York: Pitman Publishing Corporation, 1965), p. 78.

Figure 9-3 THE MANAGEMENT BY OBJECTIVES CYCLE

3. The system of MBO entails a behavior change on the part of both superior and subordinate.[13]

Advantages of MBO. The MBO system shifts the emphasis from appraisal to self-analysis and from focus on the past to the future, and the subordinates are helped in relating their career planning to the needs and realities of the organization through consultations with their superiors. These consultations, if properly conducted, should strengthen the superior-subordinate relationship and might well lead to a type of relationship in which the

[13] George S. Odiorne, *Management by Objectives* (New York: Pitman Publishing Corporation, 1965), pp. 77-79.

supervisor is concerned with what can be done to help the subordinates reach their "targets."

A major advantage is that it is possible for individuals to feel a sense of accomplishment, growth, and progress when they are being compared against their own objectives rather than against those of their peers. Other appraisal systems in which individuals are compared to each other may enable only a few to have feelings of improvement. The majority are led to believe that they are staying the same or declining. MBO also allows for greater flexibility to both the supervisor and the subordinate in setting goals and in making changes necessary to achieve these goals.[14]

Another major contribution of MBO is that of providing managers with greater clarity regarding the goals their superiors expect them to achieve. One study involving in-depth interviews with 48 managers, for example, revealed that MBO had helped these managers to know better which were the more important goals in their organization, where its top management wanted to go, and what their own roles should be. MBO, however, did not appear to bring about any change in the general relationship between subordinates and their superiors or to change leadership style.[15]

Criticisms of the MBO System. MBO is not without its critics. Some of the major pitfalls in this method are:

1. It leads many managers to assume that there is now less need for them to counsel employees because the figures give each person a running check on how he or she has done.
2. The performance data used in the results-centered appraisals are designed to measure end results on a short-term rather than a long-term basis. Thus, line supervisors may let their machines suffer to reduce maintenance costs.
3. The method does not eliminate the personal idiosyncracies that shape each manager's dealings with subordinates.
4. It may be questioned whether the understanding that is supposed to develop between supervisor and subordinate really comes about.[16]

The last point is a critical one, according to Levinson. He is of the opinion that the typical MBO effort perpetuates and intensifies hostility, resentment, and distrust between a manager and subordinate because it fails to take into account the deeper emotional components of motivation. His argument is that the MBO process neglects to provide answers to such questions as:

1. What are the managers' personal objectives?
2. What do they need and want out of their work?
3. How do their needs and wants change from year to year?

---

[14] Paul H. Thompson and Gene W. Dalton, "Performance Appraisal: Managers Beware," *Harvard Business Review,* Vol. 48, No. 1 (January-February, 1970), pp. 149-157.

[15] Henry Tosi and Stephen J. Carroll, Jr., "Improving Management by Objectives: A Diagnostic Change Program," *California Management Review,* Vol. XVI, No. 1 (Fall, 1973), pp. 57 and 65.

[16] Charles J. Coleman, "Avoiding the Pitfalls in Results-Oriented Appraisals," *Personnel,* Vol. 42, No. 6 (November-December, 1965), pp. 24-33.

4. What relevance do organizational objectives and the managers' part in them have to such needs and wants?

Therefore, he recommends that recognition of individual needs be included as an important part of the goal-setting process and that the interdependence of all managers in the organization be recognized in devising and implementing an evaluation system.[17]

DEVELOPMENT ACTIVITIES FOR MANAGERS

A management development program generally should provide a variety of development activities and experiences for participants because their development needs as determined by the requirements of their present and future positions and by their personal qualifications will vary widely. Development activities for the purposes of this discussion are grouped into two classes: those that occur on the job and those that occur off the job. This section covers some of the more common development activities and experiences in each of these two categories.

On-the-Job Activities

Management skills and abilities cannot be acquired merely by listening and observing or by reading about them in a book. They must be acquired through actual practice and experience in which a person has an opportunity to work under pressure and to learn by making mistakes and having them corrected. On-the-job experience is the method most extensively used by organizations to develop executive personnel.

In order to have developmental value, work experience should be properly planned and supervised. It should also be meaningful and challenging to the participant, otherwise the resulting experience may prove to be no better than that acquired in any regular job assignment. The experiences as noted earlier must be meaningful and interesting rather than routine make-work activities. Unfortunately, some management trainees are made to feel that they are in the way and that their boss has enough problems without trying to find work to keep them busy or taking time out to answer their questions.

On-the-job training may involve merely an assignment to a regular job in the organization with the same classification or designation as any other employee in the department. More often, however, it is likely to involve a special trainee designation or job assignment established especially for training purposes.

Coaching. If individuals are to profit fully from their work experiences, they should receive assistance from those who have acquired greater wisdom and experience so that they may recognize and correct their mistakes. They may also require assistance in learning how to apply to their jobs such skill and

---

[17] Harry Levinson, "Management by Whose Objectives?" *Harvard Business Review*, Vol. 48, No. 4 (July-August, 1970), pp. 125-134.

knowledge that they have acquired in school or elsewhere. The process of assisting individuals to perform their managerial duties and responsibilities more effectively is commonly referred to as *coaching*. Figure 9-4 illustrates how Sylvania Electric Products, Inc. believes that coaching can be conducted most effectively.

HOW CAN YOU IMPROVE DAY-TO-DAY COACHING?

- ☐ Set the right example
- ☐ Build on their strengths
- ☐ Delegate more
- ☐ Insist on completed assignments
- ☐ Let them "pinch hit"
- ☐ Seek their opinions
- ☐ Let them know how they are doing
- ☐ Broaden their viewpoints
- ☐ Use specific examples

Source: Sylvania's Plan for Management Development. Reproduced with the permission of the Sylvania Electric Products, Inc.

Figure 9-4

In contrast to the performance evaluation interviews that are conducted on a more formal and periodic basis, coaching tends to be of a more informal and continuous nature. The term "coaching" as it is used in connection with management development has much the same meaning as it has when used in connection with athletics. It involves observing subordinates for the purposes of analyzing their performance and of assisting them in improving it. Assistance may be provided in the form of a continuing flow of instructions, comments, criticisms, questions, and suggestions that the superior may offer to motivate subordinate managers to develop themselves further.

Coaching can be made more effective if the focus of attention is upon work achievements rather than upon individual inadequacies. In doing so, coaching can contribute to better relations between managers and their subordinates because the manager's role does not seem to be that of looking constantly over the subordinate's shoulder.[18] Proper coaching also requires that superiors provide the correct example for subordinates to follow and that they establish high standards of performance for themselves and their subordinates to observe. They must also demonstrate confidence in their subordinates which in turn requires that they have adequate confidence in themselves.

Understudy Assignments. The *understudy assignment* can be used either for the trainee or for the experienced manager who is being groomed to take over the superior's job. The individual in one of these assignments can relieve the superior of some of the work load while being permitted to learn as much as possible about the superior's job and the techniques for handling it.

The benefits that individuals gain from understudy assignments depend upon the time and interest that the superiors devote to them. They may also depend upon the effectiveness of the superior's managerial practices that are likely to be emulated by the understudy. If superiors permit understudies to gain experience in handling important functions, give them the help and suggestions that will enable them to develop, and set a good example, the understudy method of training can be very effective.

Rotation and Lateral Promotions. *Job rotation* is intended to provide a greater variety of work experiences with which to broaden the knowledge and understanding that the individual requires in order to be able to manage more effectively. The rotation usually is among jobs on the same organizational level and for short periods of time. These jobs may be ones that have been established especially for training purposes, or they may be regular production jobs to which the trainee is assigned as a part of a "progressive experience program."

Since it usually is not feasible to rotate managers beyond the beginning level among different jobs for training purposes, their skill, knowledge, and experience may be broadened by means of *lateral promotions* which involve horizontal movement through different departments along with the upward movement. Positions in the industrial engineering or personnel departments are frequently among those in which managers may be given some experience particularly at the lower end of the promotion ladder. Work experience in these departments brings candidates into contact with nearly every department within the organization and, thus, increases their knowledge concerning many different organizational functions. Lateral promotions, like rotational assignments, also provide an opportunity for individuals to receive guidance from a variety of managers and to observe many different management methods and techniques in action.

Project and Committee Assignments. In some organizations managers at the lower levels are assigned work on special *projects* or task force assignments in which they have the opportunity to become involved in the study of current

---

[18] Walter S. Wickstrom, *Managing by-and-with Objectives,* Personnel Policy Study No. 212 (New York: National Industries Conference Board, 1968), p. 16.

organizational problems and in planning and decision-making activities that can be both interesting and profitable for the participants.

In some companies *committees,* which are referred to as "junior boards," are established to work on projects and to submit plans and recommendations for action to the board of directors. This practice, known as *multiple management,* was introduced by the McCormick Company and derives its name from the fact that these junior boards exist in addition to the senior board. The function of the junior boards and the contributions that they may render, however, are similar to those of a committee.

Staff Meetings. Participation in *staff meetings* offers another means of increasing knowledge and understanding, thus furthering the development of management personnel. These meetings not only enable participants to become more familiar with problems and events that are occurring outside of their immediate area but also expose them to the ideas and thinking of other managers. Staff meetings, furthermore, may give managers an opportunity to make presentations to the group and to have their ideas evaluated and improved on by others in the group. The developmental value to be gained from such meetings, however, will be contingent upon how well the meetings are planned, organized, and conducted.

Off-the-Job Activities

While on-the-job experiences constitute the basic phase of a manager's development, certain methods of development away from the job can be used to supplement work experiences. Off-the-job activities include those that can help to increase the knowledge of employees, broaden their perspective, influence their attitudes, or increase their sensitivity to the reactions of others. These activities may be provided on either an individual or a group basis and may be conducted during or after normal working hours.

Many large organizations operate their own formal education programs that have curriculums and enrollments larger than many colleges. In fact, because of their excellent management training programs some corporate organizations, such as Procter & Gamble, Litton Industries, IBM, and General Electric, to mention a few, have been referred to as *academy companies.*[19] Courses in these programs may be offered by lecture-discussions or laboratory methods, or on a home-study basis. Among the subjects most frequently covered by company training courses are those dealing with human relations, supervision, personnel administration, labor relations, general economics, general management, and communications. Many of these classes permit members to contribute from their own personal experiences as well as from their professional readings.

---

[19] Robert C. Albrook, "Why It's Harder to Keep Good Executives," *Fortune,* Vol. 78, No. 6 (November, 1968), pp. 136-139, 176-180.

Case Studies. Particularly useful in classroom learning situations are *case studies*. These studies which may have been developed from actual experiences within their organization can help executives learn how to obtain and interpret facts, to become conscious of the many variables upon which a management decision may be based and, in general, to improve their decision-making skills.

Incident Method. A variation of the case method is the *incident method* in which the participants are given only a brief statement of a problem or incident. Any details or facts that may be pertinent to the problem must be drawn from the discussion leader through questioning. Whether or not the group can gain sufficient information will depend upon its ability to determine what information is relevant and to elicit it from the leader.

In-Basket Training. Another method that can be used to simulate a problem situation is the *in-basket* technique. In this technique the participants are given several documents, each describing some problem or situation, the solution of which requires an immediate decision. They are thus forced to make decisions under the pressure of time and also to determine the priority with which each problem should be considered.

Management Games. Case situations have been brought to life and made more interesting through the development of *management games*. Participants who play the game are faced with the task of making a continuing series of decisions affecting the enterprise. The simulated effects that each decision has upon each functional area within the enterprise can be determined by means of an electronic computer which has been programmed for the game. While management games do provide an exercise in decision making, they fall short of being able to duplicate the pressures and the realities of actual decision making on the job.

Role Playing. Another management development training technique is *role playing*. It consists of assuming the attitudes and behavior of and acting out the roles of individuals, usually a supervisor and a subordinate, who are involved in a personnel problem. Role playing can help participants to improve their ability to understand and to cope with the problems of other persons. It should also help them learn how to counsel others regarding their problems and how to gain the cooperation of associates. The participants may also come to recognize how, in relations with others, their attitudes and behavior may need to be improved. Thus, role playing can be an effective method for getting executives to recognize and to accept good human relations principles and for giving them an opportunity to develop skill in applying these principles.

Sensitivity Training. One of the executive training methods that has grown rapidly in popularity is *sensitivity training*. This method, pioneered by the National Training Laboratories, is used with small groups—referred to as "*T*" (training) *groups*—whose members work together for a number of days. As the term would indicate, sensitivity training has as its primary goal the development of greater sensitivity on the part of its participants including self-insight and an awareness of group processes, as well as skill in participating constructively in group activities.[20]

In recent years sensitivity training programs have tended to be modified to produce more organization- and job-oriented discussion with less probing into personal feelings and behavior. Some organizations have abandoned sensitivity training entirely.[21] The trend in management development is thus away from creating a discussion situation which Odiorne describes as:

> . . . a great psychological nudist camp in which he (the participant) bares his pale, sensitive soul to the hard-nosed autocratic ruffians in his T-Group and gets roundly clobbered. He goes away with his sense of inferiority indelibly reinforced.[22]

The above type of situation can be emotionally disturbing to some individuals because it penetrates those defense mechanisms that protect their sense of well-being. One company's experiences with T-Group training, for example, was described as follows:

> We are getting people all upset and shaken loose from past methods but we didn't give them any substitutes for the old ways.[23]

These remarks point up the importance not only of proceeding with caution in T-Group training but also for following up with the participants when they return to their jobs. Because of the hazards that T-Group training can entail, the emphasis should be upon helping the participants to identify their human-relations-skill needs and making the experience of developing these skills a "safe trip."

Professional Reading. Many larger organizations maintain extensive business and technical libraries for their personnel. Executives are encouraged to make maximum use of these facilities as a means of improving their knowledge and of keeping abreast of the latest management practices. Some organizations also have inaugurated reading acceleration courses. These courses are designed to improve reading speed and comprehension and to increase executive efficiency in the handling of paper work. Professional readers also have been employed to digest the information from the more significant articles appearing in professional and trade publications. This information is made available to management personnel by means of tape recordings or printed abstracts.

Educational and Professional Organizations. Many organizations rely upon the assistance of educational institutions and professional consultants in conducting development programs. Some organizations encourage their

---

[20] Henry Clay Smith, *Sensitivity Training* (New York: McGraw-Hill Book Company, 1973), p. 30.

[21] Bryon E. Calame, "The Truth Hurts," *The Wall Street Journal,* July 14, 1969, p. 7.

[22] As quoted by Spencer Klaw, "Inside a T-Group," *Think Magazine,* 1965.

[23] Calame, *op. cit.,* p. 1.

managers to take courses for self-improvement by paying the tuition costs or by having academic courses conducted on company premises. Educational opportunities of this type frequently can prove to be more effective and more economical than those that an organization might conduct itself.

Many colleges and universities now offer advanced and middle management programs to meet the growing demands of organizations for management development assistance. These programs may last from one to several weeks, and typically are directed toward improving the decision-making abilities of the participants. The programs also provide them with new knowledge about their organization, how it operates, and the changing external conditions affecting it to which they are required to adjust. The improvement of human relations and communication skills, as well as the development of greater self-confidence and self-awareness, also are among the benefits that may be gained from university development programs.[24]

Unfortunately many organizations participating in such programs have no formal written policies covering the criteria to be used in determining which executives are to participate and what choice, if any, executives are to be given in determining the program they are to attend. Furthermore, the participants selected for a program frequently are not given any orientation concerning what they are expected to accomplish from the program or why they were chosen to participate in it.[25] Because of the lack of well-established objectives and policies governing the use of development programs on the part of many organizations and their failure to evaluate effectively the results gained from the programs, it is questionable whether such organizations are getting full value in return for the money being spent on the programs. As the authors of one study conclude, many organizations have expressed the following position with respect to their development programs: "We don't know what we want, we're not at all sure what we are getting, but we like the results or at least are not unhappy with the results."[26]

REQUIREMENTS FOR A SUCCESSFUL PROGRAM

Not all of the management development programs that have been described glowingly in the professional literature or supported by impressive exhibits of charts, manuals, and other materials have proven to be quite so effective in practice. The true measure of a program's success, therefore, is determined not by its window dressing but by the caliber of the management which it develops and by the approval and support of the participants toward the program.

Top Management Support

To be successful a development program must receive more than mere lip service or professed support from top management, particularly from the chief

---

[24] Reed M. Powell and Charles S. Davis, "Do University Executive Development Programs Pay Off?" *Business Horizons,* Vol. XVI, No. 4 (August, 1973), p. 84.
[25] *Ibid.,* p. 83.
[26] *Ibid.,* p. 86.

executive officer. Instead it must have the full support from the top if the organization is to have the cooperation of managers at the lower level who are directly involved in coaching, encouraging, and evaluating the development of subordinates and in making development experiences available to them. Support also must include holding managers responsible for developing subordinates so that they will take the development duties of their jobs seriously.

In supporting the program top management can contribute not only budget-wise but also through participation in the program itself. Participation by top managers may include attendance at meetings and courses comprising the development program either as members, as instructors, or as discussion leaders of the groups. If top managers engage in developmental activities that contribute to their own development and renewal, their subordinates can hardly claim that they have no need to engage in them. Unfortunately members of top management in some organizations tend to view professional development as something needed by their subordinates rather than by themselves.[27]

Program Coordination

Because a program usually includes a variety of development activities involving all departments and management jobs throughout the organization, the authority for its coordination must be placed relatively high in the organization structure. Many organizations appoint a management development committee to oversee, coordinate, and enlist cooperation for the program throughout the organization. To give it prestige and enlist greater support for it, the committee may be chaired by a senior member of management. As chairperson of the committee, this manager also may function as the coordinator for the program. With a senior line executive serving as chairperson or coordinating head of the program, subordinate line managers are more likely to take their responsibilities in the program seriously. In contrast, staff executives, such as personnel managers, even though their knowledge and expertise pertaining to the program may be superior, would be less able to enlist the cooperation of line managers because they lack the authority and power of a senior line executive.

The personnel department, however, generally has certain coordinating responsibilities for management development through its handling of personnel records; arranging formal training classes, seminars, and other development activities both within and outside the organization; and processing the paper work connected with the program. The department usually is involved also in the recruitment and preliminary selection of trainees for the program in spite of the fact that the ultimate decisions regarding the selection and retention of personnel for the program generally is made by line managers.

---

[27] Chris Argyris, "The CED's Behavior: Key to Organizational Development," *Harvard Business Review,* Vol. 51, No. 2 (March-April, 1973), p. 59.

Need for Balanced Emphasis

If the management development program is to achieve its objectives, the attention devoted to the various activities contributing to the participants' development must be proportionate to their importance. Since individuals can learn to become managers or to become better managers only by engaging in the actual processes of management and assuming the risks, pressures, and decision-making responsibilities of an actual management position, their development must consist primarily of guided self-development on the job. Other development activities including participation in various courses, seminars, and training sessions within or outside the organization serve only to supplement their development on the job. One of the major weaknesses of some programs has been the tendency to overemphasize these supplemental development activities and even to view them as constituting the entire development program. Maximum value can be derived from off-the-job activities only when they are correlated properly with the development needs of individuals on the job and the practical solution of the problems encountered there. Furthermore, when participants return from management seminars, they should not be frustrated by unnecessary obstacles on the job in their attempts to take advantage of their newly acquired knowledge and enthusiasm. Money spent on development activities thus can be largely wasted unless the climate and other conditions within the organization are such as to stimulate and support the improvements that participants attempt to initiate.

A Caution on "Programitis." Some development programs suffer from "programitis" or the tendency to assume that a program which is formal and elaborate will be more likely to succeed. Objective procedures and practices established by the program may be permitted to become an end unto themselves as a part of a well-machined operation without regard to whether or not they are actually contributing to development. The assumption, therefore, is that the presence of a management development program will insure that development is being accomplished. Essential to any development program, however, is the continual questioning and evaluation of the results being achieved by it and of whether the results being achieved from off-the-job training sessions actually justify the money expended for them. Also significant is the establishment and periodic reevaluation of program objectives with respect to the type of performance that is expected of managers and how it can be most effectively developed. Particularly important is the analysis of the organizational climate in terms of whether or not it serves to stimulate managers to engage in self-development and to reward them adequately for their demonstrated improvement in competency.

Effectiveness of Current Programs. In spite of the fact that the importance of formal management development is widely recognized and emphasized in the current literature, many organizations do not have effective programs, at least on a continuing basis. As an article in Dun's concludes, ". . . over the years only a relative handful of companies have been known for doing a really outstanding job at one time."[28] Thus, the leadership in executive development has tended to pass from one company to another as the types of executives in demand have changed. For the college graduate the implications are that when seeking employment with a company that has an outstanding development program, the program's past reputation may not always be an accurate indicator of its current effectiveness.

Résumé

The growing importance of formal management development programs is reflected both by the extent of their use in organizations and by the volume of literature being written about them. Currently greater emphasis is being placed upon the use of such programs as a means of combatting obsolescence among managers and encouraging them to engage in personal renewal and job performance improvement. Less emphasis is being placed upon their use to keep the executive pipelines filled with replacement talent waiting to assume positions of greater responsibility. The increased mobility of executives, particularly the younger ones, probably has had some bearing upon this change in emphasis toward development for present rather than future assignments.

While a formal development program in itself will not insure the improvement of managerial talent, it will permit the various development activities to be better planned and coordinated so as to serve the needs of both the organization and the participants. With a formal program there should be a better understanding regarding what management talents and abilities are to be developed, and managers, furthermore, will have a better opportunity to be recognized and advanced on the basis of demonstrated ability. A formal program, if it is effective, also can serve to coordinate and integrate the off-the-job development needs of the individuals. By providing the proper development opportunities and experiences on the job, by coaching managers on improving their performance, and by evaluating their progress, such individuals should have greater assurance of realizing their potential.

DISCUSSION QUESTIONS

1. In what ways do current management development programs differ from those of a decade or more ago?
2. Why is it that some of the companies with the best development programs experience the greatest loss of young management personnel?
3. In addition to contributing to the development of its managers, what are some of the other benefits that may accrue from an MBO program?
4. The statement frequently is made that experience is the best teacher. Would you accept this statement as always being valid? Does on-the-job experience necessarily provide development?
5. A group of managers from different companies were discussing management development at a conference. One executive expressed the opinion that those executives who had the potential talent would find ways of developing

[28] "The Companies That Build Executive Talent," *Dun's*, Vol. 101, No. 5 (May, 1973), p. 51.

themselves. Another one stated that his firm had several promising young men who were qualified for promotions but could not be advanced because all positions at the higher level were filled. He stated that his company would be wasting money in training persons either for positions that they had already outgrown or for positions that would not be open for several years to come. What is your reaction to the statements of each of these two men?
6. When the participants of university-conducted advanced management seminars are asked to complete evaluation questionnaires on the program, the responses are often quite favorable. How much weight do you feel should be given to these responses?
7. What difficulties may be encountered if the responsibility and the authority for management development are assigned to the personnel department rather than to the senior line executive?

PROBLEM 9-1 THE DISILLUSIONED TRAINEE

Upon graduation from college, Larry Wong accepted a position as a management trainee with Vogue Stores, one of the nation's largest retail chains which had several stores in the city where Larry lived. Larry was hired through the college placement center by one of the store's recruiters who enthusiastically described the company's management training program for college graduates. The program, he emphasized, was designed to prepare them for management positions of major responsibilty. "The byword of our store," the recruiter stressed, "is autonomy of the individual units. We need young people who are dynamic, innovative, and on the move."

After working for the chain for nearly two years, Larry appeared back at the placement center to investigate any openings listed with it. Since the director, Dr. Canovas, was always anxious to follow-up on graduates who had been placed through the center, he invited Larry into his office to discuss his experiences in the Vogue management training program. As Larry unburdened himself, Dr. Canovas made the following notes pertaining to the former's experiences:

1. After graduates are hired they are assigned to one store for the first year, usually in the same department, where they spend at least three to six months on the floor as a salesperson.
2. During the first year, trainees have little contact with the store's top management.
3. Trainees feel like clerks on the floor and morale is poor among them.
4. While the store claims to want innovative people, they actually seem to try to fit their managers into a mold.
5. The formal development program which the trainee enters about a year after being hired consists of 12 weekly meetings of two hours each conducted by the top executives of the store.
6. The first session is conducted by the president, which is followed by sessions with the vice-president, controller, merchandise manager, and others down the organizational ladder.
7. "When we would ask these speakers questions, many of them tended to hedge their answers or give pat answers. They seemed afraid they might let some secrets out. We often suspected they were not really telling it like it is."
8. "We are not given a chance to see the broad picture of store operation nor to gain experience in other stores until the second year, when promotion assignments are given out to a position of assistant department manager in some other store."

a. Comment on this store's management training program in terms of what you consider to be favorable and/or unfavorable about it.
b. Should the program include the three- or six-month assignment as a salesperson?

SUGGESTED READINGS

Allen, Louis A. *The Management Profession.* New York: McGraw-Hill Book Company, 1964. pp. 3-97.

Bellows, Roger, Thomas Q. Gilson, and George S. Odiorne. *Executive Skills.* Englewood Cliffs, New Jersey: Prentice-Hall, Inc., 1962.

Campbell, John P., Marvin D. Dunnette, Edward E. Lawler, III, and Karl E. Weich, Jr. *Managerial Behavior, Performance and Effectiveness,* New York: McGraw-Hill Book Company, 1970.

Ellis, Albert. *Executive Leadership: A Rational Approach.* Secaucus, N.J.: The Citadel Press, 1972.

Finkle, Robert B., and William S. Jones. *Assessing Corporate Talent.* New York: Wiley-Interscience, 1970.

Humble, John W. *How to Manage by Objectives.* New York: American Management Association, 1972.

Jennings, Eugene Emerson. *The Executive—Autocrat, Bureaucrat, Democrat.* New York: Harper & Row, Publishers, 1962.

Loring, Rosalind and Theodora Wells. *Breakthrough: Women into Management.* New York: Van Nostrand Reinhold Company, 1972.

Lynch, Edith. *The Executive Suite Feminine Style.* New York: Amacom., 1973.

Odiorne, George S. *Training by Objectives.* New York: The Macmillan Company, 1970.

Reddin, William J. *Managerial Effectiveness.* New York: McGraw-Hill Book Company, 1970.

Reeves, Elton T. *Management Development for the Line Manager.* New York: American Management Association, 1969.

Schoonmaker, Alan N. *Executive Career Strategy.* New York: American Management Association, 1971.

Smith, Henry Clay. *Sensitivity Training.* New York: McGraw-Hill Book Company, 1973.

Tamarkin, Robert (ed.). *The Young Executive Today.* Chicago: Allen-Bennett Inc., 1971.

West, Jude P., and Don R. Sheriff. *Executive Development Programs in Universities.* Studies in Personnel Policy, No. 215. New York: National Industrial Conference Board, 1969.

Performance Evaluation

In the preceding chapters the policies and procedures for procuring and developing a competent and stable work force were examined. Throughout the various steps in the development of employees and managers the need for continuous evaluation was stressed. Because of the importance of its role in the development of personnel at all levels, the function of evaluation will now be considered in detail.

Performance evaluation occurs whether or not there is a formal evaluation program in an organization. Employers are constantly observing the manner in which employees are carrying out their job assignments and forming impressions as to their relative worth to the organization. Most of the larger and many smaller organizations, however, have developed a formal program that is designed to facilitate and to standardize the evaluation of employees. Such programs exist under a variety of labels. The traditional term "merit rating" is associated with an evaluation plan whereby hourly employees are rated on scales that are assigned point values. The points are then used as part of the criteria for determining wages, promotions, and similar tangible benefits.

"Merit rating" is still used in referring to evaluations of employees in jobs that are typically paid on an hourly basis. However, with the extension of performance evaluation programs to personnel in white-collar and managerial jobs and with some deemphasis on assigning points to employee performance, such terms as "performance appraisal" and "performance evaluation" have become more popular. Other titles may also be found, but they all refer to essentially the same type of program.

Although performance evaluation programs may serve many purposes, they are designed primarily to improve job performance. The success or failure of performance evaluation in an organization is dependent upon the philosophy on which it is established, the attitudes of management and supervisory personnel toward it, and their skills in achieving the objectives of such a program. Many different methods for use in assembling information about subordinates are available, but the gathering of data is only the first step in the process. The real benefits to the organization and the individual employees come through utilization of the information in interviews and appropriate personnel actions based upon the evaluation process.

THE EVALUATION PROCESS

Individuals have typically assessed the value of others in a variety of situations and will probably continue to do so. Most assessments of this type, however, are made in an informal and unsystematic manner with little thought being given to the important elements involved in the evaluative process. Formal evaluation programs, however, are different in that they have clearly stated objectives and a well-organized system for attaining them. The steps in such a system are shown in Figure 10-1 from a pamphlet prepared for Veterans Administration supervisory personnel. An essential part of such a system involves having statements of performance requirements that subordinates are

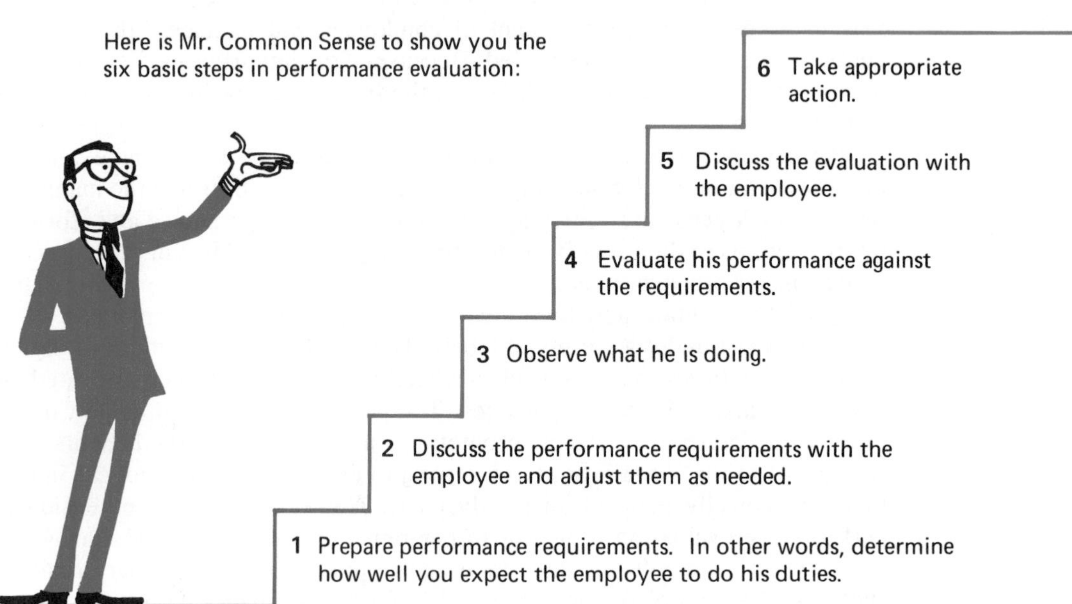

Source: Common Sense About Evaluating and Recognizing Performance, VA Pamphlet 05-29, Revised (Washington, D.C.: U.S. Government Printing Office, 1966), p. 7.

Figure 10-1 STEPS IN A PERFORMANCE EVALUATION PROGRAM

expected to meet. These statements should be discussed with subordinates and used as a basis against which to evaluate performance. It is equally important that managers and supervisors have the ability to evaluate performance against these requirements as objectively as possible and finally to discuss the evaluation with the employees and to take appropriate action.

Role of Evaluation Programs

Evaluation programs have become a major part of personnel management systems in all types of organizations. Civil service programs in government at all levels have elaborate systems for evaluating and reporting job performance, as do many nonprofit organizations. The fact that only 7 percent of the responding organizations in one study have neither an informal nor a formal performance evaluation program indicates the general acceptance of such programs. As shown in Table 10-1, employee groups most frequently covered by formal programs are professional/technical (76 percent of all organizations), first-level supervisors (76 percent), office employees (72 percent), and middle management (72 percent). For all employee groups except production and sales, formal appraisal programs are found more often in large organizations than in small ones; and except for sales and top management personnel, nonbusiness organizations are more likely to have formal programs than business firms.[1]

Objectives of Performance Evaluation Programs. The importance of performance evaluation programs to any organization is underscored by the following most frequently stated objectives:

1. Help supervisors to observe their subordinates more closely and to do a better coaching job.
2. Motivate employees by providing feedback on how they are doing.
3. Provide back-up data for management decisions concerning merit increases, transfers, dismissals, and so on.
4. Improve organization development by identifying people with promotion potential and pinpointing development needs.
5. Establish a research and reference base for personnel decisions.[2]

Reasons for the Failure of Programs. In actual practice formal performance appraisal programs have often yielded disappointing results.[3] A number of reasons have been advanced for the failure of programs to produce improvements in subordinate performance. One of the major reasons is that appraisal interviews are often used to accomplish more than one objective. For

---

[1] *Labor Policy and Practice—Personnel Management* (Washington, D.C.: The Bureau of National Affairs, Inc., 1974), par. 249:502.

[2] Winston Oberg, "Make Performance Appraisal Relevant," *Harvard Business Review*, Vol. 50, No. 1 (January-February, 1972), pp. 61-67.

[3] Ronald J. Burke, "Why Performance Appraisal Systems Fail," *Personnel Administration*, Vol. 35, No. 3 (June, 1972), pp. 32-40; James C. Conant, "The Performance Appraisal: A Critique and an Alternative," *Business Horizons*, Vol. 16, No. 3 (June, 1973), pp. 73-78.

Table 10-1 PERFORMANCE APPRAISAL PROGRAMS FOR VARIOUS EMPLOYEE GROUPS

Employee Group	Percentage of Organizations					
	Type of Industry			Size		All Organizations
	Manufacturing	Nonmanufacturing	Nonbusiness	Small	Large	
Production						
Formal Appraisal	44	38	68	49	46	47
Informal Appraisal	10	24	5	16	10	12
No Appraisal Program	46	38	27	35	44	41
Office						
Formal Appraisal	70	64	85	70	73	72
Informal Appraisal	24	22	6	23	17	19
No Appraisal Program	6	14	9	7	10	9
Sales						
Formal Appraisal	66	67	13	62	61	61
Informal Appraisal	28	22	—	24	23	24
No Appraisal Program	6	11	87	14	16	15
Professional/Technical						
Formal Appraisal	74	70	88	70	80	76
Informal Appraisal	21	17	3	22	11	16
No Appraisal Program	5	13	9	8	9	8
Supervisory (First Level)						
Formal Appraisal	75	69	85	70	80	76
Informal Appraisal	20	20	3	25	10	16
No Appraisal Program	5	11	12	5	10	8
Middle Management						
Formal Appraisal	74	69	74	64	78	72
Informal Appraisal	22	23	9	28	12	19
No Appraisal Program	4	8	17	8	10	9
Top Management						
Formal Appraisal	49	56	41	47	50	49
Informal Appraisal	29	25	18	30	22	25
No Appraisal Program	22	19	41	23	28	26

Source: Labor Policy and Practice—Personnel Management (Washington, D.C.: The Bureau of National Affairs, Inc., 1974), par. 249:502-503.

Note: This survey report of BNA's Personnel Policy Forum is based on responses from 139 organizations of which one half are manufacturing companies, one quarter are nonmanufacturing business, and one quarter are government and other nonprofit organizations. Nearly two fifths of the organizations have under 1,000 employees, and three fifths have 1,000 employees or more.

example, if an interview is used for (1) providing a written justification for salary action, and (2) motivating the employees to improve their work performance, the two purposes are in conflict. As a result, the interview essentially becomes a salary discussion in which the manager justifies the action taken, and the discussion has little influence on future job performance.

Other reasons for the failure of performance evaluation programs to yield the desired results are: (1) managers see little or no benefit to be derived from the time and energy spent in the process, (2) they dislike the face-to-face confrontation, (3) most are not sufficiently skilled in conducting evaluation interviews, and (4) the judgmental process required for evaluation is in conflict with the helping role of developing employees. Performance appraisal is seen, furthermore, as a once-a-year activity, and the evaluation interview often resembles a legal case in which the superior documents the case instead of conducting a developmental discussion.[4] While performance evaluation is one of the most complex and difficult tasks facing the manager or supervisor, it can provide many benefits to the organization and its individual members if it is established on sound principles and managed effectively.

Responsibility for Performance Evaluation. The personnel department is ordinarily charged with the responsibility for establishing and coordinating the program, but it is advisable that members from all levels within the organization as well as those from the personnel department be represented on the evaluation committee. This representation insures that the viewpoints of members of these groups are known and may be considered in developing a program that will be acceptable and workable. The evaluation committee will probably be primarily concerned with establishing and clarifying the objectives of the program. These objectives, which are agreed upon by the representatives, should be communicated to all personnel in order that they will understand the purpose of the program and its importance.

Training of Managers and Supervisors. Careful thought should also be given to the training of managers and supervisors who will be responsible for the success of the evaluation program. They must be assured of top management's interest in the program, and they must be given adequate time in which to perform the evaluations. While it may be assumed that they know something about evaluating their subordinates, a training program should include discussion of the important facets of evaluation that are considered in this chapter and their specific applications in their organization.

Criteria for Performance Evaluation

In any evaluation process it is important to consider the basis against which individuals are compared; namely, the job standards or criteria of satisfactory performance. While each person who is conducting an evaluation has some standard or guide for making comparisons, these standards or criteria must be selected in advance on the basis of study and understanding of the requirements of the job.

In production work the output of an individual in terms of quantity and quality may be compared with the standards developed from time and motion studies. Similarly in sales and other types of jobs which provide reliable and valid numerical indicators of job success, it is indefensible to rely solely on subjective evaluations. In jobs where performance cannot be evaluated primarily in terms of output or in which such intangible qualities as persistence,

---

[4] Ronald J. Burke, *op. cit.*

initiative, speed in making decisions, and similar characteristics are considered essential, the personal observations and reports of supervisory personnel are traditionally used.

In recent years, however, there has been increased use of methods in which an individual's performance is evaluated against objectives or expectancies that were established at some previous time, usually at the quarterly or semiannual review. In the case of an executive, for example, criteria of success include such factors as profitability, inventory turnover record achieved, customer service, methods improvement, cost reduction, improving market position for a product, reducing lost-time accident rates, etc. This approach illustrates the fact that the performance of persons holding nonproduction jobs can and should be assessed objectively. It also illustrates the need for establishing expectancies against which personnel can be evaluated. In some instances these expectancies or performance standards are established by the subordinates themselves in consultation with their superior, as in the case of management by objectives discussed in the preceding chapter.

Results-oriented performance appraisal is the key to the success of management by objectives. With other approaches that do not provide for as much employee participation in the setting of goals, it is still desirable to judge the subordinates by measuring their *job achievements*. Evaluating subordinates on the basis of what they have done to achieve the organizational goals is more productive than what supervisors think of them on a personal and subjective basis.[5]

PERSONNEL EVALUATION METHODS

Methods for evaluating personnel that are in use today have evolved from a procedure developed by Walter Dill Scott for rating salespersons.[6] This procedure, known as the *man-to-man rating scale,* involved comparing the performance of salespersons against named individuals whose performance represented standards at different levels. It was adapted to meet the needs of the U.S. Army in World War I, but has been replaced since with other methods that represent technical improvements and are more consistent with the purposes of evaluation. The change in emphasis and the development of newer concepts of measurement have resulted in new approaches to evaluation. However, since some of the older approaches are still used widely and provide a historical background for the newer methods, the traditional approaches will be examined first.

Traditional Methods of Evaluation

The older methods of evaluation usually attempted to quantify employee behavior on traits that were deemed to be important measures of their worth to

---

[5] Kae H. Chung, "Toward a More Results-Oriented Performance Appraisal," *Business Perspectives*, Vol. 9, No. 4 (Summer, 1973), pp. 6-12.

[6] Dr. Scott also was the senior author of one of the earliest textbooks on personnel management.

the organization. The emphasis was on attempts to measure these traits which were often stated vaguely. As a result they were usually viewed in different ways by managers, supervisors, and employees—if the latter were informed at all as to their ratings. As various inadequacies were noted in the traditional methods, experts attempted to recommend better procedures with some degree of success. For example, it was advocated that rating forms should contain characteristics that are observable, that are universal to all of the jobs in which personnel are to be rated, and that are distinguishable from other behaviors. They should also be designed in such a manner that the rater can render the most objective opinion or evaluation of the person being rated.

Regardless of what forms it may involve, an evaluation method should not be used without a thorough orientation of managers and supervisors in its objectives and procedures. They should also be made aware of errors of judgment that are inherent in most evaluation methods, such as personal bias, the tendency to overemphasize the subordinate's most recent performance, and other types of errors that will be considered later.

Graphic Rating Scale Method. The *graphic rating scale* method is the most commonly used type of rating scale. Each trait or characteristic to be rated is represented by a line or scale on which the rater indicates the degree to which the individual is believed to possess the trait or characteristic. An example of this type of scale is shown in Figure 10-2. The provision for rater comments which is found on most graphic rating scales is desirable in that it provides an opportunity for the superior to "back up" ratings with facts and thus tends to reduce the halo error discussed in Chapter 6. The halo spreads or generalizes to other areas. For example, the supervisor who values punctuality may tend to rate punctual persons high on characteristics other than punctuality.

Wherever the graphic rating scale method is used, analysis should be made of the ratings on an organization-wide basis. A program of research should include a study of the tendencies of individual raters. Some will be found to be quite lenient while others will be strict. As a result, the ratings assigned by the lenient supervisor cannot be compared with those made by the strict supervisor unless some allowance is made for the differences in their rating tendencies.

A similar problem often arises in conjunction with different jobs in the same organization. Usually those individuals in jobs that require little skill are rated lower than those persons in jobs requiring a high level of skill. Because of this tendency, it is desirable to compare the ratings of individuals holding the same job rather than to use the ratings from individuals on all jobs as a basis for comparisons.

As a result of analyzing the ratings carefully on the basis of individual raters, jobs, and departments, it is possible to arrive at a better understanding of the usefulness of the rating method in the personnel program. Often the methods can be refined by revising the rating forms, by devising scoring systems, and by establishing guidelines for the rater as to how to distribute the ratings. It is fairly common, for example, to instruct raters to conform to a pattern such as the normal frequency distribution (see Figure 7-1 on page 148) or some other recommended pattern in order to force them to recognize and report differences in the nature of the performance of their subordinates.

Appraise employee's performance in PRESENT ASSIGNMENT. Check (√) most appropriate square. Appraisers are *urged to use freely* the "REMARKS" sections for significant comments descriptive of the individual.

1. KNOWLEDGE OF WORK: Understanding of all phases of his work and related matters.	Needs instruction or guidance.	Has required knowledge of own and related work. √√	Has exceptional knowledge of own and related work.
	Remarks: Is particularly good on gas engines		
2. INITIATIVE: Ability to originate or develop ideas and to get things started.	Lacks imagination. √√	Meets necessary requirements	Unusually resourceful.
	Remarks: Has good ideas when asked for an opinion, but otherwise will not offer them. Somewhat lacking in self-confidence.		
3. APPLICATION: Attention and application to his work.	Wastes time. Needs close supervision.	Steady and willing worker. √√	Exceptionally industrious.
	Remarks:		
4. QUALITY OF WORK: Thoroughness, neatness, and accuracy of work.	Needs improvement.	Regularly meets recognized standards.	Consistently maintains highest √√ quality.
	Remarks: The work he turns out is always of the highest possible quality.		
5. VOLUME OF WORK: Quantity of acceptable work.	Should be increased.	Regularly meets recognized √√ standards.	Unusually high output.
	Remarks: Would be higher if he did not spend so much time checking and rechecking his work.		

Figure 10-2 A GRAPHIC RATING SCALE WITH PROVISION FOR RATER COMMENTS

Other Traditional Methods. While the graphic rating scale is the most commonly used method, the student should be familiar with other approaches to evaluation.

The Checklist Method. The *checklist method* is one that consists of having the rater check those statements on a list that are judged to be characteristic of the employee's performance or behavior. One such checklist developed for a salesperson included a large number of statements. A few of them are:

______Somewhat in a rut on some of the brand talks.
______Tends to keep comfortably ahead of the work schedule.
______Is a good steady worker.

_____Is weak on planning.
_____Is making exceptional progress.

The Ranking Method. The *ranking method* of evaluation requires each rater to arrange subordinates in rank order from the best to the poorest. This method has the advantage of being simple to understand and to use, and it is quite natural for the rater to think in terms of rankings. One of the main disadvantages of this method is the unwarranted assumption that the differences between ranks are the same. It has proven valuable, however, in personnel selection and in generating order of merit rankings for salary administration purposes. In these circumstances two or more people are asked to make independent rankings of the same group of individuals and their lists are averaged.

Newer Approaches to Evaluation

While the more traditional methods of evaluation are being used every day, there are newer approaches available that have become increasingly popular. As in other areas of personnel management, however, there is a resistance to change. Nevertheless, many organizations are trying new approaches, frequently in conjunction with the more traditional methods.

Forced-Choice Method. Among the newer, but less popular, approaches to evaluation is the *forced-choice method.* The typical forced-choice rating scale requires the rater to indicate by a check mark those statements that best describe the individual being rated. Since several statements equally favorable or unfavorable appear, the person completing the forced-choice report form cannot be certain whether the employee is being given a high or a low rating.

One type of forced-choice scale consists of pairs of statements, as

1a. Able to handle emergency assignments	2a. Relates well to others
1b. Definite in goals	2b. Has work well organized

The rater is presented with a series of such pairs and is instructed to indicate in each pair the statement that is most descriptive of the individual being rated. A major drawback to this method is that it cannot be used as effectively as some of the other methods in contributing to the commonly held objective of employing evaluation as a tool for developing employees by such means as the evaluation interview.

Critical-Incident Method. The *critical-incident method* involves identifying, classifying, and recording critical incidents in employee behavior.

> Briefly, an incident is "critical" when it illustrates that the employee has done, or failed to do, something that results in unusual success or unusual failure on some part of the job.
>
> Critical incidents are facts (not opinions or generalizations), but not all facts are critical. . . .

Critical facts are the employee actions that really make performance outstandingly effective or ineffective.[7]

The use of this method involves spotting critical incidents of employee performance, classifying the incidents according to the headings given in the record sheet maintained on each employee, and recording them. Before every performance review, the detailed entries under the major headings are summarized. As illustrated in Figure 10-3, space is provided under each heading on the performance record form for recording the "blue" incidents (favorable) and the "red" incidents (unfavorable).

4. ALERTNESS TO PROBLEM SITUATIONS

A. Did not see problem; B. Overlooked cause of problem; C. Failed to see special situation.			A. Saw problem as soon as it arose; B. Recognized cause of problems; C. Recognized situation that might produce problems.		
DATE	ITEM	WHAT HAPPENED	DATE	ITEM	WHAT HAPPENED
12/14	c	delay on special letter	11/12	c	furnace problem
RED			BLUE		
A special delivery letter came in about the same time as the regular mail delivery. Instead of delivering the special letter at once, this employe put it in with the regular mail.			This fellow was working late one Friday. He discovered an electric furnace had been accidentally shut off. He phoned his supervisor at home. This prompt action prevented the furnace from freezing up over the weekend.		

Source: John C. Flanagan and Robert B. Miller, *The Performance Record Handbook of Supervisors* (Chicago: Science Research Associates, 1955), p. 16. Reproduced with permission.

Figure 10-3 EXAMPLE OF RECORDED CRITICAL INCIDENTS

The Delco-Remy Division of General Motors Corporation, where this method was first developed, found that six minutes per day in recording critical incidents was the average time required for supervisors to keep the program going according to correct procedure. While recording incidents is only part of the program, these figures do indicate that the "bookkeeping" task is not as time-consuming as it may appear to be.

[7] John C. Flanagan and Robert B. Miller, *The Performance Record Handbook for Supervisors* (Chicago: Science Research Associates, 1955), p. 6.

This method, which emphasizes the importance of recording both strengths and weaknesses in specifically categorized areas, is potentially one of the most effective methods of achieving the results desired from the personnel evaluation program since it provides concrete information that can and should be discussed with the employee, preferably at the time the incident occurs. If, however, the supervisor merely records incidents and does not discuss them with the employee, or waits several months to do so, this method may be viewed by subordinates as the "little black book" approach to personnel evaluation.

Field-Review Method. As typically used, the *field-review method* provides the type of professional assistance in evaluation that managers and supervisors often need. It derives its name from the fact that a representative of the personnel department goes into the "field," that is, goes to the workplace of the supervisor to obtain information about the work of individual employees. The personnel technician will ask the supervisor detailed questions about each employee's performance and then return to the personnel department to prepare the evaluation reports. The reports are then sent to the supervisor who revises them, if necessary, and then signs them to indicate approval. This method not only provides professional assistance to managers and supervisors but makes for greater standardization in the evaluation process and helps in avoiding some of the problems that arise when each evaluator works independently.

Assessment Centers. Like the field-review method, the *assessment center* provides for personnel, other than the immediate superior, to participate in the evaluation of subordinates. Designed to identify managerial abilities, the assessment center involves participation of individuals from different departments in an organization who are brought together to work on individual and group assignments under the supervision of assessors, including the participants' superiors. In contrast to managerial selection tools such as tests, interviews, and biographical data forms, the assessment center provides a "broad band" approach to the evaluation of managerial and executive potential.[8] The assessee is observed in a variety of settings: management games, leaderless group discussions, case analyses, in-basket exercises, and interviews conducted over a two- or three-day period. At the end the observations are combined in an attempt to get an overall assessment of the participants' qualifications for promotion, and a report is usually submitted to top management to serve as a guide in making more effective personnel decisions. Feedback is usually also given to the participants so that they may know their strengths and weaknesses.

The assessment center technique was pioneered by Dr. Douglas Bray and his associates at AT&T in the mid-1950s. In the last decade it has spread to

[8] Dennis P. Slevin, "The Assessment Center: Breakthrough in Management Appraisal and Development," *Personnel Journal,* Vol. 51, No. 4 (April, 1972), pp. 255-263, as reprinted in Herbert J. Chruden and Arthur W. Sherman, Jr., *Readings in Personnel Management* (4th ed.; Cincinnati: South-Western Publishing Co., 1976), pp. 198-207.

many other companies, most of them large ones. It is estimated that 100 companies currently operate some form of center, and an equal number are in the process of developing them. Many of the companies, including AT&T, General Electric, and Sears, have conducted studies that substantiate the success of the technique.[9] In a survey of 20 companies that operate assessment centers, 22 studies indicated these centers to be more effective than other approaches. Only one study showed this approach to be equally effective as other approaches, and none showed it to be less effective.[10] While typically found in large organizations, this approach has been used successfully by smaller ones even when the program is only one day in length.[11]

Management by Objectives. The newest approach to performance appraisal is found in the management by objectives (MBO) system. As described in Chapter 9, pp. 206-209, MBO provides for the establishment of goals and a self-appraisal by the employee which is then discussed with the superior. While MBO is generally effective with higher-level personnel, many employees at lower levels may not want to be involved in their own goal setting.[12]

Work Standards Method. Instead of asking employees to establish their own goals, many organizations set work standards in terms of realistic outputs. Where the *work standards method* is used, it should provide a more objective basis for evaluating employee performance and thus be viewed more favorably by the employees. The main problem with this method is that when decisions have to be made on promotions and salary increases, it is difficult to compare employees who work at jobs with different work standards.

EVALUATION INTERVIEWS

The careful attention that is given to the establishment and functioning of the evaluation program will contribute substantially to the success of the program. For the most part, however, the success of the program is dependent upon the effective utilization of performance evaluation reports by supervisors, managers, and the personnel department. The information contained in the reports should be communicated to the employees whose performance is evaluated, and it may also be used as a basis for various types of personnel actions.

Purposes of Evaluation Interviews

The evaluation interview provides the superior an opportunity to discuss the quality of performance with the subordinate and to explore areas of possible

---

[9] James R. Huck, "Assessment Centers: A Review of the External and Internal Validities," *Personnel Psychology*, Vol. 26, No. 2 (Summer, 1973), pp. 191-212.

[10] W. C. Byham, "Assessment Center for Spotting Future Managers," *Harvard Business Review*, Vol. 48, No. 4 (July-August, 1970), pp. 150-160.

[11] John H. McConnell, "The Assessment Center: A Flexible Program for Supervisors," *Personnel*, Vol. 48, No. 5 (September-October, 1971), pp. 35-40.

[12] Winston Oberg, *op. cit*.

improvement and growth. It also provides an opportunity to identify the subordinate's attitudes and feelings more thoroughly, and thus improve communication between the parties that may lead to a feeling of harmony and cooperation.

Some managers and supervisors may be reluctant to discuss evaluations with subordinates because they feel incompetent as interviewers. They may excuse themselves by rationalizing that they might hurt the individual's feelings, or that most individuals should consider "no news" from them to be "good news," or that they are too busy to take time out for interviews. Fear of the unpleasantness aroused by criticism is also an inhibiting factor. Few persons, including supervisors, like to be viewed unfavorably by others. Since most of the unwillingness to discuss ratings with subordinates probably stems from feelings of fear and inadequacy on the part of interviewers in handling the individual who becomes upset during the interview, the best way to solve this problem is to help evaluators improve their interviewing skills.

Conducting Evaluation Interviews

The format for the evaluation interview will be determined in large part by the purpose of the evaluation. Most interviews, however, provide for feedback to employees on how well they are performing their jobs and for making plans for future development. Since there are areas about which the persons being evaluated are likely to have some opinions and feelings that should be expressed, it is recommended that employees should know when they are to be scheduled for an evaluation interview so that they, as well as the supervisor, can prepare for the discussion. Usually ten days to two weeks is about the right amount of lead time.

Using a Guide. It is also desirable for employees to have a guide to be used in planning for the interview. Figure 10-4 shows one checklist that can be used for this purpose. A checklist used by the superior in assembling information about the subordinate from personnel files and other sources would cover approximately the same areas.

Areas of Emphasis. Since a major purpose of the evaluation interview is to make plans for further development, it is important to utilize techniques that will direct the subordinate's attention to the future rather than to the past. The interviewer should (1) emphasize strengths on which the individual can build rather than stress weaknesses to be overcome; (2) avoid suggestions involving the changing of traits but rather suggest more acceptable ways of acting; (3) concentrate on opportunities for growth that exist within the framework of the individual's present position; and (4) limit plans for growth to a few important items that can be accomplished within a reasonable period of time.

While the above approach is certainly positive in nature, it does not suggest that all unpleasantness be avoided. Criticism should be expressed tactfully and in specific terms and should not be omitted for fear it will cause "hurt" feelings. Most people can take more candor than they get, and it is a mistake to shy away from straightforwardness with *all* merely because a *few* might wither before it.

EMPLOYEE SELF-APPRAISAL CHECKLIST

1. Reviewing your planned work, what seem to you to be
.... Significant contributions to the organization's goals
.... Unusually difficult problems solved
.... Major work areas for change or improvement
.... Major knowledge, skill, or experience strengths
.... Major knowledge, skill, or experience gaps.

2. Reviewing your total position responsibilities, what are
.... Significant responsibilities not yet undertaken
.... Working relationships you are pleased about
.... Working relationships which need strengthening.

3. Did you carry out any special assignments with distinction or handle emergencies skillfully? Badly?

4. How much help from your manager? Needed? Received?

5. Forward planning. What action do you feel you should take to
.... Make better use of talents
.... Improve specific performance areas
.... Add to knowledge, skill, experience
.... Improve relationships with manager, associates, direct reports
.... Change working methods or behavior?

Note: Limit your proposals to two significant development plans for discussion with the manager.

6. What help would you like from the manager in carrying out your plans?

Source: Marion S. Kellogg, *When Man & Manager Talk—A Casebook* (Houston: Gulf Publishing Co., 1969), pp. 98-99. Reproduced with permission.

Figure 10-4 EMPLOYEE SELF-APPRAISAL CHECKLIST

Most supervisors probably err on the side of reticence rather than frankness. It should not be inferred, however, that the superior should do all of the talking. The subordinate should be encouraged to express opinions and feelings as fully as necessary in order to achieve effective communication.

Interviewing Methods

The key to successful interviewing lies in a versatile and flexible approach with the procedure adjusted to the overall purposes of the evaluation, to the method of evaluation that is used, to the type of personnel (i.e., professional, clerical, factory employees), and to the specific requirements of each person being evaluated. The type of interview that would be appropriate with one of the traditional methods described previously would differ somewhat from that used in the results-centered or MBO method. Similarly, the type of personnel that one supervises will affect the approach that is used. Scientific and technical personnel, for example, tend to resent having their performance compared with that of others. The most meaningful yardstick to the scientific or technical employees is their progress in relation to their potentialities.[13] The supervisor should consider all of these factors in selecting a particular approach and should be flexible in selecting the interview approach that is most appropriate for the situation.

Maier has studied in detail the cause-and-effect relations in three types of evaluations or appraisal interviews labeled tell and sell, tell and listen, and problem-solving. These three types of interviews differ from each other in many ways as shown in Table 10-2 on page 236.

Tell and Sell Method. The skills required in the *tell and sell* method include the ability to persuade the person to change in the prescribed manner, and this may require the development of new needs in the person as well as a knowledge of how to make use of the kinds of incentives that motivate each particular individual.

Tell and Listen Method. In the *tell and listen* method the skills required include the ability to communicate the strong and weak points of a subordinate's job performance during the first part of the interview and then to thoroughly explore the subordinate's feelings about the evaluation in the second part of the interview. The superior is still in the role of a judge, but the method requires listening to disagreement and coping with defensive behavior without attempting to refute any statements. It is assumed that the opportunity to release frustrated feelings through catharsis will help to reduce or remove unpleasant ones.

Problem-Solving Method. The skills associated with the *problem-solving* approach are consistent with the nondirective procedures discussed in connection with the tell and listen method in that listening, accepting, and responding to feelings are essential. However, the objective of the problem-solving interview is to go beyond an interest in the subordinate's feelings. It thus seeks to stimulate growth and development in the subordinate by discussing the problems, needs, innovations, satisfactions, and dissatisfactions encountered in the performance of the job since the last evaluation interview. Maier recommends the latter method since the objective of evaluation normally should be to stimulate growth and development in the employee.[14]

Taking Appropriate Personnel Actions

In many instances the evaluation interview with the employee will provide the basis for noting deficiencies in employee performance and for making plans for improvement. As a result, corrective action can be taken by those

---

[13] Paul S. Strauss, "The Rating Game," *Personnel Administration,* Vol. 32, No. 1 (January-February, 1969), pp. 44-47.

[14] Norman R. F. Maier, *The Appraisal Interview* (New York: John Wiley and Sons, Inc., 1958).

Table 10-2 CAUSE-AND-EFFECT RELATIONS IN THREE TYPES OF APPRAISAL INTERVIEWS

	Tell and Sell	Tell and Listen	Problem-Solving
ROLE OF INTERVIEWER	Judge	Judge	Helper
OBJECTIVE	To communicate evaluation. To persuade employee to improve.	To communicate evaluation. To release defensive feelings.	To stimulate growth and development in employee.
ASSUMPTIONS	Employee desires to correct weaknesses if he or she knows them.	People will change if defensive feelings are removed.	Growth can occur without correcting faults. Discussing job problems leads to improved performance.
REACTIONS	Defensive behavior suppressed. Attempts to cover hostility.	Defensive behavior expressed. Employee feels accepted.	Problem-solving behavior.
SKILLS	Salesmanship. Patience.	Listening and reflecting feelings. Summarizing.	Listening and reflecting feelings. Reflecting ideas. Using exploratory questions. Summarizing.
ATTITUDE	People profit from criticism and appreciate help.	One can respect the feelings of others if one understands them.	Discussion develops new ideas and mutual interests.
MOTIVATION	Use of positive or negative incentives or both. (Extrinsic in that motivation is added to the job itself).	Resistance to change reduced. Positive incentive. (Extrinsic and some intrinsic motivation).	Increased freedom. Increased responsibility. (Intrinsic motivation in that interest is inherent in the task).
GAINS	Success most probable when employee respects interviewer.	Develops favorable attitude toward superior which increases probability of success.	Almost assured of improvement in some respect.
RISKS	Loss of loyalty. Inhibition of independent judgment. Face-saving problems created.	Need for change may not be developed.	Employee may lack ideas. Change may be other than what superior had in mind.
VALUES	Perpetuates existing practices and values.	Permits interviewer to change his view in the light of employee's responses. Some upward communication.	Both learn since experience and views are pooled. Change is facilitated.

Source: Reproduced by permission from Norman R.F. Maier, *The Appraisal Interview* (New York: John Wiley & Sons, Inc., 1958).

who are in the best position to do something about it, namely, the employee and the supervisor. Unless an evaluation interview is conducted, deficiencies could continue until they become quite serious. Sometimes underperformers do not understand exactly what is expected of them, but once they know what their responsibilities are they will be in a better position to take corrective action to improve their performance.[15] For this reason many organizations provide for frequent evaluations and interviews for new employees. It must also be recognized that occasionally it is necessary for the supervisor to refer problem cases to his or her superior or to the personnel department with a recommendation that certain types of action be taken.

Performance evaluations are of little practical benefit if the results are merely filed away. In addition to taking action on problem cases that are referred to it, the personnel department should study, evaluate, and take action on the evaluation reports as these are received. The reports should be examined for evidence that indicates the need for administrative action such as promotion, demotion, transfer, or counseling. If supervisory personnel fail to recognize the need for such action, the personnel department should bring it to their attention and recommend that appropriate action be considered for the employee in question.

Once the evaluation system has been found to be effective, it may be used to evaluate the various phases of the personnel program. It provides information that may reveal the need for improvements, especially in the selection, placement, and training policies and procedures. Performance evaluation reports have been found to be valuable as measures of employee success that may be used in validating the tests used in personnel selection. On the basis of information concerning the value (validity) of the tests, it is possible to make improvements in the testing program that will result in the selection of employees who are more likely to be successful. Performance evaluation reports may also provide information that reveals the need for correction in determining the relative worth of the job under a job evaluation program. Finally, it is important to recognize that the success of the entire personnel program is dependent upon the knowledge of employee performance in relation to the goals established for them and for the organization of which they are a part. This knowledge can best be obtained from a carefully planned and administered personnel evaluation program.

Résumé

The success of an organization is largely dependent upon the performance of its personnel. In order that the contributions of each individual to the organization may be determined, it is necessary to have a formal evaluation program with clearly stated objectives and a well-organized system for attaining them. Basically an evaluation program is designed to focus the attention of subordinates on the level of performance that is expected of them, to provide measures of the extent to which they attain their expected levels of

[15] Thomas R. Masterson and Thomas G. Mara, "Underperformers: You Can Help Them Make the Grade," *Supervisory Management*, Vol. 14, No. 11 (November, 1969), pp. 10-14.

performance, and to communicate this information to them in such a manner that they accept it and use it as a basis for making whatever changes are necessary in their performance. Where it is not possible to expect improvements in an individual's performance, the evaluation may then be used to support whatever personnel action of a corrective nature is taken.

In order that the interviews and any corrective actions may be based upon valid information, it is essential that managers and supervisors be thoroughly trained in the particular methods that they will use in evaluating their subordinates. One or more of the methods described in this chapter may be used, depending upon the specific uses to be made of the evaluations. While the graphic rating scale is still the most commonly used method, some of the newer approaches to evaluations are increasing in popularity, especially the management by objectives approach. It appeals to those who wish to be able to establish their own performance objectives and to observe the extent to which they are able to attain them.

The degree to which the performance evaluation program benefits the organization will depend largely upon the quality of the interviews that superiors conduct with their subordinates. Different interview methods may be used, but success with any of them requires the development of skills that most individuals do not possess without special training. It is essential, therefore, that a training program include instruction and practice in conducting performance evaluation interviews.

DISCUSSION QUESTIONS

1. What objective criteria could be used to evaluate the performance of people working in the following jobs: key punch operator, stenographer, carpet salesperson, tile setter, TV repairer? Would it be necessary to use any subjective criteria?
2. In many organizations the evaluator submits ratings to his or her immediate superior for review before discussing them with the individual employee.
   a. What advantages are there in this procedure?
   b. What disadvantages may result from it?
3. Consider a job in which you have worked or in which you have had an opportunity to observe others. Can you think of any critical incidents that appeared to distinguish superior from "run-of-the-mill" employees?
4. Assessment centers have become a popular method of evaluating and developing personnel for higher-level jobs with apparent successful results. Are there any potentially undesirable features of this method?
5. What would you include in a training program for superiors on "conducting meaningful evaluation interviews with employees"? What instructional methods would you use? Why?
6. How do you account for the change in performance evaluation approaches over the years from a trait-centered to a results-centered approach?

PROBLEM 10-1 JUST HOW GOOD AM I, DOCTOR?

Ms. Carlisle, a middle-aged woman with several university degrees, was employed by the federal government in a public health position prior to coming to Mentor County General Hospital. At Mentor she served as the County Mental Health Educator under Dr. Haller, Chief of the Mental Health Services Division. Ms. Carlisle's job involved giving lectures to schools, business firms, and clubs upon request and conducting training classes on mental health education for new teachers, social workers, and nurses. She was proud of her performance record which contained mainly superior ratings and nothing below excellent. She liked her boss, too, not only because he had given her an opportunity to use her talents but because he was always kind and considerate.

Performance evaluations at Mentor were made every six months, and the customary procedure was for the reports to be prepared and placed in each employee's mail box. Employees could discuss them with their supervisors if they wished to do so, but they were expected to sign them. One day Ms. Carlisle found her evaluation in her mail box and became very upset over it. Instead of superior and excellent ratings on the scale, she found excellent and good ratings. There was no explanation given for the drop in ratings, only the statement that "Ms. Carlisle continues to do good work as in the past." Ms. Carlisle asked to see Dr. Haller immediately.

The interview between Ms. Carlisle and Dr. Haller took place that afternoon. Ms. Carlisle was quite blunt and wanted to know what was wrong with her work. Dr. Haller explained that her work was fine and he could not understand why she was upset. She pointed out the difference in this last rating compared with others he had given her in the two years she had been there and asked him to explain the difference. Dr. Haller said that he thought it was a good evaluation and explained that he had changed his methods of evaluation. He refused to explain further, but assured Ms. Carlisle that her work was good and encouraged her to maintain this high standing. Ms. Carlisle did not want to sign the evaluation but later conceded, inserting "signed under protest" under her name. She then made plans for appealing the rating to the County Employees Association and the Civil Service Commission.

a. How do you account for Dr. Haller's change in methods? Or is he using this as an excuse for giving her lower ratings?
b. What effect is her appeal likely to have on her ratings? On Dr. Haller's evaluations in the future?

SUGGESTED READINGS

Chruden, Herbert J., and Arthur W. Sherman, Jr. *Readings in Personnel Management*, 4th ed. Cincinnati: South-Western Publishing Co., 1976. Part 3.

Fleishman, Edwin A. *Studies in Personnel and Industrial Psychology*, 3d ed. Homewood, Illinois: The Dorsey Press, Inc., 1973. Section 2.

Kellogg, Marion. *When Man and Manager Talk—A Casebook*. Houston: Gulf Publishing Company, 1969.

McCormick, Ernest J., and Joseph Tiffin. *Industrial Psychology*, 6th ed. Englewood Cliffs, New Jersey: Prentice-Hall, Inc., 1974. Chapter 8.

Mager, Robert F., and Peter Pipe. *Analyzing Performance Problems or "You Really Oughta Wanna."* Belmont, California: Fearon Publishers/Lear Siegler, Inc., 1970.

Miner, John B., and J. F. Brewer. "The Management of Ineffective Performance," in M. D. Dunnette, Editor, *Handbook of Industrial and Organizational Psychology*. Chicago: Rand McNally & Co., 1973.

Odiorne, George S. *Management by Objectives*. New York: Pitman Publishing Corporation, 1965.

Porter, Lyman W., Edward E. Lawler III, and J. Richard Hackman. *Behavior in Organizations*. New York: McGraw-Hill Book Company, 1975. Chapter 11.

Wesley, Kenneth N. and Gary A. Yukl. *Organizational Behavior and Industrial Psychology (Readings with Commentary)*. New York: Oxford University Press, 1975. Part 5.

Motivation and Job Satisfaction

In the preceding chapters emphasis was placed on the importance of recruiting and developing employees who have the potential to perform effectively. It should be recognized, however, that unless individuals are motivated to make sufficient use of this potential they may not achieve the level of performance that is desired from them. Managerial personnel at all levels, therefore, are challenged continually with the problem of motivating their subordinates to release their potential most effectively and thereby permit the desired goals of the organization and the needs of employees to be achieved.

Human motivation, as contrasted with animal motivation, is a more complex phenomenon, and there is still much about it that is unknown. However, being able to apply what is known about it to employment situations is essential for effective management. Today's employees are living in a period when their requirements for food and other basic necessities usually are met, with the result that the establishment of effective motivating conditions in the work environment and the reduction of frustration- and conflict-producing situations require a high degree of skill and understanding on the part of managers and supervisors.

Employee satisfaction is an important dimension of the motivational process which reflects the degree to which individuals perceive that their needs and wants are being met. The attitudes that employees hold toward various aspects of their jobs and the work environment, their own personalities, and the influences of the larger social environment all contribute to the degree of satisfaction that they experience. It should be recognized by management that satisfaction is as important to the organization as it is to the individual. Because of its possible relationship to absenteeism, turnover, and job performance, employee satisfaction warrants as much interest and concern from management as that usually given to motivating employees to better performance.

MOTIVATION: THE DYNAMICS OF BEHAVIOR

For many decades psychologists have been conducting experiments with animals and humans in an effort to understand their behavior. Likewise, in clinical and other therapeutic settings attempts are made to determine the underlying causes of behaviors that are of concern to an individual, to his or her friends, parents, supervisors, fellow workers, or to the larger society. Knowledge of the motivational process provides the basis for understanding *why* people do what they do. It involves trying to find the answer to such questions as "Why does one person strive harder than another?" and "Why do some individuals seek higher levels of responsibility?" These and similar questions are continually being raised by those who are responsible for the management of human resources.

The Motivational Process

Motivation may be defined as the state or condition of being induced to do something. Fundamentally it involves needs that exist within the individual and incentives or goals that are to be found outside of the individual. *Needs* may be thought of as something within individuals that prompts them to engage in behavior which is directed toward the attainment of *incentives* (or goals) that they perceive to be capable of satisfying their needs. The following diagram illustrates the sequence of events that comprise the motivational process.

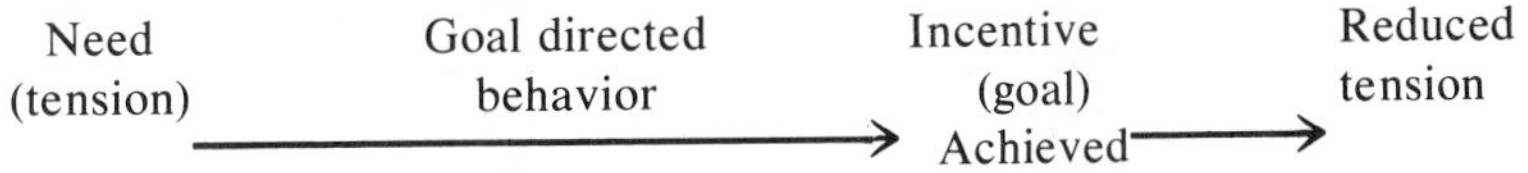

The inclusion of the word "tension" in the diagram indicates that with many motivational situations the individual literally senses a feeling of tension. This tension is most apparent with some of the physiological or tissue needs of the body but is apparent also to the individual whose personality needs direct him or her toward certain rewards or goals of a psychological nature. The preceding diagram is useful in studying the motivational process for any individual at any time. For example, if an employee has a need for economic security, behavior will be directed toward goals (savings, investment, etc.) that will tend to satisfy that need. Similarly, if an individual has a strong need for achievement, behavior will be directed toward attaining that goal. The individual may, for example, strive for a position that is higher in the organization.

From research into the nature of motivation, it has been found that the above diagram is a better representation of what happens in the case of attempts to satisfy physiological needs (hunger, thirst, etc.) rather than psychological needs (love, esteem, etc.). Psychological needs are harder to identify and to measure in intensity. Considerable evidence exists, furthermore, to indicate that there may be no limit to an individual's need for recognition or achievement. That is to say, the need for recognition or achievement persists so that the individual is continually motivated to obtain the satisfaction of it. Nevertheless, the diagram does serve a useful purpose in showing the relationships between the various parts of the motivational process and in understanding what occurs when needs are frustrated or blocked.

The Nature of Human Needs

All of the behavior that we observe around us is directed by a striving for the satisfaction of needs. Earlier theories of behavior tended to explain all behavior on the basis of a single need (e.g., Freud's libidinal drive and Jung's need or drive to assert one's ego). Modern theorists typically list several needs ranging from three (physical needs, social needs, and egoistic needs) to fifteen in number. Since human needs cannot be seen but must be inferred from human behavior, it may be expected that there will be different theories about them and different systems for classifying them.

Classification of Needs. One theory of human motivation that has had by far the greatest impact on the thinking concerned with motivation in organizations comes from the late A. H. Maslow, an American psychologist. He organized or classified human needs according to priority into the following five categories:

1. *The physiological needs*. Included in this group are the needs for food, water, air, rest, etc., that are required for maintaining the body in a state of equilibrium.
2. *The safety needs*. These include the need for safety and security, both in a physical and psychological sense. The need to be protected from external dangers to our bodies and our personalities are included in this group. Most employees, for example, desire to work at jobs that are free from physical and psychological hazards, and that provide tenure.
3. *The belongingness and love needs*. The need for attention and social activity are the major needs in this category. An individual desires affectionate relationships with people in general and desires to have a respected place in the group.
4. *The esteem needs*. These include the desire for self-respect, for strength, for achievement, for adequacy, for mastery and competence, for confidence in the face of the world, and for independence and freedom. Also included in this group is the desire for reputation or prestige or respect and esteem from other people.
5. *The need for self-actualization (realization)*. This refers to a person's desire for self-fulfillment; namely, to the tendency to become actualized in what he or she is potentially. "What one *can* be, one *must* be." This tendency might be phrased as the desire to become everything that one is capable of becoming.[1]

---

[1] Paraphrased and adapted from A. H. Maslow, *Motivation and Personality* (2d ed.; New York: Harper & Brothers, 1970).

The fact that human needs have been analyzed and categorized should not cause us to believe that we have a complete explanation of human behavior. In analyzing the motivation of an individual, attention cannot be focused on any one of the needs to the exclusion of the others. Behavior is multimotivated; therefore, several needs including both conscious and unconscious needs demand satisfaction concurrently.

Priority of Needs. According to Maslow's theory, human needs are arranged according to the priority shown in Figure 11-1. In the first place, the physiological needs are the most fundamental; they require satisfaction before other needs. Once the physiological needs are satisfied, the safety needs become predominant. At this point an individual becomes concerned over his or her physical and psychological well-being. Related to this concern is the employee's desire for security from injury as well as from adverse economic conditions and unpleasant or threatening behavior of other persons.

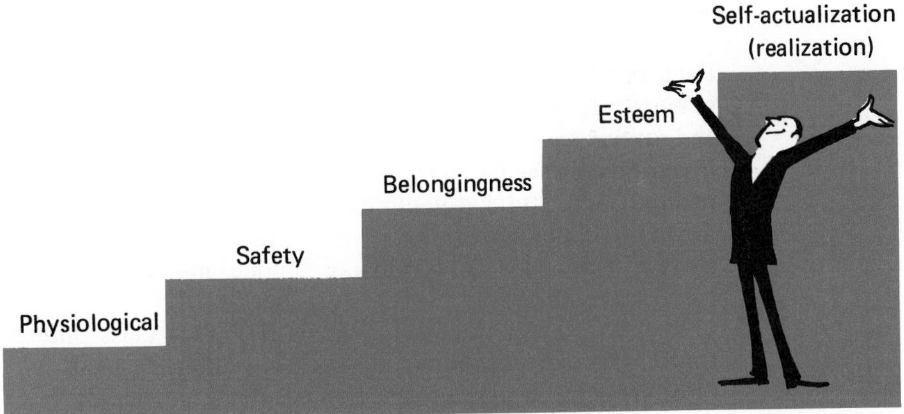

Figure 11-1 PRIORITY OF HUMAN NEEDS

If both the physiological and the safety needs are fairly well satisfied, the belongingness and love needs (the next step) will emerge as dominant in a person's need structure. The individual's behavior will turn in the direction of seeking companionship with others and in striving for a place in the group. While much of the employee's need for belongingness and acceptance may be satisfied through family relationships and friends, this need should also be satisfied to some degree on the job.

At the top of the ladder are the needs for esteem and self-realization. These needs include achievement, mastery, confidence, independence, recognition, and a realization of all that one is capable of becoming. As the lower needs are satisfied, these higher needs become dominant.

According to Maslow, as needs at one level are satisfied, needs at the next higher level come into predominance. Thus, a need does not have to be completely satisfied before the next need emerges. If, for example, the physiological and safety needs are 75 percent satisfied in an individual and the love and self-esteem needs are 25 percent satisfied, behavior will be primarily in the direction of satisfying the love and esteem needs with the physiological and safety needs taking a subordinate role. For example, a millionaire executive, in order to satisfy the need for self-realization, may work as hard or harder than the individual who works for money to meet the bare necessities of life. Maslow states that unlike motivation based on primary drives (hunger, thirst, etc.), motivation that comes from the actualization of one's potential does not decrease as these needs become satisfied. Quite to the contrary, as people experience growth and self-actualization they want more. There is a considerable amount of evidence, particularly among managerial personnel, to support this point.[2]

While a theory of motivation may serve as a useful framework to guide managers and supervisors in their understanding of subordinates, the fact remains that each individual has a different need pattern that can be understood only by studying that individual. It is often helpful, however, to be able to identify factors which may have influenced an individual's needs.

Factors Creating Differences. The differences in need patterns among a group of employees are as much to be expected as differences in interests, aptitudes, and attitudes among them. As a result of prior experiences, satisfactions, and frustrations in the life of the individual, some needs have become stronger than others. Childhood and youth experiences, previous employment experiences, and daily contacts with supervisors, fellow employees, and the family have played their part in developing unique motivational patterns within the individual employee.

Another factor influencing needs is that of class differences. Individuals from higher socioeconomic classes have different needs and aspirations than those from lower classes. The son of a bank president, for example, may feel that the job of machinist is not suitable for him, while the son of a bricklayer may feel that the machinist's job is a good choice. A person's socioeconomic class not only affects his or her occupational aspirations but also attitudes toward work, authority, education and training, responsibility, and other factors that affect on-the-job performance.

Whether one is male or female influences the development of need patterns as well as one's expectations for having certain needs satisfied. Until recently employers often ignored the needs of women or assumed that their needs were significantly different from those of men. As a result of these assumptions, female employees have often been unable to attain desired levels of need satisfaction. Lack of opportunities for advancement into jobs that provide higher wages, as well as opportunities for self-actualization, are the primary frustrations of women employees. Fortunately an increased awareness of these problem areas is developing and some improvements are being made.

---

[2] Edward E. Lawler III, *Motivation in Work Organizations* (Monterey, California: Brooks/Cole Publishing Company, 1973), p. 25.

Maslow and Other Theorists. The Maslow need hierarchy has proven to be useful in guiding managerial personnel and has served to stimulate research in this important area of personnel management. It has also served as the basis for a widely used inventory—the *Porter Need Satisfaction Questionnaire*—that has been used in a number of studies involving managerial personnel.[3] It should be recognized, however, that Maslow's need hierarchy is a theoretical formulation based largely on the work of a clinical psychologist and that it requires further validation. Maslow warned of its restrictions,[4] and experimental studies have indicated that human needs may actually be in two levels—existence and security needs at the lower level and social, esteem, autonomy, and self-actualization needs at the higher level.[5] However, research has confirmed Maslow's theory in general, i.e., that the higher-level needs will appear only when the lower-level ones are satisfied.[6]

Another comprehensive theory of motivation is that of H. A. Murray.[7] In his theory he lists more than 20 psychogenic or social needs that were later used as the basis for a personality inventory known as the *Edwards Personal Preference Schedule*.[8] The *Edwards Personal Preference Schedule* contains 225 items that measure the relative strength of the respondent's manifest needs (those of which he or she is aware, in contrast to unconscious needs) in 15 areas, among them being needs for achievement, order, affiliation, dominance, and change. It should be noted that this list represents a somewhat different organization of needs than those suggested by earlier personality theorists. Hence, one should not assume that all of the questions about motivation are answered and that human needs have been isolated as precisely as the basic elements of the physical sciences. The Murray-Edwards listing of needs has stimulated considerable research, as has that of Maslow.

There are other researchers who have written about human needs, especially as they relate to organizational behavior. Among these are David C. McClelland, who has focused on the achievement motive, and Robert W. White, who has focused on the competitive motive. More recently the work of J. S. Adams on the *need for equity*, i.e., the need to be treated fairly, has received considerable emphasis in attempts to understand employee reactions to various wage plans.[9] While the existence of different theories of motivation and various lists and categories of needs may lead the reader to question their validity, it should be recognized that human motivation is one of the most

---

[3] L. W. Porter and E. E. Lawler III, *Managerial Attitudes and Performance* (Homewood, Ill.: Richard D. Irwin, 1968).

[4] Abraham H. Maslow, *Eupsychian Management: A Journal* (Homewood, Ill.: Richard D. Irwin, Inc. and The Dorsey Press, 1965).

[5] L. K. Waters and Darrell Roach, "A Factor Analysis of Need-Fulfillment Items Designed to Measure Maslow Need Categories," *Personnel Psychology*, Vol. 26, No. 2 (Summer, 1973), pp. 185-190.

[6] Edward E. Lawler, III *op. cit.*, p. 40.

[7] Henry A. Murray, *Explorations in Personality* (New York: Oxford University Press, 1938).

[8] Allen E. Edwards, *Edwards Personal Preference Schedule* (New York: The Psychological Corporation, 1954).

[9] J. S. Adams, "Toward an Understanding of Inequity," *Journal of Abnormal Psychology*, Volume 67, No. 5 (November, 1963), pp. 422-436.

complex functions and that it will require many more hypotheses and years of research before precise understanding of it is realized.[10]

Types of Incentives

How to motivate employees to perform at the highest possible levels consistent with their abilities is a question frequently asked by managers. There is no simple answer to the question since the total organizational climate and all that it encompasses affects the manner and degree to which the needs of its members will be fulfilled. An examination of the systems established to manage employees reveals the presence of a variety of incentives that are designed to motivate individuals toward the accomplishment of organizational goals and personal goals.

Unfortunately the use of incentives is frequently carried out in a mechanistic and/or bureaucratic manner. Too often, according to Levinson, motivation is viewed as a carrot-and-stick (reward and punishment) process. This view, he says, is based upon the unconscious assumption that one is dealing with jackasses to be manipulated and controlled—the boss as the manipulator and controller, and the subordinate as the jackass. Levinson is against easy tricks for motivating subordinates since subordinates can be motivated only when their needs and aspirations have been examined in depth. To him, organizations should look more like loving families; leaders like thoughtful and caring fathers.[11]

With an awareness of the complexity of human motivation and the importance of studying the needs and aspirations of individuals more carefully, one is then in a position to examine the incentives that are commonly used.

Money. Money is an extremely complex incentive that literally means different things to different people. To the individual who is economically disadvantaged it means being provided with food, shelter, and clothing. To the wealthy it often means a source of power and prestige. Because of the different meanings that individuals attach to money, it cannot be assumed that an increase in money will necessarily result in increased productivity and job satisfaction. However, wage incentive systems that relate wages directly to output are especially effective in stimulating production if standards are developed properly and the system is administered effectively. The support and confidence of employees are important factors in determining the success of such systems. Profit-sharing, likewise, is effective as an incentive to greater production and has positive effects on employee attitudes. In a society where the satisfaction of an individual's material needs is dependent upon money either from wages or

---

[10] T. C. Chamberlin, "The Method of Multiple Working Hypotheses," *Science*, Vol. 148 (1965), pp. 754-759.

[11] Harry Levinson, *The Great Jackass Fallacy* (Boston: Graduate School of Business Administration, Harvard University, 1963), p. 10. Also see Harry Levinson, "Asinine Attitudes Toward Motivation," *Harvard Business Review*, Vol. 51, No. 1 (January-February, 1973), pp. 70-76 as reprinted in Herbert J. Chruden and Arthur W. Sherman, Jr., *Readings in Personnel Management* (4th ed.; Cincinnati: South-Western Publishing Co., 1976), pp. 309-319.

other sources, the power that money has cannot be minimized. Gellerman states that the most subtle and most important characteristic of money is its power as a symbol. Money thus can mean whatever an individual desires.[12]

Security. The appeal to the individual's needs for security of all types—physical, psychological, and economic—is seen everywhere in employing organizations. While the need for security varies among individuals, it can serve as an important incentive inducing some individuals to remain with an organization and to reach a minimally satisfactory level of performance. For others security may provide them with a sense of freedom or independence that stimulates them to participate more wholeheartedly on the job and to work toward the achievement of the organization's objectives. They are in the position of being free to direct their energies primarily toward the goals of the organization rather than toward the achievement of personal security.

Affiliation. The need for belongingness and love constitutes one of the categories of needs in Maslow's hierarchy. It may be thought of in organizational terminology as affiliation—the need to join with others in relationships that are mutually satisfying and supportive. The relationships that develop on an informal basis among members of an organization serve to meet the needs that people have for interacting with others on a satisfying and supportive basis. Although the importance of these relationships should not be minimized, managers and supervisors should do as much as possible to make relationships among those who interact with each other according to the formal organizational structure as attractive as those that develop on an informal basis. Where the organizational climate provides for the establishment and maintenance of mutually satisfying and supportive relationships among its members—new and established, young and old, male and female—higher productivity and greater employee satisfaction are more likely to occur.

Esteem. Satisfaction of the esteem needs may be realized through a variety of incentives that involve primarily prestige and power. These consist of opportunities to perform tasks that are considered to be important to the organization and to society and to have power over people and resources. The significance that the incentives in this category have is greatly influenced by the various groups in the organization and by society. Within the organization opportunities are often created for some groups of employees to receive rewards that provide esteem, whereas other groups of employees are less favored. Similarly, within the larger society some jobs are viewed as being more prestigious than others.

Authority over people and resources is a strong incentive for the individual who has intense needs for power. Such individuals strive to attain supervisory and managerial positions in order to have these needs satisfied. While any organizational structure will have a limited number of leadership positions, other opportunites may be provided to share in leadership or power functions

[12] Saul W. Gellerman, *Motivation and Productivity* (New York: American Management Association, 1963).

through participation. Participation is recognized as one of the best incentives for stimulating employee production and for providing job satisfaction. In addition to providing opportunities for the employee to participate in meetings and conferences, on committees, or through the suggestion box, greater attention can be given to participation in the making of decisions about the work itself and to the conditions under which it is accomplished within the work group. Specific approaches to employee participation of the latter type will be discussed in Chapter 14.

Self-Actualization. The incentives for satisfying the needs in this general category include the opportunity to gain a feeling of competence and achievement. Competence refers to one's ability to perform and an awareness of what one is able to do and not do. The competence motive reveals itself in adults as a desire for job mastery and professional growth. Its effectiveness as an incentive requires that the individual be provided with freedom to perform job duties through desire without close or restrictive supervision and that the opportunity to compete be given.

Also, competition is not always recommended as an approach to achieving self-actualization. For example, in France and certain other European countries employees are not likely to respond positively to competition as a motivational technique. They feel that people should be dealt with as equals and that competition is undesirable because it creates bad feelings. Germans on the other hand, prefer to work as individuals and to receive recognition directly from their supervisor rather than from the work group. Because of the strong influence that the culture of each country, and even parts of a country, has on the needs of its people and the effectiveness of the various incentives, it is important for managers to understand the backgrounds of their subordinates and to be aware of the most effective motivational approaches.[13]

In summary, the satisfaction of employee needs will be dependent upon several of the incentives being present at one time. This is illustrated by a statement by Frederick C. Ochsner, vice-president and director of corporate personnel of Texas Instruments. In explaining the causes of increased productivity, he said:

> It is a whole bunch of things acting synergistically. It's the attitudes, the team improvement program, the campus environment, the open-door management policy, the nonstructured pecking order. It's the unified goal approach—with everybody looking at his own piece of that goal.[14]

The policies and procedures to which Ochsner is referring include the types of incentives that have been discussed in this section.

[13] Herbert J. Chruden and Arthur W. Sherman, Jr., *Personnel Practices of American Companies in Europe* (New York: American Management Association, 1972), p. 71.

[14] "How Texas Instruments Turns Its People On," *Business Week* (September 29, 1973), pp. 88-90.

Incentives for Different Categories of Personnel

The modern organization is comprised of individuals whose educational and occupational backgrounds have prepared them for employment in varying types of jobs at different levels in the organization. As a result of their prior experience and their particular roles in the organization, they have acquired certain patterns of needs and aspirations that should be recognized by management if it is to create the proper motivational climate for them. It should not be assumed that the individuals who fall into a particular category are all alike. However, they often have sufficient common characteristics to warrant certain generalizations about them. This is especially true for such groups as managerial personnel; professional, scientific, and technical personnel; and blue-collar workers.

Managerial Personnel. The need for achievement is prominent among successful executives. These individuals generally perceive themselves to be hard-working and achieving persons who must accomplish in order to be satisfied. Executive positions typically provide incentive opportunities through which they may satisfy their needs. According to McClelland, who has studied the achievement motive in various groups of individuals, the business executive exhibits the following characteristics:

1. He likes situations in which he takes personal responsibility for finding solutions to problems.
2. He has a tendency to set moderate achievement goals and to take "calculated risks."
3. He wants concrete feedback as to how well he is doing.[15]

Apparently the achievement motive is attaining even greater significance than in the past. Seventy-four percent of more than 300 chief executives of companies listed in *Fortune's* Annual 500 Directory who were polled responded that they found job satisfaction a more important motivating force today than in the past. When queried about the meaning of "job satisfaction," for a substantial majority it meant reorganizing the company in some fashion to allow more executives to demonstrate their ability. Forms of organizational change mentioned included broadening the base of management, creating more executive jobs, allowing more participation in management, enhancing the challenge of the job, etc.[16]

Many organizations in recent years have experienced sharply rising rates of attrition among young managerial and professional personnel. This fact is the result not only of economic activity and shortage of talented personnel but also of the type of supervision that they receive. Supervisors often lack the knowledge and skill for developing the productive capabilities of their subordinates. According to one expert:

---

[15] David C. McClelland, "Business Drive and National Achievement," *Harvard Business Review,* Vol. 40, No. 4 (July-August, 1962), pp. 99-112.

[16] What Business Thinks," *Fortune,* Vol. 80, No. 6 (December, 1969), pp. 115-116.

> Although most top executives have not yet diagnosed the problem, industry's greatest challenge by far is the underdevelopment, underutilization, and ineffective management and use of its most valuable resource—its young managerial and professional talent.[17]

What young people need is supervision by those who are not afraid that their subordinates will outshine them and who are willing and able to help their subordinates improve their performance and career opportunities.

Professional, Scientific, and Technical Personnel. Modern organizations of all types—from those in heavy industry to those providing some type of social service—utilize the talents of certain professional, scientific, or technical personnel. Among these one will find physicians, chemists, geologists, engineers, attorneys, accountants, and many others. These individuals are different from most of the other employees of an organization not only in the type and extent of their training but also in their identification with their professional group. Furthermore, the ideals and goals of their professional group at times may be in conflict with the objectives and methods of their employing organization unless top management is of the same professional background as the employee. Professional and scientific personnel are motivated to perform at their maximum when there are opportunities for identifiable achievement, recognition, and status and when their assignments involve constructive pursuits, are diversified in nature, and lead to advancement.[18] In order that professional and scientific personnel can be advanced in an organization that is composed primarily of other categories of personnel, a dual hierarchy is often established so that the professionally oriented person can advance to positions of greater autonomy and higher salary without having to assume managerial responsibilities. For professional and scientific personnel, promotion to a managerial position is often considered a step toward loss of professional competency.[19]

Blue-Collar Workers. The fact that many blue-collar workers receive high wages does not necessarily serve to motivate them to greater productivity or provide a high level of job satisfaction. An increasing number of blue-collar workers appear to feel that they are in dead-end positions. With their self-esteem diminishing and interest in doing the job well for its own sake vanishing, many employers have attempted to enrich their blue-collar jobs.[20] This involves many approaches including job enlargement. Studies have shown that employees who were responsible for making some decisions (even if minor) reported more interest in and less boredom with their work.[21]

---

[17] Sterling Livingston, "Pygmalion in Management," *Harvard Business Review,* Vol. 47, No. 4 (July-August, 1969), pp. 81-89.

[18] William L. Campfield, "Motivating the Professional Employee," *Personnel Journal,* Vol. 44, No. 8 (September, 1965), pp. 425-428.

[19] Duane P. Schultz, "R and D Personnel: Two Basic Types," *Personnel,* Vol. 41, No. 2 (March-April, 1964), pp. 62-67.

[20] Judson Gooding, "It Pays to Wake Up the Blue-Collar Workers," *Fortune,* Vol. 82, No. 3 (September, 1970), pp. 133-135, 158-168.

[21] Melvin Sorcher and Herbert H. Meyer, "Motivating Factory Employees," *Personnel,* Vol. 45, No. 1 (January-February, 1968), pp. 22-28.

According to a Department of Labor report, one of the root causes of blue-collar discontent is the gap in status and in perquisites between the blue-collar and white-collar workers. Several companies, including IBM, Hewlett Packard, and Texas Instruments, have attempted to stamp out many of the visible distinctions between different categories of employees. It was noted in Chapter 2 that other firms have discontinued the use of "blue-collar" or "hourly" labels, and some have eliminated the hourly pay system and have placed all employees on salary. Adherence to a system of promoting from within also has helped to keep blue-collar workers from feeling that they are destined to remain at the operative level in the organization.

Disadvantaged Workers. Since the enactment of the Manpower Development and Training Act of 1962, individuals classed as disadvantaged are being trained for the industrial job market. There is still much to be learned about these people, but studies have provided some insights into their needs.

A study of *Special Training for Economic Progress* (STEP) trainees throughout South Carolina demonstrated that while there are differences between subgroups (white and black, male and female, and different geographical locations), there are certain characteristics that apply to all of them. In all groups intrinsic job factors, including the desire to do one's best and the desire for personal satisfaction, generally were found to rank higher than the extrinsic factors of pay, praise, or respect. In all cases respect or praise received from superiors was more important than that gained from peer groups. The fear of losing one's job or being reprimanded was very low, indicating that fear-inducing techniques are not likely to be effective with individuals similar to those in this study.[22]

FRUSTRATION AND CONFLICT

The motivational process as indicated earlier requires the presence of a need and accompanying behavior that is directed toward an incentive or goal that would satisfy that need. An examination of the events in the daily life of an individual confirms the fact that not all needs are satisfied fully. The individual may be prevented from reaching a particular goal or incentive, or there may be conflicting goals. Either condition may keep one in a state of dissatisfaction and tension that may interfere with job performance and ability to work harmoniously with fellow employees. Managers and supervisors should understand the forces that make for dissatisfaction and tension in their subordinates so that they may create a work environment that will be as free as possible of these conditions.

Nature of Frustration

The presence of a barrier to goal attainment and need satisfaction creates a frustrating condition with the result that the individual's initial tension is made

[22] Joseph E. Champagne and Donald C. King, "Job Satisfaction Among Underprivileged Workers," *Personnel and Guidance Journal,* Vol. 45, No. 5 (January, 1967), pp. 429-434.

to persist or become stronger. The addition of the barrier to the earlier illustration of the motivational process shown on page 241 modifies the sequence as follows:

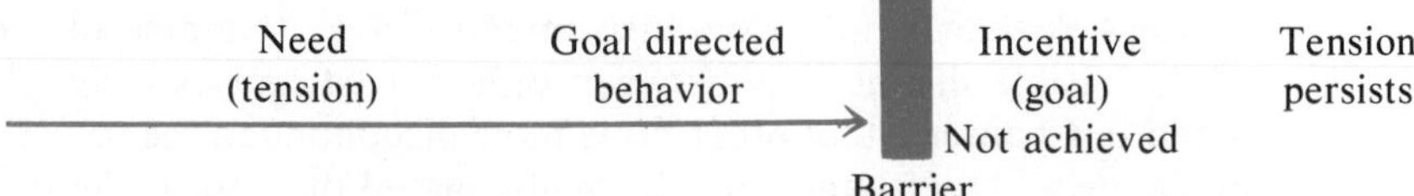

A person who is blocked from achieving a goal by some barrier is said to be frustrated. Such barriers to need satisfaction may be either external or internal. Some external barriers or obstacles to the satisfaction of needs are encountered by many employees in the form of discriminatory practices, hostile supervisors, monotonous jobs, unpleasant working conditions, economic insecurity, and similar situations. Some of the possible internal barriers that may frustrate the employee are poor habits and inadequate personality or aptitude for a particular job. A perceived inadequacy (imaginary barrier) is just as real to the person as an actual barrier, substantiating the fact that in human affairs reality is a matter of personal interpretation.

Common Reactions to Frustration

A frustrated person may respond (1) by selecting an acceptable substitute goal that is attainable, or (2) by engaging in behavior that is maladaptive.

Selecting a Substitute Goal. Striving to reach a substitute goal generally is considered to be more adaptive because it leads to need satisfaction. An example may be found in the person who has a strong need to lead others and aspires to be a manager but, because of some barrier which prohibits attainment of a managerial position, satisfies leadership needs by becoming an informal leader in the work group (a substitute goal). Many of the goals that individuals have selected for themselves which prove to be unattainable often have alternatives that can be equally satisfying and therefore should not be overlooked. The selection of a substitute or alternative goal where new barriers will not be encountered may at times require assistance from another individual, such as a superior, who is in a position to recognize alternative goals that may be available.

Engaging in Maladaptive Behavior. In the absence of a substitute goal, an individual's responses sooner or later are likely to become maladaptive in nature. Some of the maladaptive responses will be discussed later. The most common of the maladaptive responses, namely *aggression* (or hostility), will be discussed here. Aggression may be of a direct type that is expressed in the form of attacks against the person or persons perceived to be the cause of the frustration. This attack could be verbal or physical in nature. Frequently, however, where it is too dangerous or too painful to attack the frustrator directly, attacks may be made against other persons or objects. This displayed aggression may be observed in a supervisor who, when frustrated by a superior, becomes verbally abusive toward subordinates. In spite of these common aggressive reactions to frustration, one should be aware of wide individual differences in the ability to tolerate the blocking of one's needs. Some individuals quickly become tense, anxious, and angry while others are able to withstand the blocking of strong needs with minimal feelings of frustration. The latter individuals are said to have a high degree of *frustration tolerance*. Its development in the individual is not fully understood, but it appears to be a condition that is influenced by early environmental experiences.

Nature of Conflict

A person who has two or more strong motivational patterns that cannot be satisfied together is said to have a *conflict*. A conflict typically involves a choice or decision-making situation in which the needs, goals, or methods for attaining the goals are incompatible. A conflict involving needs is seen in the employee who has an urge to ask the boss for a promotion and yet is afraid to do so. The urge to ask because of the chances for promotion and the fear of being judged as not qualified represent forces tugging at each other. A conflict involving goals is illustrated by the individual who desires to be an executive and at the same time have freedom from responsibility. A conflict in methods arises when the approach to attaining the goal involves incompatible means. For example, in handling a business transaction one cannot be honest and dishonest at the same time.

Other Symptoms of Frustration and Conflict

Frustration and conflict are experienced by each individual in an organization, regardless of position in the hierarchy. Typically the person whose behavior is blocked either because of frustration or conflict feels tense and uncomfortable—a condition that is commonly referred to as anxiety. It is often accompanied by unconscious adjustment mechanisms that are also referred to as defense mechanisms.

Anxiety. *Anxiety* is a term commonly used to describe the response of the person who senses himself to be in danger. When anxiety exists, as contrasted to the existence of fear, the source of danger cannot be clearly identified, and usually the individual is not consciously aware of being in danger. Anxiety may account for various employee behaviors that are often misunderstood and misinterpreted. For example, resistance to change is fundamentally caused by the anxiety that arises from a proposed change in job, work method, or merely the relocation of a desk. Employees who resist changes, therefore, are not going out of their way to be "difficult" but, rather, are threatened or frightened at the prospects of a change. Unfortunately anxiety affects managers and supervisors as well as employees. Their anxieties often lead to failure to delegate and to a distrust of those employees who exhibit ambition or initiative.

Anxiety is accompanied by physical symptoms similar to those that one characteristically associates with fear, such as trembling, nausea, a pounding heart, and dryness in the throat. As a result of the physiological effect that anxiety has on the body, its persistence can lead to psychosomatic illnesses. In the interest of good physical and emotional health, managers and supervisors should do all that they can to reduce anxiety. It should not be inferred, however, that anxiety is always undesirable or indicative of maladjustment. A moderate degree of anxiety can serve as a drive to overcome shortcomings and is relatively harmless.

Adjustment or Defense Mechanisms. Another symptom of frustration and conflict is the *adjustment* or *defense mechanism* which is any habitual method of overcoming blocks, reaching goals, satisfying needs, or relieving frustrations. It was observed earlier that aggressive reactions commonly occur in frustrating situations but that there are also other modes of reacting to them. The choice of which adjustment or defense mechanism is used will depend primarily upon one's personality makeup and individual characteristic modes of response. Aside from the aggressive reactions that were discussed earlier, there are two other major groups of adjustment or defense mechanisms that individuals use, namely withdrawal reactions and substitute reactions.[23]

Withdrawal Reactions. *Withdrawal* or *escape reactions* include excessive daydreaming *(fantasy)* engaging in child-like behavior *(regression),* giving up *(resignation),* and in having a strong and irrational resistance to accepting the suggestions of others *(negativism).* While fantasy and regression may be seen occasionally in people at work, negativism is a very common adjustment mechanism. Responses of this latter type frequently arise in relationships with people of authority. Among employees one will find those who have negative feelings toward their supervisors. Similarly, labor leaders may have these feelings toward management; and managers, toward labor leaders. Negativism involves not only an escape reaction but also elements of aggression.

Substitute Reactions. Most of the time aggressive and withdrawal reactions are not adequate for restoring psychological equilibrium to the individual. *Substitute reactions,* on the other hand, are more common and constitute a more satisfactory method of adjustment for the individual as well as for the group. Common substitute reactions are *compensation, rationalization,* and *projection.* The office clerk who is frustrated by limited education (internal barrier) may use big words and complicated language in order to impress others; or the manager who is frustrated by having little or no authority may attempt to impress others by bossiness (compensation). The employee who aspires to be a supervisor but was passed over may say, "It would hardly have been worth the small difference in pay" (rationalization). *Projection* is the act of blaming others for one's own thoughts, feelings, or behavior. Some employees continually blame others because they sincerely believe that they

[23] Over 32 different adjustment mechanisms are referred to in different books on mental hygiene. Those discussed here are the ones that are included most frequently.

themselves are not at fault. Of the substitute reactions, projection is the least desirable since it involves distorting an important part of the real world. In its most extreme form, projection is a central part of the psychosis known as *paranoia*. To some degree everyone has paranoid tendencies.

Defense mechanisms are common modes of behavior that are used by all persons in an unconscious effort to maintain their own self-respect and the approval of others. Unless used to an extreme degree, defensive behavior is considered normal.

Reducing Frustration in Jobs

Managers and supervisors have a responsibility to be sensitive to the needs of their subordinates and to create a work environment in which these needs may be satisfied and frustration minimized. While each individual, as noted earlier, has a unique need pattern, it is well for those in managerial positions to have a general understanding of some of the possible causes of frustrations. Such causes may include changing technology and conditions of work, economic insecurity of the job, insignificance of the job and the work group, and unfulfilled expectations. Not all of the sources of frustration are under the direct control of management; however, an awareness of potential areas of employee frustration and sincere efforts to handle them effectively through better organization, planning, and communication can help to ameliorate many of the conditions that give rise to frustration. In the next chapter some recommendations will be made for creating the type of organizational climate that meets the need requirements of employees.

Minimizing Conflicts

Many of the conflicts that an individual experiences are easily resolved. Other conflicts, however, involve the core of an individual's personality and have devastating results if they are not properly resolved. Organizations frequently create conflicts within their members that can be harmful to both the individuals and the organization. One common type of conflict involves the desires that individuals have for independence on the one hand and for dependence and support on the other. Much anxiety is created over these opposing needs. Industrial as well as other types of organizations promote this type of conflict by creating conditions that foster dependency while stressing the need for members to demonstrate initiative and independence. Through a continuing program of organizational development, conditions that create frustration as well as conflict should be identified and eliminated both for the psychological well-being of the individuals and the efficiency of the organization.

JOB SATISFACTION

The satisfaction that individuals receive from their employment is largely dependent upon the extent to which the job and everything associated with it meet their needs and wants. Since much of an individual's motivation is unconscious, the employee is not clearly aware of all of his or her needs. It is more difficult, therefore, to obtain an accurate assessment of an individual's needs. *Wants,* on the other hand, are the conscious desires for things or conditions that an individual feels will provide satisfaction. Most attempts to measure job satisfaction involve studying wants through questionnaires and interviews. The manner in which an employee responds to the specific questions is dependent not only upon the conditions themselves but how the individual perceives them. The perception of them, in turn, is influenced by personality, expectations, political and social orientation, age, sex, health, family relationships, and many other factors. By discovering attitudes and opinions on matters related to the job, management can take corrective action and hopefully improve employee satisfaction.

Factors Relating to Job Satisfaction

Many organizations develop their own questionnaires or inventories for assessing employee satisfaction while others use questionnaires standardized by research organizations. Items from one of the more popular standardized questionaires will be shown in Chapter 15. In a recent study in which a large number of job satisfaction questionnaires were analyzed, the factors found to be measured most frequently were: (1) the content of the work, actual tasks performed, and control of the work; (2) supervision; (3) the organization and its management; (4) opportunities for advancement; (5) pay and other financial benefits; (6) co-workers; and (7) working conditions.[24]

Numerous studies have been made by asking employees what aspects of their job give them satisfaction and dissatisfaction. The type of job a person has, the economic and social conditions at the time of the survey, the length of time on the job, and the personal factors such as age, intelligence, education, and personality all appear to have some effect on the survey results. As revealed by a carefully controlled study conducted by an American electronics firm, nationality is also a factor. Employees in two different occupational groups (sales and service) who work in the firm's installations situated in three foreign countries were found to differ significantly in their assessments of how different job characteristics contributed to overall satisfaction.[25] Differences between members of cultures within a country may also be found. In one study, job satisfaction response patterns were examined for white and nonwhite females across three occupational levels. The results of the study suggest that the frame of reference one brings from the culture or subculture influences the way one perceives the job and those facets of it which are satisfying and dissatisfying.[26]

---

[24] W. W. Ronan, "Individual and Situational Variables Relating to Job Satisfaction," *Journal of Applied Psychology,* Vol. 54, No. 1, Part 2 (February, 1970), pp. 1-31.

[25] S. H. Simonetti and Joseph Weitz, "Job Satisfaction: Some Cross-Cultural Effects," *Personnel Psychology,* Vol. 25, No. 1 (Spring, 1972), pp. 107-118.

[26] Charles A. O'Reilly, III, and Karlene H. Roberts, "Job Satisfaction Among Whites and Nonwhites," *Journal of Applied Psychology,* Vol. 57, No. 3 (June, 1973), pp. 295-299.

Because of these different factors affecting survey results, uniform findings are not to be expected. In some surveys wages rank fairly high in the list of what people say they want in a job; in others it is of lesser importance. The same is true of security, working conditions, and other factors in job satisfaction.

In an analysis by Herzberg, the relative significance of different factors based on 16 studies including over 11,000 employees in the United States and United Kingdom was determined. Security ranked highest, wages and supervision in the middle, working conditions and communication about two-thirds down the list, and benefits last.[27]

Herzberg's Motivation-Hygiene Theory

On the basis of his analysis of job satisfaction studies, Herzberg and his associates formulated a theory of employee satisfaction and dissatisfaction commonly referred to as the *motivation-hygiene theory*.[28] The original study that was designed to test the theory involved conducting interviews with 200 engineers and accountants in nine different companies in diversified locations about job factors that had important effects on their attitudes. The respondents were asked to think of a time when they felt exceptionally good or exceptionally bad about their job, either their present job or any other jobs they have had. Following the specific questions to elicit these critical incidents, interviewers probed to get clarification on the nature of events and their personal reactions to these events.

Motivator and Hygiene Factors. Figure 11-2 portrays the original data on engineers and accountants. It will be noted that the largest percentage of the positive feelings at work were brought about by one or more of the *motivator* factors while a smaller percentage of the negative factors involved the motivators. Conversely, a larger percentage of the events describing dissatisfaction stem from *hygiene* factors or what more commonly may be thought of as a psychologically hygienic work environment (i.e., free from unhealthy working conditions).

In commenting upon motivator factors and hygiene factors, Herzberg, Mausner, and Snyderman conclude:

> Improvement in the factors of hygiene (company policy and administration, supervision, relations with supervisors, working conditions, etc.) will serve to remove the impediments to positive job attitudes. . . . When these factors deteriorate to a level below that which the employee considers acceptable, then job dissatisfaction ensues. However, the reverse does not hold true. When the job context can be characterized as optimal, we will not get dissatisfaction, but neither will we get much in the way of positive attitudes. . . .

---

[27] Frederick Herzberg, *et al., Job Attitudes: Review of Research and Opinion* (Pittsburgh: Psychological Service of Pittsburgh, 1957), p. 46.

[28] Frederick Herzberg, Bernard Mausner, and Barbara B. Snyderman, *The Motivation to Work* (2d ed.; New York: John Wiley & Sons, Inc., 1959); Frederick Herzberg, *Work and the Nature of Man* (Cleveland: The World Publishing Company, 1960).

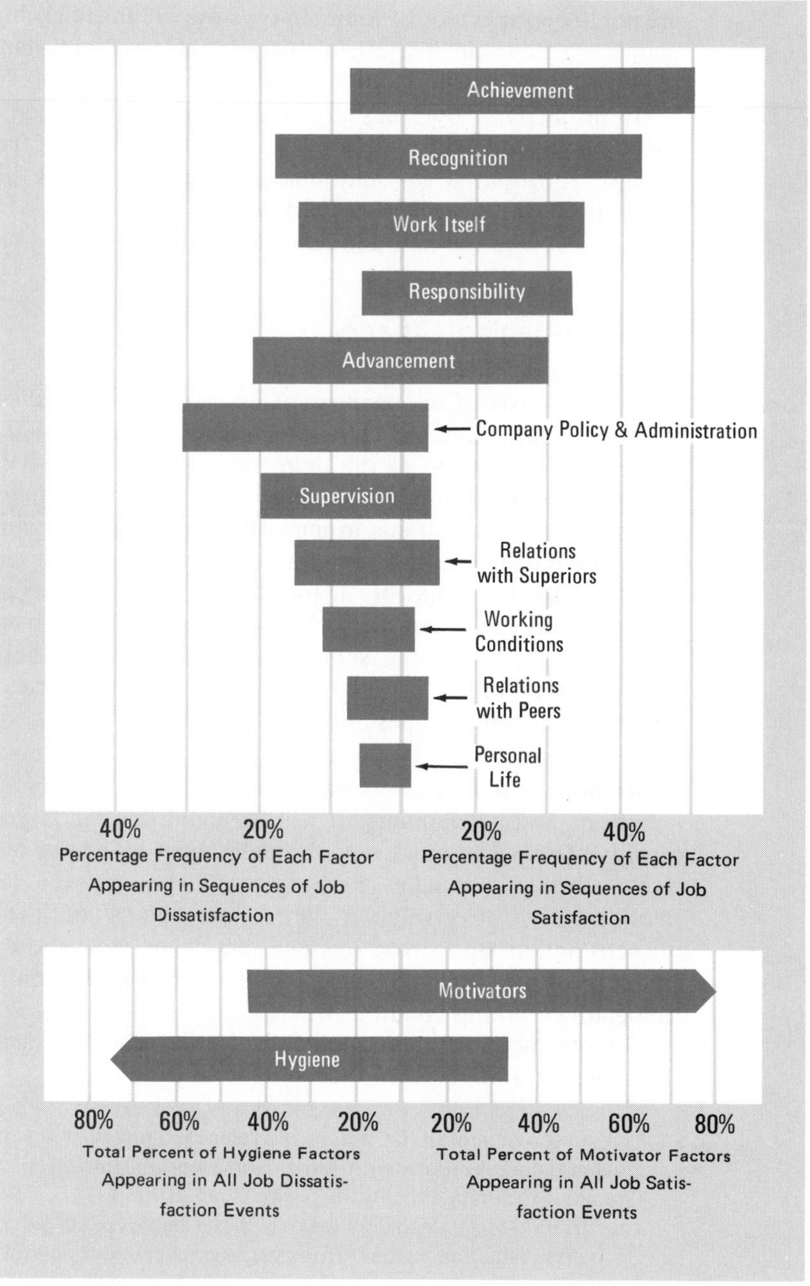

Source: Adapted from F. Herzberg, B. Mausner, and B. B. Snyderman, *The Motivation to Work* (2d ed.; New York: John Wiley & Sons, Inc., 1959). Reproduced with permission of John Wiley & Sons and *Personnel Psychology.*

Figure 11-2 COMPARISON OF MOTIVATOR AND HYGIENE FACTORS (Engineers and Accountants)

The factors that lead to positive job attitudes (the motivators) do so because they satisfy the individual's need for self-actualization in his work. . . . Man tends to actualize himself in every area of his life, and his job is one of his important areas. . . .

It should be understood that both kinds of factors meet the needs of the employee; but it is primarily the "motivators" (achievement, recognition, the work itself, responsibility, advancement) that serve to bring about the kind of job satisfaction and . . . the kind of improvement in performance that industry is seeking from its work force.[29]

The Herzberg studies indicate that the needs at the top of Maslow's hierarchy—self-realization or self-actualization—are those that provide the greatest basis for motivating employees toward higher levels of job performance at least among the various occupational groups that they have studied. It is possible that these groups by their very nature are highly achievement-oriented and are not typical of all job groups.[30] The factors of hygiene cannot, of course, be ignored or slighted, but their satisfaction alone apparently will not result in the attainment of the desired goals.

Evaluation of the Theory. The motivation-hygiene theory first postulated in 1959 has evoked collegial reactions ranging from elation to dismay; and it seems in recent years to have taken on overtones of a Holy Crusade with disciples, heretics and infidels, and a sacrifice of scientific method to polemics and righteous indignation.[31] Like any good theory, the motivation-hygiene theory has also stimulated a considerable amount of research as well as controversy. One review lists over 30 studies relating to this theory with personnel in different jobs at different organizational levels.[32] Most of the criticism centers around (1) the methods used to obtain information about satisfying and dissatisfying job events and to rate them, (2) failure to obtain a measure of overall satisfaction, and (3) disregard for the fact that one factor can cause job satisfaction for one person and job dissatisfaction for another person even in the same sample. Other studies of job motivation and satisfaction, however, support the theory for its contribution to an understanding of job attitudes.[33]

It is likely that research to test the implications of Herzberg's two-factor theory will continue to appear in the literature. It is suggested by some researchers, however, that only those studies that are reasonably close to Herzberg's in subject selection techniques, data collection, reduction and analysis methods, and interpretation can be considered relevant in evaluating

[29] Herzberg, Mausner, and Snyderman, *op. cit.*, pp. 113-114.

[30] Robert B. Ewen, "Some Determinants of Job Satisfaction: A Study of the Generality of Herzberg's Theory," *Journal of Applied Psychology,* Vol. 48, No. 3 (June, 1964), pp. 161-163.

[31] Steven Kerr, Anne Harlan, and Ralph M. Stogdill, "Preference for Motivator and Hygiene Factors in a Hypothetical Interview Situation," *Personnel Psychology,* Vol. 27, No. 1 (Spring, 1974), pp. 109-124.

[32] Robert J. House and Lawrence A. Wigdor, "Herzberg's Dual-Factor Theory of Job Satisfaction and Motivation: A Review of the Evidence and a Criticism," *Personnel Psychology,* Vol. 20, No. 4 (Winter, 1967), pp. 369-389.

[33] David A. Whitsett and Erik K. Winslow, "An Analysis of Studies Critical of the Motivation-Hygiene Theory," *Personnel Psychology,* Vol. 20, No. 4 (Winter, 1967), pp. 391-415.

the theory.[34] Other researchers argue that theory is method-bound if Herzberg's method must be used to replicate his results. In spite of the controversy, the theory does appear to have utility, especially in stimulating thinking and discussion of the factors affecting job satisfaction and dissatisfaction.

Job Satisfaction and Employee Behavior

At one time it was assumed that if management could provide satisfactory working conditions for its employees, all types of desirable ends would be achieved. It appears, however, that the relationship between degree of job satisfaction on the one hand and employee turnover, absenteeism, and performance on the other is not as simple as once believed. A comprehensive analysis of 20 studies of job satisfaction and employee behavior by Vroom does, however, provide some interesting generalizations.

Turnover and Absenteeism. In seven studies examined by Vroom, it was found that there is a consistent negative correlation between measures of job satisfaction and turnover. The higher an employee's satisfaction, the less likely resignation will occur. In view of the high cost of turnover in any organization, the importance of this finding should be apparent to managerial personnel. The relationship between job satisfaction and absenteeism is also negative but less consistent than it is for turnover. However, when unexcused absences from the job and frequency of absences are considered, rather than merely actual days lost, a strong relationship has been found. In other words, the employee with high job satisfaction is less likely to be absent frequently, particularly for unexcused reasons.

Job Performance. There is no simple relationship between job satisfaction and job performance. An analysis of 20 correlational studies using both supervisory ratings and objective performance measures in relation to job satisfaction revealed a large range of correlations with a median of .14. This correlation indicates that is is not possible to speak generally of any positive relationship between job satisfaction and performance.[35] This finding which is consistent with that of other research confirms that the relationship between satisfaction and job performance is not a simple one of satisfaction leading to better job performance. Lawler and Porter conclude that it is the other way around, i.e., job performance leads to job satisfaction, as shown in Figure 11-3. The quality of the employee's performance may result in the receiving of rewards that provide satisfaction. The rewards may be of an intrinsic nature, such as the "feeling of having done something worthwhile," or of an extrinsic nature, such as increased pay, a promotion, etc. Lawler and Porter conclude that management thus effects satisfaction through appropriately structuring the

---

[34] Earl B. French, Morton L. Metersky, David S. Thaler, and Jerome T. Traxler, "Herzberg's Two Factor Theory: Consistency Versus Method Dependency," *Personnel Psychology*, Vol. 26, No. 3 (Autumn, 1973), pp. 369-375.

[35] V. H. Vroom, *Work and Motivation* (New York: John Wiley & Sons, Inc., 1964), Chapter 6.

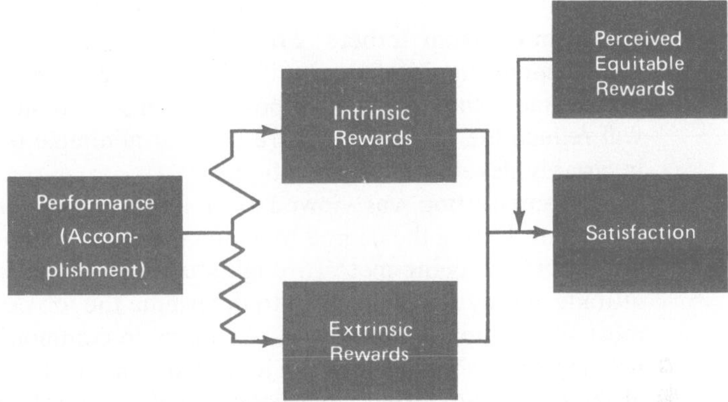

Source: Edward D. Lawler, III, and Lyman W. Porter, "The Effect of Performance on Job Satisfaction," *Industrial Relations,* Vol. 7, No. 5 (October, 1967), pp. 20-28. Reprinted with permission.

Figure 11-3 PERFORMANCE LEADS TO SATISFACTION

rewards and the ways that they will be viewed by the employee. The extent to which the employee perceives the reward to be equitable has been found to be important. If the reward is perceived as not being consistent with the rewards that others are receiving, dissatisfaction will result.[36] If it persists, such dissatisfaction may then lead the employee to reduce the effort that is put forth on the job, to be irregular in attendance, to engage in other behavior that is detrimental to the organization, and even to resign from the job. While there is yet much to be discovered about job satisfaction and its relationship to productivity, the application of what is known can contribute to the satisfaction of the individual and his or her effectiveness in the organization.

Résumé

Job performance is dependent not only upon the abilities and skills of employees but also upon their motivation. An understanding of the motivational process, including a recognition of the needs that individuals have, is essential for effective personnel management. It was observed that there are various theories of the nature of human needs but that each of them helps to contribute to knowledge of human motivation. Through an understanding of needs it is possible to determine the incentives that should be used. The incentives that may be best for an individual or a group at one time may be less desirable at another time. Employees representing different categories of personnel with educational and social backgrounds that differ

[36] Edward E. Lawler, III, and Lyman W. Porter, "The Effect of Performance on Job Satisfaction," *Industrial Relations,* Vol. 7, No. 5 (October, 1967), pp. 20-28.

significantly from others often have acquired patterns of needs that management should recognize if it is to create the proper motivational climate. Management should also take positive steps to create a work environment that will reduce the causes of frustration and minimize the conflict situations that invariably develop in organizations.

Job satisfaction was viewed as an important dimension of the motivational process reflecting the degree to which the individual perceives his or her needs and wants are being met. Through studies of individual wants, as revealed in attitude surveys, it is possible to determine the job conditions that provide the most satisfaction to employees. Contrary to common belief, however, there is no simple relationship between job satisfaction and performance. Turnover and absenteeism, however, have been found to be related to satisfaction. It has been proposed that the rewards that a person receives from his or her performance directly affect job satisfaction. Those rewards that come from management should be as consistent as possible with what the employee perceives to be the rewards that are appropriate in relation to what others receive, if satisfaction is to be experienced.

DISCUSSION QUESTIONS

1. What is the reason for different theories about the nature of human needs? Does the fact that these are different theories mean that none of them is valid?
2. Some individuals feel that attempts to motivate the employees are attempts to "manipulate" them. Is this true? What are the implications of this statement for the supervision of personnel?
3. Occasionally in a journal article a writer will state that many executives are uninformed about and even indifferent to the needs of their subordinates. Do you believe this to be true? Why or why not?
4. In an office employing 400 individuals engaged in writing insurance policies and keeping records on policies, it was announced that an electronic computer would be installed within the next few weeks and some personnel shifts would be required. Since details were not available at the time, it was stated that further information would be furnished later.
   a. How is this first announcement likely to be received by employees? What needs are likely to become predominant?
   b. What effect is the announcement likely to have on present job performance?
   c. Is this announcement likely to affect supervisor-employee relationships? How?
5. In most jobs in government the financial incentives that may be found in many business and industrial jobs are not present.
   a. What effect is this likely to have on employee behavior?
   b. How can supervisors in government agencies motivate employees?
6. What is the difference between frustration and conflict? What behavior is the supervisor likely to observe which would indicate that a subordinate is frustrated or experiencing a conflict?
7. Negativism was described in the chapter as being a common adjustment mechanism. What examples of negativism have you observed in people at work? What effect did it have on others? What steps could a supervisor take to cope with negativism in subordinates?

PROBLEM 11-1 'BIG BROTHERS' HELP HARD-CORE RECRUITS*

Lacking the extensive counseling staff which larger companies often have at their command, the executives of Homasote Company, a small New Jersey manufacturing firm, were concerned about the possible work adjustment problems ahead for an initial group of disadvantaged blacks they were considering hiring. The nature of most jobs at the Trenton firm, where insulating building board products are manufactured, does not require complex skills, so that training itself is not seen as a particularly difficult hurdle. Instead, the principal obstacle to the success of workers in their new jobs is anticipated to be the relationship between the supervisor and hard-core recruits.

Consequently, Homasote Company undertook an experimental "big brother" program to help newly-hired hard-core, unemployed persons to adjust to the life of a worker and to facilitate communication between the new worker and his supervisor. Its top management established as its goal the hiring of 10 chronically jobless individuals into the 300-person company work force, thereby hoping to make a small contribution toward solving community unemployment problems. The plan developed by the company was to assign each of the hard-core recruits to an older, more experienced worker who would serve as "big brother" during the first three months of work. Under the plan the big brothers were to act as temporary supervisors for the hard-core hires, with regular supervisors wholeheartedly agreeing to pass their orders and suggestions through them. Until the touchiest first three months were past, the big brother would be the new hire's counselor and sympathizer as well.

Selection of the big brothers did not prove to be a problem in a company the size of Homasote. The personnel director, Clement C. Marino, and other executives knew most of the employees by name and were aware of the long-service employees who would be best in getting along with the new hires. Since their support was crucial to the success of the program, the selected workers were brought together in advance and asked if they would be willing to help. Their responses were enthusiastically in the affirmative.

In practice, the relationship of big and little brother actually lasted well beyond the three months formally arranged. Homasote also discovered that the older workers played a broader role than originally expected in helping the new employees adjust. Their assistance included:

1. Getting the new hire to work. Monday mornings were particularly troublesome. By picking up their charges personally, many big brothers were able to overcome the problems of missed rides or of long trips by public transportation.
2. Orienting the new employee to the world of work. The big brother answered questions about the job, introduced the new hire to fellow workers, showed him where to find cigarettes and washrooms, etc. Every three or four weeks the big brothers reported their trainees' progress to the personnel director.
3. Bridging the communications gap. Since the foreman and the disadvantaged blacks lived in two different worlds and saw things quite differently, there was a need for interpretation. Because the big brothers were familiar with both of their worlds, they could often interpret effectively between the supervisor and the new hires.

---

* Adapted with permission from *Manpower Information Service,* Vol. 2, No. 1 (September 23, 1970). Copyright 1970 by Manpower Information, Inc., a division of The Bureau of National Affairs, Inc., Washington, D.C. 20037.

Beyond the continuing relationship with their big brothers, Homasote's new hires soon fit in with the other workers at the small, close-knit plant. Looking back on the program, company officials expressed their satisfaction with the long-term performance of the disadvantaged employees whose earliest weeks were smoothed by the big brother.

a. Why is it desirable to have big brothers or sponsors for hard-core unemployed persons who are brought into a work force?
b. What frustrations is the hard-core unemployed likely to experience in this new job?

SUGGESTED READINGS

Chruden, Herbert J., and Arthur W. Sherman, Jr. *Readings in Personnel Management,* 4th ed. Cincinnati: South-Western Publishing Co., 1976. Part 4.

Cummings, L. L. and Donald P. Schwab. *Performance in Organizations—Determinants and Appraisal.* Glenview, Ill.: Scott Foresman and Company, 1973. Chapter 3.

Davis, Keith. *Human Behavior at Work—Human Relations and Organizational Behavior,* 4th ed. New York: McGraw-Hill Book Company, 1972. Chapter 3.

Dowling, William and Leonard Sayles. *How Managers Motivate: The Imperative of Supervision.* New York: McGraw-Hill Book Company, 1971.

Gellerman, Saul W. *Management by Motivation.* New York: American Management Association, 1968.

Herzberg, F. *Work and the Nature of Man.* Cleveland: The World Publishing Company, 1966.

Herzberg, F., B. Mausner, and B. B. Snyderman. *The Motivation to Work,* 2d ed. New York: John Wiley & Sons, Inc., 1959.

Hughes, Charles L. *Goal Setting.* New York: American Management Association, 1965.

Lawler, Edward E. III. *Motivation in Work Organizations.* Monterey, California: Brooks/Cole Publishing Company, 1973.

Levinson, Harry. *The Great Jackass Fallacy.* Boston: Graduate School of Business Administration, Harvard University, 1973.

Macarov, David. *Incentives to Work.* San Francisco: Jossey-Bass, Inc., 1970.

Miner, John B. and H. Peter Dachler, "Personnel Attitudes and Motivation," *Annual Review of Psychology,* Vol. 24 (1973), pp. 379-402.

Patchen, Martin. *Participation, Achievement, and Involvement on the Job.* Englewood Cliffs, New Jersey: Prentice-Hall, Inc., 1970.

Sartain, Aaron Q., and Alton W. Baker. *The Supervisor and His Job,* 2d ed. New York: McGraw-Hill Book Company, 1972. Chapters 7 & 9.

U.S. Department of Labor, Manpower Administration. *Job Satisfaction: Is There a Trend?* Manpower Research Monograph No. 30. Washington: Superintendent of Documents, 1974.

Vroom, V. H. *Work and Motivation.* New York: John Wiley & Sons, Inc., 1964.

Williams, Whiting. *Mainsprings of Men.* New York: Charles Scribner's Sons, 1925.

Organizational Behavior

The Organizational Climate for Work

The release of human potential through the motivational process is largely dependent upon the existence of the proper conditions or climate within the organization. Every organization has a climate or personality of its own that distinguishes it from other organizations and that influences the behavior of its members. Management, therefore, should strive to create the type of climate that will permit the goals of the organization to be attained and will at the same time satisfy the psychological and social needs of its personnel. The achievement of this goal requires that top management engage continually in what is commonly referred to as *organizational development* (OD). Such development requires more than merely constructing organizational charts and detailing job responsibilities; it requires that the human dimension of the total work environment be considered. Organizational development is based upon the assumption that human resources demand equal if not greater attention than the physical resources if the organization is to function effectively. The criteria for organizational effectiveness will vary from one type of organization to another. Generally, however, these criteria may include such factors as productivity; operating efficiency; satisfaction of individual needs and wants; employee health, safety, and emotional adjustment; and the development of favorable group relationships.

There are many characteristics that distinguish one organization from another and give it a particular personality. One of these is its goals. The fact that governmental, charitable, educational, and profit-oriented organizations differ in their goals makes for different climates in these organizations. The structure of an organization, as, for example, whether it is "tall" or "flat," or whether it is line or line-and-staff, also influences the organizational climate.

Such intangibles as the methods that managers and supervisors use to direct and control the activities of their subordinates, the nature of the relationships between individuals and groups, and the interactions between persons in different levels of authority within the hierarchy are some of the other major determinants of organizational climate that will be considered in this chapter. The effect that the nature of the work itself, the size of the organization, and the quality of the physical environment have on the organizational climate will also be discussed.

APPROACHES TO MANAGING HUMAN RESOURCES

The method that managers and supervisors use to direct and control the activities of subordinates is a primary factor in determining the climate of that part of the organization for which they are responsible. In the past managers and supervisors tended to believe that employees required close supervision because they did not really want to work and it was necessary to prod them. Today such attitudes are viewed as being traditional or outdated when compared with the modern, more enlightened view of human personality that has grown out of research efforts of the behavioral scientists and has gradually filtered into the thinking of managers as well as the general public. While the extent to which employers have been influenced by modern concepts of human behavior will vary from one individual to another, an increasing number of managers recognize that the traditional views of direction and control are rapidly being replaced with modern theories that offer considerable promise for the fulfillment of individual and organizational goals. The theories of the late Douglas McGregor and of Chris Argyis and Rensis Likert have had the greatest influence on managerial attitudes.

McGregor: Theory X and Theory Y

McGregor (1960) assumed that the behavior of people is strongly influenced by their beliefs. He concluded that most business managers are *Theory X* types who believe that the average person has an inherent dislike of work, prefers to be directed, wishes to avoid responsibility, has relatively little ambition, and wants security above all.[1] This view clearly dictates that motivation will be primarily through fear and that managers or supervisors will be required to maintain close surveillance of their subordinates if the organizational objectives, and even the personal objectives of security, are to be obtained. In short, managers must protect the employees from their own shortcomings and weaknesses and, if necessary, goad them into action, as suggested by the "big boss" in Figure 12-1.

---

[1] Douglas M. McGregor, *The Human Side of Enterprise* (New York: McGraw-Hill Book Company, 1960), pp. 33-35.

Reprinted by permission of Chon Day.

Figure 12-1

The Modern View: Theory Y. According to McGregor, the Theory X approach is invalid. If managers want to improve performance and productivity, they should adopt the principles of his *Theory Y* which holds that:

1. The expenditure of physical and mental effort in work is as natural as play or rest. Depending upon controllable conditions, work may be a source of satisfaction (and will be voluntarily performed) or a source of punishment (and will be avoided if possible).
2. External control and the threat of punishment are not the only means for bringing about effort toward organizational objectives. Individuals will exercise self-direction and self-control in the service of objectives to which they are committed.
3. Commitment to objectives is a function of the rewards associated with their achievement. The most significant of such rewards, e.g. the satisfaction of ego and self-actualization needs, can be direct products of effort directed toward organizational objectives.
4. The average human being learns, under proper conditions, not only to accept but to seek responsibility.
5. The capacity to exercise a relatively high degree of imagination, ingenuity, and creativity in the solution of organizational problems is widely, not narrowly, distributed in the population.

6. Under the conditions of modern industrial life, the intellectual potentialities of the average human being are only partially utilized.[2]

Theory Y, in contrast to Theory X, emphasizes managerial leadership through motivation by objectives and by permitting subordinates to experience personal satisfaction as they contribute to the achievement of objectives.

The Theory X-Y Controversy. While McGregor has received some impressive tributes, according to Allen there are no data to support his view that most managers in business organizations were Theory X types at the time Theory Y was proposed. In order to determine the beliefs of managers today, Allen administered a questionnaire containing items central to the Theory X-Y controversy to 259 managers from 93 companies. The responses indicate that most managers today do not subscribe to the extremes of Theory X-Y; rather, they believe that both people and situations vary and that management action must vary with them. This realism is shown by their responses to five of the questions in the survey:

1. "Behavior is influenced by complex psychological, biological, social, and economic factors."	94.6% agree
2. "Most people want to do what is right, but are often blocked by characteristics of their own personalities, the influence of childhood experiences, and circumstances beyond their control."	83.2% agree
3. "People naturally tend to be more concerned with their own needs and objectives."	95.2% agree
4. "Some people lack ambition, dislike responsibility, and prefer to be led. Some are precisely the opposite, while most tend to fall somewhere in between."	71.4% agree
5. "People tend to resist change."	97.8% agree

From the findings of this study, Allen proposes a *Theory M* for management which is based on the statements listed above.[3]

Argyris's Immaturity-Maturity Theory

Many behavioral scientists have been concerned over the effects of the organizational climate on individual personality. Among those who have devoted considerable attention to this problem is Chris Argyris. He believes that organizations make demands upon its individual members that are incongruent with their needs and general orientation toward life, which essentially is to become increasingly mature. According to Argyris, the human personality in our culture exhibits developmental trends that involve progressing from immaturity to maturity. These trends from infancy to

---

[2] *Ibid.*

[3] Louis A. Allen, "M for Management: Theory Y Updated," *Personnel Journal,* Vol. 52, No. 12 (December, 1973), pp. 1061-1067.

adulthood include becoming increasingly active, being more independent of others, having deeper interests, occupying an equal or higher position in relation to peers, and developing an awareness of and control over one's self. Further, Argyris believes that organizational leaders often overlook the need of individuals to function in a mature, adult-like manner. He notes that:

> . . . we have designed organizations which have ignored individual potential for competence, responsibility, constructive intent, and productivity. We have created structures and jobs that at the lower levels alienate and frustrate the workers; lead them to reject responsible behavior, not only with impunity but with a sense of justice, and tempt them to fight the organization by lowering the quality of what they produce. . . .
>
> Problems are equally severe at management levels, where incompetent organizational structures create executive environments lacking in trust, openness, and risk taking. The attitudes that flourish best in such environments are conformity and defensiveness, which often find expression in an organizational tendency to produce detailed information for unimportant problems and invalid information for important ones. This tendency ensures ineffective problem solving, poor decision making, and weak commitment to the decisions made.[4]

Argyris has continually stressed the importance of both the organization and the individual, as well as the need for optimizing the effectiveness of both.[5]

Likert's Management Systems Theory

Another approach to building a productive and desirable organizational climate is found in a science-based management system developed by Likert and his associates at the Institute for Social Research of the University of Michigan. Basically this approach is consistent with the modern theories of McGregor, Argyris, and Herzberg (Chapter 11), but it comprises a total management system of the type discussed in Chapter 4 whose parts are mutually compatible. According to Likert, there are four different systems that may be used by the manager or supervisor: System 1, which involves an authoritative approach that is exploitative; System 2, an authorative approach that is benevolent in nature; System 3, a consultative approach; and System 4, a participative group approach. The key organizational characteristics of the different systems are defined in terms of leadership, motivation, communication, decision making, goal setting, and control processes.

System 1 involves high pressure on subordinates through tight work standards, imposes personnel and budget limitations, and obtains compliance through fear techniques. System 4, in contrast, is characterized by the manager being supportive and using group decision making and group methods of supervision—approaches that will be described in detail in the section that

---

[4] Chris Argyris, "A Few Words in Advance," in Alfred J. Marrow (Editor), *The Failure of Success* (New York: AMACOM, 1972), pp. 3-7.

[5] Chris Argyris, *Integrating the Individual and the Organization* (New York: John Wiley & Sons, Inc., 1964), p. 7.

follows. The System 4 approach produces a better organizational climate and better results in terms of productivity, costs, absences, and turnover.[6]

Likert's Organizational Profile. A considerable amount of empirical research has been carried out on the theory, mostly on organizations in the United States. More recently the theory has been tested in Brazil using the Likert *Organizational Profile*—a questionnaire that describes an organization on the dimensions of Likert's theory. One of the major findings in a study of employees in 13 Brazilian banks was that actual and ideal (Group 4) profiles were similar to those found in the United States and elsewhere: employees want participative group methods but say that their organization uses autocratic or consultative methods.[7]

Innovation of Human Resource Accounting. Likert's management systems approach emphasizes the importance of human resources in assessing the worth of an organization. Since most organizations have invested a significant amount of money in recruiting and developing their employees, the need for knowing what is happening to its investment is very important to the success of any organization. One of the features of this approach is that it recognizes the importance of *human resource accounting*. In the R. G. Barry Corporation, for example, investment in individual employees (recruiting, training, development) is carried as an asset on the company's balance sheet. Data generated by its system indicate that the replacement investment of its 96 managers is approximately $1 million, while the current "book value" is about $600,000. The firm invests around $3,000 in a first-line supervisor and upwards of $30,000 in a member of top management. The human resource accounting system provides for gathering a wide variety of data that may be used in corporate planning.[8]

A Summary of the Modern Approaches

The modern approaches to management of McGregor, Argyris, and Likert represent the viewpoints of behavioral scientists who have been closely involved in the study of organizational climates. Likert's systems approach to organizational behavior involves an integrated approach to managing human resources which takes into account the human needs and other personality characteristics emphasized by McGregor and Argyris. Consistent with the approaches of the latter two individuals, Likert's System 4 emphasizes the importance of supportive relationships and the use of group methods of supervision. The supervisor's ability to work effectively with subordinates as a group plays an important part in determining the climate for the group. There

[6] Rensis Likert, *The Human Organization* (New York: McGraw-Hill Book Company, 1967).

[7] D. Anthony Butterfield and George F. Farris, "The Likert Organizational Profile: Methodological Analysis and Test of System 4 Theory in Brazil," *Journal of Applied Psychology*, Vol. 59, No. 1 (February, 1974), pp. 15-23.

[8] R. Lee Brummet, William C. Pyle, and Eric G. Flamholtz, "Human Resource Accounting in Industry," *Personnel Administration*, Vol. 42, No. 4 (July-August, 1969), pp. 34-46.

are other factors, however, that determine the nature of the relationships within and between groups.

GROUP AND INTERGROUP RELATIONS

A group is composed of individuals, each of whom has a unique pattern of abilities, aptitudes, and personality characteristics. It soon becomes apparent to those who observe and work with various groups that a group also has its own unique personality which distinguishes it from other groups. The distinguishing characteristics of a group are the result of such factors as personalities of the individuals who comprise the group, the nature of the interpersonal relationships within the group, and the role of the group in the organization.

Within and between the work groups that have been formally organized according to the pattern of jobs and positions required for the accomplishment of the organizational mission are found subgroups that have emerged on an informal basis. Altogether these groups comprise what has already been referred to as the informal organization. In an examination of groups in an organization, attention should be given to both the groups that are formally organized by management and the informal groups. A study of the forces that are found in group behavior belongs to that area of study commonly referred to as *group dynamics*.

The study of the forces inherent in a group represents one of the more advanced areas of research in the behavioral sciences that have been explored by psychologists and sociologists with increasing interest in the years since the classic studies at the Hawthorne Plant of the Western Electric Company were conducted by Elton Mayo and his associates.[9] It is recognized by most researchers that the study of the behavior of small groups, while extremely important, presents many problems in defining the factors or variables to be studied, in measuring them, and in controlling them in relation to other factors that are part of the total group process. Nevertheless, attempts to conduct research on small groups have yielded some valuable information that has provided managers and supervisors, as well as teachers and other individuals who work with small groups, with new concepts to guide them in their leadership roles.

Leadership of Work Groups

Organizational structures provide many positions of leadership from that of chief executive down to that of the first-line supervisors. Each of these positions requires the person occupying it to exercise leadership

[9] Elton Mayo, *The Human Problems of an Industrial Civilization* (Boston: Graduate School of Business Administration, Harvard University, 1946); F. J. Roethlisberger and W. J. Dickson, *Management and the Worker* (Cambridge: Harvard University Press, 1939). See also Henry A. Landsberger, *Hawthorne Revisited* (Ithaca, New York: Cornell University, 1958).

responsibilities for such activities as making decisions, communicating orders, conducting meetings, and resolving grievances and disciplinary problems. The exact nature of these leadership responsibilities will vary according to their level in the organization and will involve different requirements that will be considered in Chapter 14. At this point the discussion will focus on first-line supervisors and their relationship to work groups. A study of work groups reveals, however, that leadership roles within the group are not limited to supervisors. Among their subordinates within the group there are likely to be individuals who lack formal authority but who function in an informal leadership role. The roles that both formal and informal leaders have in a group will determine in part the manner in which the group is to function.

Formal Leadership. The supervisor is recognized as the formal leader of the group by virtue of positional authority. Supervisory success, however, is dependent upon more than this source of authority. The University of Michigan studies reveal that the greater the supervisor's skill in using group methods of supervision, the greater the productivity and satisfaction of the work group is likely to be. In the high-producing work groups it was found that employees cooperate more and help one another in getting the work done on their own initiative. The willingness to help one another seems to come from a better team spirit and better interpersonal relationships that the supervisor has developed in the group. Likert describes the *group-centered* supervisor as follows:

> . . . endeavors to build and maintain in his group a keen sense of responsibility for achieving its own goals and meeting its obligations to the larger organization.
>
> . . . helps to provide the group with the stimulation arising from a restless dissatisfaction . . . discourages complacency and passive acceptance of the present . . . helps the members to become aware of new possibilities, more important values, and more significant goals.
>
> The leader is an important source of enthusiasm for the significance of the mission and goals of the group . . . [and] sees that the tasks of the group are important and significant and difficult enough to be challenging.
>
> As an overall guide to . . . leadership behavior, the leader understands and uses with sensitivity and skill the principle of supportive relationships.[10]

Supportive relationships with a group are similar to those used with individual employees. The supervisor may encourage the members of the group to be tolerant of the attitudes and behavior of the other members, thus creating an atmosphere in which all members are able to communicate with one another in a friendly and constructive manner. The supervisor who can develop a psychological climate that "brings out the best" in each individual and that encourages the individual to subordinate personal interests for the good of the group has achieved one of the most important objectives of supervision.

---

[10] Rensis Likert, *New Patterns of Management* (New York: McGraw-Hill Book Company, 1961), pp. 171-172.

Informal Leadership. Although the supervisor is recognized as the formal leader of the group, there may be one or more informal leaders in the group to whom the members of the group also give their allegiance. This allegiance to one or more fellow employees may result from the recognition by fellow employees of the unofficial leader's technical skill or knowledge, seniority, the type of work performed, or more frequently the ability to communicate with others and to satisfy their personal needs. The supervisor who is able to recognize the informal leaders can often develop relationships with them and, as a result, this will permit the utilization of the talents and energies of the group more effectively.

A more formal procedure for identifying informal leaders and for understanding the formation of the informal organization can be provided through *sociometry*, which is the measurement of relationships within a group. The usual procedure is to have each member of the group rank the individuals on the basis of answers to such questions as: "With which employee would you like to work? Which employee do you like the most?" or, "With whom would you most like to spend your time?" On the basis of the rankings, a *sociogram* showing the choices of individuals is prepared.[11] Once they are identified, the most effective way for management to handle informal leaders is to recognize their existence, to consider their influence, and to integrate the interests of the informal leaders and informal groups with those of the formal organization.

Role of Group Members

In examining the behavior of groups, one should not lose sight of the fact that the group is comprised of individuals each of whom has a different role. In a formalized role such as that of supervisor of a work group, the individual is expected to conform to behavior patterns that are defined by higher management. Similarly, subordinates are expected to conform to behavior patterns that are typically associated with a subordinate's role. In either role—supervisor or employee—a reasonably wide range of behavior may be considered acceptable.

In an informal group members likewise fill different roles. One person may be the leader, another may be one who fosters good feelings among the members, another may be the critic, etc. Members of the group are often assigned a role by their peers on the basis of who dominates whom. Through assertion and intimidation an accepted order of privilege, priority, and dominance may be established among the members of the group. This "pecking order," as it is commonly called, establishes a pattern that indicates the relative status of the members of the group. While members of the group usually do not verbalize it in the manner shown in Figure 12-2, they are aware of the accepted order of individuals in their group.

---

[11] B. J. Speroff, "Sociometry: A Key to the Informal Organization," *Personnel Journal*, Vol. 47, No. 2 (February, 1968), pp. 121-123.

"Don't blame me–blame Kingsley. You know the pecking order around here."

Source: Personnel (March-April, 1969), p. 22. Reproduced with permission of Sidney Harris.

Figure 12-2

Katz and Kahn have given the role concept a central place in their theory of organizational behavior.[12] Certainly the concept of role is important in understanding the behavior of supervisors. How supervisors perceive their roles in the organization will largely determine their effectiveness in leading the work group. One common fault of supervisors is their failure to perceive the nature of their role as a manager. The supervisor is ordinarily expected to perform those tasks that are typically performed by managerial personnel and not to become engaged in the same type of work as the subordinates.

Group Cohesiveness

Another characteristic of groups is their *cohesiveness,* or the extent of the loyalty of the employees toward their work group. Cohesiveness of work groups has been studied by two approaches. In one approach it is measured by the responses given by each employee to statements concerning his or her sentiments toward the group. The employee is asked questions dealing with

[12] Daniel Katz and Robert L. Kahn, *The Social Psychology of Organizations* (New York: John Wiley & Sons, Inc., 1966), p. 172.

such matters as whether the workers in the group get along together, want to stay in the group, like to stick together, enjoy helping one another, and feel that they are a part of the group. In the other approach cohesion is judged in terms of concerted group activity. Cohesive groups are those in which the members act toward a common goal. Groups that are low in cohesion are characterized by an inability to achieve a degree of unification which makes group action possible.

Factors That Influence Cohesiveness. There are several factors that influence cohesiveness. One of these is the degree of an individual's dependency on a group for need satisfaction. Another factor is size, with cohesiveness being reduced as the number of persons in the group increases. Stability is also important to cohesiveness. Wartime studies of California aircraft factories indicated that if groups were rearranged frequently then cohesiveness was reduced significantly. If groups compete with other groups, on the other hand, cohesiveness generally increases. However, excessive competition among the members of a group can reduce its cohesiveness.

Cohesiveness and Morale. Cohesiveness is the most important factor in *morale*—the condition of well-being among members of a group. Other factors determining morale are (1) the existence of goals which members of the group strive to achieve, (2) observable progress toward reaching the goals, and (3) a sense of participation among the individuals of the group in working toward the goals.[13] While "morale" is most correctly used to describe the condition of a group, it is often used in reference to individual persons. In fact, attempts to measure morale involve obtaining the opinions of the members of a group through individually administered questionnaires, interviews, and similar approaches discussed in Chapter 15. While these methods do not provide a measure of group behavior, they frequently reveal certain information pertaining to the state of morale of a group.

Conformity vs. Innovation

There is a constant struggle in organizations between the pressures for conformity and those for innovation. If it is to survive, it is necessary for an organization to require some degree of conformity through adherence to certain established procedures and policies. It is also essential, however, for an organization to encourage innovation if it is to progress. The development and implementation of new and better solutions to problems can be encouraged by the presence of an organizational climate and a positive program that will maximize the creation of new ideas.[14]

[13] Milton L. Blum and James C. Naylor, *Industrial Psychology* (New York: Harper & Row, 1968), pp. 391-413.

[14] John F. Patrick, "Organization Climate and the Creative Individual," *Public Personnel Review*, Vol. 31, No. 1 (January, 1970), pp. 31-35, as reprinted in Herbert J. Chruden and Arthur W. Sherman, Jr., *Readings in Personnel Management* (4th ed.; Cincinnati: South-Western Publishing Co., 1976), pp. 347-356.

It should be recognized, however, that innovation and conformity are also under the control of the informal groups in an organization. These groups typically have their own beliefs and attitudes toward the work, supervision, and other important matters that their members are expected to assume. Such *attitude conformity* may serve the interests of management—e.g., a group has a tradition of adhering carefully to company rules and exerts group pressure on an individual who has fallen into the habit of breaking certain rules. However, group requirements for attitude conformity may sometimes be contrary to management's interests—e.g., an employee is punished by the group for producing significantly more than the amount upon which the group has informally agreed. Although a group may influence its members to restrict production, it may also influence its members to increase production. The latter action requires understanding and cooperation between management and its employees that can most effectively be achieved through work group participation. The attitudes and skills that managers and supervisors should possess in order to have effective employee participation in deciding such matters will be discussed in Chapter 14.

Relationships Between Groups

In every organization there will be interaction between the various groups that exist within it. How to establish conditions between groups that will enhance the productivity of each and result in favorable human relations is a problem with which management is continually confronted. One of the major problems between groups to be resolved is that of handling competition. Competition sometimes may cause one group to regard a competing group as the enemy while it views itself as faultless. As a result, hostility toward the other group is likely to increase while interaction with it decreases.

It is natural for supervisors to be interested primarily in their own groups. However, every supervisor should be trained to recognize the importance of cooperation between groups in the organization. Schein suggests that the organization planner who wishes to avoid intergroup competition and conflict need not abandon the concept of division of labor but should observe the following conditions in creating and handling different functional groups:

1. Relatively greater emphasis given to *total organizational effectiveness* and the role of departments in contributing to it; departments measured and rewarded on the basis of their *contribution* to the total effort rather than their individual effectiveness.
2. *High interaction* and *frequent communication* stimulated between groups to work on problems of intergroup coordination and help; organizational *rewards given partly on the basis of help* which groups give to each other.
3. Frequent *rotation of members* among groups or departments to stimulate high degree of mutual understanding and empathy for one another's problems.
4. *Avoidance of any win-lose situation;* groups never put into the position of competing for some organizational reward; emphasis always placed on

pooling resources to maximize organizational effectiveness; rewards shared equally with all the groups or departments.[15]

THE PHYSICAL ENVIRONMENT

The climate of an organization is largely determined by management's attitudes toward people and by the nature of the relationships among employees and among groups. There are, however, other factors that contribute to the climate either directly or indirectly through their influence on human behavior. The nature and layout of the work, the size of the organization, and conditions affecting health and safety will be considered.

Nature of the Work

The nature of the work, its organization, and its flow have considerable influence on the behavior of individuals and of groups. In the assembly line, for example:

> . . . There is little in the way of a group to which the employee can belong in a meaningful way. Perhaps the most important counterweight to anonymity and lack of belonging or purpose, if they exist in a factory, is the sense of belonging to a small work group. But the development of groups requires frequent and easy interaction (i.e., some form of verbal or nonverbal communication) between the members, and this is not found on the assembly line. For one thing, the noise in many sections of the plant interferes with interaction; so does the fact that most jobs, while simple, cannot be performed automatically, requiring constant attention as they do if the operator is to keep up with the line. Most jobs are performed singly, or with only occasional help from one "partner" performing similar work on the other side of the line.[16]

The physical environment thus creates a type of climate in which employees are prevented from interacting satisfactorily because of the noise and the requirement for keeping up with the line.

An example of how the work flow affects the behavior of employees is found in a study of the restaurant industry. It revealed that there are many opportunities for friction arising primarily out of who initiates orders and to whom. Whyte reports that in one restaurant supplymen seeking to originate action (in getting food supplies) for cooks who were older, of greater seniority, more highly skilled, and much more highly paid caused friction between the two groups.[17] Another problem area was found in the relationships between waitresses and countermen. In this industry, at least, men have found it difficult to take verbal orders from women. It was found that when waitresses wrote out

---

[15] Edgar H. Schein, *Organizational Psychology* (2d ed; Englewood Cliffs, New Jersey: Prentice-Hall, Inc., 1970), p. 102.

[16] Arthur N. Turner, "Management and the Assembly Line," *Harvard Business Review,* Vol. 33, No. 5 (September-October, 1955), pp. 40-48.

[17] William Foote Whyte, *Men at Work* (Homewood, Ill.: Richard D. Irwin, Inc., 1961), pp. 125-135.

slips and placed them on top of a warming compartment that separated them from the countermen, less friction occurred. The written order in itself, however, was not enough to eliminate friction because opportunities for verbal interaction still existed. When conditions were changed so that the waitresses and the counterman actually could not see each other, there was still less friction. Finally, the spindle—the round, metal wheel on which the waitress may fasten her order and from which the cook may take the orders—(see Figure 12-3) became the solution to the problem. It can be concluded from the study, therefore, that the layout of the work, the status of the different groups that are required to interact with each other, and the manner in which orders are initiated have been found to be important factors in determining the nature of relationships among people at work.

Source: Elias H. Porter, *Manpower Development* (New York: Harper & Row, Publishers, 1964), p. 5. Reproduced with permission.

Note: The introduction of the spindle breaks up the face-to-face relation between the waitress and the cook.

Figure 12-3 THE SPINDLE

Organization Size, Shape, and Structure

Increases in the size and complexity of organizations can influence their members significantly. One of the major problems created by organizational growth is the development of feelings of alienation of the type discussed in Chapter 2. In the large organization where information is passed through many channels, individuals at either end of a communication chain feel uninformed, unable to influence their own destiny in the organization, and unable to confirm their own concepts of self, ability, and relationship. Since it is not always possible to reduce the size of organizations without taking certain economic risks, other approaches to reducing feelings of alienation must be explored.

One recommendation is that the induction of new employees include the opportunities to experience a consistent concern from people in the organization whom they trust and to permit contact with seniors who identify with the organization and who demonstrate integrity.[18] Through association with individuals who are interested in them and are able to communicate with them, the new employees may achieve the beginning of a sense of identification. It is important that the supervisor be alert to the needs of new employees and devote a reasonable period of time to developing the type of relationship that will foster mutual respect and understanding and provide for a free flow of communication.

In addition to the size, the shape of an organization (i.e., tall or flat), and the type of organizational structure (i.e., line-and-staff or functional) were shown earlier in Chapter 3 to affect the behavior of people at work and their attitudes toward their jobs and the organization.

Health and Safety

In modern society employers are expected to provide working conditions that protect the health and safety of their employees. This requires providing a work environment that safeguards employees from such hazards as atmospheric contaminants, high noise levels, unguarded machinery, radiation, and others. State laws and administrative procedures have traditionally prescribed the safeguards that must be taken by employers and have provided for inspections in order to determine compliance. In an effort to assist and encourage the states in their attempts to assure safe and healthful working conditions, Congress enacted the Occupational Safety and Health Act of 1970 (OSHA).

Administration of OSHA. Responsibilities for implementing OSHA are divided between the Department of Labor and the Department of Health, Education, and Welfare (HEW). The Department of Labor is charged with setting, promulgating, and enforcing standards for industrial safety and health. Enforcement is accomplished through the agency's authority to enter places of employment and conduct inspections for compliance purposes. Citations can be issued and penalties imposed if violations are found. HEW's major role in connection with OSHA is to undertake the research for furnishing criteria or the technical basis for developing new work place safety and health standards. Safety and health standards and regulations which are published in the *Federal Register* cover every conceivable health and safety problem for all employers engaged in business affecting interstate commerce. The act provides for the exclusion of certain groups that are covered by comparable safety and health acts.[19]

---

[18] Robert Graham and Milton Valentine, "Alienation Through Isolation," *Personnel Administration,* Vol. 32, No. 2 (March-April, 1969), pp. 17-20.

[19] Miners are covered by the Federal Coal Mine Health and Safety Act. Title IV of this act provides Black Lung benefits to coal miners and their survivors. See "The Flap over Black Lung Benefits," *Occupational Hazards,* Vol. 35, No. 2 (February, 1973), pp. 59-63. Black lung is a disabling lung disease contracted from breathing coal dust.

OSHA Standards and Regulations. The OSHA standards and regulations are published in great detail and fill many volumes. They cover standards for the work place, machinery and equipment, material, power sources, processing, as well as worker-employee standards for protective clothing and first aid and administrative requirements. Since even an outline of the standards would be too lengthy to reproduce, a list of the most frequent OSHA violations shown in Figure 12-4 provides one with an appreciation for the scope of the problem areas that are covered by the standards. An examination of the list may also serve to remind one of the potential hazards to be found off the job at home and elsewhere.

Investigations Under OSHA. Any employees (or their representatives) who believe that a violation of a job safety or health standard exists which threatens

1. Uncovered junction boxes.
2. Wiring showing at splices.
3. Lights swinging..
4. Improper solvent grounding & bonding.
5. Inadequate recordkeeping.
6. Fire extinguisher, not tested, no durable tag.
7. Fire extinguisher, not mounted, not mounted properly.
8. No first aid facilities.
9. No toilet facilities within 200 feet.
10. No washing facilities for personal cleanliness.
11. Inadequate housekeeping.
12. Misuse of compressed air for cleaning.
13. Faulty cylinder storage.
14. No properly-trained first aid personnel.
15. Gas cylinders not capped.
16. Exits not identified, exit route not identified.
17. Acetylene oxygen storage improper.
18. Workers not guarded by shields or goggles.
19. Inadequate ventilation .
20. Inadequate lighting.
21. Occupational noise exposure.
22. Failure to post the Job Safety and Health poster.
23. Misuse of electrical cords and cables.
24. Walking and working surfaces.
25. Guarding floor and wall openings and holes.
26. Scaffolding, no guardrails.
27. Machine guarding, fully enclosed.
28. Failure to red tag.
29. Aisles not designated.
30. Aisles not cleared.
31. Hand and portable powered tools not grounded.
32. Improper stacking of materials.
33. Absence of handrails.
34. Unclean toilet facilities.
35. Grinder work rest not adjusted properly.
36. Battery charging areas.
37. Wheel chocks for trailers.
38. Fans not guarded properly.
39. Dockboards not in compliance.
40. Absence of personal protective equipment.
41. Fire extinguisher not readily available.
42. Lack of illumination in stairway.
43. Deposit on sprinkler head.
44. Broken ladder.
45. Unsecured ladder.
46. Lack of signs requiring safety glasses.
47. Lack of safety shoes, glasses, and hard hats.
48. Dip tank, no fusible lid.
49. No Smoking signs not posted.
50. Ladder, no cage or wells.
51. R. R. derails not in use.
52. Safety cables and stop buttons, red.
53. Respirators not U.S. Bureau of Mines approved.

Source: National Loss Control Service Corporation, Long Grove, Illinois 60049. Reproduced with permission.

Figure 12-4 FREQUENT OSHA VIOLATIONS

physical harm, or that an imminent danger exists, may request an inspection. Where an investigation by a Labor Department safety inspector reveals a violation, the employer is issued a written citation describing the specific nature of the violation. The citation, which must be posted at or near each place where a violation occurred, fixes a reasonable time for the abatement of the violation. After issuance of a citation, the employer is notified of the penalty, if any, to be assessed. Willful or repeated violation of the act's requirements by employers may incur monetary penalties of up to $10,000 for each violation.

Record Keeping Requirements. Employers are required to keep and make available to the federal government records on certain activities and reports on work-related deaths, injuries, and illnesses. Employers may also be required to maintain accurate records of employee exposures to potentially toxic materials or harmful physical agents which are required to be measured or monitored.

The costs of keeping such records are borne by the employers, but they are minor when compared with the costs of complying with OSHA standards. For example, one estimate in the construction industry is that the law will boost construction costs anywhere from 10 to 20 percent. With construction being a $100-billion-a-year industry, one large contractor estimated a 10 percent hike would add $10 billion to the price of construction.[20] Another specialist in labor and personnel relations notes that the expense of meeting the new standards is a one-time cost producing a safer and more healthful working environment that should result in a decrease in lost wages, reduced insurance costs, lower medical expenses, and higher productivity.[21]

Personnel Problems. Since OSHA holds employers responsible for making their employees wear safety equipment, employers must engage in more safety training and be prepared to discipline employees for noncompliance with safety rules. As a result, many grievances have been filed by employees who have refused to work in unsafe conditions and who have been subjected to management discipline.[22] It is also reported that some disgruntled union personnel have filed complaints directly with OSHA and then deliberately sabotaged the employer, creating violations only minutes before the inspector arrived. Such incidents are made possible by the fact that OSHA does not provide for employee responsibility for any safety violations discovered by the OSHA inspector.[23] The burden of compliance rests solely with the employer. However, the employee does have the responsibility of complying with established safety rules, and deliberate refusal to comply becomes grounds for termination under the federal law.

---

[20] "Where the Safety Law Goes Haywire," *Nation's Business,* Vol. 60, No. 6 (June, 1972), pp. 40-47.

[21] Fred K. Foulkes, "Learning to Live with OSHA," *Harvard Business Review,* Vol. 51, No. 6 (November-December, 1973), pp. 57-67.

[22] *Ibid.*

[23] Edward J. Kehoe, "The Federal Occupational Safety and Health Act: Its Impact on Management, Safety, and Public Relations," *Public Relations Journal*, Vol. 28, No. 8 (August, 1972), pp. 25-27.

Causes of Accidents. The OSHA requirements for keeping records of work-related injuries and illnesses are desirable because all factors which led or contributed to an accident or illness should be identified and reported on prescribed forms. From such records analyses can be made and corrective action taken where causes may be identified. In some cases accidents result primarily from unsafe equipment. In others, human factors appear to be responsible.

The term *accident prone* is often used to describe those individuals who have more than their share of accidents. According to Kerr, only about 15 percent of individual accidents can be accounted for by accident proneness. This leaves 85 percent of the accidents unaccounted for. To cover the 85 percent of the accidents that cannot be explained by the accident proneness theory, Kerr proposes two theories. The first theory states that accidents tend to occur in an unrewarding psychological work environment that is not conducive to a high level of alertness. The richer the climate in economic and psychological opportunities, the higher the level of alertness. This theory proposes that if the work climate provides the freedom to set reasonably attainable goals, the workers feel themselves to be significant participants, and this in turn leads to habits of alertness, problem raising, and problem solving. Studies on the effect of psychological climate on accident behavior lend considerable support to this theory.

The second theory holds that unusual, negative, distracting stress upon the individual increases the tendency to have accidents. Negative stresses include diseases, toxic materials, temperature excesses, poor illumination, excessive noise level, and excessive physical work strain.

Kerr states that it seems wise to emphasize that both of these theories should assist in escaping the defeatism of the overemphasized proneness theory and in better understanding and controlling of accidents.[24] These theories lend further support to the importance of the organizational climate on human behavior.

Résumé

The study of an organization reveals that it has its own unique "personality" or climate that distinguishes it from other organizations. Because of the effect that the climate has on the satisfaction of the psychological and social needs of its personnel and on the attainment of the organization's goals, management should give careful attention to its quality. In order to maintain and improve the quality of the organizational climate, the forces that interact to determine it should be isolated and studied. Several forces were observed to contribute to its "personality." The primary purpose for the organization's existence, its size, and its structure play important roles in determining its uniqueness. Less tangible factors, however, have an even greater influence.

[24] Willard A. Kerr and Florence W. Dunbar, *Theory and Problems of Industrial Psychology* (Brookport, Illinois: William James Press, 1966), pp. 292-296.

The attitudes that managers and supervisors have about human personality and the methods they use to direct and control the activities of subordinates are of primary importance in determining the climate of that part of the organization for which they are responsible. While the Theory X view of human behavior is still held by some employers, the modern theories that have grown out of the research activities of behavioral scientists have had a significant impact upon the attitudes of a significant number of employers. These theories emphasize the importance of understanding human personality in order that the needs of employees and the organization may be brought into harmony in the achievement of goals that are mutually satisfying.

The relationships within and between the groups that comprise an organization also contribute to its climate. Through knowledge of the characteristics that are common to groups, supervisors should be in a better position to understand the forces that help to create the climate at their level in the organization. They should also be able to develop more effective and harmonious relationships between groups of employees. Other factors of a physical nature contribute to the climate either directly or indirectly through their influence on human behavior. Among these are the nature and layout of the work and conditions affecting employee health and safety.

DISCUSSION QUESTIONS

1. Some managers feel that effective leadership is primarily dependent upon the quality of the relationships established between the leader and the individuals in the group and that too much emphasis is given to "group relationships."
   a. What is your opinion? What support can you cite for its validity?
   b. Can you think of any jobs where the supervisor must give close attention to group relationships as well as to individuals?
2. One common fault of supervisors is their failure to perceive the nature of their managerial roles?
   a. Why does this occur?
   b. What should management do to change their perceptions?
3. Some writers have been critical of large corporations because they view them as demanding conformity from employees. Do you agree with them? What specific evidence can you cite that would support your opinion?
4. The next time you go into a restaurant, sit where you can observe the interpersonal relationships between the counterman (or cook) and the waiters or waitresses. Make a note of what you see and hear and bring it to class. (In making your observations be as objective as possible, and look for pleasant exchanges as well as unpleasant ones.)
5. When it was enacted in 1970, OSHA was heralded as the most important new source of protection for the U.S. worker in this half of the 20th century. What opinions about the effectiveness or the ineffectiveness of the act or its implementation have you heard from acquaintances who have been affected by it?
6. Describe the climate of an organization with which you have had considerable experience. Use the characteristics discussed in this chapter in your description.

PROBLEM 12-1 DON'T BOTHER ME

In a government facility employing some 60 professional engineers, there were 8 clerk-stenographers assigned to perform the clerical work. These latter personnel were in a clerical pool headed by a lead clerk who had been with the facility for about 25 years. A new chief who was assigned to the facility decided, as one of his first undertakings, to make a survey of the activities of the professional engineers and the clerks. The results of this survey revealed that all of the engineers spent a considerable amount of time performing various clerical functions such as typing, xeroxing, filing changes to manuals, making travel arrangements, etc. Apparently the lead clerk had made it clear to each engineer, when he joined the staff, that the clerks had their own work to do and that the engineers would be expected to do as much as they could to lighten the load of the clerks.

Recognizing the fallacy of having highly paid employees perform routine clerical functions, the new chief attempted unsuccessfully to change the arrangements. After six months of trying to change the lead clerk's attitude, he forced her to take an early retirement. One of the engineering positions that had become vacant was then converted to the position of office manager and staffed by a woman who was a new employee brought into the facility. The new office manager was advised that it was the responsibility of her staff to assume as much of the professional staff's clerical load as possible. These instructions were communicated to all of the clerks as a reminder of their duties and responsibilities. Some friction developed at first, but as the work load increased and additional clerical help were hired the clerical staff began to provide the services required by the engineers.

a. How was it possible for the clerks to develop the perception of their role that they possessed initially?
b. What could management have done to prevent this situation from developing?

SUGGESTED READINGS

Chruden, Herbert J., and Arthur W. Sherman, Jr. *Readings in Personnel Management*, 4th ed. Cincinnati: South-Western Publishing Co., 1976. Part 4.

Hampton, David R., Charles E. Sumner, and Ross A. Webber. *Organizational Behavior and the Practice of Management*. Glenview, Illinois: Scott, Foresman and Company, 1968.

Hodge, Billy J., and Herbert J. Johnson. *Management and Organizational Behavior—A Multidimensional Approach*. New York: John Wiley & Sons, Inc., 1970.

Katz, Daniel, and Robert L. Kahn. *The Social Psychology of Organizations*. New York: John Wiley & Sons, 1966.

Likert, Rensis. *New Patterns of Management*. New York: McGraw-Hill Book Company, 1961.

———. *The Human Organization*. New York: McGraw-Hill Book Company, 1967.

Luthans, Fred, and Robert Kreitner. *Organization Behavior Modification*. Glenview, Illinois: Scott, Foresman and Company, 1975.

Margolis, Bruce L., and William H. Kroes. *The Human Side of Accident Prevention: Psychological Concepts and Principles Which Bear on Industrial Safety*. Springfield, Illinois: Charles C. Thomas Publisher, 1975.

Mayers, May R. *Occupational Health*. Baltimore: The Williams and Wilkins Company, 1969.

McGregor, Douglas. *The Professional Manager*. New York: McGraw-Hill Book Company, 1967.

Schein, Edgar H. *Organizational Psychology*, 2d ed. Englewood Cliffs, New Jersey: Prentice-Hall, Inc., 1970.

Zedeck, Sheldon, and Milton R. Blood. *Foundations of Behavioral Science Research in Organizations*. Monterey, California: Brooks/Cole Publishing Company, 1974. Chapter 2.

Communication

Good communication is essential to the effective operation of any organization. Because of its pervasive nature, communication is often referred to as the network that binds together all of the members and activities within an organization. Through the transmission of information, ideas, attitudes, and feelings, the personnel and their activities may be coordinated in the pursuit of organizational goals and individual satisfaction. Within the organization the communication process is in action continuously between individuals and groups, both up and down and laterally.

In the past management has measured the effectiveness of its communication primarily in terms of how well it was telling its story. Currently, however, there is an increasing recognition of the importance and value of also obtaining feedback from employees. This form of communication, commonly called "two-way" communication, is the only approach to the development of mutual understanding between management and employees. Without understanding there is no communication. The achievement of mutual understanding requires that managerial and supervisory personnel be aware of the dynamic nature of the communication process and that they develop a climate that encourages the continuous exchange of information and feelings among the members of the organization. Through their efforts to establish effective formal communication and to keep communication channels open to all members, the formal organization will be strengthened and at the same time individual needs, especially for affiliation and esteem, will be satisfied.

Although their main concern will be with establishing and keeping formal communication operating effectively, managerial and supervisory personnel will find that the informal communication that develops between the members of the organization requires their attention and understanding if they are to be effective leaders. Through an awareness of the nature of such communication between employees outside of formal channels, managers and supervisors will have a better understanding of employee attitudes toward their jobs and relationships among employees, and they will be in a better position to recognize and reduce the barriers to communication. It should be noted, however, that one's effectiveness as an employee, regardless of the job, is determined in some degree by his or her ability to communicate with the supervisor, fellow employees, and others. Basically, then, effective communication is a responsibility of every person in the organization.

NATURE OF COMMUNICATION IN AN ORGANIZATION

When communication is studied within the context of organizations, it quickly assumes a complexity that permits only partial understanding and is found to be one of the most difficult organizational processes to measure.[1] Nevertheless, its importance requires that serious attempts be made to understand it as fully as possible. According to Miller,

> Communication may thus be conceived of as the dynamic process underlying the existence, growth, change, the behavior of all living systems—individual or organization. Communication can be understood as that indispensable function of people and organizations through which the organization or the organism relates itself to its environment and relates its parts and its internal processes one to the other.[2]

Behavioral scientists who study communication emphasize the *flow* of communication and the *effects* of communication. In measuring the flow they are concerned with who initiates and who receives the communication, what type of information is communicated, and which network or channel is used (and how) for communication. Networks may range from very formal, e.g., those that follow lines of authority, to very informal, e.g., those who eat lunch together. The effects of communication are usually measured in terms of attitude and performance. Communication can affect the morale of the group and attitudes that its individuals have toward their jobs, their leadership, and their peers. Likewise, individual and group performance can be affected by it.[3]

The Communication Process

In any communication there are steps through which an idea or concept passes from its inception by one person (the sender) until it is acted upon by another person (the receiver). Through an understanding of these steps and of

---

[1] Karlene H. Roberts and Charles A. O'Reilly III, "Measuring Organizational Communication," *Journal of Applied Psychology,* Vol. 59, No. 3 (June, 1974), pp. 321-326.

[2] J. G. Miller, as quoted in Lee Thayer, *Communication and Communication Systems* (Homewood, Illinois: Richard D. Irwin, Inc., 1968), p. 17.

[3] Sheldon Zedeck and Milton R. Blood, *Foundations of Behavioral Science Research in Organizations* (Monterey, California: Brooks/Cole Publishing Company, 1974), pp. 36-42.

some of the possible barriers that may occur, more effective communication may be achieved.

Steps in the Communication Process. As shown in Figure 13-1, the first step is *ideation* by the sender. This is the intended content of the message the sender wants to transmit. In the next step, *encoding,* the ideas are organized into a series of symbols designed to communicate to the intended receiver(s). Suitable words or phrases that can be understood by the receiver(s) as well as the appropriate media to be used—memorandum, conference, etc.—are selected. The third step is *transmission* of the message as encoded through selected channels in the organizational structure. The fourth step is where the *receiver* enters the process by tuning in to receive the message. If it is an oral message, failure to listen or to concentrate results in the message being lost. The fifth step is *decoding,* as, for example, changing words into ideas. At this step the decoding may not agree with the idea that the sender originally encoded because of the difference in perceptions between the receiver and the sender as to the meaning of words, or semantics. Finally, the receiver *acts* or responds by filing the information, asking for more information, or taking other action.[4] There can be no assurance, however, that communication has taken place unless there is some type of *feedback* to the sender in the form of an acknowledgment that the message was received.

Nonverbal Communication. While the preceding analysis has been in terms of the communication of verbal symbols, it should be recognized that nonverbal communication is occurring simultaneously. In face-to-face communication the

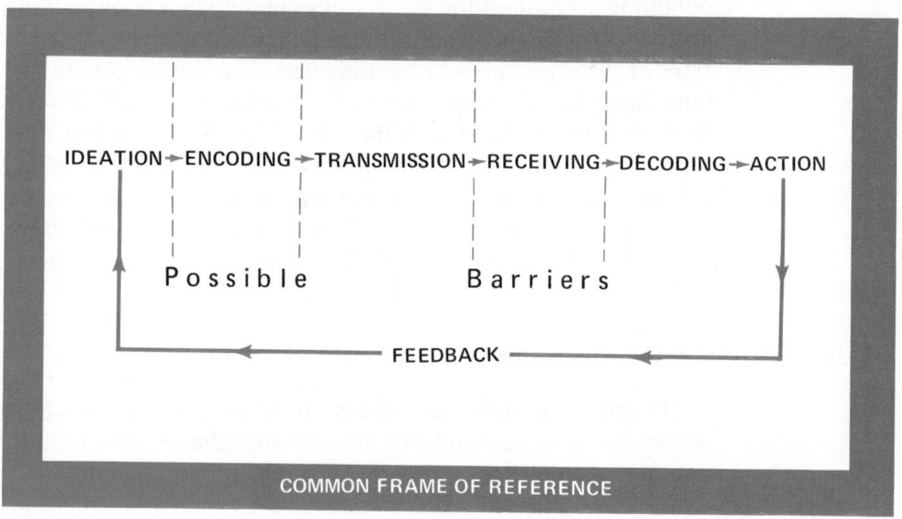

Figure 13-1 THE COMMUNICATION PROCESS

[4] Keith Davis, *Human Behavior at Work, Human Relations and Organizational Behavior* (4th ed.; New York: McGraw-Hill Book Company, 1972), pp. 386-387.

parties are also responding to facial expressions, gestures, bodily positions, and other nonverbal stimuli that are just as important to the communication process as the words that are being spoken. These expressions, gestures, and bodily positions together constitute our *body language,* as it is commonly called, and it conveys to others our attitudes and feelings.[5] Often the body language is consonant with the words being spoken. However, when it contradicts verbal communication, it tends to reduce the credibility of what one says.

Similarly, problems are created when there is a discrepancy between verbal communication and overt behavior.[6] The boss who, for example, says "My door is always open" but is invariably busy when employees request a conference is guilty of transmitting conflicting messages. Whenever the meaning of a nonverbal message conflicts with that of the verbal, the receiver is likely to find the nonverbal more believable.[7]

Requisites for Effective Communication

Communication even between friends is at best difficult and at times impossible to achieve in spite of their relationship. It may be expected, therefore, that where hierarchical relationships exist, as in an organization, and where interpersonal feelings are sometimes more negative than positive, the communication process will require even more attention and effort if it is to yield the level of understanding necessary for efficient operations. In spite of the complexity of the process, there are some fundamentals that should be heeded by managers and supervisors.

Feedback and Listening. In any communication there must be feedback from the receiver to the sender. Furthermore, the recipient must be made to feel free to respond fully. Unfortunately feedback procedures too often are established but are not utilized because managers may send out nonverbal signals of indifference or tend to listen very ineffectively to what people are saying. Listening, thus, is probably the most important and yet the most neglected dimension of communication.

Ineffective listening is not the only deterrent to keeping the feedback loop open. Recipients are sometimes embarrassed or reluctant to admit that the message is not clearly understood by them. In such instances affirmative head nodding and verbal responses do not necessarily mean that the message has been properly decoded. For this reason it is often desirable that more conclusive methods be utilized to determine whether the decoded message corresponds to the idea that is in the mind of the sender. Supervisors, for example, should encourage their subordinates to request clarification of

---

[5] Julius Fast, *Body Language* (New York: M. Evans and Company, Inc., 1970).

[6] Norman B. Sigband, *Communication for Management* (Glenview, Illinois: Scott, Foresman and Company, 1969), p. 20.

[7] An interesting theoretical and pictorial presentation of this subject may be found in Jurgen Ruesch and Weldon Kees, *Nonverbal Communication* (Berkeley and Los Angeles: University of California Press, 1956) and in James H. Campbell and Hal W. Hepler, *Dimensions in Communication* (2d ed.; Belmont, California: Wadsworth Publishing Company, Inc., 1970).

instructions whenever it is needed. Above all, they should listen carefully and acknowledge their understanding of what their subordinates are attempting to communicate to them.[8]

Sincerity. In planning communications with subordinates, managers should recognize that their sincerity or insincerity soon will become apparent. This is true not only in face-to-face relationships where nonverbal behavior may not coincide with what is said but also in other types of communication. All too often management has plans for one type of action, but in communicating its plans to the employees, management attempts to hide the nature of the action or attempts to tell the employees what it believes they want to hear. It does not take many episodes of this type for employees to question the sincerity of management's intentions. If management has a record of fair and honest dealings with employees, its communication is more likely to be accepted.

Understanding Human Needs. There is a close relationship between motivation and communication that must always be considered. Since it is human nature to listen to someone who has something to say about those things in which we are interested, management's attention to employees' needs, interests, and attitudes can go a long way toward facilitating employee receptivity. For example, the manager is very likely to have an interested audience when prospects for continued employment are discussed with employees at a time when there are rumors of widespread unemployment in the industry. Similarly, the supervisor who calls a meeting of subordinates at a time when they are "griping" about working conditions will be appealing to the needs of employees to express themselves and will thus facilitate communication and morale.

Proper Timing. The importance of the proper timing of a communication should not be overlooked. An announcement made at one time may be received enthusiastically by the employees. The same announcement made at another time may create havoc. For example, the premature announcement of the merger of two companies, both of which are considerably overmanned, is likely to create many problems. On the other hand, if the announcement is made after new contracts have been received or after arrangements have been worked out for placing excess personnel in other related jobs, it may be received and accepted more readily.

Appropriate Channels and Media. For maximum effectiveness in communication, the channels and media to be used should be appropriate. The manager may choose to use formal organizational channels, informal channels, or both. Of the media a choice may be made from various types of written or oral communication. The decision both as to channels and media should be based upon such considerations as the importance of speed, the necessity for

---

[8] For a list of obstacles to feedback to superiors, see John Anderson, "Giving and Receiving Feedback," *Personnel Administration,* Vol. 31, No. 2 (March-April, 1968), pp. 21-27.

feedback from subordinates, and knowledge of the degree of their acceptance of the communication.[9]

FORMAL COMMUNICATION

Formal communication takes place between personnel through the lines of authority that are established by management. These lines constitute the nerve system of the organization which provides the channels through which procedures and practices, job instructions and rationale, and feedback about subordinate performance are transmitted *downward* from higher management to subordinate personnel.[10] They also establish the channels through which *upward communication* occurs, i.e., subordinates can be encouraged to express their ideas, attitudes, and feelings about themselves, their jobs, organizational policies and practices, and similar matters of concern to them.

It is important that management seek to create favorable conditions including the appropriate social climate that will be conducive both to upward communication and *lateral communication*. This latter type of communication among personnel at approximately the same levels in the organization is essential in order to coordinate their activities and facilitate their interaction in the performance of their job responsibilities. A free flow of communication, downward and laterally, is dependent not only upon an organizational structure and climate that promotes effective formal communication but also upon the use of media that are most appropriate for different levels in the organizational structure.

Written Communication from Management

It is essential that methods be established so that top and middle management personnel are able to communicate effectively with subordinate personnel as well as among themselves, and that personnel at lower levels also are able to communicate among themselves. While managers at all levels will make considerable use of oral media, most of their communication will be through the written word.

The personnel department, like other staff departments, will ordinarily be responsible for preparing communications that are essential to the performance of its functions. A few of the written media that relate directly to the personnel program will be considered below.

Job Descriptions and Procedural Manuals. One of the most important media for communication with the employee is the job description. It enumerates in detail the duties that the employee is expected to perform, the equipment to be used, and other important information necessary for successful job

[9] Arlyn J. Melcher and Ronald Beller, "Consideration in Channel Selection," *Academy of Management Journal,* Vol. 10, No. 1 (March, 1967), pp. 39-52.

[10] Daniel Katz and Robert L. Kahn, *The Social Psychology of Organizations* (New York: John Wiley & Sons, Inc., 1966), p. 239.

performance. Manuals in which operating procedures and rules and regulations are described should be made available to employees in order that a reasonable degree of uniformity, efficiency, and safety may be achieved.

Handbooks. Handbooks are often used to convey information of immediate concern to the employee. Employee services, sick leave provisions, insurance coverage, stock ownership plans, and other benefits are usually described in detail. An authoritative and condensed discussion of these topics is not only valuable to the employee but management may also reach the employee's family through this medium, thereby increasing their understanding of and appreciation of the organization.

Newspapers and Magazines. A widely used medium for downward communication within an organization and for reaching the families of employees is the newspaper or magazine, sometimes referred to as the *house organ*. News about employees and their families is still the backbone of many internal publications, but the trend is toward transmitting information that is vital to the continuing, efficient operation of the organization. According to Tingey, a successful publication is one that reports on internal technological matters, the internal social environment, the external environment (free enterprise system, inflation, taxation, productivity), and the organization's social responsibilities and dynamics.[11]

Most employee publications in the United States do not adequately cover items of worker discontent. In Sweden, however, the Swedish Employers Federation has encouraged an open press which employees have used to express their opinions on vital matters. The personnel manager of a large shipyard is quoted as saying,

> "We have learned it's a lot better that criticism about the company come out in the open and up for discussion than having people go around grumbling and discontented. Nothing stops the workers or the union from saying what they think, but nothing stops me from coming back with a reply."[12]

Written Communication from Employees

Most of the communication between employees and management will take place through face-to-face communication. It is important, however, that procedures be established whereby an employee is able to communicate with higher management on matters of personal concern. In addition to correspondence and grievance procedures, the following methods may be used to facilitate upward communication.

The Question Box. One type of communication program, sometimes referred to as the *Question Box,* provides employees with a system for obtaining

---

[11] Sherman Tingey, "Six Requirements for a Successful Company Publication," *Personnel Journal,* Vol. 46, No. 10 (November, 1967), pp. 638-642.

[12] "Letting Workers Let Off Steam," *Business Week,* (April 28, 1973), p. 112.

answers to their questions from management. IBM, for example, has established a "Speak Up Program," which is designed to provide answers to complaints, comments, and questions. Employees use a special form that is mailed directly to the home office. If an employee signs the form, an answer is mailed directly to the employee's home. Employees are also given an opportunity to indicate a preference for discussing the matter with a qualified person. IBM has found that over 90 percent of the letters received are signed and about 8 percent ask for interviews.[13] While this medium for communication bypasses the individual's superior, it does insure that employees will receive answers to questions for which the supervisor may not be able to obtain the answer.

The Suggestion Program. The *suggestion program* is a type of upward communication that is widely used to stimulate participation of employees in the larger and more important aspects of the operations by rewarding them for suggestions that may be used to benefit the organization. The suggestions may cover such areas as work methods and procedures, equipment design, safety devices, and other matters related to the effectiveness of the organization. In order for the program to be successful, the support of managers and supervisors is essential. They should recognize the importance of receiving new ideas and make every effort to insure that employees do not develop a reluctance to participate for fear of ridicule or falling into disrepute with management. The message in the cartoon (Figure 13-2) reflects the feelings that employees sometimes develop about a suggestion program.

Face-to-Face Communication

Modern organizations require extensive use of face-to-face as well as written communications. Face-to-face communication not only is faster but it permits immediate feedback to occur by enabling the participants to indicate the extent of their information and to suggest alternative actions. Such communication is essential in an age of rapidly changing technology where many minds can contribute to the solution of complex problems and where individuals are able and expect to participate in problem-solving or decision-making sessions. The more common types of face-to-face communication are those that take place between superiors and subordinates and in committee meetings and conferences.

Superior-Subordinate Communication. The communication that occurs between superiors and subordinates is probably the most important because of its effect on the subordinate's attitudes and behavior. Communication can be used (1) to advise subordinates what is to be done, (2) to increase goal aspirations and hence motivation, (3) to communicate the consequences of their performance to employees, and (4) to provide for employee feedback to

[13] International Business Machines, *Fact Book on Speak Up!* (Armonk, New York: International Business Machines, Publications Services Department, January, 1969).

Courtesy of Publishers-Hall Syndicate.

Figure 13-2

management.[14] Communication can also be used to advise subordinates on matters that are of interest and concern to them, and to counsel with them on problem situations. In order to meet these responsibilities, the superior is required to have or to know where to get complete and accurate information, as well as the ability to transmit it, and the facility for listening for facts and feelings. Furthermore, the superior must also constantly "listen" for the other person's nonverbal communications.[15]

By becoming a good listener and encouraging subordinates to communicate fully, the superior will have a better opportunity to obtain the type of information that is needed. The information from subordinates may include that pertaining to problems or difficulties as they relate to accomplishing the work, their feelings and attitudes toward the organization and the department, as well as ideas and suggestions to improve the overall operations.[16]

Committees. Upward, downward, and lateral communication may be facilitated through the use of committees of the type discussed in Chapter 3.

---

[14] L. L. Cummings and Donald P. Schwab, *Performance in Organizations—Determinants and Appraisal* (Glenview, Illinois: Scott, Foresman and Company, 1973), pp. 51-52.

[15] Norman B. Sigband, "Listen to What You Can't Hear," *Nation's Business*, Vol. 57, No. 6 (June, 1969), pp. 70-72.

[16] Burt K. Scanlan, "Improving Organizational and Personal Communication," *Supervision*, Vol. 32, No. 6 (June, 1970), pp. 3-6.

The success of committees, however, is largely dependent upon the ability of both the membership and the chairperson to handle their assignments. In one organization where the leadership of committees is rotated among the members of committees, the following suggestions have been developed.

1. Never compete with the group members.
2. Listen to the group members.
3. Don't permit anyone to be put on the defensive.
4. Use every member of the group.
5. Keep the energy level high.
6. Keep the members informed about where they are and what is expected of them.
7. Keep your eye on the expert.
8. Remember that you are not permanent.
9. Do not manipulate the group.
10. Work hard at the technique of chairmanship.[17]

In conducting committee as well as other types of meetings, the individual who has the chairperson's role should use a leadership style that fits the purpose of the meeting or a given portion of the meeting. The leadership style to be used when the purpose of the meeting is to give information should be different from that used to collect information or to sell the members on a decision that the leader has already reached. Figure 13-3 illustrates varieties of communication that are possible between a leader and the members of the group.

Conferences. The committee and the conference are similar types of meetings with the exception that the committee implies a more or less stable membership and some regularity in meeting. The conference, on the other hand, usually is a one-time or infrequent meeting called in order to keep people informed, to solve problems and make decisions, to consult and ascertain attitudes, and to provide a participation medium and climate.

The face-to-face contact in conferences enables the participants to achieve a level of understanding that is not possible with the written word or with the information or instructions passed through many intermediaries. As in a committee, the members are in a position to consider each other's ideas, to weigh the pros and cons of each suggestion, and to arrive at a decision in which each member has played a part.

INFORMAL COMMUNICATION

Informal communication takes place between persons in an organization whose relationship to one another may be independent of their authority and job functions. It occurs as the result of their desires to socialize and to pass on information that they believe their colleagues may not possess. While these

[17] George M. Price, "How to Be a Better Meeting Chairman," *Harvard Business Review,* Vol. 47, No. 1 (January-February, 1969), pp. 98-108.

Your leadership style should fit the purpose of the meeting

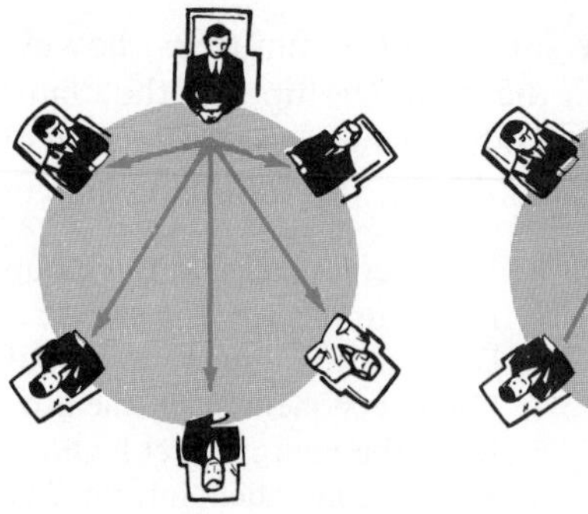

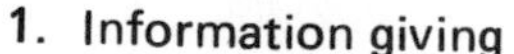

1. Information giving

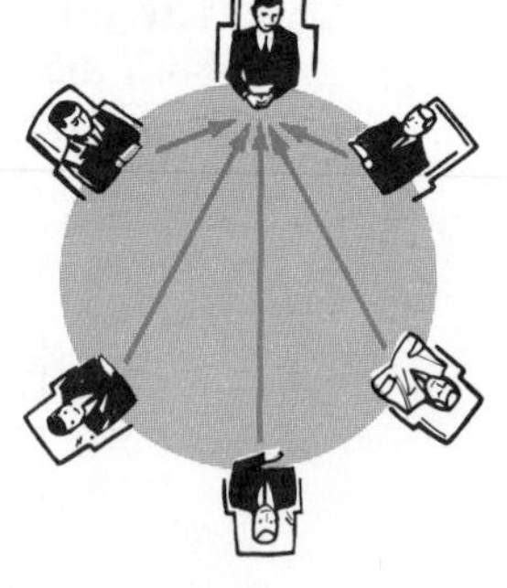

2. Information collecting

3. Decision making

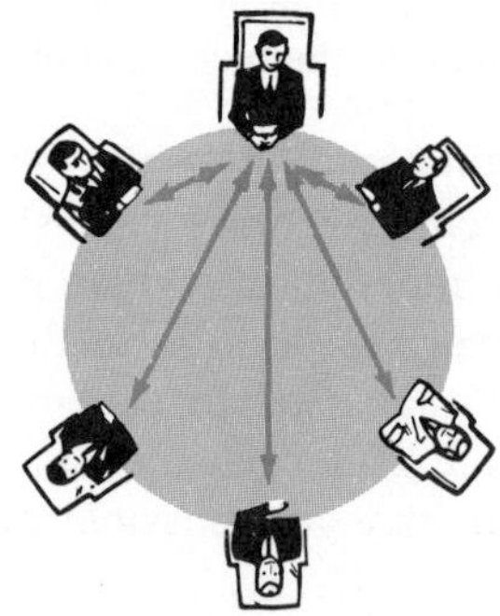

4. Decision selling

5. Problem solving

Reprinted with special permission of *Factory* (April, 1960). Copyright Morgan-Gramppian, Inc., 1960.

Figure 13-3 DIFFERENT MEETINGS REQUIRE DIFFERENT LEADERSHIP STYLES

contacts follow patterns that are independent of the formal organizational structure, they nevertheless provide an important channel of communication, frequently referred to as the *grapevine* because it fans out through the organization without regard to the formal structure or channels of communication.

Charting Informal Communication

Informal communication in an organization provides clues as to whether or not the formal communication channels are functioning effectively. By studying informal communication, adjustments may be made in the formal organization to facilitate communication and the achievement of organizational objectives. One approach to studying informal communication is to observe the composition of informal groupings of employees. The superior can usually notice who talks with whom during free periods, which persons eat lunch together, and other types of contacts in which there is communication. A more formalized approach is to use sociometric techniques that were discussed in Chapter 12. Through an awareness of such preferences in interpersonal relationships, a supervisor may develop an understanding of the nature of the communication that flows among the individuals and its effect on their attitudes toward their jobs, the work group, and the organization.

Coping with the Grapevine

In most instances the grapevine provides for a rapid transmission of information and misinformation and, therefore, presents a challenge to the planned communication of management. According to Hershey, however, there are some controls that can be used to minimize the number and severity of rumors that are passed from one person to another over the grapevine. He recommends:

> . . . keeping the channels of communication open, presenting positive and truthful facts about all topics, and thus building faith in the credibility and source of management communication. Since communication processes are so imperfect, managers should attempt to analyze rumors, understand them, and take positive steps to prevent their occurrence.[18]

Since the grapevine satisfies a need that employees have for communication, it can have some positive value to the organization. Because of the limited research information concerning the grapevine and the difficulty of making generalizations about its operation, however, its value must be determined by studying it in each individual organization.[19]

BARRIERS TO COMMUNICATION

While there are several avenues by which understanding may pass from one person to another as well as many media for promoting understanding, these avenues and media do not necessarily lead to the desired goal. The groupings of people into a complex organization impose additional conditions and factors affecting human relationships which may constitute potential barriers to communication. In order for communication to be effective, it is essential for the manager or supervisor to recognize these potential barriers and to plan communication so that these barriers may be overcome or at least minimized.

Differences Between Individuals

A major barrier in communicating with large numbers of individuals in an organization is the simple fact that no two individuals are alike. Individuals are born with different potentialities; they have had different experiences

---

[18] Robert Hershey, "The Grapevine—Here to Stay But Not Beyond Control," *Personnel,* Vol. 43, No. 1 (January-February, 1966), pp. 62-66.

[19] Harold Sutton and Lyman W. Porter, "A Study of the Grapevine in a Governmental Organization," *Personnel Psychology,* Vol. 21, No. 2 (Spring, 1968), pp. 223-230.

during their childhood and youth, and as adults they have had employers and supervisors who have exerted a variety of influences upon them.

Differences in Perception. One result of prior experiences is that each employee brings to the job his or her own unique way of looking at things, or, in other words, a personal *frame of reference*. This frame of reference determines the way in which whatever is seen or heard will be interpreted. If, for example, the supervisor is perceived as a "parent figure," the employee may accept or reject everything the supervisor says, depending upon personal experiences. Similarly, employees who have been "let down" by previous supervisors are likely to view a new supervisor as someone not to be trusted.

Differences in Age. Older persons, i.e., anyone over 30 according to many young people, often find it difficult to "tune in" on the same wavelength or frame of reference of youth and thus have problems in communicating with them. Managers and supervisors should learn enough about each individual to know what meaning will be applied to their messages and what emotional overtones will be inferred. Feedback in a live interview is the key to open communication. In communicating with young people it is essential to remember that they are not only of a different generation biologically but communication-wise may be several generations away. The consensus of authorities is that a "generation" is now about five years.[20] As a result of technical changes and the rapid development and dissemination of knowledge, the ability to communicate with individuals whose training is of an earlier period is made more difficult.

Differences in Emotional States. Closely tied to perception and influencing it are the motivational and emotional states of the individual. The manner in which an individual interprets a situation will be largely influenced by one's condition at the moment. Haire points this out in a vivid example:

> During World War II, an aerial-gunnery student was taking a training flight over the Gulf of Mexico. The pilot, enjoying the ride and the scenery, pointed over the side of the plane, in a friendly spirit, to call the student's attention to a speedboat below. The gesture was clear to him, but the student referred it to his own acute terror of being in the air, and interpreting it to mean that his worst fears were realized, he parachuted over the side.[21]

Such misinterpretations frequently occur in the supervisor's attempts to communicate with employees where perceptions, motivations, and emotions of the sender and receiver are subject to continuous interactions. It has been suggested that one way to understand communication is to view it as a people process rather than as a language process. One way to improve communication is to reduce the defensive behavior that occurs when an individual is threatened.

---

[20] Thomas F. Stroh, *Managing the New Generation in Business* (New York: McGraw-Hill Book Company, 1971), pp. 103-119.

[21] Mason Haire, *Psychology in Management* (2d ed.; New York: McGraw-Hill Book Company, 1964), p. 91.

Differences in Listening Ability. We can learn more about how the world looks to others or what motivational and emotional states they may be experiencing by *listening*. In addition, Carl Rogers suggests going one step further. Instead of following our natural tendency to judge, to evaluate, to approve (or disapprove) the statement of the other person, we should listen *nonevaluatively*.[22] This means that we should try to understand the other person's frame of reference or point of view; and once this is achieved, we have then overcome a major barrier to communication and mutual understanding is possible. Nonevaluative listening fosters understanding by encouraging the other person not only to listen more carefully but to present more information. When the other person experiences the openness and freedom of a nonthreatening environment, that person may also have a clearer perception of what he or she is saying.[23]

Differences in Interpretation (Semantics). Words, like gestures, can be interpreted in various ways thus creating a barrier to communication. Since there is not necessarily a connection between the symbol (the word) and what is being symbolized (the meaning), the communication may be received quite differently than was intended. The word "profit," for example, to the executive may represent a measure of success and a return deserved by a company; whereas to the employee it may represent some of the funds that he or she should have received in the form of higher wages. In selecting words the communicator should consider the audience and its likely interpretation of the words being used.

The general semanticists who are concerned with more than the meanings of words point out that the structure of our language leads to misrepresentation of the true nature of events.[24] People have a propensity for thinking in terms of opposites. For example, an employee is either lazy or industrious, guilty or innocent, or can or cannot accept authority. But even when there are words to describe degrees of laziness, innocence, and the many other behaviors with which managers are concerned, there is a tendency to use "either-or" thinking and language. For a more scientific approach to describing human behavior and thus for more effective communication, it is essential that more precise language be used and either-or descriptions avoided.

Difference in Status. The position of the individual in the organizational structure will also influence the quality of communication that takes place. Persons of equal status, such as two supervisors, will probably find it easier to share information and feelings than a supervisor and a subordinate. In the latter instance, the differences in rank in the organizational hierarchy can create barriers.

---

[22] Carl R. Rogers and F. J. Roethlisberger, "Barriers and Gateways to Communication," *Harvard Business Review,* Vol. 30, No. 4 (July-August, 1952), pp. 46-52.

[23] Norman B. Sigband, "Listen to What You Can't Hear," *op. cit.*

[24] Gerald H. Graham, "Improving Superior-Subordinate Relationships Through General Semantics," *Public Personnel Review,* Vol. 30, No. 1 (January, 1969), pp. 36-41.

Dilution of Information. A careful study of the communication efficiency of 100 representative business and industrial organizations reveals a tremendous loss of information as it passes from the board of directors downward through channels. It was found that by the time information had flowed downward through channels the plant manager had received only 40 percent of what had been transmitted to him, and the general supervisor had received 30 percent. An average of 20 percent of the communication sent downward through the five levels of management finally reached the worker level.[25] Thus, in downward communication every effort must be made by executive and managerial personnel to reduce the amount of unnecessary *dilution* of information that takes place in order that subordinates may have as much information as possible for intelligent and enthusiastic job performance.

Filtering of Information. When communicating with superiors, on the other hand, subordinates are even more likely to give only partial information and will frequently color events in such a manner as to conceal mistakes, failures, and other types of news that the boss may find unpleasant. This conscious manipulation of the ''facts'' to color events is called *filtering*. It is motivated primarily by the subordinate's desires to appear competent in the eyes of the boss because the boss controls and evaluates the subordinate's performance. Because of its effects on the success of the organization, management should take positive steps to reduce filtering as much as possible. Some large organizations have established special ''audit groups'' to improve the quality of information transmitted in the system. The audit groups monitor communications in the organization and report directly to higher command levels.[26]

Barriers Created by the Psychological Climate

Organizations, like individuals, have "personalities." One organization may be permissive in that individuals have the freedom to express themselves and are encouraged to participate in many of the important activities. Another organization may be autocratic, that is, individuals are expected not to express their opinions and are otherwise discouraged from engaging in participative activities except in rare instances. In one company or department may be found individuals who are cheerful and friendly because the boss is relaxed; whereas in another company or department individuals are disgruntled and uncooperative primarily because of a neurotic boss. Thus, the setting or climate in which individuals work influences their attitudes and behavior as well as the effectiveness of communication in the organization.

Personalities of Managers. Members of top and middle management can influence communication considerably. Their perceptions of their own roles and their attitudes and sensitivity toward subordinates are important factors in

---

[25] From a booklet published by Savage-Lewis, Inc.

[26] William G. Scott and Terence R. Mitchell, *Organizational Theory: A Structural and Behavioral Analysis* (Rev. ed.; Homewood, Illinois: Richard D. Irwin, Inc., 1972), pp. 159-161.

their own ability to communicate. Members of top management in many large organizations have found that, in addition to being skilled in communication themselves, it is desirable for them to have a communication specialist who may continuously assess the quality of communication in their organizations and suggest steps that may be taken to improve it.[27] Unfortunately such specialists, in their zeal to please management, often ignore the relationship between the communication practices of an organization and their impact on the feelings of dignity and self-worth of the organization's members.[28]

Effect of Special Groups upon Climate. Within an organization there may be special groups or subgroups composed of individuals of various professions or occupations which have different value systems. Their differing values create barriers to communication that are frequently impossible to overcome. The accountants, for example, may not understand the attitudes that the research people have toward fiscal matters, just as the lawyers may not be able to understand the executives' attitudes toward government regulation of business. Differences in backgrounds and in the developing of "occupational personalities" may thus have profound effects on communication within the organization.

Barriers in the Mechanics of Communication

The barriers to communication that have been discussed represent those that are usually more difficult to overcome because they involve surmounting the idiosyncracies of human personalities or complex interrelationships of people in groups. Another category of barriers that is somewhat easier to hurdle includes those that are due to lack of proper facilities or means of communication. Included in this group are those due to deficiencies in planning, clarity, and reading skills.

Lack of Definite Plans. In spite of the fact that the formal structure of the organization should be followed in communicating orders and information, it is fairly common for confusion to arise over the simple mechanics of who will do the communicating and when. If, for example, new work methods are to be introduced, should the announcement come from the president or the vice-president in charge of production? From there and on down the organizational structure, consideration should be given as to who will handle the various matters to be considered in relation to the change. Coordination between executives and managers is essential to having a presentation that will be complete and in proper focus in relation to the total operation of the organization.

Lack of Clarity. Regardless of the educational or intellectual levels of the persons with whom one is attempting to communicate, understanding is less

---

[27] Frederick M. Nathan, "Staff Role in Communication," *Personnel Administration,* Vol. 32, No. 4 (July-August, 1969), pp. 59-62.

[28] Richard V. Farace and Donald MacDonald, "New Directions in the Study of Organizational Communication," *Personnel Psychology,* Vol. 27, No. 1 (Spring, 1974), pp. 1-19.

likely to occur if the material presented is not clear. Both the spoken and the written word may be misunderstood if the communicator uses words of many syllables or uses long, complex sentences. This type of speaking or writing has been labeled *gobbledygook* and should be eliminated through training and experience in plain talk and writing. The absurdity of gobbledygook is illustrated by a story about a plumber who was trying to communicate with a government agency in Washington.

> A New York plumber wrote the Bureau that he had found hydrochloric acid fine for cleaning drains, and was it harmless? Washington replied: "The efficacy of hydrochloric acid is indisputable, but the chlorine residue is incompatible with metallic permanence."
>
> The plumber wrote back that he was mighty glad the Bureau agreed with him. The Bureau replied with a note of alarm: "We cannot assume responsibility for the production of toxic and noxious residues with hydrochloric acid, and suggest that you use an alternate procedure." The plumber was happy to learn that the Bureau still agreed with him.
>
> Whereupon Washington exploded: "Don't use hydrochloric acid; it eats hell out of the pipes!"[29]

Many organizations have improved their communication by following the suggestions of Rudolf Flesch who has developed methods for improving the readability of written material.[30] There is still considerable room for improvement, however. In one analysis by Davis of employee handbooks in 29 organizations that were written in 1949 and 1964, the average improvement in readability was quite small. Those employers who had the most readable handbooks in 1949 also had the most readable ones in 1964. Only 11 of the 29 handbooks, analyzed by the Flesch formula, were found to be sufficiently readable to reach those who lacked a college degree and who constitute the majority in most organizations.[31]

Lack of Reading Skill. While clarity of communication may be improved, barriers may still exist in the form of individual deficiencies in reading skills. Those who for one reason or another do not have the level of reading comprehension required for handling various types of communication are often at a disadvantage. By detecting such deficiencies through tests at the time of employment and by conducting special reading improvement programs, the skill levels may be improved. In fact, even good readers can learn to read faster and with greater comprehension through training.[32] Many organizations sponsor or encourage attendance at such programs as a part of their communication improvement program.

---

[29] From *Power of Words,* Copyright 1953, by Stuart Chase. Reprinted by permission of Harcourt Brace Jovanovich, Inc.

[30] *The Art of Plain Talk* (1946), *The Art of Readable Writing* (1949), *How to Test Readability* (1951), and *How to Make Sense* (1954) (New York: Harper & Brothers).

[31] Keith Davis, "Readability Changes in Employee Handbooks of Identical Companies During a Fifteen-Year Period," *Personnel Psychology,* Vol. 21, No. 4 (Winter, 1968), pp. 413-420.

[32] Francis P. Robinson, *Effective Study* (4th ed.; New York: Harper & Row, 1970), especially Chapter 10; and Wayne Otto and David Ford, *Teaching Adults to Read* (Boston: Houghton Mifflin Company, 1967).

Other Barriers. The choice of media is often a barrier to communication. If persons who need to have information are not on the routing list or if they are not readily reached through one type of media, communication may suffer. The format for written communication may also be a barrier. Some persons, unless instructed, may assume that a mimeographed document is not as important as one that is individually typed; whereas in many instances the reverse is true. Similarly, the misuse or overuse of a medium may cause people to ignore what comes over it, for they may come to have attitudes such as "it's not important" or "just more of the same." These and the other barriers mentioned need to be avoided if communication is to be effective.

Résumé

The life of an organization is found in the people who occupy the positions and in the communication that they have with one another. If there is a free flow of information and attitudes from one person to another and from one level to another in the organizational hierarchy, the organization will most likely be strong and productive. If, on the other hand, communication is blocked at many points and information and attitudes fall on "deaf ears," the whole structure may be nothing more than a hollow shell pictured by names in boxes on an organizational chart. The chart has meaning only when the persons occupying the positions are able to interact successfully with one another in the accomplishment of the organizational objectives.

Effective communication is dependent upon all of the persons in an organization, particularly managers and supervisors whose responsibility it is to develop a climate in which communication can flow freely. Their ability to make use of feedback, to understand human needs, and to select the appropriate channels and media largely determines the success of their communications with subordinates. In modern organizations communication is viewed as a two-way process which requires the establishment of procedures that will facilitate upward communication. While provision should be made for subordinates to communicate with higher management in writing, the most important type of communication is that which takes place on a face-to-face basis between superiors and subordinates. The effectiveness of communication at this level is essential to the well-being of the organization.

In its effort to develop and improve formal communication, management should not overlook the important role that informal communication plays in the organization. Understanding its role and being aware of the paths it takes can provide a basis for improving formal communication and even for making changes in the organization itself so that communication barriers may be reduced. Barriers to communication, however, are inevitable. The many differences that exist between individuals, the psychological climate of the organization, and the lack of proper facilities are always influencing communication. Minimizing the effects of the barriers requires continuous attention by managers and supervisors if the communication process is to bind the members of the organization together.

DISCUSSION QUESTIONS

1. Many Americans are not good listeners.
   a. How do you account for this fact?
   b. What effect may this deficiency have on an individual's progress in a job and in other areas of life?
   c. What can one do to improve his or her listening ability?
2. In our everyday language, especially when we talk about people, we use labels such as "businessman," "union leader," "good-looking secretary," "blue-collar worker," etc. What effect does this have on communication? Does the use of these labels facilitate or hinder communication? Explain.
3. The late Neil McElroy, once Chairman of the Executive Committee of the Board of the Procter & Gamble Company, in a talk before a meeting of the National Industrial Conference Board said: "Starting with the foremen, we insist that each member of supervision be wholly responsible for that portion of the operation assigned to him. If questions are to be answered, he answers them. If company news is to be passed along, he tells it to his people. He is the Company management to the people under him."
   a. What is your opinion of this policy?
   b. What does it assume about the communication skills of foremen?
   c. What effect would it have on the formal organization of the company?
4. In some organizations supervisors are encouraged to assist employees in their preparation of suggestions to be submitted to management, and the supervisor as well as the employee is rewarded for suggestions that are accepted. How would this procedure affect the quality of communication in an organization?
5. What problems have you experienced in your attempts to communicate with individuals who are younger or older than you? Have you been able to make any improvements in such communication? What approaches have you used?
6. In a Ph.D. dissertation at Yale University, A. F. Wessen reported that in one large hospital 75 percent of the doctors' conversations were with other doctors, 60 percent of the nurses' conversations were with other nurses, and 60 percent of the conversations of the workers of other groups tended to be with others in their own groups.
   a. How do you account for these findings? Do you believe they are typical only of hospital personnel?
   b. What significance do they have as far as the attainment of organizational objectives are concerned?
   c. What action could be taken to encourage greater interaction among personnel of different groups?
7. Many companies make arrangements for their executives and managers to attend special courses devoted to improving reading speed and comprehension. How would this action benefit a company? What is there about the nature of modern management that necessitates such action?
8. How is the internal communication of a company related to its communication with customers and the community? Discuss.

PROBLEM 13-1 FACTS AND INFERENCES*

Read the following story and take for granted that everything it says is true. Read carefully because, in spots, the story is deliberately vague. Don't try to memorize it since you can look back at it at any stage.

Then read the numbered statements about the story and decide whether you consider each one true, false, or questionable. Circling the "T" means that you feel sure the statement is definitely true. Circling the "F" means you are sure it is definitely false. Circling the "?" means you cannot tell whether it is true or false. If you feel doubtful about any part of a statement, circle the question mark.

Take the statements in turn, and do not go back later to change any of your answers. Do not reread any of the statements after you have answered them. Such altering or rereading will distort the test.

---

* From the "Uncritical Inference Test" by William V. Haney. Copyright 1961. Reproduced with permission of William V. Haney.

The Story

John Phillips, the research director of a midwestern food products firm, ordered a crash program of development on a new process. He gave three of his executives authority to spend up to $50,000 each without consulting him. He sent one of his best men, Harris, to the firm's west coast plant with orders to work on the new process independently. Within one week Harris produced a highly promising approach to the problem.

Statements About the Story

1. Phillips sent one of his best men to the west coast plant .... T F ?
2. Phillips overestimated Harris's competence .... T F ?
3. Harris failed to produce anything new .... T F ?
4. Harris lacked authority to spend money without consulting Phillips .... T F ?
5. Only three of Phillips' executives had authority to spend money without consulting him .... T F ?
6. The research director sent one of his best men to the firm's west coast plant .... T F ?
7. Three men were given authority to spend up to $50,000 each without consulting Phillips .... T F ?
8. Phillips had a high opinion of Harris .... T F ?
9. Only four people are referred to in the story .... T F ?
10. Phillips was research director of a food products firm .... T F ?
11. While Phillips gave authority to three of his best men to spend up to $50,000 each, the story does not make clear whether Harris was one of these men .... T F ?

Discussion Questions

a. Why is it important to distinguish between facts and inferences?
b. In what ways can executives use their knowledge about facts and inferences in communications with subordinates?

SUGGESTED READINGS

Bassett, Glenn A. *The New Face of Communication*. New York: American Management Association, 1968.

Breth, Robert D. *Dynamic Management Communications*. Reading, Massachusetts: Addison-Wesley Publishing Company, 1969.

Chruden, Herbert J., and Arthur W. Sherman, Jr. *Readings in Personnel Management*, 4th ed. Cincinnati: South-Western Publishing Co., 1976. Part 4.

Davis, Keith. *Human Behavior at Work, Human Relations and Organizational Behavior,* 4th ed. New York: McGraw-Hill Book Company, 1972.

Haney, William. *Communication and Organizational Behavior, Text and Cases*. Homewood, Illinois: Richard D. Irwin, Inc., 1972.

Hay, Robert D. *Written Communications for Business Administrators*. New York: Holt, Rinehart & Winston, Inc., 1965.

Hayakawa, S. I. *Language in Thought and Action,* 2d ed. New York: Harcourt, Brace, and World, 1964.

Sigband, Norman B. *Communication for Management*. Glenview, Illinois: Scott, Foresman and Company, 1969.

Stroh, Thomas F. *Managing the New Generation in Business*. New York: McGraw-Hill Book Company, 1971. Chapter 7.

Leadership and Supervision

In preceding chapters references were made to the responsibility and authority that managers and supervisors have for carrying out their assigned functions. Their ability to perform these functions depends to a considerable degree upon the understanding that they and their superiors have of the leadership process and the degree to which they are able to develop and to use the skills needed for effective leadership.

The leaders of an organization—managers and supervisors alike—are a part of the total organizational setting and as a result are in a position to influence as well as be influenced by it. While it is generally expected that leaders will exercise a role different from that of their followers and display more initiative and concern for the achievement of the organizational goals, there has been increasing recognition of the need for *all* members of the organization to participate to some degree in the leadership function, even though formal authority has not been officially delegated to them. Thus, the present-day managers or supervisors are expected to solicit participation and at the same time retain the responsibility for the actions of their subordinates in this area. This trend toward greater participation by individuals and by the work group requires not only that managers be technically competent but also that they possess human relations skills and insights that enable them to share the leadership functions effectively. Because of the important leadership role that first-line supervisors have within their organization, a large part of this chapter will be devoted to a description of their role in motivating and controlling performance, developing employee participation, facilitating employee adjustment, and working effectively with others in the organization.

THE LEADERSHIP ROLE

The leadership positions which encompass the levels in the organizational hierarchy from top to bottom involve forms of responsibility and authority that are typically delineated by means of organizational charts, manuals, and job descriptions. Such authority and responsibility provide the basis for carrying on the activities of the organization in an orderly and systematic manner. Since authority is inherent in the positions rather than in the persons who occupy them, it is commonly referred to as positional authority. This *positional authority* enables the manager or supervisor to carry out assigned job duties efficiently. Too frequently, however, the authority that is delegated to a position is so limited that the individual is unable to carry out the assignments in a manner consistent with his or her talents.

There are times when managers and supervisors possess positional authority on which they do not have to rely because of the respect and cooperation that they command through their *personal authority*. In 1916, Henri Fayol, a French industrialist and organization theorist, said:

> Distinction must be made between a manager's official authority deriving from office and personal authority, compounded of intelligence, experience, moral worth, ability to lead, past services, etc. . . . In the make-up of a good head, personal authority is the indispensable complement of official authority.[1]

Today we recognize that what Fayol referred to as personal authority would relate primarily to the leader's personality characteristics and social skills.

Concepts of Leadership

Over the years many attempts have been made to identify the characteristics of effective leadership in terms of personal traits as, for example, intelligence, alertness, dominance, originality, etc. It was assumed at one time that leadership effectiveness could be explained by traits which were presumed to differentiate leaders from nonleaders. More recently, however, it has been recognized that leader identification based solely upon this assumption has proven to be of little value since there is little agreement as to which are the most desirable traits; and effective leaders were found to be different in the traits they possessed. However, some experts believe that trait research is not completely fruitless and further research in this area should not be abandoned.[2]

A behavioral theory of leadership which followed the *trait theory* historically proposed that what makes leaders effective is what they do, such as how they communicate, give directions, motivate, delegate, plan, conduct

---

[1] Aaron Q. Sartain and Alton W. Baker, *The Supervisor and His Job* (2d ed.; New York: McGraw-Hill Book Company, 1972), p. 259.

[2] E. E. Ghiselli, "Managerial Talent," *American Psychologist*, Vol. 18, No. 10 (October, 1963), pp. 631-634.

meetings, etc. The value of this theory is the implication that individuals can be trained to do the right things, independently of their personality traits. It should be recognized, however, that the leader's inner personality "spills over" into his or her behavior which, in turn, affects that person's success as a manager or supervisor.[3]

In the study of leadership, increased attention has been given to the situation in which leaders function. This approach involves determining the significant leadership characteristics in situations that are highly similar as, for example, having subordinates with similar backgrounds or performing the same type of work. The *situational approach* recognizes the importance of the subordinates' roles as that of the leader. As implied by the comment in Figure 14-1, both roles are important.

Conditions Affecting Leadership

All leaders in an organization, from the chief executive officer to the first-line supervisors, perform such functions as planning and organizing,

"How do you know the fault is in my 'leading'? Maybe the fault is in your 'following'!"

Source: Reprinted with the permission of *The Saturday Evening Post* and Dana Fradon © 1966, The Curtis Publishing Company.

Figure 14-1

[3] James Owens, "The Uses of Leadership Theory," *Michigan Business Review,* Vol. 25, No. 1 (January, 1973), pp. 13-19.

communicating orders and instructions, motivating and controlling the performance of subordinates, resolving conflicts between individuals and groups, settling grievances, and taking disciplinary action. These functions, however, may be performed in a variety of ways depending upon several factors.

Nature of the Organization. A supervising nurse in a hospital, for example, will have different conditions under which to perform than a principal in a public school. Similarly, an office manager in a government agency will be in a work setting that is different from that of a supervisor of a railroad track gang. These differences in the nature of the organization and the personnel being supervised often require that somewhat different leadership approaches be used.

Level of the Leader's Position and Specific Job Requirements. The level at which a formal leadership position is located also affects the pattern of competencies required for effective performance. Figure 14-2 illustrates the relative importance of technical, conceptual, and human relations abilities at different levels from first-line supervisors to top management. It may be observed that the technical ability needed by first-line supervisors is relatively greater than that required at the higher levels. Conversely, conceptual ability increases from first levels of supervision to the higher levels. Human relations ability, however, does not vary appreciably with the level of supervision.

Leader-Member Relations. According to Fiedler, the factor that would seem most important in determining one's leadership influence is the degree to which the group members trust and like the leader, and are willing to follow his or her guidance. The trusted and well-liked leader obviously does not require special rank or power in order to get things done.[4]

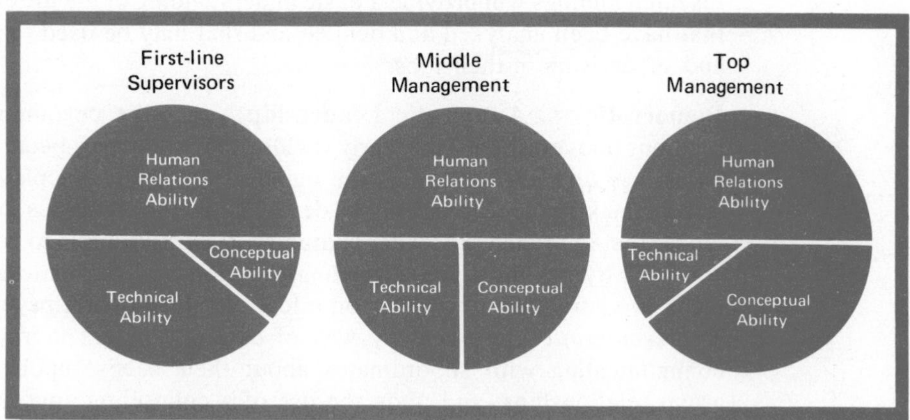

Figure 14-2 LEADERSHIP ABILITIES REQUIRED AT DIFFERENT LEVELS IN THE ORGANIZATION

[4] Fred E. Fiedler, "Engineer the Job to Fit the Manager," *Harvard Business Review*, Vol. 43, No. 5 (September-October, 1965), pp. 115-122.

Task Structure. Another important factor isolated by Fiedler is the *task structure*. By this term is meant the degree to which the task (1) is spelled out step by step for the group and, if so, the extent to which it can be done "by the numbers" or according to a detailed set of standard operating instructions, or (2) must be left nebulous and undefined. Vague and ambiguous or unstructured tasks make it difficult to exert leadership influence, because neither the leader nor the subordinates know exactly what has to be done or how it is to be accomplished.[5]

Position Power. Finally, Fiedler points out the power of the leadership position, as distinct from any personal power the leader might have. Can the leader hire or fire and promote or demote? Is the leader's appointment for life, or will it terminate at the pleasure of the group? It is obviously easier to be a leader when the position power is strong than when it is weak.[6] It may be concluded that the ability of leaders to influence other people to work together effectively in a common task is dependent upon their own abilities and environmental factors that are largely outside of their control.

Leadership Approaches

There are different leadership approaches or styles that managers and supervisors use in achieving organizational goals with and through their subordinates. The method that is used to motivate and control employee performance has been studied most thoroughly, although other aspects of leadership have also been examined. While it is not possible to examine all of the different aspects of the leadership function, a look at some of the major research findings will provide a basic understanding of the different approaches that have been analyzed and defined and that may be used to guide managers and supervisors in their jobs.

Democratic vs. Autocratic Leadership. Since the beginning of the human relations movement in the early 1930s, the trend has been away from the *autocratic approach* in which the manager or supervisor plays the dominant role in making decisions and in determining the activities of subordinates. Under that approach the leader characteristically attempts to control employee behavior by relying upon disciplinary action and legalistic approaches and tends to view human behavior on a logical rather than a psychological basis. The *democratic approach*, by way of contrast, places more emphasis upon communicating with subordinates about their needs, upon building strong group relationships, and upon the use of a counseling approach in resolving personnel problems. Basically the democratic approach emphasizes the human element in achieving organization objectives, whereas the autocratic approach

[5] *Ibid.*
[6] *Ibid.*

stresses the importance of structure, controls, authority, and discipline in the management of personnel.[7]

Employee- vs. Production-Centered Supervisors. By the mid-1940s researchers were devoting more attention to the systematic study of leadership. Studies conducted by the Survey Research Center of the University of Michigan in widely different kinds of work groups and organizations were designed to determine the types of leader characteristics that would prove to be most effective. One of the major findings of the studies was that the *production-centered supervisors,* i.e., those who are concerned primarily with production, are less effective in terms of actual productivity records than the *employee-centered supervisors,* who give their attention to the people who do the work but who also have high performance goals and enthusiasm for achieving them. While the job- or production-centered supervisors feel that they do not have time for employees until they have attained a satisfactory level of production, the employee-centered supervisors recognize the individual needs of their subordinates. It was found that the employees who work for the employee-centered supervisors felt that the supervisors were personally interested in them, found them available for discussion, and viewed them as nonthreatening individuals.[8]

Structure and Consideration. Another approach to supervision is illustrated by the Ohio State leadership studies. One of the studies identified two major dimensions of supervisory behavior: consideration and structure. These two characteristics which were found to be independent of each other are described as follows:

> *Consideration* includes behavior indicating mutual trust, respect, and a certain warmth and rapport between the supervisor and his group. This does not mean that this dimension reflects a superficial "pat-on-the-back," "first name calling" kind of human relations behavior. This dimension appears to emphasize a deeper concern for group members' needs and includes such behavior as allowing subordinates more participation in decision making and encouraging more two-way communication.
>
> *Structure* includes behavior in which the supervisor organizes and defines group activities and his relation to the group. Thus, he defines the role he expects each member to assume, assigns tasks, plans ahead, establishes ways of getting things done, and pushes for production. This dimension seems to emphasize overt attempts to achieve organizational goals.[9]

---

[7] In addition to the democratic and autocratic leaders, there is a third type known as the *laissez-faire leader* who permits subordinates to do what they choose and imposes very few limitations. This approach is seldom effective and not likely to be found in most organizations. Most of the discussion of leadership patterns, therefore, centers around the concepts of democracy and autocracy.

[8] Rensis Likert, *New Patterns of Management* (New York: McGraw-Hill Book Company, 1961).

[9] Edwin A. Fleishman and Edwin F. Harris, "Patterns of Leadership Behavior Related to Employee Grievances and Turnover," *Personnel Psychology,* Vol. 15, No. 1 (Spring, 1962), pp. 43-46.

Flexibility in Leadership Style

One of the characteristics of managers who fit the democratic, employee-oriented, or consideration pattern is that they recognize the importance of employees as members of a group and encourage them to participate in the making of decisions concerning job problems. Such managers also recognize that group members cannot always participate in decision making and that they must decide when and to what extent it is possible for them to do so. The most effective managers are those who recognize the important forces that are involved in the leadership of a group and are flexible in the approach that they use in carrying out their leadership responsibilities. They are able to use the wide variety of leadership approaches available to them in determining the degree to which the work group may participate in the making of decisions. As shown in Figure 14-3, boss-centered leadership (the most autocratic type) is at one end of the continuum, and subordinate-centered leadership (the most democratic type) is at the other end.

Each type of action is related to the degree of authority used by the boss and to the amount of freedom available to subordinates in reaching decisions. At the one extreme the manager or supervisor maintains maximum control; whereas at the other extreme minimal control is exercised. In between the two extremes are intermediate stages with varying degrees of "use of authority by the manager" and "area of freedom for subordinates." These two categories are equal or balanced on the continuum in Figure 14-3 when the leadership behavior is: "manager presents tentative decision subject to change."

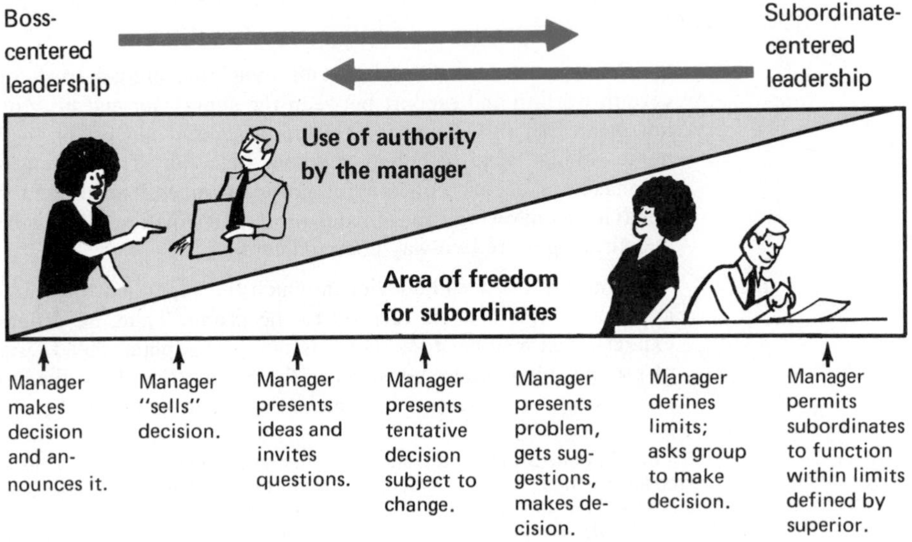

Source: R. Tannenbaum and W. H. Schmidt, "How to Choose a Leadership Pattern," *Harvard Business Review,* Vol. 36, No. 2 (March-April, 1958), pp. 95-101 and Vol. 51, No. 3 (May-June, 1973), pp. 162-170. Reproduced with permission.

Figure 14-3 CONTINUUM OF LEADERSHIP BEHAVIOR

Each situation or problem calling for a decision requires the superior to determine the approach to be used. The choice should be made on the basis of an evaluation of forces within the superior, within the subordinates, and in the situation. *Forces within the superior* include such matters as confidence in subordinates and his or her own inclinations as to how to handle the particular situation that calls for a decision. *Forces within the subordinates* include their interest in the problem, their understanding and identification with the goals of the organization, their knowledge, and their desire and expectancy to share in the decision making. *Forces in the situation* include such factors as the type of organization, the effectiveness of the group, the problem itself, and the pressure of time.[10] As problems arise, it is the responsibility of the manager or supervisor to determine whether employees should be permitted more or less freedom in making the necessary decisions concerning these problems. There is, however, a need for any organization which operates in a democratic society to recognize the values of increased employee participation.

THE SUPERVISOR'S ROLE IN THE ORGANIZATION

The discussion up to this point has been concerned with management positions at all levels from the top down to and including first-line supervisors. Since persons holding positions as first-line supervisors are directly responsible for supervising the largest portion of an organization's human resources, the remainder of this chapter will focus upon their role in performing these responsibilities. Much of what is said about the supervisor's role as a leader, however, also applies to that of persons in positions of higher management.

Engaging in Various Activities

The first-line supervisor may supervise a few or a large number of subordinates, depending largely upon the type of work for which his or her unit is responsible. The duties may also vary considerably according to the objectives, policies, functions, and other characteristics of the organization. However, several studies made of supervisors reveal some similarities in how they spend their time at work. The results from these studies show the following pattern.[11]

Planning and scheduling	15%
Assigning jobs	10%
Checking work	20%
Coaching and training	20%

[10] Robert Tannenbaum and Warren H. Schmidt, "How to Choose a Leadership Pattern," *Harvard Business Review,* Vol. 36, No. 2 (March-April, 1958), pp. 95-101, and Vol. 51, No. 3 (May-June, 1973), pp. 162-170, as reprinted in Herbert J. Chruden and Arthur W. Sherman, Jr., *Readings in Personnel Management* (4th ed.; Cincinnati: South-Western Publishing Co., 1976), pp. 287-298.

[11] Howard F. Shout, *Start Supervising* (Washington, D.C.: The Bureau of National Affairs, Inc., 1972), p. 49.

Handling problems	10%
Observing and improving	5%
Meetings and telephone	5%
Record keeping	15%

While this pattern will vary with the kind of work and the organization involved, it does reveal the varied activities of the supervisor.

Serving as a "Linking Pin"

An awareness of the supervisor's position in the organizational structure is also important to understanding the forces affecting the supervisor's ability to function effectively. The supervisor has been described as a *linking pin* who belongs to two groups within the organization as illustrated in Figure 14-4. The supervisor is the superior in one group and a subordinate in the other. As shown by the arrows, the supervisor is a link between these two groups.

In order to function effectively, however, a supervisor must have sufficient influence with his or her superior. Too often this is the exception rather than the rule. Over 30 years ago, F. J. Roethlisberger wrote a classic article, "The Foreman: Master and Victim of Double-Talk." In the article he emphasized the dilemma of the supervisors and documented the conflicting expectations that management had of them. Surveys indicate that the condition not only still exists but has become worse. The supervisors of today are being held

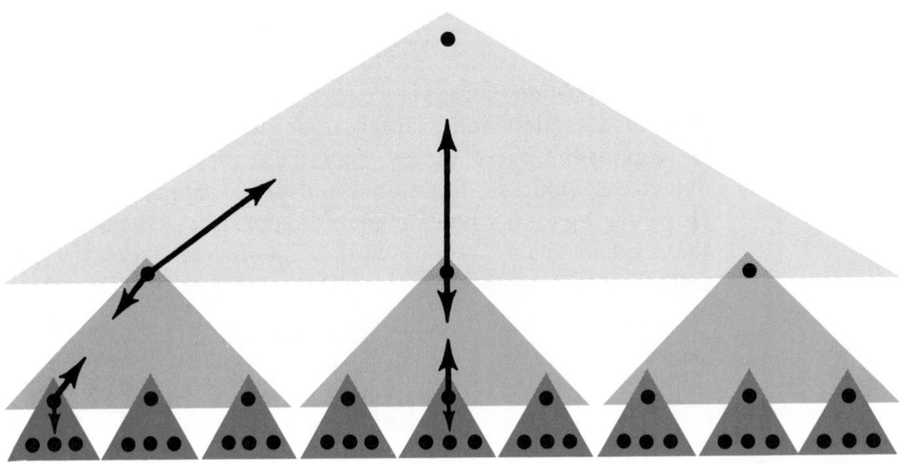

Source: Rensis Likert, *New Patterns in Management* (New York: McGraw-Hill Book Company, 1961), p. 113. Reproduced with permission.

Figure 14-4 THE LINKING PIN

responsible for functions which over which they no longer have any real authority or control.[12] Unless higher management and staff departments, such as the personnel department, help to strengthen the influence that supervisors have, their ability to carry out their functions that are critical to the success of the organization will suffer.

Motivating and Controlling Employee Performance

Probably the most important functions performed by the supervisor are those of motivating and controlling employee performance. It is the supervisor's responsibility to create conditions and incentives that will motivate employees to achieve the objectives established for their jobs and for the department. The supervisor must then determine the extent to which the goals are being achieved, whether or not prescribed quality standards are being maintained, and whether or not employees are conforming to organizational policies, procedures, and regulations.

Concern for Human Relations. It was once the common practice for management to view the supervisor primarily as a "driver" or a "bull of the woods." Little concern was given by management to the methods that were used to achieve results as long as they were achieved and the directives of higher management were followed. Over the past several decades, however, supervisors have found that their power has been reduced largely as a result of increased reliance upon staff specialists, increase in the strength of unions, and a growing expectation on the part of subordinates that they should be treated with respect and dignity. As a result of social changes, unskilled laborers are as aware of their rights to work at a job free from threats and coercion as those who are in professional and managerial jobs. Today's supervisor is expected to promote good human relations with individual employees as well as with the work group and, at the same time, meet production standards and requirements.

Promoting effective human relations is frequently one of the more difficult aspects of supervision since effective human relationships depend upon attitudes as well as skills. Employees are quick to sense whether the supervisor's skills in human relations are based on sincerity or whether they are "management devices." While it is desirable for supervisors to develop their human relations skills, these are no substitute for sincerity. According to Sartain and Baker, the most fundamental factor in effective supervision is *trust and confidence* on the part of both parties—supervisor and subordinate—in each other.[13]

---

[12] John A. Patton, "How to Solve the Foreman's Dilemma," *Foundry,* Vol. 102, No. 4 (April, 1974), pp. 58-61, as reprinted in Herbert J. Chruden and Arthur W. Sherman, Jr., *Readings in Personnel Management* (4th ed.; Cincinnati: South-Western Publishing Co., 1976), pp. 299-308. An interesting discussion of the problem may also be found in the article "As a Ford Foreman, Ed Hendrix Finds He Is Man in the Middle," *The Wall Street Journal,* July 25, 1973.

[13] Sartain and Baker, *op. cit.,* pp. 173-175.

Concern for Ethical Values. Effective human relations also depend upon sincerity and a concern for ethical values. While it is not always easy to obtain agreement as to what is right and what is wrong, supervisors should be encouraged through examples by top management to give careful attention to ethical values in the performance of their duties. Particularly in motivating and controlling the performance of subordinates, supervisors should make a special effort to consider the human values that are involved. One way to emphasize its importance is to have a formal code of ethics like the one shown in Figure 14-5.

Concern for Employee Efficiency. The supervisor has a responsibility to see that subordinates contribute their full potential. When the duties, responsibilities, and formal relationships are properly planned, organized, and

CODE OF ETHICS FOR SUPERVISORS

1. Set an example of what you expect from others.
2. Emphasize the future rather than the past or present.
3. Look for, and deal with, causes rather than symptoms.
4. Admit, and learn from, making a mistake.
5. Don't pass the buck.
6. Consider both the long-run and short-run results.
7. Everyone involved should benefit.
8. Legal and ethical means should be used to achieve legal and ethical ends.
9. The dignity of every individual should be respected.
10. Try to understand others, and make yourself understood by them.

Source: From an address by Robert D. Gray presented at the 1970 Management Conference, Hawaii Employers Council, March 10, 1970. Reproduced with permission of the California Institute of Technology.

Figure 14-5 CODE OF ETHICS FOR SUPERVISORS

controlled, employees are better able to direct their energies into productive and satisfying activities, and frustrations are minimized. As observed earlier, it is also desirable to plan for employees to have as much opportunity as possible for self-direction. However, this should not be construed as meaning that there are no controls on employee performance and behavior.

Establishment of Work Rules. A part of effective personnel planning is the establishment of sound work rules and other controls to govern the behavior of all employees in a reasonably uniform manner. Rules concerning working hours, coffee breaks, general safety, and other items that are essential to the maintenance of a good working environment should be established, communicated, and enforced. Similarly, in order to determine the extent to which subordinates are meeting their individual and/or group job standards, records should be kept of their performance and compared against the standard.

Use of Work Measurement. Where wages are linked to individual or group productivity, *work measurement,* including time and motion studies, may be used as a basis for determining standards of output either in the factory or the office. Today the use of work measurement in the office probably exceeds that in the factory. This trend reflects the rapid increase in the number of office jobs as compared with those in the factory and the desire of management to have control over the ever-rising overhead costs.

The effectiveness of work measurement approaches, however, is largely dependent upon supervisory understanding and cooperation. One study made of work measurement in banks revealed that many supervisors did not understand how the data could be used. They viewed work measurement as a form of control imposed from higher management, and they identified so closely with their subordinates that they were unable to use it effectively. Work measurement has the potential for contributing to a number of planning as well as controlling purposes, but its effective use is dependent upon supervisory understanding and commitment.[14]

Concern for Employee Behavior. The supervisor's responsibility for maintaining high levels of efficiency in the work group requires that appropriate corrective action be taken with individuals who do not possess the abilities for the job, are insufficiently motivated, or engage in behavior that impairs their performance or that of their fellow employees. Excessive absenteeism, tardiness, and such unacceptable behavior as gambling, stealing, and appearing at work under the influence of alcohol or drugs likewise require attention by the supervisor. According to various reports, both alcoholism and drug addiction are on the increase with the result that employers are required to take positive steps to handle the problems that create and are created by such behavior.[15]

---

[14] Donald L. Caruth, "The Trouble with Work Measurement Is . . . ," *Michigan Business Review,* Vol. 24, No. 1 (January, 1972), pp. 7-15.

[15] "Drunk Employees Rise but Labor-Short Firms Often Don't Fire Them," *The Wall Street Journal,* October 2, 1969, "The Rising Problem of Drugs on the Job," *Time* (June 29, 1970), and "Alcoholism: New Victims, New Treatment," *Time* (April 22, 1974).

The Problem of Alcoholism. Since the late 1940s when the first industrial alcoholism programs were started, some 200 companies including General Motors, Hughes Aircraft, Illinois Bell Telephone, Consolidated Edison of New York, du Pont, Standard Oil of New Jersey (now Exxon Corp.), Eastman Kodak, and Allis-Chalmers have reported considerable success with their respective programs. Many of these firms have written the plans into their union agreements, and others cover treatment and rehabilitation under company medical insurance plans.[16]

The immediate supervisor is the key to early detection and proper handling of alcoholism, but most supervisors are reluctant to confront employees about drinking. A better approach is to have the supervisor keep a record of attendance, production, and undesirable behavior. The record is then discussed with the individuals, and assistance in any problem that may be affecting their work is offered. While there are various clinics for the treatment of alcoholism, Alcoholics Anonymous is reported to be the most effective single outside agency.[17]

The Problem of Drug Addiction. A survey of Chicago's *Industrial Relations Newsletter* concluded that three out of every four United States companies with over 50 or more employees have a serious drug problem. Drug usage by employees not only affects the production but also accounts for much of the tools, office machinery, and other goods stolen from corporations and stores each year. Detecting the on-the-job addict is a more difficult task than spotting an alcoholic, and for legal reasons caution must be used in accusing an employee of addiction or even examining a personal locker.[18] Supervisors should, however, look out for such symptoms as absenteeism, tardiness, unexplained absences from the work area, frequent telephone calls, and frequent and lengthy visits to the washroom. Frequent changes in mood during the day, unsteady gait, and trembling of hands or mouth are a few of the behavioral signs of drug abuse of which supervisors should be aware.[19]

Drug abusers will seldom seek help from a supervisor because they know that in all likelihood the supervisor cannot relate to their problem. This can reduce the supervisor's effectiveness in his or her own mind and in the minds of the subordinates. For this reason, as well as for the reason of coping with employee drug abuse per se, it is critical that supervisors be encouraged by management to learn about drugs and drug abuse. Management should instruct supervisors about what the organization is going to do about the drug problem and what management expects supervisors to do.[20]

---

[16] "The Rising Problem of Drugs on the Job," *Time* (April 22, 1974), p. 79.

[17] *Labor Policy and Practice—Personnel Management* (Washington, D.C.: The Bureau of National Affairs, Inc., 1974), pp. 245:151-154.

[18] *Time, op. cit.*

[19] *Labor Policy and Practice—Personnel Management, op. cit.*

[20] Carl D. Chambers and Richard D. Heckman, *Employee Drug Abuse: A Manager's Guide for Action* (Boston: Cahners Publishing Co., Inc., 1972).

Developing Employee Participation

Another important role of the supervisor is to provide employees with the experience of participating in the making of decisions. As noted earlier, the continuum of leadership (page 312) provides for different degrees of employee participation. Changing work methods, scheduling coffee breaks and vacations, and handling excessive use of sick leave are a few of the problems that supervisors have successfully passed on to the work group for its decision. As a supervisor learns to trust the group and to recognize that it, too, can make good decisions, he or she is usually willing to let the group participate in decisions about more important matters. In any case it should be realized that the supervisors may make the decisions or submit to the group for decision only those matters or problems that fall within their jurisdiction or *area of freedom*.

Ways of Encouraging Participation. The supervisor of a group of employees, according to Maier, has two roles when the group is involved in the decision-making process: (1) *discussion leader,* with responsibility for conducting a good discussion about the problem under consideration, and (2) *expert,* with certain information that should be made available to the group. The skills needed for the democratic type of discussion must be consistent with a permissive approach in which each member of the group is encouraged to present opinions and feelings; however, no one should be permitted to dominate or to utilize the discussion for selfish purposes. Before attempting to use the group-decision approach, it is suggested that supervisors develop some competency in leading discussions, including the ability to:

1. State a problem in such a way that the group does not become defensive, but instead approaches the issue in a constructive way.
2. Supply essential facts and clarify the areas of freedom without suggesting a solution.
3. Draw persons out so that all members will participate.
4. Wait out pauses.
5. Restate accurately the ideas and feelings expressed, and in a more abbreviated, more pointed, and more clear form than when initially expressed by a member.
6. Ask good questions so that problem-solving behavior is stimulated.
7. Summarize as the need arises.[21]

Values of the Participative Approach. Research conducted with various groups has revealed that the *participative approach* has several values. One of its major values lies in the *acceptance* of the decision by the members of the group. People are more likely to accept the decisions that they feel responsible for, as a result of having participated in making them. Furthermore, experience has shown that the *quality* of decisions made by groups has generally been high.

[21] Norman R. F. Maier, *Psychology in Industrial Organizations* (4th ed.; Boston: Houghton Mifflin Company, 1973), pp. 130-135.

For example, groups that participate in setting goals often place higher demands upon themselves than the supervisors and methods engineers would have made upon them. If quality of decision is of primary concern—as it must be in certain instances—the supervisor should make the decision without involving the work group. Studies have shown, however, that once supervisors were trained in the use of the group decision approach, the majority of problems requiring decisions were viewed primarily as involving acceptance of the decisions rather than quality.[22]

Other values of the group decision approach are increased employee satisfaction and morale, and the development of a climate in which employees can contribute to accomplishing organizational goals while fulfilling their own higher-level needs. More recently this approach has been viewed as a way of providing a manager or supervisor with more time to carry on lateral relationships within the organization and with the types of skills needed for accomplishing effective coordination within the organization.[23]

A Caution on Implementing the Participative Approach. Before proceeding too far with participative approach, managers and supervisors should evaluate not only their own inclinations but the needs and interests of the work group. In one company's Puerto Rican operations, the attempt to have employees sit in on problem-solving sessions resulted in the departure of workers. The manager learned that the employees who left had decided that if management was so dumb that it had to consult with its employees, the company was in bad shape and would soon fail.[24]

In a study conducted by the authors of personnel management practices in Europe, it was found that many Europeans, especially the adults of middle and older ages, interpret the participation of employees as a sign of weakness on the part of management. It was inferred that the supervisor using this approach doesn't have the answer to a problem or is trying to "pass the buck." The younger employees, however, tended to be less willing to submit to autocratic leadership, which has been traditional in Europe, with the result that employers gradually are being forced to become more democratic.[25]

Facilitating Employee Adjustment

From the time that employees are recruited until they are separated from an organization, a large portion of their lives is influenced by the personnel policies and procedures, by their supervisors, and by their relationships with fellow employees. All of these influences, together with past and present life experiences, determine the nature of their adjustment to the job as well as to

[22] *Ibid.*

[23] Joel K. Leidecker and James L. Hall, "A New Justification for Participative Management," *Human Resource Management,* Vol. 13, No. 1 (Spring, 1974), pp. 28-31.

[24] Alfred J. Marrow, *The Failure of Success* (New York: American Management Association, 1972).

[25] Herbert J. Chruden and Arthur W. Sherman, Jr., *Personnel Practices of American Companies in Europe* (New York: American Management Association, 1972), p. 9.

other areas of their daily lives. Because emotional adjustment is very important to employees, their families, the organization, and to society at large, it should be one of the areas of primary concern to the supervisor. The supervisor should recognize changes in behavior, such as excessive absenteeism, tardiness, hostility, moodiness, withdrawal, and decline in job performance, as indicators that the individual requires understanding and assistance. Similarly, the worrier, the crank, the bully, the chronic complainer, and the other types of "problem employees" that frequently demand the supervisor's attention are people who are having difficulties in adjusting to the world about them. In most instances these individuals are also problems to themselves and feel uncomfortable about their own behavior.

Since supervisors interact with their subordinates frequently, they are usually in the best position to observe changes in their subordinates' behavior and to assist in identifying and resolving their problems. The supervisor, however, must have some knowledge and skill in counseling and, above all, know when and how to make referrals to professional persons if the counseling role is to be performed satisfactorily.

Counseling Methods. In attempting to help an employee who has a problem, the supervisor may use a variety of counseling methods. All of them, however, depend upon active listening, which is not easy for many persons. Sometimes the mere furnishing of information may prove to be the solution to what at first appeared to be a knotty problem. More frequently, however, the problem cannot be solved as easily as this because of frustrations or conflicts that are accompanied by strong feelings such as fear, confusion, or hostility. In such cases the supervisor may be inclined to furnish advice to the employee and in most instances, but not necessarily all, advice-giving falls short of what is required in the situation.

The Nondirective Approach. The maximum degree of assistance can often be realized by the use of the *nondirective approach* in which the employee being counseled is permitted to have maximum freedom in determining the course of the interview.

The importance of nonevaluative listening as a communication skill was described in Chapter 13. Nonevaluative listening is also a primary technique used in nondirective counseling. Fundamentally the approach is to listen, with understanding and without criticism or appraisal, to the problem as it appears to the troubled person. The counselee is encouraged through the counselor's attitude and reaction to what is said or not said to express feelings without fear of shame, embarrassment, or reprisal. As the interview progresses, the counselor should strive to reflect the feelings of the employee by restating them. For example, if the employee has discussed several situations which indicate feelings of being treated unfairly, the counselor at the conclusion of this particular statement would probably say, "You feel that you have been treated unfairly." While questions may be used at appropriate places in the interview, the interviewer should use general questions that stimulate the employee to pursue an examination of those areas which are troublesome. Questions that call for "Yes" or "No" answers on the part of the employee should be avoided.[26]

Values of Nondirective Counseling. The free expression that is encouraged in the nondirective approach tends to reduce tensions and frustrations. After an employee has had the opportunity to release pent-up feelings through catharsis, he or she is in a better position to view the problem area more objectively and with a problem-solving attitude. The permissive atmosphere allows the individual to try to "work through" the entanglements of the problem and to see it in a clearer perspective, often to reach a more desirable solution. The supervisor should not feel, however, that a nondirective approach must always be used. There are times when a directive approach will be more suitable, such as when an employee asks for specific information or when it is essential that the supervisor express his or her opinions or inform the subordinate of rules that may have been violated.

Use of Professional Counselors. Since the supervisor may not have the skill or time in which to handle the more complex personal problems of employees, there should be an established system for making referrals to trained counselors in the personnel department or medical department. Such referrals should be made on the basis of the severity and complexity of the problem. Likewise, if the problem area is one over which the supervisor has little or no influence, as for example the employee's family relationships, it may be advisable for the supervisor to refer the employee to the medical or personnel department where specialists are available or may be contacted. Needless to say, the act of referring an employee for professional assistance requires the exercise of considerable skill and tact. In many cases it is best to recommend that the employee consult a private physician or psychologist.

THE SUPERVISOR'S ABILITY TO RELATE TO INDIVIDUALS

Those individuals who occupy supervisory positions seemingly are required to be "all things to all people." They must strive to satisfy higher management by the productivity and profitability of their departments and by having a minimum number of grievances, accidents, and other problems. They must recognize the importance of effective human relations and attempt to achieve the objectives of management while satisfying the needs and wants of their subordinates. This latter accomplishment requires that they establish good relationships with subordinates as well as their superiors and fellow supervisors

[26] For a detailed discussion of nondirective techniques, see Carl R. Rogers, *Counseling and Psychotherapy* (Boston: Houghton Mifflin Company, 1942), and his *Client-Centered Therapy* (Boston: Houghton Mifflin Company, 1951). Specific applications of this method to business are discussed in Norman R. F. Maier, *Psychology in Industrial Organizations* (4th ed.; Boston: Houghton Mifflin Company, 1973), Chapter 20, and in William A. Ruch, "The Why and How of Nondirective Counseling," *Supervisory Management,* Vol. 18, No. 1 (January, 1973), pp. 13-19.

and, most important, that they recognize the uniqueness of individual personalities as influenced by their prior experiences at work, at home, and in the larger society.

Contemporary Employees

The individuals who comprise today's labor force in the United States are in many ways different from those who were in the labor force during the 1960s, the 1950s, and in previous decades. In the first place, they are more knowledgeable than their predecessors. Through more years of formal education, television viewing, travel, and other experiences they have acquired a vast amount of information. In addition to becoming more knowledgeable about their physical environment, they have developed an awareness of the psychological and social dimensions of life and expect their superiors to be skillful in human relations. The employees of today expect that attention will be given to their feelings and their desires to participate as fully as possible in decision making. With their limited authority, today's supervisors are compelled to use all of the human relations skills at their command to achieve results. The use of these skills in managing sophisticated individuals requires a high degree of sensitivity, integrity, and competence. Otherwise they may be accused by subordinates of manipulation and insincerity in their relations with them.

Young Employees

There were 23 million persons in the 16-24 age group out of a total of 91 million, or roughly 25 percent, in the civilian labor force in the United States in 1974.[27] Most of the differences between today's workers and those of past generations that were discussed earlier are magnified when young employees (16-24) are compared with their older fellow workers. The former are, on the average, more knowledgeable about their physical, psychological, and social environment; more reluctant to accept authority; more critical of authority figures; and more are likely to view the job and the organization as only one of several important aspects of their lives.

In recent years many young people have become disenchanted with business and industrial organizations, preferring to affiliate with government agencies and other nonprofit organizations that are more attuned to their interests and values. However, young adults view critically any organizations that they may perceive as being part of "the establishment." While there is much to be done to make organizations more viable for the majority of its members, recommendations for improving the supervision of young employees have emphasized the importance of job design, employee involvement, and communication.[28] Job enlargement has proven to be an effective motivator in

---

[27] U.S. Department of Labor, Bureau of Labor Statistics, *Employment and Earnings*, Vol. 21, No. 7 (Washington, D.C.: U.S. Government Printing Office, January, 1975).

[28] John S. Morgan, *Managing the Young Adults* (New York: American Management Association, 1967).

many instances for those young employees who want and can cope with it. Employee participation of the type described in the preceding section has in general yielded positive results; it does so most effectively with the brighter young employees. Communication is not only the most important but also the most difficult aspect of supervising young employees. In addition to the generation gap, there is also the perennial communication gap. It is essential that special attention be given to providing effective communication in accordance with the principles discussed in the preceding chapter. This requires that each young employee be considered a unique individual. The supervisor is urged to learn what each individual wants to do and what he or she aspires to be in the future. With such understanding the supervisor may guide the growth and development of the young employee to the mutual benefit of the employee and the organization.[29]

Disadvantaged Employees

Those organizations that have been able to utilize disadvantaged persons successfully have found that the quality of supervision is a major factor in permitting them to do so. While the importance of selection and training of such persons for their jobs cannot be minimized, the quality of the supervisor's contact with them is critical to their success. The ability to understand them and their way of life and to guide and counsel them into the behavioral patterns that the organization expects of its employees represent a challenge of a magnitude that many have not experienced previously. For example, tardiness and absenteeism are often unbelievably high for disadvantaged persons until special efforts are made to find causes and to help the individuals correct them. The disadvantaged generally require close supervision, and it may be necessary for the supervisor to repeat instructions, orders, and rules many times.[30]

The first six months on the job for the hard-core unemployed appear to be important for their initial and future job success. When the hard-core unemployed perceive a supervisor as considerate or supportive, they tend to perform more successfully; whereas when a supervisor is perceived as attempting to highly define or structure the work activities, they tend to perform less successfully.[31]

Coping with a State of Alienation. One of the major problems is the state of alienation that exists between the disadvantaged person and others at work. Characteristics of ghetto life that are brought to the job result in the newly assigned disadvantaged person being rejected by other employees. An important part of the supervisor's job is to help them in building an image that is

---

[29] Thomas F. Stroh, *Managing the New Generation in Business* (New York: McGraw-Hill Book Company, 1971), p. 67.

[30] Lawrence A. Johnson, *Employing the Hard-Core Unemployed* (New York: American Management Association, Research Study 98, 1969), p. 168.

[31] Richard W. Beatty, "Supervisory Behavior Related to Job Success of Hard-Core Unemployed Over a Two-Year Period," *Journal of Applied Psychology,* Vol. 59, No. 1 (February, 1974), pp. 38-42.

more acceptable to others in the organization. Obviously this requires considerable skill, tact, patience, and understanding—qualities that are not found in all supervisors. In a study of supervision of disadvantaged workers in several different companies, one of the most significant findings was that a supervisor of disadvantaged employees should, wherever possible, be one who has volunteered for that assignment. In the same study it was also reported that the supervisor should possess such qualities as willingness to listen to others, respect for all, use of good judgment, and keen job interest.[32]

Providing Counseling and Other Services. Many organizations have found that counseling and other supportive services, such as medical, legal, day care, and transportation, are essential supplements to what the supervisor is able to do to bring these individuals up to the required performance standards. While counselors have been reported to be essential to the success of programs for hard-core individuals in Boeing, Eastman Kodak, Westinghouse, United Air Lines, and Bankers Trust Company, there is always the possibility that the employee will become overly dependent upon the counselor and that normal relationships between employees and their supervisor will not develop.[33] Like other attempts that are made to assist the supervisor, the overuse of staff counselors may prove to be detrimental to the fulfillment of his or her role.

Women Employees

The fundamental problems of supervising female employees stem primarily from the minds of male supervisors who often have stereotyped notions of why the working woman seeks employment and what she expects from her job.

Research on Job-Related Attitudes and Beliefs. A recent study of the job related attitudes and beliefs of a nationwide sample of working women and working men conducted by the Institute of Social Research, University of Michigan, has dispelled some of the commonly held stereotypes such as: women work only for "pin money"; they are more often satisfied than men with intellectually undemanding jobs; or they are less concerned that the job help them realize their full potential. The study did, however, show several noticeable differences in the attitudes of women toward their jobs. The women were much less inclined than men to say that they would continue to work if they could be freed from the economic necessity to do so. Women were also more concerned with their physical work surroundings, with hours of work, and with travel to and from work than were men; and they were less likely to say that taking the initiative on a job was important to them. Much of the difference in attitudes and beliefs is attributed to early childhood socialization which prepares males and females to fulfill different work and family roles as

---

[32] Robert L. Finkelmeier, "The First-Line Supervisor Who Directs the Disadvantaged Worker," *Training and Development Journal,* Vol. 27, No. 2 (February, 1973), pp. 26-30.

[33] Leonard Nadler, "Helping the Hard-Core Adjust to the World of Work," *Harvard Business Review,* Vol. 48, No. 2 (March-April, 1970), pp. 117-126.

adults. Other social forces, such as educational and professional training or the demands of the job itself, also have some influence on job related attitudes.[34]

The Civil Rights Act of 1964 has been helpful in correcting discrimination in the hiring of women but there are still gross inequities in many organizations with respect to women's opportunities in supervisory and managerial positions. The Institute for Social Research study revealed, however, that while both men and women were equally concerned about being in jobs where the chances for promotion are good, significantly more women than men said that they never wanted to be promoted. It was discovered that the attitudes of women toward promotion were strongly tied to their *expectation* of being promoted. "That women in general were less interested than men with promotions on their present job was mainly a result of their resignation to their expectations that they were *not* going to be promoted," the researchers concluded.[35]

Reactions of Male Managers. Largely through the efforts of women as individuals and as members of various organizations identified with the Women's Liberation Movement, managers and supervisors are gradually becoming more aware of the problems that face women at work and in the larger society in realizing their potential as full persons. However, studies show that in the face of objective data, many male managers continue to react to women in terms of stereotypes.[36] It is recommended that managers attempt to overcome their stereotypes and that, meanwhile, they should develop policies and procedures for identifying women as well as men for promotion to higher-level jobs. They should also provide women with supervisory and managerial training opportunities of the types discussed in Chapter 15.

Résumé

The talents and enthusiasm of the members of an organization are of little value unless they are carefully directed toward the objectives established for the organization. Providing the type of leadership that will result in the most effective utilization of personnel is a primary responsibility of managers and supervisors. However, because of their position in an organization, first-line supervisors have one of the most important leadership roles. They have many responsibilities, but of primary importance is the part they play in developing

---

[34] Newsletter, Institute for Social Research, The University of Michigan, Autumn, 1972, pp. 4-5; Joan E. Crowley, Teresa E. Levitin, and Robert P. Quinn, "Seven Deadly Half-Truths About Women," *Psychology Today,* Vol. 6, No. 10 (March, 1973), pp. 94-96.

[35] Newsletter, ISR, *loc. cit.*

[36] Sheila Tobias, "Male Chauvinism in Employment," *Journal of College Placement,* Vol. 33, No. 4 (April-May, 1973), pp. 51-57. For an interesting anthology of articles concerning changing institutions and attitudes that are allowing women to grow, see Barbara Stanford (Editor), *On Being Female* (New York: Pocket Books, 1974). Also see M. Barbara Boyle, "Equal Opportunity for Women Is Smart Business," *Harvard Business Review,* Vol. 51, No. 3 (May-June, 1973), pp. 85-95, as reprinted in Herbert J. Chruden and Arthur W. Sherman, Jr., *Readings in Personnel Management* (4th ed.; Cincinnati: South-Western Publishing Co., 1976), pp. 57-73.

efficient employees, in motivating and controlling their performance, and in facilitating their adjustment. The manner in which supervisors perform these functions may vary from one individual to another, but the effective supervisor is one who is aware of the important factors in the leadership role and is flexible in relationships with individuals and with the work group. The ability of the supervisor to provide for group participation in decision making was cited as one of the leadership skills that could be developed and would contribute to personal as well as organizational success.

Supervisors who are able to relate to subordinates, particularly those with backgrounds different from their own, can go a long way toward making them effective leaders. It should be recognized, however, that the effectiveness of supervisory personnel is a function not only of their own personal characteristics but their status which is determined primarily as a result of management's attitudes toward supervisory personnel. The personnel department also has an important role in helping to preserve the superior's status, and personnel workers should recognize the value of the supervisor's contribution to the entire organization and especially to the personnel department.

DISCUSSION QUESTIONS

1. Why should a supervisor be flexible in leadership style? Of what value is the continuum of leadership behavior illustrated on page 312?
2. Assume that upon graduation from college you are employed by a company that promotes you to a supervisory position within a year or so. Shortly after your promotion an employee who has been with the company for several years is transferred to your work group. As you begin to explain his new job to him, he tells you that he has been around for quite a while and understands everything.
   a. What would you do?
   b. Why may the employee have responded as he did?
3. What are the major advantages and disadvantages of the supervisor serving as a counselor to subordinates with problems not directly related to the job?
4. One of the important skills in using the group-decision approach is the ability to state a problem to a group in such a manner that the members of the group will not feel threatened and become defensive. How would you state the problems in the following situations that concerned you as a supervisor?
   a. Employees have taken sick leaves far in excess of what they had taken at the same time a year ago.
   b. Some members of the group are not producing as much as they are able to produce, and other members of the group have to make up for their deficiencies in order to get the work accomplished.
   c. Employees are failing to heed safety rules and are taking dangerous short cuts in their work.
5. What types of professional persons are available in your community to help individuals with complex personal-emotional problems? How can you determine their competency? Do you know of any employers who have such professional persons in their organizations?
6. What are some of the early childhood socialization experiences that contribute to the attitudes of men and women in the U.S. about the role of women in organizations? What changes have you observed in the last few years in the attitudes of men toward women and in the women toward themselves?
7. Study the approaches used by different instructors under whom you have studied to motivate students, control their classroom behavior, and encourage or discourage discussion. How do these approaches relate to the descriptions of autocratic and democratic leaders found on page 310?

PROBLEM 14-1 SUPERVISION BY TV CAMERA*

In an attempt to study the performance of his workers, a furniture manufacturer installed a closed circuit television system. Employees who were not meeting production standards were observed continuously by the television for as long as an entire shift. These observations were recorded on video tape and were used to demonstrate to the employees any deficiencies in their performance. The employees were fully informed when such studies were to be made.

If the employee being observed was one who had been performing at a substandard level, he or she was permitted to observe the video tape and get instructions on how to improve. As a result of viewing the tapes and being instructed by time study personnel on how to improve, a number of the substandard operators were able to improve both their performance and their earnings.

The surveillance, however, caused some employees to quit their jobs; and at least one female employee became so nervous that she had to ask permission to leave the plant for the remainder of her shift. These incidents led the employees to protest the installation of the equipment.

a. A spokesman for the employees accused management of spying and of invading the privacy of the employees. Would you agree with this accusation? Why or why not?
b. TV surveillance is most commonly used by management to detect or deter suspected pilferage by employees. Is this practice sound from an ethical and/or legal standpoint? Discuss.

SUGGESTED READINGS

Chruden, Herbert J., and Arthur W. Sherman Jr. *Readings in Personnel Management*, 4th ed. Cincinnati: South-Western Publishing Co., Inc., 1976. Parts 3 and 4.

Davis, Keith. *Human Behavior at Work, Human Relations and Organizational Behavior*, 4th ed. New York: McGraw-Hill Book Company, 1972. Section 2.

Fiedler, Fred E. *A Theory of Leadership Effectiveness*. New York: McGraw-Hill Book Company, 1967.

Filley, Allen C. *Interpersonal Conflict Resolution*. Glenview, Illinois: Scott, Foresman and Company, 1975.

Goldstein, Arnold P., and Melvin Sorcher. *Changing Supervisory Behavior*. New York: Pergamon Press, Inc., 1974.

Haimann, Theo, and Raymond Hilgert. *Supervision: Concepts and Practices*. Cincinnati: South-Western Publishing Co., 1972.

Levinson, Harry. *Emotional Health and the World of Work*. New York: Harper and Row, 1964.

Maier, Norman R. F., Allen R. Solem, and Ayesha A. Maier. *Supervisory and Executive Development, A Manual for Role Playing*. New York: John Wiley & Sons, Inc., 1957.

Miner, John B. *The Management of Ineffective Performance*. New York: McGraw-Hill Book Company, 1963.

---

* Adapted with permission from BNA *Bulletin to Management*, No. 1100, March 11, 1971. Copyright © 1971 by The Bureau of National Affairs, Inc., Washington, D.C. 20037.

Morgan, James E., Jr., *Principles of Administrative and Supervisory Management*. Englewood Cliffs, New Jersey: Prentice-Hall, Inc., 1973.

Morgan, John S. *Managing the Young Adults*. New York: American Management Association, 1967.

Pfiffner, John M., and Marshal Fels. *The Supervision of Personnel,* 3d ed. Englewood Cliffs, New Jersey: Prentice-Hall, Inc., 1964.

Richards, Max D., and William A. Nielander. *Readings in Management,* 4th ed. Cincinnati: South-Western Publishing Co., Inc., 1974. Section C.

Sartain, Aaron Q., and Alton W. Baker. *The Supervisor and His Job,* 2d ed. New York: McGraw-Hill Book Company, 1972.

Shulman, Lee M., and Joan Kennedy Taylor. *When To See a Psychologist*. Los Angeles, California: Nash Publishing Corporation, 1969.

Stogdill, R. M., "Personal Factors Associated With Leadership: A Survey of the Literature," in C. A. Gibb (Editor) *Leadership*. Baltimore: Penguin Books, 1969.

Williams, Richard L. and Gene H. Moffat. *Occupational Alcoholism Programs*. Springfield, Illinois: Charles C. Thomas Publisher, 1975.

Administering Change

One of the major sources of problems faced by organizations is the rapid rate of change that is taking place in modern civilization. Discoveries in the sciences, improvements in technology, and changes in social behavior create conditions that can have a vital effect on organizations. If they are to continue to function effectively, it is essential that organizations and the personnel who comprise them be capable not only of adapting to change but also of planning for it. While functions of management traditionally have included the forecasting and anticipating of future problems and requirements, the modern concept of organizational development (discussed briefly in Ch. 3) connotes a more scientific and professional approach to these functions. Organizational development among other things emphasizes the need to improve the capabilities of an organization by placing particular emphasis upon the training of managerial and supervisory personnel. Such training should provide them with skills and attitudes that enable them to assist subordinates to cope with the ever-changing conditions occurring within their organizations in a manner that will permit a high level of performance and personal adjustment to be achieved.

Within an organization changes are taking place continually with respect to the structure, functions, and work load of the organization and with respect to the numbers and types of jobs that are to be staffed within the organization. Changes are occurring also in terms of the qualifications, capacities, attitudes, and behavior of the personnel who are available to staff these positions. Many of these changes may in turn necessitate changes in the placement of employees by means of transfers, promotions, demotions, or even layoffs. Regardless of their nature, however, placement changes should be accomplished so as to place employees in the jobs for which they are best suited and most needed, thus contributing to their adjustment and to effective performance of the organization.

ORGANIZATIONAL DEVELOPMENT

Organizational development (OD) means different things to different specialists in this area, but basically it is a method for facilitating change and development in *people* (e.g., styles, values, skills), in *technology* (e.g., greater simplicity, complexity), and in *organizational processes and structures* (e.g., relationships, roles). The objectives of organizational development can generally be classified as those optimizing human and social improvement or as those optimizing task accomplishment, or more likely a blend of the two.[1] These objectives are achieved through the OD process which is a change strategy that is (1) planned, (2) organization-wide, (3) managed from the top, and (4) oriented toward increased organizational effectiveness and health through planned intervention in the organization's processes, using behavioral-science knowledge.[2] The process of organizational development involves a change-agent—an OD practitioner who may be a paid consultant or a member of the organization.[3] These agents are primarily concerned with "initiating, creating, and confronting needed changes so as to make it possible for organizations to become or remain viable, to adapt to new conditions, to solve problems, to learn from experiences, and to move toward greater organizational maturity."[4]

Achieving Change

Earlier approaches that were used in analyzing the overall effectiveness of organizations—such as Operations Research—tended to be concerned with technological and structural aspects of an operation with lesser attention being given to its human aspects. In the newer approaches to organizational development, the emphasis is more likely to include such personnel-oriented variables as: identification of appropriate missions and values, human collaboration and conflict, control and leadership, coping with resistance to change, utilization of human resources, communication between hierarchical ranks in the organization, and management and career development.[5] While most OD practitioners emphasize the human factor in changing systems, there are growing numbers of them who believe that the technological aspects must

---

[1] Frank Friedlander and L. Dave Brown, "Organization Development," *Annual Review of Psychology, 1974* (Palo Alto, Calif.: Annual Reviews, Inc., 1974), pp. 313-341.

[2] Richard Beckhart, *Organization Development: Strategies and Models* (Reading, Mass.: Addison-Wesley Company, 1969).

[3] The International Association for Applied Social Scientists is an accrediting agency for OD practitioners. Several professional organizations also have OD divisions.

[4] Gordon L. Lippitt, *Organizational Renewal* (New York: Appleton-Century-Crofts, 1969), p. 1.

[5] Warren G. Bennis, *Changing Organizations* (New York: McGraw-Hill Book Company, 1966), p. 87.

also be considered.[6] Since this book is primarily concerned with the management of personnel, the discussion will center around the human factors that are involved in making changes.

Developing a Favorable Climate. One of the basic factors affecting the success of any type of change is the quality of the climate of the organization. It is essential that employees feel secure and know that their interests are protected when changes affecting them are to occur. A history of fair and honest treatment by management lays the groundwork for such feelings of security. Wherever feasible, as many employees as possible should participate in planning for the change; and a program for communicating the details of the change and for keeping employees advised of its progress should be included. In any proposed change, employees must be convinced that they will benefit from the change or at least not be adversely affected by it. If possible, changes should be introduced gradually in order to permit employees more time to adjust to the change. The use of financial incentive systems that permit those persons who are involved to share in any of the financial benefits that may stem from the change will also contribute to getting the change accepted.

Obtaining Feedback from Subordinates. According to one proposed model, as a start on implementing change occurs, provision should be made for obtaining feedback from subordinates, which can lead to modification of the change if needed. Figure 15-1 shows how the feedback information is integrated into the changes proposed by the initiator and into the implementation of the new procedures. Fundamental to this model is the provision for utilizing rather than ignoring the ideas and attitudes of the individuals involved and for letting feedback integration and utilization become the "pacer" of change.[7]

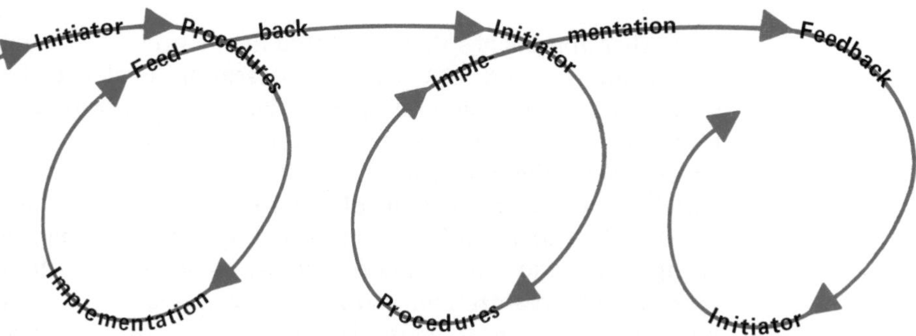

Source: Joseph W. Hollis and Frank H. Krause, "Effective Development of Change," *Public Personnel Management,* Vol. 2, No. 1 (January-February, 1973), pp. 60-70. Reprinted by permission of the International Personnel Management Association, 1313 East 60th St., Chicago, Illinois 60637.

Figure 15-1 IMPLEMENTING CHANGE—FEEDBACK IS INTEGRATED FOR FURTHER IMPROVEMENT

[6] Leslie E. This, *Organizational Development: Fantasy or Reality* (Washington, D.C.: Society for Personnel Administration, 1967), p. 9.

[7] Joseph W. Hollis and Frank H. Krause, "Effective Development of Change," *Public Personnel Management,* Vol. 2, No. 1 (January-February, 1973), pp. 60-70.

Overcoming Resistance to Change. In spite of all that may be done to develop a climate that is favorable to change, some degree of resistance can be anticipated. This resistance may be based on economic fear—the fear of experiencing a reduction in pay, or temporary, or even permanent unemployment. Employees also may fear that the change will impair their status or reduce the recognition or satisfaction that they have been receiving from their work or that they will fail at the new endeavor.

Social causes for resistance to change may be due to the reluctance of employees to break established social ties or to the fear that new social relationships will not be as rewarding as former ones. Individuals who have difficulty in meeting and becoming acquainted with others may be afraid that they will not be accepted by individuals with whom they may be placed as a result of the change. Employees who are a part of a closely knit group may object to change if they feel that the change is being imposed upon them, without their consultation, for the benefit of the organization or others outside of their group.

In any situation where resistance is encountered, positive as well as negative motivational conditions may exist, as illustrated in Figure 15-2, in connection with a proposed change in work methods. It will be noted that while more pay represents positive motivation for the new method, boredom, fear of management, and dislike of the time-study specialist are negative factors that may offset whatever positive motivational force is exerted by more pay.

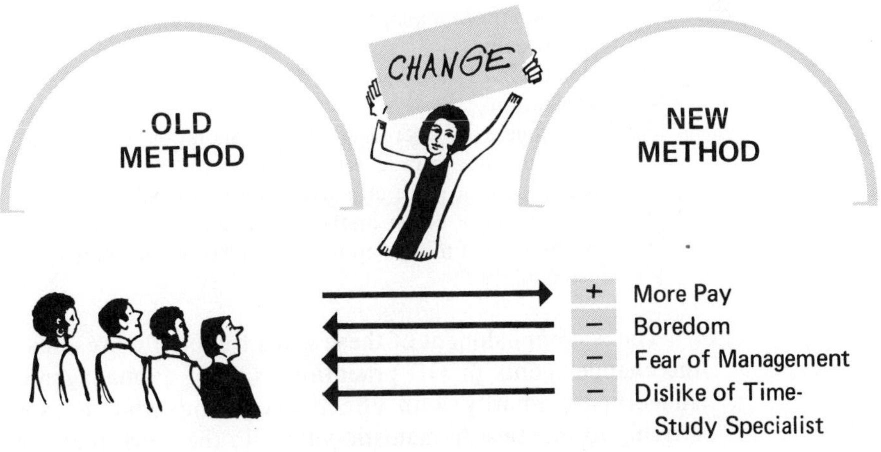

Source: Norman R. F. Maier, *Psychology in Industrial Organizations* (4th ed.; New York: Houghton Mifflin Company, 1973), p. 345. Reproduced with permission.

Note: The forces (represented by arrows) are those set in motion when a supervisor suggested a change in work methods. The direction of the forces (to right or left) is determined by the positive (plus signs) and negative (minus signs) motivational conditions aroused or removed, and they act upon the crew (circle) determining whether or not they will move from left to right. The left and right arcs at the top represent the "old" and "new" methods, respectively.

Figure 15-2 INTERACTING FORCES IN A PROPOSED CHANGE

By conducting discussions with the members of a group, it may be possible for them to weigh the pros and cons of the interacting forces in a proposed change. Getting negative factors out in the open in a discussion makes them easier to analyze and often lowers the resistance to change.[8]

Agents of Change. According to one author it is desirable, wherever possible, to encourage work groups to be their own *agents of change,* i.e., to be responsible for effecting a change in values and competence in interpersonal relationships.

> When a group and its various subgroups have harmonious relationships and well-understood objectives and goals, the group itself may become the prime mover in getting a change effected. Impetus for change that comes from within the group itself is probably the strongest and most effective way of producing it.[9]

The agents for change may be individuals or groups within the organization (internal agents) or may be a professional consultant (external agent) hired to study and to resolve its problems. Most change-agents are specialists in one of the behavioral science disciplines such as psychology or sociology.

Goals of Change-Agents. While each change-agent may have certain goals in mind that are unique for the client organization, some of the goals that are sought most frequently are:

1. Improvement in manager's interpersonal relationships with other members of the organization.
2. Recognition of the importance of human feelings in the management of the organization.
3. Development of increased understanding between and within working groups in order to reduce tensions.
4. Development of more effective team relationships.
5. Development of better methods of resolving conflicts.
6. Development of mutual confidence and trust and wide sharing of control and responsibility.[10]

The accomplishment of these goals frequently presents ethical problems to the change-agents or OD practitioners who, as management consultants, are concerned primarily with effectiveness and who, as social reformers, are striving to increase humanistic values in the work place. Many of the ethical dilemmas in OD relate to power, freedom, and professional responsibility of change-agents.[11]

---

[8] W. J. Reddin, "How to Change Things," *Executive* (June, 1969), pp. 22-26.

[9] Edgar G. Williams, "Changing Systems and Behavior," *Business Horizons,* Vol. 12, No. 4 (August, 1969), pp. 53-58.

[10] Adapted from Bennis, *op. cit.,* p. 118.

[11] Richard E. Walton and Donald P. Warwick, "The Ethics of Organization Development," *The Journal of Applied Behavioral Science,* Vol. 9, No. 6 (1973), pp. 681-698, as reprinted in Herbert J. Chruden and Arthur W. Sherman, Jr., *Readings in Personnel Management* (4th ed.; Cincinnati: South-Western Publishing Co., 1976), pp. 329-346.

Methods for Implementing Goals. Most change-agents would probably agree with the goals listed on the preceding page. However, the methods for implementing these goals will vary among the change-agents. Those methods that are most widely used involve:

1. Obtaining as much information as possible about the organization through employee attitude or opinion surveys, individual interviews, and discussions followed by discussions of the findings with managerial and supervisory personnel.
2. Conducting laboratory training programs.
3. Sponsoring clinically oriented seminars that focus on mental health and adjustment to the work situation.
4. Providing opportunities for managerial and supervisory personnel to participate in transactional analysis workshops.

Use of Attitude Survey Data

One of the most economical approaches to obtaining data for use in making organizational changes is through surveys. These surveys are usually conducted on a company- or plant-wide basis and usually involve the administration of a questionnaire or inventory that has been especially designed for the purpose. Such questionnaires are intended to measure employee opinions concerning various aspects of their work situation. On the basis of information obtained from questionnaire surveys, management may then take action to change the conditions that make for dissatisfaction or attempt to change employee attitudes toward them.

Planning the Survey. Careful planning of the survey is essential to its success. The objectives of the survey should be clearly determined and discussed by representatives of the various groups concerned, namely, managers, supervisors, employees, and the union. The suggestions from these various groups, as well as from counselors and other members of the personnel department, not only can be helpful but also will serve to enlist the cooperation of the personnel involved and help guarantee the success of the survey.

The confidence and cooperation of the employees are especially important. Management can increase the confidence of employees in management's intentions for conducting a survey by giving assurances that the responses will be made on an anonymous basis and that no punitive action of any kind will be taken. It is also essential that employees be advised that the results will be published and that action will be taken to correct unsatisfactory conditions wherever possible.

Designing the Questionnaire. The questionnaire or inventory that is used in a survey should cover all phases of the employment situation that are believed to be related to employee satisfaction and dissatisfaction. One commercially available questionnaire used by several large companies is the *SRA Attitude Survey*.[12] It consists of a questionnaire known as the Core Survey that contains

[12] Published by Science Research Associates, Inc. (259 East Erie Street, Chicago, Illinois 60611), 1970.

78 items sampling 14 job categories as listed in Figure 15-3 on page 337. There are also provisions for supplementary items of concern to individual organizations as well as for use with supervisors and salespersons.

Types of Questions. The questionnaire method of appraising employee attitudes may include different types of questions or items. Agree-disagree items, multiple-choice questions, a checklist of items, and open-ended questions to which the respondents comment in their own words are commonly used. The *SRA Attitude Survey* mentioned above contains items to which the employee responds with "agrees," "disagrees," or "undecided." A few typical items from this inventory are:

> If I have a complaint to make, I feel free to talk to someone up-the-line.
> My boss sees that employees are properly trained for the job.
> Changes are made here with little regard for welfare of employees.
> Poor working conditions keep me from doing my best in my work.[13]

It should be recognized, however, that for many items it is difficult for respondents to answer the questions with an "agree" or "disagree." The use of a scale with four or five response positions may be desirable.

Administering the Questionnaire. The conditions under which the attitude questionnaire is administered are of vital importance to the success of the survey and to the morale of the participants. The planning of the survey should give special attention to this phase in order that employees will be fully oriented and will understand the purpose of the survey. The usual procedure is to administer the questionnaire to employees in large groups during working hours. This approach gives the employees a greater assurance of anonymity and insures that each employee who is at work will participate.

Analyzing the Data. A tabulation of results broken down by departments, male versus female workers, hourly rated workers versus piece-rate workers, and other meaningful categories is the starting point in analyzing the data. The next step is to make comparisons with some standard. If data are available from previous surveys, comparisons can be made. Comparisons may also be made between departments of the organization. Furthermore, where standardized questionnaires such as the *SRA Attitude Survey* are used, it is possible to compare the attitudes of personnel in one branch of an organization with that of personnel in another branch. Because of the extensive use of this inventory, the opinions of employees in an organization may be compared against national figures (norms).

Organizations that are operating on an international basis and employing personnel that are native to the various countries may wish to assess the attitudes and opinions of its workers. Interpretation of findings from a survey should take into consideration the effect that the particular culture will have on employee attitudes. For example, in a study of employee attitudes in Japan and

[13] *Ibid.*, reproduced with permission of Science Research Associates, Inc.

	CATEGORY	QUESTIONS ASKED
1	JOB DEMANDS	Work pressure, fatigue, boredom, work load, hours of work.
2	WORKING CONDITIONS	Annoyances, management's concern for conditions, equipment adequacy, safety measures, effect of these on efficiency.
3	PAY	Adequacy, comparison with pay of others in the company and in other local companies, administration of pay system.
4	EMPLOYEE BENEFITS	All benefits, comparison with benefits in other companies, knowledge of program, administration of benefits.
5	FRIENDLINESS, COOPERATION OF FELLOW EMPLOYEES	Bossiness, friction.
6	SUPERVISORY-EMPLOYEE INTERPERSONAL RELATIONS	Friendliness, fairness, treatment of suggestions, credit for good work, concern for welfare, follow-through on promises.
7	CONFIDENCE IN MANAGEMENT	Belief in management's integrity and its concern for employee welfare, adequacy of personnel policies, friendliness.
8	TECHNICAL COMPETENCE OF SUPERVISION	Administrative skill, knowledge of job, ability to train employees, decision making, work organization.
9	EFFECTIVENESS OF ADMINISTRATION	Competence of higher levels of management, efficiency of company operations, cooperation among departments.
10	ADEQUACY OF COMMUNICATION	Freedom to express opinion and suggest improvements; complaint-handling; information about operations and plans.
11	SECURITY OF JOB AND WORK RELATIONS	Security from arbitary discharge and layoff, recognition of length of service, handling of job changes.
12	STATUS AND RECOGNITION	Standing with the company, fair appraisal of work done, respect for judgment.
13	IDENTIFICATION WITH THE COMPANY	Pride in the company, interest in its future, sense of belonging and participation with the company.
14	OPPORTUNITY FOR GROWTH AND ADVANCEMENT	Opportunities to use one's skills, to grow and develop on the job, to get ahead in the organization.

Figure 15-3 CATEGORIES IN THE SRA ATTITUDE SURVEY

the United States, marked differences were found between native employees in the two countries, both of which are industrial. Japanese employees are more willing to identify themselves positively with the company than are employees in the United States. More than two thirds of the Japanese workers believed that their job lives were at least equally as important as their personal lives, whereas the response pattern was almost reversed by United States participants.[14]

Despite the obvious advantages of employee attitude surveys, many have questioned the reactions of employees toward the surveys. To find out what employees actually thought, over 2,000 marketing and administrative employees were queried about surveys through a questionnaire. Three out of four marketing employees and two out of three administrative employees responded that the opinion surveys were useful to the company. Managers of these groups were even more positive. While two out of three marketing employees and one of two administrative employees thought management would take the survey seriously, only half of both groups expected that something constructive would come out of it. These findings reinforce the admonitions about the need for employee feedback and meaningful follow-up action.[15]

Taking Corrective Action. The findings of the attitude survey should be presented to department heads for their information and corrective action as well as to top management. It is not enough, however, to assume that advising a department head of deficiencies to be corrected is sufficient. It should be the responsibility of one individual or a committee to review progress continously to insure that necessary action is being taken.

As corrective action is taken, employees should be advised through company publications, memoranda, and other media that such action is a result of the survey findings. This proof to the participants that their ideas and opinions are wanted and will be respected helps to guarantee the success of future surveys and facilitates other types of communication within the organization, thus making a contribution to employee satisfaction and adjustment.

Laboratory Training for Managerial and Supervisory Personnel

Laboratory training, as the term is used in organizational development, refers to a type of training that is also known as "sensitivity," "group dynamics," or as "T-group" training (see Chapter 9). Of 241 companies reporting some interest in the behavioral sciences that were surveyed by the National Industrial Conference Board, 42 percent use some form of sensitivity training.[16]

---

[14] Arthur M. Whitehill, Jr., "Cultural Values and Employee Attitudes: United States and Japan," *Journal of Applied Psychology,* Vol. 48, No. 1 (February, 1964), pp. 69-72.

[15] William Penzer, "Employee Attitudes Toward Attitude Surveys," *Personnel,* Vol. 50, No. 3 (May-June, 1973), pp. 60-64.

[16] Harold M. Rush, *Behavioral Science: Concepts and Management Application,* Studies in Personnel Policy No. 216 (New York: National Industrial Conference Board, Inc., 1969).

The Managerial Grid. Another type of laboratory training—the Managerial Grid—was reported to be used by 33 percent of the 241 companies in the NICB study. Basically the Grid is an analytical training approach which is closely related to the consideration and structure dimensions of leadership discussed earlier. In their book, *The Managerial Grid,* Blake and Mouton analyze managerial styles in detail, using the grid shown in Figure 15-4 as a basis for expressing the relationships between Concern for People (Consideration) and Concern for Production (Structure). The grid depicts five different patterns (the number 1 in each instance represents minimum concern, 9 stands for maximum concern), although 81 mixtures of these two concerns might be pictured.

By referring to the Grid and identifying their behavior on the two dimensions or areas of concern, namely for production and for people, the managers or supervisors are better able to understand the approach that they use with their subordinates. The Grid itself, however, only provides the conceptual framework that must be implemented through participation in

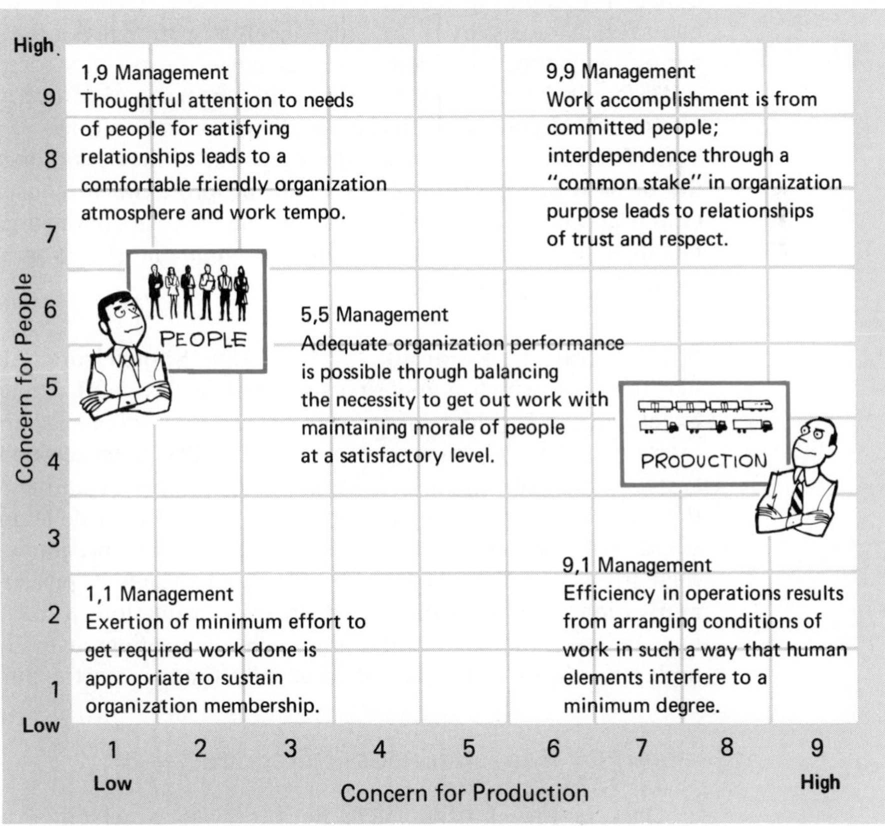

Source: Robert R. Blake and Jane S. Mouton, *The Managerial Grid* (Houston: Gulf Publishing Company, 1964), p. 10. Reproduced with permission.

Figure 15-4 THE MANAGERIAL GRID

seminars if it is to be effective. In the Grid seminars managerial and supervisory personnel learn to identify the personal and organizational changes that are needed and to become more effective in their interpersonal relationships and in their work with groups.

Phases of a Grid Program. Participation in a Grid program involves six phases. Prior to attending a Grid seminar which usually runs for a week (phase 1), each participant is required to read Blake and Mouton's book along with other behavioral science literature. At the seminar simulation exercises based on problem cases from different organizations are discussed and solutions proposed. As they conduct their discussions, the participants evaluate each other's managerial style. Upon returning to their organizations (phase 2), the participants are encouraged to apply what they have learned to the development of their respective work teams.

The first two phases—referred to as management development phases—are followed by four subsequent phases, referred to as organization development. These phases involve intergroup development where conflicts and tension between groups are identified and resolved (phase 3); the setting of organizational goals by a top management policy-making team that is concerned with broad problems such as cost control, profit improvement, labor relations, etc. (phase 4); the use of special task forces to measure the attainment of goals that cut across the organization (phase 5); and finally, the "stabilization phase" in which strong points of the operation are established as the desired approaches (phase 6). While professional consultants assist in a Grid program, its purpose is to involve the members of the organization itself as much as possible. Thus, the change-agents in the program are primarily members of the organization.

Special Training Programs for First-Line Supervisors. Although programs like the Grid which involve personnel at all levels of management from top executives to first-line supervisors are on the increase, there is a continuing interest in special training programs for the latter group. Such programs typically are concerned with keeping supervisors up to date on all phases of their work and providing opportunities for them to develop a better understanding of themselves in their leadership role. The programs typically involve regularly scheduled meetings in order that the many phases of their work—motivation, communication, performance evaluation, to mention but a few—may be covered. By the time the cycle of meetings over this wide range of topics has been completed, it is usually time to start a new cycle.

Laboratory Training for Nonsupervisory Personnel

Only in recent years have nonsupervisory personnel been included in those organizational development programs that originally were designed for managerial and supervisory personnel. After Grid seminars had been conducted for managerial and professional staff personnel for four years in one corporation, middle management personnel recommended that Grid seminars be conducted for both wage and salaried employees.[17] Grid seminars were conducted on site during regular working hours with participants going through the same program as their superiors. After an evaluation study was conducted at the end of the program, outside researchers concluded that wage earners were able to understand and to apply the concepts and methods learned in Grid seminars. The programs were found to help these employees to contribute to improvement of plant climate and to the solution of problems relating to production and other matters. In addition, they appear to have a newly found self-confidence, a deeper sense of involvement and commitment, and a feeling of working better as a team. Specific advantages in terms of gain in dollar savings were also shown.[18]

Clinically Oriented Seminars

Another approach to organizational development is the use of clinically oriented seminars. About 1954 the Menninger Foundation established a division of industrial mental health for the purpose of training executives (1) to increase the effectiveness of their subordinates as well as of themselves, (2) to better understand human motivation, and (3) to improve their communication skills. The program emphasizes the understanding of normal behavior and covers such topics as psychological structure, unconscious expectations, adjustment mechanisms, dependency, personality development, rivalry, and conflict. The emotional problems executives encounter involving such feelings as fear, anger, and self-doubt, are discussed freely in order that they may be able to understand themselves better. Similar programs are sponsored by organizations like The Levinson Institute. In week-long sessions considerable emphasis is given to the major crises and stresses that executives face, both at home and at work, and some methods of coping more effectively with them.

Surveys indicate that widespread stress is adversely affecting more and more people in business. Of 2,800 managers and supervisors surveyed, almost 30 percent reported job-related health problems. Only 7 percent of these job-related health problems were classified as physical whereas 93 percent were reported as the result of stress—strain, tension, and pressure.[19] Stress in itself is neither good nor bad: it's how one copes with it and how one responds when the pressure becomes overwhelming. Recognition of the need for professional psychological or psychiatric assistance is growing among executives, and more of them are seeking such help and are being more tolerant of subordinates who seek it. In too many cases, however, the harried executive seeks relief in pills or alcohol.[20] Through participation in clinically oriented seminars, executives are frequently awakened to the need for a change in attitudes and habits. They may then be ready to seek the assistance of such professionals as clinical

[17] Robert R. Blake, Jane S. Mouton, Richard L. Sloma, Barbara Peek Loftin, "A Second Breakthrough in Organization Development," *California Management Review,* Vol. 11, No. 2 (Winter, 1968), pp. 73-78.

[18] *Ibid.,* p. 78.

[19] *The Changing Success Ethic,* An AMA Survey Report, 1973.

[20] "The Executive Under Pressure," *Business Week* (May 25, 1974), pp. 119-130.

psychologists, psychiatrists, physical fitness experts, as well as physicians. Those physicians described by Dr. Nittler who use a preventative approach with emphasis upon nutrition and healthful living are frequently identified with organizational programs for executives.[21]

Transactional Analysis Workshops

A newer approach to improving the quality of organizational life is through a behavioral technique called *transactional analysis,* commonly referred to as "TA." This technique was developed originally by Eric Berne as a simplified approach to psychotherapy.[22] According to Berne, three primary "ego states"—Parent, Adult, and Child—exist in all of us. In each social situation or *transaction,* one of the ego states predominates. The one that is predominant depends upon many factors including early life experiences, the circumstances under which the transaction takes place, and the other person's ego state. To know which ego state is predominant in a given transaction, one needs to analyze posture and facial expressions (body language), as well as verbal expressions and vocal tone. The behavioral characteristics for the three ego states are given in Figure 15-5. A study of them will reveal that the labels—Parent, Adult, and Child—reflect the type of behavior one thinks of as being characteristic of parents, adults, and children. TA's fundamental strength

What the Parent does	What the Adult does	What the Child does
Nurtures	Processes information	Invents
Criticizes	Takes objective action	Expresses curiosity
Restricts	Thinks, then acts	Acts on impulse
Judges	Organizes	Acts selfishly
Blames	Plans	Loves
Encourages	Solves problems	Imagines/brainstorms
Supports	Estimates risks	Acts belligerently
	Ferrets out assumptions	Complains
Source—the relationship between you and your parents.	*Source*—the emergence of independent thinking in early life and its subsequent development.	*Source*—the best and worst of your young self.

Source: Charles Albana, "Transactional Analysis on the Job," *Supervisory Management,* Vol. 19, No. 1 (January, 1974), pp. 2-12. Reproduced with permission.

Figure 15-5 EGO-STATE CONTRIBUTIONS TO BEHAVIOR

[21] Alan H. Nittler, *A New Breed of Doctor* (New York: Pyramid House, 1972).
[22] Eric Berne, *Transactional Analysis in Psychotherapy* (New York: Grove Press, 1961).

"is that it is essentially a language that translates past psychological ideas into easily understood concepts that even lay people can handle."[23]

There are many specific applications of TA to various activities within organizations—e.g., supervising personnel, developing better relations with customers, counseling employees—but in all of them the major contribution of TA is the improvement of interpersonal communication and feelings. In TA workshops managers, supervisors, and employees learn how to understand themselves and others through a study of TA principles and practice in analyzing various interpersonal transactions.

At the beginning the participants are asked to identify reactions to common situations by indicating whether they are Parent, Adult, or Child reactions such as the following:

A clerk loses an important letter.[24]	(circle one)
1. "Why can't you keep track of anything you're responsible for?"	P A C
2. "Check each person who may have used it in the last two days and try to trace it. Perhaps Mrs. Smith can help you."	P A C
3. "I can't solve your problems. I didn't take your old letter."	P A C

With an understanding of P-A-C reactions, participants then go on to analyzing such basic transactions as: (1) complementary transactions, i.e., where people are on the same wavelength and there is good communication, (2) crossed transactions, i.e., where individuals attempting to communicate with each other are shut off by what one or both say, and (3) ulterior transactions, where individuals say one thing but mean another. In the workshop more advanced and specialized exercises may then be used.

Although TA originally started as a treatment approach and is now widely used by professional therapists for that purpose, it is equally popular for use in developing individuals for more effective functioning in organizations. As Harris, author of *I'm O.K, You're O.K.* has stated: "It is a teaching and learning device rather than a confessional or an archaelogical exploration of the psychic cellars."[25] TA is also valuable in laying bare the psyche of corporations as well as of individual executives by revealing the patterns or

[23] Dr. Donald Bower as quoted in "Business Tries Out 'Transactional Analysis'," *Business Week* (January 12, 1974), pp. 74-75.

[24] The answers are as follows: (1) P, (2) A, (3) C. This example is from Dorothy Jongeward and Muriel James, *Winning with People—Group Exercises in Transactional Analysis* (Reading, Massachusetts: Addison-Wesley Publishing Company, 1973), p. 38. For a detailed discussion of TA as applied to organizations, see Dorothy Jongeward, *Everybody Wins: Transactional Analysis Applied to Organizations* (Reading, Massachusetts: Addison-Wesley Publishing Company, 1973) and Charles Albanó, "Transactional Analysis on the Job," *Supervisory Management,* Vol. 19, No. 1 (January, 1974), pp. 2-12; No. 2 (February, 1974), pp. 12-27; No. 3 (March, 1974), pp. 14-20; and No. 4 (April, 1974), pp. 22-36.

[25] Thomas A. Harris, *I'm O.K.—You're O.K.: A Practical Guide to Transactional Analysis* (New York: Harper & Row, 1969), p. xvii.

"scripts" by which organizations are managed. Jongeward states that corporations that play the parent role "may be locked into this autocratic pattern, spending their energies maintaining the old script rather than keeping up with the times." The script can be altered by making people think about their relationships with others and giving them some kind of framework to evaluate and improve them.[26]

CHANGES INVOLVING EMPLOYEE PLACEMENT

In order for an organization to be able to remain viable, to adapt to new conditions, and to serve its members and society effectively, the employees within it, as noted earlier, must be required to make changes and adjustments. Although many of the changes will be of a minor nature requiring minimal readjustment, others will be of a major nature, at least as far as their jobs and personal lives are concerned. Among these, changes in job placement may be required in order to accommodate changes that are occurring in production loads or processes in the organization. Such changes also may be required to allow for changes that have occurred in the qualifications, performance, or behavior of the employee. Job changes in other instances may be made in an effort to find a job which is better suited for the employee.

A change of jobs may constitute a transfer, a promotion, or a demotion depending upon whether the new job to which the employee is assigned involves more, less, or the same amount of responsibility, status, and pay. When the employee is removed from employment in any job, the action may be in the form of a layoff or discharge.

Transfers

A transfer involves the placement of an individual in another job for which the duties, responsibilities, status, and remuneration are approximately equal to those of the previous job. A transfer may require an employee to change work group, work place, work shift, or organizational unit; and it may even necessitate moving to another geographic area. Transfers make possible the placement of employees in jobs where there is greater need for their services; they often permit employees to be placed on jobs which they prefer and can perform more effectively; and they sometimes enable employees to join a work group in which they can work more cooperatively. Transfers can also provide employees with training and development experiences. Employment in a variety of jobs and departments can help individuals to prepare for jobs at higher levels as well as increase their effectiveness at present levels.

Control of Transfers. Since some loss of efficiency is likely to occur while the employees who are transferred are learning and adjusting to their new jobs, some degree of control should be maintained over transfers. Accurate sales,

[26] "Business Tries Out 'Transactional Analysis'," *op. cit.*

production, and manpower planning and the exercise of greater caution in the selection and placement of personnel, furthermore, can reduce the need for transfers. The transfer of "problem employees" in particular must be carefully controlled since too often such action does not remove the cause of the problem but may merely pass the problem on to some other supervisor. In some instances a problem which exists between a supervisor and an employee may be the result of a clash in personalities for which both have a measure of responsibility.

Transfer requests must also be kept under control to prevent some individuals from continually changing jobs in hopes of finding an occupational Utopia. Employees who are always seeking to change jobs may not need a change of environment as much as they need counseling. If too many transfer requests originate within a particular department, however, it could indicate that the fault lies at least partially with the supervisor or with the conditions within the department rather than with the employees.

Resistance to Transfers. It is not uncommon for employees to resist being transferred to another job. Even if the new job is considered to be equally desirable, a transfer can necessitate certain changes in well-established habits. Supervisors also may object to losing their personnel to another department through transfers. This reaction may stem from an inclination to hoard human resources and from the desire to avoid losing individuals who have received a considerable amount of training. Resistance may be particularly strong if a supervisor is required to supply personnel to departments in which the supervisors have failed to provide adequate training programs for developing the potential of their subordinates.

Some of the resistance to transfers can be reduced by communicating to personnel the reasons why the transfers are necessary and the bases upon which personnel are selected for transfer. Supervisors also may offer less resistance if they are given some voice in selecting the individuals who are to be transferred.

Promotions

A *promotion* involves a change of assignment from a job of a lower level to one of a higher level within the organization. The new job normally is one that provides an employee with an increase in pay and status, and is more demanding in terms of skill or responsibility.

Purposes of Promotions. Promotions permit an organization to utilize more effectively any skills and abilities that individuals have been able to develop during the course of their training and employment. The opportunity to gain a promotion can serve as an incentive for individuals to improve further their capacities and their performance. Promotions can also serve as a reward and as evidence of appreciation for past achievements. If the promotion program is administered properly, it can serve to improve employee efficiency and morale and to attract new employees to the organization. In the past a promotion invariably meant the assumption of supervisory responsibilities, but today it may not. It is fairly common now for organizations to establish alternative methods by which employees may be promoted. Where scientists, engineers, and other specially trained personnel are utilized, a dual-track system may be provided for promotional opportunities to jobs that may not include supervisory responsibilities.

Bases for Promotion. The benefits to be derived from a promotion program are contingent upon having objective criteria available for selecting individuals for promotion. The use of such criteria permits promotion decisions to be made fairly and enables employees to understand the basis for them.

Merit and Seniority. The two principal criteria for determining promotions are merit and seniority. While the term *merit* more correctly applies to an individual's record of performance, it also is commonly used in reference to abilities. In its broader sense, merit can be said to refer to both past performance and ability; for it is in this sense that merit is used as a criterion for determining that an individual is qualified to meet the requirements of a higher-level job. Evidence of merit may be provided by performance ratings, personal history records, and scores on job-relevant tests. *Seniority* refers to the length of service that an employee has accumulated. While seniority lends itself to more objective measurement than merit, its determination can create various problems that will be discussed later in this chapter.

In giving recognition to merit and seniority, the problem generally is *not* one of deciding which of the two factors to consider; rather, the problem is to determine the degree of recognition which should be given to each of the factors. Rarely is either merit or seniority considered to the exclusion of the other, although employers generally prefer to give more weight to merit. Even when not restricted by a labor agreement, however, management may find itself giving considerable recognition to seniority because of the difficulty of effectively measuring relative merit and of effectively communicating to employees that the measurement is accurate and fair. Recognition for seniority also increases the assurance that there is no discrimination, or what might be perceived to be discrimination, on the basis of age, sex, or minority group membership in promotion decisions.[27]

In considering candidates for promotion, performance in their present job may not necessarily provide an accurate basis for predicting success in a job at a higher level. This fact is especially true if an employee is being promoted into a different type of job, such as when an operative employee is promoted to a supervisory job. To the extent that the functions of the job for which a candidate is being considered are different, it is important that merit be judged in terms of meeting the requirements of the higher-level job as well as in terms of meeting those of the present one.

---

[27] *Labor Policy and Practice—Personnel Management* (Washington, D.C.: The Bureau of National Affairs, Inc.), par. 207:13.

Tests. Tests also can be used in making decisions on promotions in some instances as long as they are professionally developed and are related to skills necessary to accomplish the job. Tests of supervisory knowledge and attitudes are generally of questionable value because the "correct" response is usually apparent to the candidate for a supervisory job. The use of job-knowledge tests in promoting, as well as hiring, individuals in government agencies is fairly well recognized. While very few business firms use job-knowledge tests in evaluating persons for promotion, this approach should receive more attention than it has because of the contributions that it can make through the assurance that individuals have the requisite knowledge for handling the demands of a higher-level job.

In determining the qualifications of potential candidates for supervisory positions, several sources of information may be used. Their supervisors and co-workers are in a good position to assess their potentiality for supervisory work. Performance evaluation reports, test scores, training records, assessment center reports, and other data that may be found in personnel files may also provide information about candidates, and a review of the files may reveal individuals who should have been considered but were overlooked.

Need for a Thorough Evaluation. Too often a thorough appraisal is not made before promoting individuals. This tendency has led one student of occupational patterns to formulate the *Peter Principle,* which states that "in a hierarchy every employee tends to rise to his level of incompetence," and *Peter's Corollary* which states that "in time, every post tends to be occupied by an employee who is incompetent to carry out his duties."[28] The consequences of not evaluating individuals as carefully as should be done is likely to lead executives to give some thought to the suggestion made by the one in Figure 15-6.

Encouraging Employees to Accept Promotions. In our society an individual is under considerable pressure to seek and accept promotions; however, there are many individuals who will refuse to accept a promotion. In order to interest qualified individuals in promotions, management must make a promotion worthwhile in terms of the pay, status, and other benefits received. By giving candidates proper encouragement, coaching, training, and the opportunity to perform the duties of the job for which they are eligible to be promoted, management can do much to build confidence and enthusiasm for accepting the promotion. It may be well, however, for management not to be overly insistent that an individual seek and accept a promotion.

Demotions

A *demotion* consists of a change in assignment to a job on a lower organizational level and involving less skill, responsibility, status, and pay.

[28] Laurence J. Peter and Raymond Hull, *The Peter Principle*. (New York: William Morrow and Company, 1969) considers why things always go wrong. How to make things go right is discussed in Laurence J. Peter, *The Peter Prescription* (New York: William Morrow and Company, 1972).

"If there is validity in the Peter Principle, why don't we just demote everyone one rung and have a perfect organization?"

Source: Business Week. Reprinted with permission.

Figure 15-6

Employees may be demoted because of a reduction in the number of positions of the type they are occupying or because their performance has not been satisfactory. Demotions also may be used as a disciplinary action to punish employees for their failure to correct their deficiencies or to comply with existing policies, rules, or standards.

Demotion Problems. A demotion can create more personnel problems within an organization than other assignment changes because of the psychological effects that such action may have upon the demoted employee or upon fellow workers. It is difficult for most employees to accept and adjust to the loss of pay and status that usually results from a demotion. It is important, therefore, that an employee who is demoted be given whatever assistance is possible.

Alternatives to Demotion. Sometimes an alternative course of action may be preferable to a demotion. When the abilities and skills of a long-service employee decline below the job requirements, the problem may be solved by transferring some of the duties to other jobs while allowing the title and pay of the job to remain the same. In other instances the problem is resolved by "kicking the person upstairs" to a job with an impressive title and relatively little authority or responsibility. If an employee's difficulties are due to a hostile attitude or to an emotional disorder, a demotion may serve only to aggravate the problem. If these difficulties cannot be overcome by means of counseling or similar corrective action, early retirement or discharge may be a better solution to the problem than demotion.

Layoffs

In Chapter 5 the advantages of stabilized employment to both the organization and employees were discussed. In spite of its efforts to avoid the layoff of employees, an organization may find it necessary to reduce the size of its work force as a result of a reduction in its work load, the elimination of certain jobs through reorganization, depressed economic conditions, or the improvements made in production efficiency. While a reduction in the work force sometimes necessitates the permanent termination of the services of some employees, it can at times be accomplished by laying them off temporarily pending the resumption of normal activity.

Nature of Layoffs. The procedures by which layoffs are to be accomplished and the nature of the reemployment of those affected by layoffs are usually covered in considerable detail by the labor agreement in those organizations that are unionized. Adequate protection of job rights and equitable treatment of members whenever layoffs are necessary are among the benefits that individuals seek first from their union. Organizational policy as well as provisions in the labor agreement, therefore, should establish and define clearly the employment rights of each individual and the basis upon which layoff selections will be made and reemployment effected. The rights of employees during layoffs, the conditions concerning their eligibility for recall, and their obligations in accepting recall should also be clarified. It is common for labor agreements to preserve the reemployment rights of individuals receiving a layoff for periods of up to two years, providing that they do not refuse to return to work if recalled sooner.

Determination of the Order of Layoffs. The determination of the order of layoff for employees usually is based upon seniority and/or ability. Under some labor agreements seniority may be the primary consideration, as illustrated by the following provision:

> In all cases of layoffs or rehiring the principle of straight seniority by departments shall be observed and the length of service shall govern provided the employees shall have the skill, industry and ability to do the work they are required in a satisfactory manner.[29]

[29] Agreement between the Allen Manufacturing Co. and the United Auto Workers.

In other organizations such factors as ability and fitness may take precedence over seniority in determining layoffs. For example, a labor agreement may provide that:

> . . . in all cases of decreases in forces or recalls after layoff, the following factors as listed below shall be considered; however, only where both factors "a" and "b" are relatively equal shall continuous service be the determining factor:
>
> a. Ability to perform the work.
> b. Physical fitness.
> c. Continuous service.[30]

The practice of using job seniority as the basis for deciding which workers to lay off may well affect women and minority workers who, in many organizations, have less seniority than other groups. In a U.S. District Court a ruling was given in favor of a group of blacks who were laid off. The judge held that the company's procedures were discriminatory because the black workers' low seniority stemmed from the company's previous failure to hire blacks.[31]

In the case of organizations that are not unionized, definite policies and procedures should be established for conducting layoffs so as to insure that employees will receive fair and consistent treatment and be able to anticipate their vulnerability to layoff. Even when provisions governing layoff are contained in a labor agreement, it is still desirable to establish policies and procedures that can serve to supplement and clarify the terms of the agreement. Employees who are terminated temporarily or permanently are usually entitled to unemployment compensation from various sources that are described in Chapter 22.

Seniority Considerations

It has become customary for employers to give some degree of recognition to seniority even among employees who are not unionized. Unions generally advocate recognition of seniority because they feel that their members should be entitled to certain job rights that are proportionate to the years that they have invested in their jobs.

Whenever seniority provides a basis for determining or even influencing personnel decisions, the judgment and discretion of management is reduced accordingly. Decisions based on seniority are relatively easy to make since they require merely computing the amount of service that an individual has accumulated and, by referring to established policies and rules, determining entitlements to be derived from such seniority. One of the major disadvantages,

---

[30] Agreement between the U.S. Steel Corp. and the United Steel Workers.

[31] " 'Last Hired, First Fired' Takes It on the Chin," *Business Week* (March 9, 1974), p. 166. Also see "Who's Next? Courts' Protection Against Job Layoffs Sought by Minorities," *The Wall Street Journal,* November 5, 1974.

however, of overemphasizing seniority is that the less competent employees receive the same rewards and security as the more competent ones.

In order to be able to compute the amount of an employee's seniority, it is first necessary to establish certain provisions governing the conditions under which it can be accumulated and applied. These provisions, which are usually covered in detail by the labor agreement, should clarify: (1) the organizational unit within which seniority rights may be accumulated and applied, (2) the conditions under which these rights may be accumulated and retained, (3) the rights and benefits that are to be determined by seniority, and (4) the groups that may be excluded from seniority provisions.

Importance of Placement Policies and Procedures

Since changes in job placement can have a significant effect upon organizational efficiency and upon the morale and the lives of employees, it is important that such changes give recognition to the needs of both the organization and the employees. Carefully prepared policies and procedures can help both to acquaint personnel with the circumstances under which changes in assignments are permitted and to prevent inequities and abuses from occurring as a result of such changes.

In order for changes in job placement to be coordinated and controlled most effectively, they should be processed through the personnel department. While department managers must have authority to make changes in employee job assignments if they are to be held responsible for the efficiency of their departments, they must make these changes in accordance with established policies and procedures. If they do not do so, it is within the functional authority of the personnel department to prevent the changes in placement from being executed. If some form of staff control were not provided, operating departments occasionally might make changes in job assignments that would ignore the rights of individual employees or the pertinent text of the labor agreement.

Since personnel in other departments may be eligible to fill a job vacancy or to receive a layoff, some centralized system of locating and screening eligible personnel is necessary. The personnel department often uses computerized skills files to locate qualified personnel to fill openings. The location of employees for promotion or transfer also may be accomplished by means of a job-bidding system. Success with such a system is contingent upon management being able to notify promptly all candidates who might be eligible about job vacancies and also to prevent employees from bidding indiscriminately.

In administering changes in job placement, it is to be expected that certain problems will be encountered both by individual employees and by the organization. By giving individual consideration and attention to employees in helping them to solve their adjustment problems, management can do much to maintain their morale and efficiency during assignment changes.

Résumé

Every organization must be dynamic and undergo changes continually if it is to be effective. It should not only be capable of adapting to changing forces but its management also should be making plans for change on a continuous basis. The modern concepts of organizational development emphasize the importance of change in creating an organization that is viable and adaptable. In the modern approach the human factor is recognized as being of primary importance. It emphasizes the need for employee acceptance of change and for constantly renewing the organization so that it offers more challenging and rewarding opportunities for its members.

External agents for change generally emphasize the importance of learning as much as possible about the organization through employee attitude surveys and taking whatever corrective action is necessary. Since the changes that contribute the most are those that start at the top of the hierarchy, management training is considered an important part of any organizational development program. Through Grid seminars, T-group training, clinically oriented seminars, and TA workshops, managers become involved in developing a better understanding of themselves and the nature of their relationships with others in the organization. This leads into a broader consideration of those factors that relate directly to the achievement of the existing organizational goals and the setting of new goals that may be feasible as a result of a renewed organization.

In order for an organization to change, it is necessary for its members to make changes in their jobs. Several types of changes in job placement—transfers, promotions, demotions, and layoffs—were discussed. The condition and basis for making these changes should be thoroughly understood by all personnel, and sufficient control should be maintained by the personnel department to insure that changes in placement are made in a fair and consistent manner.

The program governing job changes should determine the recognition to be given to ability and seniority, and information pertaining to this subject should be communicated to employees. Since employee initiative and efficiency can be jeopardized if too much recognition is given to seniority, it is advisable for management to resist the inclusion of restrictive seniority; it should not be considered to the exclusion of ability. It is particularly important that management recognize that a change of jobs can provide a very critical experience for an employee which requires the understanding and assistance of managerial and supervisory personnel as well as the personnel staff.

DISCUSSION QUESTIONS

1. Why do employees resist change? Under what circumstances may they seek to have change accomplished?
2. Some executives are against conducting attitude surveys because they feel that asking employees to express their opinions will create unnecessary problems and result in employees becoming dissatisfied with working conditions.
   a. What do you think of this point of view?
   b. As a personnel manager, how could you influence them to change their point of view?

3. Four types of organizational development methods were discussed in this chapter: attitude surveys, laboratory training for managers and supervisors, clinically oriented seminars, and transactional analysis workshops. What contributions can each of these methods make to an organization? If you were restricted to using only one method, which would you select? Why?
4. Of what value would periodic consultations with a psychiatrist or clinical psychologist be to an executive? Who should pay for this service?
5. The personnel manager has received a request from an employee to be transferred to another department because the employee feels that his current supervisor is standing in the way of his advancement. The employee has requested that his supervisor not be advised of his interview for fear that the supervisor might make future conditions unbearable. The personnel manager has heard a few other complaints about this supervisor, but none of them have been raised formally.
   a. What action should the personnel manager take?
   b. Should he disclose the request to the supervisor?
6. What explanation and justification can you give for the fact that seniority tends to be more of a determining factor in those decisions involving layoff than in those decisions involving promotion?
7. In recent years the failure of many organizations to consider women for promotion on an equal basis with men has been well documented and disseminated. What are the underlying reasons for this discrimination? What are some of the typical stated reasons?

PROBLEM 15-1 THE OFFICE MOVE

A personnel research staff of a large government agency employed several technical writers and specialists in addition to the personnel needed to perform administrative and clerical functions. One of the technical writers, Priscilla Clemington, in her middle forties, had been with the organization for over a year. During that time she had made a distinguished record for herself as a result of her superior performance and her skill in working with specialists in the preparation of technical manuals. She was friendly, well poised, and in other ways revealed her keen interest in the work and in the people with whom she worked. Unlike many employees, she seldom talked about herself, and it was generally believed that she was enjoying life to the fullest. Only those who had interviewed her at the time she was considered for the job knew that she had just divorced her husband and that she was returning to work in order to earn a living.

One day while Priscilla was working away from the office, the manager decided that some physical rearrangements within the office were necessary for achieving greater efficiency. She called in her immediate subordinates, one of whom was Priscilla's chief, and discussed the need for making changes. All agreed that the changes were necessary, and the manager called the moving crews who reported promptly and rearranged the office according to plan. In the process of relocating furniture, Priscilla's desk and filing cabinet were moved about six feet from where they had been. Priscilla was, however, still next to the same people as before, and the lighting in the new location was superior to that in the old spot. It was anticipated that she would be pleased at the change and that she would feel that others were concerned about her interests.

About half an hour before closing time Priscilla returned from the place where she had been working for the day and quickly noticed that her desk had been moved and that things were not the way they were at the time she left the office that morning. She immediately burst into tears and left the office. Her supervisor tried to console her, but she would not listen to the latter's reasons for the change. Priscilla then left for the day feeling very despondent.

a. How do you explain Priscilla's attitude and reaction following her return to the office?
b. What important lessons in human relations might one draw from this incident?

SUGGESTED READINGS

Argyris, Chris. *Management and Organizational Developments: The Path from xa to yb.* New York: McGraw-Hill Book Company, 1971.

Chruden, Herbert J., and Arthur W. Sherman, Jr. *Readings in Personnel Management,* 4th ed. Cincinnati: South-Western Publishing Co., 1976. Part 4.

French, Wendell L., and Cecil H. Bell, Jr. *Organization Development.* Englewood Cliffs, New Jersey: Prentice-Hall, Inc., 1973.

Gruenfeld, Elaine F. *Promotion: Practice, Policies, and Affirmative Action.* Ithaca, New York: New York State School of Industrial & Labor Relations, Cornell University, 1975.

Hage, Jerald, and Michael Aiken. *Social Change in Complex Organizations.* New York: Random House, 1970.

Jones, Garth N. *Planned Organizational Change.* New York: Frederick A. Praeger, 1969.

Levinson, Harry. *Executive Stress.* New York: Harper & Row, 1970.

Luthans, Fred, and Robert Kreitner. *Organizational Behavior Modification.* Glenview, Illinois: Scott, Foresman and Company, 1975.

Morgan, John S. *Managing Change.* New York: McGraw-Hill Book Company, 1972.

Owens, Robert G. *Organizational Behavior in Schools.* Englewood Cliffs, New Jersey: Prentice-Hall, Inc., 1970.

Porter, Lyman W., Edward E. Lawler, III, and J. Richard Hackman. *Behavior in Organizations.* New York: McGraw-Hill Book Company, 1975. Chapters 15, 16.

Schein, Edgar H. *Process Consultation: Its Role in Organization Development.* Reading, Massachusetts: Addison-Wesley Publishing Company, 1969.

Tagliere, Daniel A. *People Power and Organizations.* New York: AMACOM, 1973.

Wasmuth, William J., Rollin H. Simonds, Raymond L. Hilgert, and Hak Cong Lee. *Human Resources Administration: Problems of Growth and Change.* Boston: Houghton Mifflin Company, 1970.

Management-Labor Relations

The Union and Personnel Management

The power of employees to bargain with their employer on an individual basis and to protect themselves from arbitrary or unfair treatment is a limited one. Because of this fact many employees find it to their advantage to bargain collectively with their employer through a union. This method of bargaining, moreover, is protected and encouraged by government legislation not only for persons in private employment but increasingly for those in public employment as well.

Because personnel decisions are subject to the terms of the labor agreement and to challenge by the union, the management of personnel becomes more complicated when employees unionize. Rather than acting unilaterally, employers may find it necessary to consult first with officials of the union before taking actions affecting its members. Caution also must be observed by management to insure that personnel policies and practices affecting employees conform to the terms of the labor agreement with the union.

If employees are not unionized, the employer's personnel policies and practices can affect employee desires to unionize. Employers, therefore, must be concerned with unions either because they are required to negotiate with them or because there is always the possibility that their employees may decide to unionize. It is essential that all employers and their managers have knowledge and understanding regarding the purposes and objectives of unions, the attitudes and feelings of the union leaders, and the processes by which unions organize employees and negotiate agreements with employers. It is the purpose of the next three chapters to discuss the subject of union-management relations and the processes by which union agreements are negotiated and grievances pertaining to them are resolved. It is hoped that these chapters will provide the reader with a better understanding of unions and their role in the management of personnel.

THE FUNCTIONS OF A UNION

A major function of a union is to negotiate and administer the *labor agreement* with the employer covering the conditions of employment for its members.[1] Its function also is to protect members from unfair or arbitrary treatment, and to assist them in resolving grievances that they believe may exist in connection with their employment. In these capacities the union can affect significantly the organization's personnel program and its relations with employees. By providing employees with a greater sense of security, power, and importance in their relations with superiors that they otherwise would not have as individuals, a union can exert a significant influence upon their attitudes and behavior. Through such influence it can affect appreciably employees' motivations and their response to supervisory efforts to improve efficiency.

Impact of the Union upon the Employer

When a union is recognized and certified as the bargaining agent for employees who are members, the employer is required to use time that was previously devoted to other personnel functions to negotiate the labor agreement and to discuss with union representatives the problems and grievances relating to its administration. Additional and more accurate personnel financial records also may be necessary in order to support the employer's position during contract negotiations or grievance hearings. Decisions such as those relating to wages, hours, and working conditions, instead of being made unilaterally by the employer, are likely to be subject to union consultation and/or challenge.

On Managerial Control Over Personnel Policies. Greater care will have to be exercised by the employer in the development and enforcement of personnel policies and regulations so as to insure that employees throughout the organization are treated in a manner that is fair and consistent. Since a union is quick to detect and to challenge any inconsistencies in personnel actions or inequities in the treatment of personnel that may occur between departments, its presence is likely to lead to more centralized control over personnel policies and practices.

On Managerial Authority. Management's ability to resolve problems with employees directly and quickly is reduced when employees are unionized. First-line supervisors in particular often find their status and authority reduced

[1] Although the terms contract and agreement tend to be used interchangeably, the term agreement is the more technically correct one since it lacks the requirement of specific performance—of compelling employees to work against their will.

and their relations with subordinates made more difficult because their decisions may be challenged by the *union steward*.[2] Not only must supervisors assume the added responsibility of administering the labor agreement but they also may find their efforts to maintain efficiency and discipline within the department subject to union grievances. Should decisions be reversed very often through the grievance procedure, supervisors may find it preferable to ignore rather than face certain personnel problems that arise within their departments and to overlook certain violations committed by subordinates.

On Managerial Prerogatives. Unions typically seek to achieve participation in those decisions that affect the employment, security, and welfare of their members. Specifically, the union may try to extend its right of participation in such management decisions as those relating to the location of a new plant, the subcontracting of certain work, the introduction of new production equipment and methods, the scheduling of the work load, the establishment of production standards, and the determination of job content. While the employer may seek to claim these decisions as exclusive *prerogatives of management,* it is likely to find that such prerogatives are subject to challenge and erosion by the union. These challenges can be exerted not only at the bargaining table but also through the grievance procedure and by means of pressures exerted on the job in the form of walkouts and slowdowns.

Appeal of the Union to Its Members

Undoubtedly some employers sincerely believe that a large proportion of their employees belong to a union because they are compelled to do so as the result of the union agreement or pressures from co-workers. This belief is largely erroneous, however, since few if any union leaders today have the power necessary to compel a majority of the employees in any organization to remain in the union very long against their will. The majority of members in most unions undoubtedly belong because of the benefits they believe are to be gained from doing so. Furthermore, many of those who are required by the terms of the labor agreement to join a union as a condition of employment will accept the union after they are involved in it as a member.[3]

Psychological Satisfaction. According to Stagner and Rosen, a union comes into being when a large number of employees have or think that they have needs, such as those discussed earlier in the chapter on motivation, the realization of which are being frustrated by the employer. The union thus provides a vehicle for the satisfaction of their needs even though these needs may vary considerably among employees.[4] Union membership also can

---

[2] The steward is the union counterpart of the company supervisor who works on the job with the members and represents them in resolving any problems that may arise in their relations with the company.

[3] Ross Stagner, *Psychology of Industrial Conflict* (New York: John Wiley & Sons, 1956), pp. 339-344.

[4] Ross Stagner and Hjalmar Rosen, *Psychology of Union-Management Relations* (Belmont, California: Wadsworth Publishing Company, Inc., 1965), p. 40.

provide certain employees with a means for releasing pent-up frustrations, for building self-confidence, or for putting dormant leadership capacities to work. It also may provide employees with new sources of interest, an outlet for their idle time, and a means of satisfying their desires for status, recognition, and group associations. Through their union employees may have an opportunity to become better acquainted and to fraternize with other persons who have similar desires, interests, problems, and gripes. Identification with the union can give employees added feelings of security and equality in relations with their boss. Union members need not hesitate to challenge actions of the boss or to express sentiments freely since they know the union is obligated to provide protection from possible retaliatory action by the boss.[5]

Economic Benefits. Although unions serve to satisfy psychological needs, the benefits of union membership mentioned most frequently are the economic ones. By bargaining collectively with an employer, employees have far greater strength than they would ever have as individuals in their demands for higher wages, improved fringe benefits, greater job security, and a shorter workweek. Many unions also provide various personnel benefits and services for their members which include vacation retreats, social and recreation centers, as well as health clinics, legal aid, income tax services, retirement homes, and even housing developments.

THE GROWTH OF ORGANIZED LABOR

Unions have existed in the United States since the Colonial Period, although their organization and role have changed substantially since then. Originally unions were local in scope and functioned largely as fraternal societies to provide mutual help and assistance for the members. Today the vast majority of local unions are a part of national organizations, most of which are affiliated within the AFL-CIO federation; and since their goals are those of improving the conditions of employment for members, they are referred to as *business unions*.

Early Unionizing Efforts

The early-day union seldom was able to exert much pressure upon employers. If the business panics and recessions did not curb their membership, the employer was able to do so by discharging the union members, by maintaining a blacklist of active unionists with other employers, by refusing to deal with union representatives, or by requiring new employees to sign a *yellow dog contract* in which they agreed not to join a union. If employers were unable to curtail union growth by these means, they could obtain court injunctions forbidding union organizing or strike activities, or they could charge unions

[5] For an interesting article on the conflict between the personal needs of employees and their organizational environment, see Chris Argyris, "Organizational Leadership and Participative Management," *The Journal of Business*, Vol. XXVII, No. 1 (January, 1955), pp. 283-298.

with criminal action under the prevailing *conspiracy doctrine*. This doctrine held that union efforts to bring economic pressure to bear upon an employer were illegal acts of conspiracy.

A major advancement for organized labor was achieved with the reversal of the conspiracy doctrine in the Commonwealth *vs.* Hunt case of 1842. In reversing its earlier interpretations with respect to this doctrine, the judiciary undoubtedly gave recognition to the change that was occurring in public opinion toward unions. By this date public opinion was beginning to demand that improvements for the workers be made in the area of social welfare and in employment conditions. As compared with today's employment conditions, those at that time and even as late as the 1930s were often deplorable.

The effort of unions during the 1800s, in addition to seeking better employment conditions, was directed toward the promotion of social and political reforms, the achievement of universal suffrage, and the extension of free public education. During this period unions also began to assume the role of minority pressure groups, intent upon generating favorable public opinion upon rewarding political candidates and parties friendly to their cause, and upon withholding support from unfriendly political candidates and parties.

The Growth of Contemporary Unions

While setbacks experienced by unions caused their early growth to be slow, they still were able to achieve some progress. As early as the Colonial Period the local unions within some communities began to affiliate through local labor councils similar to those found in most communities today for the purpose of coordinating their activities and promoting the interests of labor within the region. By the middle 1800s local unions representing certain crafts were able to unite and form what are now termed *national unions*.

Knights of Labor. The first union federation to achieve significant size was the *Knights of Labor,* formed about 1869. This union welcomed individuals and local units into its ranks from all crafts and occupational areas. The Knights also actively engaged in several business cooperatives and in political activity. Although the union experienced a significant growth in size, its decline was hastened by the heterogeneous character of its membership, the lack of internal unity, the loss of several strikes, and the unfavorable public opinion which certain unfortunate events and unfavorable publicity generated.

American Federation of Labor. The experiences of the Knights of Labor provided some important organizing lessons for its successor, the *American Federation of Labor* (AFL), which was formed in 1886 through the affiliation of some 25 *craft unions*. This federation under the able leadership of Samuel Gompers was able to profit from the mistakes of the Knights of Labor and to survive subsequent depressions and employer opposition. While the organization grew slowly at first and reached a membership of only 548,000 by 1900, it expanded rapidly to 1,676,000 members within the next four-year period.

The American Federation of Labor, as the term *federation* implies, is a loosely-knit group of autonomous national unions which constitute the real power of the organization. The national unions originally were composed mainly of skilled craft workers; and although certain unskilled groups were also admitted, most of the craft unions were oppposed to the admission of industrial workers into the AFL ranks. Industrial workers were shunned because of leadership inertia and the fear among certain craft groups that their status would be weakened by the admission of lesser skilled workers from the mass-production industries. It was not until the *Congress of Industrial Organizations* (CIO) began vigorously to organize industrial workers that the AFL as a whole became receptive to the admittance of industrial workers from the mass-production industries.

Congress of Industrial Organizations. The CIO was formed by John L. Lewis, President of the United Mine Workers, in cooperation with seven other presidents whose unions also had been expelled from the AFL as a result of their campaign to organize the mass-production industries. Once established, the CIO unions, which are referred to as *industrial unions,* embarked upon vigorous organizing drives to recruit industrial workers. The CIO placed particular emphasis upon training personnel to conduct these organizing drives, and upon educational and communication programs to explain union objectives and viewpoints to members, prospective members, and the general public. Organizing, training, communication, and research activities were performed also by the AFL unions, but not to the degree that they were by the CIO.

In soliciting members the CIO made a special effort to recognize the problems of minority groups and to avoid racial and religious discrimination within its ranks. It also engaged actively in political action at the local and national levels, a practice to which Samuel Gompers and the AFL earlier had been opposed.

Competition for members led to bitter jurisdictional conflicts between the AFL and the CIO union groups in their drives to organize different companies and occupational areas. The two groups, however, united in 1955 into a single AFL-CIO organization. A diagram showing the structure and composition of this new organization is contained in Figure 16-1. Based upon data compiled by the Bureau of Labor Statistics, membership in this organization totals about 16.5 million.[6]

Unaffiliated Unions. Although the majority of the national and international labor unions belong to the AFL-CIO, a number of unions representing about 4.4 million members are unaffiliated.[7] Among the more important of these unions are the United Mine Workers, United Transportation Workers, United Auto Workers, and Teamsters, the latter of which is the largest union in the

[6] U.S. Department of Labor, Bureau of Labor Statistics, *Directory of National Unions and Employee Associations,* (Washington, D.C.: U.S. Government Printing Office, 1974). p. 66.

[7] *Ibid.,* p. 67.

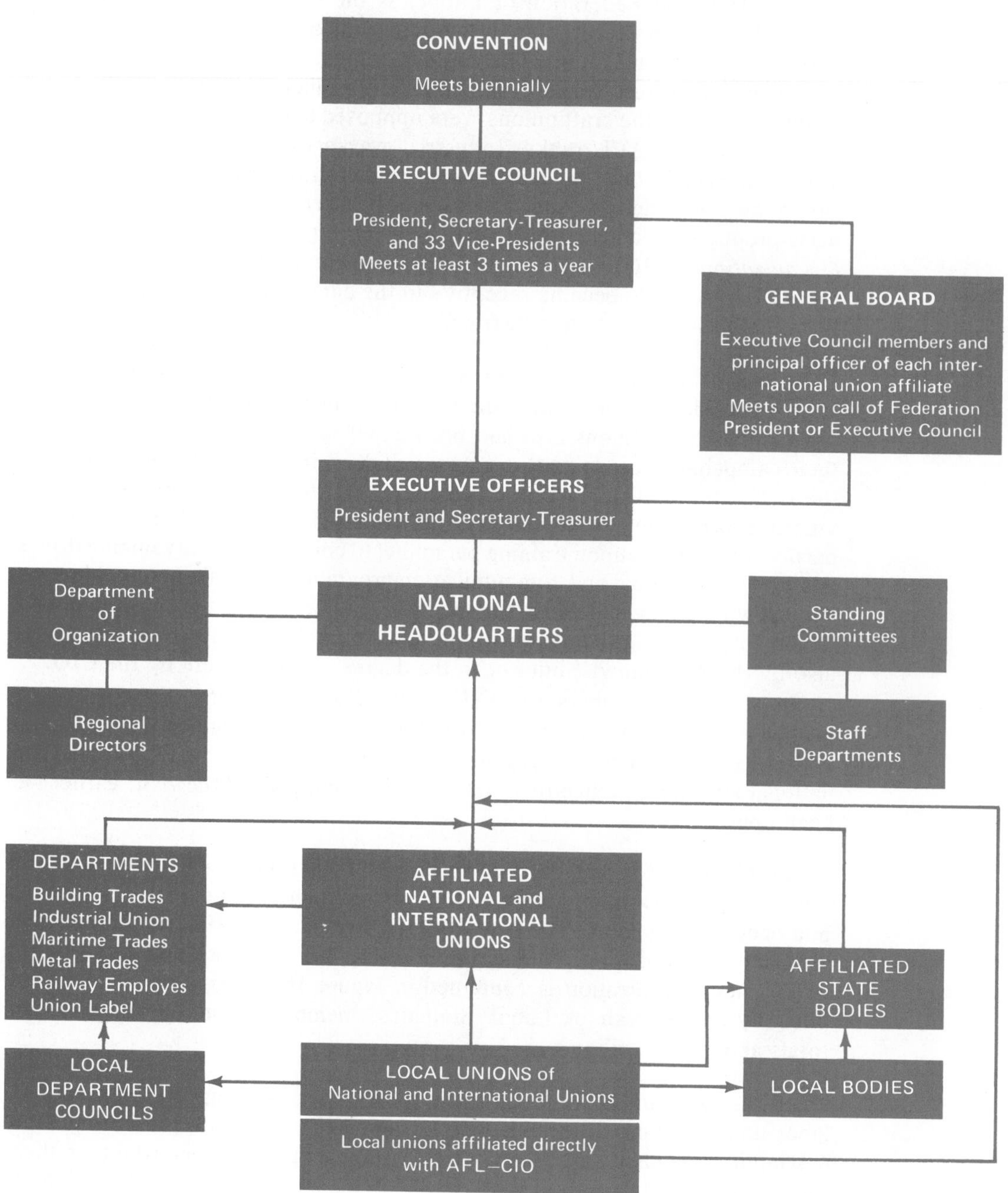

Source: *Directory of National Unions and Employee Associations*, Bureau of Labor Statistics, 1974.

Figure 16-1 STRUCTURE OF THE AFL-CIO

United States. Those unions whose membership is limited to employees within a particular company are called *company unions*. This term was once used to refer to unions that were subject to domination by a company as a result of its ability to exercise control over employees who were officers of the union; however, employer interference in the internal affairs of a union is now forbidden by law.

ORGANIZATION AND LEADERSHIP OF UNIONS

In terms of the size of their staffs and their revenues, many unions are large organizations which require the same caliber of management, leadership and financial control as any business or government organization of comparable size. Full-time personnel who are employed on national union headquarters staffs include attorneys, accountants, engineers, statisticians, as well as administrative and clerical employees. Many unions offer various types of management and leadership development programs similar to those described earlier in Chapter 9 in order to improve the performance of union officers at all levels within the organization.

The National Union

The constitution of the *national union* establishes the rules and conditions under which the local unions may be chartered and permitted to retain their membership in the national organization. While the degree of control that the parent organization maintains over its locals will vary, most national unions have regulations governing the collection of dues and initiation fees, the administration of union funds, and the admission of members by the local. They also may require that certain standard provisions be included in labor contracts with employers. In return for the controls that it may exercise over the locals, the national union may provide them with professional and financial assistance during organizing drives and strikes as well as assistance in the negotiation and administration of labor contracts. The national unions also prepare various printed materials for use by the locals in their educational and public relations activities. Of 177 national unions reporting in a survey, 144 issued a total of 166 publications.[8]

The negotiation of agreements that are purely local in scope usually are handled by the officers of the local. If assistance is needed in contract negotiations, however, a national representative may be called in by the local union. Because they are likely to have acquired greater experience and insight in labor relations, national representatives often can detect weaknesses in a local union's position and thus help its leaders to avoid bargaining difficulties.

---

[8] *Ibid.*, p. 92.

The Local Union

The *local union* is one with which the members have direct contact. It represents the interests of the members and seeks to insure that management decisions affecting these interests are fair and in compliance with the terms of the labor agreement. Most important, it assists members in rectifying any treatment that they may consider to be unjust.

In most cities the local unions are organized into a regional labor council to promote the interests of labor by supporting member unions that are engaged in local organizing efforts or strike activities. The labor council may campaign for favorable opinion from the public and government officials in support of the labor dispute that local unions may have with employers.

The officers of a local union typically include the president, vice-president, secretary-treasurer, business representative, and various committee chairpersons. Depending upon the size of the union, one or more of these officers, in addition to the business representative, may serve on a full-time basis. The remaining officers are members who have regular jobs and who serve the union without remuneration except perhaps for token gratuities and allowances to cover official expenses. Although the business representative often is a dominant power, in some unions this power may be in the hands of the secretary-treasurer or the president.

Business Representative. Negotiating and administering the labor agreement and working to resolve problems that may arise in connection with it are major responsibilities of the business representative. In performing these duties business representatives must be all things to all persons within their unions. They frequently are required to assume the role of counselor in helping the members with their personnel problems. They also are expected to dispose satisfactorily of the members' grievances that cannot be settled by the stewards, and also to help the employer correct members who are creating disciplinary problems.

Administering the affairs of the local organization is another significant part of the business representative's job. This task may include maintaining headquarters facilities, supervising an administrative staff, collecting dues, and recruiting new members. The handling of internal and external publicity for the local, coordinating social activities, and arranging for business and committee meetings also are generally a part of the business representative's duties.

Union Steward. The *union steward* is the representative of the union who represents the interests of members in their relations with their immediate supervisors and other members of management. In some industries, such as the auto industry, the steward has the title of *district committeeman*.[9] In these industries, the committeeman, whose salary is paid by the company, devotes full

[9] Since the titles of steward and committeeman make reference to the sex of the position holder, it is quite probable that these titles in the future will be changed in many unions to conform to the trend of eliminating sex designation in job titles.

time to reconciling disputes involving union members in the performance of their work that may arise in connection with the interpretation and administration of the labor agreement.

In describing the role of a district committeeman named Charlie Bragg in an assembly plant of the Ford Motor Company, one author expressed these observations:

> He might be called, in fact, 'the fixer'—the man to whom workers can turn in times of trouble. . . . Unofficially, Mr. Bragg *is* the union to his people and often the only union representative they deal with, and he is every bit as important to them as is Leonard Woodcock, the UAW president.
>
> To some extent, the content of Mr. Bragg's work on a typical day is deceptive. While his fellow workers spend their time monotonously piecing together over 300 cars, their union representative seems to spend much of his time roaming around, slapping people on the back, chit-chatting, and poking his head into unfinished cars to check things out. But it's all done for a purpose: finding problems.
>
> "The main function of a committeeman is to settle problems right on the floor," Mr. Bragg says. "I'm a mediator, a foot-soldier out there. Without the committeeman, Ford couldn't run this plant."
>
> Ford might dispute this assertion, but there is no denying that Mr. Bragg's meanderings uncover problems—or that he is the man on the spot. For while Mr. Woodcock and other union leaders are making speeches on such lofty topics as 'dignity in the work place' or 'shared decision-making,' it is Charlie Bragg and the men like him who are fighting disciplinary actions, getting supply racks fixed, arranging days off, getting bathrooms cleaned and drinking fountains unclogged. (On an average day, Mr. Bragg handles about 20 individual problems.)
>
> In the course of attacking such problems, Mr. Bragg avoids threats and confrontations. His prime goal, he says, is keeping his constituents happy. But he also must remain on working terms with their supervisors, who, he feels, must regard him as tough, but flexible. Indeed, he uses his ultimate weapon—the formal, written grievance—sparingly; and he says he tries hardest to avert, rather than win, disciplinary cases. "A grievance can just lie around for weeks," he says. "Meanwhile, the problem might be corrected anyway. What I want to do is take care of the problem and do it quickly."[10]

It is evident from the preceding quotation that stewards and committeemen, if they perform their positions effectively, serve as a very important link between union members and their employer. Their attitudes and actions can have an important bearing upon union-management cooperation and upon the efficiency and morale of the employees they represent.

Union Leadership

To be able to interpret effectively the behavior of union leaders, one must understand the nature of their backgrounds and ambitions and recognize the

---

[10] Walter S. Mossberg, "On the Line: As Union Man at Ford, Charlie Bragg Deals in Problems, Gripes," *The Wall Street Journal,* July 26, 1973, p. 1. Reprinted with permission of *The Wall Street Journal,* © Dow Jones & Company, Inc. (1973). All Rights Reserved.

political aspects of the offices they occupy. The leaders in many of the national unions have been able to develop political machines that enable them to suppress opposition and to perpetuate themselves in office. Tenure in office for the leader in a local union, however, is less secure. In the local union, officers periodically must run for reelection and, if they are to remain in office, they must be able to convince a majority of the membership that they are serving them effectively. At the local level, furthermore, it is not uncommon for opposition to develop toward those in office from members with political ambitions who seek to defeat the incumbent and to assume the office for themselves.

Sources and Motives of Union Leaders. Most labor leaders enter the labor movement at an early age and work their way up within the organization. Many seek leadership roles because of their dedication to the labor movement. The opportunity to realize the satisfaction of leadership responsibilitity as well as to gain status, recognition, and freedom from tight supervisory control, furthermore, can serve to make a union office attractive for some members. Regardless of their origins or motivations, most union leaders if not thoroughly dedicated to "the cause" of the labor movement at least give lip service to it.[11] Unfortunately for the union movement as a whole, however:

> Talented young people shun the labor movement, finding in it little of the idealism, creativity, or passion for change that impelled an earlier generation of activists to seek posts as organizers in the founding days of the CIO. A movement born as a voice of dissent has become a mainstay of the status quo in a period when even the staidest institutions—education, corporate and governmental—have felt obligated to take a critical look at all their most cherished precepts and scrap those made obsolete by changing technology and mores.[12]

Some unions recognize that the practice of obtaining leaders largely from the ranks can serve to weaken the organization. Therefore, they are seeking to induce persons with a college education to become union officers rather than just staff specialists, the role that college graduates traditionally have assumed. The growing need of unions for college-trained leaders is indicated by the following statement by a union representative:

> Over the years, the management guys have become much smarter and better educated. The guys for the unions have got to get smarter too. The old technique of grinding a cigar on the plant manager's desk doesn't work any more—you have to talk their language.[13]

Some union leaders also point out that the presence of college-educated staff specialists in the union makes it imperative for the union officers to be

---

[11] Bevars D. Mabry, *Labor Relations and Collective Bargaining* (New York: The Ronald Press Company, 1966), pp. 57-61.

[12] A. H. Raskin, "The Labor Movement Must Start Moving," *Harvard Business Review*, Vol. 48, No. 1 (January-February, 1970), p. 110.

[13] *The Wall Street Journal*, June 5, 1967, p. 1.

better educated in order that they will not be forced to lean too heavily upon the staff for guidance. In their words:

> A union leader relying on experts can be at a big disadvantage. A lot of experts just tell the union leader what he wants to hear because they want to keep their jobs.[14]

Leadership Approaches in Unions. Employers as well as members of the general public are prone to equate the authority of the union leader with that of an executive in a public or private enterprise. Consequently, they may exaggerate the power and influence that these leaders may be able to exercise over union actions. As Bok and Dunlop point out, many employers assume that their failure to achieve harmonious employee relations within their organization is the result of some opportunistic union leader leading their employees astray.[15] Although some blame for strikes and other forms of labor strife may be attributed to their leaders, Bok and Dunlop suggest that the rank-and-file members can and often do exercise a very strong influence over these leaders, particularly with respect to the negotiation and administration of the labor agreement. The leader who ignores the demands of these members may risk (1) being voted out of office, (2) having them vote the union out as their bargaining agent, (3) having them refuse to ratify the union agreement, or (4) having them engage in wildcat strikes or work slowdowns.[16]

According to another study, however, union leaders play an administrative role that, as far as their relations with subordinates are concerned, is similar to that of administrators in other types of organizations.[17] Union leaders, for example, tend to view themselves as being more capable and dependable than their followers. Because they may have reservations about the capacities of the members for sound judgment, they actually may be fearful of the consequences of their participation. However, since they recognize the value of participation in building the loyalty and morale of members, union leaders may resort to participative techniques in the belief that it will produce better support for their decisions but not necessarily better decisions. This attitude of union officers toward participation, in the study cited, was found to be more apparent in industrial than in craft unions.[18]

GOVERNMENT REGULATION OF LABOR RELATIONS

Relations between the union and the employer are governed by state and federal laws. These laws have evolved through common law and legislation and through legal interpretations rendered by the National Labor Relations

---

[14] *Ibid.*, p. 14.

[15] Derek C. Bok and John T. Dunlop, "How Trade Union Policy Is Made," *Monthly Labor Review*, Vol. 93, No. 2 (February, 1970), p. 17.

[16] *Ibid.*, p. 18.

[17] Raymond E. Miles and J. B. Ritchie, "Leadership Attitudes Among Union Officials," *Industrial Relations*, Vol. 8, No. 1 (October, 1968), p. 115.

[18] *Ibid.*

Board and by the courts. These laws relating to labor relations have evolved from those of preventing union bargaining to accepting it, to encouraging the peaceful settlement of labor disputes, and ultimately to encouraging and protecting employees in their efforts to unionize and bargain collectively.

Early Legislation Affecting Labor

The first federal legislation relating specifically to labor relations was the Arbitration Act of 1888 which sought to encourage the voluntary settlement of labor disputes of the railroad industry where the government's regulatory power was established clearly by the United States Constitution. The Erdman Act of 1898 and others of minor significance which followed during the next two decades represented further efforts to achieve the settlement of labor disputes and the improvement of labor relations in the railroad industry. The first significant piece of labor legislation to be passed by Congress was the Railway Labor Act of 1926 which defined specifically the legal right of railroad employees to organize and to bargain collectively. It also established a Mediation Board to help resolve disputes. This act represented the beginning of a more positive role by the federal government which in the next decade was to be extended to other industries.

Although the Sherman Antitrust Act of 1890 was directed toward the control of business monopolies and not unions, a nationwide union boycott of an employer was held to be illegal under the provisions of the act in the famous *Danbury Hatters* case. While Sections 6 and 20 were included in the Clayton Act of 1914 to exempt unions from the provisions of the Sherman Antitrust Act, these did not protect them from any civil damage suits by employers that might result from economic sanctions taken against them by unions.

Extension of Labor Legislation

It was not until the 1930s that the federal government became actively involved in the regulation of labor-management relations in other than the railroad industry. During this decade, however, several Supreme Court decisions interpreted more liberally the constitutional authority of the federal government to regulate interstate commerce as applying also to those companies whose products or services were marketed in more than one state. These decisions made federal labor legislation applicable to most industries except those engaged only in operations of an intrastate nature. As a result of such legislation, various weapons that employers formerly had been able to use to combat employee unionization were severely curbed.

The first act to be enacted in the 1930s was the Norris-LaGuardia Act, also known as the Anti-Injunction Act. Passed in 1932, this act served to limit the powers of the federal courts to enjoin union picketing, boycotts, and strike activities. Injunctions previously had served as an effective weapon against union activities since those union leaders who failed to comply with an injunction could be charged with contempt of court by the judge issuing the injunction and given a fine or jail sentence without jury trial. The act also contained provisions making unenforceable the *yellow dog contract* in which an applicant agreed not to join a union as a condition of employment.

Following the Norris-LaGuardia Act, the National Labor Relations Act (NLRA), better known as the Wagner Act, was passed in 1935, and subsequently was held to be constitutional by the United States Supreme Court. This act had a very drastic effect upon management-labor relations, and it placed the protective power of the federal government firmly behind employee efforts to organize and to bargain collectively through unions of their choice.

The Taft-Hartley Act (Labor-Management Relations Act)

The Wagner Act was amended and supplemented by the Taft-Hartley Act in 1947. However, most of the basic provisions of the Wagner Act were retained in the amendment. One of these basic provisions was Section 7 guaranteeing employee bargaining rights as follows:

> Employees shall have the right to self-organization, to form, join, or assist labor organizations, to bargain collectively through representatives of their own choosing, and to engage in concerted activities, for the purpose of collective bargaining or other mutual aid or protection. . . .

Unfair Practices of Employers. Other provisions of the Wagner Act that were retained include those of defining certain unfair labor relations practices of employers. These practices by which employers previously had been able to discourage or combat employee unionizing efforts are defined as follows:

1. To interfere with, restrain, or coerce employees in the exercise of their rights guaranteed in Section 7.
2. To dominate or interfere with the formation or administration of any labor organization, or to contribute financial or other support to it.
3. To discriminate in regard to hiring or tenure of employment or any term or condition of employment so as to encourage or discourage membership in any labor organization.
4. To discharge or otherwise discriminate against an employee because he has filed charges or given testimony under this act.
5. To refuse to bargain collectively with the duly chosen representatives of his employees.

As a result of the protection that the Wagner Act afforded them, unions were able to recruit nearly 10 million new members in the decade that followed. Because their bargaining power also increased significantly during this period, certain restraints on union labor relations practices were considered to be necessary and were provided for in the Taft-Hartley Act.

Unfair Labor Practices by Unions. The Taft-Hartley Act specified the following activities by unions to constitute unfair practices:

1. Restraint or coercion of employees in the exercise of their Wagner Act rights.
2. Restraint or coercion of employers in the selection of the parties to bargain in their behalf.
3. Persuasion of employers to discriminate against any of their employees.
4. Refusal to bargain collectively with an employer.
5. Participation in secondary boycotts and jurisdictional disputes.
6. Attempting to force recognition from an employer when another union is already the certified representative.
7. Charging excessive initiation fees.
8. "Featherbedding" practices requiring the payment of wages for services not performed.

Enforcement of the Taft-Hartley Act. The Wagner Act established the National Labor Relations Board (NLRB) to determine bargaining units, to conduct union representation elections by secret ballot, and to prosecute certain antiunion activities (i.e., unfair labor practices) of employers that were forbidden by the act. Although certain changes in the Board's structure were made by the Taft-Hartley Act, the functions of the Board continued to remain basically the same except that it was given the added responsibility of prosecuting unfair labor practices by unions.

Other Provisions of the Taft-Hartley Act. One of the major effects of the Taft-Hartley Act was to relax the restrictions that the Wagner Act had placed upon an employer's freedom of speech. It gave them the opportunity to express their views regarding unions and unionizing efforts provided that no attempt was made to threaten or coerce or bribe employees concerning their membership in a union or their decision to join or not to join one.

Among other things the Taft-Hartley Act denied supervisors legal protection in forming their own unions. The closed shop and the preferential hiring shop were forbidden, as was the practice of deducting union dues from the members' wages without having prior written consent. The act attempted, although without too much success, to reduce jurisdictional disputes and the mishandling of union welfare funds. The right of employers to sue a union for damages arising from the union's violation of the labor agreement or from unfair labor practices committed by it was clarified. The rights of individual members to submit their grievances directly to an employer without going through the union also was established.

The Taft-Hartley Act enlarged the conditions under which court injunctions might be issued in labor disputes as well as the opportunities for the NLRB to obtain court injunctions against certain illegal strikes and other unfair labor practices by the unions. The act also provided that the President of the United States, through the Attorney General, may seek an injunction against strikes or lockouts affecting the nation's health and welfare for a period of 80 days. If the dispute has not been settled after the injunction has been in effect for 60 days, the NLRB is required to take a secret vote among the employees involved in the dispute to determine if they are willing to accept the employer's "final offer." These injunction provisions of the act represent the basis for the "slave labor" charges that unions have leveled against it.

The Landrum-Griffin Act

As provisions of the Taft-Hartley Act were put into practice and tested in the courts, the need for changes became evident. Investigations by Congress into corrupt practices occurring within the field of union-management relations revealed that the existing statutes were inadequate to protect the rights of individual union members, to protect the equities of members in union welfare funds, or to prevent racketeering or unscrupulous practices from being committed by certain employers and union officers. As a result of these reasons, Congress passed the Landrum-Griffin Act which is officially entitled the Labor-Management Reporting and Disclosure Act of 1959.

Bill of Rights of Union Members. One of the most important provisions of the act is the so-called *Bill of Rights of Union Members,* which requires that every union member must be given the right to: (1) nominate candidates for union office, (2) vote in union elections or referendums, (3) attend union meetings, and (4) participate in union meetings and vote on union business. Members who are deprived of this right are permitted under the act to seek appropriate relief in a federal court which may include obtaining an appropriate injunction. Union members are also granted the right to examine union accounts and records in order to verify information contained in union reports and to bring suit against union officers to protect union funds.

Control of Trusteeships. The act establishes certain ground rules governing the use of trusteeships by labor organizations in order to protect the rights of members within the trusteed locals.[19] The use of trusteeships at times in the past has been subject to abuses by national unions. Members can now bring civil action against the national union to gain relief from trusteeships that have been installed in violation of the act.

Reporting and Bonding Provisions. Under the act unions are required to submit a financial report annually to the Secretary of Labor. Union officers are required to be bonded for an amount not less than 10 percent of the union funds that they are responsible for handling.

Employers must report any expenditures that are made in attempting to persuade employees to exercise their bargaining rights. Labor consultants, similarly, must report agreements with employers involving efforts to persuade employees to exercise their bargaining rights or to supply information about union activities during a labor dispute.

Taft-Hartley Amendments. Some of the amendments to the Taft-Hartley Act contained in the Landrum-Griffin Act provide for the tightening of the ban on secondary boycotts and prohibit *"hot-cargo" agreements.*[20] The

[19] A trusteeship is established when the national union takes the authority for administering a local union away from its officers and places it in the hands of a trustee appointed by the national organization.

[20] A *hot-cargo agreement* is one in which an employer agrees not to discipline employees for refusing to handle nonunion products or unfair products, which are termed "hot-cargo."

Landrum-Griffin Act also prohibits picketing for the purpose of "shaking down" employers, of forcing them to recognize a union, or of compelling their employees to join a union.

Unions were granted some minor concessions under the act. Economic strikers were granted the right to vote in representation elections during the first year of their strike. Unions in the construction industry were permitted the right to sign prehire contracts with employers that require union membership as a condition of employment when the work force is recruited. This provision in effect legalizes a closed shop agreement.

CURRENT UNION PROBLEMS AND GOALS

The many conflicts and strains that are occurring within this nation's social structure are having a significant effect upon union policies and practices and upon the attitudes and behavior of their members. Union problems resulting from today's rapidly occurring social, economic, and technological changes are very different from those that confronted unions during and prior to the 1930s. The backgrounds and attitudes of the union members are also different. Unions, therefore, like any organization, must be adaptable and dynamic and be capable of solving these contemporary problems if they are to survive and fulfill their intended purposes.

Changing Character of the Union Member

During earlier days of the labor movement, unions tended to consist of members who knew firsthand what employment conditions could be like without unions and what personal sacrifices were required to organize and make a union survive. As subsequent generations entered the unions, their memberships have contained fewer and fewer individuals who are truly dedicated to the union cause. Furthermore, union members no longer may be categorized as being from a "down-trodden" working class but rather they are identified with the large American middle class population. One writer describes this socioeconomic change and the problems that it presents for their unions and union leaders as follows:

> Sweeping changes are occurring in the composition of organized labor that the unions' structure and hierarchy have failed to reflect. The new generation of workers has little or no recollection of that profound shaper of the labor movement, the Great Depression; by best estimates nearly half of all union members are under 40, and one-fourth under 30. Furthermore, these younger members are predominantly suburbanites, property-owners and tax-payers with a political and psychological orientation quite unlike that of their aged leaders. The new union members are much more interested in air-pollution control and property-tax relief than in such old-time legislative goals as repealing right-to-work laws or broadening construction unions' picketing rights. Yet labor's lobbying aims, while beginning to show some updating, still

concentrate overmuch on those worn-out symbols dear to the hearts of the traditionalist leaders.[21]

Improvements in the affluence and life styles of union members have reduced substantially the homogeneity that formerly existed, and in turn the unity within union ranks. The migration of members to the suburbs as a result of their increased affluency has weakened their ties with the union hall. An AFL-CIO study, for example, complained that although union members are likely to live 30 miles from their jobs rather than in neighborhoods near the plant, they still are able to get to work regularly but only infrequently to the union halls.[22] This new attitude has been referred to as "crabgrass unionism" by those who complain that many union members now live in an environment where it is "far more prestigious to be a Boy Scout leader than a union leader."[23] The loss of potential leaders within the membership to community projects as well as to civil rights, ecology, and other movements, if it becomes significant enough, may serve to further weaken union leadership.

Unions to some extent have become victims of their own successes in that they have reached the point of having satisfied most of the needs that their members expect them to satisfy, with the result that their leaders are being forced to help the members recognize new needs that the union can satisfy for them.[24] According to one federal mediator, "The biggest problem that they (unions) have today is that they are running out of demands they can afford to make. Somehow, some way, they must maintain their protest function if they are to survive."[25]

Internal Problems Confronting Unions

The civil rights and the women's liberation movements have given rise to some very significant problems for both unions and their leaders in the area of civil rights. Members of the black and other disadvantaged groups have become frustrated because they believe that they have not been accorded fair and equal opportunity to participate in the gains being realized by organized labor as a whole. In particular, many minority groups complain that because of racial prejudices they have been denied their share of membership opportunities in the craft and other unions representing the higher paying jobs with the result that membership opportunities for them have been restricted primarily to unions representing jobs of lower skill and pay. Minorities also resent the fact that members of their group have had a very limited chance to become officers even in those unions that have large minority group representations. According to one report,

---

[21] James P. Gannon, "The Labor Movement: Sinew Turned Fat," *The Wall Street Journal*, June 3, 1969.

[22] "Trouble Plagues the House of Labor," *Business Week* (October 28, 1972), p. 76.

[23] *Ibid.*

[24] Stagner and Rosen, *op. cit.*, p. 40.

[25] As quoted in Stagner and Rosen, *op. cit.*, p. 40.

Only two of the 35 members of the AFL-CIO's prestigious executive council are black. The International Brotherhood of Teamsters and the United Steelworkers, which have very substantial black memberships, have no blacks on their executive boards. The United Auto Workers, about one-third black, has only one black officer among nine, and two blacks on its 26-man board.[26]

Militancy Among Black Union Members. Frustration over alleged injustices by unions, whether real or perceived, has led to militant actions by black labor leaders, aimed at increasing black leadership and control in labor organizations and in enlarging the membership and employment of black workers in the crafts and other jobs with higher pay. It has led also to the organization of some very militant labor groups, and has spurred a drive among black union members to form a separate black labor federation. Compounded with the problem of increasing militancy among black members that confronts union leaders is the reaction of some white workers to this militancy.[27] The increasing polarization between white and black workers presents a very serious danger to the welfare of unions as well as society unless constructive action can be taken rapidly to reduce some of the frustrations and hostility that is developing within the black and other minority groups. As one author points out, however,

> The real threat to the white worker does not come from the black's desire for an equal place in the sun but from the fact that he does not have one. Every union leader recognizes this, but few are working overtime at convincing their members of it. Until they do, their rank and file will be potential prey for any populist demagogue seeking to weld them into a reactionary political force.[28]

Women's Demand for a Greater Role. Like minority groups, women are demanding greater representation in the unions. Although there are approximately 4.3 million women in U.S. unions, and women make up at least half of the membership of 26 unions, very few of them hold international union positions or sit on international boards.[29] As a result of these conditions, women members from at least 58 international unions have organized a "Coalition of Labor Union Women" (CLUW) to push more aggressively for a bigger role in labor affairs, higher wages, and improved working conditions for female workers.

External Problems Confronting Unions

In addition to internal problems, organized labor also is being confronted with problems from the outside.

Increased Competition from Foreign Manufacturers. One major problem has been the loss of jobs as the result of competition from manufacturers

---

[26] "Black Unionists Want More Say," *Business Week* (May 18, 1974), p. 71.
[27] James P. Gannon, "Black Unionists," *The Wall Street Journal,* November 29, 1968.
[28] A. H. Raskin, *op. cit.,* p. 117.
[29] "Women Push for Union Power," *Business Week* (March 30, 1974), p. 102.

abroad. Since the mid-1960s there has been a rapid increase in the importation of steel, consumer electronics, autos, wearing apparel, textiles, and shoes with a corresponding loss of jobs for workers producing these products in the companies within the United States.[30] Some of these goods have been produced by foreign subsidiaries of American corporations which have been accused by labor of "exporting the jobs of American workers." Although the dollars gained by foreign countries from exports to the United States are used to purchase imports from this country, this fact does not make the losses of jobs to foreign competition any easier for those workers bearing the burden. Furthermore, many of the workers in the labor-intensive industries which have been the hardest hit by foreign competition are middle-age and either women or minorities, or both, who cannot be easily retrained, reshuffled, and reslotted.[31] As a result of the problems being created for their members, particularly in the industries affected, unions are demanding some form of protection against foreign imports. Such protection, however, is likely to create higher prices for the American consumer already heavily burdened by inflation and who, consequently, is not sympathetic toward the drive for protection.

Decline in Public Support. Perhaps the greatest problem confronting unions has been the decline in public support for the labor movement. Polls conducted by Opinion Research Corporation, for example, revealed that:

> Public opposition to the continued growth of unions in membership and power has risen. Seventy-one percent of the public polled felt that unions were either too big or big enough. . . . Increasingly labor's efforts are being interpreted as being against the public interest, with 59 percent of those surveyed blaming union demands and steadily rising labor costs for 'causing the United States to price itself out of world markets'.[32]

Many individuals also blame labor for contributing to inflation, which affects all persons who buy the products labor produces, including the many persons who do not share in the wage increases gained by union members. Thus, millions of individuals on fixed salaries, pensions, or on the welfare rolls become the victims of the vicious circle of wage-price increases.

The failure of many unions to support the civil rights and the women's liberation movements, or even to cooperate in expanding employment opportunities to members of these groups, has caused labor to lose some of their support. Many liberal intellectuals who vigorously supported the labor movement in the 1930s now criticize organized labor for being ultra-conservative, with the result that their sympathy for the movement has given way to antagonism. While many leaders still outwardly express confidence that the labor movement continues to enjoy widespread public acceptance, others have privately conceded that there is a declining public acceptance of their movement which can lead only to legislation unfavorable to labor.

[30] Irwin Ross, "Labor's Big Push for Protectionism," *Fortune* (March, 1973), p. 94.
[31] *Ibid.*, p. 95.
[32] "Truth Plagues the House of Labor," *op. cit.*, p. 67.

Unionization of White-Collar Groups

Another major problem confronting organized labor has been that of maintaining a satisfactory growth rate. The magnitude of the problem is shown by Figures 16-2 and 16-3 which illustrate how the growth rate of union

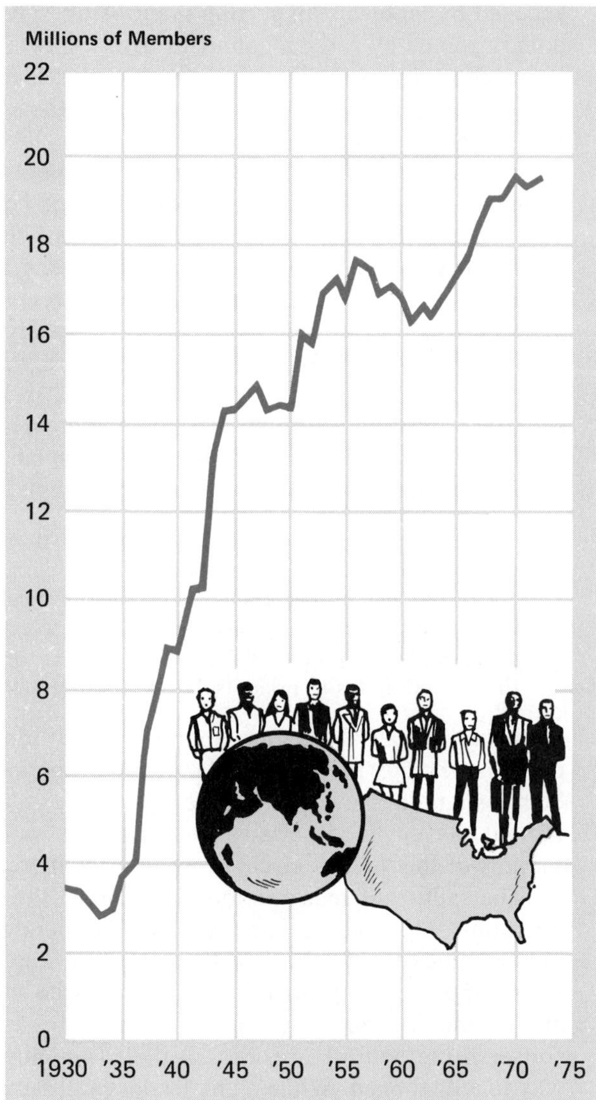

Source: Directory of National Unions and Employee Associations, Bureau of Labor Statistics, 1974, p. 71.

* Excludes Canadian membership but includes members in other areas outside the United States. Members of AFL-CIO directly affiliated local unions are also included. For the years 1948-52, midpoints of membership estimates, which were expressed as ranges, were used.

Figure 16-2 MEMBERSHIP* OF NATIONAL UNIONS, 1930-72

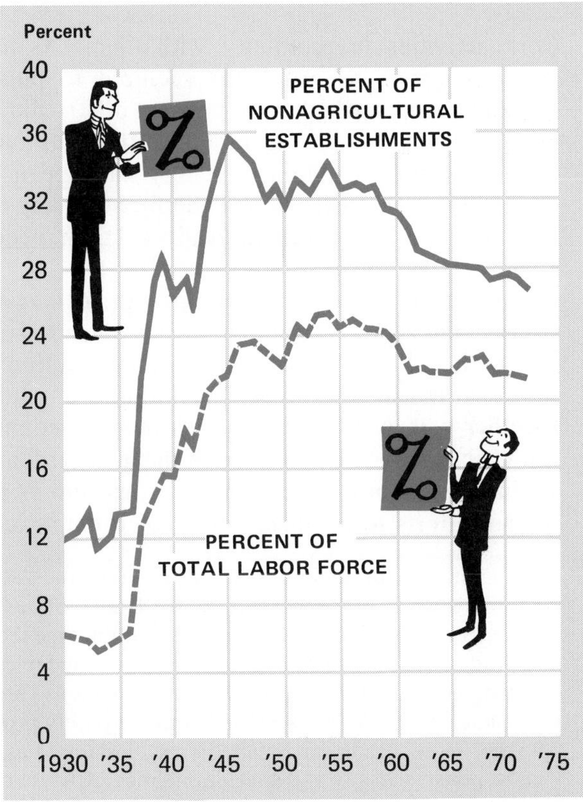

Source: Directory of National Unions and Employee Associations, Bureau of Labor Statistics, 1974, p. 72.

* Excludes Canadian membership.

Total labor force includes employed and unemployed workers, self-employed, members of the Armed Forces, etc. Employment in nonagricultural establishments excludes the Armed Forces, self-employed, as well as the unemployed, agricultural workers, proprietors, unpaid family workers, and domestic servants.

Figure 16-3 UNION MEMBERSHIP* AS A PERCENT OF TOTAL LABOR FORCE AND OF EMPLOYEES IN NONAGRICULTURAL ESTABLISHMENTS, 1930-72

membership has leveled off both in terms of total numbers and in terms of the total labor force. This trend reflects the impact that laborsaving devices have had in eliminating both jobs and members for the union. It reflects also the past failures on the part of unions to draw membership from among the white-collar ranks where the labor force is growing the most rapidly. The fact that efforts to unionize the white-collar groups have proven quite successful in European countries and that forces favorable to such unionization exist in this country would indicate that American white-collar employees offer unions the greatest possibility for growth.

Forces Affecting Unionization. Traditionally white-collar employees tended to identify themselves with the owners or managers and to perform similar work activities in proximity with them. As a group they enjoyed certain privileges (such as not being required to punch a time clock) and socioeconomic status which blue-collar workers did not possess. Those improvements for which union members in the shop have had to bargain vigorously or even strike to obtain generally have been extended to the white-collar group. For these reasons and the fact that any union drives to organize them were not attuned psychologically to their needs and thinking, white-collar employees had been slow to unionize.

In recent years, however, growth in the size of organizations in which white-collar groups are employed has tended to impersonalize their work and to isolate them from and reduce their identification with management. The lack of job security during layoffs resulting from automation or declining sales, together with growing difficulties being encountered in attempting to resolve grievances, have helped to push them toward unionization. A study by Archie Kleingartner, for example, reveals that unions are becoming more successful in their efforts to organize white-collar employees. As he indicates:

> Unions for their part have taken various steps to increase their appeal among white-collar workers. In the United States this may include establishing separate white-collar departments within large industrial unions, hiring college graduates as organizers, sponsoring radio and television programmes, changing a name, decentralizing activities, etc. Unions catering to professional workers made special attempts to deal with the purely professional problems as well as the more traditional job items. Adaptations of this sort represent a responsiveness to the special qualities of white-collar workers.[33]

Unionization of Professional Groups. The professional white-collar groups have been receiving greater attention currently as the result of strikes that have been conducted by teachers, engineers, nurses, and members of other well-established professions. Unionization and strikes by such groups can be regarded as being particularly significant because professionalism traditionally has been regarded as being incompatible with unionism. Professionalism thus has been associated with such prestigious free-lance occupations as law and medicine, whereas unionism has been associated with manual workers. Still, the desire among various occupational groups to attain professional status and recognition has caused them to establish professional societies, formulate codes of ethics, develop licensing procedures, and publish journals in an effort to become accepted professionals. Unfortunately the fact that members of many new professional groups are predominantly employees rather than self-employed has required them to bargain individually with an employer over the conditions of their employment.[34] Their lack of success in bargaining often has forced them to seek collective action as a group either by unionizing or by forcing their professional societies to become their bargaining agent. As a result

[33] Archie Kleingartner, "The Organization of White-Collar Workers," *British Journal of Industrial Relations,* Vol. VI, No. 1 (March, 1968), pp. 79-93.

[34] Archie Kleingartner, "Professionalism and Engineering Unionism," *Industrial Relations,* Vol. 8, No. 3 (May, 1969), pp. 225-226.

of these developments, both unions and professional societies, such as those representing teachers or nurses, have competed for the membership by each attempting to demonstrate that it can be the more militant and achieve the greater gains.

Problems with Collective Bargaining in Government

During the past decade, unions have been engaged actively in organizing employees of the federal, state, and local governments. Their successes have forced professional and other associations representing employees within government to become more militant and aggressive and to assume the characteristics of a union. The growth in memberships of such employee associations has led to demands for a greater role in determining the conditions of employment, including the right to bargain collectively and even to strike to achieve these conditions. As yet, however, collective bargaining by government employees is authorized in only a few states and, even where this is the case, certain restrictions may be imposed regarding what conditions of employment can be negotiated. In certain other states, employees have the right only to "meet and confer" with representatives of management for the purpose of developing "memoranda of understanding."[35]

Political Foundation of Labor Relations in Government. Government employees typically are not able to negotiate with their employers on the same basis as their counterparts in private enterprise. Because of inherent differences that exist between the public and private sectors, it is doubtful that they will ever be able to do so. One of the significant differences between the public and private sectors is that labor relations in industry have an economic foundation whereas in government they have a political one. Since employers in the private sector must stay in business in order to sell their goods or services, their employees are not likely to make demands that could bankrupt the enterprise. When a strike occurs, it is a test of economic staying power in which the customer may have alternative or substitute sources of supply.

Governments, on the other hand, must stay in business because alternative services usually are not available. Since their payrolls must be met from public taxes or fees, unions representing their employees in the public sector are not reluctant to press for financial gains that will be paid by the public. Moreover, public employees exert influence not only as union members but as pressure groups and voting citizens as well.[36] However, it is a fact that in the private sector certain industries may provide products or services over which they have monopolistic control and therefore are able to pass wage increases on to the consumer just as governmental agencies pass them on to the public. The disruption of company services, moreover, may in certain instances be sufficiently detrimental to the public welfare to precipitate government

[35] David T. Stanley, *Managing Local Government Under Union Pressure* (Washington, D.C.: The Brookings Institution, 1971), pp. 11-12.

[36] *Ibid.*, pp. 19-20.

intervention, and then the bargaining deadlock becomes a political as well as an economic issue.[37]

Problems Relating to Managerial Authority. Another difference between the public and private sectors with respect to collective bargaining concerns the source of management authority. In a company the authority flows downward from the board of directors and ultimately from the stockholders who elect them. The management can resist union demands for a greater participation in management on the grounds that management requires flexibility to achieve profit goals and meet its obligation to the board of directors and to the stockholders.

In the public sector, however, authority flows upward from the public at large to their elected representatives and to the appointed or elected managers. While the chief executives in private enterprises commit their company to the labor agreement they have negotiated, the chief executive of a government agency cannot do so because new revenues or changes in existing statutes are likely to be required to meet the new terms of the labor agreement. Such changes require legislative approval and in some cases ratification by the voters. Decisions by these managers are subject to public scrutiny and debate; their performance is judged in part by their ability to stay within the budget, to prevent taxes from rising, and, if possible, to locate new sources of revenue that the majority of voters will not have to bear. Both the public and legislative bodies, furthermore, become involved in evaluating a public manager's performance. This fact can make the jobs of these managers very difficult, particularly when their ability to resist union encroachment upon management decisions affecting public services may constitute a major criterion upon which the managers' performance is to be judged.[38]

Union Relations in Europe

Since many American companies operate in foreign countries, particularly in Europe, American managers become involved either directly or indirectly with unions and union officials in these countries. Unfortunately, because the role of these unions in the social and political structure of a foreign country is different from that in the United States, American managers abroad are often required to make substantial adjustments in the approach to union relations that they used at home, frequently with some difficulty. One of the major difficulties encountered by American managers stems from the fact that they tend to see the foreign union in the image of its American counterpart, when in effect the goals, structures, and the conditions under which the foreign union operates are substantially different.[39]

---

[37] *Ibid.*, p. 20.

[38] Archie Kleingartner, "Collective Bargaining Between Salaried Professionals and Public Sector Management," *Public Administration Review*, Vol. 33, No. 2 (March-April, 1973), p. 169, as reproduced in Herbert J. Chruden and Arthur W. Sherman, Jr., *Readings in Personnel Management* (4th ed.; Cincinnati, Ohio: South-Western Publishing Co., 1976), pp. 395-409.

[39] "European Labor Gets Tougher," *Business Week* (October 18, 1969), p. 65.

Unions in most European countries have existed longer than those in the United States; thus, they enjoy greater acceptance among workers and within society as a whole. Workers join unions because it is the accepted thing to do, not because they are required to do so by terms of the labor agreement. Unions in many European countries are affiliated closely with one of the political parties so that when employers deal with the unions they may, in effect, be dealing with the government through the union. Furthermore, in countries such as France, Italy, and the United Kingdom, strikes and demonstrations often are fomented by the union for the purpose of pressuring the political party in power rather than just for reasons involving the employer.

The unionization of white-collar groups is more prevalent in Europe than in the United States, and in a number of countries even management personnel belong to a union. In some countries, through strikes and demonstrations, unions have seriously impaired productivity and even the economic and political stability of the government. In other countries such as Sweden and Switzerland, however, unions have contributed significantly to the achievement of labor peace and to the improvement of efficiency. In these countries unions are sufficiently enlightened to recognize that such labor peace is essential in order for the nation to produce goods that can be sold competitively on the world markets. Furthermore, labor peace is due in no small part to the fact that the unions no longer must fight for recognition since their presence is thoroughly accepted by the employers and by society as a whole. As a result, unions can concentrate their attention on conditions of employment and in cooperating with employers rather than on fighting to retain membership or employer recognition.

It is typical in Europe for the labor agreement to be negotiated at the national level by an association representing employers. This agreement may be augmented by further negotiations with individual employers at the local level. Unfortunately in some countries, such as Italy and Great Britain, the labor agreement in the past has not been binding on the union—a situation which can create confusion and frustration for the employer. Efforts are being made in Great Britain to change this condition. While European countries generally lack an established body of law governing union-management relations similar to the Taft-Hartley Act, many of them do have laws requiring union consultation and participation in matters affecting the workers as well as providing job protection, released time for union officers, or certain facilities for their use.[40]

Résumé

Unions in our society are fully accepted organizations to which employees are legally entitled to belong for the purpose of bargaining collectively with

[40] Herbert J. Chruden and Arthur W. Sherman, Jr., *Personnel Practices of American Companies in Europe* (New York: American Management Association, 1972), pp. 115-135.

employers over conditions of employment. The union not only can provide certain economic benefits for its members but also can contribute to the satisfaction of their various psychological and social needs.

Although unions have existed in this country since the Colonial Period, it was not until about the middle 1930s that they began to achieve significant bargaining power. Much of the power has been gained as the result of the Wagner Act which has helped to protect and to encourage union organizing and bargaining activities. In more recent years the passage of the Taft-Hartley and the Landrum-Griffin acts has served to establish certain controls over the internal affairs of unions and their relations with employers.

Most local unions with whom members have direct contact operate under a charter granted by the national organization. The majority of these national organizations in turn are affiliated with the AFL-CIO. While the bargaining strength of a particular union is affected considerably by the amount of its membership and treasury resources, it is affected also by the caliber of its leaders. Good management and leadership is as important to a union as it is to a business organization. From the standpoint of their financial operations and the number of people that they employ, many unions are, in fact, big business. To be effective, therefore, union leaders must be skillful in administration and leadership and in politics as well if they are to remain in their elected offices. Today's labor leaders are confronted with many problems, some of which are equally critical and even more complicated than those which were encountered prior to the Wagner Act. Union leaders must cope with problems created by the reduction of blue-collar jobs and the growth of white-collar ones. There also are many internal problems within their unions that must be resolved. As a result of changes in the attitudes and backgrounds of individuals who comprise the current membership of unions and as a result of growing demands from minority groups for greater membership proportions and participation, the leaders of most unions are being challenged constantly. The demands of certain groups, such as public and professional employees, to engage in collective bargaining also serve to challenge union leaders to develop policies and practices within their organizations that will serve the needs of these groups.

DISCUSSION QUESTIONS

1. In what ways is an organization's personnel program affected by the unionization of its employees?
2. Why are college graduates needed for union leadership positions? What are the positions in unions in which college graduates typically have been placed?
3. In what respect is today's union member different from his predecessor 40 years ago and what are the effects of this difference?
4. What impact is the civil rights movement having upon unions and their operation?
5. Why do attitudes toward organized labor on the part of certain segments of our society tend to become less favorable than formerly?
6. In what ways do union-management relations in the public sector differ from those in the private sector?

PROBLEM 16-1 THE ANNIVERSARY WATCH

Jerry Rose, the business representative for Local No. 25 of the International Brotherhood of Plastics Workers, had relied heavily upon Mrs. Marconi, his secretary, to handle the operation of the local's office. Mrs. Marconi had served several previous business representatives during the nearly 20 years that she had been employed by the union. Although she sometimes tended to be a little domineering in her relations with union members, it was generally agreed that she had been of great service to the union.

In recognition of the fact that she was about to complete her twentieth year of service with Local 25, Rose decided to purchase an attractive wrist watch with an appropriate inscription engraved upon it for presentation to her as an anniversay gift. The cost of the gift totaled about $100.00 and was paid for from the local's discretionary fund. When Jerry Rose announced at the monthly union meeting that he had purchased the watch and that it was to be presented to Mrs. Marconi at a luncheon ceremony the next week, several of the members objected to the gift. They complained, in effect, that they felt it unfair to use the dues taken from their hard-earned wages to buy an expensive "luxury gift." One member complained that he did not feel that it was right for him to be contributing to such a gift for Mrs. Marconi when he had never been able to afford a decent watch for his own wife. After about an hour of heated discussion, the issue was put to a vote with the majority present supporting Rose's purchase of the gift. As might be expected, news reached Mrs. Marconi through the grapevine about the impending gift and about the controversy that it had created. While she never mentioned the fact, Rose could tell that she was aware of the objections raised about the gift by the way that she reacted to the watch when it was presented to her. The controversy over the watch also had dampened Rose's enthusiasm for the gesture, and he wondered if the gift did not now constitute a waste of the members' dues.

a. How do you explain the attitude of the members who objected to the gift?
b. Does this case indicate any possible problems that one might encounter in working for a union or for some type of fraternal organization? What motivates people to work for a union?
c. If you did not have the hindsight provided by this case, would you have taken the same action as Rose?

SUGGESTED READINGS

Beirne, Joseph A. *Challenge to Labor; New Roles for American Trade Unions.* Englewood Cliffs, N.J.: Prentice-Hall, Inc., 1969.

Chruden, Herbert J., and Arthur W. Sherman, Jr. *Readings in Personnel Management,* 4th ed. Cincinnati: South-Western Publishing Co., 1976. Part 5.

Foner, Phillip S. *Organized Labor and the Black Worker, 1619-1973.* New York: Praeger Publishers, 1974.

Kassalow, Everett M. *Trade Unions and Industrial Relations: An International Comparison.* New York: Random House, 1969.

Labor Law Reporter, 4th ed. Chicago: Commerce Clearing House, Inc. Vols. 1, 2, 4, 4A, 5, and 6.

Labor Policy and Practice. Washington, D.C.: The Bureau of National Affairs, Inc. Vols. 1-5.

Murphy, Richard J., and Morris Sachman. *The Crisis in Public Employee Relations in the Decade of the Seventies*. Washington, D.C.: The Bureau of National Affairs, Inc., 1970.

Roberts, Harold S. *Labor Management Relations in the Public Service*. Honolulu, Hawaii: University of Hawaii Press, 1969.

Serrin, William. *The Company and the Union*. New York: Alfred A. Knopf, 1973.

Silverberg, Louis G. *How to Take a Case Before the National Labor Relations Board,* 3d ed. Revised by Kenneth C. McGuiness. Washington, D.C.: The Bureau of National Affairs, Inc., 1967.

Stanley, David T. *Managing Local Government Under Union Pressure*. Washington, D.C.: The Brookings Institution, 1972.

Stieber, Jack. *Public Employee Unionism: Structure, Growth, Policy*. Washington, D.C.: The Brookings Institution, 1973.

U.S. Department of Labor, Bureau of Labor Statistics. *A Brief History of the American Labor Movement,* Bulletin 1000. Washington, D.C.: Superintendent of Documents, 1970.

Van De Vall, Mark. *Labor Organizations*. Cambridge: Harvard University Press, 1970.

Union-Management Relations

Basic to every union-management relationship is the labor agreement which establishes in writing the conditions of employment, including wages, hours, fringe benefits, and job security under which the union's members will agree to work. Such an agreement often is achieved only after a long period of negotiation during which serious deadlocks may occur. These deadlocks can be resolved through the use of economic power or through the assistance of outside mediators, or, in exceptional instances, through government intervention. Once negotiated, the agreement serves to determine the role of each party and the rights it is to possess during the life of the agreement.

Most agreements contain provisions for resolving disputes that may arise over the interpretation or enforcement of its provisions. Because of the effects an agreement can have upon the management of the employer's organization and upon the union and its members, the negotiators for each party should be fully equipped to bargain in terms of their skills and experiences and in terms of having done their "homework" for the bargaining sessions. The discussion in this chapter will be concerned with the bargaining tactics and strategies involving the negotiation of an agreement, as well as with the more important provisions it may contain and their effects upon union-management relations.

UNION RECOGNITION

Before it can negotiate an agreement with an employer, a union must first be recognized by the employees whom it represents as their official bargaining agent. To gain recognition may require an extensive membership drive by the union in which hostility, bitterness, and even violence may develop before the union is able to gain a sufficient proportion of the employees to have the legal right to negotiate in their behalf.

Unionizing Campaigns

Organizing campaigns may be directed toward employees working for private companies, government organizations, or nonprofit institutions, including those in the blue-collar, white-collar, or professional positions. These campaigns may be conducted not only by labor unions of the traditional type but also by organizations representing various groups of employees in both professional and nonprofessional categories.

Whether or not a unionizing campaign is successful and peaceful will depend upon many factors. Probably most important to its success or failure is the factor of climate and morale that exists within the employer's organization and the desire of the employees to have a union come in. Management policies and practices with respect to such things as wages, overtime, promotion, seniority, discipline, grievance, job security, and working conditions can be extremely important factors in either encouraging or discouraging employees to unionize. It is most important that employers develop an awareness of the attitudes, sentiments, and feelings, as well as the desires and ambitions their employees may have toward these elements of their employment situation. Employers who are able to maintain such an awareness as a result of effective two-way communications should be better able to initiate corrective action and thus remove many of the dissatisfactions which employees may otherwise seek to overcome through union membership and action.[1]

The ease with which the union is able to organize an employer also may help to determine whether or not its campaign will remain peaceful. If the union campaign generates vigorous employer opposition, the union may escalate the campaign by pulling members off the job and by trying to prevent nonunion employees from continuing to work. Should operations continue in spite of such pressures, violent action may be taken against the employer's property, against employees seeking to continue working, or against law enforcement personnel who provide protection. Similarly, if the union senses that its position is a weak one, it may seek to gain support of more employees by stepping up a written and verbal campaign against the employer of the type illustrated by Figure 17-1. Such campaigns, however, may serve to increase the bitterness and the determination of the employer to resist unionization.

Union Recognition Procedures

A union organizing campaign may be subject to competition from rival unions. The employer's organization as a result may become a battleground in the conflict between the two unions while employees attempt to decide which, if either, of the unions they should join. However, if a majority of employees

[1] Matthew Goodfellow, "How the Union Organizer Rates Your Company," *Supervision*, Vol. XXXV, No. 3 (March, 1973), p. 6.

"THE PROGRESSIVE LOCAL UNION"

You hear that word 'paternalism' around the plant a lot these days. And for good reason. 'Paternalism' is what the employer believes in and practices.

The word's getting around about what 'paternalism' really means. 'Paternalism' means "DADDY (the boss) knows best."

It means DADDY will give you all sorts of presents (like picnics and smoking privileges) so long as you forget you are adults and let him fire you whenever he pleases, promote just his pets and pay you whatever he decides.

PATERNALISM IS A TRICK TO TRY TO KEEP THE UNION OUT. That's pretty obvious when you stop and think about it. The employer knows that when the employees form a union, he won't have things all his own way. The employer knows that a union contract will guarantee promotions on a fair basis; he knows that under a union contract he won't be able to fire somebody just because he doesn't like the way his hair curls.

The employer knows that a union means COLLECTIVE BARGAINING for higher wages, better working conditions and increased benefits for the employees.

The real objective of 'paternalism' is to fool the employees into thinking all good things come from the generous nature of the employer. The real aim of 'paternalism' is to keep the union out. Spoon-feeding is great for babies; but it's not for adults.

Let the employer know that you're big enough to make some of your own decisions—and you CAN MAKE THEM THROUGH YOUR UNION.

SIGN YOUR AUTHORIZATION CARDS!
MAIL IT TODAY!

Figure 17-1 EXAMPLE OF A UNIONIZING CAMPAIGN "HANDOUT"

decide to form or join a union and no other union is competing for their membership, the employer can simply agree to recognize the union and negotiate an agreement with it. If, however, the employer believes that a majority of employees do not want to belong to a union or if more than one union is attempting to gain recognition, the employer can insist that an election be held to determine which union, if any, the employees prefer to have represent them.

Union elections are conducted by the National Labor Relations Board or by a state labor agency if the election is subject to the latter's jurisdiction. The petition to hold an election usually is initiated by the union although employers, under certain conditions, have the right to petition for one.

If the petition to hold a representation election is not contested, the election can be conducted by secret ballot without holding a pre-election hearing. An election conducted under these conditions is known as a *consent election*. Should the request for representation be contested by the employer or should more than one union be seeking recognition, a formal election must be held which is preceded by pre-election hearings to determine voting choices to appear on the ballot. Since the ballot provides for the choice of "no union," it is possible, when more than one union appears on the ballot, for none of the available choices to receive a majority of the votes. In such instances, a *runoff election* must be conducted between the two choices receiving the largest number of votes. If a union receives a majority of the votes in the initial or the run-off election, it is certified by the NLRB as the bargaining agent for a period of at least a year, or for the duration of the labor agreement.

The Bargaining Unit

Employer recognition gives a union the right to represent employees within a particular bargaining unit which may include all or part of the employer's organization. The *bargaining unit* may be defined as "a group of employees recognized by an employer, or designated by an agency, as appropriate for representation by an employee organization for purposes of bargaining."[2] The determination of the bargaining unit or units can be very important to certain occupational groups within an organization. If a single bargaining unit is established for the organization as a whole, for example, then white-collar and skilled groups of employees must be represented by the same union as the semiskilled production-line workers. When more than one bargaining unit is established, however, it may be possible for white-collar and skilled groups of employees to belong to unions that more closely represent their occupational interests or to refrain from belonging to any union. The existence of more than one bargaining unit within an organization can compound the collective bargaining and union relations problems of the employer as well as reduce the strength of the union representing the majority. It may also help to stimulate interunion rivalry within the organization and to precipitate jurisdictional disputes.

The bargaining history of a company and the wishes of the majority of its employees are among the major factors that are considered by the NLRB in determining the bargaining units. The Taft-Hartley Act, however, requires that under certain conditions separate bargaining units be established for

[2] Paul Prasow, *Unit Determination in Public Employment—Concepts and Problems*, Institute of Industrial Relations, Reprint No. 198 (Los Angeles: University of California, 1969), p. 60.

professional and craft groups. This requirement is designed to help insure that the special problems and interests of these smaller groups will not be submerged in a large industrial union.

Achieving Cooperation

Employer recognition of a union is merely the first step toward the development of a satisfactory working relationship between the two parties. How soon thereafter, if ever, the two parties begin to cooperate and work together will depend upon the bitterness generated during the organizing campaign and the extent to which each party is willing to forget past differences and try to achieve a level of mutual understanding. The stages through which the bargaining relationship may evolve, according to one author, are (1) conflict, (2) containment, (3) accommodation, and (4) cooperation.[3]

The *conflict* stage exists when the employer attempts to drive out or keep out the union and the union reciprocates with equally aggressive action to strengthen its position. The *containment* stage is one of "armed truce" in which the employer recognizes, perhaps grudgingly, the futility of attempting to drive out the union, and the union begins to recognize that its own welfare is contingent upon the employer's survival. Mutual suspicion and distrust from earlier conflict, however, still may remain. The *accommodation* stage is reached when both parties attempt to achieve an agreement by utilizing reason and persuasion to gain a general accord, rather than economic strength to impose a settlement on the weaker party that will create lingering ill will and feelings of injustice.[4] The *cooperation* stage is the ultimate one that may never be reached in some employer-union relations. It is one in which both parties recognize the mutual need to cooperate in protecting the competitive position and future of the enterprise upon which they depend. At this stage recognition of the responsibility that both parties have to the whole society may exist.

Thus, according to the late Walter Reuther of the UAW, the goal of both parties should be to:

> . . . recognize that in a free society, bargaining decisions should be based upon facts and not upon economic power. I hope the day will come in America when, in collective bargaining problems and other problems that bear upon the economic interest, decisions can be based upon the power of economic persuasion rather than upon the persuasion of economic power. In the exercise of naked economic power we make arbitrary decisions, which too frequently are in conflict with the basic needs of the whole of our society.[5]

---

[3] Bevars B. Mabry, *Labor Relations and Collective Bargaining* (New York: The Ronald Press Company, 1966), pp. 66-67.

[4] David L. Cole, "Focus on Bargaining: The Evolving Techniques," *AFL-CIO American Federationist,* Vol. 81, No. 5 (May, 1974), pp. 14-20, as reprinted in Herbert J. Chruden and Arthur W. Sherman, Jr., *Readings in Personnel Management* (4th ed.; Cincinnati: South-Western Publishing Co., 1976), pp. 381-394.

[5] *Ibid.*

COLLECTIVE BARGAINING

Collective bargaining is the process by which the employer and the union negotiate the conditions under which the members within the bargaining unit are to be employed. These conditions are described in the labor agreement that results from such bargaining. Although the collective bargaining process ends officially with the signing of the agreement, it actually continues during the life of the agreement as the two parties work together in resolving problems that were not anticipated during negotiations or that have arisen because certain terms of the agreement have not proven to be entirely clear. During this period the parties may begin gathering data and developing a line of reasoning to support changes when the next agreement is negotiated.

Preparing for Negotiations

Careful preparation which includes planning the strategy and assembling data to support bargaining proposals can permit collective bargaining to be conducted on a more orderly, factual, and positive basis with a greater likelihood of achieving desired goals. Ideally, preparation for the negotiation of the agreement should start soon after the last agreement has been signed. Not only will this practice provide more time in which to collect, organize, and assimilate the needed factual material but it will also permit negotiators to review and to diagnose mistakes and weaknesses evidenced during the preceding negotiations while the experience is still current in their minds. Hopefully, these reviews can provide a basis for negotiating future agreements more effectively.

Sources of Bargaining Information. In preparing for negotiation, internal data relating to grievances, disciplinary action, transfers and promotions, layoffs, overtime, individual performance, and wage payments obtained from this source can be useful in formulating and supporting the employer's bargaining position. The supervisors and executives who must live with and administer the agreement can be a very important source of ideas and suggestions concerning changes that are needed in the agreement. Their contacts with union members and representatives provide them with a firsthand knowledge of many of the complaints that the union negotiators are likely to raise and the changes in the agreement that these negotiators may demand. Since conditions outside of an organization can have an important effect upon bargaining demands and strategy, the compilation of data concerning such factors as general economic conditions, cost of living trends, profit outlook for business, community wage patterns, and fringe benefits and wage rates of other employers can prove invaluable as a basis for supporting arguments presented by a negotiating party.

Bargaining Strategies. It is advisable for negotiators to develop a plan covering their bargaining strategy. This plan should take cognizance of the proposals that the union is likely to submit, based on the most recent agreements with other employers and the demands that remain unsatisfied from previous negotiations. It should also consider the goals that the union is striving to achieve and the extent to which it may be willing to make concessions or to resort to strike action in order to achieve these goals.

The employer's negotiating team will be better able to adhere to their planned course of action if their positions are carefully prepared as a written document. In some bargaining situations the union and the employer will exchange such documents in advance of actual negotiation. Even when this is not the case, the process of reducing proposals to written form can help a negotiating team to identify the relative importance of each proposal and the chances of obtaining them.[6]

Certain elements of strategy are common to both the employer and the union. Generally, the initial demands presented by each side are greater than those that it actually may hope to achieve so as to provide room for concessions. Each party, furthermore, usually will avoid giving up the maximum that it is capable of conceding in order to allow for further concessions, should this become necessary in order to break a bargaining deadlock.

Union strategy often involves the making of *bridgehead demands*—demands in some new area which the union hopes to achieve in some future agreement rather than in the current negotiations. Demands by unions for pensions, welfare benefits, and guaranteed employment that initially were quite modest in nature but which were expanded substantially in subsequent agreements are examples of bridgehead demands.

The Bargaining Process

Legally, *collective bargaining* has been defined as:

> . . . the performance of the mutual obligation of the employer and the representative of the employees to meet at reasonable times and confer in good faith with respect to wages, hours, and other terms and conditions of employment, or the negotiation of an agreement, or any contract incorporating any agreement reached if requested by either party, but such obligation does not compel either party to agree to a proposal or require the making of a concession.[7]

The conditions under which negotiations take place, the experience and personalities of the participants on each side, the goals they are seeking to achieve, and the strength of their relative positions are among the factors that tend to make each bargaining situation unique. Some labor agreements can be

---

[6] Frank P. Doyle, "When It's Your First Time to Negotiate with Labor," *Administrative Management,* Vol. 34, No. 2 (February, 1973), pp. 20-22, 90, as reprinted in Herbert J. Chruden and Arthur W. Sherman, Jr., *Readings in Personnel Management,* (4th ed.; Cincinnati: South-Western Publishing Co., 1976), pp. 368-373.

[7] From the National Labor Relations Act, Sec. 8(d).

negotiated informally within a matter of a few hours particularly if an agreement's terms are based upon the pattern that has been established by the industry. Other agreements, however, may require months of negotiation before a final settlement can be reached.

After negotiators have had extensive experience in bargaining with each other, they often acquire the ability "to read their opponents' minds" and to anticipate their actions and reactions. Inexperienced negotiators bargaining together for the first time, on the other hand, may misinterpret actions and statements of their opponents with the result that they may precipitate a deadlock unintentionally. Regardless of the variations in collective bargaining practices that may occur, however, there are certain rules and rituals that must be observed, and there are certain stages through which negotiations must progress if they are to produce results.

Opening the Negotiations. The initial meeting of the bargaining teams is a particularly important one because it may establish the climate that will prevail during the ensuing negotiations. A cordial attitude with perhaps the injection of a little humor can contribute much to a relaxation of tensions and help the negotiations to begin smoothly. The first meeting usually is devoted to establishing the bargaining authority possessed by the representatives of each side and to determining the rules and procedures to be used during negotiations. If the parties have not submitted their proposals in advance, these may be exchanged and clarified at this time.

It is particularly advisable for the employer's negotiators to request the union counterparts to explain fully each proposal and their reasons for seeking it. The union's responses may help to reveal the amount of thought it has devoted to each proposal and the importance it attaches to it. Those proposals that have been submitted merely because some individual or group demanded them at a union meeting or that are to be used as concessions for trading purposes are more likely to become evident with the union negotiators' explanations, thereby enabling the employer's negotiators to deal with them accordingly.

Analysis of Proposals. The negotiation of an agreement can have certain of the characteristics of a poker game in which each side attempts to determine its opponent's position while not revealing its own. A party normally will try to avoid disclosing the relative importance that it attaches to each proposal in order that it will not be forced to pay a higher price than is necessary to achieve those proposals that are of the greatest importance. Thus, as in the case of the seller who will try to get a higher price for his product if he thinks the prospective buyer strongly desires it, the negotiator will try to get greater concessions in return for granting those that his opponent wants most.

The proposals that each side submits generally may be divided into those that it feels it must achieve, those that it would like to achieve but on which it will compromise, and those that it is submitting primarily for trading purposes. Proposals that are submitted for trading purposes, however, must be realistic in terms of the opponent's ability and willingness to concede them. Unrealistic proposals, such as a union demand that its officers be provided transportation to and from work, may serve only to antagonize the opponent and can precipitate a deadlock, particularly if the employer's negotiators, by reacting vehemently, convey the impression that the proposals are being taken seriously. Unrealistic demands, as one author emphasizes, "can have a nasty way of becoming real issues." [8]

Resolving the Proposals. The proposals submitted by either side, regardless of the degree of importance that is attached to them, must be disposed of if an agreement is to be consummated. These proposals may be withdrawn, or they may be accepted by the other side in their entirety or in some compromise form. In negotiations the proposals may be discussed in the order of their appearance in the agreement or in some other sequence. The sequence in which the proposals are to be discussed can in itself become a subject for collective bargaining since it can affect bargaining results for either or both sides. If the discussion of the more important proposals can be deferred until the last, these proposals may serve as leverage for gaining agreement on proposals of lesser importance which precede them. Since its members are more willing to strike over major issues, the union is likely to try to have such issues discussed near the end of the bargaining agenda.

In order for each bargaining issue to be resolved satisfactorily, the point at which agreement is reached must be within limits that the union and the employer are willing to concede. Stagner and Rosen term the area within these two limits the *bargaining zone*. In some bargaining situations such as the one illustrated in Figure 17-2, the solution desired by one party may exceed the tolerance limit of the other party; thus, that solution is outside of the bargaining zone. If that party refuses to modify its demands sufficiently to bring them within the bargaining zone or if the opposing party refuses to extend its tolerance limit to accommodate the demands of the other party, a bargaining deadlock will result.[9]

Bargaining Pressures and Deadlocks

The knowledge that the opposing side is able and willing to use economic pressures to enforce its demands may help to induce the other side to make greater efforts to achieve a compromise.

Pressures from the Union. The union may exert economic pressures by striking, by picketing, or by boycotting the employer's products and encouraging others to do likewise. The mere threat and ability to engage in such activities can serve as a form of pressure.

---

[8] Doyle, *op. cit.*, p. 22.

[9] Ross Stagner and Hjalmar Rosen, *Psychology of Union-Management Relations* (Belmont, California: Wadsworth Publishing Company, Inc., 1965), pp. 95-97.

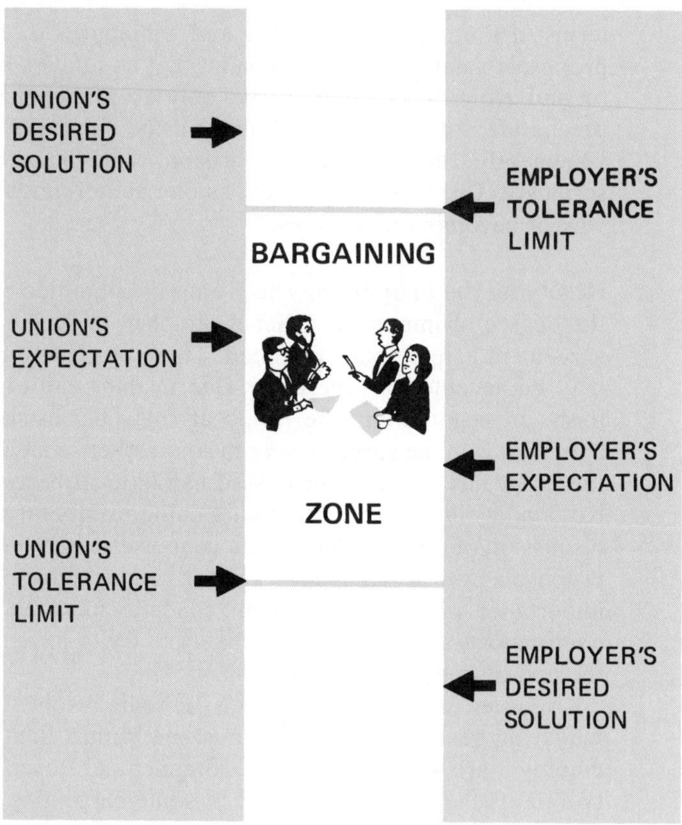

Source: Ross Stagner and Hjalmar Rosen, *Psychology of Union-Management Relations* (Belmont, California: Wadsworth Publishing Company, Inc., 1965), p. 96. Reproduced with permission.

Figure 17-2 TOLERANCE LIMITS THAT DETERMINE THE BARGAINING ZONE

Strikes. A *strike* involves the refusal of a group of employees to perform their jobs. Since a strike can have a serious effect upon the union and its members, the prospects for its success must be analyzed carefully by the union before the strike is called. Most important in this analysis is the estimate of the members' willingness to endure the personal hardships resulting from a strike, particularly if it proves to be a long one. Also of critical importance is the extent, if any, to which the employer will be able to continue operating through the use of non-union personnel and new employees hired to replace the strikers. The greater the ability of the employer to continue operating, the less will be the union's chances for gaining the demands it is attempting to enforce through the strike. Failure to achieve such a desired settlement can result in the employees either voting the union officers out of office or the union out of the organization. Other factors the union must consider are the effects that losing a strike may have upon its power in future relations with the employer. The degree of support the union may expect from the public and the likelihood of government intervention also must be considered by the union.

Employers, on the other hand, must weigh the cost of taking a strike against the long- and short-term costs of acceding to union demands. They also must consider the effects that either course of action may have on union demands in negotiating future agreements. The extent to which they will be forced to close operations and the length of time that they and the unions will be able to endure a strike also must be considered.

Unions usually will seek strike authorization from their members to use as bargaining leverage in the hope of gaining concessions that will enable them to continue negotiating. A strike vote by the members, thus, does not mean that they actually want or expect to go out on strike; but, rather, it is intended as a vote of confidence to strengthen the position of their leaders at the bargaining table.

Picketing. When a union goes on strike, it is general practice for the union to *picket* the employer by placing persons at plant entrances to advertise the dispute and to discourage persons from entering or leaving the premises. Even when the strikers represent only a small proportion of the employees within the plant, they can cause the shutdown of an entire plant if a sufficient number of the plant's employees refuse to cross their picket line. Also, a picket line may serve to prevent others from crossing it to deliver and pick up goods.

Picketing carried on by nonemployees is called *stranger picketing,* and it is sometimes used by unions in an effort to unionize an employer. Because peaceful picketing has traditionally been regarded as a form of free speech, the courts have been reluctant to curb it even when it has been used unfairly. If a strike fails to stop an employer's operations, the picket line may serve as more than a passive weapon. Employees who attempt to cross the line may be subjected to verbal insults and even physical violence. *Mass picketing* in which large groups of pickets try to block the path of people attempting to enter a plant may then be used. However, the use of picket lines to exert physical pressure and to incite violence may harm more than help the union cause.

In addition to picketing, at least one union, the United Farm Workers, has resorted to the use of *marches* to enlist public sympathy for their cause. While this tactic, borrowed from earlier civil rights and anti-war movements, is not characteristic of those tactics used by most unions within the United States, it has been used rather frequently by unions in Europe. Such marches and demonstrations in Europe, however, are intended more to bring pressure upon the government for political change than to enforce bargaining demands. Equally unorthodox as far as the United Farm Workers are concerned has been the enlistment of students, civil rights workers, and members of the clergy to participate in picketing, demonstrations, meetings, and marches.

Boycotting. Another economic weapon of unions is the *boycott*. This action can hurt an employer if conducted by a large enough segment of organized labor. In contrast to a strike, a boycott may not end completely with the end of the strike. Many former customers may have developed a bias toward a company's products or a change in buying habits during the boycott that are not easily reversed. For example, even though a manufacturer of work clothes is able to operate during a strike, it could suffer a substantial loss of sales because of the refusal of union members throughout the nation to buy the garments that it manufactures. Most unions levy heavy fines against members if they are discovered patronizing an employer who is the subject of a union boycott. The refusal of a union to allow its members to patronize a business enterprise where there is a labor dispute is a *primary boycott*. This type of boycott under most circumstances is legal. A union may go a step farther, however, and attempt to induce third parties, primarily suppliers and customers, to refrain from business dealings with the employer with whom it has a dispute. A boycott of this type is called a *secondary boycott* and generally is illegal under the Taft-Hartley Act.

Since they are not covered by the Taft-Hartley Act, the United Farm Workers have been able, with varying degrees of success, to utilize the secondary boycott to restrict the sale of lettuce, grapes, or wines produced by growers from whom the union is attempting to gain recognition. In at least one court decision, it has been ruled that the use of pickets at a store to discourage the purchase of a particular product (in this instance Washington State apples) did not constitute a secondary boycott because it was held that the union was merely urging customers to refrain from purchasing apples rather than from patronizing the store.[10]

Employer Response to Strikes. An employer who is struck by a union has the option of continuing to operate in the face of union opposition or ceasing operations.

Continued Operations. Because of the nature of its operations, its products or services, its ownership or financial resources, or various other factors, an organization may find it more advantageous to continue to operate. In a study by Hutchinson, some of the advantages gained from continuing to operate that were most frequently cited by the managers involved with strikes were the following:

1. Unions were taught a lesson and the prestige of their leaders was lowered.
2. Managers learned things about their operations that they had not known before the strike.
3. Terms more favorable to the company were gained as a result of the strike.
4. Cost reduction and efficiency improvement initiated during the strike continued after it ended.
5. Vital services were continued during the strike.[11]

Some of the disadvantages of operating during the strike were reported to be the following:

---

[10] NLRB v. Fruit and Vegetable Packers, Local 760, Supreme Court of the United States, 1964, 377 U.S. 58, 84, S.Ct. 1063, 12L Ed. 2d 129.

[11] John G. Hutchinson, *Management Under Strike Conditions* (New York: Holt, Rinehart, and Winston, Inc., 1966), p. 29.

1. Loss of orders and revenues during (or before or after) the strike.
2. Bitterness between nonstrikers and strikers resulting during and after the strike.
3. Public relations image suffered.
4. Strike created long-term bitterness that might affect future negotiation.
5. Property damage and/or personal injuries were caused by the strike.[12]

Plant Shutdown or Lockout. An alternative response by an employer may be to shut down the plant in an effort to force the union to cease harassing activities or to accept certain conditions demanded by the employer. Such action is called a *lockout*. In recent years the lockout has perhaps been used more frequently by employer associations to support members who have been struck by a union. In such instances the lockout is invoked by the other employers on the grounds that "a strike against one is a strike against all." Lockouts also may be used by employers to combat union slowdowns, damage to their property, or violence within their plant that may occur in connection with a labor dispute even though a strike may not be in progress. Employers, however, are reluctant to resort to a lockout because of the loss of revenue during the shutdown and because of their fear that such action might generate unfavorable public opinion or result in legal action against them.

Overcoming Bargaining Deadlocks. If a strike or lockout occurs, it usually is not long before both parties begin to feel its effects. The company may suffer the loss of profits, customers, and public goodwill or may risk unfavorable government action. The union leaders may risk the possibility of losing members, of being voted out of office, or of having the employees vote the union out of the company. Unions also may experience the loss of public goodwill, may become involved in unfavorable legal action, or may suffer from subsequent legislation that is passed to regulate their activities. As the losses to each side increase, therefore, the participants usually become more anxious to achieve a settlement.

Conciliation, Mediation, and Arbitration. When the two parties are unable or unwilling to continue negotiations, an outside third party such as a conciliator or a mediator can be helpful. A *conciliator* provides a catalytic service by reestablishing communications between the two parties and thereby helping them to reach their own solution without making any direct recommendations. A *mediator,* by definition, exercises a more positive role in helping to resolve a deadlock by suggesting compromise solutions. In practice, however, the functions of conciliation and mediation often overlap. The conciliator may see fit to offer suggestions and thus perform the role of a mediator, or the mediator may attempt to let the two parties work out their own solutions and thus act merely as a conciliator. Since both the union and management usually are under pressure to achieve a settlement by the time they enter the picture, conciliators (or mediators) can help them to retreat from their deadlocked position without suffering a loss of face.

---

[12] *Ibid.,* p. 34.

In arbitration both parties to the dispute agree to permit an *impartial umpire* or *arbitrator* to consider the relative merits of their respective positions and to resolve the dispute through the award made for the case. Most arbitration cases arise in connection with the administration of the agreement rather than in connection with the negotiation of it. In collective bargaining the parties generally prefer to make those concessions that may be necessary to achieve agreement on a voluntary basis. Even concessions made in response to economic pressure from strike action usually are preferred because the decision is reached by either or both parties and not imposed upon them by a third party.

Government Intervention. In some situations deadlocks may have to be resolved directly or indirectly as the result of government intervention, particularly if the work stoppage is a threat to the national security or to the public welfare. Government intervention may include plant seizure or the threat of seizure, the issuance of injunctions, or the cancellation of government contracts. The threat of punitive legislation or of public condemnation of either or both sides also can have a persuasive effect in achieving a settlement. Government pressure also may be exerted through the appointment of a *fact-finding board* to investigate a bargaining deadlock. Although these boards do not have power to force the parties to reach a settlement, they do provide additional information that can serve to fix the responsibility for the deadlock. The influence of this information upon public opinion can place one or both parties under considerable pressure to reach an agreement.

Strikes in the Public Sector. Strikes by government employees have created a problem for lawmakers and for the general public. Because of the essentiality of the services they provide, public policy is opposed to strikes by public employees. Generally state legislatures have not granted them the right to strike and, with few exceptions, court decisions relating to this issue have held that public employees have no right to strike in the absence of permissive legislation.[13] This position goes back to the concept of government sovereignty and "the right of kings" which holds that "government employees have only those rights given to them by their sovereign."[14]

Despite the *de jure* absence of any right to do so, public employees in practice do strike, and often with impunity. These strikes occur both in jurisdictions that permit collective bargaining and in those that do not.[15] As a result of this fact, various possibilities are being explored for resolving collective bargaining deadlocks. One is that of *compulsory binding arbitration* for employees, such as police officers and firefighters, and similar jobs where strikes cannot be tolerated. One plan proposed in connection with such

---

[13] Kenneth McClennan and Michael H. Moskow, "Public Education," in Seymour L. Wolbein (editor), *Emerging Sectors of Collective Bargaining* (Morristown, N.J.: General Learning Corporation, 1970), p. 252.

[14] David T. Stanley, *Managing Local Government Under Union Pressure* (Washington, D.C.: The Brookings Institution), p. 17.

[15] Charles M. Rehmus, "Labor Relations in the Public Sector in the United States," *International Labour Review,* Vol. 109, No. 3 (March, 1974), p. 213.

arbitration is the "final offer selection" in which the arbitrator has no power to compromise but must select one or other of the final offers submitted by the two parties.[16] This plan can serve to discourage one or both parties from avoiding making concessions in hopes that they will come out ahead should the arbitrator make a settlement by "splitting the difference" between the two deadlocked positions. Instead, the arbitrator's award is more likely to go to the party that has moved the closest toward a reasonable position for a settlement.

THE LABOR AGREEMENT

After an agreement has been reached through collective bargaining, it must be reduced to writing and signed by the representatives of both parties. This written document, which typically tends to expand with each succeeding agreement, may vary from a few typewritten pages to a printed document well in excess of 100 pages, depending upon the size of the employer and the union that it covers.

Sections of the Agreement

The labor agreement is divided into articles or sections covering the major subjects that it encompasses, with appendixes covering certain of these subjects in greater detail. The sections of the labor agreement shown in Figure 17-3 are typical of those found in agreements. This figure reveals that a major portion of the labor agreement is concerned with conditions of employment. These conditions include wages, hours, fringe benefits, and various provisions covering discipline and other personnel actions. According to a Bureau of National Affairs survey, 92 percent of the labor agreements also contain provisions governing seniority and 99 percent contain procedures for the processing of employee grievances.[17]

Management Rights

Union members expect and usually are able to achieve with each successive agreement improvements in employment conditions which will tend to increase operating costs unless offset by corresponding improvements in operating efficiency. Management, therefore, is under pressure to improve efficiency by whatever means it can develop including the improvement of scheduling, tightening of work standards and work rules, and eliminating labor that is considered to be unnecessary. Such economy measures, however, may precipitate demands from the union for the right to participate in these decisions because of the effect they can have upon the job security of union members. These demands inevitably lead to controversy and even to conflict between the union and the employer regarding the question of whether or not

---

[16] *Ibid.*, p. 214.

[17] *Collective Bargaining: Negotiations and Contracts*, Vol. 2, (Washington, D.C.: The Bureau of National Affairs, 1971), pp. 51:1, 75:1.

Section No.	Subject Covered
1.	Purpose and Intent of the Parties
2.	Scope of the Agreement
3.	Management
4.	Responsibilities of the Parties
5.	Union-Membership and Checkoff
6.	Adjustment of Grievance
7.	Arbitration
8.	Suspension and Discharge Cases
9.	Rates of Pay
10.	Hours of Work
11.	Overtime — Holidays
12.	Vacations
13.	Seniority
14.	Safety and Health
15.	Military Service
16.	Severance Allowance
17.	Savings and Vacation Plan
18.	Supplemental Unemployment Benefits Program
19.	S.U.B. and Insurance Grievances
20.	Prior Agreements
21.	Termination Date
	Appendixes

Source: Agreement between the United States Steel Corporation and the United Steelworkers Union.

Figure 17-3 CONTENT OF THE LABOR AGREEMENT

the right to make such decisions can be considered an exclusive *management right* or *prerogative* in which the union does not have the right of participation.

Management thus establishes as the status quo a set of conditions with or without the union's consent. In so doing, it seals off certain areas from bilateral determination with the union and reserves them exclusively for management determination. Since virtually every so-called inherent right can and has been challenged successfully by unions, the ultimate determination of what can be sealed off from negotiation will depend upon the relative bargaining power of the two parties.[18]

Traditionally the *reserved rights theory* has held that:

> . . . management's authority is supreme in all matters except those it has expressly conceded in the collective agreement, or in those areas where its authority is restricted by law. Put another way, management does not look to the collective agreement to ascertain its rights; it looks to the agreement to find out which and how much of its rights and powers it has conceded outright or agreed to share with the union.[19]

Employers subscribing to the preceding theory may consider it preferable not to mention management rights in the labor agreement on the grounds that they possess such rights already and that to mention them would create an issue with the union. Many employers, however, consider it advisable to include a clause in the agreement defining the rights of management to reduce confusion and misunderstanding and to remind union officers, union stewards, and employees that management never relinquishes its status quo. In one survey 99 percent of the labor agreements that were included contained a statement on management rights.[20] The following is an example of such a statement:

> It is the intention hereof that all of the rights, powers, prerogatives, authorities that the company had prior to the signing of this agreement are retained by the company except those, and only to the extent that they are specifically abridged, delegated, granted, or modified by the agreement.[21]

Management rights also refer to the *functional* role of management and its procedural right to direct the work force—to give the orders with which employees are expected to comply. Protests to these orders are left to be resolved through the grievance procedure except when the orders are detrimental to employee health, safety, or morals.[22] It is therefore management rather than the union that assigns members to their work stations; determines when layoffs and recalls shall occur and how production is to be scheduled; and initiates other decisions of a similar nature.

Union Security

Security is equally as important to the union as management rights are to the employer. Union security determines the extent to which the jobs within its representation area will be manned by union members and the extent to which

---

[18] Paul Prasow, "The Theory of Management Reserved Rights—Revisited," Proceedings of the 26th Annual Meeting of the *Industrial Relations Association*, p. 74.

[19] Paul Prasow and Edward Peters, "New Perspectives on Management's Reserved Rights," *Labor Law Journal* (January, 1967), pp. 5-6.

[20] *Collective Bargaining: Negotiations and Contracts*, Vol. 2, *op. cit.*, p. 65:1.

[21] AMBAC Industries, Inc., Electrical Products Division and Electrical Workers (IUE), p. 65, dated 8/2/73.

[22] Prasow, *op. cit.*, p. 76.

the union will be able to maintain disciplinary control over its members. Nearly 83 percent of the labor agreements included in one survey now provide for some form of union security such as those described in this section.[23]

Union Shop. The *union shop* which exists in 62 percent of the agreements provides that any person who is hired, if not a union member at the time, must join the union within a prescribed period—usually 30 days—or be terminated.

Modified Union Shop. While the *modified union shop* is similar to the union shop, it may permit certain employees to be exempt from joining the union; for example, those who were employed before a certain date, those who are Christmas workers, students in work study programs, or those who object to union membership on religious grounds. This shop is much less common than the union shop and appears in only about 11 percent of the agreements.

Maintenance-of-Membership Shop. The *maintenance-of-membership shop* which appears in only about 7 percent of the labor agreements requires that employees who voluntarily join a union must remain members in good standing during the life of the agreement. It also may provide an escape period during which those who may wish to do so may drop their membership before it becomes effective.

Agency Shop. The *agency shop* which is contained in 9 percent of the agreements does not require employees in the bargaining unit to join the union, but it does require that they pay dues to the union which serves as their bargaining agent within the organization.[24] This type of shop at one time was ruled to be illegal by the NLRB, but it now has limited adoption primarily in those states that have "right-to-work laws" forbidding compulsory union membership.

Closed Shop. Another type of shop is the *closed shop* which would require that an employer hire only those who are union members. Although this type of shop is forbidden by the Taft-Hartley Act, it exists for all purposes in certain industries, such as the maritime and construction fields, where employers obtain their personnel through union hiring halls.

Simple Recognition Shop. Unions failing to achieve one of the forms of security that have been mentioned above may operate through a *simple recognition shop* under which the employer recognizes it as the exclusive bargaining agent for all employees within the bargaining unit.

Dues Checkoff. About 86 percent of all agreements also provide for the *checkoff.* Under this provision the employer withholds the union dues from the paycheck of each union member who signs an affidavit agreeing to such deduction.[25] While this provision requires the employer to perform an

[23] *Collective Bargaining: Negotiations and Contracts,* Vol. 2, *op. cit.,* p. 87:1.
[24] *Ibid.*
[25] *Ibid.,* p. 87:3.

accounting function for the union, it eliminates the need for union officers to come onto the employer's premises to collect from delinquent members. It also eliminates the possibility of the employer being forced to discharge a capable employee who has been expelled from the union for nonpayment of dues.

Wording of the Agreement

The wording of the labor agreement can be very important in preventing difficulties from arising over its interpretation. The fact that the language of an agreement may be subject to different interpretations makes it essential that each provision be discussed thoroughly to insure that both parties are agreed upon its precise meaning. Prasow and Peters cite the following contract provision as an example of one that inevitably will be subject to differences in interpretation: "An employee who does not work the day before the holiday or the day after the holiday will not be paid for the holiday."[26] Depending upon the voice intonation patterns of the persons reciting this statement, some listeners will interpret it to mean that the employee need work only one day, either before or after the holiday, in order to qualify for holiday pay. Others will interpret the statement to mean that the employee must work both the day before and the day after the holiday in order to qualify for holiday pay. As a means of eliminating the ambiguity existing in the statement, therefore, it should read: "An employee who does not work *either* the day before the holiday or the day after the holiday, etc." or "An employee who does not work *both* the day before the holiday *and* the day after the holiday, etc."

When differences of opinion arise over the interpretation of a provision in the agreement, a solution may be achieved by going back and reviewing the minutes of the bargaining sessions pertaining to it to determine what the intent of the parties may have been when the provision was agreed upon. If the differences in the interpretation of a provision cannot be resolved, however, they may be submitted to an arbitrator whose interpretation becomes the binding one.

TRENDS IN UNION-MANAGEMENT COOPERATION

In recent years union-management relations have been characterized by greater accommodation and cooperation. Conditions of open warfare and conflict have become less prevalent as rationalism and give-and-take bargaining have tended to replace emotionalism and sheer economic pressures as the basis for achieving bargaining agreements. Increasingly employers are recognizing that the negotiation of a labor agreement is facilitated by the existence of a sound personnel management program. They also have learned the futility of attempting to destroy a union and of permitting themselves to always be on the defensive when negotiating with the union. Although some employers have

[26] Paul Prasow and Edward Peters, "The Semantic Aspects of Collective Bargaining," *ETC: A Review of General Semantics,* Vol. 25, No. 3 (September, 1968), pp. 292-293, as reprinted by the Institute of Industrial Relations, University of California, Los Angeles. Reprint No. 193.

been curtailed by their union in attempting to take advantage of technological advancements, an increasing number of them have been able to work out a system for introducing laborsaving devices that preserves the job rights of union members.

Reasons for the Growing Cooperation

The growing cooperation between unions and management in the private sector does not stem from any emerging spirit of altruism on the part of either side. Rather it is due to an increasing awareness on the part of union leaders and even the rank-and-file members of a fact that management has long recognized: namely, that a company must remain competitive if it and the jobs it provides are to continue in existence.

In recent years, increasing numbers of companies have been forced either to go out of business or to transfer their production to subsidiaries abroad because of growing foreign competition. Many workers forced out of their jobs by this competition have found it difficult and even impossible to get new jobs. This fact has not gone unnoticed by union members still holding jobs who recognize that the same thing may happen to them. Consequently, many union members are exhibiting a more conciliatory attitude by making concessions that would once have been militantly opposed. The president of one union has this explanation for the change in attitude: "It's a question of preserving jobs. If what you get in your bargaining puts the company out of business, you haven't gained anything and our people realize this."[27]

The willingness of union leaders to accept changes in work rules also is becoming more prevalent. As one union leader admits, "We've got outmoded work rules, hell yes. You know it, I know it, and the company knows it. What we've come down to is whether we are willing to make some changes in hopes of keeping jobs. I'm optimistic that we'll work something out."[28]

Some union members have even shown a willingness to accept a reduction in wages in order to save their jobs. A young refrigerator assembly man, for example, who was forced to accept a 25¢ per hour wage cut and forego wage increases for a two-year period, had this reaction: "Look at it this way. I was on layoff almost six months and all the time it looked like the company was going broke. Hell, I'm just happy to have a job to come back to, whatever the pay. It's sure a lot better than being out on the street and earning zero."[29]

Union-Management Cooperation

Possible areas of cooperation between employers and unions are often outlined in the labor agreement, such as provisions for the payroll deduction of union dues. Union participation in determining and administering time

---

[27] Everett Groseclose, "Conciliatory Mood: Increasingly Workers Give Up Some Benefits So as Not to Lose Jobs," *The Wall Street Journal,* January 26, 1972, p. 1.
[28] *Ibid.*
[29] *Ibid.*

standards, in reducing waste, in promoting safety, or in handling various other operating problems also may be provided for in the agreement. Unions, in addition, may assist employers in solving certain of their personnel problems. Fines and reprimands and other forms of disciplinary action by the union can do much to discourage "quickie strikes," substandard performance, or violations of company rules by its members. Petty and unwarranted grievances can also be screened and resolved by union officers, and this serves to keep the grievance machinery available for the handling of the more serious cases.

More recently there has been a trend to negotiate for labor agreements which will be effective over a longer period of time. About 65 percent of the agreements surveyed by the Bureau of National Affairs were of three years' duration. Longer-term agreements permit greater stability to be achieved in labor relations since both parties can plan ahead more effectively and also have more time to work together in solving mutual problems without being subjected to the typical collective bargaining pressures and tensions. Some unions and employers have established joint committees to work together in resolving such mutual problems as those relating to cost reduction, automation, or quality improvement, thereby reducing the number of problems that must be made the subject of collective bargaining.

One of the landmark examples of union-management cooperation was that worked out between the International Longshoremen's and Warehousemen's Union and the Pacific Maritime Association in the late 1950s. At that time shipowners either were having or threatening to have cargoes unloaded in Mexico or Canada to avoid the high costs in the ILWU contract ports. These high costs were the result of provisions in the labor agreement requiring unnecessary work and manpower. Cargo arriving on pallets, for example, had to be unloaded and put back on the pallets by longshoremen. Regulations governing the size of crews, furthermore, hampered the mechanization of cargo handling. In 1958, however, the ILUW agreed to accept cost-cutting mechanization and to ease crew size requirements if the employers would split the savings achieved with the union. The union's share of the savings went into a trust fund and was used to provide earlier retirement benefits or financial assistance for those suffering the loss of employment as a result of technological improvements. The resulting relaxation of union restrictions on cargo handling caused production to soar and resulted in man-hour savings of as high as 80 percent of that required under former conditions.[30]

In certain European countries, such as Sweden and Switzerland, the state of union-management cooperation is considerably more advanced than it is in the United States. The following statement appearing in one Swedish labor agreement illustrates the stage to which cooperation between the unions and employers has progressed:

> The central organization of the Swedish labour market fully realizes how important it is to have its disputes settled as far as possible without resort to open conflict. It is of major interest to those gaining their income from industry

[30] "The Unions Beginning to Bend on Work Rules," *Business Week* (September 9, 1972), p. 105.

> and trade that work be allowed to continue; they are mainly the persons who suffer losses through open conflicts. For this reason, their own organizations must naturally deem it to be their chief mission to employ all possible means for settling disputes in a peaceful way; both parties also realize that the results gained through an open conflict very rarely stand in proportion to the costs and other sacrifices connected with the conflict. The fact that the organizations themselves fully realize the responsibility they assume when resorting to open conflict is believed to be evidenced by developments in the Swedish labour market in recent years. The guiding principle of the two parties has in this instance been to preserve undisturbed labour peace in view of its importance to industry and trade and to the national economy.[31]

This advanced state of cooperation probably is due to the fact that unionism is accepted extensively in Sweden by both employers and the general public. Since Sweden is a highly organized society, unions represent persons from all walks of life including college students, clergymen, physicians, engineers, and other white-collar groups in addition to the blue-collar workers. Unemployment benefits, furthermore, are disbursed through the unions. Swedish unions thus operate from a position of strength because their existence is assured and there is no need for them to struggle for membership, recognition, or survival.

Résumé

One of the first goals of employees in their drive to unionize is to gain recognition and security provisions that are essential in order to negotiate an agreement with an employer. The right of employees to unionize, to bargain collectively with an employer over their conditions of employment, and to exert economic pressures to enforce these demands has become firmly accepted by American society. A growing body of law, furthermore, has been developed to protect these rights, to facilitate collective bargaining, to minimize conflicts, and to prevent abuse by either side in the maintenance of a bargaining relationship. While some employers may resent sharing with a union the authority to make various decisions relating to the operation of their organizations, the existence of unions and their participation in these areas has become an established fact. It, therefore, is to the best interests of every employer who must deal with a union to develop the ability to bargain effectively and to maintain a satisfactory relationship with union leaders. Even those employers who are not unionized can hardly afford to ignore the subject of union relations or the laws pertaining to it since there is always the possibility that they may become the subject of a unionizing effort.

Because it is the union-management conflict that normally attracts the public's attention, it is easy to overlook the fact that most relationships between unions and management are peaceful ones. Such relationships, however, do not "just happen" but, rather, have developed as the result of the

[31] Basic Agreement Between the Swedish Employers' Confederation and The Confederation of Swedish Trade Unions (as amended in 1947, 1958 and 1964).

skill and effort that have been exerted by representatives of both sides. While representatives with such abilities may be able to drive a hard bargain, they also are able to understand the position and problems of the opposing side and to avoid unrealistic demands and needless antagonism. They also are more likely to achieve an agreement which is clear and understandable and less likely to be the subject of disputes and conflict in the course of its administration. The evolution of a bargaining relationship into one that is peaceful and cooperative thus can work to the mutual benefit of both parties, as experience in some European countries such as Sweden has proven.

DISCUSSION QUESTIONS

1. Why may it be advantageous for the employer to request the union negotiator to explain what each of its proposals entails and the reasons for making each proposal?
2. Of what significance is the "bargaining zone" in the conduct of negotiations, and what determines the limits of this zone?
3. What is the purpose of picketing, and why have the courts been reluctant to curb its use?
4. What are some of the possible reasons why an employer may take a strike that inevitably will result in substantial losses in terms of customers and profits?
5. Why is a company more likely than the union to press for an agreement of more than a year's duration? Under what conditions will the union be more likely to agree to a longer-term agreement?
6. At an election conducted among the 20 employees of the Exclusive Jewelry Store, all but two of them voted in favor of the Jewelry Workers Union which subsequently was certified as their bargaining agent. In negotiating its first agreement, the union demanded that it be granted a union shop. The two employees voting against the union, however, informed the management that they would quit rather than join the union. Unfortunately for the store, the two employees were skilled gem cutters who were the most valuable of its employees and would be difficult to replace. What position should the company take with regard to the union shop demand?
7. What are some of the reasons for the growing cooperation between employers and unions for the elimination of certain work rules that previously restricted production?

PROBLEM 17-1 WHO'S HARASSING WHOM?

The Peter Pan Toy Company employed nearly 200 permanent personnel and slightly over 100 temporary personnel during the peak period. Few employees were members of a local of the International Novelty Makers Union since most of them belonged to an independent union within the company. For a number of years the Novelty Makers Union had attempted unsuccessfully to recruit enough members from within the company to become the exclusive bargaining agent for its employees. Finally the Novelty Makers Union decided to conduct a major organizing campaign utilizing some professional and financial assistance from the international union. The campaign included passing out at the plant entrances organizing literature which violently condemned the company's management for being antiunion in its personnel practices. Pickets who were stationed at each of the plant's entrances also began to interfere with the movement of people in and out of the plant, including those who were tour party visitors and those having business to conduct with the company, as well as nonstriking employees.

In an effort to curb this growing nuisance, the company decided to seek a court injunction forbidding the pickets from interfering with persons entering or leaving the plant. In order to gain supporting evidence for its injunction request, the company employed a photographer to record instances of picket interference. When the union discovered the presence of the photographer who was hired to film their activities, they immediately filed an unfair labor practice against the company with the NLRB, alleging that the company was "attempting to harass and interfere with the legitimate efforts of the union to organize its employees."

To what extent, if any, do you believe that there was justification for:

a. Picketing by the union.
b. Use of the photographer by the company.
c. Unfair labor practice charge filed by the union.

SUGGESTED READINGS

Chamberlain, Neil W., and James W. Kuhn. *Collective Bargaining,* 2d ed. New York: McGraw-Hill Book Company, 1965.

Cohen, Sanford. *Labor in the United States,* 3d ed. Columbus, Ohio: Charles E. Merrill Publishing Company, 1970.

Davey, Harold W. *Contemporary Collective Bargaining,* 3d ed. Englewood Cliffs, N.J.: Prentice-Hall, 1972.

Dunlop, John T., and Neil W. Chamberlain (eds.). *Frontiers of Collective Bargaining.* New York: Harper and Row, 1967.

Hutchinson, John G. *Management Under Strike Conditions.* New York: Holt, Rinehart and Winston, Inc., 1966.

Prasow, Paul, and Edward Peters. *Arbitration and Collective Bargaining.* New York: McGraw-Hill Book Company, 1970.

Sloane, Arthur A. and Fred Witney. *Labor Relations,* 2d ed. Englewood Cliffs, N.J.: Prentice-Hall, 1972.

Stagner, Ross, and Hjalmar Rosen. *Psychology of Union-Management Relations.* Belmont, California: Wadsworth Publishing Company, Inc., 1965.

Stanley, David T. *Managing Local Government Under Union Pressure.* Washington, D.C.: The Brookings Institution, 1972.

Warner, Kenneth O., and Mary L. Hennessy. *Public Management at the Bargaining Table.* Chicago: Public Personnel Association, 1967.

Wolfbein, Seymour L. (ed.). *Emerging Sectors of Collective Bargaining.* Morristown, N.J.: General Learning Corporation, 1970.

Woodworth, Robert T., and Richard B. Peterson. *Collective Negotiation for Public and Professional Employees.* Glenview, Illinois: Scott, Foresman and Company, 1969.

Reducing Labor Relations Problems

No matter how carefully and conscientiously the union and the employer may negotiate the labor agreement, differences between the two parties over its administration and enforcement are almost certain to arise. It is inevitable that occasionally some employees may feel that they have been subjected to certain personnel actions affecting them that are contrary to the terms of the labor agreement or to established personnel policy. Such actions may include those involving work assignments, job classification, remuneration, or disciplinary penalties. In some instances employees may merely develop some vague or nebulous belief that their boss is not providing them fair or consistent treatment. Whether their beliefs are valid or not, the fact that these exist in their minds becomes a problem that must be resolved. If left unresolved, they often can become aggravated and lead to serious difficulties with the union, declines in efficiency and morale, or the loss of competent personnel.

Grievance procedures for resolving problems that may arise in connection with the administration of labor agreements or with decisions affecting individuals or groups within the union are provided for in most agreements. Otherwise, without grievance procedures the union would be forced to resort to strikes, slowdowns, or other economic pressures in order to correct what is considered to be an injustice. Typically, therefore, in a private enterprise a union's grievances are initiated in response to actions that it believes the employer has taken or failed to take in living up to the terms of the labor agreement or the policies of the organization.

Ideally, personnel management should prevent the causes of grievances or disciplinary actions from arising in the first place. The effectiveness with which managers can perform such functions as selection, training, performance evaluation, and other personnel processes that have been discussed in earlier chapters can contribute significantly to the prevention of grievance and disciplinary actions. Sound personnel policies and procedures, furthermore, can help facilitate an early and satisfactory solution to those grievances and disciplinary problems that do occur. The discussion in this chapter will be concerned with the nature of grievances and disciplinary actions that may arise in the management of employees, the possible underlying causes of these problems, and the means by which they may be resolved most effectively.

EMPLOYEE GRIEVANCES

It is inevitable that some employees will become dissatisfied with the treatment they receive. These dissatisfactions, regardless of whether they are expressed or suppressed, valid or invalid, are referred to in personnel management terminology as *grievances*. Although some students of labor relations restrict the term grievance to those dissatisfactions that result from actual or alleged violations of the union agreement or formal personnel policy, and refer to all other employment dissatisfactions as *complaints,* the term grievance in this book is used in the broader sense to include all forms of dissatisfaction including those that arise in an organization that is not unionized.

Symptoms of Grievances

Grievances are likely to be resolved more readily if they can be recognized and acted upon promptly. While employees who are candid and articulate may have little difficulty or hesitation in revealing their grievances, many employees are not so inclined. Employees of the latter type may either be unable to detect accurately the nature of their grievances or they may be unwilling to disclose it. Their grievances therefore are often revealed only through various symptoms that indicate their presence.

Although the personnel department may be able to detect certain grievance symptoms through the analysis of statistical data that it compiles or through its direct communications with employees, the employee's immediate supervisor is in the best position to detect these symptoms. It is the supervisor who provides the direct link between the employee and management and who is in continual contact with employees and is available to listen to their grievances. It is important, therefore, for supervisors to create the type of climate and rapport within their departments that will encourage subordinates to speak up and discuss anything that may be bothering them without fear of provoking resentment. Since some individuals may have difficulty in expressing themselves or in identifying accurately the exact cause of their dissatisfaction, the supervisor should try to become skillful in drawing out these people and in helping them to express their feelings. As a result of this assistance, employees may be able to uncover the true nature of their grievances through verbalizing their feelings.

Usually the more difficult grievances that confront a supervisor are those that the employee is unable or unwilling to express. These grievances may be evidenced by such symptoms as sullenness, moodiness, tardiness, indifferent attitudes, insubordination, or decline in quality and quantity of work. Determining what is causing these symptoms and the extent to which they may be the result of dissatisfactions relating to the employee's job can challenge even the most competent supervisor. The supervisor who can avoid placing the wrong interpretation on these symptoms, such as viewing them as a personal attack, and who follows the clinical approach of diagnosing the causes of underlying symptoms will have better results in resolving grievances.

Causes of Grievances

The fact that grievances may result from one or more causes can make their diagnosis difficult. Often there are factors that have contributed to the grievance other than those recognized or stated by the employee. Some of the causes of grievances that may or may not be stated include those relating to the labor agreement, to the employee's job, and to personal problems of the individual.

Causes Relating to the Labor Agreement. Many grievances involving the agreement result from omissions or ambiguities in its provisions that cause each party to interpret differently the meaning of a particular provision or how a particular personnel decision should be made. In other instances one of the two parties may use the grievance procedure as a means of gaining changes in the agreement that it either neglected or was unable to achieve at the bargaining table. In addition, union representatives sometimes may solicit grievances relating to the agreement for the purpose of demonstrating to employees what the union can do for them or what changes should be negotiated into the next agreement. Union officers also at times may solicit grievances against an employer to divert the attention of members from weaknesses or leadership deficiencies existing within the union. Furthermore, the Supreme Court, by ruling that members have a right under certain conditions to sue the union for failing to process their grievances, has made union officers more prone to process grievances which formerly might have been dropped.

Causes Relating to the Job. Many grievances, including those that appeal disciplinary action, often stem from failure of employees either to meet the demands of their jobs or to gain satisfaction from performing them, or both. Employees who are placed in the wrong job or who lack adequate orientation, training, or supervision are more likely to perform unsatisfactorily, to become dissatisfied with their employment, and to become grievance or disciplinary problems. It should be noted, however, that grievances do not tend to be any more prevalent in one kind of work than in another.[1] The factor determining

[1] Phillip Ash, "The Parties to the Grievance," *Personnel Psychology*, Vol. 23, No. 1 (Spring, 1970), p. 16.

work-related grievances, therefore, is not the nature of the work but how well the individuals are suited to and able to meet the demands of their jobs.

Another source of grievance lies in supervisory practices. The supervisor's attitude and behavior toward individual workers and the union may provide a fertile source of grievances. Supervisors who play favorites, fail to live up to promises, or who are too demanding are likely to encounter many grievances from workers. In addition to establishing good relationships with employees, it is the supervisor's responsibility to be familiar with the labor agreement and with company rules in order that he or she may protect the rights of the employees as well as those of the employer.

Causes Relating to Personal Problems. There are some individuals who will become dissatisfied regardless of the nature of their job or employer because of personal problems to which they are unable to adjust. Personal problems such as poor health, family illness, marital discord, or financial difficulties are typical of some that employees bring with them to the job. The frustration resulting from these problems may cause employees to find fault with their jobs or with others around them.

Grievances stemming from personal problems usually cannot be resolved merely by changing jobs or conditions of employment. They can be resolved only if the supervisor tries to help employees by having nondirective type discussions which enable the latter to release their frustrations and to recognize the true cause for these frustrations and their personal roles and responsibility in solving them. Most important, in contacts with employees, supervisors must exercise maximum patience and avoid creating additional frustrations.

Characteristics of Grievants

Several studies have been conducted to determine what differences in characteristics, if any, may exist between those employees who submit a high frequency of grievances (the grievers) and those who submit few if any grievances (the nongrievers). Ash, for example, found that in comparison with the nongrievers, the grievers were more likely to be younger, veterans, native white Americans, and those having less service with the company. In general the grievers were individuals who had not yet settled down. The fact that members of minority groups were found to have low grievance rates, however, may have been due more to their insecurity and unwillingness to jeopardize their jobs than to a high level of job satisfaction.[2]

A study by Sulkin and Pranis produced findings somewhat similar to those of Ash. In this study grievers were found to be more prevalent among those employees who were younger, better educated, and lower paid.[3]

Still another study concerning the personality characteristics of grievers and nongrievers revealed that the basic difference between the two groups was that

---

[2] *Ibid.*, pp. 13-37.

[3] Howard A. Sulkin and Robert W. Pranis, "Comparison of Grievants with Non-Grievants in a Heavy Machinery Company," *Personnel Psychology,* Vol. 20, No. 2 (Summer, 1967), pp. 111-119.

grievers tended to be more "thin-skinned" and had their feelings hurt more easily. This finding suggests that some people may tolerate a certain condition without filing a grievance, whereas others will protest.[4] While one cannot hope to remake such individuals, an awareness of the fact that there is this basic personality difference between grievers and nongrievers may prove helpful in working with the former individuals. It should also be recognized that many grievers can be quite productive and render a significant contribution to the organization, which is an important reason for trying to understand and work with them.

Reducing Grievances

Although there will always be grievances wherever people are employed, competent managers can do much to prevent those situations that precipitate grievances. Whenever employee attitudes and feelings indicate that dissatisfactions may be developing, management should attempt to uncover the causes and take whatever corrective action may be feasible. In some instances the appropriate corrective action may require a change in work procedures or employment conditions. In other instances the appropriate corrective action may be achieved through proper communication; for example, proper communication may be achieved in an interview if a single employee is involved or by an announcement in which management states its position if grievances seem to be developing in a group of employees.

The degree of consideration shown to employees is an important factor in minimizing grievances. One study, for example, showed that the grievance rate was definitely associated with consideration. Consideration, it will be recalled, includes behavior indicating mutual trust, respect, and a warmth between supervisors and their groups as well as encouragement of more two-way communication. Structure refers to the supervisor's overt attempts to achieve organizational goals (see page 311). An examination of Figure 18-1 shows that, regardless of structure score, supervisors with low consideration scores had high grievance rates. Conversely, those with high consideration scores had low grievance rates. The grievance rate of those with medium consideration scores is observed to vary with the amount of structure.[5] It would appear, therefore, that the attitudes and behavior of supervisors play an important role in the tendency of employees to file grievances.

FORMAL GRIEVANCE PROCEDURES

Virtually all organizations whose employees are unionized have *grievance procedures* for resolving disputes. These procedures, which are set forth in the agreement, provide for the union to represent the interests of its members (and

[4] Ross Stagner, *The Psychology of Industrial Conflict* (New York: John Wiley & Sons, Inc., 1956), pp. 394-395.

[5] E. A. Fleishman and E. F. Harris, "Patterns of Leadership Behavior Related to Employee Grievances and Turnover," *Personnel Psychology,* Vol. 15, No. 1 (Spring, 1962), pp. 45-53.

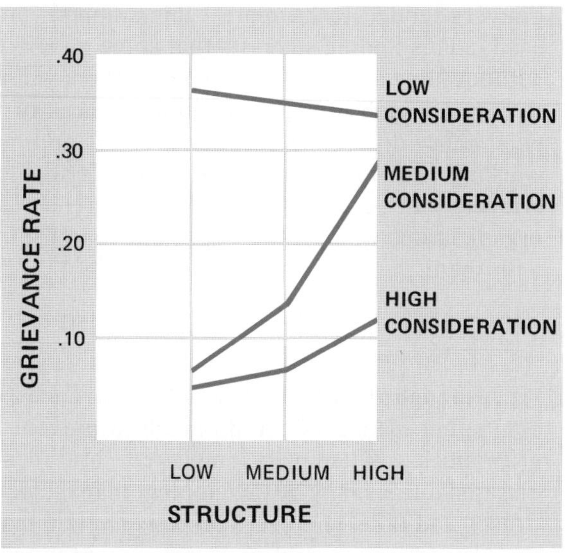

Source: E. A. Fleishman and E. F. Harris, "Patterns of Leadership Behavior Related to Employee Grievances and Turnover," *Personnel Psychology,* Vol. 15, No. 1 (Spring, 1962), pp. 45-53. Reproduced with permission.

Figure 18-1 COMBINATIONS OF CONSIDERATION AND STRUCTURE RELATED TO GRIEVANCES

in some situations nonmembers as well) as a grievance is processed through successive steps. When a grievance cannot be resolved by the two parties at one of these steps, most agreements provide for it to be submitted to a third party, usually an arbitrator, who constitutes the final step in the grievance procedure. The third party then renders a decision or *award* resolving the dispute that is binding on both parties.

In the case of nonunionized organizations, voluntary procedures may be established by management to facilitate the hearing and hopefully the resolving of employee grievances. Grievance procedures also are to be found in certain nonprofit organizations and in some government jurisdictions which are unionized. These procedures typically involve a series of steps in an appeals system. The creation of the office of *ombudsman* to improve communication and to reconcile differences between aggrieved parties and those in the organization against whom they have grievances also is becoming more common in educational and other nonprofit organizations.

Procedures in Unionized Organizations

Grievance procedures in unionized organizations describe how the grievance is to be initiated, the number of steps that are to comprise the procedure, and the identity of representatives from each side who are to be involved in the hearings at each step. Limitations as to the number of working days within which an unresolved grievance must be taken to the next step in the hearing procedure, and the method, if any, for disposing of unresolved grievances at the final step in the procedure are also usually set forth.

Initiating the Formal Grievance. An employee's grievance begins when he or she perceives to have received treatment that is contrary to established organizational policies and practices or to accepted standards of fairness, or that violates some provisions of the labor agreement or some civil law. In order for this grievance to be considered formally, however, it must be expressed orally and/or in writing.

If good communication exists between the employee and his or her immediate supervisor, the supervisor would be the logical person to whom the grievance should be presented and discussed initially. Should the employee be unable to communicate effectively with the supervisor, he or she may choose to take the grievance first to the steward who in turn will present and discuss it with the supervisor. Since grievances are often the result of an oversight or a misunderstanding on the part of one or both parties, the majority of them are resolved at this initial step of the formal grievance procedure. Figure 18-2 illustrates, for example, that a high proportion of grievances are resolved at the first step in the General Motors Corporation, just as they are in most organizations.

The extent to which it is possible to resolve grievances at the initial step will be determined in large measure by the ability and willingness of the supervisor to discuss problems with employees and their stewards. Good personnel management recognizes the importance of the supervisors' roles and trains them in the handling of grievances. Training should include familiarization with the terms of the labor agreement and the development of counseling skills. Through the skillful handling of grievances on an oral rather than a written basis, a true problem-solving approach may be facilitated. According to McKersie, who compared the old grievance system at International Harvester with the new one (in effect since 1959), the oral handling approach to grievances has these values:

1. Problems are settled where they arise and by the people concerned, and not at some higher level in the organization.
2. Grievances are considered while the facts are still fresh. Since details cannot be recorded, the parties have to grapple with the problem before the facts of the situation get away from them.
3. Employee complaints can be much more intelligently handled in oral discussion rather than in an exchange of written documents. Many foremen at International Harvester, as is the case with other companies, find it difficult to understand the written word, especially complicated contractual language. It is much easier for the interested parties to get to the bottom of the situation with an oral investigation than it is with the submission of depositions.[6]

[6] Robert B. McKersie, "Avoiding Written Grievances by Problem-Solving: An Outside View," *Personnel Psychology,* Vol. 17, No. 4 (Winter, 1964), pp. 367-379.

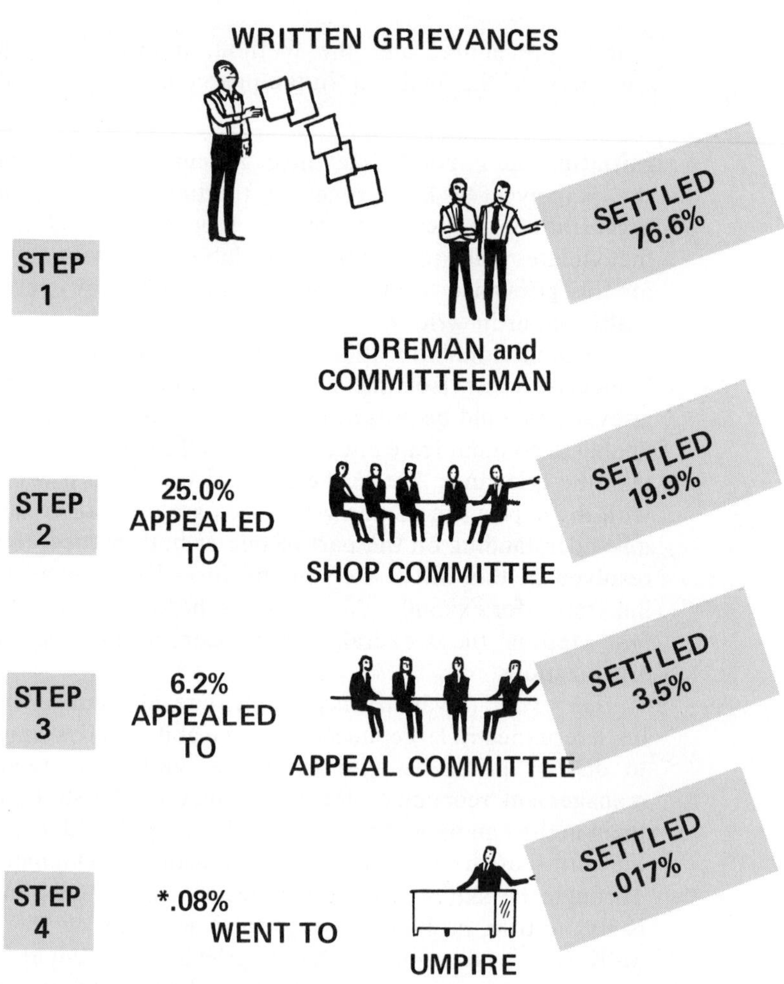

Source: Disposition of written grievances during 1973 under the General Motors-United Auto Workers National Agreement. Reproduced with permission of the Personnel Department, General Motors Corporation.

* An unsettled grievance will not necessarily be carried to the final step, hence the small unaccounted for difference at this point in the handling of written grievances.

Figure 18-2 DISPOSITION OF WRITTEN GRIEVANCES

Processing the Grievance. In spite of efforts to resolve grievances, it is not always possible to do so satisfactorily at the first step. In some instances a solution may not be possible because of honest differences of opinion between the employee and the supervisor or because the supervisor just does not have the authority to take the action required to satisfy the grievant. Personality conflicts, prejudices, emotionalism, ordinary stubbornness, or other factors also may provide the barrier to a satisfactory solution.

Most labor agreements require that grievances carried beyond the initial step must be stated in writing, usually on a multicopy form similar to the type shown in Figure 18-3. Requiring a written statement reduces the chance for various versions of the grievance to be changed because of any lapses in memory. It also forces the employees to be more rational and to think more

GRIEVANCE STATEMENT

EMPLOYEE: Roland Smith CLOCK NO: 65891 SHIFT: Swing

JOB CLASSIFICATION: Bench Mach. PLANT: 2 DEPT.: 616

DEPT. FOREMAN: R. M. Lancaster

STATEMENT OF GRIEVANCE: I received only a 7-cent wage increase on my eighth-month review. Everyone else in my department has received the top of the rate in the past. A man who was hired later than I received the top of the rate. I am doing the same type, quality, and quantity of work as others in this classification who have received the top of the rate. When I hired in, the supervisor told me that I would receive the top of my rate on the eighth-month review. This was not the case. I feel that I have been discriminated against and should receive back pay to my eighth-month review for top rate of Bench Machinist.

EMPLOYEE: Roland Smith (Signature) DEPT. STEWARD: Oscar Block (Signature)

RECEIVED BY: R. M. Lancaster (Supervisor or Foreman) TIME: 9:30 a.m. DATE: 1/16/–

Prepare in quadruplicate for distribution

1. Original and one copy (Labor Relations)
2. Department
3. Chief Steward

UNION FILE NO. ______

LABOR RELATIONS NO. ______

Figure 18-3 GRIEVANCE STATEMENT

carefully about their grievances. Grievances which stem from trivial complaints or feelings of hostility thus are less likely to be pursued beyond the first step.

In preparing the written statement of a grievance, the employee usually obtains assistance from the union steward representing members in the work area. Because of their familiarity with the provisions of the union agreement and their experience in evaluating the validity of complaints, union stewards can provide a valuable service. If the steward is of the opinion that the complaint is valid, he or she can help the employee formulate the complaint in language that is appropriate for the official grievance form. On the other hand, if the steward feels that the employee does not have a valid grievance, he or she can discuss the grievance with the employee in an attempt to get at the real cause of the latter's dissatisfaction. If the relationship between the steward and the supervisor is a cooperative one, the steward, as a result of discussions with the aggrieved employee, may be able to assist the supervisor in resolving what the employee perceives to be the problem without the necessity of processing the grievance formally. A good steward can also assist the supervisor by screening out chronic complainers or grievers; as a result, the steward places the union in a stronger position to gain satisfactory consideration on those grievances that are of major importance.

Number of Steps in the Grievance Procedure. The number of steps in the grievance procedure will be affected by the size and structure of the organization and by the organization of the union. Figure 18-4 illustrates some of the variations in grievance procedures that may exist as a result of differences in the size of an employer's organization. In developing a grievance procedure the most important consideration, however, is not its specific structure but rather how well it serves the needs of an organization in enabling grievances to be processed expeditiously and resolved in a manner mutually satisfactory to both parties.

Methods of Resolving Grievances. In attempting to resolve a grievance, representatives of management and the union must maintain a flexible attitude and be prepared to discuss the problem in a give-and-take manner if their efforts are to be generally successful. A grievance cannot be viewed as something to be won or lost but, rather, as an attempt to resolve a human relations problem. Neither side, furthermore, should expect to have all of the grievances decided in its favor.

If a grievance cannot be resolved through established grievance procedures, the following alternative courses of action are available. One of the parties may back down from the position that it has been holding, thereby resolving the problem. Or, if the agreement provides for arbitration by outside parties as most of them do, the grievance can be submitted to arbitration. If, however, the agreement does not contain arbitration provisions and the deadlock cannot be broken, the union will either have to drop the grievance or resort to some form of economic pressure such as a strike or a slowdown.

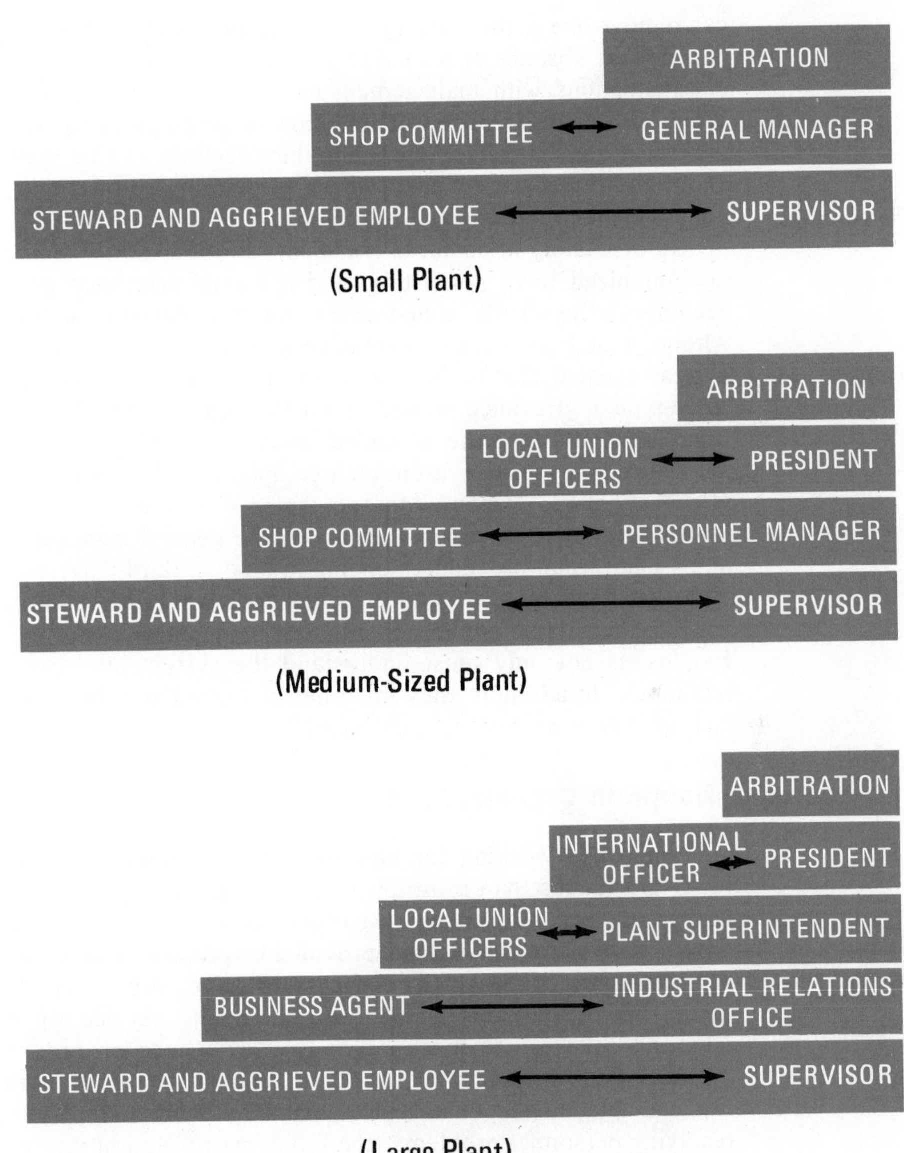

Source: C. Wilson Randle, *Collective Bargaining* (4th ed.; Boston: Houghton Mifflin Company, 1966), p. 235. Reproduced with permission.

Figure 18-4 GRIEVANCE PROCEDURES IN ORGANIZATIONS OF DIFFERENT SIZES

Procedures in Nonunion Organizations

Even though formal grievance procedures are confined largely to those organizations that are unionized, such procedures can and should be developed in those organizations that are not unionized. A formal procedure, furthermore, can remove one of the primary reasons employees have for seeking to unionize; namely, the absence of formal channels through which they may redress their dissatisfactions with management decisions that they consider to be unfair. While a formal procedure will not eliminate all employee dissatisfactions, it can provide a "safety valve" through which feelings can be vented more readily and higher management made more acutely aware of employee reactions to employment conditions and to the quality of supervision at the working level.

Unfortunately in business organizations the majority of companies that are not unionized have not established a formal grievance procedure that will accomplish the results comparable to those achieved by unionized companies. Although there has been no extensive study of the subject, an informal study by Trotta revealed that there is a trend for nonunion organizations to establish some type of grievance procedure for their employees.[7] In some instances this trend involves only the so-called open door policy or a policy statement allowing employees to present their complaints to higher levels of management. However, of the 34 nonunion companies surveyed, Trotta found that 18 had formal grievance procedures involving the general manager at the final step, and 4 had formal procedures ending in binding third-party arbitration.[8]

Regardless of the details of the grievance procedure, the important consideration in a nonunion organization is the climate existing within it. Employees not only must understand the system but also have no fear of retaliation. In addition, they must not be placed at a disadvantage because of lack of skill in presenting their cases.[9]

Procedures in Nonprofit Organizations

Employees working for nonprofit organizations do not necessarily have fewer grievances than those in profit-making organizations; in fact, they may have more because wages and other conditions of employment frequently are less satisfactory than those provided by profit-making firms. Consequently, it is becoming increasingly common to have formal grievance procedures established in charitable foundations, community service organizations, hospitals, and colleges. Even churches have grievance procedures for resolving disputes and differences of opinion occurring within their organization. For example, in response to a demand for more democratic procedures in resolving personnel problems, the following resolution was developed within the Roman Catholic Church:

> Therefore, BE IT RESOLVED, that the National Conference of Catholic Bishops, properly aware of the urgency of the problem recommends to its members experimentation with procedures such as are outlined in the Agenda Report on what is called Due Process, adapted where necessary to local

[7] Maurice S. Trotta, *Arbitration of Labor-Management Disputes* (New York: AMACOM, Division of American Management Association, 1974), p. 218.

[8] *Ibid.*

[9] Robert E. Sibson, "Handling Grievances Where There Is No Union," *Personnel Journal,* Vol. 35 (June, 1956), pp. 56-58.

circumstances, and to the prompt implementation on the diocesan, provincial and regional levels of this and other well-conceived plans which may become advisable for that secure protection of human rights and freedoms which should always be among the goals of the church.[10]

Procedures in Governmental Organizations

Typically the grievances of employees in the public sector are resolved through established civil service appeal systems. In contrast to grievances in the private sector which frequently are the result of actions taken by management, grievances in the public sector are generally initiated to prevent management from taking punitive action until the employee has the opportunity for "due process," during which he or she hopes to have the pending disciplinary action prevented. Thus, in the private sector employees generally cannot use the grievance procedure to prevent management from taking discharge or other disciplinary action. Instead they use it to have such actions reversed and possibly to receive reimbursement for all or part of the losses suffered from these actions should these be reversed through the grievance process. Under the typical civil service appeals system, on the other hand, management is prevented from effecting a discharge until the employee has carried the grievance through the appeals system and has failed to have the discharge reversed. Of course, in the case of severe charges against an employee in government, such as those of a criminal nature, the individuals are suspended from their jobs, possibly without pay, until their case is processed through the appeals system.

In government jurisdictions where employees are unionized, the resolution of grievances may be complicated by the presence of two grievance procedures: one provided by the civil service system and the other by the union agreement. In such instances civil service regulations and the terms of the union agreement must clarify the extent to which an employee can opt for one of the two procedures, conceivably by waiving the right of protection under the other procedure.

GRIEVANCE ARBITRATION

Arbitration is a process by which a grievance is resolved by an impartial third party who hears all of the facts pertaining to it and recommends a solution for both parties to follow. While it was noted in the preceding chapter that arbitration may be used to resolve bargaining deadlocks, it is used mostly to settle disagreements arising in the administration of the agreement. Provisions governing arbitration generally are set forth in the labor agreement and usually describe the subjects that may be arbitrated, who is to do the arbitration, the method by which arbitrators are to be selected, and the restrictions, if any, that are placed on their authority.

---

[10] *On Due Process*, National Conference of Catholic Bishops, 1969, as published in Trotta, *op. cit.*, p. 214.

Sources of Arbitrators

Arbitration may be accomplished by means of an arbitrator (or umpire), or by means of a *tripartite board* made up of representatives of management and labor plus an impartial chairperson who is acceptable to both sides. Typically arbitrators are professional people, such as attorneys, professors, or clergymen, whose professional activities or sympathies are not identified with either party, thereby permitting them to occupy a position of neutrality. Although some arbitrators make arbitration a full-time profession, the majority perform this service in addition to other professional work. Organizations such as the American Arbitration Association, the Federal Mediation Service, and state mediation services maintain lists of qualified individuals from which an arbitrator can be selected in the event the two parties are unable to agree upon one by themselves.

The Arbitration Process

Although a document known as the *submission agreement* may be drawn up to describe formally the issue or issues for arbitration, these issues are frequently presented orally to the arbitrator by the two parties at the beginning of the hearing. If they have been prepared, minutes and memoranda covering the meetings held at earlier stages of the grievance procedure are sometimes submitted prior to the formal hearing to inform the arbitrator of the issues to be resolved by arbitration.[11]

In arbitrating a dispute it is the responsibility of arbitrators to insure that each side receives a fair hearing during which it may present all of the facts it considers pertinent to the case. Since they are attempting to solve a human relations rather than a legal issue, the procedures for conducting arbitration hearings and the restrictions governing the evidence that may be introduced during these hearings are more flexible than those permitted in a court of law. Hearsay evidence, for example, may be introduced provided it is considered as such when evaluated with the other evidence presented during the hearing. Arbitrators also may question witnesses or request additional information relating to the case from records or witnesses which have not been presented by either side. They thus seek to obtain facts which will give them the insight and basis required to render a just solution to the case.

The Arbitration Award

Depending upon the importance of the case, the hearings may be conducted in either an informal or a very formal manner not unlike that of a court trial in which a transcript is kept of the proceedings. After hearing the case an arbitrator customarily has 30 days in which to ponder the evidence and to

[11] Harold W. Davey, "What's Right and What's Wrong with Grievance Arbitration: The Practitioners Air Their Views," *The Arbitration Journal*, Vol. 28, No. 4 (December, 1973), pp. 219-220.

prepare a decision. This decision, referred to as the *award,* should be accompanied by a written review of the case in support of the award. This review statement can be as important as the award itself since it helps to preserve face for the unsuccessful party and soften its disappointment. (The term unsuccessful is used deliberately since arbitration should not be viewed as a win-lose situation.)

Unlike decisions in a court of law, those in arbitration, at least in theory, are supposed to be reached on the basis of the facts of the case rather than on the basis of precedents established by previous cases. The reason for this is that no two cases are exactly alike; therefore, each case should be decided upon individual merits. In practice, however, precedents do have some influence at times upon the decision of an arbitrator who may seek guidance in a particular case from decisions of other arbitrators in somewhat similar cases. These decisions, which are compiled and published by the American Arbitration Association and by such labor services as the Bureau of National Affairs, Commercial Clearing House, and Prentice-Hall, can help an arbitrator to stay in line with contemporary standards of industrial jurisprudence.

Criticisms of Grievance Arbitration

One of the major problems relating to arbitration, according to some critics, is that "most grievance arbitration has acquired characteristics which contradict the objectives and needs of the parties and thereby threaten its future."[12] Specifically, arbitration is criticized for taking too much time, for becoming too expensive, and often creating frustration for the aggrieved employee and/or the supervisor in the dispute. Busy schedules and other commitments on the part of the arbitrator, the union, and management officials, as well as a backlog of cases, frequently result in unnecessarily long delays in resolving disputes that may be relatively simple in nature. Extravagant amounts of time devoted by the arbitrator to a case as a result of reading lengthy transcripts or briefs, or of attempting to write an impressive opinion, are some of the factors contributing to the added expense and delay in resolving grievances. Furthermore, the cost and time required in preparation of briefs by each side or the preparation of a transcript of the hearings often are excessive as well as unnecessary.

In an endeavor to expedite cases and reduce their costs, a new streamlined process has been used experimentally in the steel industry, where grievants have the option of using a new process in place of the traditional one. Under the new process, panels have been created from which arbitrators are designated to handle cases on a rotating basis. Arbitration hearings must be held within 10 days of the appeal, and the award must be made within 48 hours after the hearing. No briefs or transcripts are utilized, and cases for each side are presented by local plant and local union representatives rather than the usual labor "pros" who are attorneys or labor relations specialists. The arbitrator

[12] Ben Fischer, "Arbitration: The Steel Industry Experiment," *Monthly Labor Review,* Vol. 95, No. 11 (November, 1972), p. 7.

receives a fee of $25 to $75 from each party and only for the hearing day. So far, the new expedited procedure appears to be succeeding in producing decisions more rapidly and at less cost.[13]

Arbitration of Discrimination Grievances

Arbitration of grievances pertaining to discrimination of the type forbidden by the Civil Rights Act of 1964 may well create a new problem for arbitrators. Rather than resorting to legal actions permitted by the act, those individuals who believe themselves to be victims of discrimination in their employment may in the future seek to resolve their grievances by processing them through the established grievance procedure. This course of action can save costly litigation for both the grievant and the employer. However, whether or not the union can and will represent the grievant effectively in such cases, particularly if it has been a contributing party to the discrimination, may be open to question. Furthermore, should some civil rights group seek to intervene in behalf of the grievant at one of the steps in the grievance procedure, a legal question conceivably may arise with respect to the union's contractual role of being the exclusive agent in representing members in their relations with the employer. Finally, grievances involving discrimination create a new set of issues which many arbitrators may not be too well equipped to handle because the standards they have acquired in resolving the typical union-management disputes and the body of industrial jurisprudence upon which they must rely for decisions frequently are not applicable to discrimination cases.[14]

Limitations of Arbitration

It is almost axiomatic that no decision rendered by a third party in a labor dispute can solve the problems that involve interpersonal relationships or contract interpretations as effectively as can the parties themselves, regardless of the labor-management hierarchy level.[15] Unfortunately one of the two parties to an arbitration case may allow a weak case to go to arbitration because it wants the arbitrator to be the one to concede the case to the other party. For example, it is not unusual for the union to take a weak case to arbitration in order to demonstrate to the members that the union is willing to exhaust every remedy in looking out for their interests. Union officers also are not likely to refuse to take to arbitration the grievances of members who are popular or politically powerful in the union, even though their cases are weak. The fact that a union member can bring suit against union officers for failure to process a grievance also has helped to make many officers reluctant to refuse to process even those grievances against which they believe an arbitrator will rule unfavorably.

---

[13] *Ibid.*, p. 9.

[14] Richard I. Block, "Arbitrating Discrimination Grievances—A New Approach," *Michigan Business Review*, Vol. 22, No. 5 (November, 1970), pp. 26-32.

[15] Thomas Rime, Jr., "Arbitration: How to Avoid It," *Personnel* (May-June, 1970), p. 29.

Management, on the other hand, may take a weak case to arbitration in order to demonstrate to the union officers that management "cannot be pushed around." Also, rather than risk the displeasure of superiors by telling them that a certain personnel policy is unworkable or unsound, managers at a lower level may simply let a grievance involving such a policy go to an arbitrator whose award will demonstrate its unsoundness. Plain hardheadedness and mutual antagonism also may force many grievances into arbitration because neither party is willing to make concessions to achieve agreement even if it may recognize that it is in the wrong.

Compulsory Arbitration

The type of arbitration discussed thus far is the result of mutual agreement between the two parties and is referred to as *voluntary arbitration*. There also is *compulsory arbitration* in which the two parties are forced by legislation to submit their differences to an arbitrator in order to resolve them. Compulsory arbitration has never proved very satisfactory as a means of achieving labor peace. Demands for it generally have been raised only when strikes threatened to cripple the economy or security of the nation. Compulsory arbitration is rarely successful because an outsider cannot contrive an agreement that will be satisfactory to both management and the union leaders and members. Since compulsory arbitration is invoked for the purpose of gaining a labor truce, the arbitrator is likely to concentrate on coming up with some truce formula rather than on achieving a lasting agreement between the two parties. This truce formula quite often is one that tends to split the differences between the two parties regardless of how reasonable or unreasonable the positions of either party may be. This fact can serve to discourage give-and-take collective bargaining because the weaker party is likely to hold back making concessions in hopes that the arbitrator will award to it what it has been unable to gain through negotiation. When applied to the public sector, furthermore, there are those who believe that compulsory arbitration will cause public officials to avoid making unpopular decisions by leaving them to the arbitrator to make.[16]

EMPLOYEE DISCIPLINE

The discussion up to this point has been concerned with the methods by which the employees and/or the union may resolve their disagreements with management through a formal grievance procedure. It has been noted that although management also is free to utilize this procedure in resolving dissatisfactions with employees or the union, the more common practice is for it to take direct corrective action against an employee since most labor agreements permit management to do so for *just cause*. Unfortunately there is no precise definition or clear-cut standard to use in determining conclusively what constitutes just cause. Each cause therefore must be judged on its

[16] Walter G. Seinsheimer, "What's So Terrible about Compulsory Arbitration?" *The Arbitration Journal,* Vol. 26, No. 4 (December, 1971), p. 223.

particular merits, relying upon the doctrines and concepts of industrial jurisprudence that arbitrators have developed collectively over the years through their awards.

Basic Concepts Underlying Disciplinary Actions

The concept of corrective or progressive discipline holds that an employee be discharged only as a last resort after every possible effort has been made to help that person correct deficiencies in performance and/or behavior.[17] Corrective measures may include not only special instructions, counseling, and written warnings, but also progressively more drastic punitive measures such as demotions or suspensions, without pay, carried out prior to the final recourse of discharge.

Other factors to be considered in evaluating the justification for an employer's disciplinary action may include the following:

1. Degree of severity of the offense.
2. Length of service with the company.
3. Provocation, if any, that may have led to the offense.
4. The number of previous offenses.
5. The nature of the previous offenses.
6. Previous warnings or other disciplinary action for previous offenses.
7. Company rules: Are they clear? Are they reasonable? Have they been communicated to the employee?
8. Have company rules and regulations been consistently applied?
9. Past disciplinary actions for similar offenses by other employees.
10. Employee's pattern of conduct.
11. Supervisory practices.
12. Is the penalty reasonable and appropriate to the offense?[18]

Although the preceding factors, as well as other guidelines, can aid an arbitrator in determining whether or not there was just cause, in the final analysis the arbitrator must rely upon a personal sense of justice and fair play in reaching a decision. Under these conditions, it is not surprising when arbitrators have honest differences of opinions on the meaning of just cause due to differences in their value judgments and in the weights they may attach to the various circumstances to be considered in evaluating such cause.

The Disciplinary Program

The purpose of a disciplinary program is to provide the means for securing employee performance and behavior that is necessary in order for organizational goals to be achieved. While one of its purposes is to provide corrective action, a more important purpose is to prevent the need for such action in the first place. The need for corrective action perhaps can best be reduced through the positive efforts of the personnel program that help

[17] Trotta, *op. cit.*, p. 236.
[18] Trotta, *op. cit.*, p. 237.

motivate employees to put forth the performance, behavior, and cooperation that are required of them. Positive measures thus represent the "carrot" rather than the punitive "stick" approach to motivation.

Preventing Disciplinary Problems. Each of the processes of the personnel management program that has been described in the chapters thus far, if performed effectively, can reduce the need for corrective disciplinary action. Grievances and disciplinary actions can be reduced, for example, if each job is staffed with a person who understands and has the qualifications to match the requirements of the job. Programs that provide for accurate job descriptions, employee orientation, training, communication, and performance evaluation can contribute to the prevention of disciplinary problems. In addition, good selection procedures can help to prevent the employment of individuals whose personal qualifications or emotional problems make them unsuited for the organization or a potential source of disciplinary problems. Effective leadership and supervision discussed in earlier chapters can also help to reduce grievance and disciplinary problems.

The Supervisor's Role. The primary responsibility for preventing or correcting disciplinary problems rests not with the personnel department but with the supervisor who is in the position of immediate authority over the employee. He or she is the person best able to observe evidences of unsatisfactory behavior or performance and to take early corrective measures, often by merely having an informal discussion with the employee. Such discussions frequently may be sufficient to correct the situation without having to take disciplinary action. Occasionally, however, it may become necessary for supervisors to use their disciplinary powers. They should approach a disciplinary situation with a humanistic as well as a legalistic attitude. The causes underlying it are as important as the behavior itself, and any attempt to prevent further recurrence will require an understanding of these causes. It is often difficult for supervisors to maintain an objective attitude toward infractions of employees; but if they can approach such problems with a problem-solving attitude, they are more likely to come up with a diagnosis that is nearer the truth than would be possible if the approach of a trial lawyer were used.[19]

In attempting to uncover reasons for employee misbehavior, the supervisor must keep in mind the fact that employees may not be aware of certain work rules. It is essential, therefore, that supervisors, before initiating any disciplinary actions, consider whether or not they have given their employees

---

[19] For purposes of identifying personality characteristics with choice and actual implementation of various styles of discipline, Shell and Cummings have developed a scale for measuring attitudes toward discipline ranging from pure humanitarian to pure legalistic. See "Enforcing the Rules: How Do Managers Differ?" *Personnel,* Vol. 43, No. 2 (March-April, 1966), pp. 33-39. Also see Project 18-2 in Herbert J. Chruden and Arthur W. Sherman, Jr., *Practical Study Experiences in Personnel Management* (5th ed.; Cincinnati: South-Western Publishing Co., 1976).

careful and thorough indoctrination in the rules and regulations relating to their jobs.

Need for Fair Treatment. Definite policies and procedures for handling disciplinary matters are essential for insuring fair treatment of offenders. Each supervisor should be furnished with a written policy and a standardized procedure, including recommended penalties for specific infractions of the rules that may serve as a guide in determining what type of disciplinary action should be taken. While it is usually recommended that disciplinary action be handled on an impartial basis without regard for the specific circumstances involved, most individuals rebel against the imposition of inflexible rules. Rather than being forced into the rigid enforcement of rules and not being supported by management, supervisors will often ''turn their heads'' and fail to take any action on employee behavior that, according to the rule book, should be formally recognized and appropriately disciplined. In fact, this inaction on the part of supervisors, which has become commonplace, is referred to as the *indulgency pattern*.

Investigation of Disciplinary Problems. Before taking disciplinary action against an employee, that person should be interviewed for the purpose of soliciting information that may reveal the attitudes, behavior, and other reasons that might be the cause for an infraction. Even though the supervisor may be angry over what has happened, every effort should be made to approach the employee in an objective and understanding manner. Unless the employee is to be discharged and there is assurance that the action will not be reversed by the grievance procedure, the supervisor will be faced with the task of soliciting cooperation and good performance after any disciplinary action has been taken. Therefore, it is particularly desirable that the supervisor avoid ''taking personally'' certain forms of employee behavior that may represent a reaction to frustration. Supervisors should react in terms of the situation and the individual involved rather than in terms of their own ego needs. It should not be inferred that disciplinary action should be avoided at all costs, but rather that it should be based on understanding and good judgment and not upon vindictiveness or emotional reaction.

A record of offenses and disciplinary action taken, including formal reprimands, is usually maintained in the employee's personnel file. This not only provides a complete work history of each employee but also serves as a basis for determining disciplinary action and evaluating the company's disciplinary policies and procedures.

Maintenance of proper records also provides management with valuable information about the worth of its rules and regulations. Those rules that are violated most frequently should receive particular attention. The need for them may no longer exist or some alteration may need to be made that will facilitate their enforcement. If the rule has little or no value, it probably should be revised or rescinded. Otherwise employees are likely to feel that management is overly restricting their behavior.

Upholding Disciplinary Action

The more severe the disciplinary action that is taken, the greater the likelihood will be that the union will challenge it through existing appeals procedures. These procedures, as described previously, may include those established by the labor agreement or, in the case of a government organization, civil service appeal boards. Appeals may also include taking action in the civil courts. Should the disciplinary action be reversed through any of these avenues of appeal, the grievant may then acquire a sense of power that will make him or her even more difficult to control. The supervisor who initiated the disciplinary action, furthermore, may feel that he or she has suffered a loss of face and authority, and therefore may be inclined to ignore disciplinary offenses in the future rather than risk having the corrective action reversed.

The Role of Supervisors. Supervisors must be able to distinguish between what does and does not constitute a valid disciplinary case. Furthermore, they must learn how to document their cases against employees so that the evidence supporting their actions will not be refuted by evidence that the union presents at the arbitration hearing. Union representatives during arbitration hearings, for example, may be able to refute a supervisor's charge that an employee should be discharged for incompetency by citing the fact that this employee had received a merit increase and favorable comments from the supervisor within recent months.

The Role of Arbitrators. In considering the facts in a disciplinary case, arbitrators or other persons hearing the appeal usually will seek to determine the extent, if any, to which the disciplined employee was at fault and the extent, if any, to which management may also have been at fault. If the case involved a violation of rules, arbitrators must determine whether such considerations as those enumerated in Figure 18-5 have been observed in the enforcement rules. They will examine in particular whether the rules had been effectively communicated to all employees and understood by them, whether they had been enforced previously, and whether the employee being disciplined for a rule violation had actually received any prior warning concerning the violation of the rule. Similarly, if the disciplinary action was taken for unsatisfactory performance, the arbitrator will want to determine whether or not there were any standards against which the employee's performance could be judged consistently. The arbitrator also will look for evidence to indicate that the disciplined person had received the training and assistance necessary to achieve these standards, had been warned about poor performance and given every opportunity to improve it, and that ineffective management was not the cause for the unsatisfactory performance.

The Role of Unions. One of the union's most important functions is that of protecting members against disciplinary actions of the employer. The union

7 Laws for Making Plant Rules That Will Stick

1. Make the rule reasonable

2. Stay out of private lives

3. Don't keep rules in your hat

4. Correct—don't punish

5. Make the punishment uniform

6. Don't double up punishment

7. Grant the benefit of the doubt

Source: From an article by Paul A. King, "Tips to Successful Discipline," *Factory Management and Maintenance,* Vol. 116, No. 6 (June, 1958), p. 78. Reproduced with permission.

Figure 18-5

representatives, therefore, are virtually certain to grieve many disciplinary actions that were justified as well as those that were unjustified. If a mature relationship exists between it and management, however, the union may be able to cooperate in reducing many of the causes for disciplinary actions and resulting grievances. At times the supervisor may be able to avoid a disciplinary problem by requesting the steward to have a talk with a problem employee who may be more responsive to a warning from the steward than from the supervisor. By advising and consulting with the steward regarding disciplinary problems and impending actions, the supervisor may be able to prevent the problem from leading to antagonism with the union.

DISCIPLINARY DISCHARGES

Discharge is the most drastic administrative action that can be taken. It is used against an employee who has committed a serious offense or has a record of repeated violations of company rules. It is also used to remove workers who cannot be utilized effectively in any job because of incompetence or inability to perform adequately or to get along with others. It was once a popular type of disciplinary action, but in recent years the trend has been for companies to resort to discharge action less frequently because of restrictions imposed upon them by the unions and by law. The shortage of trained personnel in many fields has also made discharge an unpopular way of handling problems with employees who have valuable talents but who may present behavior problems that occasionally disrupt the organization or infuriate the managers.

Discharge Procedures

The development of the labor agreement and provisions for the arbitration of grievances have led to more centralization of the labor relations function in many organizations. Because of the requirement that penalties be assessed under rules in harmony with the principles of the labor agreement and because there must be some consistency if a penalty is to stand the test of arbitration, disciplinary powers in some instances have been taken from the supervisor and placed in the hands of staff specialists or higher managers. Even where this has not been done, the supervisor must rely upon the staff for advice in how to handle disciplinary cases and avoid conflict with the union. Otherwise, if a grievance results, the supervisor may find that his or her action will not be supported by higher authority in the organization.[20]

Although it may not be regarded as a favor at the time by employees who are discharged, sometimes the organization actually may be doing them a favor by forcing them to leave employment situations for which they are unsuited. Instead of following the line of least resistance and remaining in a position where there is no future opportunity, the discharged employee is forced to seek

[20] Dallas L. Jones, "The Supervisor and the Disciplinary Process in a Unionized Setting," *Personnel Administration,* Vol. 26, No. 1 (January-February, 1963), pp. 42-48.

new employment where hopefully the future is brighter. The blow of being discharged also has been known to help shock some individuals into correcting undesirable behavior traits that were a factor in causing their discharge.

Dehiring of Executives

The task of discharging an employee can be a very unpleasant one which often is avoided, especially if the superior has socialized with that employee. Rather than face up to the task squarely, various subterfuges may be used to get employees, particularly at the executive level, to realize that there is no longer a place for them within the organization. Certain tactics, such as removing some of their more important responsibilities or status symbols, reducing their salary, or giving them a less desirable work place, are among some that have been used to encourage an executive's resignation.

Some companies have been successful in utilizing executive recruitment firms to find a position elsewhere for their discharged executives through the process that is known as *disemployment, outplacement,* or *dehiring.* An increasing number of companies are also utilizing the services of *outplacement consultants* to assist the executive being terminated. In addition to helping mollify the anger and grief of the terminated executive, outplacement consultants can help this individual to regain self-confidence and to begin seriously the search for a new job. Since many terminated executives have been out of the job market for many years, they may lack current knowledge and skill about looking for a job. The outplacement specialist can coach the executive in how to develop contacts and to probe for job openings through systematic letter writing and telephone campaigns, as well as in how to handle employment interviews and salary negotiations.[21] While the specialists may charge from 10 to 15 percent of the fired executive's gross salary, companies apparently believe that this service is worthwhile. For example, one executive's reaction to the use of consultants was: "Not only do they advise you not to be overly generous in severance pay but they get the man thinking about a new job so he doesn't vent his venom and inflict turmoil on the company."[22]

Some executives, however, do not look with favor on the use of outplacement consultants. One of them had this comment to make: "This business of having a consultant come in after the man has been fired is terribly cold and calculating. Why, it's like calling in an undertaker to pick up the body."[23] Still other executives believe that a competent executive should have enough contacts and talent to find a new job independently, and that a corporate personnel department with competent personnel should have the talent necessary to do the firing without assistance from the outside.

---

[21] "How Consultants Make Firing Easier," *Business Week* (July 20, 1974), p. 67.
[22] *Ibid.*, p. 68.
[23] *Ibid.*

Legal Restrictions on Discharge

In addition to restrictions created by the various appeal systems, there are also certain curbs imposed by federal and state laws that limit the employer's freedom to discharge employees. The Taft-Hartley Act, it will be recalled from Chapter 16, makes it an unfair practice for an employer to discharge or otherwise discriminate against an employee because of his or her union activities. If the employee to be discharged is a union leader or activist, the case against that individual must be particularly strong to withstand any charges of discrimination by the union.

State fair employment practice laws and the Civil Rights Act of 1964 which were discussed in Chapter 6 forbid discrimination on the basis of race, religion, color, and sex (in the case of the latter act) in personnel decisions involving employees. The federal government and some states also forbid employment discrimination on the basis of age. These various antidiscrimination laws make it essential that management review discharge decisions carefully to insure that there is no evidence of bias or prejudice being exercised by the supervisor who has initiated the decision. Furthermore, in the selection and training of individuals for supervisory and managerial positions, a major objective must be to help them eliminate personal prejudices which may influence personnel decisions.

Future Trends in Discharge Practices

In many foreign countries employment is regarded as a rather permanent condition so that employees are discharged or laid off only as a last resort. A number of European countries require that employees who are terminated be paid substantial indemnity or separation payments, with the result that it may be less costly to retain than to discharge a marginal performer. In Sweden, for example, a law known as the Employment Security Act now requires that employee discharges be supported by factual evidence that will hold up in the labor court. Employees must be given a written notice one month prior to their discharge if they are under 25 years of age, and six months prior to discharge if they are over 45. Employees who object to their discharges may appeal to the labor court. If they are found to have been discharged unjustly and if the employer refuses to reinstate them, they may be eligible to receive damages equal to as much as 32 months of wages if they have over 10 years of service.[24]

Companies in Europe that discharge or lay off employees in any noticeable number soon develop an unfavorable public image that impairs their recruitment efforts. Many United States companies, when they began to establish subsidiaries in Europe, thus soon acquired a ''hire and fire'' reputation because they were following the same discharge practices that their parent company used in the States. This image has been difficult for these

[24] *Sweden Now,* Vol. 8, No. 3, 1974, p. 5.

subsidiaries to lose even though their employment practices have since improved substantially.

Laws, union agreements, and social pressures are forcing employers to modify their discharge practices in the United States because their freedom and right to discharge at will is gradually being reduced. Public concern over environmental health and product-safety issues may build further support for laws to protect employees who disagree with their employers or who may expose violations or negligence of the employer with respect to these areas.[25] There is every reason to anticipate that the trend will continue toward providing greater job security for managers and other personnel in the United States in the direction of conditions that now exist in Europe.

Résumé

It is inevitable that grievances will develop from time to time among employees. Whether or not the causes of these grievances are legitimate, they can become the source of serious personnel problems if they cannot be expressed and resolved quickly. If employees are represented by a union, the labor agreement will establish the formal procedure through which a grievance may be presented and carried to higher authority when it cannot be resolved at the initial step. Most agreements also provide for arbitration as a means of resolving those grievances that cannot be settled through the formal grievance procedure.

In nonunion organizations it is especially important to establish procedures through which grievances may be expressed and resolved without fear of retaliation from superiors. These procedures not only permit injustices to be recognized and rectified but also provide an outlet through which frustrations may be vented since these employees do not have a union representative to look after their interests and personal welfare.

Rather than wait for dissatisfactions to evolve into formal grievances, it is much better for management to eliminate, as far as possible, the causes for such dissatisfactions. If an effective personnel program is developed which will provide for effective selection, training, motivation, evaluation, and remuneration of employees and will permit them to be treated as individuals with respect and consideration, many of the causes for grievances can be prevented. In spite of these preventative measures, however, certain problems are likely to arise that will require some form of corrective disciplinary action. This action, which should be taken only as a last resort, must be fair and consistent in accordance with established policies and procedures. Any necessary disciplinary actions should be administered only after the case has been reviewed thoroughly to insure that the individuals being disciplined are completely responsible for their actions, that every possible effort has been made to make them aware of their deficiencies and what is expected of them,

[25] *The National Observer,* April 19, 1972, p. 1.

and that they are being helped to improve performance and/or behavior. Not only will the respect of employees and the union be increased by the proper handling of disciplinary problems but also any action that is taken is less likely to be reversed subsequently through the grievance procedure or through arbitration.

DISCUSSION QUESTIONS

1. Why is it desirable for every organization, regardless of whether or not it is unionized, to have formal grievance procedures? What are the precautions, if any, that should be observed in the handling of grievances in a nonunion organization?
2. What action should management take if it finds that an unusually large number of grievances are filed by employees in a particular department?
3. How do discharge appeal procedures in government organizations differ from those of company organizations?
4. What are some of the criticisms being raised against the current arbitration process procedures and what is being done to improve these procedures?
5. Do you favor federal legislation that would require the use of compulsory arbitration of nationwide strikes that endanger the nation's welfare? To what extent do you feel that this type of arbitration does or does not provide the solution to the problem?
6. If you were the arbitrator of a discharge case, what facts would you analyze carefully in deciding whether to uphold or reverse the employer's actions?
7. An employee of the Ajax Washing Machine Company had a sick sister and father. Because of this, his job attendance was poor. In a six-month period he was able to work only 60 days. The company decided to discharge him. Was it fair in its decision? Is it likely that the union will contest this action? Discuss.

PROBLEM 18-1 THE DISTRAUGHT FATHER

Phil Baylor had been employed in the accounting department of the Blakewell Supply Company for over five years. He was quiet and dependable and performed his work in a highly competent manner. Blakewell, the owner, therefore, was very surprised when an audit of his company's books revealed a shortage of $2,200 in Baylor's accounts. He was even more surprised when Baylor confessed to having embezzled the money over the past year, a few hundred dollars at a time. Baylor, it seems, had need of money to help defray the medical expenses for one of his children who was suffering from leukemia. Although the company's health insurance policy covered family medical costs, it did not provide sufficient funds to cover all the expenses Baylor had incurred in the treatment of his child.

In conferring with his office manager over the incident, Blakewell continued to repeat the question, "Why didn't Phil come to us and tell us he needed money instead of stealing it from us?" Then, shaking his head, he added, "He should have known that we have helped our people out in the past with their emergency needs. Besides, we might have been able to get some financial assistance from one of the community organizations. Now what are we going to do?"

a. What action would you advise Blakewell to take?
b. What are some of the conditions within the company that may have helped to create this disciplinary problem?

SUGGESTED READINGS

Baer, Walter E. *Discipline and Discharge Under the Labor Agreement*. New York: American Management Association, 1972.

————————. *Labor Arbitration Guide*. Homewood, Illinois: Dow Jones Irwin, Inc.

Black, James M. *Positive Discipline*. New York: American Management Association, 1970.

BNA Editorial Staff. *Grievance Guide,* 4th ed. Washington, D.C.: The Bureau of National Affairs, Inc., 1972.

Chruden, Herbert J., and Arthur W. Sherman, Jr. *Readings in Personnel Management,* 4th ed. Cincinnati: South-Western Publishing Co., 1976. Part 5.

Elkouri, Frank, and Edna Asper Elkouri. *How Arbitration Works*. Washington, D.C.: The Bureau of National Affairs, Inc., 1973.

Fleming, R. W. *The Labor Arbitration Process*. Urbana, Illinois: University of Illinois Press, 1965.

Prasow, Paul, and Edward Peters. *Arbitration and Collective Bargaining*. New York: McGraw-Hill Book Company, 1970.

Scott, William G. *The Management Conflict—Appeal Systems in Organizations*. Homewood, Illinois: Richard D. Irwin, Inc. and The Dorsey Press, 1965.

Stagner, Ross, and Hjalmer Rosen. *Psychology of Union-Management Relations*. Belmont, California: Wadsworth Publishing Co., Inc., 1965.

Stone, Morris. *Labor Grievances and Decisions*. New York: Harper and Row, 1965.

Trotta, Maurice S. *Arbitration of Labor-Management Disputes*. New York: American Management Association, 1974.

Updegraff, Clarence M. *Arbitration and Labor Relations*. Washington, D.C.: The Bureau of National Affairs, Inc., 1970.

U.S. Bureau of National Affairs. *Grievance Guide*. 4th ed. Washington: U.S. Government Printing Office, 1972.

Remuneration and Security

Wage and Salary Administration

The money employees receive for their services is important to them not only financially for what it will buy but also psychologically for what it will provide them in terms of status and recognition within and outside the organization. Since money represents a quantifiable measure of their worth, employees are quite sensitive about the amount of pay they receive in return for their contributions on the job and how this amount compares with what other employees are receiving for their contributions. Employees therefore want their wages to be equitable both in terms of what is being demanded of them on the job and in terms of what other employees are paid in return for the demands of their respective jobs. In order for these wage payments to be equitable, the system for determining them must give consideration to both the relative worth or demands of each job and also to the qualifications and performance of the employees in these jobs. At the same time the system must facilitate the control of labor costs. Finally, it must take into account the prevailing rates being paid for similar jobs within the community, the condition of the local labor market, living costs, and the various federal and local laws governing wage payments.

IMPORTANCE OF FINANCIAL COMPENSATION

For years employers have been experimenting with different systems, plans, and even gimmicks in an attempt to relate effectively the pay of employees to their work contributions. While it is possible to measure employee contributions in a fairly objective manner, these measurements nevertheless are subject to human judgments and error and to various forms of pressure. Such pressures may include those for wage increases exerted by employees individually or collectively through their union. Pressures also occur in the form of competition from other employees in the labor market for individuals possessing certain skills and within an organization to reduce labor costs in order to cope with competition. In the case of public organizations, pressures to reduce labor costs result from limitations in tax revenues and from competition with other public agencies for these revenues.

Importance to Employees

It is essential that the wages employees receive for their contributions not only be equitable but, as a result of effective communication, be perceived by them as being equitable. According to the *theory of equity,* employees want a relationship to exist between their *input*—what they contribute through their jobs in terms of skill, effort, and other factors—and their *outcome*—what they receive from their jobs in terms of pay and other rewards.[1]

Reducing Cognitive Dissonance. If the outcome does not conform to employees' expectations, they are said to experience a feeling of inequity, which is commonly described by behavioral scientists as *cognitive dissonance.*[2] Thus, if employees believe they are contributing more to the organization and/or are more qualified than other employees who are receiving the same or more pay, they may experience this cognitive dissonance and seek to reduce it.[3] They may attempt to reduce it by lowering their contributions, or input, by means of greater absenteeism, poorer workmanship, less cooperative attitude, or reduced initiative. Or they may try to increase the outcome from their jobs by demanding more pay, more job recognition or satisfaction, or other rewards. If there is an objective system for determining the worth of each job and each person's performance and for making that person aware of this determination, employees are less likely to perceive themselves as being victims of inequity.

Personal characteristics, however, also may affect employee perceptions of equity. One study, for example, revealed that employees who are higher performers, less educated, higher paid, and older generally felt less inequity over their pay. Such employees, more than others, also viewed the organization as doing a better job in setting standards for pay increases.[4]

Communicating Salary Decisions Effectively. In order for employees to recognize that they are being treated equitably in terms of their monetary outcomes, effective communication must exist in an organization. An effective communication system must facilitate feedback from employees concerning

---

[1] J. Stacy Adams, "Wage Inequities, Productivity, and Work Quality," *Industrial Relations,* Vol. 3, No. 1 (October, 1963), p. 7.

[2] For a discussion of the subject, see Leon Festinger, *A Theory of Cognitive Dissonance* (New York: Row, Peterson & Company, 1957).

[3] *Ibid.*

[4] Jay R. Schuster and Thomas J. Atchinson, "Examining Feelings of Pay Equity," *Business Perspectives,* Vol. 9, No. 3 (Spring, 1973), p. 19.

the relative importance that they attach to the various financial and nonfinancial rewards or outcomes they expect to receive in return for the respective contributions or inputs which they perceive are being demanded of them.

Research indicates, for example, that there may be differences among the production, white-collar, and technical groups within an organization in terms of the input demands of their jobs. Among such groups differences may also exist with regard to the basis upon which their pay is determined, as well as the desired outcomes or rewards they perceive should be derived from their work.[5] Furthermore, there is evidence to indicate that money and its role mean different things to different groups comprising the working population.[6] In one study, for example, salary decisions that were based upon performance evaluation were found to be perceived as inequitable and those based on maturity curves (where seniority is given substantial weight) were perceived as equitable. This study also confirmed the importance of the perceptions of employees with respect to their feelings of equity regarding their remuneration.[7] Good communication, however, can contribute to a better knowledge of what the various groups perceive they should be giving and receiving on the job and can help the employer to provide compensation and other reward systems that are better tailored to the actual desires and expectations of employees comprising each of these groups.

Importance to the Employer

In many organizations wages are a major cost of operation, particularly in those that are not able to utilize laborsaving equipment extensively. In the less automated industries, such as shipbuilding and auto manufacturing, labor may represent more than 40 percent of the total costs; whereas in the more highly automated industries, such as cigarette making and petroleum, labor may constitute only 6 to 7 percent of the total costs. Increases in labor costs will affect production costs more in those industries where labor constitutes a major cost of production than they will in the more highly automated ones.

It must be recognized that labor costs are contingent not only upon the amount of money paid out for wages but also upon the productivity gained from employees in return. Thus, the labor of employees who are paid the highest wage rates may be less costly if their contributions on the job equals or exceeds the amount of their pay. Conversely, the labor of employees who are paid the lowest wage rates may be more costly if their performance is worth less than the amount of their pay. How much employees contribute in return for their wages, however, will depend upon how effectively wages can serve to motivate them as well as upon the contributions of other aspects of personnel management to efficiency.

---

[5] D. W. Belcher and T. J. Atchinson, "Equity Theory and Compensation Policy," *Personnel Administration,* Vol. 33, No. 3 (July-August, 1970), pp. 25-29.

[6] Paul F. Wernimont and Susan Fitzpatrick, "The Meaning of Money," *Journal of Applied Psychology,* Vol. 56, No. 3 (June, 1972), p. 226.

[7] R. H. Finn and Sang M. Lee, "Salary Equity: Its Determination, Analysis and Correlates," *Journal of Applied Psychology,* Vol. 56, No. 4 (August, 1972), pp. 292-293.

Importance to the Community

Prevailing compensation rates are important to the community because they help to determine the prosperity and standard of living existing within it. Higher wage levels make greater tax revenues possible to pay for better schools, hospitals, and various other public services. They also contribute to the purchasing power of employees and to the economy and general level of prosperity for the community as a whole. In many economically depressed regions both here and abroad, the living standards and general welfare of the region have been improved substantially as the result of well-paying jobs created by new industry moving into the area. Moreover, in spite of charges of exploitation that sometimes have been leveled against them, often unjustly, foreign subsidiaries of American companies have helped to raise the pay levels and living standards in many regions abroad where they have located and to provide much needed goods and services for the local population. Various impoverished areas within the United States also have reaped similar benefits from new industry.

Regions that have lower wage rates or declining payrolls, on the other hand, are affected adversely by the fact that people lack the money required to achieve satisfactory living standards or adequate community services. Business recessions, cuts in federal spending, and increases in foreign competition which force substantial layoffs by employers also can affect the economy of a community adversely. Political decisions governing these and other issues, therefore, will affect local employment and payrolls and may bring about differences in reactions from one community to another.

DETERMINING COMPENSATION PAYMENTS

A compensation system should contribute to the achievement of the overall objectives of the organization by motivating employees toward this end and by providing adequate controls that help to keep labor costs and employee productivity commensurate with each other.

Basis for Determination

The most common systems by which employees are compensated are those based upon increments of time. Work performed in blue-collar jobs traditionally has been paid on an hourly or daily rate basis and commonly is referred to as *daywork*. Of the employers included in one survey, 93 percent reported using this basis for compensating their plant employees.[8]

Employees compensated on the basis of daywork are classified as *hourly employees* or *wage earners*. Those employees whose compensation is computed on a weekly, biweekly, or monthly basis, on the other hand, are classified as *salaried employees*. Traditionally the hourly employees are paid

[8] "Wage and Salary Administration," *Personnel Policies Forum*, Survey No. 97 (Washington, D.C.: The Bureau of National Affairs, Inc., July, 1972), p. 14.

only for the time that they work; whereas salaried employees are compensated for each pay period (weekly or longer) even though they may occasionally work less than the regular number of hours comprising the pay period.

In the past, salaried employees usually have received certain benefits not provided to hourly employees, although more recently hourly employees also have been able to acquire additional fringe benefits such as supplemental unemployment allowances, paid holidays, vacations, and sick leave. As a result of these developments, the distinction between hourly and salaried employee classifications has been reduced considerably. Furthermore, some companies, such as IBM and Hewlett-Packard, have eliminated the classification of hourly worker and now consider all personnel to be salaried employees.

Daywork. Daywork is easy to understand and administer, and enables wage payments to be computed rapidly. Time standards and records of individual output, although useful for purposes of control, are not essential for computing payments under this system. Daywork, furthermore, may be the only system that can be used when employees are learning a new job, when it is not practical to develop accurate time standards for them, or when there are frequent fluctuations in the rate of output which are not within the control of the employees. Daywork also is generally the more desirable system when emphasis is to be placed upon the quality as well as the quantity of production. Although some unions have accepted piecework or other financial incentive systems, daywork generally tends to be the system preferred by most of them and is the only system under which some will agree to work.

The principal weakness of daywork is that the wages employees receive are not related directly to their work contributions during a particular pay period. An employee's wage payment may be just as large if only 90 units were produced for example, as it would be if 100 units were produced during the same period. The stimulation of performance beyond the minimum requirements, therefore, must be achieved through the use of forms of motivation other than direct financial incentives. The unit labor costs of production also are more difficult to predict under day-wage rates since the number of units that employees produce during an hour tends to vary, while the hourly wage remains constant, thus causing unit labor costs to fluctuate with the rate of output.

Piecework. In order to provide employees with a financial incentive that may increase their productivity, they may be paid according to the number of units that they produce under a system of *piecework*. Piece rates are determined by dividing the hourly wage rate for the job by the standard number of units that an employee is expected to produce in an hour. This standard represents the amount that an employee, working at a normal pace, should be able to produce and is determined by time and motion study or some other objective system of work measurement. There are also other incentive systems besides the piecework system that may be used in place of or in conjunction with daywork to reward employees for the extra effort that they exert. Some of these systems are discussed at greater length in the next chapter.

Factors Affecting Wage Rates

There are many factors which help to determine directly or indirectly the wage rates that are established for the various jobs. These factors include the condition of the labor market, the prevailing wage rates, living costs, the ability of the employer to pay, union bargaining power, and the relative worth of the job. (Government regulations, another factor, are discussed on pages 462-466.) Although the effect of each factor may be difficult to determine precisely, each must be considered as a part of a collective force that is referred to as the *wage mix*.

Condition of the Labor Market. Prior to the existence of labor unions and wage laws, labor was regarded by employers primarily as a commodity to be procured at the lowest rate possible. Wage rates were contingent largely upon the factors of labor supply and demand which served to determine what job seekers could get for their services. Today the wages for certain jobs requiring specific qualifications still may be affected by the availability and demand for personnel with these qualifications. However, restraints created by such factors as government regulations and union bargaining power may prevent the forces of supply and demand from operating freely. Unions, for example, by means of strike threats can prevent employers from lowering wage rates even when high unemployment may create an oversupply of labor for certain types of work. Government regulations also may prevent an employer from paying less than an established minimum rate or more than an established wage ceiling.

Prevailing Wage Rates. It is essential that an employer maintain current data on the wage rates being paid by other employers in the community for comparable jobs. Data pertaining to community wage rates may be obtained from surveys conducted by the personnel department and by local employer groups. Data obtained from community surveys typically include not only employee wage rates but also fringe benefits which in turn must be converted into an equivalent hourly rate for purposes of comparison. Community wage data will help to insure that the job rates of an employer are not permitted to drift too much above or below those of other employers in the region. If rates get too far above existing community levels, an employer's labor costs may become excessive; but if rates drop too far below existing community levels, difficulties in recruiting and retaining competent personnel may result.

Cost of Living. Because of continued inflation during and since World War II, wage rates have had to be adjusted upward periodically in order for employees merely to maintain their purchasing power. These adjustments have been accomplished informally or by means of formulas that tie wage increases to the rises in the *consumer price index* (CPI). One survey revealed, for example, that only 15 percent of the manufacturers responding have a formal plan for adjusting wages in response to changes in the cost of living. Another 73 percent, however, provide some form of cost-of-living adjustments but not in accordance with any formal plan.[9] Some unions have negotiated successfully for *escalator clauses* in their labor agreements which provide for quarterly adjustments in wages in accordance with changes in the CPI. The escalator clause in the General Motors agreement, for example, provides that a one-cent-per-hour change is to be made in the wage rate for each 0.4 change in the CPI prepared by the Bureau of Labor Statistics.

One problem of tying wages or other forms of income, such as pensions, Social Security benefits, or welfare payments, to changes in a consumer price index is that no single index can take into account the differences in spending patterns of the individuals in the various income groups. In order to make the CPI representative of the consumption pattern of a larger segment of the population, beginning in April, 1977, the Bureau of Labor Statistics will enlarge the index coverage, which is now based on the spending patterns of urban wage earners and clerical workers, to include executives, professionals, self-employed persons, the unemployed, and retirees. Organized labor, however, is opposed to this expansion of the CPI coverage which would change the nature and weightings of the goods and services that comprise the "market basket" upon which the CPI currently is based. This opposition stems from the fear that such changes would cause the new index to understate rises in the cost of living for urban workers.[10]

In order to curb any major decrease in wages resulting from declines in the cost of living, many unions negotiate to incorporate the cost-of-living increases they received during their previous labor agreement in the basic wage rate provided for in the new agreement. Some unions, however, prefer to bargain for general wage raises that include increases in the cost of living rather than to have increases determined by an escalator clause. Increases achieved through bargaining are less vulnerable to declines in the cost of living. Furthermore, the union officers can take full credit for getting the increase which would not be possible if it were derived by means of a cost-of-living formula.

Ability to Pay. Ability to pay has frequently been used as a collective bargaining argument by the unions in attempting to prove that company profits are sufficient to support their wage demands. A company's ability to pay is influenced by such economic conditions as its competitive position within its industry and the prosperity that exists within the geographic region in which it is located. In the case of government and nonprofit organizations, such ability may be contingent upon adequate tax or other revenues. It is also contingent upon the productivity of employees within an organization as determined by their willingness to work, by the existence of laborsaving equipment, and by how effectively employees are managed.

Although employers may use inability to pay as an argument for not meeting wage increases being granted by other organizations, unions are reluctant to accept the argument particularly if they feel that this inability is due to inefficient management. It is not uncommon, therefore, for a union to take the position that its members should not be expected to subsidize either inefficient

[9] *Ibid.*, p. 18.

[10] "Labor Bristles at a Broader CPI," *Business Week* (April 6, 1974), p. 18.

management or the continued existence of a submarginal enterprise, or the cost of government in the case of public employees.

Collective Bargaining. If the employer is unionized, wages and other conditions of employment are determined primarily through the process of collective bargaining. Each of the various factors that are a part of the wage mix may be used in arguments by the union and the employer in support of their bargaining positions. Even though bargaining arguments based upon prevailing wage rates, cost of living, ability to pay, or any other factors affecting wage determination may favor either one party or the other, the wage rate that is agreed upon finally is likely to be due as much to the comparative economic pressures that the two parties are able to exert upon each other as it is to the logic of their arguments.

Relative Worth of the Job. Since employees expect wages and other outcomes of their jobs to be consistent with the demands or input of these jobs, this input-outcome relationship as noted earlier must be consistent and equitable. Various systems of job evaluation have been developed for determining the relative worth of the jobs within an organization and for providing a tangible and objective basis by which demands or input required in each job may be measured and the outcome for the employees—at least the wage portion of it—can be related more equitably to their input.

JOB EVALUATION SYSTEMS

The relative worth of a job may be determined by comparing the job with others within the organization or by comparing it with a scale. Each method of comparison, furthermore, may be made on the basis of the jobs as a whole or on the basis of the factors comprising the jobs. These four methods of comparison are illustrated by Figure 19-1 and provide the basis for the principal systems of job evaluation. In the order of their popularity, these systems include the point, factor comparison, grade, and ranking systems.[11]

Basis for Comparison	Scope of Comparison	
	Job as a Whole (Nonquantitative)	Job Parts or Factors (Quantitative)
Job vs. Job	(1.) Job Ranking System	(4.) Factor Comparison System
Job vs. Scale	(2.) Job Grade System	(3.) Point System

Figure 19-1 COMPARISON OF JOB EVALUATION SYSTEMS

[11] Elizabeth Lanham, *Administration of Wages and Salaries* (New York: Harper & Row, Publishers, 1962), pp. 165, 189.

Point System

The *point system* developed initially by Western Electric and adopted by the National Electric Manufacturers Association (NEMA) and the National Metal Trades Association (NMTA) has been successfully used by the United States Steel Corporation, the Johnson Wax Company, and many other companies both large and small.[12] The principal advantage of the point system is that it is relatively simple to understand and to use. It also provides a more refined basis for making judgments than either the ranking or grade systems and thereby can produce results that are more valid and less easy to manipulate. This system permits jobs to be evaluated quantitatively on the basis of the factors or elements that comprise the demands of the job. The skills, efforts, responsibilities, and working conditions that a job usually entails are typical of the more common major factors that serve to make one job more or less important than another. The point system requires the use of a *point manual* that contains a description of the factors and the degrees to which these factors may exist within the jobs. A manual also must indicate—usually by means of a

Table 19-1 POINT VALUES FOR JOB FACTORS

Factors	1st Degree	2nd Degree	3rd Degree	4th Degree	5th Degree
Skill					
1. Job Knowledge	14	28	42	56	70
2. Experience	22	44	66	88	110
3. Initiative and Ingenuity	14	28	42	56	70
Effort					
4. Physical Demand	10	20	30	40	50
5. Mental or Visual Demand	5	10	15	20	25
Responsibility					
6. Equipment or Process	5	10	15	20	25
7. Material or Product	5	10	15	20	25
8. Safety of Others	5	10	15	20	25
9. Work of Others	5	10	15	20	25
Job Conditions					
10. Working Conditions	10	20	30	40	50
11. Hazards	5	10	15	20	25

Source: National Metal Trades Association.

[12] Herbert G. Zollitsch and Adolph Langsner, *Wage and Salary Administration* (2d ed.; (Cincinnati: South-Western Publishing Co., 1970), pp. 187-188.

table (see Table 19-1)—the number of points that are allocated to each factor and to each of the degrees into which these factors are divided.[13]

Nature of the Point Manual. A variety of point manuals have been developed by companies, trade associations, and management consultants. Those manuals prepared by the National Metal Trades, the National Electric Manufacturers, and the Administrative Management Society are among the ones most widely utilized. An organization that seeks to use one of these or other manuals should make certain that it is suitable to its particular jobs and conditions of operation and, if necessary, should modify it to fit its needs. In many instances it may be preferable for the organization to develop a manual of its own.

Construction of a Point Manual. The job factors and subfactors in the point manual should include those that are significant in measuring the worth of the jobs. The inclusion of those factors that are of a minor nature, that overlap, that are not clearly definable, and that are not present in varying degrees among the job factors should be avoided. The trend is for point systems to utilize fewer factors in support of the belief that a large number is unnecessary for effective job measurement. The number used ordinarily ranges from five to fifteen with the average being approximately ten.

The job factors and subfactors that are illustrated in Table 19-1 represent those covered by one particular point manual. Each of the factors listed in this manual has been divided into five degrees. The number of degrees into which the factors comprising a manual are to be divided, however, can be more or fewer than this number, depending upon the relative weight assigned to each factor and upon the ease with which the individual degrees can be defined or distinguished.

After the job factors comprising the point manual have been divided into degrees, a statement must be prepared defining each of these degrees as well as each factor as a whole. The definitions should be concise and yet distinguish the factors and each of their degrees. Figure 19-2 represents a portion of a point manual used by the Allis-Chalmers Manufacturing Company to describe each of the degrees for the factors of experience and of initiative and ingenuity. These descriptions enable those persons conducting an evaluation to determine the degrees of the factors that exist in each job being evaluated.

The final step in developing a point manual is that of determining the number of points to be assigned to each factor and to each degree within these factors. Although 500 points quite often are the maximum point value for a manual, there is nothing to prevent the figure from being 400, 800, 1,000, or some other point total.

---

[13] Table 19-1 is taken from the point manual developed by the National Metal Trades Association and reproduced with their permission. The figure represents the table for assigning the point values for the various job factors covered by the manual and the degrees into which these factors have been divided.

EXPERIENCE

This factor measures the length of time, with the specified job knowledge, that is required to obtain and develop the skills necessary to effectively perform the work. Where previous experience is required, time spent in related work or lesser classifications, either within the Company or other organizations, will be considered as contributing to the total experience required to effectively perform the work. Consideration must be given to continuous progress by the average individual, allowing sufficient practice time to encounter and satisfactorily resolve representative deviation in the work assignments that could normally be expected.

First Degree: Up to and including three months.
Second Degree: Over three months up to one year.
Third Degree: Over one year up to three years.
Fourth Degree: Over three years up to five years.
Fifth Degree: Over five years.

INITIATIVE AND INGENUITY

This factor measures the complexity of job duties in terms of the amount of initiative and ingenuity required for successful job performance. Consider the variation and involvement of the methods, procedures, and practices; the degree of independent action and original thought required; the extent of supervision received; and the availability of standards, precedents, and shop practices.

FIRST DEGREE: Instructions are received orally or written in nontechnical terms which can be understood and carried out with a minimum of initiative and judgment. Work is of such a nature that details left to the control of the employee are limited; operations are highly repetitive and minimum of responsibility for maintaining tolerances exists.

SECOND DEGREE: Instructions may require explanation to the extent of using a single view or plan drawing. Procedures are normally detailed: the majority of work is similar in its overall requirement; however, minor variations exist in completing individual details which require the use of some judgment or initiative. Tolerances are easy to maintain, using scales, gauges, solid frame micrometers, templates, and related means of checking.

THIRD DEGREE: Instructions may require explanation to the point of using multiple view or related part drawings. Work is of a varied nature within a well-defined field under standard practices and precedents. Operations can normally be accomplished by several methods or procedures requiring a selection to fit individual variations. Judgment or initiative are required within the limits of established standards. Tolerances are considered close and somewhat difficult to maintain.

FOURTH DEGREE: Instructions available for job performance are few and of a general nature. Basic planning of successive steps together with consideration for related operations is necessary. Duties vary to the extent that assignments normally require drawing upon past parallel solutions for general guidance. Mental resourcefulness, initiative, and judgment are required to solve problems. Tolerances, sizes, clearances and balancing, testing, and related procedures are considered difficult to maintain.

FIFTH DEGREE: Instructions, precedents, and standards for performance of the job are seldom available. Considerable planning and consideration of a variety of factors difficult to evaluate are necessary for successful completion of work. Duties involve the development of new procedures, processes, or methods with a minimum of technical guidance. Requires a high degree of imagination, ingenuity, and independent action.

Source: Reproduced with the permission of the Allis-Chalmers Manufacturing Co.

Figure 19-2 SAMPLE MANUAL DESCRIPTIONS FOR JOB FACTORS AND FOR THEIR DEGREES

Job evaluation under the point system is accomplished by comparing the job specifications, factor by factor, against the various factor degree descriptions contained in the manual. Each factor within the job being evaluated is then assigned the number of points that is appropriate on the basis of the degree descriptions contained in the manual. When the points for each factor (or subfactor) have been determined from the manual, the total point value for the job as a whole can be calculated. The relative worth of the job is then determined by the total points that have been assigned to it.[14]

[14] For further description of the point method, see Henry A. Sargent, ''Using the Point Method to Measure Jobs,'' in Milton L. Rock (editor), *Handbook of Wage and Salary Administration* (New York: McGraw-Hill Book Company, 1972), pp. 2-31—2-41.

Factor Comparison System

The *factor comparison system* was originated by Eugene Benge about 1926.[15] Like the point system, it permits the job evaluation process to be accomplished on a factor-by-factor basis. It differs from the point system, however, in that the specifications of the jobs to be evaluated are compared against the specifications of key jobs within the organization which serve as the job evaluation scale. Thus, instead of beginning with an established point scale, a factor comparison scale must be developed as a part of the job evaluation process. The factors of skill, mental effort, physical effort, responsibility, and working conditions are typical of those that may comprise the factor comparison scale.

Developing the Factor Comparison Scale. The first step in the development of the factor comparison scale is that of selecting the *key jobs* with which the remaining jobs are to be compared. These key jobs should include jobs of varying difficulty for which complete and accurate descriptions and specifications have been developed. The wage rates for these jobs, furthermore, should be consistent both internally and externally and not be the subject of any grievance action. Usually 15 to 20 key jobs are a sufficient number for a factor comparison scale.

The next step in the factor comparison system is that of determining the proportion of the key job's current wage being paid to each of the factors of which these jobs are comprised. Thus, the proportion of a key job's wage rate that is allocated to the skill factor, for example, will depend on the importance of this job requirement in comparison with its requirements for mental effort, physical effort, responsibility, and working conditions. Table 19-2 illustrates how the rate for six key jobs has been allocated according to the relative importance of the basic factors that comprise these jobs.

Table 19-2 WAGE RATE APPORTIONMENT TABLE

Job	Wage Rate	Skill	Mental Effort	Physical Effort	Responsibility	Working Conditions
Machinist Planner	$6.55	$3.30	$1.80	$ .25	$ .75	$ .45
Punch Press Operator	5.80	3.20	.55	.35	.60	1.10
Tank Sealer	5.30	1.50	1.05	.75	.55	1.45
Storekeeper	4.60	2.50	.60	.55	.35	.60
Tank Cleaner	3.70	1.40	.30	.60	.50	.90
Oiler, Maintenance	3.50	1.30	.35	.40	.45	1.00

[15] For further information about the factor comparison system, see Zollitsch and Langsner, *op. cit.*, pp. 179-184, and Eugene J. Benge (ed.), "Using Factor Methods to Measure Jobs," *Handbook of Wage and Salary Administration* (New York: McGraw-Hill Book Company, 1972), pp. 2-42—2-55.

This money allocation must be accomplished in such a way as to permit the jobs to rank correctly with respect to each of the factors on the basis of the portion of the wage that has been allocated to that factor. Thus, since the job of machinist planner listed in Table 19-2 requires more skill than that of a punch press operator, the money allocation for this factor must be greater for a machinist planner than for punch press operator. If the apportionment of the punch press operator's wage in this example were $3.40 for skill (because less had been allocated to some other factor or factors), this situation would then have caused the punch press operator's job to incorrectly outrank the $3.30 that had been allocated to the skill column for the machinist planner.

To correct this situation, either a large proportion of the machinist planner's wages would have to be allocated to the factor of skill by reducing the allocation to one or more of the other factors, or the amount allocated to skill for the punch press operator job would have to be reduced by increasing the allocation to one or more of the other factors of this job. Any increases or decreases of the wage apportionment for a particular factor of a job will necessitate a change in apportionment of the money allocations of at least one of the other factors of that job. In some instances it may not be possible to correct inconsistencies in the ranking of key jobs on the basis of certain factors; therefore, such jobs must be eliminated from the comparison scale. The remaining key jobs can then be placed at the appropriate location on the comparison scales for each factor as illustrated in Figure 19-3 on pages 452-453.

Evaluating Jobs with the Factor Comparison Scale. The locations of the key jobs on the factor comparison scale and the specifications of these jobs provide the bench marks against which the other jobs are evaluated. As an example of how the scale is used, let us assume that the job of ***automatic screw machine operator*** is to be evaluated through the use of the factor comparison scale shown in Figure 19-3. By comparing the specification covering the skill requirement for an ***automatic screw machine operator*** with the skill requirements of the other jobs on the table, it was decided that the skill demands of the job placed it about half way between those of a storekeeper and a punch press operator. The job therefore was placed at the $2.85 point on the scale. The same procedure was used in locating the job at the appropriate point on the scale for the remaining factors. As additional non-key jobs are added to the scale and are available for comparison, it is possible that minor adjustments, upward or downward, may be made in the location of certain jobs on the scale. Further, as more non-key jobs are added to the scale, the jobs to be evaluated become easier to place on the scale because there are more jobs on the scale against which comparisons can be made.

The evaluated worth of the jobs added to the scale is computed by adding up the money values for each factor as determined by where the job has been placed on the scale for each factor. Thus, the evaluated worth of an ***automatic screw machine operator*** of $5.05 would be determined by totaling the monetary value for each factor as follows:

Skill	$2.85
Mental Effort	.50
Physical Effort	.30
Responsibility	.65
Working Conditions	.75
	$5.05

Advantages and Disadvantages of the Factor Comparison System. Some of the advantages claimed for the factor comparison system are:

1. It can be custom tailored to fit the particular jobs of a company.
2. It enables jobs to be compared against other jobs, including those of a similar nature, in determining their relative value.
3. It permits adequate weight to be allowed for factors that exist to an unusually high degree within a job because there is no maximum or minimum value to be assigned to any of the factors.
4. The evaluation of jobs by means of the scale can be conducted with relative ease.

Some of the disadvantages of the system are:

1. It may be difficult to locate a sufficient number of key jobs to comprise the scale.
2. Any inequities in the rates of the key jobs or errors in the specifications of these jobs will affect the system's accuracy.
3. The existence of monetary values in the system may tend to introduce certain bias on the part of those using it.
4. The system tends to be rather complicated and difficult for some employees to comprehend with the result that they do not have full confidence in its accuracy.

Variations of the System. In some systems percentages are substituted for monetary values in order to avoid the possibility of bias caused by making comparisons in monetary values. Points also may be used as a substitute for the monetary values. The profile method to be discussed in connection with the evaluation of management positions on page 455 represents still another variation of the factor comparison system.

Job Grade System

In the *job grade* or *classification* system, jobs are classified and grouped according to a series of predetermined wage classes or grades. While this system has the advantage of simplicity, it is less precise than the point and factor comparison systems because the job is evaluated as a whole. The federal civil service job classification system is probably the best known system of this type. The descriptions for each of the job classes constitute the scale with which the specifications for the various jobs are compared. The number of classes that are required for the system will depend upon the range of duties,

Hourly Rate $	Skill	Mental Effort	Physical Effort	Responsibility	Working Conditions
–3.30	Machinist Planner				
–3.20	Punch Press Oper.				
–3.10					
–3.00					
–2.90					
–	Screw Mach. Oper.				
–2.80					
–2.70					
–2.60					
–2.50	Storekeeper				
–2.40					
–2.30					
–2.20					
–2.10					
–2.00					
–1.90					
–1.80		Machinist Planner			
–1.70					

Figure 19-3 FACTOR COMPARISON SCALE (Page 1)

responsibilities, skills, and other requirements that exist among the jobs to be evaluated by the system. Generally it is necessary to provide separate systems for office, factory, sales, and supervisory jobs. The classes shown in Figure 19-4 might be established for jobs in the shop and service groups, for example.

Ranking System

The simplest and oldest system of job evaluation is the *job ranking* or *order-of-merit* system by which jobs are arrayed on the basis of their relative worth. One technique that is used to rank jobs consists of having the raters arrange cards containing the specifications for each job in the order of

Hourly Rate $	Skill	Mental Effort	Physical Effort	Responsibility	Working Conditions
1.60					
1.50	Tank Sealer				
					Tank Sealer
1.40	Tank Cleaner				
1.30	Oiler Maintenance				
1.20					
1.10					Punch Press Oper.
		Tank Sealer			
1.00					Oiler Maintenance
.90					Tank Cleaner
.80					
			Tank Sealer	Machinist Planner	Screw Mach. Oper.
.70					
				Screw Mach. Oper	
.60		Storekeeper	Tank Cleaner	Punch Press Oper.	Storekeeper
		Punch Press Oper.	Storekeeper	Tank Sealer	
.50		Screw Mach. Oper.		Tank Cleaner	
				Oiler Maintenance	Machinist Planner
.40			Oiler Maintenance		
		Oiler Maintenance	Punch Press Oper.	Storekeeper	
.30		Tank Cleaner	Screw Mach. Oper.		
.25			Machinist Planner		
.20					

Figure 19-3 (Page 2)

importance of the jobs that the cards represent. Differences in the rankings made by the raters can then be reconciled into a single rating.

The basic weakness of the job ranking system is that it does not provide a very refined measure of each job's worth. Since the comparisons must be made on the basis of the job as a whole, it is quite easy for one or more of the factors of a job to bias the ranking that the evaluator gives to a job, particularly if the job is complex. Furthermore, the rankings merely indicate the relative importance of the jobs but not the differences in the degree of importance that may exist between jobs.

Union Reactions to Job Evaluation

Unlike wage rates that are determined by negotiation and thereby reflect the bargaining achievements of the union officers, those rates established through

SHOP AND SERVICE EMPLOYEES

S-1 Repetitive work under immediate supervision and involving no unusual hazard or extra effort; requires no previous training.
Example: Watchman; Janitor.

S-2 Repetitive work under general supervision; repetitive work under immediate supervision, but involving unusual hazard or extra physical or mental application; no special training before employment, and very short training on the job.
Example: Guard; Routine inspection or assembly; Box maker.

S-3 Semiskilled work requiring exercise of judgment by employee in making decisions; specialized training or experience in operating tools required.
Example: Difficult assembly and inspection; Rough carpentry; Operation of machine tools to moderate tolerances.

S-4 Skilled work involving broad knowledge of a recognized trade; read and interpret difficult blueprints; responsibility for materials and equipment; set up and operation of a variety of machine tools to close tolerances.
Example: Machinist; Plumber; Carpenter; Steamfitter; Electrician; Supervision of S-2 or S-3 work.

S-5 Supervision of S-3 or S-4 work; precision work; highest degree of skill and experience; requires knowledge of two or more skilled trades.
Example: Tool and die maker; Instrument maker; Pattern maker; Lens grinder.

Source: Robert D. Gray, *Classification of Jobs in Small Companies,* Bulletin No. 5, Industrial Relations Section (Pasadena: California Institute of Technology, 1944), p. 21.

Figure 19-4 EXAMPLE OF A JOB GRADE SYSTEM

job evaluation are based upon a system. Because of this fact, the role of the union negotiators in wage determination is reduced. Thus, in the opinion of many union leaders, job evaluation serves to restrict bargaining on wage adjustments and to freeze the wage structure.[16] Other complaints of union officers concerning job evaluation are that it often is used as the sole criterion in establishing wage scales rather than as a guide, that job evaluation plans are not kept current, that they are not understood by employees, that they fail to give equitable evaluation to "human elements" of the job, and that they are based upon "ideal" rather than normal performance. The results of one study, however, have indicated that dissatisfaction among union officials toward job evaluation has decreased from that revealed in a study four years earlier, with some officials even expressing their satisfaction toward it. This reduction in dissatisfaction, among other things, probably stems from improved communication between management and unions concerning wage and salary administration.[17]

[16] Harold D. Janes, "Issues in Job Evaluation: The Union View," *Personnel Journal,* Vol. 51, No. 9 (September, 1972), p. 677.

[17] *Ibid.,* p. 679.

Evaluation of Management Positions

Because they usually are more complicated and involve certain demands not found in jobs at the lower levels, some organizations do not attempt to include management positions in their job evaluation programs. Those that do evaluate these positions, however, may extend their regular system of evaluation to include such positions, or they may develop a separate evaluation system for management positions. Any one of the four systems of job evaluation that have been discussed may be used to evaluate management positions, particularly if certain modifications are made.

Several systems have been developed especially for the evaluation of management positions. One of the better known of those which are gaining acceptance is the *profile method*. The profile method combines certain features of the point, factor comparison, and ranking systems. The three basic factors or components that comprise the evaluation "profile" in one system include knowledge (or know-how), mental activity (or problem solving), and accountability.[18] The profile for each position is developed by determining the percentage value to be given to each of the three broad factors. Jobs are then ranked on the basis of each factor, and point values that go to make up the profile are then assigned to each job on the basis of the percentage-value level at which the job ranked.[19]

THE RATE STRUCTURE AND ITS ADMINISTRATION

Job evaluation does not determine the wage rate but only the basis for its determination. The evaluated worth of each job in terms of its rank, class, points, or monetary worth must be converted into an hourly, daily, weekly, or monthly wage rate. The wage rate that is established for a particular job also must give recognition to such external factors as labor market conditions, prevailing wage rates, living costs, union negotiated rates, and legal minimums that were mentioned earlier in this chapter. Figure 19-5 provides a schematic chart showing the processes that may be involved in wage determination and the sources of data that may be utilized.

The Wage Curve

The relationship between the relative worth of the jobs and their wage rates can be represented by means of a *wage curve* or *conversion line*. This curve may indicate the rates currently paid for jobs within the organization, or the new rates resulting from job evaluation, or the rates for similar jobs currently

---

[18] See Edward N. Hay and Dale Purves, "The Profile Method of High Level Job Evaluation," *Personnel*, Vol. 28, No. 2 (September, 1951), pp. 162-170.

[19] For another description of the profile method, see Charles W. G. VanHorn, "The Hay Guide Chart—Profile Method," in Milton L. Rock (editor), *Handbook of Wage and Salary Administration* (New York: McGraw-Hill Book Company, 1972), pp. 2-86—2-97.

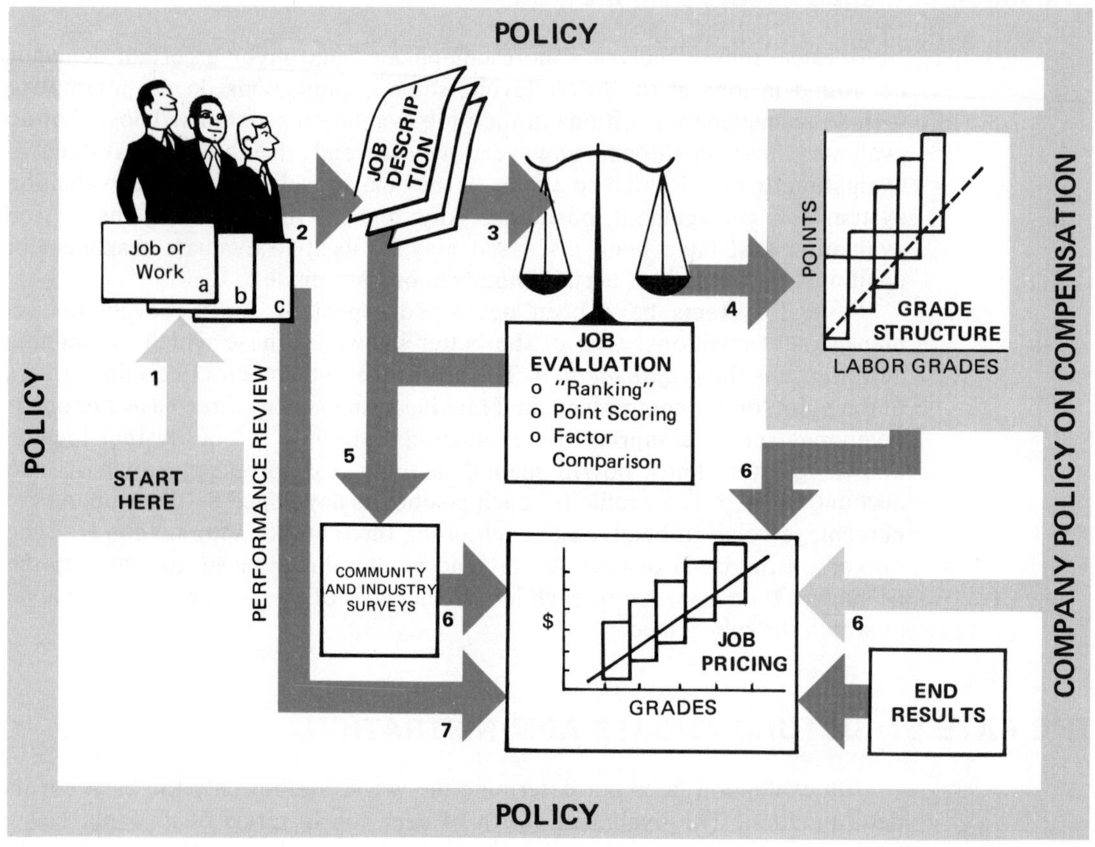

Source: Bureau of Industrial Relations Seminar (Ann Arbor, Michigan: University of Michigan). Reproduced with permission of Dr. Gerard Carhalvo.

Figure 19-5 A WAGE ADMINISTRATION SYSTEM

being paid by other organizations within the community as revealed by a wage survey. A curve may be constructed graphically by preparing a scattergram consisting of a series of dots that represent the current wage rates. A freehand curve is then drawn through the cluster of dots in such a manner as to leave approximately an equal number of dots above and below the curve, as illustrated by Figure 19-6. This wage curve will then determine the relationship between the value of a job and its wage rate at any given point on the line. The curve also can be constructed by means of an algebraic formula using what is known as the *least squares method*.[20]

[20] A description of the least squares method may be obtained from any basic textbook in business statistics.

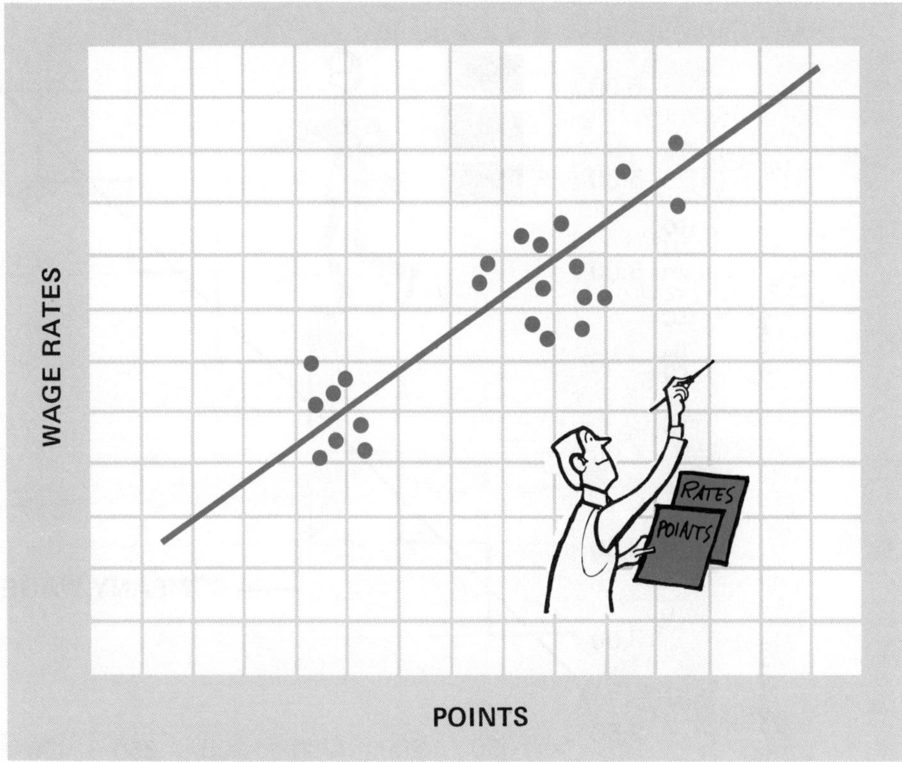

Figure 19-6 FREEHAND WAGE CURVE

Wage Classes

Generally it is preferable from an administrative standpoint to group the jobs into *wage classes* or *grades* and to pay all jobs within a particular class the same rate or rate range. When the grade or classification system of job evaluation is used, jobs are grouped into classes as a part of the evaluation process. When the point and factor comparison systems are used, however, wage classes must be established at selected intervals representing either the point or evaluated monetary value of these jobs. The graph in Figure 19-7 illustrates a series of wage classes which are designated along the horizontal axis at 50-point intervals.

The rates for wage classes also may be determined by means of a *conversion table* similar to the one illustrated in Table 19-3. The classes within a wage structure may vary in number with the average number being somewhere between 10 and 15.[21] The number of classes utilized is determined by such factors as the slope of the wage curve, the number and distribution of the jobs within the structure, and the company wage administration and promotion

[21] Lanham, *op. cit.*, p. 228.

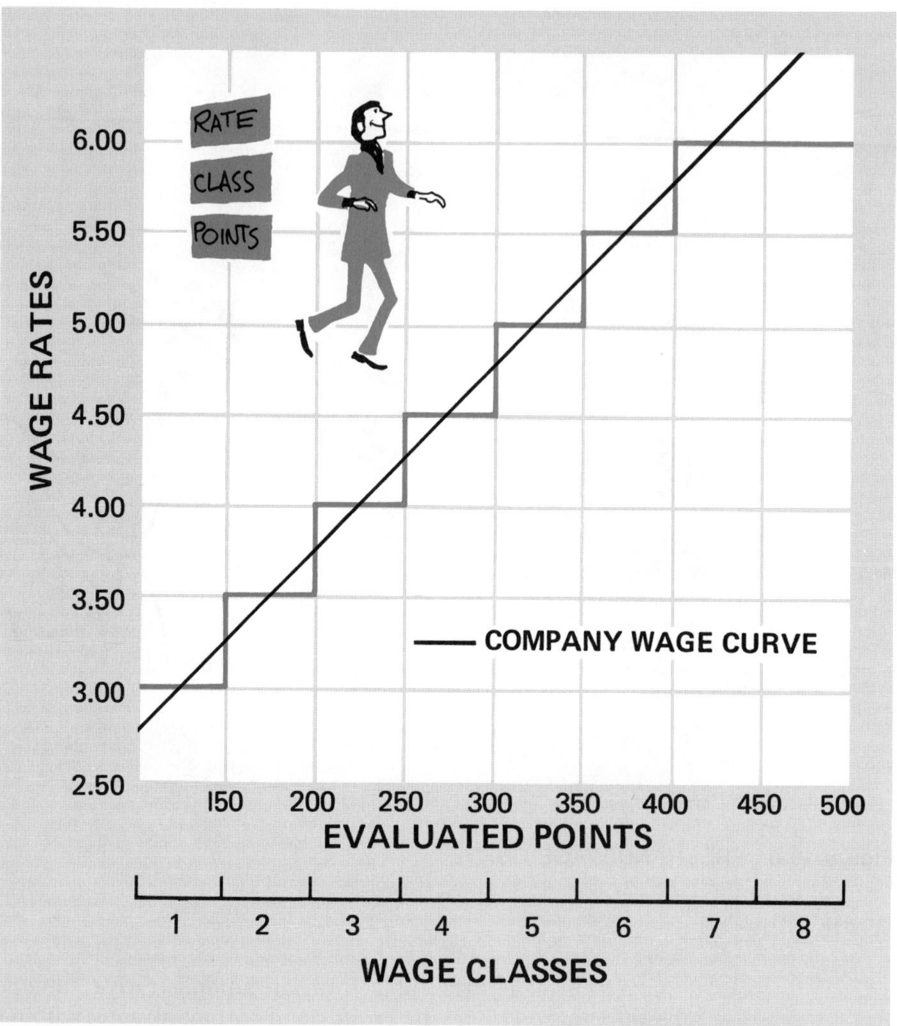

Figure 19-7 SINGLE RATE STRUCTURE

Table 19-3 POINT CONVERSION TABLE

Wage Class	Point Range	Hourly Rate Range
1	101-150	$2.75-$3.50
2	151-200	3.25- 4.00
3	201-250	3.75- 4.50
4	251-300	4.25- 5.00
5	301-350	4.75- 5.50
6	351-400	5.25- 6.00
7	401-450	5.75- 6.50
8	451-500	6.25- 7.00

policies. The number utilized should be sufficient to permit difficulty levels to be distinguished but not so great as to make the distinction between two adjoining classes insignificant.[22]

Rate Ranges

Although a single rate may be created for each wage class as in Figure 19-7, it is more common to provide a *rate range* for each of them. The rate ranges may be the same for each class as provided in Table 19-3, or proportionately greater for each successive wage class as in Figure 19-8. Proportionately greater

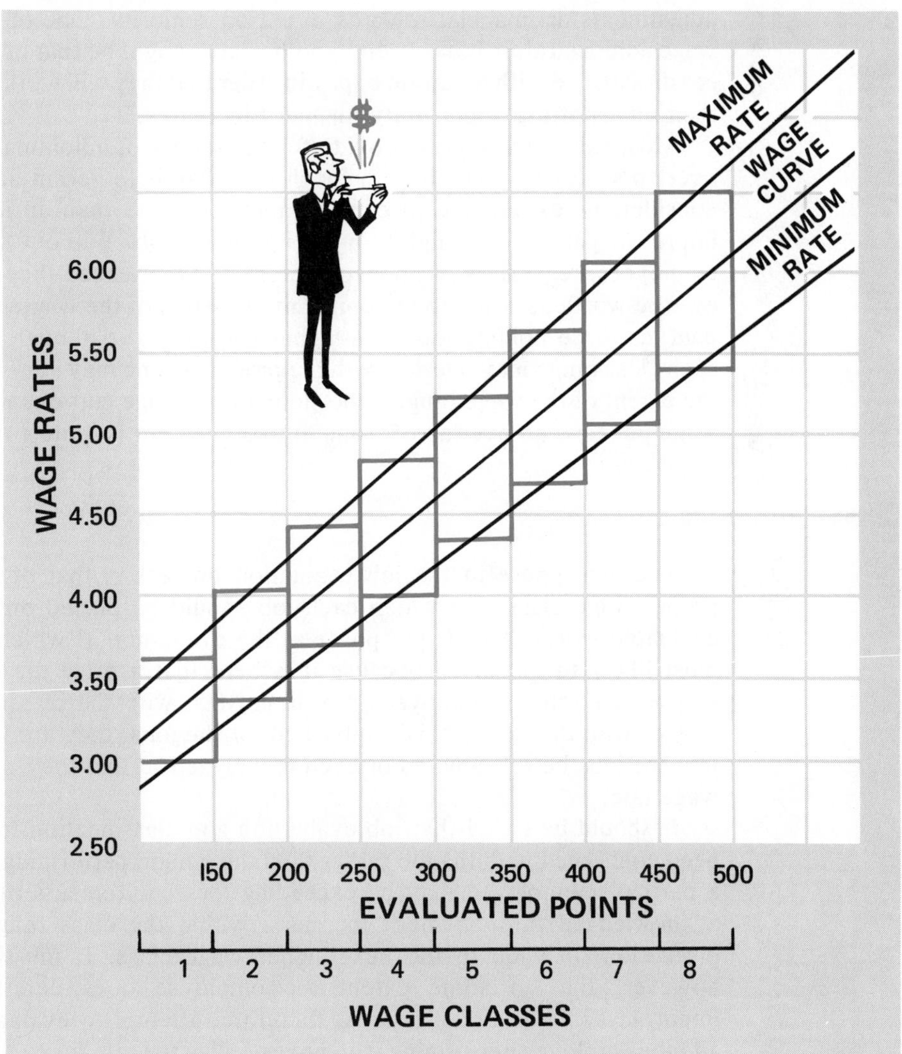

Figure 19-8 WAGE STRUCTURE WITH INCREASING RATE RANGES

[22] *Ibid.*

ranges of a percentage amount reflect the proportionately greater demands of the jobs in each higher class and thus provide a greater incentive for employees to accept a promotion to a job in a higher class.

Ranges generally are divided into a series of steps that permit employees to receive increases periodically on the basis of merit or seniority or a combination of the two factors up to the maximum rate for the range. If increases are to be based upon merit, wage policies should insure that the increases are actually earned on the basis of specific achievement. Merit increases also should be separated and distinguished from economic adjustments or financial rewards based on seniority. One of the goals of the wage administrator, it has been hypothesized, might be that of making employees dissatisfied with their rate of pay in order that they will work harder and avail themselves of the opportunity for merit increases.[23]

Most salary structures provide for the ranges of adjoining wage classes to overlap somewhat. The reason for this overlap is to permit an employee with considerable experience to earn as much or more than an inexperienced or unproved person in a slightly more important job. Without some overlap no employees, regardless of how competent or experienced they might be, could ever be worth as much to the company, in terms of the wages they were being paid, as those holding jobs in a higher wage class. Although the amount that each class range may overlap with the preceding one may vary in accordance to the extent of the wage ranges, the slope of the wage curve, and the company's wage policies, an overlap of from 30 to 50 percent is quite common.

Classifying Jobs

The final phase in the job evaluation process is that of determining the proper wage class into which each job should be placed on the basis of its evaluated worth. This is the phase of the evaluation at which complaints are most likely to be raised because it is here that a price tag is placed on an employee's job. If employees are dissatisfied with the classification of their jobs or with the rate that is established for the jobs, they are likely to demand that the jobs be reevaluated or even reanalyzed so that they will earn a higher wage rate.

It should be noted that job evaluation and classification traditionally have been concerned with the job rather than the person performing it. The fact that a particular employee may be exceeding the requirements of the job can be acknowledged through merit increases within the class range or through a promotion to a job in the next higher wage class. It must be recognized, however, that to some extent the employee does determine the job's importance. Some organizations, therefore, attempt to evaluate both the job and the employee performing it and to establish the rate for each position on the basis of a combination of these two factors.

---

[23] David W. Belcher, "Ominous Trends in Wage and Salary Administration," *Personnel,* Vol. 41, No. 5 (September-October, 1964), p. 44.

Wage Policies and Procedures

In order to insure that decisions affecting wages are made in a consistent and equitable manner, formal policies and procedures must be developed to govern these decisions. If the wage structure contains a wage range for each wage grade, policies and procedures must be established to determine (1) the step within the range at which employees are to be placed when hired or promoted, and (2) the basis upon which employees are to be advanced within the range or from one step to another. These policies and procedures also should provide the means for reviewing periodically the structure and the classification of jobs within the structure for the purpose of correcting errors or eliminating inequities. The procedures, furthermore, should establish the machinery that is necessary for processing employee grievances and complaints pertaining to wages.

Wage Compression. Since World War II there has been a trend for companies to grant across-the-board increases to all employees in order to satisfy union bargaining demands to cover rising costs of living, or to keep wage rates in line with those of other companies; or because of a combination of these factors. Such increases have been either a flat amount, that is, a certain number of cents an hour for all jobs, or a percentage amount based upon the existing wage rate for each job. Flat increases have tended to be more commonplace and, as a result, jobs in the lower wage classes are receiving a larger percentage increase than those in the higher wage classes. This latter condition has had the effect of compressing the traditional rate differentials between the more highly skilled and the less highly skilled jobs with the result that some skilled wage earners no longer enjoy the same financial differential that they once did. If this trend continues long enough, it can severely curtail the incentive for employees to train themselves for jobs requiring greater skill. Percentage increases, on the other hand, have the advantage of preserving wage differentials based upon the relative worth of the jobs within an organization whenever wage increases are given.

The rate structure can be distorted by hiring applicants who are in scarce supply for jobs at rates higher than the evaluated worth of the jobs, or at a rate higher than that of persons who have been employed in these jobs for a period of time.[24] It can be distorted also by raising the rates of certain employees above the maximum limits of the range established for a particular classification. If an organization can afford to do so, it is better for it to raise the entire rate structure rather than to impair an objective rate structure by making special exceptions to the structure for certain jobs. Similarly, an organization can do much to preserve its rate structure if it makes any rate increases for union personnel or blue-collar workers applicable to other groups of personnel that comprise its payroll.

---

[24] For a more detailed discussion of the problem, read Sami M. Kassem, "The Salary Compression Problem," *Personnel Journal,* Vol. 50, No. 4 (April, 1971), pp. 313-317.

Compensation of Government Employees. The method of compensating employees in governmental jurisdictions basically is the same as it is in private enterprise. Job evaluation is utilized commonly in government to determine the relative worth of jobs. Wage surveys—at least those covering key jobs—usually are included in the wage determination process. Most wage structures in government provide for salary ranges that overlap between adjoining wage classes. The typical salary range consists of five or six steps within a wage class and is about 5 percent greater than the range for the preceding class.

In the past, unions and other employee organizations have not exercised a significant influence upon wage determination. Since the 1960s, however, when the unionization of government employees grew rapidly, more states have been passing legislation permitting employee organizations to "meet and confer," or even to engage in collective bargaining with government officials at the state and local levels to determine wages and other conditions of employment.[25]

Unlike the private sector, production incentive systems are rarely used in government and year-end bonuses are unknown. Automatic cost-of-living adjustments have been installed in some jurisdictions with mixed success. Some of the additional forms of pay available to government workers have included longevity pay (particularly after a number of years at the top of a wage range) and payment for unused sick leave either in the form of added vacation time or as credit toward retirement.[26]

Federal government employees are divided into two broad groups for compensation purposes: *General Service* (G.S.) employees and *Wage Board* (W.B.) employees. The salary structure for G.S. employees is divided into 18 grades, the rates for which the government endeavors to keep in line with those for the same kind and level of work in the private sector. The Wage Board employees are for the most part in the skilled trades. Their wage rates are adjusted periodically by federal wage boards in each locality to reflect the prevailing rates for similar work, which in turn are influenced heavily by local union agreements.[27]

GOVERNMENT REGULATION OF WAGE PAYMENTS

Since the 1930s wage and salary administration, like the other areas of personnel management, has become the subject of many laws enacted by the states and by the federal government. These laws cover such subjects as minimum wage rates, overtime premiums, restrictions on child labor, methods of computing and disbursing wage payments, tax withholdings, and payroll records. During World War II and the Korean War, and again in late 1971, regulations were put into effect freezing existing wage rates and restricting the wage increases that could be granted to employees.

---

[25] Kenneth O. Warner and Keith Ocheltree, "Designing Compensation Programs for Public Employees," in Milton L. Rock (editor), *Handbook of Wage and Salary Administration* (New York: McGraw-Hill Book Company, 1972), pp. 8-36—8-37.

[26] *Ibid.*, pp. 8-42—8-43.

[27] *Ibid.*, pp. 8-37—8-38.

The three principal federal laws affecting wages are the Fair Labor Standards Act, the Walsh-Healy Act, and the Davis-Bacon Act. These laws were enacted during the 1930s to prevent the payment of abnormally low wage rates and to encourage the spreading of work among a greater number of workers. The latter objective was accomplished by forcing companies to pay a premium rate for overtime work, that is, for all hours worked in excess of a prescribed number. This federal wage legislation with certain amendments has continued to exert an important influence upon wage policies and practices.

Fair Labor Standards Act

The Fair Labor Standards Act (FLSA), which is commonly referred to as the Wage and Hour Act, was passed in 1938 and subsequently has been amended many times. It covers those employees who are engaged in the production of goods for interstate and foreign commerce, including those whose work is closely related to or directly essential to such production. The act's coverage also includes employees of certain retail and service establishments whose sales volumes exceed a prescribed amount and, most recently, agricultural workers. The major provisions of the FLSA are concerned with minimum wage rates and overtime payments, child labor, and equal rights.[28]

Wage and Hour Provisions. The minimum wage prescribed by the law has been raised many times from its original figure of 25 cents per hour to the rate of $2.30 per hour effective in 1976. This minimum rate applies to the actual earning rate before any overtime premiums have been added, but it may include the reasonable cost of any facilities that are furnished, such as lodging.

An overtime rate of one and a half times the base rate must be paid for all hours worked in excess of 40 during a given week. The base wage rate from which the overtime rate is computed must include incentive payments or bonuses that are received during the period. For example, if a person who is employed at a stated rate of $3 an hour works a total of 45 hours in a given week and receives a bonus of $45, that person is actually working at the rate of $4 an hour. (The $45.00 bonus divided by the 45 hours required to earn it equals $1.00 per hour which, when added to the regular pay rate of $3.00 per hour, brings the employee's earning rate to $4.00 per hour for the week.) Total earnings for the week would amount to $190.00 computed as follows:

Regular time	40 × $4.00	= $160.00
Overtime	5 × $6.00	= 30.00
Total		= $190.00

If the bonus is paid on a monthly or quarterly basis, earnings for the period must be recalculated to include this bonus in the hourly rate for overtime

[28] Because the act is likely to be subject to future amendments, an employer should consult the appropriate publications of the labor services previously mentioned or the Wage and Hour Division of the United States Department of Labor in order to obtain the latest information regarding its provisions, particularly the minimum wage rate.

payments. If employees are given time off in return for overtime work, it must be granted at 1½ times the number of hours that were worked as overtime.

The fact that employees are paid on a piece-rate basis does not exempt the employer from paying a premium for overtime work. Employees still must be paid overtime based upon rates that are computed by dividing earnings from piecework by the total number of hours of work required to earn this amount. For example, if an employee produced 1,250 units of work at 10 cents per unit during a 50-hour week, the earning rate would be $2.50 per hour computed as follows:

$$\frac{1{,}250 \text{ units} \times 10¢}{50 \text{ hours}} = \$2.50 \text{ per hour}$$

Since the 10 hours in excess of a 40-hour week constitute overtime, total earnings for the week would be $137.50 computed as follows:

Regular time	40 × $2.50 =	$100.00
Overtime	10 × $3.75 =	37.50
Total		$137.50

Under the FLSA, employee wage payments must include credit for the proper amount of the working time. This time may include periods when employees are not engaged in actual production activities, such as when waiting for repairs, for work to arrive, or for loading and unloading operations to be accomplished. Employees must also be paid for the time consumed by rest periods, trips to the washroom, required travel during the workday, short meal periods, fire drills, compulsory physical examinations, or medical treatment of job injuries. In counting the number of hours worked by employees, credit also must be given for any time required to be spent outside of normal working hours in order to hold their jobs or achieve advancements.

Child Labor Provisions. The FLSA forbids the employment of minors between 16 and 18 years of age in hazardous occupations, such as mining, logging, woodworking, meat-packing, and certain types of manufacturing. Minors under 16 cannot be employed in any work destined for interstate commerce except that which is performed in a nonhazardous occupation for a parent or guardian or for an employer under a temporary permit issued by the Department of Labor.

The feature of the FLSA that perhaps creates the most confusion concerns the exemption of certain groups of employees from coverage by the act or from certain of its provisions. The act now provides more than 40 separate exemptions, some of which apply only to a certain group of personnel or to certain provisions of the act such as those relating to child labor or to overtime.[29]

[29] Many employers find the major labor reference services such as those published by The Bureau of National Affairs, Inc., by Prentice-Hall, Inc., and by the Commerce Clearing House to be helpful sources of information concerning these exemptions and other provisions of the act.

Equal Rights Provisions. One of the most significant amendments to the FLSA was the Equal Pay Act passed in 1963. This act states:

> No employer shall discriminate between employees on the basis of sex by paying wages to employees less than the rate at which he pays wages to employees of the opposite sex for equal work on jobs which require equal *skill, effort,* and *responsibility,* and *similar working conditions.*

The federal Age Discrimination Act of 1967 extends the equal rights provisions by forbidding wage discrimination based upon age for employees in the 40 to 65 age group. Neither of these acts, however, prohibits wage differentials based on factors other than age or sex such as seniority, merit, or a measure of performance.

In spite of the Equal Pay Act, the achievement of parity by women in the labor market has been slow in coming. One study conducted in the early 1970s indicated, for example, that women on the average were earning $3,458 less per year than their male counterparts doing the same work.[30] On the other hand, as a result of legal suits initiated under the Equal Pay Act, many women have succeeded not only in gaining levels of pay equal to those received by men performing the same job but also in obtaining a reimbursement with interest for the amounts they have been underpaid during the two-year period preceding their suits. Moreover, according to Department of Labor estimates, back pay claims awarded to women during the fiscal year ending in 1972 totaled about $18 million. This figure is likely to continue to become larger each year until there is greater compliance with the Equal Pay Act.[31]

Walsh-Healy Act

The Walsh-Healy Act, which is officially called the Public Contracts Act, was passed in 1936 and covers workers employed on government contract work for supplies, equipment, and materials in excess of $10,000. The act requires contractors to pay employees at least the prevailing wage rates established by the Secretary of Labor for the area and overtime of 1½ times the regular rate for all work performed in excess of 8 hours in one day or 40 hours in one week, depending upon whichever basis provides the larger premium. For example, an employee working 4 days of 12 hours each during a given week would be entitled to receive 16 hours of overtime and 32 hours of regular time for the week. In computing overtime payments under the Walsh-Healy Act, as under the FLSA, the wage rate used must include any bonuses or incentive payments that may be a part of the employee's total earnings. The Walsh-Healy Act also contains restrictions covering the use of child and convict labor.

---

[30] Teresa E. Levitin, Robert P. Quinn, and Graham L. Staines, "A Woman Is 58% of a Man," *Psychology Today* (March, 1973), p. 90.

[31] "Flexing a Muscle—Women, Government, Unions Increasingly Sue Under Equal Pay Act," *The Wall Street Journal,* August 22, 1971.

Davis-Bacon Act

The Davis-Bacon Act, which is also referred to as the Prevailing Wage Law, was passed in 1931 and is the oldest of the three federal wage laws. It requires that the minimum wage rates paid to persons employed on federal public works projects worth more than $2,000 be at least equal to the prevailing rates and that overtime be paid at 1½ times this rate.

Résumé

Wage and salary administration is an extremely important function of personnel management because of its far-reaching effects, not only upon employees and their performance but also upon the employer's cost of operation and upon the economy of the community. For employees wages are important because they constitute both a financial and a psychological return from their work. Because wages serve to determine their relative worth within the organization as well as their standard of living in society, employees tend to be sensitive about the amount they are being paid as compared to what others are being paid for their work. It is essential, therefore, that the wages of employees be determined on an objective basis that will insure them equitable treatment and enable them to recognize this fact.

Several systems have been developed, including the point, factor comparison, classification, and ranking systems, by which the relative worth of jobs may be measured objectively for purposes of wage determination. Data pertaining to the evaluated worth of each job, when combined with that obtained from wage surveys and other sources, provide the basis for a wage structure into which these jobs may be classified. This structure may establish a rate range for each of the job classes in order to provide rate increases for employees in their jobs on the basis of either merit or seniority, or both. In organizations that are unionized, the type of wage structure as well as the rates that are established for each job will be determined to a large extent by collective bargaining. In such instances job evaluation will serve largely as an aid to bargaining and financial control for the employer. Whether or not they are unionized, employers must also take cognizance of such factors as the prevailing wage laws, condition of the labor market, trends in living costs, and economic conditions when determining the amount to be paid for each job. Moreover, decisions relating to these wage payments must be guided by established wage payment policies and procedures that will insure consistent and equitable treatment for each employee.

DISCUSSION QUESTIONS

1. What is the equity theory and how does it relate to wages and salary administration?
2. Why is it that many jobs requiring a college degree pay less money than some of those which require only a high school diploma and a minimal amount of training?
3. Should the Consumer Price Index be changed to reflect the spending patterns of pensioners

and professional workers as well as the wage earner? Since pensioners as a group have much lower incomes than wage earners, would it not be beneficial to the wage earners if the former group was included in the CPI population base? Explain.

4. During collective bargaining, unions sometimes have responded to a company claim of inability to pay with the statement that the union should not be expected to subsidize inefficient management. To what extent do you feel that a union response of this type has or does not have merit?

5. Since employees may differ in terms of their job performance, would it not be more feasible to determine the wage rate for each employee on the basis of his or her relative worth? Comment on the advantage or disadvantages of this system.

6. Why do union leaders as a group tend to look upon job evaluation systems with disfavor?

7. One of the objections to granting wage increases on a percentage basis is that the lower paid employees who are having the most trouble ''making ends meet'' get the least increase while the highest paid get the largest increase. Is this objection a valid one?

8. How do compensation plans for employees in government tend to differ from those for employees in the private sector?

9. An employee covered by the FLSA earns $4.00 per hour, works 50 hours during a given week, and receives a production bonus of $10.00. What are the gross earnings for the week?

PROBLEM 19-1 PAID INITIATIVE?

Among the products manufactured by the Jupiter Electronics Company were electronic equipment testing consoles. During the production of an order for one particular model, it became necessary to make certain modifications in its electrical circuits. While it was the normal procedure for blueprints to be prepared first for the technicians to follow, the urgent need to meet a delivery deadline made it necessary to proceed with the console modifications without the benefit of the blueprints. The nature of the modifications desired was explained to the technicians by their supervisor who expressed confidence in their ability to utilize their talent and initiative in getting the job done. The ten technicians working on the project accepted the assignment as a challenge and were able to complete the order within the established deadline, thus saving the company from being forced to pay a penalty that otherwise would have resulted from a delay in the delivery.

About a week after the completion of the modifications project, however, the technicians who worked on the project filed a grievance through their union demanding that their jobs be reclassified to the next higher grade and that the reclassification be retroactive to the time that they began work on the project. In support of their grievance the technicians called attention to the fact that their job description called only for an ability to do work with the aid of blueprints. In being required to work without the aid of blueprints and to utilize their initiative in making the modifications, the technicians maintained that they were doing the work of junior engineers, the next higher grade.

a. Should the company accede to the technicians' demands?
b. What are the implications of this case from the standpoint of job descriptions? What are the implications with respect to employee training?
c. How do you account for the fact that the employees filed a grievance when they had willingly accepted the additional responsibilities at the time the job was assigned?

SUGGESTED READINGS

Baumback, Clifford. *Structural Issues in Collective Bargaining*. Lexington, Mass.: Heath Lexington Books, 1971.

Belcher, David W. *Wage and Salary Administration*, 2d ed. Englewood Cliffs, New Jersey: Prentice-Hall, Inc., 1962. Chapters 1-6, 12, 13.

Benge, Eugene J., Samuel L. H. Burk, and Edward N. Hay. *Manual of Job Evaluation*. New York: Harper & Brothers, 1941.

Bird, Caroline. *Everything a Woman Needs to Know to Get Paid What She's Worth*. New York: David McKay Company, Inc., 1973.

Burgess, Leonard R. *Wage and Salary Administration in a Dynamic Economy*. New York: Harcourt, Brace & World, Inc., 1968.

Jaques, E. *Measurement of Responsibility: A Study of Work Payment and Individual Capacity*. New York: Halsted Press, 1972.

Lanham, Elizabeth. *Administration of Wages and Salaries*. New York: Harper & Row, Publishers, 1963. Pp. 1-106.

Moore, Russell F. (ed). *Compensating Executive Worth*. New York: American Management Association, 1968.

Nash, Allan N., and Stephen J. Carroll, Jr. *The Management of Compensation*. Monterey, California: Brooks/Cole Publishing Company, 1975.

Patton, John A., C. L. Littlefield, and Stanley A. Self. *Job Evaluation, Text and Cases*, 3d ed. Homewood, Illinois: Richard D. Irwin, Inc., 1964.

Porter, Lyman W., Edward E. Lawler III, and J. Richard Hackman. *Behavior in Organizations*. New York: McGraw-Hill Book Company, 1975. Chapter 12.

Position-Classification in the Public Service. Chicago, Illinois: Public Personnel Association.

Rock, Milton L. (ed.). *Handbook of Wage and Salary Administration*. New York: McGraw-Hill Book Company, 1972.

U.S. Department of Labor. *Postwar Trends in Labor Compensation*. Washington, D.C.: U.S. Government Printing Office, 1967.

Worldwide Executive Compensation. New York: Business International, 1967.

Zollitsch, Herbert G., and Adolph Langsner. *Wage and Salary Administration*, 2d ed. Cincinnati: South-Western Publishing Co., 1970.

Financial Incentives

The preceding chapter emphasized how important it is to compensate employees on a consistent and equitable basis. Most organizations, it will be recalled, attempt to do so by developing a wage structure through which the pay of each employee can be related to the relative worth of his or her job and to the other factors that may serve to determine the wage rate for the job. Above-average performance in the job is then recognized by raising the employees' rate of pay within the established rate range, if one exists, or by promoting them to higher paying jobs. Unfortunately under this method certain delays occur between the times that these rewards are deserved and the times that they are granted. Furthermore, because seniority is often a major factor in their determination, raises and promotions in actual practice may provide employees with very little incentive to improve job input or performance.

In an effort to relate the financial rewards or outcomes of the employee more tangibly and directly to performance, various types of financial incentive systems have been developed by management, primarily in the private sector. When utilized properly, financial incentives can provide employees with a source of motivation, the cost of which can be more than offset by improvements in productivity and cooperation.

THE FUNCTION OF FINANCIAL INCENTIVES

Financial incentive plans generally existed before there were job evaluation and fringe benefit plans. Whereas the latter plans have become the subject of increasing attention, financial incentive plans, at least for jobs below the management level, have been declining in importance. This decline has been due in a large measure to the problems encountered by many organizations with financial incentives, particularly for hourly workers. These problems generally result not from the fact that financial incentives as such are not feasible or beneficial but rather from the improper use and administration of incentives. Management frequently has failed to understand fully how money functions as a motivator and how it relates to other forms of motivation including leadership.[1]

In spite of certain unsatisfactory or discouraging experiences with them, financial incentives have something to offer if both their shortcomings and their requirements for success are recognized. Furthermore, money still is valued strongly by most individuals in an organization because it can serve to satisfy both their psychological and economic needs. The major problem in any incentive system, therefore, is one of relating increases in incentive payments to the improvements in the behavior and performance being sought from employees and of making them fully aware of such relationships.

Origin of Incentive Systems

The scientific management movement gave rise to financial incentive systems by providing objective performance standards through which employee output could be measured and rewarded. Frederick W. Taylor and his contemporaries in the movement believed that employees would exert greater effort if they were paid a financial incentive based upon the number of units of work they produced. Taylor developed a type of incentive plan called the *differential piece rate* whereby employees were paid at one piece rate if they produced less than the standard amount of output and at a higher piece rate if their output exceeded this standard. This plan thus stimulated employees to achieve or to exceed established standards of production. Taylor's incentive system was followed by a variety of financial incentive plans which bore the names of such leaders in management as Gantt, Emerson, Halsey, Rowan, and Bedeaux. While the plans varied somewhat in terms of the system that was used to calculate the incentive payments, they all attempted to relate employee wages more closely to their productivity. These attempts were directed toward the development of not only more accurate standards and measures of performance but also more effective formulas for computing incentive payments.

Factors Influencing Reactions to Incentives

The motivational value to be derived from financial incentives will be affected by one or more of the different factors discussed below.

Economic Factors. Some employees have a greater need to earn more money than others and therefore will make the effort and the sacrifices that are

[1] Edward E. Lawler, III, "The Mythology of Management Compensation," *California Management Review,* Vol. IX, No. 1 (Fall, 1966), pp. 11-22.

required to earn it. The amount of the payment the employee may be able to earn will also affect its incentive value. An incentive system would be more likely to offer a greater inducement if it enabled employees to double their income rather than to increase it, say, by 25 percent. Its incentive value also would be greater if there were a reasonable probability, such as one chance in two, of earning the incentive. If the probability is too high or too low, the inducement it provides for most employees to work harder generally is reduced.[2]

Employees also may differ in terms of their reaction to delays in the payment of the incentive. Generally, for employees in the lower socioeconomic levels, the sooner the incentive is paid to them, the greater the motivational effect it will have upon them. For them the incentive comes from having the money to spend *soon*. Furthermore, those in the lower wage groups have more immediate need for the money, and its incentive value for them may be diminished if the payment is deferred for too long a period. By way of contrast, managers and professional employees who earn at a higher level usually are better able to accept the deferment of their wages and can be motivated by the fact that incentive money is accruing to their accounts. It should be recognized, however, that even members of this latter group may derive a greater incentive from cash than from deferred payments during that period of life when the financial obligations involved in raising a family are at a peak.

Psychological Factors. Since financial incentives also serve to satisfy psychological needs, the influence they may have upon a particular employee will be affected by the priority that person attaches to each of the various basic needs that were discussed in Chapter 11. Because money in our society is considered to be one of the measures of achievement, its value as a motivator will be governed by the extent to which it satisfies an employee's need for recognition, for self-realization, and for other forms of achievement.

The need for group acceptance may discourage some employees from earning too much incentive pay if it incurs the disapproval of others. An employees's reaction to incentives thus may be influenced by the attitudes and reaction of the group in which he or she works, which in turn may be dominated by the informal leaders within the group. If the group favors competition among members and stimulates their desire to earn higher wages, then financial incentives are more likely to prove successful. However, if the group informally establishes certain production limits or "bogeys" which members are under pressure to observe, a financial incentive system may do relatively little to stimulate increased production.

Group pressures to hold the rate of production within established limits may be prompted by the fear of its members that their incentive rates will be reduced or that they will work themselves out of a job if they produce at their maximum capacities. Another cause for pressures to control production rates may be the fear of the less efficient members that they will be placed in an

[2] David C. McClelland, "Money as a Motivator: Some Research Insights," *The McKinsey Quarterly* (Fall, 1967), pp. 17-18.

unfavorable light by the more productive "pacesetters" or "rate busters." The latter group may be subjected to the "silent treatment" or to various forms of embarrassment and abuse. A situation like this can be very effective in discouraging their desire to earn more incentive pay.

Requirements for a Successful System

The success of any incentive system must be judged in terms of its total impact upon the organization. Thus, increases in production generated by incentives may be at the expense of higher operating costs, lower quality, decreased employee cooperation, or a combination of these factors. It is essential, therefore, for the total effects of an incentive system to be recognized so that it can be tailored to the specific objectives that the organization is seeking to achieve.

Confidence in Management. A financial incentive system will be more likely to succeed if there is a favorable climate and an effective personnel program which has the support of management at all levels. Employees who have faith and trust in the integrity of management are more likely to view an incentive system as serving rather than jeopardizing their best interests. If they lack confidence in management, they may regard an incentive system as a device for gaining more effort from them in return for less money.

Positive Relationship Between Incentive Payment and Job Input. The concept of equity discussed in the previous chapter applies to financial incentives. Employees must be able to perceive a positive relationship between the outcome they receive in the form of incentive payments and their job input. Such perception, however, is contingent upon the existence of standards by which performance may be judged and upon a clear knowledge on the part of employees as to what constitutes acceptable performance. Commitment on the part of employees to achieve this performance is essential for effective motivation and requires mutual understanding and confidence between employees and their supervisors, which in turn requires open channels of two-way communication.[3] Incentive payments must never become a guarantee that bears little relationship to input but, rather, they should be a reward that always must be earned. The larger the financial rewards, the sooner they are paid; and the more objectively they are related to performance and behavior, the more equitably they are likely to be perceived by employees. The equity of incentive wages also will be more recognizable if the payment of them is separate from the regular paycheck.

---

[3] A. W. Charles, "Theory Y Compensation," *Personnel Journal,* Vol. 52, No. 1 (January, 1973), pp. 12-18, as reprinted in Herbert J. Chruden and Arthur W. Sherman, Jr., *Readings in Personnel Management,* (4th ed.; Cincinnati, Ohio: South-Western Publishing Co., 1976), pp. 439-449.

Managerial Problems Created by Incentives

A financial incentive system also can be a source of new problems. First of all, certain grievances and labor disputes may arise. When an incentive program is installed, employees may challenge those standards, measures, and performance records as well as company policies and practices that relate to efficiency and to their incentive pay.

Another managerial problem is created by the fact that a financial incentive program places management in the position of being obliged to provide and maintain facilities that will enable employees to earn incentive payments consistent with their efforts. Any deficiencies that exist with regard to these facilities or to the management of them will be recognized and quickly become the subject of complaint.[4] If not corrected promptly, such deficiencies can have an adverse effect upon employee efficiency and morale.

A financial incentive program, moreover, is likely to create an additional cost of maintaining with accuracy those records that are necessary to administer the program. It will also require that management devote more attention to communication since the motivational value to be derived from incentives will be contingent upon the ability of employees to associate their contributions with the incentive payments that they receive. If a complicated financial incentive system is used, the task of educating and keeping employees informed about its operations can be substantial. In this regard one management consultant concludes that "top management too often wants to establish a pay plan in the terms it understands rather than the terms the worker understands."[5]

INCENTIVE PLANS FOR PRODUCTION PERSONNEL

Financial incentive systems for production personnel may provide that the incentive payment constitute their entire wages or that it be merely a supplement to their regular wages. The amount of the incentive payment may be related directly to the number of units produced (as in the case of piecework), to the achievement of established quotas or goals (as in the case of bonuses), or be based upon improvements in company efficiency or profit records (as in the case of profit sharing and committee participation plans).

Piecework Systems

Under the straight *piecework system* wage payments are determined by multiplying the number of units produced by the piece rate for one unit, as expressed by the following formula:

---

[4] Wilfred Brown, *Piecework Abandoned* (London: Heinemann, 1962), p. 10.

[5] "Tips on Effective Incentive Systems," *Steel* (August 10, 1964), as reprinted in *Management Review,* Vol. 53, No. 10 (October, 1964), pp. 69-70.

N	×	U	=	W
(Number of Units)	×	(Unit Rate)	=	(Wages)

The piecework system can provide maximum financial motivation for employees, particularly for those individuals who have a strong desire to increase their earnings, because the amount of wages that they receive is directly proportionate to their output. The wage payment for each individual is simple to compute, and the plan will permit a company to predict its labor costs with considerable accuracy since these costs are the same for each unit of output. The piecework system is more likely to be successful when units of output can be measured readily, when the quality of the product is less critical, when the job is fairly standardized, and when a constant flow of work can be maintained.[6] Employees normally are not paid for the time that they are idle unless the idleness is due to conditions for which the company is responsible, such as delays in work flow, defective materials, inoperative equipment, or power failures. In the case of delays of this type, employees are paid a ''down time'' allowance for the idle period that is equal to what their average piece-rate earnings would otherwise have been for the period.

Declining Use of Piecework. In spite of its incentive value, piecework is not nearly as prevalent in industry as is daywork, and its usage is declining. One reason for this fact is that production standards upon which piecework must be based can be difficult to develop for many types of jobs. In some instances the cost of determining and maintaining this standard may exceed the benefits to be gained from piecework. Jobs in which individual contributions are difficult to distinguish or measure, or in which the work is mechanized to the point that the individual exercises very little control over output, also may be unsuited to the use of piecework, as may be those jobs in which employees are learning the work or in which high standards of quality are of paramount importance.

In his book describing the Glacier Project (conducted over a 15-year period at the Glacier Metal Co. Ltd. during which time piecework was being abandoned), Wilfred Brown concluded that the system tended to stimulate envy and greed. While he concedes that piecework stimulates a systematic study of work and the exposure of production problems as well as encourages inventiveness on the part of the operators working under it, he did not find that it causes people to work faster. He also concludes that piecework does not result in greater output or concentration on the work being performed but, rather, causes pressure to be exerted on the piece rate that results in the loosening of time standards.[7]

Employee and Union Reactions to Piecework. Deep-seated suspicion and resentment on the part of certain groups of employees and labor organizations toward piecework is another factor that has restricted its usage. There is still an underlying fear among some union leaders that management will use piecework

---

[6] David W. Belcher, *Wage and Salary Administration* (2d ed.; Englewood Cliffs, New Jersey: Prentice-Hall, Inc., 1962), pp. 384-385.

[7] Wilfred Brown, *op. cit.*, pp. 8-28.

or systems similar to it to achieve a *speed up* (gaining more production from the workers for the same amount of money). Another fear is that the system may induce employees to compete against each other and thereby cause a loss of jobs for those who are revealed to be less productive. Some leaders, furthermore, believe that the system will cause employees to work themselves out of a job or cause craft standards of workmanship to suffer.

In spite of opposition by some unions, piecework has had a history of success in the garment, leathergoods, and cigar-making industries where it has been used to the mutual benefit and satisfaction of management and the union. It should not be assumed, therefore, that union leaders as a group are opposed to the use of piecework. If the union has confidence in and a good working relationship with management and if it feels that its members stand to gain from the system, it will accept piecework.

Production Bonus Systems

Under a *bonus system* incentive payments, as indicated by Figure 20-1, are supplementary to the basic wage. This system has the advantage of providing employees with more pay for exerting greater effort while, at the same time, providing them the security of a basic wage. A bonus payment may be based

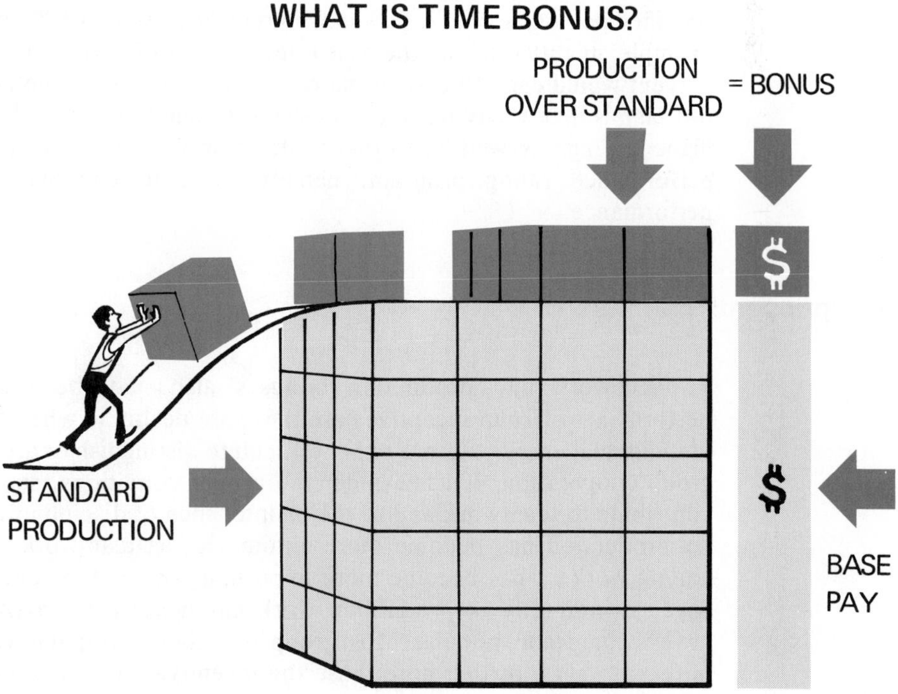

WHAT IS TIME BONUS?
PRODUCTION OVER STANDARD = BONUS
STANDARD PRODUCTION
BASE PAY

upon the number of units that an individual or a group produces, as in the case of piecework. Thus, under a bonus system an employee who is paid at the rate of $3 an hour plus a bonus of 10 cents per unit would receive $34 in wages for producing 100 units during an 8-hour period as computed below.

(Hours	×	Time Rate)	+	(Number of Units	×	Unit Rate)	=	Wages
(8	×	$3)	+	(100	×	10¢)	=	$34

Bonuses also may be based upon the amount of time that an employee is able to save in completing a task as compared with the standard time established for it. For example, if one-half hour has been established as the standard time required to complete one unit of production, an employee who is able to complete 20 units during an 8-hour day will accomplish the equivalent of 10 hours of work during an 8-hour period. In this type of situation, plans such as the *100 Percent Premium Plan* permit the employee to receive the entire two-hour savings as a bonus. Under other plans, such as the *Halsey Plan,* the employee may receive only a portion of the two-hour savings as a bonus. The theory behind this latter practice is that the time which an employee saves is due in part to those persons who contribute indirectly to production.

Some wage incentive plans give consideration to factors other than output alone. One such plan is the *measured day plan* which permits employees to earn a bonus based upon the amount that their merit rating scores exceed a specified percent score. A person who receives a score of 70 percent or less, for example, might earn only the base rate; whereas one who receives a score of 80 percent would earn 10 percent more than the base rate. The main weakness of this plan is that it may place the supervisor under considerable pressure to give higher ratings as well as to divert attention from the primary objective of a performance rating program, namely, to help employees improve their performance.

Group Incentive Plans

Piecework and production bonuses also may be based upon group performance. Group incentives are the more desirable when the contributions of individual employees are either difficult to distinguish or are contingent upon group cooperation. If used under the proper conditions, such incentives can contribute to teamwork and to the maintenance of discipline within the group. As production has become more automated, as teamwork and coordination among workers has become more important, and as the contribution of those engaged indirectly in production work has increased, group incentive plans have become more popular. Most group incentive plans that have been developed in recent years, furthermore, base the incentive payments on such factors as improvement in company profits or efficiency or upon reductions in labor costs. These plans, in contrast with those based solely upon output, can motivate employees for the total aspect of their contributions on the job.

Standards for Production Incentives

The success of incentive systems for production work is contingent upon the development of accurate work standards. These standards are essential not only in order to relate incentives to employee effort but also to maintain the confidence of employees in the system. If standards are set too "loose" (too low), the result may prove costly to management because employees are not required to put forth effort that is commensurate with the income they receive. Loose standards, moreover, are difficult to tighten without creating a loss of employee morale and cooperation. Standards that are set too "tight" (too high), on the other hand, may limit the employees' opportunities to earn incentive wages and provide them with very little inducement to work harder. Such standards also may become a source of grievances and ill will.

Determining Time Standards. One of the most common methods for determining time standards is making actual time measurements of the work being performed by means of a stop watch. The observed time that has been recorded then must be *leveled* to allow for the degree of skill and effort being exerted by the worker. For example, if the person being timed were judged to be working faster and more efficiently than is required to maintain an average work pace, the observed time for completing a work cycle would be increased by an appropriate amount of time. Conversely, if the person studied were judged to be working slower or less efficiently than what is considered normal, the observed time for completing a work cycle would be reduced accordingly. The figure that is achieved after the observed time for a work cycle is leveled thus represents the amount of time that is required for an employee of average skill and effort to complete the cycle while working at a normal pace.

After the observed time has been leveled, further allowances must be made for work interruptions that may be required for employees to care for personal needs, to service equipment, or to wait for additional work to arrive. The time figure that is obtained after making these adjustments constitutes the standard time required to perform the task being observed.

Computing the Incentive Wage Rate. Although time standards establish the amount of time required to perform a given amount of work, they do not by themselves determine what the incentive rate should be. The incentive rates must be based upon hourly wage rates that would otherwise be paid for the type of work being performed under the incentive system. If, for example, the standard time for producing one unit of work in a job paying $4.50 per hour were computed to be 10 minutes, the piece rate would be 75 cents per unit. This piece rate is computed as follows:

$$\frac{60 \text{ (Minutes per Hour)}}{10 \text{ (Standard Time per Unit)}} = 6 \text{ Units per Hour}$$

$$\frac{\$4.50 \text{ (Hourly Rate)}}{6 \text{ (Units per Hour)}} = 75¢ \text{ per Unit}$$

INCENTIVES FOR WHITE-COLLAR PERSONNEL

While the use of the piece rates, production bonuses, and other incentive systems in production jobs is declining, the use of incentive systems covering other groups of personnel is not. Financial incentives in the form of commissions and bonuses for sales personnel, for example, continue to be used extensively. Various types of bonuses also continue to be an important part of compensation systems for executive and professional personnel.

Incentives for Sales Personnel

The enthusiasm and drive that must be exerted in most types of sales work require that salespeople be highly motivated. This, in part, explains why financial incentives are utilized widely in this area. Motivation is particularly important for outside salespeople who cannot be supervised closely and, as a result, must exercise a high degree of self-discipline. Incentive systems for salespeople are made complicated by the wide differences in the nature of sales which may range from order-taking by a person on a route to providing technical consultation and services by a sales engineer. Depending on the nature of the job, a salesperson's performance may be measured not only by the dollar volume of sales but also by the ability to gain new accounts, to promote new products or services, or to provide various forms of service and assistance to customers which do not produce sales revenues immediately.

Like those for other groups of workers, incentive systems for salespeople in themselves do not provide the solution to motivation. To be successful, incentives for them must have an organizational climate that enlists employee acceptance and trust. Also required are accurate performance standards upon which incentives can be based and in which salespeople have confidence. A financial incentive system which fails to satisfy these requirements may create more problems than it is worth.

Problems Relating to Sales Incentives. The development of financial incentives for salespeople is difficult since their performance often is affected by external influences beyond their ability to control. Economic and seasonal conditions, sales competition, and changes in customer demands are among the external forces that can affect the dollar volume of their sales. Sales volume, therefore, may not serve as an accurate indicator of the effort they have expended. In developing incentive systems for salespeople, employers are confronted with the problem of how to reward extra sales effort and at the same time compensate salespeople for activities that do not contribute directly or immediately to sales achievement. Employers also have the problem of providing some degree of income stability for them.

Types of Compensation Systems. Compensation systems for sales personnel include primarily the *straight commission,* the *straight salary,* and the *combination salary and incentive bonus* plans. According to a survey of 200 companies conducted by the National Industrial Conference Board, the trend is toward the use of combination plans involving a fixed salary plus an incentive commission or bonus. This survey disclosed that among the companies participating only 3 percent were using the straight commission and only 14 percent a straight salary; whereas 83 percent were using a combination of salary plus an incentive.[8] In another study of 444 manufacturers, the combination plan was found to be the one most commonly used although by a smaller percentage of companies. The results of this study revealed that 9 percent of the companies were using the straight commission, 26 percent the straight salary, and 65 percent the combination salary plus an incentive.[9]

Disadvantages of the Straight Commission Plan. Although the straight commission does provide maximum incentive and is easy to compute and understand, its comparative lack of popularity is perhaps explained best by the following disadvantages cited by Smyth and Murphy:

1. Emphasis is on sales volume rather than on profits (except in those rare cases where the commission rate is a percentage of the profit on the sale).
2. Salespeople are too independent of the company and have very little feeling of company loyalty.
3. Territories tend to be milked rather than worked.
4. It is difficult to get missionary work and special selling tasks performed.
5. Customer service after the sale is likely to be neglected.
6. Earnings are often excessive in good business periods.
7. Earnings tend to fluctuate widely between good and poor business periods, and turnover of trained sales personnel tends to increase in periods of poor business.
8. Salespeople are tempted to grant price concessions.
9. Salespeople are tempted to overload their customers with inventory.[10]

Advantages of the Combination Plan. By way of contrast, Smyth and Murphy cite the following advantages for the combination plan which indicate why it is utilized so widely:

1. The right kind of incentive compensation, if linked to salary in the right proportion, has most of the advantages of both the straight salary and the straight commission forms of compensation.
2. A salary-plus-incentive compensation plan offers great design flexibility and therefore can be more readily designed to help maximize company profits.
3. The plan can develop the most favorable ratio of selling expense to sales.
4. The field sales force can be motivated to achieve specific company marketing objectives in addition to sales volume.[11]

---

[8] David A. Weeks, *Incentive Plan for Salesmen,* Studies in Personnel Policy, No. 217 (New York: National Industrial Conference Board, 1970), p. 3.

[9] Reprinted by permission of the publisher from Richard C. Smyth and Matthew J. Murphy, *Compensating and Motivating Salesmen* (New York: American Management Association, © 1969), p. 2.

[10] *Ibid.,* p. 22.

[11] *Ibid.,* p. 24.

Incentives for Executive Personnel

Financial incentives for executive personnel are confined largely to the private sector and are utilized more in some industries than in others. They are used extensively in what have been referred to as *natural incentive industries* which include the appliance, office equipment, textile, chemical, and pharmaceutical industries. Conversely, in the past relatively few incentive plans have been found among the *marginal incentive industries* which include public utilities, banking, mining, railroads, and life insurance.[12]

Differences Between Natural Incentive and Marginal Incentive Industries. According to Patton, the natural incentive industries tend to be those in which numerous short-term decisions influencing profit are made, the results of which can be judged within a year. Individuals rather than committees have full responsibility to make key decisions and their performance is measured against such criteria as budget variances and market-share data that can reflect the difficulty of accomplishing their objectives. Companies in these industries demand a great deal from their executive people and are not hesitant to remove the poor performer or to hire top people from the outside—a condition that serves to attract the more assertive person who is interested in self-development rather than in security.[13]

In the marginal incentive industries, by way of contrast, a few long-term decisions generally have the most important profit impact. In these industries it may take years to prove the profitability, for example, of a new mine, a new insurance policy package, or of a new banking system. Inter-functional support among departments as well as committee decisions are prevalent, and the focus of attention is on the performance of the whole organization rather than upon individual segments of it. Perhaps most significant, however, is the fact that executives within these industries are subject to a lower stress factor, and promotions from within are the byword and are influenced heavily by seniority. The resulting climate, therefore, according to Patton, serves to attract individuals who favor security over assertive self-advancement.[14] The operating conditions and the organizational climate that prevail within companies of these two groups of industries present a significant contrast that serves to explain the prevalence of financial incentives within the first industrial group and the absence of them in the latter.

Recent Developments in the Marginal Incentive Industries. There is some indication that conditions in the marginal incentive industries may be changing. Recently some companies in the insurance and banking fields have initiated incentive plans. Citicorp, one of the most innovative banks in America, was one of the first to move ahead of competitors by adopting a management

---

[12] Arch Patton, "Why Incentive Plans Fail," *Harvard Business Review,* Vol. 50, No. 3 (May-June, 1972), pp. 59-60.

[13] *Ibid.*

[14] *Ibid.*

incentive plan in 1973. It has been followed by Chase Manhattan Bank and the CNA Financial Corporation.[15] Aetna Life has been one of the first insurance companies to establish a financial incentive plan which may become a trend that others in the marginal incentive industries will follow.[16]

Objectives of Incentive Plans. Financial incentives for executives should serve to stimulate an enthusiasm for their work, a loyalty toward their company, and a motivation which enables them to utilize their energies and abilities fully in contributing to organizational objectives. Among the specific objectives to be achieved through incentive plans for executives are the improvement of profits and return on investment, the reduction of costs, the achievement of greater individual and group effort and cooperation among company units, and the realization of satisfactory organizational growth. Executive incentive plans, furthermore, must facilitate the recruitment of good executive talent and induce executive personnel to continue their professional growth and development. Above all, the plan should serve to encourage competent executives to remain with the company by providing them with opportunities to build an estate and to enjoy income tax advantages that they might otherwise experience as owners of a business. These principal goals of executive compensation have led to the development of a multitude of plans involving different methods of relating compensation to the contributions of executives. Many such plans contain provisions for deferring the payment of all or part of the incentive earnings until retirement and for the acquisition of stock in the company.

It is important, however, for executives who remain with the organization for a given period of time, such as five or more years, to acquire a vested right in their deferred compensation. This is the right to withdraw their deferred compensation should they quit before reaching retirement. Otherwise deferred plans may become what Crystal terms the "Golden Handcuffs" that force executives to remain, not because of choice, but rather because of their reluctance to forfeit the compensation they have accumulated.[17]

Decisions to be Resolved. The creation of an incentive system for executives requires a number of decisions to be resolved.

Determining Who Are Eligible. Probably the most basic decision, and one which can be exceedingly difficult to make, is that of determining which executives are to be included in the plan. Theoretically the plan should include those executives whose duties and responsibilities give them an opportunity to contribute substantially to the attainment of organizational goals. Because of overlapping responsibilities among executive positions, it can be difficult to determine exactly which executives should be included in the plan.[18]

---

[15] John C. Perkam, "Payoff in Performance Bonuses," *Dun's Review,* Vol. 103, No. 5 (May, 1974), p. 53.

[16] *Ibid.*

[17] Graef S. Crystal, *Financial Motivation for Executives* (New York: American Management Association, 1970), pp. 38-40.

[18] *Ibid.,* p. 129.

Although there are pressures in the case of nearly every incentive plan to expand the number of positions covered by it, this number preferably should be restricted to those positions that demonstrably contribute to company profits. According to Patton, when more than one percent of a company's total employment is included in an incentive program, the credibility of individual performance evaluations tends to suffer; therefore, ideally the optimum number should not exceed one half of one percent.[19]

Determining the Amount of Incentive Payments. As in the case of eligibility for participation, determining the amount of incentive payments often is based upon what the executive is considered to have contributed to the profits or to the return on investment realized by the company. Payments determined by a formula based either on a percentage of total profits or upon a percentage of profits in excess of a specific return on stockholders' investments are among those commonly found in incentive plans. Some plans also seek to adjust the payments to reflect a company's performance relative to the industry. In other instances the payments may be tied to an annual profit plan whereby the amount of incentive payments is determined by the extent to which an agreed-upon profit level is exceeded.[20] Payments also may be based upon the performance ratings or upon the achievement of specific objectives agreed upon between executives and the board of directors.

Incentives for executives, as for other personnel, should not be permitted to become a guarantee. Those executives whose performance is deserving should be able to receive up to the maximum reward and those who are less deserving should receive smaller rewards or even none at all. In order for rewards to have maximum motivational value, Crystal recommends that they range up to as high as 50 to 60 percent of an executive's regular salary. He also suggests that the amount of the bonuses be permitted to rise sharply as the company closes in on its objective so as to recognize the fact that the last increments of performance are the hardest to achieve and also the most profitable.[21]

Types of Incentive Plans. Since there is no one incentive plan that is suitable for all situations or for all executives, a number of different types of plans have evolved to meet the particular needs of different organizations and of their executives. These different plans enable organizations not only to achieve specific motivational objectives but also to provide the participants with the maximum tax shelter possible under current income tax regulations. While cash bonuses are an important part of executive compensation packages, also utilized are stock options, performance share plans, and self-designed pay plans.

Bonus Payments. Bonuses which are earned by executives in addition to their regular salary may be paid in cash or deferred until the executive has retired or otherwise terminated employment. A study by the National Industrial Conference Board indicated that the use of bonuses is quite prevalent

---

[19] Patton, *op. cit.*, p. 65.
[20] *Ibid.*, p. 62.
[21] Crystal, *op. cit.*, p. 128.

and on the increase in several groups of industries that were covered. Conducted among six major types of businesses, this study revealed that of the participating firms approximately two thirds of the manufacturing and one half of the retailing firms provided bonuses for their executives. In contrast, only 46 percent of the fire and casualty insurance companies, 23 percent of the banks, 16 percent of the life insurance companies, and 8 percent of the gas and electric utilities provided bonuses for their executives. In each of these industries, 50 to 70 percent of the plans provide for the entire bonus to be paid as soon as practical after the year in which it was earned.[22]

According to another study by McKinsey & Company, the *Tax Reform Act of 1969* which now limits the maximum income tax rate on earned income to 50 percent is helping to make the cash bonus more attractive to executives.[23] Cash payments, furthermore, have the advantage of providing immediate benefits to those executives who are at the period in life when financial obligations and their need for extra money are at a maximum. Deferred incentive systems, on the other hand, have the advantage of making it easier to accumulate funds for retirement. Furthermore, in the case of those deferred plans approved by the Internal Revenue Service, the personal income tax on incentive payments is postponed until they are withdrawn at retirement age, at which time the executive is likely to be in a lower income tax bracket.

Stock Options. A *stock option* is a right to purchase a specified amount of stock at a certain price within a stated period of time. The option price normally is less than the market price at the time that it is offered. The difference between the option price and the market price for the stock at any given time constitutes the value of the option. Although some company stock option plans permit supervisors and middle-level managers to participate, 10 percent of the companies included in one survey limit stock options to their top executives, and about 30 percent limit these options to middle-level executives and above.[24] Persons in the upper executive levels, however, are more likely to have the income and/or the capital necessary to exercise an option and to benefit from any income tax advantages that the option may provide.

Stock options may be provided by means of either a *qualified* or *nonqualified plan,* depending upon whether or not the plan meets the requirements of the Internal Revenue Service for favorable capital gains treatment. In order for the plan to qualify, stock options must be issued at 100 percent of market value and the stock purchased with the option must be held for at least three years and for not more than five years before being sold. Any income realized from exercising the option is taxed at a capital gains rate not to exceed 35 percent on all gains over $50,000. This increase in the capital gains tax from the former 25 percent rate level and the reduction of the maximum tax on current income to 50 percent have tended to make qualified stock option

[22] Harland Fox, *Top Executive Compensation* (New York: National Industrial Conference Board, 1972), p. 11.

[23] "Top Men Demand New Kinds of Pay," *Business Week* (January 23, 1971), p. 65.

[24] Harland Fox, *"Qualified Stock Options for Executives,"* (New York: The Conference Board, undated), p. 1.

plans less attractive.[25] Although gains from stock appreciation are treated as ordinary income in a nonqualified option plan, under certain conditions plans of this type have proven to be more advantageous than qualified plans. As a result of this situation, some companies have provided what are termed *tandem stock options* in which an executive may participate in either a qualified or nonqualified plan but, under recent IRS rulings, not in both.

Performance Share Plans. Under *performance share* or, *phantom stock, plans* executives do not actually receive shares of stock; rather, the current market value of the shares of stock is credited to their accounts at no cost to them. After a given period of time—usually three or five years—they are paid a bonus in either cash or stock equal to the increase in the market value of the stock during the period. If the stock has declined in value, the executives receive no bonus, but neither do they suffer any loss as they otherwise would if they had owned the stock.

One of the criticisms of performance share plans is that they can become a giveaway or bonanza for participants unless the goals upon which the payouts are based are established at a level sufficiently high to force the participants to "stretch out" in achieving them. In contrast to stock options, performance share plans are charged directly to current earnings—a condition which some experts consider to be an advantage since it forces companies to be selective in choosing participants.[26]

The Self-Designed Pay Plan. Because of differences in the financial needs and income tax obligations of executives, some companies have established a *self-designed pay plan,* or "cafeteria plan," whereby the participants can choose the form in which their incentive payments are to be received. In one survey of U.S. executives, 75 percent of the respondents indicated a preference for the cafeteria plan, a fact which indicates that it may be utilized more in the future.[27]

Incentives for Professional Personnel

During the past 25 years the demand for certain classes of professional and technical personnel has increased so substantially that employers have been forced to compete vigorously for their services. This competition not only has led to improvements in the status, treatment, and compensation of these personnel but also has spurred the development of incentive bonuses for them. Bonuses, however, still are less common for professional than for executive personnel.

---

[25] V. Henry Rothschild, II, and Jack B. Salwen, "Stock Option Plans in Transition," *The Conference Board Record,* Vol. X, No. 6 (June, 1973), p. 17.

[26] "Performance Shares: Popular—But Under Fire," *Business Week* (May 5, 1973), p. 56.

[27] Wilbur G. Lewellen and Howard P. Lanser, "Executive Pay Preferences," *Harvard Business Review,* Vol. 51, No. 5 (September-October, 1973), p. 119.

The motivation of professional personnel also may be accomplished by means of advancement opportunities that permit ability to be recognized and rewarded. Unfortunately in the past, professional employees usually were forced to assume an administrative assignment in order to advance beyond a certain point in the salary structure. Consequently, when these personnel were promoted, their professional talents ceased to be utilized fully with the result that the company perhaps lost a good scientist and gained a poor administrator. In an effort to avoid this type of situation, some companies have extended the salary range for personnel in scientific positions so that it equals or nearly equals the range for a department administrator. The extension of the range, therefore, provides a double-track wage system whereby the scientist who does not aspire to an administrative position can have an equal opportunity to gain salary advancement as a scientist.

There also has been a trend for some companies to make use of *maturity curves* as a basis for providing salary increases to professional personnel. These curves, such as the ones shown in Figure 20-2, provide for the annual rate of salary to be based upon experience and performance. Separate curves are established to reflect different levels of performance and to provide for annual increases. The curves representing the higher levels of performance tend to rise to a higher level and at a more rapid rate than the lower performance curves.

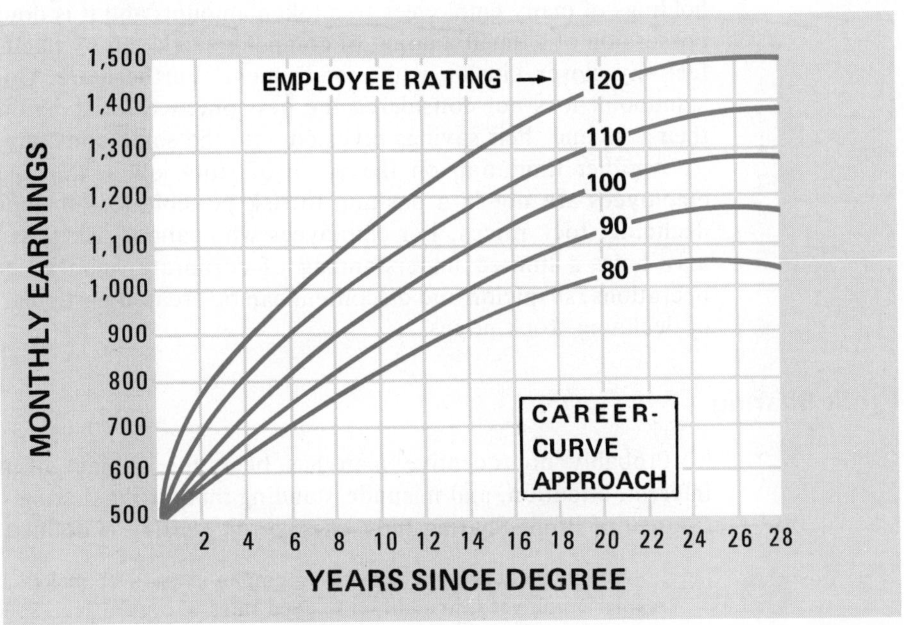

Source: Robert D. Sibson, *Wages and Salaries* (New York: American Management Association, 1960), p. 170. Reproduced with permission.

Figure 20-2 PROFESSIONAL MATURITY CURVES

ORGANIZATION-WIDE INCENTIVE PLANS

In recent years there has been a trend for companies to attempt to secure greater cooperation, efficiency, and loyalty from their personnel by providing them with an opportunity to participate in the financial gains derived from their efforts. Such participation has been accomplished indirectly through company-wide stock ownership, profit sharing, and employee committee participation plans.

Stock Ownership Plans

If a company is publicly held, its employees, like the general public, are always free to acquire its stock through regular brokerage channels. Some companies, however, permit their employees to acquire such stock at less than the quoted market price. Installment buying and payroll deduction provisions frequently are used to facilitate employee stock purchases. Stock ownership plans are intended to make employees more interested in the success of the company and more conscious of its problems and objectives. These plans also help to provide a new source of capital and to spread the ownership of the company among employees.

Stock ownership plans, of course, have their limitations in terms of their incentive value. Lack of funds with which to purchase stock may restrict the holdings of many employees to a token amount, and it is doubtful whether the possession of a small amount of company stock can by itself make employees feel any closer kinship with management. Furthermore, from an investment standpoint it is not considered the best practice for individuals to have both their jobs and their savings invested with the same company.

Another limitation on the value of stock ownership plans is that many employees are not in a position to risk possible loss in their equity through declining stock prices. For employees who cannot risk possible loss and who may have a limited understanding of corporate finances and stock market operations, suspicion and discontent can be created particularly during periods of declining stock prices.

Profit Sharing

Probably no incentive plan has been the subject of more widespread interest, attention, and misunderstanding than profit sharing. According to the Council of Profit Sharing Industries, *profit sharing* is defined as:

> Any procedure under which an employer pays or makes available to all regular employees, in addition to good rates of regular pay, special current or deferred sums based upon the profits of the business.[28]

---

[28] Constitution and By-Laws of the Council of Profit Sharing Industries (1957), Article 2, Section I.

Profit-sharing plans are intended to provide employees with the opportunity to increase their earnings by contributing to the improvement of their company's profits. Their contributions may be directed toward improving product quality, reducing operating costs, improving work methods, and building company goodwill rather than just toward increasing their rate of production. Profit sharing can help to stimulate employees to think and feel more like partners in the business and thus to concern themselves with the welfare of the organization as a whole. Its purpose, therefore, is to motivate the "whole person" rather than just specific aspects of his or her performance.

Variations in Profit-Sharing Plans. Profit-sharing plans differ as to the proportions of profits shared with each employee and as to the form of payment. The amount that is shared with employees may range from 5 to 50 percent of the net profit. Generally, however, most plans provide for the sharing of about 20 to 25 percent of the net profit. As is the case with executive compensation plans, profit distributions may be carried out in a variety of ways. The distribution may be made to all employees on an equal basis, or it may be based on their regular salary or on some formula that takes into account either or both of the factors of seniority and merit. The payments may be disbursed in cash, they may be deferred, or they may be made on the basis of a system involving a combination of these two forms of payment.

Cash payments keep employees more aware of the current earnings of the company and of their contributions to them, and therefore tend to have more incentive value than a deferred plan. They also allow employees complete freedom of choice in disposing of their share of profit, that is, to achieve an immediate improvement in their living standards or to invest the income for later needs.

Deferred payments, on the other hand, can serve as a source of retirement income, disability payments, separation payments, or loans in the event of an emergency. Profits distributed in this manner can provide the company with a more flexible method of accumulating a retirement fund, or it can serve to supplement the benefits of a regular pension plan. If *deferred profit-sharing plans* meet the requirements of the Internal Revenue Service, they also can provide certain income tax advantages for the employees over the cash plans.

Considerations Relating to Profit Sharing. Most authorities in the field are agreed that in order to have a successful profit-sharing program a company must first have a sound personnel program, good labor relations, and the trust and confidence of its employees. Profit sharing thus is a refinement of a good personnel program and a supplement to an adequate wage scale rather than a substitute for either one. As in the case of all incentive plans, it is the underlying philosophy of the management rather than the mechanics of the plan that may determine its success. Particularly essential to the success of a profit-sharing plan are the provisions it affords for psychological as well as financial participation since employees today are seeking greater involvement in connection with decisions affecting their welfare.

In spite of the potential advantages of profit sharing, it is also subject to certain weaknesses. As one author points out, the profits shared with employees may be the result of inventory speculation or many other factors that are beyond the influence of the employees. Conversely, company losses may occur during years when employee contributions have been at a maximum. When these bad years occur, employees may become less assertive in their attempts to reduce costs. The fact that the payment of profit shares is rendered only once a year or deferred until retirement reduces the motivational benefits to be gained from these payments.

Union Reaction to Profit Sharing. Union attitudes toward profit sharing are so varied as to prevent generalizations. Some union leaders look upon profit sharing as a company device designed to weaken union power, to divert the loyalty of the members from the union, and to avoid giving employees any outright wage increases. Other unions are not opposed to profit sharing provided they are consulted in the adoption of the plan and provided that any share of profit received by employees is in addition to the negotiated union rates. Some have made it a bargaining demand.

Just how strongly the latter unions actually want profit sharing is open to speculation. It is quite possible that the demands for a profit-sharing plan in some instances have been raised primarily for bargaining purposes, to be traded for other concessions from the company, since unions traditionally have sought to gain more for their members regardless of a company's profit outlook. The question of whether the union demands for profit sharing represent a desire to develop a new approach to management-union relations or just a strategic bargaining move, therefore, will require time to be answered.

Committee Participation Plans

In order to relate employee bonuses more closely to the effort and cooperation that they may put forth, during the years when company profits are poor as well as in years when they are good, some rather unique plans have been developed. Two such plans, which bear the names of their originators Joe Scanlon and Allen W. Rucker, are somewhat similar in that they place heavy emphasis upon employee participation and teamwork. The financial incentive formulas of these plans, while important, are not necessarily the primary factors that have contributed to their success.

Scanlon Plan. According to one of Scanlon's associates, effective employee participation, which includes the use of employee committees, is the most significant feature of this plan. This participation should involve not only an opportunity for employees to communicate their ideas and opinions, but also to influence decisions affecting their work and their welfare within the organization.[29] The primary mechanisms for participation are committees, the

[29] Robert K. Goodman, J. H. Wakeley, and R. H. Ruh, "What Employees Think of the Scanlon Plan," *Personnel,* Vol. 49, No. 5 (September-October, 1972), p. 23.

most important of which is the screening committee, composed of management and union officials and members. The committee's function is to review the production figures at the end of each month in order to determine the bonus or deficit that has been incurred. In addition, the committee may discuss problems relating to the administration of the plan and review suggestions relating to company efficiency that have been submitted to it by the various production committees.[30]

The financial incentives under the plan are normally distributed to all employees (a significant feature of the plan) on the basis of an established formula. This formula is based upon increases in employee productivity as determined by improvements that are realized with respect to a "norm" that has been established for labor costs. The norm which is subject to review reflects the relationships of the payroll to the sales value of the company's products. The plan also provides for the establishment of a reserve, into which 25 percent of any earned bonus is paid for the purpose of covering deficits encountered during the months when labor costs exceed the norm. After the portion for the reserve has been deducted, the remainder of the bonus is distributed with 25 percent going to the company and 75 percent to the employees. Any surplus that has been accumulated in the reserve at the end of a year is distributed to employees on the basis of the same formula.

In one survey of 21 plants having Scanlon Plans, opinions expressed by employees indicated that the intent of the plan was being realized. This intent is not to provide a giveaway program but rather a system that defines a new set of roles for participants and a unique way of assessing organizational efficiency. It compensates employees for improvements in organizational efficiency as a result of hard work.[31]

Rucker Plan. The Rucker plan, also known as the Share of Production Plan (SOP), normally covers hourly factory workers and executives. The financial incentive is based upon the historic relationship of the total earnings of hourly employees to the production values that they create. The bonus that is paid to employees is based upon any improvement in this relationship that they are able to realize. Thus, for every one percent increase in production value that is achieved, the workers covered by the plan receive an additional bonus of one percent of their total payroll costs. As in the case of the Scanlon Plan, maximum use is made of committees in administering the plan.

Lessons to be Gained. Perhaps the most important lesson to be gained from the Scanlon and Rucker plans is that any management that expects to gain the cooperation of its employees in improving efficiency must permit them to participate psychologically as well as financially in the company. If employees are to contribute maximum effort, they must be able to gain a feeling of involvement and identification with their company which is not provided

---

[30] Fred G. Lesieur, *The Scanlon Plan: A Frontier in Labor-Management Cooperation.* (Boston: Massachusetts Institute of Technology—The Technology Press and New York: John Wiley & Sons, Inc., 1958), pp. 46-48.

[31] Goodman, *et. al., op. cit.*, p. 27.

for them under the traditional manager-employee relationship. Consequently, it is important for companies to realize that while employee cooperation is essential to the successful administration of a financial incentive system, the development of an incentive system will not by itself necessarily stimulate their cooperation.

Résumé

Even though money may not be the primary return that employees seek from their work, it can provide an effective source of motivation if utilized properly. If a specific incentive system is to induce greater effort from employees, it must have a favorable organizational climate in which it is to operate and be geared to their particular financial and psychological needs. Furthermore, it is important that employees view their incentive payments as being equitable and not constituting a threat to their sense of economic security.

Because of differences in personal needs and the nature of the jobs being performed, it may be advisable to have separate plans for specific groups of personnel. In some of these plans, incentive payments are related directly to performance; whereas in others they are related to the performance of the organization as a whole. Furthermore, payments may be disbursed as cash or deferred until after an employee's retirement. While incentive plans are common for sales and executive personnel, their use with blue-collar personnel is less common. Increasingly those incentive plans being developed are organization-wide in scope and seek to encourage cooperation and to motivate the total contribution of employees. Plans of this type, such as profit sharing, also are used to create tax shelters for the participants by deferring the distribution of the incentive payments until retirement. Unfortunately, when too much consideration is given to the tax-saving features of a plan, its actual motivational value and its contribution to organizational objectives may be reduced in the process.

DISCUSSION QUESTIONS

1. What are some of the possible reasons that employees might have for not favoring financial incentives?
2. Why have many financial incentive plans for blue-collar workers failed?
3. Why do some companies provide more than one financial incentive plan?
4. A company that paid its production employees entirely on a piece-rate system pointed with pride to the fact that it permitted its employees "to go into business for themselves." To what extent do you feel that this claim is true or untrue?
5. If the standard time for producing one unit of a product were 4 minutes, what would the piece rate per unit be if the rate for this particular type of work were $3 an hour?
6. What are some of the problems likely to be encountered in developing an incentive system for sales personnel?
7. What are some of the reasons that financial incentives are not as common in banks, insurance companies, and public utilities as they are in manufacturing and retailing?
8. What are the reasons for the success of the Scanlon Plan?

PROBLEM 20-1 THE CHRISTMAS BONUS

During the previous eight years the Security Investment Company had given each of its employees a year-end bonus in an amount equal to from one- to two-weeks' pay. Consequently, over the years the employees had become accustomed to using this bonus as a means of meeting their Christmas season expenses. Because of unusually poor earnings one year the company recognized that even if it did not pay a bonus to its employees it would be fortunate to avoid encountering a deficit. Since management recognized that a majority of its employees had worked hard during the year and were counting on receiving a bonus, it was reluctant to forego the bonus payment even if a deficit had to be incurred. Management also recognized that the company's bonus record was usually mentioned during employment interviews particularly when it hired clerical help whose salaries were not too high. As the first of December approached, management was faced with the problem of making a decision regarding the payment of the bonus.

a. What decision do you feel management should make concerning the bonus, and when and how should the information concerning it be communicated to the employees?
b. What problems does this case indicate may arise in connection with the use of financial incentives?
c. What future policy should the company establish concerning the bonus?

SUGGESTED READINGS

Belcher, David W. *Wage and Salary Administration,* 2d ed. Englewood Cliffs, New Jersey: Prentice-Hall, Inc., 1962. Chapters 14, 15, 19.

Brown, Wilfred. *Piecework Abandoned*. London: Heinemann, 1962.

Crystal, Graef S. *Financial Motivation for Executives*. New York: American Management Association, Inc., 1970.

Fox, Harland. *Qualified Stock Options for Executives*. New York: The Conference Board, undated.

———. *Top Executive Compensation,* 1972 ed. New York: The Conference Board, 1972.

Incentive Plans for Salesmen, Studies in Personnel Policy, No. 217. New York: National Industrial Conference Board, 1970.

Jehring, J. J. *Profit Sharing for Small Business*. Evanston, Illinois: The Profit Sharing Research Foundation.

Rock, Milton L. (ed.). *Handbook of Wage and Salary Administration*. New York: McGraw-Hill Book Company, 1972. Chapters 31-40.

Von Kaas, H. K. *Making Wage Incentives Work*. New York: American Management Association, Inc., 1971.

Employee Security

As a return or outcome from their work, employees seek not only personal satisfaction and financial rewards but security as well. Particularly as they become older and less employable, or when they are disabled and unable to work, financial security is of extreme importance to them. Closely related to financial security is psychological security or a sense of well-being that results from feeling able to cope with both the financial problems and the personal adjustment that may occur during their employment or after their retirement from it.

The professionalization of personnel management has resulted in greater concern being given to the welfare and financial security of employees during their employment and following their retirement. Increased concern for employee security also has been due to competition for qualified personnel, government legislation, and union bargaining. Government-sponsored programs such as the Social Security program, furthermore, have enabled employees to achieve income security to supplement that provided by employers. This chapter will cover not only the role of employers in providing for the security needs of employees but also the role of government programs in connection with financial security.

FORMS OF INCOME SECURITY

If employees are to achieve some degree of financial security, it is essential that they be employed on a fairly continuous basis. As noted in Chapter 5, employers can provide greater employment stability through effective planning that will lead to more constant work loads and, in turn, more constant work force requirements. In spite of these preventive efforts, however, layoffs and terminations at times are unavoidable so that provisions must be made to provide individuals with some income in order to satisfy their financial needs at least partially, until they regain employment. Provisions also must be made to minimize income loss to an employee who becomes unable to work due to illness, disability, or old age.

Unemployment Income

A major source of income for employees who suffer a loss of employment is that provided through the federal Social Security program. Under some union agreements employees who are laid off also may receive supplemental unemployment benefits paid by the employer from a special fund established for this purpose. As yet, such benefits are paid only by a relatively small number of employers.

Unemployment Compensation. Employees who have been working in employment covered by the Social Security Act and who are laid off may be eligible for unemployment compensation during their unemployment for a period up to 26 weeks. Eligible persons must submit application for *unemployment compensation* with their state employment agency, register for available work, and be willing to accept any suitable employment that may be offered to them. While the term ''suitable'' permits individuals to enjoy considerable discretion in accepting or rejecting job offers, they must, nevertheless, make weekly contact with the employment office in order to receive their weekly checks.

The amount of the compensation that workers are eligible to receive, which varies among states, is determined by their previous wage rates and previous periods of employment. Funds for unemployment compensation are derived from a federal payroll tax based upon the wages paid to each employee, up to an established maximum. The major portion of this tax is refunded to the individual states which, in turn, operate their unemployment compensation programs in accordance with minimum standards prescribed by the federal government. A separate account record is maintained for each employer; and when the required reserve has been accumulated within this account, the amount of tax is reduced. Because of this sliding tax rate, the employer has an added incentive not to lay off personnel since the unemployment compensation that these personnel will receive will deplete the reserve account and cause the payroll tax rate to increase again.

Supplemental Benefits. The payment of unemployment benefits by the employer began in 1955 when the United Auto Workers successfully negotiated a *Supplemental Unemployment Benefits* (SUB) plan with the automobile industry which established a pattern for other industries. The SUB plan permits an employee who is laid off to draw, in addition to state unemployment compensation, weekly benefits from the company that are paid from a special fund created for this purpose. Many SUB plans in recent years have been liberalized to permit employees to receive weekly benefits when the length of their workweek is reduced and to receive a lump sum payment if their employment is terminated permanently. The amount of these benefits is determined by length of service and wage rate. Employer liability under the plan is limited to the amount of money that has been accumulated within the fund from employer contributions based on the total hours of work performed by union members. In those states that forbid workers from receiving SUB payments simultaneously with state unemployment compensation payments, the benefits from each of the two sources may be drawn on alternate weeks; or the SUB payments may be accumulated and paid after all state unemployment compensation payments have been received.

In certain European countries, such as Italy and Belgium, employers are required by law to pay employees who are terminated what are known as *indemnity payments*. The amount of the payment is governed by years of service and the income level of the employee. In the case of management personnel, the amount of the payment may range from the equivalent of several months' to more than a year's salary. This fact in certain instances can make it more economical for an employer to retain rather than discharge an executive.[1]

Disability Income

There are several ways in which employees may be compensated during periods when they are unable to work because of illness or injury. Most of those in public employment as well as many in private industry, particularly in white-collar jobs, receive a set number of sick-leave days each year to cover absences for physical reasons. Where it is provided, unused sick leave generally can be accumulated up to at least a given amount to cover prolonged absences. Accumulated annual vacation leave may be used as a source of income when sick-leave benefits have been exhausted. Group insurance which provides for income protection is also becoming more common. Loss of income during absences resulting from job-incurred injuries can be reimbursed, at least partially, by means of workmen's compensation insurance.

Nature of Workmen's Compensation Laws. The first *workmen's compensation* law in the United States was enacted in Maryland in 1902, but it was declared unconstitutional. The first laws to be held constitutional were passed in 1911 by four states—California, New Jersey, Washington, and Wisconsin. Since that time every state has adopted some type of workmen's compensation act. Both state and federal workmen's compensation legislation is based on the theory that the costs of industrial accidents should be considered as one of the costs of production and should ultimately be passed on to the consumer. Individual employees should not be required to stand the expense of their treatment or loss of income nor should they be required to

[1] Herbert J. Chruden and Arthur W. Sherman, Jr., *Personnel Practices of American Companies in Europe* (New York: American Management Association, 1972), p. 112.

resort to complicated, delaying, and expensive legal procedures. The provisions of the newer legislation thus represent a radical change in the philosophy of employer responsibilities toward the employee.

Compulsory or Elective Coverage. Workmen's compensation laws may be classified as *compulsory* or *elective*. Figure 21-1 indicates those states in which such compensation is compulsory and those in which it is elective. Under a compulsory law, every employer subject to it is required to comply with its provisions for the compensation of work injuries. These acts are compulsory for the employee also. An elective law is one in which the employers have the option of either accepting or rejecting the act, but in case they reject it, they lose the customary common law defenses—assumed risk of employment, negligence of a fellow servant, and contributory negligence.[2] Although most employers elect to be covered by the act, some do not. In the latter case the employees may be unable to obtain compensation unless they sue for damages. The elective laws also permit the employee to reject coverage, but in practice this is rarely done.

Coverage and Benefits. Workmen's compensation laws typically provide that injured employees will be paid a disability benefit that is usually based on a percentage of their wages. Each state also specifies the length of the period of payment and usually indicates a maximum amount that may be paid. In addition to the disability benefits, provision is made for payment of medical and hospitalization expenses to some degree, and in all states death benefits are paid to survivors of the employee. Unlike the former employee liability laws, it is not necessary for an injured employee to file a suit in a court in order to benefit under workmen's compensation laws. Commissions are established to adjudicate claims at little or no expense to the claimant. In general, the commissions have been increasingly liberal in the awards made to injured employees.

Recommended Reforms. Because of wide variations in the nature and the adequacy of the coverage and benefits provided by state compensation laws, organized labor for some time has been requesting Congress to establish minimum federal compensation standards. Other provisions being sought by labor include increasing weekly benefit payments to at least 80 percent of the employee's take-home pay, and the periodical adjustment of benefit levels to protect disabled workers against inflation.[3]

Supporting labor's request is a report by the National Commission on State Workmen's Compensation Laws to the effect that these laws generally are inadequate and inequitable. Among the recommendations of the Commission

---

[2] These three defenses are defined as follows: (1) the *doctrine of contributory negligence* states that the employer would not be liable if the injury of the employee was due wholly or in part to his own negligence, (2) *the doctrine of the assumption of risk* holds that when an employee accepts a job, he assumes the ordinary risks of the job, and (3) the *fellow-servant rule* provides that if the employee was injured as a result of the negligence of a fellow employee, the employer would not be liable for his injury.

[3] "Federalizing Workmen's Compensation," *Business Week* (February 16, 1974).

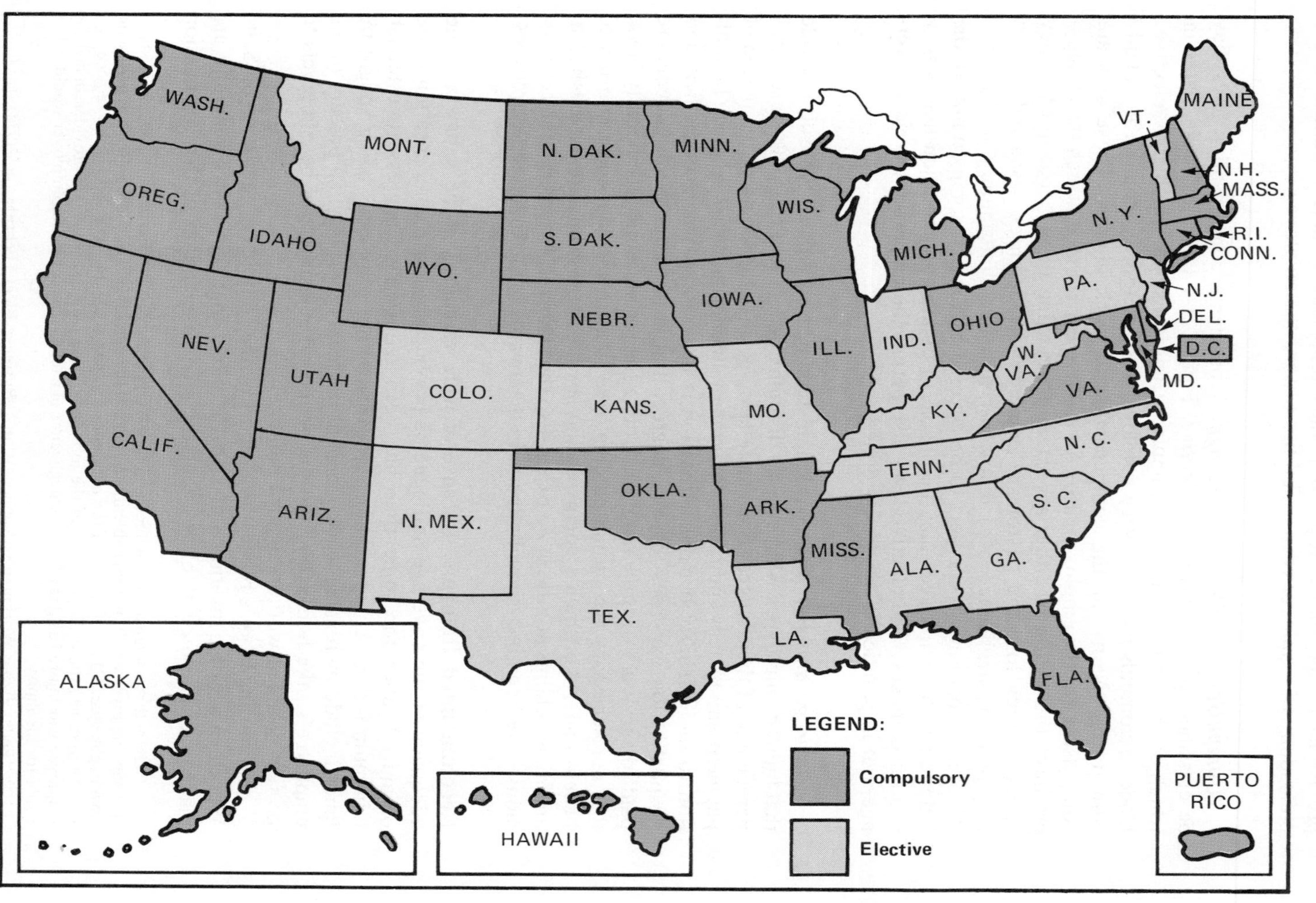

Source: State Workmen's Compensation Laws: A Comparison of Major Provisions with Recommended Standards, Bulletin 212 (Washington, D.C.: U.S. Department of Labor, 1971 revision), p. 3.

Figure 21-1 COMPULSORY VS. ELECTIVE WORKMEN'S COMPENSATION LAWS BY STATES are mandatory compensation insurance in all states and the elimination of all exemptions from coverage for employers having fewer than a required number of employees or for certain types of employment. Other recommendations call for the end of arbitrary limits on benefit payments as well as full coverage for work-related diseases.[4]

Trends in Workmen's Compensation. While workmen's compensation plans originally provided only for the coverage of physical injuries, they have gradually been extended in many jurisdictions to cover emotional impairments. For example, a person who suffers the loss of several fingers in a machine may develop a severe neurosis about working with any moving equipment. Even when there is recovery from the physical injury, that person may be emotionally incapable of performing the former job or other similar jobs. In this type of case, the courts have granted workmen's compensation—even where there is a lapse of as much as five years between the physical injury and the emotional upset. Similarly, those emotional illnesses that occur before they precipitate a physical injury have been found to be compensable. For example, it has been held by courts in several states that job-induced strain, stress, anxiety, or pressure that leads to a heart attack is compensable.

More recently, mental illness that can definitely be linked to job conditions has been found to be compensable in cases that were tried in Kansas, California, Texas, Louisiana, Massachusetts, West Virginia, Colorado, New York, and Michigan. In one case, a train dispatcher was awarded compensation for a nervous breakdown which developed under the pressure of routing trains and having people shout at him over loudspeakers. In another case, an assembly-line employee was awarded partial temporary disability compensation for a neurosis attributed to the emotional pressures resulting from his superior's criticism coupled with his inability to perform the job correctly.

Financing Workmen's Compensation. The workmen's compensation benefits prescribed by law in the various states generally are financed by the employers. A few states require the employees to make small contributions, but these funds meet only a small part of the expense involved in paying the benefits. While payment of the benefits is an operational expense for the employer, the consumer ultimately pays the cost of benefits.

Two methods of providing for workmen's compensation risks are commonly used. One method is for the state to operate an insurance system that employers may join and in some states are required to join. Another method is for the states to permit employers to insure with private companies, and in some states employers may be certified by the commission handling workmen's compensation to handle their own risks without any type of insurance.

[4] "Federalizing Workmen's Compensation," *Business Week* (September 16, 1972).

Under most state and private insurance plans the employer and the employee gain by maintaining good safety records. Employers are rated according to accident experience, and their casualty insurance costs are determined on this basis. Under many compensation plans employees are encouraged to follow safe practices. In some states employees' benefits under the law are reduced by a specified percentage if they are found to have willfully failed to use safety devices provided by the employer, willfully failed to obey safety rules, or were injured as the result of intoxication. A method that provides workers with reasonable compensation for injury but at the same time penalizes those who are willfully negligent in the observance of safety practices should help to promote safe practices. Since employers also lose in the event of an accident, their continuing attention to fostering safety likewise pays dividends.

Retirement Income

The source of retirement income upon which the greatest number of individuals are dependent is that provided by the federal Social Security program, which is discussed later in this chapter. In most government as well as certain private employment, however, benefits are provided for employees by means of pension plans. Such plans have been in existence since 1875 when the first known plan was initiated by the American Express Company. A few years later the Baltimore & Ohio Railroad also developed a pension plan for its employees, and it was followed by other railroads until the majority of the workers in this industry were covered by some form of plan. Personnel in the civil and the armed services of the federal government were also among the first groups to receive pension benefits. In industry most of the early pension plans included only the executive and other salaried employees.

Prior to the 1948 NLRB decision in the *Inland Steel Case,* employers were not required to bargain with their unions on the subject of pensions.[5] Employers who did not want to establish pensions were able to forestall union demands for them on the grounds that decisions involving pensions were an exclusive prerogative of management. In the NLRB decision which was later upheld by the Supreme Court, however, it was ruled that employers could not refuse to bargain over pensions; and as a result of this decision the way was cleared for union pension drives. Shortly thereafter a number of the major unions succeeded in negotiating pension benefits with some of the nation's largest companies, including those in the steel, automobile, and other manufacturing industries. The successes achieved by these unions helped to establish a precedent for unions in other industries to demand similar benefits from their employers.

Pension plans continue to grow as indicated by a Bureau of National Affairs study which revealed that over 90 percent of the production workers in

[5] Inland Steel Company *v*. NLRB, NLRB 77, 1 (1948).

manufacturing were covered by a pension plan, about 9 percent of which were financed entirely by the employer.[6]

Determining Pension Size. There are a number of factors that affect the amount of pension employees receive. The most important factor is the amount of funds the employer is able and willing to allocate for pensions. The share of this fund that is to comprise a particular individual's pension usually is determined by such factors as years of service, the earning level attained by the employee, retirement income needs, and, in some instances, the amount of that person's Social Security payments. The size of the pension also will be affected by the amount, if any, that the employee is contributing to it. The effect of continued inflation upon the purchasing power of payments provided under each of the various types of plans is increasingly becoming a major factor to be considered.

Based upon a study conducted by the Department of Labor, the plan used most commonly to determine the amount of an employee's pension is one in which the payment is based upon a percentage of the employee's earnings (frequently based on an average over several years) multiplied by the number of years of employment with the organization.[7] A survey conducted by the Bureau of National Affairs also indicated that this formula was the most common for computing pensions, having been used by 44 percent of the respondents. The next most common formula, used by 26 percent of the respondents, was based upon a specific number of dollars ($5.00 was a figure reported by several respondents) multiplied by the number of years of credited service completed. Cost-of-living escalator provisions for adjusting benefits to inflation were reported to be used by 12 percent of the companies participating in the survey. On the other hand, pension payments were reported by 13 percent of the companies to be reduced by the amount of an individual's Social Security benefits.[8]

Another but much less common type of plan is one in which the payment is a flat amount without relationship to earnings or years of service. In some instances the payment may be related to the employee's Social Security payments and provide the difference between these and a flat amount of money. A final plan for calculating pension benefits is the money-purchase plan. Under this plan the amount of each employee's pension is determined by the funds that have been accumulated in the pension account and the size of the insurance annuity payments that can be purchased with this amount.

Pension Plan Abuses. Any pension plan constitutes only an empty promise unless adequate funds are set aside and invested properly so that the necessary

[6] BNA Policy and Practice Series, *Compensation* (Washington, D.C.: The Bureau of National Affairs, Inc., 1975), pp. 343:11-343:13.

[7] Donald J. Staats, "Private Pension Plans: How Benefits Are Computed," *Management Review*, Vol. 54, No. 10 (October, 1965), pp. 33-36.

[8] *Pensions and Other Retirement Benefits*, P.P.F. Survey No. 103 (Washington, D.C.: The Bureau of National Affairs, Inc., October, 1973), p. 6.

money will be available to make the payments provided for by the plan. In the past, many private pension plans have proven to be illusory because employees covered by them have received benefits much smaller than had been promised or received no benefits at all. Such conditions led to the passage of the Pension Reform Law, officially entitled the Employee Retirement Income Security Act of 1975, after extensive Congressional hearings and investigations covering private plans. These investigations revealed that between one third and one half of the 35 million workers would never receive any pensions under existing plans.[9] One of the major reasons for this fact was that many of these plans failed to provide employees with *vested rights;* that is, an irrevocable interest or equity in the benefits they had earned through their years of service. Even those plans that provided vested rights often did so only after a number of years or only on a partial basis. In pension plans that did not include provisions for vested rights, those employees who quit or were terminated prior to reaching retirement age suffered the loss of pension benefits regardless of how close they were to retirement age or how many years they had worked for the company.

Congressional investigation also revealed that many employees received no benefits or only a fraction of their entitled pension benefits upon retirement because the plan had been terminated as the result of the company closing down or being acquired by another company. The failure to estimate accurately the employer contributions necessary to pay the benefits provided by the plan, the lack of funds to meet these obligations, or the loss of funds due to declines in the value of fund investments also caused many employees to receive pensions smaller than those promised, if any at all.

Federal Regulation of Pension Plans. While the Pension Reform Law does not require employers to establish pension plans, it does provide certain controls and standards governing pension plans including minimum funding standards so as to offer greater assurance that money will be available to provide a pension when an employee retires. The soundness of the actuarial assumption upon which the fund is based must be certified by an actuary at least every three years. Employers who already have pension plans are given up to 40 years to fund these plans in accordance with prescribed standards, and new plans must be funded fully for past service liabilities covering all employees within 30 years. Standards of conduct and accountability for persons administering the funds are also provided.

To insure against the failure of plans to provide established benefits, a Pension Benefit Guaranty Corporation has been formed. It is supported by premiums from employers to assure that employees will receive their pensions even if the plan becomes insolvent. A particularly important requirement of the pension act is that all pension plans must provide for the vesting of employee equity according to one of three prescribed options. One option, for example, provides full vesting for employees after 10 years of service.

---

[9] Jacob K. Javits, "The Scandal of Our Pension Plans: What's Wrong and What We Can Do About It," *Family Weekly* (November 11, 1973).

Employees who are not covered by a private pension plan can now establish an *Individual Retirement Account* (IRA) to which they contribute and can deduct from federal income tax an amount up to 15 percent of their earned income, or $1500, whichever is less. For a number of years, self-employed persons have been able to contribute a tax-deductible 15 percent of their income up to a maximum of $2,500 per year to their own pension funds under the *Keogh Plan*. The Pension Reform Act has raised this maximum to $7,500 per year.

Methods of Funding Pensions. Pension funds may be derived from employee as well as employer contributions. The *noncontributory plan* in which funds are provided entirely by the employer, however, is the type preferred and most commonly negotiated by organized labor. This type of plan eliminates the need to take a portion of an employee's wages after income taxes have been deducted from it. Employer contributions to the pension fund may be determined by an established formula, or they may be contingent upon company profits as a part of a profit-sharing plan. In some labor contracts, such as those negotiated by the United Mine Workers, employer contributions to the welfare and pension fund come from production royalties.

Pension funds should be invested where they will receive adequate protection and yet earn a satisfactory return. The earnings derived from a trust fund can be used either to increase the amount of money that is available for pension benefits or to reduce the amount of money that the employer must contribute to the fund, or both. During inflationary periods a major investment problem is that of preserving the purchasing power of the pension funds as well as the dollar value of the funds.

At one time pension fund managers considered blue-chip common stocks as one of the best hedges against inflation because they assumed that rises in the prices of goods and services would be accompanied by rises in the prices of common stocks. However, this assumption proved to be invalid during the 1973-74 inflationary period because the stock market at that time suffered one of its severest declines. A loss of approximately 20 percent of $30 billion dollars occurred in private pension fund investments.[10] Losses of this type serve either to increase the cost of pensions to employers by forcing them to increase their contributions to offset the fund losses, or to reduce pension benefits for employees. Inflationary periods also place employers under pressure to increase pension payments to those employees who have been retired for several years during which time the purchasing power of their pensions has been eroded drastically.

Management of Pension Funds. Pension funds may be administered through either a trusteed plan or an insured plan. Under a *trusteed plan* the money required to meet pension obligations is accumulated in a trust fund. The amount of money that must be accumulated to provide employees with the monthly payment they are entitled to receive at retirement age must be determined by

---

[10] "Why Pension Funds Are Running Scared," *Business Week* (August 3, 1974).

actuarial calculations which take into account the age and sex of the employee and the number of years remaining until retirement. An *insured plan* is one in which payments are provided from insurance annuities which are purchased for the employees. The responsibility for investing and administering the funds being accumulated to meet pension obligations is assumed by an insurance company rather than a bank, trust company, or committee designated to serve as the trustee.

Portability of Pensions. A weakness of most private pension plans is that they lack the portability which would enable employees, when changing employment, to maintain equity in a single pension. Even when employees acquire vested pension rights, several changes in employment over their working life can result in the accumulation of equity in more than one fund. Although some unions and employer associations have developed portable pension plans that enable employees to accumulate equity in the same pension plan even though they change employers, such plans are not widespread. Undoubtedly future legislation will be passed to facilitate and encourage the development of portable pension systems. Until such legislation occurs, however, the Individual Retirement Account provides the greatest degree of portability.

Pension Philosophy. The philosophy underlying pensions has undergone a substantial change in recent years. Originally pensions were based upon a "reward" philosophy in which their primary purpose was to retain personnel within the organization until they reached retirement age.[11] The pension thus represented a reward to employees for remaining with the organization until they retired. Employers believed that those employees who quit or who were terminated prior to retirement time did not deserve the reward of a pension. However, as a result of the vesting requirements negotiated into most union contracts and more recently by law, pensions are now based upon an "earnings" philosophy.[12] Under this philosophy a pension is regarded as deferred income which employees accumulate during their working lives and which belongs to them after a specified number of years of service whether or not they remain with the employer until retirement.

SOCIAL SECURITY

Because of the inadequacies of private pension plans, the retirement benefits provided under the federal Social Security program constitute the major source of income for the majority of retirees in the United States. However, one should recognize that Social Security is not a pension system but rather an insurance system designed to indemnify those covered by it against loss of earnings resulting from various causes. Therefore, a person

---

[11] Howard H. Hendricks, "Can Private Pension Plans Measure Up to Expectations?" *Personnel Journal*, Vol. 50, No. 4 (April, 1971), p. 293.

[12] *Ibid.*

who earns more than a prescribed amount in gainful employment following retirement from a particular job is ineligible for any retirement benefit under Social Security because this retirement has not resulted in a sufficient loss of income. Under a pension system the amount an individual may earn in another job following retirement from a previous one usually has no effect upon pension payments.

In addition to indemnifying those covered against the loss of earnings due to retirement, the Social Security insurance is intended to indemnify them against losses caused by unemployment and by disability; it also indemnifies their families against loss of income in the event of their death. Thus, as in the case of other types of insurance against loss, Social Security does not pay off unless a loss of earnings actually is incurred. It is entirely possible, therefore, for individuals who continue working until their death to receive nothing back from Social Security.

Coverage and Financing

In order to receive benefits for oneself and/or one's family under the Social Security Act, an individual must have been engaged in some form of employment that is covered by it. Most employment by private enterprise, most types of self-employment including farming, active military service after 1956,[13] and employment in certain nonprofit organizations and governmental agencies are subject to coverage under the act. Some groups of employees, however, including railroad workers and United States civil service employees who are covered by their own systems, and other occupational groups are under certain conditions exempted from the act.[14]

The Social Security program is supported by means of a tax levied against the earnings of those covered by it up to a maximum limit. This tax must be matched by the employer. Self-employed persons are required to pay a tax on their earnings at a rate which is higher than that paid by an employee but less than the combined rates paid by an employed person and his or her employer. In recent years upward adjustments have been made periodically, both in the tax rate and in the maximum amount of earnings subject to the tax, to cover improvements in the benefits provided under the program. Additional increases are scheduled to occur at specific times in the years ahead, and it may be expected that further liberalization of the program by Congress will push the taxes required to support it still higher.[15]

---

[13] Active military service completed between 1940 and 1956 inclusive was granted Social Security credit gratuitously based upon monthly earnings of $160 per month. If this credit is used for Social Security benefits, however, it cannot be counted toward any other federal service pension.

[14] For a more detailed account of exempted groups, see the current editions of *Labor Course*, or *Tax Course* (Englewood Cliffs, New Jersey: Prentice-Hall, Inc.).

[15] Since the Social Security Act is subject continually to amendment, readers should refer to the literature provided by the nearest Social Security office for the most current details pertaining to the tax rates and benefit provisions of the act. The current edition of the booklet *Your Social Security*, prepared by the Social Security Administration, is an excellent general source of information.

Retirement Benefits

In order to be eligible to receive retirement benefits, a person must have reached retirement age, must be retired, and be fully insured. Whether or not an individual is fully insured is determined by the number of quarters in which he or she has received a prescribed amount of earnings. A calendar quarter is a three-month period beginning January 1, April 1, July 1, or October 1. For most kinds of employment a person must earn at least $50 in wages in order to obtain a quarter of coverage. Those persons who are self-employed must earn at least $400 a year, for which they receive four quarters of coverage. The exact number of quarters that a person must obtain in order to be classed as *fully insured* will depend upon date of birth or, if one dies or becomes disabled before reaching retirement age, upon the date of death or disability. In no case can an individual become fully insured with less than six quarters of coverage and in no case will more than 40 quarters be needed regardless of date of birth.

From the standpoint of meeting the *test of retirement*, eligible persons under the age of 72 must be retired. This test of retirement refers to the maximum amount of money that can be earned from gainful employment without suffering any reduction in Social Security payments. The amount of money is limited to earnings from work and excludes investment, pension, or other retirement income.

Since retirement benefits are computed on the basis of average earnings, a person's benefits are reduced by each year in which he or she does not work in covered employment. In determining this average, however, an individual is entitled to drop out the five years in which there has been the least or no earnings. Thus, if an individual worked in covered employment during only 10 years of a 20-year period, that person's average earnings would be computed on the basis of a 15-year period—that is, 20 years less the 5 years that can be dropped.

Retirement benefits consist of those benefits which an individual is entitled to receive in his or her own behalf, plus additional benefits for eligible dependents. These benefits are based upon the individual's average monthly earnings and can be determined from a prepared benefit table. There are also both minimum and maximum limits to the amount that individuals and their dependents can receive. Dependents for whom benefits may be claimed include the following:

1. Wife over 65 (or 62 at a reduced amount).
2. Wife caring for an unmarried child who is under 18 years of age or disabled.
3. Unmarried child who is under 18 or disabled.
4. Parents who are dependent upon a covered individual for more than 50 percent of their support.
5. Unmarried children between the ages of 18 and 22 who are attending school.

Disability Benefits

The Social Security program provides benefit payments to workers who are too severely disabled to engage in gainful employment. In order to be eligible for such benefits, however, an individual's disability must have existed for at least 6 months and must be expected to continue for at least 12 months. Those eligible for disability benefits, furthermore, must have worked under Social Security for at least 5 out of the 10 years before becoming disabled. Disability benefits, which include auxiliary benefits for dependents, are computed on the same basis as retirement benefits and are converted to retirement benefits when the individual reaches the age of 65.

Survivors Benefits

Survivors benefits represent a form of life insurance that is paid to members of a deceased person's family who meet the requirements for eligibility. As in the case of life insurance, the benefits that the survivors of a covered individual receive may be far in excess of their cost to this individual. Survivors of individuals who are currently insured as well as those who are fully insured at the time of death are eligible to receive certain benefits, provided the survivors meet other eligibility requirements. A *currently insured person* is one who has been covered during at least 6 out of the 13 quarters prior to death. In the case of a currently insured person, the benefits are paid only to a widow or a dependent divorced wife with dependent children who are under 18 or are disabled, and these benefits cease when the youngest child reaches 18 or marries. These benefits include allowances for the widow and for each unmarried child of the deceased person who is under 18, who is under a disability that began before the child reached 18, or who is under 22 and a full-time student.

When she reaches retirement age, the widow of a fully insured person whose survivors benefits were terminated earlier can become eligible to draw Social Security benefits if she meets prescribed conditions. Dependent parents of a person who was fully insured at the time of death also may be able to qualify for survivors benefits.

Health Insurance or "Medicare"

Health insurance is the most recent addition to the Social Security Program. This insurance provides for *hospital insurance* and for *medical insurance* for persons over 65. Hospital insurance is financed by employer and employee contributions and covers most of the expenses of hospitalization for a given period. It also covers a major portion of the cost for out-patient care, for post-hospital home care, or for nursing home care. The health insurance provisions of "Medicare" are provided to individuals who have been covered by the Social Security Program and, in addition, are available to those persons who have not been covered previously providing that they make application to the program. Medical insurance coverage requires the payment of a monthly fee by those who elect to be included. This coverage pays a major portion of the doctor's fees for medical services, including office calls, home visits, surgery, and various laboratory services.

SECURITY IN LATER LIFE

Financial security becomes increasingly important to employees as they grow older because of greater difficulty in finding jobs in the event they become unemployed. Financial losses, furthermore, are difficult if not impossible to replace because relatively few years of earning power remain for them. As their need for financial security increases, so may their fears and anxieties about it. Anxieties may increase further as they become more aware of the fact that the time is rapidly approaching when they will be faced with the financial and other personal adjustments that retirement is likely to entail for them.

Older employees constitute a group with whom management must be especially concerned. Anxieties, for example, may cause older persons to perceive that they are in danger of being replaced by younger employees, of being forced into retirement, or even worse, of being terminated before becoming eligible to receive retirement benefits. As a result of these perceptions, older employees often tend to become more cautious and to avoid making decisions or taking any actions that might reflect unfavorably upon them. Unfortunately such behavior may have the very effect upon their reputation and value as employees that they seek to avoid. Consequently, as employees approach retirement age, they may require greater reassurance that they are making an important contribution to the organization; that they are wanted, needed, and respected by fellow employees; and that they are not in danger of being forced out of their jobs. While being provided with such reassurances, older employees should be assisted in preparing for their retirement and in making the necessary adjustments prior to and following this event.

Preparation for Retirement

As a result of experiences gained during the course of their lives, people learn how to adjust to a variety of personal problems, disappointments, and even tragedies. However, since retirement is something that most persons experience only once in their lifetime, they have no opportunity to gain experience in adjusting to it. As one author states, "It is a curious fact that we spend years in preparing for an occupation but often retire from it with little or no preparation."[16] Thus, they must rely upon those experiences received secondhand from others who have preceded them to retirement. These experiences which include the successes and mistakes of others in retirement, along with the knowledge from psychology, medicine, finance, and other fields, are accessible through the literature and various preretirement courses and programs.

Preretirement Programs. In an effort to assist employees in adjusting more readily to retirement, the majority of the larger organizations have inaugurated

[16] Jerome W. Bettman, "Repotting Time," *California Health* (July, 1972), p. 3.

preretirement programs. A primary contribution of such programs is to make employees who are approaching retirement more aware of this fact, and in some instances to jolt them into thinking and doing something about it. Although some organizations begin their counseling with employees as early as five years prior to retirement, others do not provide it until a year or less prior to retirement time. The shorter period, however, is not likely to allow individuals sufficient time to change their habit patterns. Generally preretirement counseling covers all or most of the following areas:

1. Health problems of older people.
2. Use of leisure time and recreation.
3. Community resources for older people.
4. Housing and living arrangements.
5. Revenue-producing hobbies and activities.
6. Family adjustment problems.

Preretirement programs may include provisions for certain adjustments in the employees' work assignments. The gradual reduction of their duties and work loads, for example, may serve not only to facilitate their replacement but also to help them "ease into retirement" with a minimum of difficulty. There are several ways in which employee work loads may be lightened and their active careers with an organization "phased out" gradually. One is to extend the length of vacation periods, and another is to reduce the workweek during the last few years of their employment. If a replacement is being groomed for the job, that person may gradually assume more of the responsibilities connected with the job. Regardless of what measures are used, however, a systematic plan for gradually reducing the work load of retiring employees can help to make the transition easier for them and for the organization.

Adjustment to a reduction in income as a result of retirement is another critical step that an employee must take. Through preretirement counseling, therefore, employees should be encouraged to make downward adjustments in their spending habits and to eliminate their debts well in advance of retirement. Assistance in financial planning and budgeting, through meetings arranged by the personnel department, may help employees to avoid financial mistakes and the accompanying hardships.

A number of companies have prepared booklets, pamphlets, and other literature to use in their preretirement programs. Some companies also purchase subscriptions to senior-citizen magazines for employees nearing retirement. These magazines include *Aging*, published by the U.S. Department of Health, Education, and Welfare; *Harvest Years*, published by the Harvest Years Publishing Company; *Modern Maturity*, published by the American Association of Retired Persons; and *Retirement Planning News*, published by the Retirement Planning Council, Inc.[17]

[17] The interests of older persons are the special concern of the Office of Aging, Department of Health, Education, and Welfare, that issues many publications related to the problems of senior citizens.

Problems Relating to Preretirement Programs. While there are those who maintain that preretirement programs represent an intrusion into the personal lives of employees, the fact that a growing number of organizations are now providing assistance in this area would seem to indicate their value. Certain weaknesses found in these preretirement programs, however, can serve to help employers improve their programs. Some of these weaknesses are:

1. Preretirement programs in some instances have given employees the impression that such programs are being conducted for the purpose of "easing them out of the organization" through encouraging them to seek early retirement.
2. Many employees in the 55-65 age group who stand to profit most from the programs are reluctant to attend because they want to avoid giving any appearance of being "over the hill."
3. Much of the material in the program, although interesting, comes too late in life to be used profitably.
4. Many programs do little to involve the employee's spouse in retirement preparation or to prepare the spouse for the changes that retired life will create for both.[18]

Determining the Age for Retirement

A basic problem relating to retirement to be resolved by an organization is that of determining the age at which retirement is to occur. Many employers adhere to a policy of *compulsory retirement* at an established age, at least for certain classes of employees. Some organizations, however, maintain a flexible retirement policy that permits employees to keep working beyond the normal retirement age (generally 65) for as long as they continue to be reasonably efficient and physically able to work.

Compulsory Retirement Policy. Undoubtedly one of the reasons for a compulsory retirement policy is that it spares management the unpleasantness of having to inform individuals, particularly friends, that they should retire or of forcing individuals, like the one shown in Figure 21-2, to retire. A compulsory retirement age thus insures the retirement of those who have outlived their usefulness.

Even more important, compulsory retirement creates opportunities for executives at lower levels to gain promotion and, as a result, encourages them to remain with the organization. As the board chairman of one corporation has stated, "There is nothing more deadening to a person who has a boss five years older than he but who still has 10 years to go in his job. People shouldn't stay in the same job too long. It's not good for the individual or the organization."[19] Compulsory retirement policies increase the infusion of new ideas.

---

[18] Ronald Chen, "The Problem of Retirement," *Public Personnel Review*, Vol. 28, No. 3 (July, 1967), p. 188.

[19] "The Growing Trend to Early Retirement," *Business Week* (October 7, 1972), p. 74.

"Of course, tomorrow's papers will report that after a long and fruitful career, he decided to hand over the reins to a younger man."

Source: Courtesy of *True, The Man's Magazine* (September, 1964), p. 73, and Donald Reilly.

Figure 21-2

"Top managers in business are recognizing that a man has a few years to inject new ideas into a corporation, a few more to implement them, and then he tends to sit back. He may even sit on new ideas developed by younger managers."[20]

Flexible Retirement Policy. One of the arguments against compulsory retirement is that it ignores the fact that the mental and physical condition of employees is not just a function of age, and that some individuals are capable of rendering valuable contributions to the company well beyond the normal retirement age. Thus, a flexible retirement age prevents the organization as well as society from being deprived of the contribution that individuals still may be able to render. It also permits employees who have not accumulated adequate pension benefits or who fear the adjustment problems of retirement to continue working. Flexibility also may be increased by permitting early retirement for employees who suffer a disability, a mental or physical decline, or who prefer to quit working before the normal retirement age.

Increasing numbers of executives are choosing early retirement. One of the reasons for this fact is that many executives have found their greatest challenge to be one of getting to the top after which they had little left to challenge them in the future. Consequently, some of them engage in what has been referred to as "repotting" in that they retire from one career and begin a new one in which

[20] *Ibid.*

they can again progress upward. Early retirement for many blue-collar workers, on the other hand, means "getting away from something you've learned to hate."[21]

Adjustment to Retirement

The initial reaction to retirement often is a very favorable one. It is viewed as providing a release from pressure and an opportunity to enjoy self-chosen activities and hobbies, or to spend more time with relatives and friends. With the passage of time, however, retirement tends to be regarded less favorably because it fails to provide the means by which human needs can be satisfied fully.

Individuals vary considerably in terms of their desire for retirement and their ability to adjust to it. Generally persons, such as the one pictured in Figure 21-3, who have been absorbed in their job and who have built their life around it may find it difficult if not impossible to make a suitable adjustment to retirement. This fact holds true, particularly in the case of persons in management positions and in professional careers. It is their work that enables

Source: The Next Promotion (Hartford, Conn.: The Connecticut Mutual Life Insurance Company). Reproduced with permission.

Figure 21-3

[21] *The Wall Street Journal,* May 22, 1972.

such individuals to feel "worth something," a feeling that helps them to cope with the challenges of daily life and gives them the posture necessary to engage in the problems of survival.[22] The following statement by one executive typifies this feeling:

> Retirement to me is a disappointment. I feel useless, unasked to do the things I worked so hard to learn to do in my work years. I've lost a lot of the old zest I had for living when I went to work every day.[23]

Retirement for this person was a state of quiet frustration.

New Sources of Satisfaction. One of the major problems of adjusting to retirement for many persons, therefore, is developing ways of replacing those sources of satisfaction derived from the job. As Hepner points out, individuals must make adjustments and seek out new sources of satisfaction for themselves—no one else can do it for them. Unfortunately there is a tendency for some retirees at this point in life to let down and say to themselves, "I'm tired of looking after others—let some one look after me now."[24] Adherence to this attitude can cause retirees to suffer from "atrophy of disuse" through failure to be mentally and physically active. As a means of keeping active and adjusting to retirement, Hepner recommends that retirees develop and pursue projects that will provide an outlet for their accumulated knowledge and experience. Such projects have the value of giving the retiree an objective to pursue as well as a source of personal discipline and satisfaction. Various forms of research and consulting work as well as self-employment in the service fields can be possible projects for individuals to pursue. For example, the Small Business Administration has recruited a group of retired executives to provide assistance to individuals starting businesses of their own. Other groups of executives have been organized to provide technical assistance to governments and businesses in developing countries abroad.

Influence of Expected Retirement Income. For employees below the management level who often have had jobs with lower incomes involving little or no satisfaction or challenge, the greatest adjustment may be of a financial nature. In a study of United Auto Workers Union members conducted by the University of Michigan Survey Research Center, it was found that the expected retirement income had the greatest influence upon the worker's decision to retire, with job satisfaction and leisure preference being less important. Factors found to be associated with satisfaction following retirement were the ability to keep relatively active and involved with life, the enjoyment of good health, and the feeling of being financially secure. The study concluded that workers

---

[22] Morton D. Bogdonoff, "The Human Need for an Appointment with Tomorrows," *Archives of International Medicine*, 1969, pp. 635-636.

[23] Harry W. Hepner, "Corporate Executives Who Retire," *Michigan Business Review*, Vol. XXII, No. 3 (May, 1970), p. 13.

[24] Harry W. Hepner, *Retirement—A Time to Live Anew* (New York: McGraw-Hill Book Company, 1969), p. 24.

actually are enthusiastic about the prospect of early retirement and satisfied with the experience when they do retire.[25] Very likely the favorable reaction to retirement among the respondents is due to lack of satisfaction derived from mass-production work and to the fact that retirement income for them is becoming more adequate. Problems of adjustment to retirement, furthermore, are much less for individuals who have become alienated from their work and welcome the opportunity to leave their jobs. Even these individuals, however, must find activities to occupy their time and help them to feel wanted and worthwhile.

Résumé

Security is one of the major outcomes individuals seek from their employment. It is concerned in a large measure with the possible loss of income as the result of layoffs, disability, or retirement, as well as with the loss of the feeling of being needed and worthwhile. Until recent years it was considered to be mainly the responsibility of the government through the various insurance programs to provide financial assistance to employees and their families who suffered a loss of income. Unemployment insurance, survivors benefits, disability benefits, and old age assistance under the Social Security program, therefore, have been the major sources of assistance contributing to the financial security of employees. In addition, state workmen's compensation insurance also has provided financial assistance to those suffering from job-incurred injuries.

More recently, there has been a growing sense of responsibility among employers for the welfare of their employees. As a result of this fact as well as various external pressures, many employers have begun to initiate unemployment and retirement benefits to supplement those received by employees through government insurance programs. Although private pension plans have been growing rapidly in number since World War II, the majority of employees have not benefited from such plans because they do not remain with an employer for the required period to become eligible for benefits. Congressional concern over this deficiency in private plans has resulted in legislation that will enable a larger proportion of employees to receive private pensions.

In addition to financial security, psychological security can be a problem for employees in the older age groups. Such individuals often need reassurance that they are wanted and needed in the organization and not in danger of being terminated before becoming eligible for a pension. Many of them also can benefit from assistance in preparing for their retirement and in making the adjustment to retired life. These adjustments must be made by everyone who lives to retirement age. Although only the individual can accomplish the adjustment, any assistance received enables that person to understand the

[25] "Early Retirement Continues to Attract Auto Workers; Satisfaction with Retirement Experiences Still High," *I.S.R. Newsletter*, University of Michigan (Autumn, 1970), p. 4.

problems of adjustment and make the transition to retirement more satisfactory.

DISCUSSION QUESTIONS

1. What are some of the deficiencies of contemporary workmen's compensation laws?
2. What are some of the trends that are occurring with respect to the types of disabilities for which employees may receive workmen's compensation?
3. What major improvements are provided by the Pension Reform Act for employees covered by private pension plans?
4. What are some of the problems that an organization must seek to overcome when establishing a pension plan for its employees?
5. How do the retirement benefits under Social Security differ from a regular pension plan?
6. Distinguish between a currently insured worker and a fully insured worker in terms of requirements for coverage and benefits received.
7. What are some of the adjustment problems that employees are likely to encounter upon their retirement? Can a company actually do much to help its employees resolve these problems?
8. What factors may affect an individual's desire for retirement and the ability to adjust to it?

PROBLEM 21-1 YOU TELL HIM!

A special meeting of the executive committee of the Central City Gas and Electric Company had just been called to order by its president, J. D. Wood. All members of the committee were present except Sid Heller, the treasurer, who had not been notified of the meeting for reasons to be disclosed. Wood began: "I've called this meeting this morning to discuss a rather delicate problem we have on our hands, namely, the problem of what action to take in the case of our long-time colleague and friend, Sid Heller. What are we going to do with him?"

Heller, age 66, had been employed by the company for well over 40 years, longer than any other member of management. Starting as a clerk in accounting, he had risen gradually to his present position of treasurer. In his prime Sid had been held in high regard both within and outside the company. Furthermore, he had always gone out of his way to help and take under his wing the younger people entering management. In fact, J. D. Wood and each of the other members of the executive committee, earlier in their management careers, had received counsel and encouragement from Heller and had been entertained in his home. Unfortunately Heller had slowed down considerably during the past few years with the result that the assistant treasurer had been forced to assume many of his job responsibilities. Heller actually should have retired by this time if he had known what to do with his life in retirement.

In response to Wood's opening question, Tony Lopez, vice-president for sales, replied, "I think we should ask him to retire." Fred Schmidt, controller, entered the discussion at this point saying, "Yes. That might be a good idea, but who's going to tell him. Do you want the job, Tony?" "Thanks, but no thanks," was Tony's reply. About this time Wood took over again, "Well, gentlemen, I certainly don't have the heart to tell him to retire. Perhaps we should start by formulating a company policy on retirement. Maybe we should formulate a policy making retirement mandatory at 65." "Yeah," interrupted Tony, "but what would such a policy do to my department? At least two of my best people are 65 or nearing that age and why should I have to lose them?"

After considerable discussion and little progress, Wood decided to wind up the meeting, stating, "Gentlemen, I am appointing Tony, Fred, and Will Ball, our personnel manager, to study the matter and come up with some sort of policy statement on retirement. I'll call another meeting next week to consider their recommendations. The meeting is adjourned.''

a. What action, if any, should the executive committee take with respect to Sid Heller?
b. Does the action taken in appointing a special committee to study the problem represent the most effective solution at the moment?
c. What are some of the possible reasons for having a policy making retirement mandatory at some particular age such as 65?

SUGGESTED READINGS

Chruden, Herbert J., and Arthur W. Sherman, Jr. *Readings in Personnel Management*, 4th ed. Cincinnati: South-Western Publishing Co., Inc., 1976, Part 6.

Corporate Retirement Policy and Practice, Studies in Personnel Policy, No. 190. New York: National Industrial Conference Board, 1964.

Geist, Harold. *Psychological Aspects of Retirement*. Springfield, Ill.: C. C. Thomas, 1968.

Hepner, Harry W. *Retirement—A Time to Live Anew*. New York: McGraw-Hill Book Company, 1969.

Kent, Donald P. *Aging: Fact and Fancy*. OA No. 224, U.S. Department of Health, Education, and Welfare, Welfare Administration, Office of Aging, 1965.

U.S. Department of Health, Education, and Welfare. *Planning for the Later Years*. Washington, D.C.: U.S. Government Printing Office, 1965.

Employee Benefits

In the preceding chapter a variety of employee benefits were described. In this chapter other types of benefits or wage supplements will be examined, following a discussion of historical trends in employee benefit programs and factors to be considered in planning these programs. For a long time employee benefits were generally referred to as "fringe benefits" and, while the term is still used, it is misleading from the standpoint of costs. The cost of employee benefits, or supplementary nonwage payments, may range from 14 percent to over 60 percent of wages, depending upon the organization and/or industry, with the average cost of employee benefits now at 32.7 percent of wages or payroll payments.[1] Even these figures do not include the costs of many of the services commonly furnished to employees which contribute to their welfare.

In other countries the average cost of benefits is even higher. European union leaders have been able to negotiate benefit packages that are substantially greater than those found in the United States. In Italy, for example, the mandatory fringe benefits exceed 82 percent of the employee's basic wage.[2]

Because of the increasing costs of employee benefits, which have been rising steadily since the 1920s, many employers are concerned not only about their cost but are questioning their value to the individuals and to the organization. Before unions achieved their present status, benefits were extended to employees largely as a result of management's desire to keep employees

---

[1] *Employee Benefits*, 1973 (Washington, D.C.: Chamber of Commerce of the United States of America, 1974), p. 5.

[2] Herbert J. Chruden and Arthur W. Sherman, Jr., *Personnel Practices of American Companies in Europe* (New York: American Management Association, 1972), p. 19.

satisfied and to counteract the efforts of unions to organize their personnel. Union leaders, however, learned that they could bargain for additional fringe benefits when it was not possible or feasible to ask for substantial wage increases. Therefore, benefits began to be initiated more as a result of collective bargaining or as the result of the need for nonunion employers to compete with unionized ones for competent personnel. Collective bargaining agreements continue to affect the nature of benefit programs, but there are other factors which will be discussed that influence the trends that these programs are following.

TRENDS IN EMPLOYEE BENEFITS

The emphasis on benefits, reflected by the amount of money spent to provide them, has been growing steadily over the past several decades to the present and is reflected in many different types of benefits. While these benefits may be categorized in different ways, they are often grouped into five major categories:

1. Legally required benefits (unemployment insurance, Social Security, and workmen's compensation).
2. Private welfare and security programs (pension plans, life and health insurance payments).
3. Pay for time not worked (holidays, vacations, sick leave, rest periods).
4. Extra compensation plans (profit sharing, savings plans, suggestion awards).
5. Employee services (subsidized cafeterias, discounts on purchase of company products, educational assistance).[3]

Each organization will have its own benefit package made up of specific items in the above categories. These items have often been added in piecemeal fashion in response to various forces in society.

History of Employee Benefits

While the major increase in employee benefits has occurred since the middle 1940s, there were benefits prior to that time. Many employers, as early as the 1920s, recognized the fact that their employees were entitled to have a desirable place in which to work as well as some degree of security in their employment and, thus, provided various types of fringe benefits on a more or less informal basis. In some instances this action was undoubtedly motivated by a sincere belief by employers that employees were entitled to more of the benefits of capitalism than was represented by their wages. Other employers were motivated by a belief that employees, because of their lesser economic and educational status, lacked the ability to manage their own personal affairs and

[3] Robert M. McCaffery, *Managing the Employee Benefits Program* (New York: American Management Association, 1972), p. 13.

needed someone to "look after" them. Frequently referred to as paternalistic, employers of this type assured employees that they would be taken care of in time of need or emergency and that they should feel secure. This paternalistic approach was not entirely unsuccessful. However, with the growth of unions during the 1930s and 1940s and the increasing education and employment opportunities, employees began to recognize that their contributions to the employer and to society were worthy of reward and should not be left to the initiative of a benevolent employer. Union leaders, in their desire to obtain better working conditions for their members and to attract new members, pushed for additional fringe benefits at a time when employers were already attempting to use benefits to "keep employees in the fold" and dissuade them from the advances of the union. As a result, employees were assured of receiving benefits either through the employer's initiative, the union's initiative, or both. Employee benefits were at this stage in their history at the end of the 1930s.

Influence of World War II. One of the most important factors in the development of employee benefits was the concern over inflation and the imposing of a ceiling on wages by the federal government during World War II. Under regulations that were established, employers could not increase wages and, therefore, did not have the customary appeals with which to attract new employees who were badly needed to replace those individuals who were called into the Armed Forces. The easiest way to overcome the restriction on wages was for an employer to provide special inducements in the forms of nonwage supplements, such as pension and welfare programs, paid vacations, sick leave, and health and life insurance. Although these benefits helped the employer to obtain needed personnel during the war, most employers found themselves obligated to continue the benefits after the war because employees and their unions were unwilling to give them up. The continued competition among employers for competent employees during the postwar period was also an important factor in their retention.

Post World War II period. Following the removal of the wage freeze after World War II, union leaders concentrated their efforts on obtaining wage increases which they felt were long overdue. The inflationary results of World War II were apparent to everyone, and the unions were able to make an effective case for increasing wages in order that their members could maintain a satisfactory standard of living. As the costs of living began to level off about 1948, the unions' arguments for increased wages became less significant since the public began to look with disfavor upon continuing rounds of wage and accompanying price increases. It was generally accepted by the public, however, that employees should have better standards of health and welfare in their employment than they were receiving. Thus, fringe benefits became a bargaining issue that the unions could pursue realistically. Interpretations by the National Labor Relations Board and the Supreme Court to the effect that employers were obligated to bargain for pensions were also major factors that stimulated the spread of this type of fringe benefit.

Recent Developments. The growth of employee benefits has occurred during a period in the economic history of the United States when profits have been high and labor unions have been free to make employee benefits a major bargaining effort. The number and types of benefits are evident when one studies the summaries of labor negotiations. While pressure from organized labor is expected to continue, there are other trends and developments that are predicted to have a major influence on employee benefits. A force equal to that of labor is expected from the increased leisure time available to workers. This is both a benefit and a stimulant for more benefits with a leisure orientation. Flexible working hours are now fairly common, free concert and theater tickets are distributed regularly, and organization-owned facilities are available to most employees. Several other major stimulants may appear and have a significant impact on benefits such as higher levels of affluence, new medical advances, increasing frustration and militancy among the blacks, and further social legislation.[4]

It is difficult to make specific predictions of what employees will want and expect in benefits, but Foltman suggests the possibilities listed in Figure 22-1. Foltman also predicts that more emphasis will be placed on the psychological and economic theories pertaining to fringe benefits. Long-standing assumptions will be challenged and theory pertaining to lifetime compensation problems rather than to single moments in time will become available.[5]

The "Cafeteria" Approach. Though not yet widespread, the "cafeteria" approach to benefits on Foltman's list is likely to be one of the next steps in the evolution of employee benefits. It recognizes that individual situations differ because of such factors as age, family status, and life style. This approach utilizes the data-handling capabilities of computers and allows each employee to have an individual combination of benefits within some overall limit.[6] An individual combination of benefits, or *variable benefits* as they are also called, requires overcoming two barriers: the cost of implementation and managerial resistance to change. Werther is of the opinion that the cafeteria or variable benefits approach offers an opportunity for improved organizational atmosphere, more controllable costs, and greater individual autonomy and satisfaction.[7]

Psychological Fringe Benefits. Another predicted trend in this area is for such psychological factors as recognition, job satisfaction, and self actualization to become bargainable issues in the evolution of employee

[4] T. J. Gordon and R. E. LeBleu, "Employee Benefits—1970-1985," *Harvard Business Review*, Vol. 48, No. 1 (January-February, 1970), pp. 93-107.

[5] Felicia F. Foltman, "Implications of Fringe Benefits in the 1970's," *The Arizona Review*, Vol. 17, Nos. 6-7 (June-July, 1968), pp. 1-5.

[6] J. H. Foegen, "The High Cost of Innovative Employee Benefits," *California Management Review*, Vol. 15, No. 3 (Spring, 1973), pp. 100-104.

[7] William B. Werther, Jr., "A New Direction in Rethinking Fringe Benefits," *MSU Business Topics*, Vol. 22, No. 1 (Winter, 1974), pp. 35-40, as reprinted in Herbert J. Chruden and Arthur W. Sherman, Jr., *Readings in Personnel Management* (4th ed.; Cincinnati: South-Western Publishing Co., 1976), pp. 505-514.

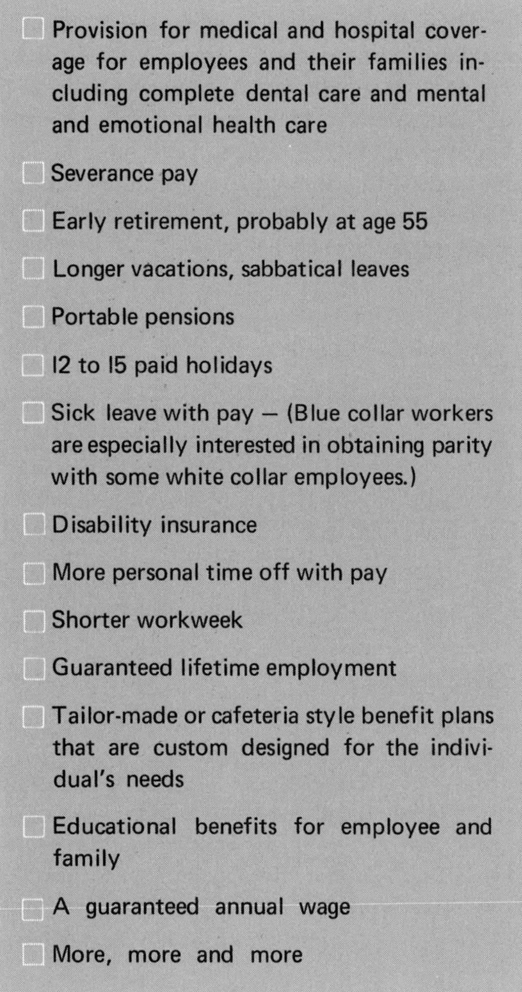

- Provision for medical and hospital coverage for employees and their families including complete dental care and mental and emotional health care
- Severance pay
- Early retirement, probably at age 55
- Longer vacations, sabbatical leaves
- Portable pensions
- 12 to 15 paid holidays
- Sick leave with pay — (Blue collar workers are especially interested in obtaining parity with some white collar employees.)
- Disability insurance
- More personal time off with pay
- Shorter workweek
- Guaranteed lifetime employment
- Tailor-made or cafeteria style benefit plans that are custom designed for the individual's needs
- Educational benefits for employee and family
- A guaranteed annual wage
- More, more and more

Source: Felicia F. Foltman, "Implications of Fringe Benefits in the 1970s," *The Arizona Review*, Vol. 17, Nos. 6-7 (June-July, 1968), p. 5. Reprinted with permission.

Figure 22-1 POSSIBLE FRINGE BENEFITS OF THE FUTURE

benefits. According to Foegen, bargained psychological "fringe on the fringe" is just around the corner. While these intangibles are more difficult to use as bargaining issues, Foegen states that union imagination in recognizing worker needs and in finding innovative ways to meet them should not be underestimated.[8]

[8] J. H. Foegen, "Fringe on the Fringe," *Personnel Administration*, Vol. 35, No. 1 (January-February, 1972), pp. 18-22.

Cost of Fringe Benefits

According to one Chamber of Commerce study (1973)[9] with 742 reporting companies, payments for fringe benefits averaged 32.7 percent of the payroll. The percentage shown after each one of the five categories of benefits in Table 22-1 represents a breakdown of the 32.7 percent. The average cost of these benefits was $3,230 a year per employee. Industry payments varied widely, and larger firms tended to pay higher benefits than smaller firms. The highest payments were made in the Northeast, followed by the East North Central, Western, and Southeastern states.

Table 22-1 FRINGE BENEFIT COSTS

Fringe Benefit Category	Percentage of Payroll
Pension and other agreed-upon payments, including pension-plan premiums and payments not covered by insurance-type plan, life insurance premiums, death benefits, sickness, accident, and medical-care insurance premiums, hospitalization insurance, etc., separation or termination pay allowances, discounts on goods and services purchased from company by employees, free meals . . . (Employer's Share)	10.5
Payments for time not worked, including paid vacations and bonuses in lieu of vacation, payments for holidays not worked, paid sick leave, and payments for State or National Guard duty, jury, witness and voting pay allowances, payments for time lost due to death in family or other personal reasons, etc.	9.2
Legally required benefits, including old-age and survivors insurance, unemployment compensation, workmen's compensation, railroad retirement tax, railroad unemployment insurance, state sickness benefits insurance, etc. . . (Employer's Share) . . .	7.5
Paid rest periods, lunch periods, wash-up time, travel time, clothes-change time, get-ready time, etc.	3.5
Profit-sharing payments, Christmas or other special bonuses, service awards, etc., and special wage payments ordered by courts, payments to union stewards, tuition refunds, etc.	2.0
	32.7

Source: Employee Benefits, 1973 (Washington, D.C.: Chamber of Commerce of the United States of America, 1974), p. 8.

[9] *Employee Benefits, 1973, op. cit.,* p. 5. The Chamber of Commerce has been publishing fringe benefit data since 1947 and the Bureau of Labor Statistics since 1953. For a report of BLS activities in this area, see Alvin Bauman, "Measuring Employee Compensation in U.S. Industry," *Monthly Labor Review,* Vol. 93, No. 10 (October, 1970), pp. 17-24.

Among the 742 reporting companies were 155 companies that had reported data to the Chamber of Commerce since 1953. Analysis of their reports showed that the employee benefit payments increased from 21.6 percent in 1953, to 28.0 percent in 1963, and to 36.3 percent in 1973.[10] This increase is sufficient to point out the importance of insuring that an employee benefit program is making a maximal contribution to the total personnel program of an organization.

BUILDING AN EFFECTIVE BENEFITS PROGRAM

In order to be effective to a maximum degree, considerable attention should be given to the planning and development of the benefit program. Too often a particular benefit is provided because other employers are doing it, because someone in authority thinks it is a good idea, or because of pressure from the union. The type of contribution that fringe benefits will make to the personnel program will depend upon the extent to which attention is given to certain basic principles that are discussed in this section.

Developing the Objectives

An employee benefit program, like any other phase of the personnel program, should be based upon a statement of objectives which serves as guidelines for building the program. The objectives should be concerned with satisfying employee needs and expectations and meeting employer requirements. Objectives for any single organization will depend upon many factors including size, location, degree of unionization, profitability, industry patterns, and management's perception of employee needs. Most importantly, the objectives have to be compatible with the philosophy and policies of the organization.[11]

Unless an organization has already adopted the cafeteria or variable benefits approach, an optimum combination or mix of benefits should be developed into a package. This involves the careful consideration of the various fringe items possible, the relative preference shown for each by management and the employees, the estimated cost of each, and the total amount of money available for the entire benefit package. By developing an optimum combination of benefits, the organization is more likely to achieve goals that are in harmony with its personnel policies.

Inviting Employee Participation

One of the prime requisites of a successful benefits program is that it receive the support of employees. Therefore, it is advisable that before a new benefit is introduced, the need for it should first be determined through some type of survey of the employees. Many organizations establish committees composed

---

[10] *Ibid.*

[11] Robert M. McCaffery, *op. cit.*, p. 19.

of representatives of management and the employees that study needs and make recommendations concerning the benefits and services which are desired.

While most benefit plans are based upon mass participation and their success and value depend primarily upon the application of group principles, the parts of the plans that are not required by law can often be tailored to specific groups within an organization. However, the more options there are to participate or not to participate in certain benefits, the more complicated the benefits program can become. There are, for example, some sophisticated employees who have the background, interest, and time necessary for choosing intelligently. Yet there are many indications that most employees of all categories do not wish or do not feel able to choose among a number of options.[12] Whether or not options are permitted, the fact that employees participate in designing fringe benefit programs helps to insure that management is moving in the direction of satisfying employee wants. It also provides a basis of communication about any problems associated with benefits, such as abuse of sick leave privileges or the overextending of the coffee break period.

Communicating the Benefits

The true measure of the success of a benefit program is the degree of trust, understanding, and appreciation which it gains from the employees.[13] Effective communication is the key to the attainment of these objectives. In communicating with employees about benefits, the information about complicated insurance and pension plans should be made clear to the employees so that there will be no misunderstanding as to what the plans will not provide as well as what they provide. Since employees are not usually skilled in technical or legalistic language, care must be taken to present the information in an understandable manner, using various media on a continuous basis.

A study of 202 large companies reveals that each of them used an average of three different methods for communicating information about benefits to employees.[14] Articles in in-house publications and personalized annual reports about benefits were the most popular methods, although other methods were used with considerable frequency. The personalized annual report to each employee provides employees and their families with information of personal concern to them. It also advises them of what it costs the employer to provide the specific benefits described in the report.

Many employers attempt to acquaint their supervisory personnel with the intricacies of benefit programs and provide various handouts as well as audio-visual materials that supervisors may use. Figure 22-2 from a supervisory

---

[12] E. S. Willis, "Problems in Selecting Employee Benefits," *Monthly Labor Review,* Vol. 92, Part 1, No. 4 (April, 1969), pp. 61-62.

[13] Robert M. McCaffery, *op. cit.,* p. 175.

[14] Richard M. Coffin and Michael S. Shaw, *Effective Communication of Employee Benefits* (New York: American Management Association, 1971), p. 121.

Source: Social Security Administration, U.S. Department of Health, Education, and Welfare, *Fringe Benefits* (Washington, D.C.: Superintendent of Documents, July, 1964), p. 13.

Figure 22-2 COMMUNICATION OF FRINGE BENEFIT PROVISIONS

manual on fringe benefits developed by the United States Department of Health, Education and Welfare is used in a presentation to remind department employees that they need not spend labored hours with calculators and complicated formulas in computing their basic annuity under the United States Civil Service Commission retirement system.

Controlling Costs

A major problem confronting most organizations is the increasing cost of providing benefits. Since many of the benefit items represent a fixed rather than a variable cost, management must decide whether or not it can meet the fixed costs under less desirable economic conditions. It is generally recognized that if an organization is forced to discontinue a benefit, the negative effect may exceed any positive effects that may have accrued from providing it.

In addition to the actual costs of employee benefits are the costs of administering the program. For the larger organization the overhead costs may be negligible. However, in the smaller organization the personnel costs of managing the benefit program may be sizable in proportion to the number of employees served. This situation points up an apparent need for fringe benefit consultants who would establish and assist in administering such programs in small business firms.

As a matter of sound administration as well as for collective bargaining purposes, it is important for an employer to maintain complete records of its costs for fringe benefits. Such costs should be communicated to employees in order that they may understand that the paycheck tells only part of the wage story.

Recognizing Problem Areas

It is generally assumed that benefits contribute to higher morale among employees and thus are worth the cost. With continuing pressure from the unions for additional benefits, however, some employers have begun to question their value and to scrutinize each item with care. Employees have also questioned the value of some of the benefits, and they may actually prefer to have higher wages instead of the benefits. Under most conditions the individual employee is forced to take the whole package whether or not it meets his or her individual needs.[15] The employee may prefer a wage increase to insurance, or additional days of vacation with pay to having long lunch periods or supplemental unemployment benefits. In addition to restricting the individual's freedom of choice, there are also other problems that arise in connection with benefit programs.

Continued Demands for Additional Benefits. What may be considered a luxury at one time may be viewed later as a necessity. This has been true particularly of many employee benefits. Not too long ago vacations with pay were limited almost exclusively to executives and white-collar personnel. This situation no longer exists. Similarly, employer contributions to welfare funds to provide financial security for technologically displaced and retired workers have become bargaining issues in recent years. Although it is difficult to predict what the future will hold as far as benefits and services are concerned, it may be assumed that employees, through their union representatives, will continue to ask for more benefits. As soon as patterns are set in one industry and/or company, they tend to spread to other industries and/or companies with the result that an organization often experiences considerable difficulty in maintaining its own planned program. With established policies, however, an organization can resist some of the pressures for conformity that it encounters.

New Sources of Grievances. As additional benefits and services accrue to the employee as a result of bargaining, new potential problem areas are introduced.

---

[15] For an interesting article relating fringe benefits to psychological needs, see John Metzer, "Are Fringe Benefits An Answer?" *Personnel Administration,* Vol. 29, No. 4 (July-August, 1966), pp. 41-44.

The food service is a common target for complaints, some of which are perhaps justified. Health services are likewise criticized at times by employees who feel that they should receive better attention from the physicians and nurses. In fact, any of the benefits and services that are provided may become the subject of criticism and formal grievance action.

Charges of Paternalism. In its desire to let employees know what the company is doing for their welfare, management may create the impression of being paternalistic. Benefits that are interpreted by employees as constituting gifts from a beneficient employer are seldom received enthusiastically by these employees. Most employees feel that they have earned these benefits and services and that they are rightfully entitled to them regardless of how the employer feels about the matter. This does not mean that employees do not appreciate benefits and services but, rather, that they prefer to feel that they have earned or are entitled to them.

Some Larger Problems. While every employer is concerned with immediate problems, there are some far-reaching problems arising from benefits that sooner or later affect not only the employer but society as a whole. One of the most important and obvious problems is the effect that employee benefits have on inflation. If the costs of these benefits can be paid from profits or from increased productivity, there would be no problem; but often the costs must be passed on to the consumer in the form of higher prices. The consumer, in turn, to meet the price must eventually demand a higher wage. With benefits becoming an increasingly greater percentage of payroll costs, they may be more important than wages. Since benefits tend to be paid across the board, the higher they become in relation to wages the more they will tend to negate the values of the objective standards of job evaluation. There is also the problem of increased benefits in such areas as unemployment compensation. With supplementary unemployment benefits some workers can now collect 65 percent of their previous take-home pay. As unemployment benefits increase, and it is predicted they will, and as they approximate normal wages, there is the possibility that people will prefer not to work especially in jobs or under conditions where it is difficult to obtain need satisfaction. Finally, as employee benefits increase there is the tendency to freeze employees in their jobs since the benefits would be lost to them if they were to change employment. This tendency to freeze labor mobility may, in the long run, be detrimental to the economy.

Neglect of Other Personnel Functions. With increasing attention being given to benefits by the unions, there is always the possibility that executives and personnel managers will focus their attention on them and neglect other phases of the personnel program that may be more important. Similarly, overemphasis on benefits may result in employees being more concerned about their security for the future than they are in "turning out a day's work." The many cartoons and jokes about the job applicant barely out of high school or college who wants a detailed description of a company's retirement program and other benefits reflect the importance attached to job security and employee benefits. Employers recognize the interest in benefits and induce applicants by emphasizing them in employment advertisements. Employers should, however, be aware of the fact that benefits are likely to discourage movement of marginal personnel who are strongly motivated by security, status quo, and certainty as opposed to uncertainty. It is essential, therefore, that the recruiting, selection, development, and evaluation functions of the personnel program produce the type of work force to whom an organization can afford to provide employee benefits.[16]

TYPES OF EMPLOYEE BENEFITS

Several types of employee benefits were examined in the preceding chapter. All of them involved a direct or indirect payment of money to the employee. In addition to benefits that are designed to increase the financial security of employees, most organizations have other types of benefits that involve providing a service. Like any employee benefit, these represent a cost to the employer and an economic gain to the employees since the latter would normally spend part of their wages in payment of these services if obtained from sources outside the organization. Therefore, the contribution of these benefits to the organization as well as to the employees should be assessed as carefully as the types of benefits discussed in Chapter 21. While specific programs will include their own benefit mix, some of the more popular service-type benefits will be considered here.

Health Services

Virtually all organizations of any size provide some form of health service such as first aid, treatment of minor illness by nurses, and routine services administered or supervised by a physician. The extent of the services will vary considerably, but they are generally designed to handle minor illnesses and injuries and to provide preventative measures against such nonoccupational illnesses as polio, colds, and influenza. In a number of organizations, health services have been expanded to meet the requirements of the federal Occupational Safety and Health Act. Preemployment and periodic employee examinations, for example, require more sophisticated audiometric and visual tests than have been used previously. Other changes in health services include the addition of alcohol and drug abuse referral services, and an increase in in-house counseling programs.[17]

---

[16] F. K. Dempsey, Jr., "Too Many Benefits Spoil the Employee," *Administrative Management*, Vol. 28, No. 10 (October, 1967), pp. 45-46.

[17] *Labor Policy and Practice—Personnel Management* (Washington, D.C.: The Bureau of National Affairs, Inc., 1974), pp. 245:11-18.

One of the main objectives of company health programs is to educate personnel in the principles and practices of good physical and mental health. The success of the program is dependent upon stimulating interest among employees. This may be done through the use of posters and films and through talks and interviews with employees. Supervisors should recognize that while many individuals are not inflicted with an illness, neither are they enjoying the quality of health to which they are entitled and from which both they and the organization would benefit. Over-indulgence in smoking and the use of alcohol, lack of exercise and proper rest, and poor nutrition keep many individuals from attaining the level of efficiency and the feeling of well-being that others enjoy. Many individuals, for example, are nervous and irritable and low in efficiency during the morning because they did not have a breakfast that contained sufficient protein to sustain them throughout the morning. A doughnut or roll or other high-carbohydrate food does not give the sustaining energy that is necessary even for sedentary jobs.[18] Surveys show that income is no determiner of eating habits. Many Americans, including those in executive groups, are overfed but undernourished.[19]

Insurance Programs

One of the oldest and most popular employee benefits is the group life insurance program which provides death benefits to beneficiaries and which may include accidental death and dismemberment benefits. As a rule, the amount of life insurance coverage for an individual employee depends solely on salary level; however, in manufacturing industries there are many plans which provide the same amount of insurance regardless of salary. The trend continues toward union-negotiated, company-financed plans; however, in some organizations employees still pay the cost or it is shared by the employees and the employer.

Group medical, surgical, and dental plans and prepaid drug programs are also popular services provided by the employer through a master or group policy written by an insurance company, by an association such as the Blue Cross or Blue Shield, or through some type of prepaid medical practice such as the Kaiser Foundation Health Plan.

About 9 out of 10 persons in the United States under the age of 65 are covered by private health insurance, chiefly group insurance plans connected with employment.[20] Plans negotiated by unions with the employers account for almost half of the employees covered by health benefit plans in private industry. Despite the ever-increasing expenditures by employers and employees for health benefits, the unions have continued to find the plans

[18] Adelle Davis, *Let's Eat Right to Keep Fit* (New York: Harcourt Brace Jovanovich, Inc., 1970), Chapter 2.

[19] "Our Daily Bread," *The Wall Street Journal*, January 6, 1971.

[20] Donald M. Landay, "Negotiated Health Plans," *Monthly Labor Review*, Vol. 92, No. 5 (May, 1969), pp. 3-10.

inadequate. They are currently stressing two major lines of improvement: (1) broadening the scope of benefits to cover more kinds of health care, and (2) increasing the efficiency of expenditures to get more service of higher quality for the money spent. The unions are negotiating for increased benefits in the areas of dental and visual care, prescription drugs, and mental health care.[21]

Financial Services

Credit unions have been established in many organizations to serve the financial needs of the employees. The credit union encourages thrift by offering interest or dividends on deposits (usually in the form of $5 shares) at a higher rate of interest than that paid by most commercial banks. It also serves as a lending institution from which the employee may borrow money at a rate of interest usually not exceeding 1 percent a month on the unpaid balance of the loan. While employers often provide office space and a payroll deduction service, the credit union is an activity operated by employees under federal and state legislation and supervision. The popularity of credit unions is reflected by the fact that in 1972 there were 23,160 credit unions in the United States with 26 million members and combined assets of $24.6 billion.[22]

While the credit unions are lending institutions and in most instances are able to help an employee who needs financial assistance, there are occasional instances in which companies assist employees by granting loans at a low rate of interest or interest free. Some companies make loans to assist in the purchase of homes and provide other financial assistance that will contribute to employee welfare and morale. For top-level executives an increasing number of companies are now providing financial counseling on such matters as estate planning, investment strategy, and the details of executive compensation benefits.[23]

Counseling Services

While most organizations expect supervisors to counsel subordinates, it is recognized that there will occasionally be employees with problems that require the services of qualified counselors. A large percentage of organizations refer such individuals to outside counseling services such as church organizations, family counseling services or marriage counselors, and mental health clinics. Some organizations, however, have a qualified person, such as a consulting psychologist, a counselor, or another qualified individual to whom employees may be referred. One company goes so far as to provide 24-hour counseling service. The Utah Copper Division of the Kennecott Copper

[21] *Ibid.*

[22] *Credit Union Yearbook, 1973* (Madison, Wisconsin: Credit Union National Association, 1973).

[23] "Personal Business," *Business Week* (September 1, 1973), p. 62.

Corporation has a program under which employees or members of their families can dial INSIGHT on a Salt Lake City area telephone day or night. Arrangements are made on the spot for an appointment in the employee's home, the INSIGHT office, or wherever the employee would be comfortable. Smaller organizations that cannot afford to undertake extensive counseling programs on their own often benefit from working with community institutions.[24]

Legal and Accounting Services

Many organizations make the services of professional persons on the staff available to employees at no expense. Attorneys and accountants, employed in most of the larger organizations, possess knowledge and skills that can be used to the advantage of employees. An attorney can contribute immeasurably to employee effectiveness by providing help in drawing up a will, giving advice on contracts, and assisting employees in locating qualified personnel to handle complicated legal cases. Similarly, the talents of an accountant can be made available, at least on a limited basis, to employees who need assistance in completing tax returns or who have minor problems in connection with the returns.

In 1973 Congress amended the Taft-Hartley Act to permit unions to bargain for legal insurance as an employer-shared benefit. Some 2,500 plans were operating in 1974, bringing legal services routinely to millions of people who have not been able to afford them.[25]

Recreational Services

The fact that many organizations have a recreational program is some indication of the general desirability and need for it. The extent of the program, however, and the specific types of recreation should be determined largely by the expressed desires of the employees.

Most organizations offer some type of sports program in which personnel may participate on a voluntary basis. Bowling, handball, volleyball, golf, baseball, and tennis are quite common because a large number of employees may engage in these activities on an intramural basis. In addition to the intramural program, many organizations have teams that represent them in athletic contests with other local organizations.

While sports normally are provided only for employees, many social functions are for employees and their spouses or entire families. The company picnic is a typical institution among business firms that may be attended by personnel at all levels in the organization and their families. Dances, banquets, cocktail hours, and other social events also provide an opportunity for

---

[24] *Labor Policy and Practice—Personnel Management, op. cit.*, (1974) pp. 245:101-106, 152-154.

[25] "New Fringe Benefit: Prepaid Legal Service," *Business Week* (January 12, 1974), p. 34.

everyone to get better acquainted and to strengthen interpersonal relationships. It is desirable that employees have a major part in the planning of such programs and events if they are to be successful. However, the employer should retain control of all events associated with the organization because of possible legal responsibility. The California Supreme Court, for example, ruled that employers who encourage or allow office drinking parties on or away from the company premises may be liable for resulting consequences of overindulgence.[26]

Other Services

In addition to the services described above, other services have become popular with employees and serve to meet their needs. The services discussed in this section are merely typical of those provided and do not constitute an exhaustive list.

Purchasing Assistance. Various methods may be used by the company to assist employees in purchasing merchandise more conveniently and at a savings. One type of enterprise is known as the "company store" or commissary and in its present form represents a real service to the employee, especially in remote areas where the community or a substantial part of it is owned by the company. Most companies sell their own products at a discount to the employees, and in some instances certain items of other manufacturers are procured through the purchasing department for the employee at a discount.

Housing, Moving, and Transportation. The days of "company houses" are now relatively rare, except for mining or logging operations, construction projects in remote areas, or the armed forces. There are, however, a variety of housing services provided by nearly all organizations that move employees from one office or plant to another in connection with a transfer, promotion, or plant relocation. These services include helping employees find living quarters, paying for travel and moving expenses, and protecting transferred employees from loss in disposing of their homes.[27] Some firms now subsidize increased mortgage rates, and others purchase the transferred employee's old home.[28] To facilitate transportation to and from the job, parking spaces are provided; a service that enables employees to form car pools readily may also be established.

Child Care Facilities. The increased employment of women with dependent children has created an unprecedented demand for child care facilities. In the

---

[26] 117 Cal Reporter 65 (1974).

[27] *Labor Policy and Practice—Personnel Management, op. cit.,* (1975) pp. 245:401-404.

[28] "Easier Moves—Housing Worries Spur Companies to Increase Relocation Benefits," *The Wall Street Journal,* November 12, 1974.

past mothers typically had to make their own arrangements for sitters or with nursery schools for preschool children. It is not uncommon today, however, to find community centers established for the benefit of working mothers by nonprofit organizations and even day care centers set up on company premises. AVCO Economic Systems Corporation in Boston and KLH Research and Development Corporation in Cambridge operate such facilities. Many hospitals have operated day care centers for children of their employees. Unions have also promoted such facilities for the benefit of their members.[29]

While several women's organizations have been involved in day care projects for many years, they have recently made great strides in their nationwide efforts to establish more day care centers. Among these groups are the National Council of Negro Women, National Council of Jewish Women, the Black Women's Community Development Institute, and the YWCA.[30]

Food Service. In the larger organizations the most common arrangements for providing food services for employees are lunch rooms with several different vending machines and/or employee cafeterias. In addition, vending machines are typically located in various office and plant areas close to employee working stations. This makes food and beverages readily available when they are desired. Their presence, however, often creates housekeeping problems and some employers complain that employees spend too much time at the machines. (In earlier days, the drinking fountain was the subject of employer complaints.) Perhaps a more serious problem with the machines is that they often do not provide the types of snack foods that are most suitable from a nutritional standpoint. In response to customer suggestions, some vendors are attempting to provide a more balanced selection of food items.

Related to the matter of food service is the coffee break—an employee benefit that has become almost universal since World War II. Its purpose is to offset the lag in energy that often occurs in midmorning and midafternoon as the result of, in many cases, improper nutrition and lack of exercise. A survey of more than 600 representative business firms in Ohio disclosed that nearly nine out of ten firms provided coffee breaks, two breaks a day of 10 to 15 minutes in length are standard, workers are paid for the time spent in breaks, and more and more unions demand that the agreements specify coffee breaks as employee benefits.[31]

Résumé

In recent years employees have come to expect a variety of benefits that are supplements to their regular wages. These benefits that now cost

---

[29] *Personnel Management—Policies and Practices,* New Ideas, No. 393 (Englewood Cliffs, New Jersey: Prentice-Hall, Inc., 1971).

[30] U.S. Department of Labor, *Day Care Facts,* 1973.

[31] *Labor Policy and Practice—Personnel Management, op. cit.,* (1974) p. 245:205.

employers, and ultimately the consumers, billions of dollars a year represent a sizable portion of the wage costs in American industry. While benefits were originally initiated by management, they have more recently become bargaining demands of the union. As a result, organizations have been forced to add certain benefits that may not be in harmony with its overall personnel policies. While it is expected that unions will continue to ask for additional benefits, management should take the initiative, in consultation with its employees, to determine the benefits that will satisfy the employees and provide incentives to greater efficiency. The costs and the potential problems that may arise from benefits should also be considered.

In this and the preceding chapter a wide variety of benefits were described. Many of them are designed to increase the financial security of employees while many others provide some type of service that will contribute to employee satisfaction. Regardless of the type of benefit, management expects that the cost of these benefits will be offset by increased efficiency, reduced turnover, and other tangible benefits to the organization.

DISCUSSION QUESTIONS

1. Many companies are concerned about the rising cost of employee benefits and question their value to the company and to the employees.
   a. In your opinion what benefits are of greatest value to employees? To the company? Why?
   b. What can management do to increase the value of benefits to the company?
   c. How do benefits in other companies affect a company's benefit program?
2. Sometimes at company picnics, and similar "short-sleeved" events, a few employees are likely to lose their inhibitions temporarily and express their opinions and feelings quite freely to management personnel.
   a. What advantages are there in such types of events? What disadvantages?
   b. Should executives fraternize with employees? What types of events are least likely to result in incidents that would be embarrassing to both executives and employees?
3. Employees often fail to consider benefits when wages are discussed and compared with those of persons doing similar work in a different company. What should a company do to make employees aware of the financial value of benefits to them?
4. Employee benefits were found to cost over $3,230 a year per employee in 742 United States companies surveyed by the Chamber of Commerce. What would you think of a plan that called for removing all benefits, except those required by law, and giving the employees this amount in cash as part of wages? Discuss the advantages and disadvantages of such a plan.
5. Abuse of sick leave is so common that many companies question its value and resent its costs.
   a. What can management do to reduce its abuse under most sick leave plans?
   b. Would it be appropriate for a company to send a visiting nurse to the employee's home?
   c. Can you suggest a plan that would provide security for employees but would discourage them from using sick leave when they were not ill?
6. An article in *The Wall Street Journal* captioned "A Union Plot Succeeds at Stanford University" tells of the Service Employees International Union negotiating employee

access to a plot of university land for vegetable gardening. In what ways would this benefit the employees? Does this type of benefit suggest any possibilities for other unusual types of benefits?

7. The coffee break was described as an employee benefit that has become almost universal since World War II. What are the advantages and disadvantages of it to the employer? To the employee?

PROBLEM 22-1 THE SHORT FRIDAY

Friday, December 22, started like any other day at the Meyer's Meat Products Company. Since it was the last working day before Christmas, spirits were high among employees in the plant; and as the morning progressed these spirits soared still higher, with the aid of flasks that appeared from pockets and lunch boxes. After a while, individuals were forced to decide whether they should try to maintain their capacity to work or foster the goodwill of those co-workers who insisted upon sharing their bottled cheer with all persons whom they contacted. In most instances, the urge to foster goodwill was stronger than the urge to continue working. The rapid developments within the plant caught the production supervisor, Harry Stone, somewhat off guard; and as employees became more unruly, Stone grew more hesitant as to what action he should take for fear of what they might do to him. Finally, he decided to consult with James Shultz, the general manager and one of the company owners, about the problem that was developing. As the two entered the plant area they were just in time to witness one of the workers being thrown, clothes and all, into the curing vat that was used in the processing of hams. The soggy appearance of the pair who were administering the dunking indicated that they had previously been accorded similar treatment.

The arrival of Shultz, with an enraged look on his face, helped to quiet conditions momentarily. Partly because he feared his rising blood pressure and partly because he feared that he, too, might get dunked in the pickling vat, Shultz managed to keep his temper under control. His only reaction was to order the workers to clean up their work places and leave the company premises immediately. While it had been customary to close the plant early on the last workday before Christmas, the 10:30 a.m. shutdown on the 22nd of December constituted a new record for the company.

a. In order to avoid a repetition of the situation that developed at this plant, what preventive action should Shultz take in future years?
b. Should disciplinary action be taken against those who brought liquor into the plant?
c. What are the inherent dangers of permitting celebrations such as this to occur on company premises?

SUGGESTED READINGS

Allen, Donna. *Fringe Benefits: Wage or Social Obligations*. 2d ed. Ithaca: New York State School of Industrial and Labor Relations, Cornell University, 1969.

Chruden, Herbert J., and Arthur W. Sherman, Jr. *Readings in Personnel Management*, 4th ed. Cincinnati: South-Western Publishing Co., 1976, Part 6.

Coffin, Richard M., and Michael S. Shaw. *Effective Communication of Employee Benefits*. New York: American Management Association, 1971.

Deric, Arthur J. (ed.). *The Total Approach to Employee Benefits*. New York: American Management Association, 1967.

Employee Benefits, 1973. Washington, D.C.: Chamber of Commerce of the United States, 1974.

McCaffery, Robert M. *Managing the Employee Benefits Program*. New York: American Management Association, 1972.

Assessment and Research

23

Appraisal and Research

The importance of establishing policies and procedures that will result in the development of an effective personnel program has been emphasized throughout this book. It should be recognized, however, that management cannot be certain that its personnel objectives are being achieved merely because it has established a program for this purpose. The program should be audited periodically to assure that its objectives are being accomplished.

Personnel program audits or appraisals typically involve obtaining statistical data relative to employee turnover, grievances, absences, accidents, and similar indicators of the overall effectiveness of the program. In larger organizations, however, assessment of the personnel program is likely to go beyond the compilation of personnel statistics and to include research in the behavioral sciences. Such research involves more intensive investigations so as to obtain in-depth information about the program. It is also usually more sophisticated in terms of theory and methodology.

While statistical information from a personnel program appraisal and the findings from organizational research studies will often provide the basis for making improvements in the personnel program, successful personnel management requires that managers familiarize themselves with the practices of other organizations and with the findings from studies conducted by professionals. The findings from research studies are widely disseminated through journals, special reports, professional meetings, and even the daily newspapers, so that information which can be used to improve personnel policies and procedures is virtually available to everyone. The management of an organization, therefore, should utilize findings from personnel research studies along with the information obtained from appraisals of its own program.

APPRAISAL OF THE PERSONNEL PROGRAM

It is a universal practice to conduct a periodic audit or appraisal of the financial condition of an organization in order that any deficiencies may be noted and necessary action taken to correct them. Such an appraisal may uncover not only the presence of deficiencies but may also reveal strengths which were not recognized. One might assume that an important function like personnel management would receive the same careful evaluation as the fiscal aspects of an organization in order that strengths and weaknesses could be known and used as a basis for intelligent action. Various studies indicate rather clearly, however, that a comprehensive appraisal of the personnel program is conducted in only a small percentage of organizations. Nevertheless, there is a growing interest in human resource accounting in which the human assets are evaluated just as are the other assets of an organization. In determining the value of its human resources, an organization needs to consider all of the costs that enter into recruiting and developing employees. Similarly, the costs of absenteeism and turnover must also be considered.[1] While most organizations are not yet at this stage in their thinking about human resources, many of them do conduct appraisals of specific personnel functions.

Personnel Appraisal Practices

According to replies from members of BNA's *Personnel Policies Forum,* well over four out of five Forum companies evaluate the effectiveness of certain functions of their personnel-industrial relations departments. Methods of evaluation are varied, and most employers use more than one method. As shown in Table 23-1, the chief method of evaluating the personnel function is by comparing results against previously set goals. In 25 percent of the companies, appraisal is done through periodic audits of policies and procedures. Other methods used include the analysis of various data on such matters as turnover, grievances, personnel costs, training, and accidents, and the conducting of surveys, meetings, discussions, and interviews of the types described in earlier chapters.[2] Included in this group are attitude surveys (discussed in Chapter 15), performance appraisal summaries (Chapter 10), interviews and group conferences between management and employees (Chapter 14 and 15), and formal grievance procedures (Chapter 18). These nonstatistical approaches are often more valuable in correcting problem areas in that they may reveal the causes of problems rather than merely indicate their existence. However, statistical data that reach top management can serve to stimulate corrective action.

Methodological Problems. Too frequently the appraisals that are conducted are limited in their scope and lack the type of comprehensive coverage of the

[1] William C. Pyle, "Monitoring Human Resources—on Line," *Michigan Business Review,* Vol. 22, No. 14 (July, 1970), pp. 19-32.

[2] *Labor policy and Practice—Personnel Management* (Washington: The Bureau of National Affairs, Inc., 1975), pp. 251:201-202.

Table 23-1 CHIEF METHODS OF EVALUATING THE PERSONNEL FUNCTION *

	All Companies	Larger	Smaller
Evaluating Departmental Results Against Goals	33%**	37%	23%
Periodic Audit of Policies, Procedures	25	25	26
Surveys, Meetings, Discussions, and Interviews	20	19	23
Analysis of Turnover Figures	16	15	19
Analysis of Grievances	8	9	10
Analysis of Cost of Performing Various Personnel Functions	6	7	5
Analysis of Training Effectiveness	5	5	5
Analysis of Accident Frequency	5	6	4
Feedback from Managers	5	5	5

Source: Labor Policy and Practice—Personnel Management (Washington, D.C.: The Bureau of National Affairs), pp. 251:201-202. Reproduced with permission.

* Figures total more than 100 percent because most companies use more than one method.
** Includes 7 percent of companies specifying a "management-by-objectives" program for personnel department.

personnel functions that should be undertaken. There are many reasons for this lack of full appraisal, especially in the initial stages of a program. In the first place, the specific objectives of the various personnel programs—i.e., recruitment, selection, training, safety, etc.—are rarely defined with any degree of clarity. Even where the objectives are clearly stated, there is the problem of conducting a scientifically designed study with control groups that are treated like the experimental group, with the exception that they are not exposed to the new personnel procedure or program. There are also problems in documenting the results of personnel practices because numerous environmental and human factors are intermixed.

Attitudinal Problems. Attitudes and values which impede the validation of personnel programs are described by Gordon as follows:

> If management is convinced of the potential value of a new personnel program, a controlled validation study is likely to be viewed as a needless waste of time and an intolerable delay in providing all employees with the program's promised rewards. Management is especially prone to overlook the principle of evaluation when the company is confronted by impending personnel problems which demand immediate action. Under these circumstances, management is reluctant to deprive any employees (viz., a control group) of the supposed benefits of the new personnel program. Consequently, scientific evaluation becomes impossible.
>
> Another potential source of the neglect of validation is a failure on management's part to appreciate fully all of the costs associated with the use of invalid personnel programs. The initial outlay of funds for new personnel programs usually pales in significance when contrasted with expenditures required for the purchase of new hardware and equipment.

One additional factor which accounts for numerous failures to attempt validation of personnel programs is related to the anxiety engendered by the notion of an evaluation. The term "evaluation" may suggest the idea of a test of the judgment and skills of the people responsible for recommending the development or purchase of the new program, as well as the people responsible for conducting the program. Many personnel specialists appear to be plagued by lingering doubts that their "heads will roll" should the validation fail to reveal that the experimental program has produced worthwhile results. Obviously, in this type of psychological climate there is little inclination or incentive for "risking" a test of the validity of a new program.[3]

To overcome these methodological and attitudinal problems, organizations will have to commit themselves to major policy changes. This will enable them to create an environment in which the validation of personnel programs will become standard operating procedure that has the support and full cooperation of top management.

Conducting an Appraisal Program

The first step in conducting an appraisal of the personnel management function is to identify the personnel functions about which more information is desired. After the major functions and principal subfunctions have been identified, the next step is to assess each of them in the light of the following questions:

1. What is the philosophy underlying the function?
2. What principles of management are being followed in carrying it out?
3. What policies have been established for this function?
4. What procedures have been established? Are they in line with the philosophy, principles, and policies?
5. Are the procedures, policies, management principles, and philosophy of each function consistent with those of other, related functions?[4]

Once the first two steps are completed, the next step is to determine the sources of information. Since appraisal is a form of research, it is important that the findings be based on as objective, reliable, and valid data as can be obtained. Various existing records in the organization may provide the necessary information concerning some of the activities. Figure 23-1 on pages 540 and 541 shows the wealth of information available from organization records and some suggested methods for analyzing it.

According to Odiorne, several approaches may be used in analyzing data:

1. Compare personnel programs with those of other companies, especially the successful ones.
2. Base an audit on some source of authority, such as consultant norms and behavioral science findings, or simply use a personnel textbook as a guide.

[3] Michael E. Gordon, "Three Ways to Effectively Evaluate Personnel Programs," *Personnel Journal*, Vol. 51, No. 7 (July, 1972), pp. 498-504, 510.

[4] Robert D. Gray, "Evaluating the Personnel Department," *Personnel*, Vol. 42, No. 2 (March-April, 1965), pp. 43-52.

RECORD	SOME METHODS OF ANALYSIS
Employee turnover record	Analyze record for causes of employee's termination of service. Correlate data with sources of applicants, tests used in selection and placement, sex of employees, length of service, departments, and occupations. Check to see if turnover should be reduced. Also ascertain methods for cutting turnover. Compare with other firms.
Absenteeism record	Check for possible causes of absenteeism. Correlate with age, occupation, and length of service of employees to see if any pattern is disclosed. Other items such as religion and community events may also be analyzed.
Accident frequency and severity	Compare departmental records for indications of problems in certain departments. See if time of day or length of day affects accident rates. Also compare with other firms. Show savings in reduced number of accidents.
Scrap-loss record	Discover whether scrap loss is reduced by better training or different types of training. Compare with past scrap records. See if use of tests in placement of employees reduces this figure. Compare records to see if employee-rating plans help reduce scrap costs.
Employee requests for transfers	Correlate with training received, sex, length of service, placement methods, type of work, and supervision received.
Grievance records	Analyze subject, handling, cause, costs, and employee characteristics to effect reduction in number of grievances. Show savings in time lost in handling grievances. Check frequency of grievances to locate trouble spots and to make necessary changes in company policies or union agreement.
Personnel inventories	Compare the number of employees required to handle certain functions with the number used for the same functions in other concerns. Check ages of personnel to see if young replacements are available for key jobs. See if employees are being trained for advancement. Also prepare for possible draft calls for employees.

Source: Thomas J. Luck, *Personnel Audit and Appraisal* (New York: McGraw-Hill Book Company, 1955), pp. 31-32. Reproduced with permission.

Figure 23-1 USING COMPANY RECORDS TO CHECK PERSONNEL PRACTICES (Page 1)

RECORD	SOME METHODS OF ANALYSIS
Time standards and output records	Compare with other companies and with past records to judge effects of methods in improvements and training.
Job specifications	Compare minimum personnel specifications before and after job analysis to see if savings have been effected in hiring employees with lower personal and job-skill requirements. See if better placement and less training time are required since the system was installed.
Costs of recruitment of employees	Study sources from which employees were drawn and correlate with success on the job to see if some sources should be dropped or other sources added.
Test scores before and after training	Check to see if there is an improvement in employee's knowledge as a result of training. Correlate with success on the job in order to check validity of tests and value of training.
Personal employee records	Determine by sampling if records are up to date and if they are used in making transfers and promotions.
Costs of training methods	Compare unit costs with other firms and costs before and after changes. Balance costs against savings from increased output, lower overhead, reduced accidents and turnover, etc.
Employee use of services such as publications, cafeteria, recreation centers	Determine whether percentage of employees using services is increasing or decreasing. Decide whether the service should be continued or changed. Check possible interrelationships of grievances and services, output and services.
Arbitration awards	Classify the subject, contract clause, and employees involved to determine needed changes in personnel policies or practices.
Payroll data	Compare with other companies in the vicinity and in the industry to see if wages are in line. Check effects of wage incentives on output, quality, and inspection costs.
Health records	Analyze causes of illness to check defects in working conditions. Compare with general population and other firms. Compare with morale scales to see if health has affected morale or morale has injured health.
Suggestion records	Study to determine what percentage of employees are handing in suggestions, what type of suggestions. Check to see if more employees should participate. Estimate savings achieved.

Figure 23-1 (Page 2)

3. Rely upon some ratios or averages, such as ratios of personnel staff to total employees.
4. Use a compliance audit to measure whether the activities of managers and staff in personnel management comply with policies, procedures, and rules.
5. Manage the personnel department by objectives and use a systems type of audit.[5]

While Odiorne recommends approach No. 5 above (management by objectives), the other approaches for analyzing the effectiveness of a personnel program have proven useful.

Yardsticks for Appraisal

Most of the organization records listed in Figure 23-1 yield statistical data that are readily available in most organizations. Where EDP facilities are being utilized, such information can be kept current and may be obtained at moderate cost.[6] On the basis of such information, problem areas may be identified and corrective action taken. Many of the types of data provided by the records listed in Figure 23-1 were considered in preceding chapters. The first three records on the list, which are those used most frequently in auditing personnel functions, have been discussed only incidentally. Because of their importance, further attention will be given to employee turnover, absenteeism, and accidents.

Turnover. Turnover refers to the amount of movement of employees in and out of an organization, ordinarily expressed in terms of the *turnover rate*. The turnover rate for a department or an organization can be an important indicator of the efficiency with which the various personnel functions are performed by managerial and supervisory personnel as well as by the personnel department.

Formulas for Turnover Rates. The U.S. Department of Labor suggests the following formula for computing turnover rates:

$$\frac{\text{number of separations during the month}}{\text{total number of employees at midmonth}} \times 100$$

Thus, if there were 25 separations during a month and the total number of employees at midmonth was 500, the turnover rate would be

$$\frac{25}{500} \times 100 = 5\%$$

According to a BNA *Personnel Policies Forum* survey, more than one half of the companies figuring turnover rates use this formula. Of the remaining

[5] George S. Odiorne, "Yardsticks for Measuring Personnel Departments," *The Personnel Administrator,* Vol. 12, No. 4 (July-August, 1967), pp. 1-6.

[6] W. F. Rabe, "Yardsticks for Measuring Personnel Department Effectiveness," *Personnel,* Vol. 44, No. 1 (January-February, 1967), pp. 56-64.

companies most use a similar formula which results in figures comparable to those based on the Labor Department formula.[7] Separate rates for different departments or divisions of an organization may be computed, and separate rates may be computed for different types of turnover such as quits, discharges, deaths, retirements, layoffs, and transfers.

Another method is one in which the rate is based upon unavoidable separations. If S equals the total separations in the selected period and US the unavoidable separations, the formula becomes:

$$\frac{(S - US)}{N} \times 100 = T$$

Unavoidable separations include termination of temporary employment, promotions, transfers, and separations due to illness, death, or marriage.[8] This latter method yields what is probably the most significant measure of a personnel program's effectiveness since it can serve to direct attention to that portion of employee turnover that can be reduced. It also represents that portion of turnover that management has the most opportunity to control through its personnel program by means of better selection, training, supervisory leadership, improved working conditions, better wages, and opportunities for advancement. It cannot be used, however, when comparing a company's turnover rate with the figures reported in the *Monthly Labor Review*.

Methods for Studying Turnover. The turnover rate is not the only factor to be considered, however. The quality of personnel who leave an organization is important since turnover among competent and desirable employees is a serious matter as compared with turnover among incompetent and undesirable employees. In an effort to determine why employees become dissatisfied and quit, many companies conduct exit interviews. A skillful interviewer can often obtain the type of information that will be helpful in correcting conditions that are undesirable.

Another way in which to obtain information concerning the reasons why employees leave an organization is to mail a questionnaire to them after a short interval has lapsed since the date of their termination. The questionnaire shown in Figure 23-2 illustrates the type of questions that may be asked of former employees. Because it is received after the initial anger (if any) has subsided and because the former employee already has the security of another job, a more honest evaluation is likely to be reflected on the questionnaire. The fact that this method is conducted anonymously rather than in a face-to-face confrontation with a member of the personnel staff is also likely to result in favor of a candid response.[9]

---

[7] *Employee Absenteeism and Turnover*, PPF Survey No. 6 (Washington, D.C.: The Bureau of National Affairs, Inc., May, 1974), pp. 7-12.

[8] *Labor Policy and Practice—Personnel Management* (Washington, D.C.: The Bureau of National Affairs, Inc., 1975), pp. 241:211-212.

[9] Julius Yourman, "Following Up on Terminations," *Personnel*, Vol. 42, No. 4 (July-August, 1965), pp. 51-55.

CONFIDENTIAL COMPANY X QUESTIONNAIRE

DO NOT SIGN. Answer by a checkmark where choice of answer blank is offered. If you need more room for your comments, write "Over" and continue on the back of this sheet.

1. When you were first employed at Company X, were the duties and responsibilities of your job clearly explained to you? YES ___ NO ___ UNCERTAIN ___
   COMMENTS ___
2. Were the conditions of work, salary, and other benefits, hours of work, etc. clearly explained to you? YES ___ NO ___ UNCERTAIN ___ COMMENTS ___
3. Did you know who was your immediate supervisor—the one person to whom you reported and from whom you were to receive instructions? YES ___ NO ___ UNCERTAIN ___
   COMMENTS ___
4. When you needed information to do your job, were you able to get it easily, usually? YES ___ NO ___ UNCERTAIN ___ COMMENTS ___
5. When you had a suggestion about doing your work, could you discuss it easily with your supervisor? ALMOST ALWAYS ___ USUALLY ___ SOMETIMES ___ RARELY ___
   PRACTICALLY NEVER ___ COMMENTS ___
6. Frankly, what was the real (most important) reason for your leaving the company? ___
7. Could anything have been done to prevent your leaving? PROBABLY NO ___
   PROBABLY YES ___ UNCERTAIN ___ COMMENTS ___
8. Have you secured another job? YES ___ NO ___ If "Yes," how does it compare with your last job with us? COMMENTS ___
9. Add here any other comments you wish to make about your work at Company X, your feelings as an employee, or suggestions for making Company X a better place to work. ___

THANK YOU FOR YOUR COOPERATION. PLEASE RETURN QUESTIONNAIRE IN ENCLOSED ENVELOPE. DO NOT SIGN YOUR NAME.

Source: Julius Yourman, "Following Up on Terminations," *Personnel*, Vol. 42, No. 4 (July-August, 1965), pp. 51-55. Reproduced with permission.

Figure 23-2 A TYPICAL POST-EXIT QUESTIONNAIRE

The methods for studying turnover described thus far may be viewed as focusing on the negative elements of turnover. It has been suggested that managers stop the rituals of finding out why people leave and start investing resources in the positive management of retention. If managers reinforce the right reasons for employees staying and avoid reinforcing the wrong reasons, they can improve not only traditional turnover statistics but also set goals for retention. As a prerequisite to the development of a program to manage retention, these questions must be answered:

Why do employees stay?
What are their values for working and for living?
What are their ages, sexes, marital statuses, and so on?
What are the right and wrong reasons for employees staying on their jobs?
How dissatisfied is dissatisfied?

This approach requires an in-depth study of an organization with considerable emphasis upon employee attitudes and feelings.[10]

Another method for studying turnover makes use of biographical data, a methodology discussed earlier in Chapter 7 in connection with personnel selection. In one study of a central petroleum products credit card issuing and billing office employing 700 persons, biographical information from the employees' application forms was related to turnover. Through this procedure it was possible to determine personal characteristics of the employees associated with turnover. Such factors as age, proximity to work, and military service were found to be related in one way or another, thus providing information with which to explore further the characteristics to look for in job applicants in order to maximize length of employment. Since the factors will vary from one job to another and from one organization to another, the specific information obtained in this study should not be generalized as to other situations.[11] The use of biographical information has proven valuable in many instances. However, the journal literature contains reports of many studies that were not cross-validated and therefore overstate the validity and usefulness of the weighted application blank.[12]

While management should be concerned with determining the causes of turnover in its organization, reference to findings from other organizations in the same industry and by type of job will provide a basis for comparison. The Bureau of National Affairs, for example, surveyed the members of its *Personnel Policies Forum* for causes of turnover among production, office, and management personnel. Their findings, as shown in Figure 23-3, indicate the relative ranking of turnover causes. The relative ranking was determined by totaling the weighted rankings given each factor by Forum companies.

Absenteeism. The extent to which employees are absent from their work may serve to indicate the effectiveness of the personnel program of an organization. A certain amount of absenteeism is due to unavoidable causes. There will always be some who must remain away from work because of sickness, accident, serious family problems, and for other legitimate reasons. Considerable evidence, however, indicates that there are many other absences which could be avoided. It is advisable, therefore, for management to determine the seriousness of its absenteeism problem by maintaining individual and department attendance records and by computing absenteeism rates. While there is no universally accepted definition of absence nor a standard formula for computing absence rates, the method most frequently used is the one used by the Bureau of Employment Security of the United States Department of Labor. The general formula suggested by this office is:

---

[10] Vincent S. Flowers and Charles L. Hughes, "Why Employees Stay," *Harvard Business Review*, Vol. 51, No. 4 (July-August, 1973), pp. 49-60.

[11] Gerald L. Shott, Lewis E. Albright, and J. R. Glennon, "Predicting Turnover in an Automated Office Situation," *Personnel Psychology*, Vol. 16, No. 3 (Autumn, 1963), pp. 213-219.

[12] Donald P. Schwab and Richard L. Oliver, "Predicting Tenure with Biographical Data: Exhuming Buried Evidence," *Personnel Psychology*, Vol. 27, No. 1 (Spring, 1974), pp. 125-128.

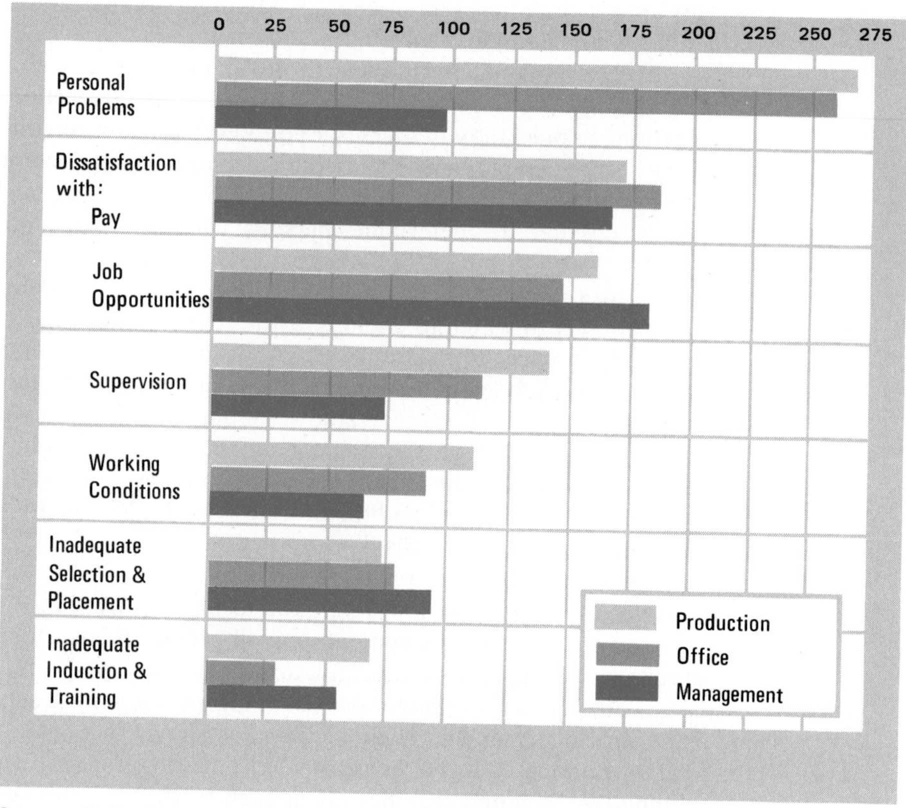

Source: Labor Policy and Practice—Personnel Management (Washington, D.C.: The Bureau of National Affairs, Inc., 1975), p. 241:222. Reproduced with permission.

Figure 23-3. COMPANY VIEWS ON THE RELATIVE RANKING OF TURNOVER CAUSES

$$\frac{\text{number of man-days lost through job absence during period}}{(\text{average number of employees}) \times (\text{number of workdays})} \times 100 = \text{rate}$$

If 300 man-days are lost through job absence during one month with 25 scheduled working days at a company that employs 500 workers, the absentee rate among the employees for that month would be determined as follows:

$$\frac{300}{500 \times 25} \times 100 = 2.4\% \text{ absenteeism rate}$$

As used by the Department of Labor, "job absence" is defined as the failure of employees to report on the job when they are scheduled to work, whether or not such failure to report is excused. Scheduled vacations, holidays, and pre-arranged leaves of absence are not counted as job absence.

The Bureau of Labor Statistics of the U.S. Department of Labor receives data on job absences from the Current Population Survey of Households conducted by the Bureau of the Census, and the analyses of data are published periodically. These analyses permit the identification of problem areas—industries, occupations, or groups of workers—with the highest incidence of absence or with rapidly increasing rates of absence.

Comparison with other organizations may be made by referring to Bureau of Labor Statistics data reported in the *Monthly Labor Review* or by such personnel reporting services as the Bureau of National Affairs, Prentice-Hall, and Commercial Clearing House. It is interesting to note that only 40 percent of the companies participating in BNA's *Personnel Policies Forum* indicated that their companies compute employee absenteeism rates on a regular basis. This should not be construed to mean that absenteeism is not controlled nor are efforts made to reduce it. The types of programs used for reducing absenteeism include systems for better recording of absences, disciplinary procedures, employee counseling, rewards for good attendance records, and special contests or other promotional efforts.[13]

Accidents. Accident frequency and severity records provide an index of the effectiveness of the safety program. Such records should be broken down by department in order that machines or jobs that may be especially hazardous or personnel who tend to be unsafe may be identified. By maintaining accident records an organization may compare itself with other organizations in the same industry who report their data to the United States Public Health Service or the National Safety Council. Figure 23-4, for example, contains recent data on frequency and severity rates for a wide variety of industries. The injury frequency rates are presented on the left-hand side of the chart and the severity rates on the right-hand side. A steel company, for example, that wished to compare its accident statistics with this chart would find that for that industry there were 4.45 disabling injuries per 1,000,000 man hours and 626 days charged for work injuries per 1,000,000 man hours' exposure (or 141 days per individual case). The frequency rate for steel companies of 4.45 is less than the average of 10.55 for all industries as indicated by an arrow on the chart. The severity rate of 626 for steel companies is also less than the average of 654 for all industries. The National Safety Council report also includes other breakdowns of work accident data that may be used as a basis of comparison.

Special Appraisals

The data that are routinely collected and compiled for use in appraising or auditing various functions of the personnel program are not likely to provide all the information needed for a comprehensive coverage of the program. Where there are new programs or special emphases, it will be necessary to devise plans whereby essential information about their effectiveness may be obtained. Affirmative action programs are an example of new programs that require special audit procedures. Slevin has devised a series of action checklists that

[13] *Employee Absenteeism and Turnover, op. cit.*, pp. 2-5.

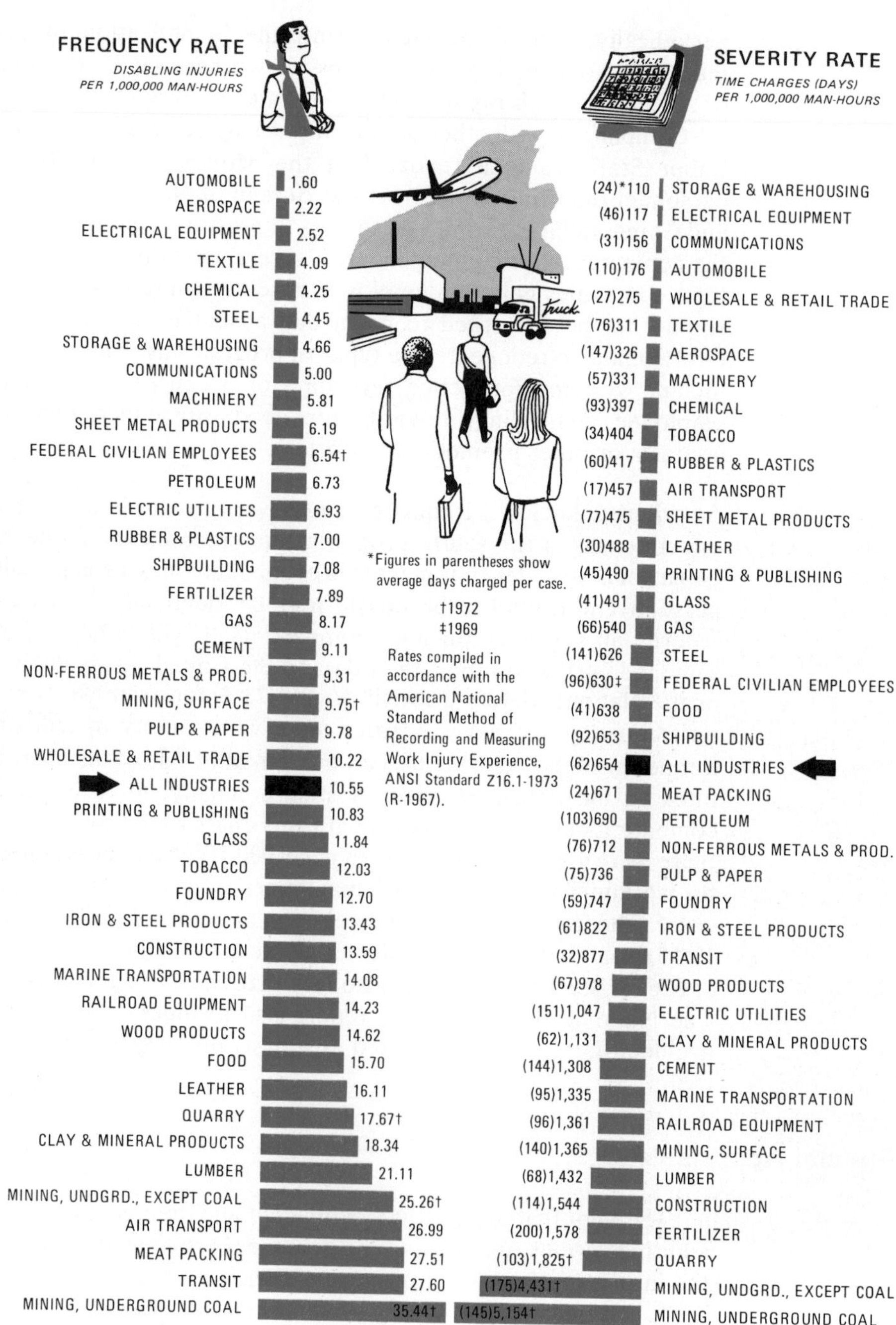

Source: Accident Facts, 1974 Edition. (Chicago: National Safety Council, 1974), p. 26. Reproduced with permission.

Figure 23-4 INJURY RATES BY INDUSTRY OF COMPANIES REPORTING TO THE NATIONAL SAFETY COUNCIL are designed for auditing a program to utilize women more fully. The checklists are titled as follows:[14]

1. Top management commitment audit
2. Administration audit
3. Recruitment audit
4. Selection audit
5. Attitude audit
6. Promotion policies audit
7. Periodic program review

The checklist for auditing the promotion policies is shown in Figure 23-5.

Promotion Policies Audit	yes	no
1. Are these instances of unequal pay for equal work?	☐	☐
2. Are women afforded the same potential career paths as men in your organization?	☐	☐
3. Have you developed targets for the proportion of women in each job category and done manpower planning for the next five years?	☐	☐
4. Do you have a system (such as the assessment center) for identifying qualified women?	☐	☐
5. Are your annual performance appraisals sexually unbiased?	☐	☐
6. Does a woman who does not feel she is being promoted rapidly enough have an appeal procedure with her supervisor?	☐	☐
7. Does a woman who does not feel she is being promoted rapidly enough have an appeal procedure with the action plan administrator?	☐	☐
8. Are women participating sufficiently in attendance at management training and development seminars sponsored by your organization?	☐	☐
9. Are women participating sufficiently in other management development efforts, such as job rotation, etc.?	☐	☐

Action steps

If question one is answered "yes," the situation can be changed by top management mandate. If questions two through nine are answered "no," substantial long-term effort in effecting the required organizational change will be required of the administrator. Much of this may be accomplished through the attitude change techniques described in the "attitude audit." However, in many cases, specific administrative action may be taken. Some examples are:

a. review of all job classifications in which either sex is not represented in reasonable numbers.

b. review of salary and promotion progress of men and women who were hired at the same time into similar jobs to see if their progress has been dissimilar.

c. review of each employee's record to make sure that he or she has reached the highest possible level given the employee's capabilities and the organization's needs.

d. institution of a method of job posting so that all employees are aware of vacancies as they occur and that promotion into these vacancies is based on qualifications, not sex.

e. review of layoff and rehiring procedures to ascertain that they do not discriminate on the basis of sex.

f. review of all union contracts. Make sure that there are no discriminatory clauses and that there is a policy statement that discrimination is a violation of the contract.

Source: Dennis Slevin, "Full Utilization of Women in Employment: The Problem and an Action Program," *Human Resource Management,* Vol. 12, No. 1 (Spring, 1973), pp. 25-32. Reproduced with permission.

Figure 23-5 AN AUDIT CHECKLIST

[14] Dennis Slevin, "Full Utilization of Women in Employment: The Problem and an Action Program," *Human Resource Management,* Vol. 12, No. 1 (Spring, 1973), pp. 25-32.

Human Resource Accounting

A favorite statement of corporate presidents in the annual report reads, "Our employees are our most important—or most valuable—asset." Yet, as one looks at the remainder of the report one might ask, "Where is the human asset on these statements that serve as reports of the firm's resources and earnings?"[15] The exclusion of human asset data from annual reports is a serious omission. At the present time only one company—the R. G. Barry Corporation's experiment with human resource accounting—has made its way to the prominent published literature. The Barry system (see page 271 in Chapter 12) purports to measure investments in management personnel on the basis of both historical and replacement costs that are shown on the firm's financial statements. Others have questioned whether human resources should be given a monetary value and have suggested that another approach might be to have an audit by behavioral science professionals for the purpose of determining the state of the human system in the organization. Regardless of the approach to be used, further study is needed to develop methods for taking account of an organization's and, ultimately, society's investment in human resources.[16]

Taking Corrective Action

The value to be derived from information obtained from appraisals lies in the use made of it to correct deficiencies in the personnel program. Analysis of the information may reveal that changes in procedures for carrying out some of the personnel functions need to be revised. It is even possible that whole programs should undergo a thorough revision if they are to meet the objectives that have been established for them. Finally, the policies themselves for the various functions should be examined to determine their adequacy as part of the overall personnel policy. Changes in policies and in operating procedures that may be indicated by appraisal findings are often resisted by managerial and supervisory personnel. Nevertheless, if the personnel appraisal is to be of any value to the organization, positive action must be taken by management to correct deficiencies as they are discovered from an analysis of available information.

PERSONNEL RESEARCH

Although every organization should have an appraisal system that will provide it with accurate and current information concerning the adequacy of its personnel program, it should also attempt to improve its program through the

---

[15] R. L. Brummet, E. G. Flamholtz, and W. C. Pyle, "Human Resource Measurement—A Challenge for Accountants," *The Accounting Review*, Vol. 43, No. 2 (1968), pp. 16-24.

[16] John G. Rhode and Edward E. Lawler, III, "Auditing Change: Human Resource Accounting," in Marvin D. Dunnette (editor), *Work and Nonwork in the Year 2001* (Monterey, California: Brooks/Cole Publishing Company, 1973), pp. 153-177.

use of personnel research data. There is a wealth of information that can be used in planning and improving a personnel program.

Behavioral science research is being conducted at various colleges and universities, and considerable information on human behavior is coming from governmental agencies as well as private institutions and from companies that employ psychologists, sociologists, cultural anthropologists, and workers in related fields as members of their staffs. Although research will probably never be able to provide solutions to all of the personnel problems of organizations, the fact that more and more problems are being studied by experts who use the scientific approach in the study of human problems is an encouraging development.

Contributions of Personnel Research

It was noted earlier in the book that understanding of human behavior has lagged considerably behind understanding of the physical environment for various reasons. One reason is that a person is a complex organism whose behavior is usually much more difficult to analyze than material or physical items. A second and probably more important reason is that all persons are inclined to feel that, as a result of their experiences, they have learned about human nature and that they understand its complexities as well as the next person.

While experiences that one has are undoubtedly quite valuable, they may not always result in improved ability to handle personnel problems effectively. The findings from carefully designed and conducted research studies, however, provide a sounder basis for solving the personnel problems that arise in an organization. Some organizations have the talent available for conducting research studies and are able to conduct their own research. All of them, however, can make use of the findings from studies conducted by experts and reported in the professional literature.

Personnel Research in Organizations. It is estimated that approximately 150 business firms employ staff behavioral scientists who conduct personnel research within their organizations. Data are not available from governmental organizations and other nonprofit organizations, but many of them also have specialists engaged in personnel research. Since a number of the individuals conducting research also have other responsibilities, it is difficult to assess the extent of research activities. However, 34 companies and two associations were included in a study because of their professional reputations and published results in personnel research. Among the participants in the study were Xerox, Sears, IBM, General Electric, Corning Glass, Exxon Corp., Western Electric, General Motors, American Telephone and Telegraph, J. C. Penny, and Inland Steel. Only half of the 36 participating organizations reported that they had attempted any long-range project planning; the other half generally gave as their reason the fire-fighting aspect of much of personnel research.[17] According

[17] William C. Byham, *The Uses of Personnel Research*, AMA Research Study 91 (New York: American Management Association, 1968).

to both Byham and Berry, the general lack of long-range planning and goal setting is a major obstacle to effective personnel research. In response to questions about future research projects, the personnel executives that Byham interviewed mentioned these areas: selection of minority groups, placing and training the disadvantaged, turnover, training and development evaluation, management appraisal, and opinion surveys.[18]

Use of Consultants. Organizations that have their own personnel research staffs use outside consultants only rarely. Those that contract with a consultant usually are rewarded with fresh ideas and approaches. It is preferable for an organization to engage a consultant on a retainer basis in order that the organization may have a continuing relationship with one professional who can gain a familiarity with the organization and thus be in a better position to suggest needed projects. Extreme care should be exercised in hiring consulting firms or individuals to insure that they are qualified to conduct research.

Research Organizations. Throughout this book the findings from the research efforts of a number of different research organizations have been reported. The primary function of these organizations is to conduct research and to make their findings available to all who are interested in them. Many such organizations may be found at universities. Probably the largest university research center in the behavioral sciences is the Institute for Social Research at the University of Michigan. Its two main divisions—the Survey Research Center and the Research Center for Group Dynamics—have published well over 2,000 articles, reports, and books as a result of their research activities. A number of state universities have centers for the study of labor and industrial relations including those in California, Minnesota, Illinois, and New York. Organizations sponsored by industry, such as the American Management Association and the National Industrial Conference Board, publish research studies that benefit managers in their personnel relations. Since World War II, agencies of the federal government, particularly in the Department of Defense, have conducted research or have contracted with private research organizations for a wide variety of projects, the results of which are generally available to the public.

Research Methods

In the "Space Age" the word "research" has become very common, and most educated persons have a fairly accurate understanding of what is meant by the term. Students of personnel management should, however, have a knowledge of the steps that must be followed in conducting sound personnel research. With such knowledge students not only may be able to plan research studies of their own but also will have a frame of reference from which to read the reported research of others. Students should be able to read a report with

[18] Dean F. Berry, *The Politics of Personnel Research* (Ann Arbor: University of Michigan, Bureau of Industrial Relations, 1967).

understanding, to evaluate it critically, and to apply the information to current problems that are encountered at work. A knowledge of the types of studies, the steps in the experimental method, and some of the tools used in personnel research are essential to understanding its significance.

Types of Studies. Various approaches may be used to obtain information, to analyze it, and to arrive at a conclusion that has some value in predicting and controlling the behavior of people at work. The type of approach that may be used depends on such factors as the nature of the problem, the available data, and what is likely to be accepted by those persons who are being studied. While the experimental approach (to be discussed later) represents the most refined type of study, there are others that are often found to be useful in personnel research. *Surveys,* in which facts are obtained on a topic or problem from a variety of sources, are often used in research on wages, fringe benefits, and labor relations. *Historical studies* are sometimes used to trace the development of problems with a view to understanding them better and to isolating possible causative factors. *Case studies,* like those found at the end of this book, may be developed for the purpose of exploring all the details of a particular problem that is believed to be representative of other similar problems. All of these types of studies have their place. It should be recognized, however, that they lack the precision of the experimental method.

The Experimental Method. The observation of events in a restricted setting is characteristic of the experimental method. The *experimental method* employs the scientific approach which requires that observations meet three requirements: (1) they must be empirical, (2) they must be observable, and (3) they must be repeatable. In addition, experimental observations are made under controlled conditions. While it is sometimes difficult to consider personnel research as being scientific, it should be remembered that what makes a study scientific is not the subject matter but the manner in which one deals with it. A brief examination of the following steps in the scientific method should reveal its applicability to the study of human behavior:

1. Define and delimit the problem. Do not attempt to work on too large an area at one time.
2. Find out through reference to books and journals what others have done on this and related problems.
3. State your problem in the form of a hypothesis or assumption. For example, the hypothesis "workers who are supervised too closely produce less than those workers who receive more general supervision" or "older employees use more sick leave than younger employees" may be tested.
4. Decide on such details as which workers will be used as subjects, how many subjects are needed, the types of control groups, the statistical techniques to be used, etc.
5. Collect the necessary data. This may involve administering questionnaires or tests, conducting interviews, studying available records (personnel, production, etc.).
6. Interpret the data. At this point the hypothesis is either accepted or rejected.

7. Cross-check or verify your findings, if possible, by using another method of gathering data or another group of subjects (if all available subjects were not used in the original study).
8. Publish the findings and distribute. If the report is being prepared for top management, it should be reduced to the essentials and should include positive recommendations that management may either accept or reject on the basis of the findings plus other factors that must usually be considered.

By following these steps systematically one will obtain meaningful answers to questions that are the bases for the hypotheses to be tested. Before conducting research of any type, however, one should become familiar with studies that are reported in journals and should learn to evaluate them. The checklist for evaluating scientific articles in Figure 23-6 may prove useful for this purpose.

Use of Statistics in Research. In all types of studies it is usually desirable to quantify the data being collected. This facilitates analysis and summarization of the data and permits generalizations to be made through the use of statistics. Because of the increasing need for the personnel specialist to understand and to know how to use statistics, it is recommended that the student learn all that he or she possibly can about statistics. The old idea that "intuition is enough" has given way to a more scientific approach, which includes the use of statistical concepts.[19]

The personnel specialist should not only be familiar with business statistics but should at least examine a book in psychological statistics since most personnel research that is reported in the various professional journals employs psychological statistics. (See suggested readings at end of this chapter.) It would also be desirable for the personnel specialist to become familiar with the rapid advancements that are being made in the applications of electronic data processing (EDP) equipment to personnel research. The availability of computers and other electronic equipment not only facilitates the accomplishment of research studies but also will inevitably stimulate more research in areas where heretofore only feeble attempts could be made to study the many complexities of human behavior in the work situation. In the final analysis, however, it is the researcher who has to do the research, not the computer.[20]

Use of PERT and CPM in Personnel Operations. As new techniques of work control are developed, managers should consider the possibilities of adapting them for personnel projects. For example, some companies have used PERT (Program Evaluation and Review Technique) to integrate planning, evaluate program status, and identify potential trouble spots. The Sandia Corporation has applied the method to its college recruitment. Prerecruitment

---

[19] Stephen Habbe, "Statistics and the Personnel Director's Job," *Management Record,* Vol. 21, No. 6 (June, 1959), pp. 198-201.

[20] John R. Hinrichs, "The Computer in Manpower Research," *Personnel Administration,* Vol. 33, No. 2 (March-April, 1970), pp. 37-44.

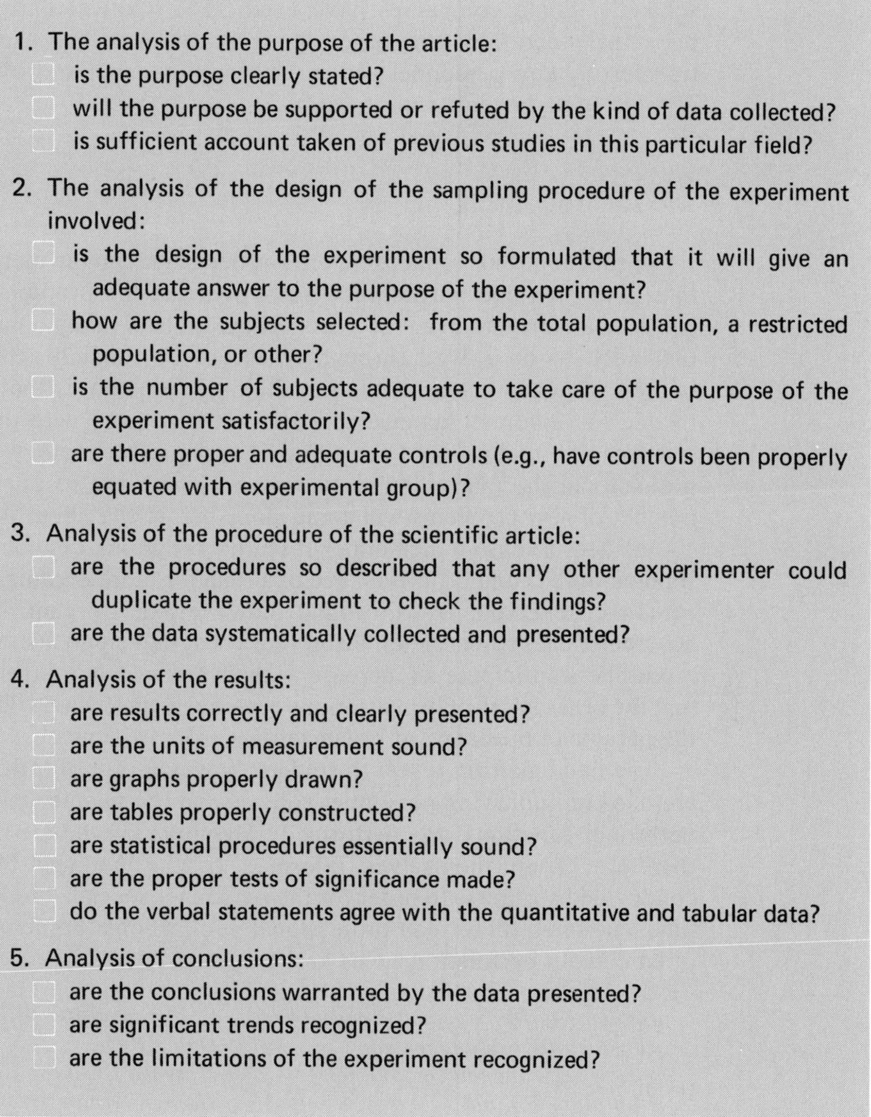

1. The analysis of the purpose of the article:
   - ☐ is the purpose clearly stated?
   - ☐ will the purpose be supported or refuted by the kind of data collected?
   - ☐ is sufficient account taken of previous studies in this particular field?
2. The analysis of the design of the sampling procedure of the experiment involved:
   - ☐ is the design of the experiment so formulated that it will give an adequate answer to the purpose of the experiment?
   - ☐ how are the subjects selected: from the total population, a restricted population, or other?
   - ☐ is the number of subjects adequate to take care of the purpose of the experiment satisfactorily?
   - ☐ are there proper and adequate controls (e.g., have controls been properly equated with experimental group)?
3. Analysis of the procedure of the scientific article:
   - ☐ are the procedures so described that any other experimenter could duplicate the experiment to check the findings?
   - ☐ are the data systematically collected and presented?
4. Analysis of the results:
   - ☐ are results correctly and clearly presented?
   - ☐ are the units of measurement sound?
   - ☐ are graphs properly drawn?
   - ☐ are tables properly constructed?
   - ☐ are statistical procedures essentially sound?
   - ☐ are the proper tests of significance made?
   - ☐ do the verbal statements agree with the quantitative and tabular data?
5. Analysis of conclusions:
   - ☐ are the conclusions warranted by the data presented?
   - ☐ are significant trends recognized?
   - ☐ are the limitations of the experiment recognized?

Source: Harry W. Hepner, *Psychology, Applied to Life and Work* (4th ed.; Englewood Cliffs, New Jersey: Prentice-Hall, Inc., 1966), p. 603. Reproduced with permission.

Figure 23-6 A BRIEF CHECKLIST FOR EVALUATING SCIENTIFIC ARTICLES

activity was broken down into 23 specific tasks that had to be accomplished during the summer months prior to actual campus recruitment, such as analyzing results of prior recruiting efforts, analyzing work load, selecting salary projections, and establishing salary guides. The data were fed to a computer which came out with deadlines that had to be met to keep on schedule. Some companies have used CPM (Critical Path Method) in their personnel operations. A large chemical company has used this method in transferring key personnel and in moving personnel and offices of a product division to its headquarters location.[21]

Continuing Need for Research

Throughout this book reference has been made to the many research studies that have provided partial answers to some of the problems that have faced personnel managers over the years. There are still many unanswered problems that need to be solved through research. Fortunately, there is heightened interest in personnel research, but the basic problem is that research in areas related to personnel management has not kept pace with that in the physical sciences and technology. The rapid changes in technology have created new problems in the management of personnel with the result that an increasing number of new problems will come along before the old problems are solved.

In the surveys of personnel research programs conducted by Berry and Byham, both found little evidence of a rush for more organizations to engage in personnel research. Byham found, however, that organizations that already have personnel research units and those that make considerable use of outside researchers anticipate an increase in their research activities.[22] It is also likely that the other types of organizations previously described will continue to study the personnel problems of organizations.

The findings from research studies, however, are of little value unless they are used in improving personnel policies and the manner in which the various personnel functions are performed. Members of the personnel staff must, therefore, keep themselves informed of the findings from the research conducted by others. In order for the personnel specialist to keep abreast of the times, it is helpful to read professional publications. Some of the journals that often contain pertinent articles are:

Academy of Management Journal
Administrative Management
Advanced Management Journal
Arbitration Journal
Business Horizons
Business Topics
Business Week
California Management Review
Canadian Personnel and IR Journal
Civil Service Journal
Compensation Review
Conference Board Record
Dun's Review
Harvard Business Review
Human Organization
Human Resource Management
Industrial and Labor Relations Review
Industrial Psychology
Industrial Relations
Journal of Applied Behavioral Science
Journal of Applied Psychology

[21] Geneva Seybold, *Personnel Audits and Reports to Top Management,* Personnel Policy Study No. 191 (New York: National Industrial Conference Board, 1964), p. 113.

[22] Berry, *op. cit.,* p. 238, and Byham, *op. cit.,* p. 20.

Journal of Business
Journal of Industrial Psychology
Labor Law Journal
Management Review
Management Science
Michigan Business Review
Monthly Labor Review
MSU Business Topics
Nation's Business
Occupational Mental Health
Organizational Behavior and Human Performance
Organizational Dynamics
Personnel
Personnel Administrator
Personnel Journal
Personnel Psychology
The Personnel Woman
Public Personnel Management
Studies in Personnel Psychology
Supervision
Supervisory Management
The Wall Street Journal
Training and Development Journal
Training in Business and Industry

Most organizations make at least some of these journals available to the personnel staff in order that it may have access to the current thinking and findings from research studies. Where journals are not provided by the employer, one should find a library where these may be read on a systematic basis. Only through continued study can one hope to keep abreast of the changes that are occurring more rapidly than ever before.

Résumé

The need for appraising the work of the personnel department has been considered in this chapter along with the need for making use of available information obtained from research studies. While those who are engaged in the management of a particular function usually believe that they are doing the best they can "under the circumstances," they should try to recognize that improvements can always be made if facts rather than opinions are used in guiding their decisions.

Several sources of factual information with which to conduct an appraisal of the personnel program are available. While the use of information on turnover, absenteeism, and accidents has been considered in detail, many other types of data are available for statistical analysis. Wherever possible, however, in-depth analyses should be made of the personnel functions not only to correct undesirable situations but also to provide information for planning for future operations.

Every organization should have a personnel appraisal system, and it should also make use of the wealth of information that is available from research that is reported in the literature. Members of the personnel staff should be able to evaluate published research findings and to use them for the benefit of the organization. Although the term "research" is academic to some people, for the practical person it represents an effort to do things better. It represents also a problem-solving attitude. Personnel workers who adopt this attitude will probably be among those who are viewed by management and their colleagues as being "out in front" in the field.

DISCUSSION QUESTIONS

1. Some companies employ specially trained consultants to conduct audits of their personnel program.
   a. What are the advantages and disadvantages of using consultants for this purpose?
   b. Consultants often compare the audit findings from a company with other companies with which they are familiar. Of what value are such comparisons?
2. What are the reasons for the failure of organizations to conduct thorough appraisals of their various personnel procedures and programs?
3. Analyze the data in Figure 23-3 (page 546) on the causes of turnover.
   a. If you were a supervisor of office personnel, of what value would the findings be to you?
   b. How do you account for the differences among production employees, office employees, and managers in the personnel problems category?
4. How is absenteeism related to the various personnel functions that have been discussed in the various chapters of this book? How far should a manager go in attempting to control it?
5. Identify the types of problems that are likely to arise when human resource accounting methods are put into practice in a corporation. How may they be solved?
6. One of the first steps in conducting personnel research is the formulation of specific hypotheses. Formulate five hypotheses for studies that could be conducted by a personnel department. Have other members of the class criticize your hypotheses.
7. Using the checklist in Figure 23-6 (page 555), evaluate one of the research articles that appear in one of the journals listed on pages 556-577.
8. Examine recent copies of the journals listed on pages 556-557. Write a brief résumé of the types of articles that are found in these journals. Which journals appear to be of most value to you at this stage in your career? Have you considered subscribing to one or more of them to enhance your professional growth in this area of management?

PROBLEM 23-1 TWO WAYS TO REDUCE ABSENTEEISM *

Two plans to reduce absenteeism were among those submitted to the National Foundry Association's "Idea of the Year." Each of them approached the problem from a different point of view and each has proved to be successful.

At Pohlman Foundry in Buffalo, New York, management felt that there were a limited number of ways in which the problem of absenteeism could be resolved and that money still offered the greatest incentive. The union president and the union steward were well aware of the absenteeism problem. In fact, management was approached by the union to explore the possibility of receiving increased economic benefits under the contract since their members were lagging behind the gains of other employees in the area. Consequently, the union and management worked out a new four-year agreement in which over 21 percent of the total economic package is in the form of an attendance bonus plan. The bonus for good attendance starts at 6¢ per hour and increases in varying increments during the life of the contract up to a maximum of 20¢ per hour during the last year. The details of the bonus plan are too detailed to describe in this problem, but basically they provide that employees not be penalized for sickness or bereavement leave. The attendance bonus is computed weekly and paid by a separate monthly check.

At Dalton Foundries, Inc., in Warsaw, Indiana, a systematic procedure has been developed to enable consistent application of corrective discipline. Each reason for

* Adapted with permission from an article by William M. Pohlman and Kenneth L. Davidson, "2 Ways to Reduce Absenteeism," *Foundry* (June, 1971), pp. 126-129.

absence, tardiness, extended break or lunch period has been assigned a point value, or demerit. For example, jury duty is assigned 0 points; sickness verified by a physician, 0 points; sickness without verification, 3 points; tardiness or overstaying break period or lunch period, 3 points, etc. Accumulated demerits are used to take corrective action as follows:

7-10 points	first written warning
11-17 points	second written warning plus one day off
18-24 points	third written warning plus three days off
25 points & over	suspension pending discharge

In the last case, the employee will report within five days to the industrial relations manager who will determine the appropriate action.

a. What is the basic difference in the two approaches? How can both approaches be successful in reducing absenteeism?
b. Should employees be given a bonus for being present for work regularly?

SUGGESTED READINGS

Bassett, Glenn A., and Harvard Y. Weatherbee. *Personnel Systems and Data Management*. New York: American Management Association, 1971.

Berry, Dean F. *The Politics of Personnel Research*. Ann Arbor: University of Michigan, Bureau of Industrial Relations, 1967.

Byham, William C. *The Uses of Personnel Research*. AMA Research Study 91. New York: American Management Association, 1968.

Guilford, J. P., and Benjamin Fruchter. *Fundamental Statistics in Psychology and Education,* 5th ed. New York: McGraw-Hill Book Company, 1973.

Kolstoe, Ralph H. *Introduction to Statistics for the Behavioral Sciences*. Homewood, Illinois: The Dorsey Press, 1969.

Litterer, Joseph A. *The Analysis of Organizations*. New York: John Wiley & Sons, Inc., 1965.

Luck, Thomas J. *Personnel Audit and Appraisal*. New York: McGraw-Hill Book Company, 1955.

Peskin, Dean B. *The Doomsday Job—The Behavioral Anatomy of Turnover*. New York: AMACOM, 1973.

Seashore, Stanley E., and David G. Bowers. *Changing the Structure and Functioning of an Organizaton,* Report of a Field Experiment. Ann Arbor: University of Michigan, Survey Research Center, 1963.

Seybold, Geneva. *Personnel Audits and Reports to Top Management,* Studies in Personnel Policy No. 191. New York: National Industrial Conference Board, 1964.

Strother, George B. (ed.). *Social Science Approaches to Business Behavior*. Homewood, Illinois: The Dorsey Press, Inc. and Richard D. Irwin, Inc., 1962.

Whyte, William F., and E. Hamilton. *Action Research for Management*. Homewood, Illinois: Richard D. Irwin, Inc., 1965.

Personnel Management in Perspective

Throughout this book an attempt has been made to present a philosophy of personnel management and to consider various objectives, policies, and procedures that are consistent with that philosophy. It is recognized that the philosophy presented may in some respects have appeared to be idealistic when compared with the current practices of many organizations. This fact, however, does not necessarily invalidate the philosophy that was expressed, but, rather, it may indicate that such practices of these organizations may have become outmoded or may not have been implemented effectively. Personnel management as practiced is often a process of meeting immediate operational needs (the "putting out of fires") rather than a total, integrated approach to the use of human talents. In times past a relatively loose, informal approach to the utilization of personnel was often adequate. In recent years, however, there has been an increasing challenge for management to reassess its philosophy of personnel management and its practices for carrying out this philosophy. The next decade will present new and exciting challenges that will require the attention of executives, managers, and personnel researchers. Legislators, judges, and government officials, as well as educators, union officials, and the many professional and technical persons whose areas of responsibility and interest involve various aspects of personnel relations will likewise be engaged in the task of helping to meet the demands of a rapidly changing society.

In the six decades during which personnel management has developed into an important functional area of organization management, there have been many economic, technological, and social changes that have influenced the role that human beings will have at work. Concurrent with these changes have been changes in the composition of the labor force, in legislation, and in the concepts concerning the utilization of human resources. The field of personnel management has been and will continue to represent the dynamic interaction of many forces that require careful study and analysis followed by appropriate action at each point in its day-to-day emergence.

In the preceding chapters the objectives, policies, and procedures for carrying out the functions of personnel management have been considered in detail. As the discussion of this area of management is brought to a close, it is appropriate to examine the personnel management function in the perspective of today's events and to speculate about its role in the organization of tomorrow. Career opportunities in personnel and the paths to follow in preparing for them will also be considered.

PERSONNEL MANAGEMENT TODAY

It has been emphasized that all managers and supervisors are responsible for performing a wide variety of personnel functions. Except where studies have been made in individual organizations, however, it is difficult to assess the nature and quality of their performance in personnel matters. Most of the reported studies, therefore, are concerned with the effectiveness of the personnel manager and the personnel department. From such studies it is possible to obtain some information about the role and status of personnel management today and yesterday, especially those aspects of it that are performed by personnel managers and their staffs.

The Role of Personnel Managers

Since the success of an organization is dependent largely upon the quality of its personnel, it is essential that the personnel manager be given the responsibility and authority to provide the professional leadership that is necessary to achieve a high level of efficiency in the personnel department, and ultimately in the entire organization.

What Personnel Managers Do. Attempts have been made to determine the types of activities in which personnel managers engage. In a survey of 419 personnel managers below the vice-presidential level, Ritzer and Trice found the percentages of time that they actually spend on each activity, of time that they feel they should spend, and the differences as shown in Table 24-1.

Ritzer and Trice point out that personnel managers are apparently satisfied for the most part with the manner in which they distribute their time. However, the biggest difference appears to be in "planned personnel department activities." This seems to reflect their desire to work on longer range and broader questions relating to the personnel function.[1]

---

[1] George Ritzer and Harrison M. Trice, *An Occupation in Conflict—A Study of the Personnel Manager* (Ithaca, New York: New York State School of Industrial and Labor Relations, 1969), pp. 19-20.

Table 24-1 ACTIVITIES OF PERSONNEL MANAGERS

Activity	Actual %	Should %	Difference
Supervising Subordinates	17	14	−3%
Planning Personnel Department Activities	16	20	+4%
Representing Company to Outside Organizations	5	6	+1%
Representing Company to the Union	10	9	−1%
Gathering Information Both Inside and Outside the Organization	10	6	−4%
Providing Information and Advice for Decision Making by Others	17	19	+2%
Making Decisions on Personnel Matters for Other Departments in the Company	13	11	−2%
Involved in Professional Functions	4	5	+1%
Others	8	10	+2%

Source: George Ritzer and Harrison M. Trice, *An Occupation in Conflict—A Study of the Personnel Manager* (Ithaca, New York: New York State School of Industrial and Labor Relations, 1969), p. 19. Reproduced with permission.

Effectiveness of Personnel Managers. While it is difficult to obtain an objective assessment of the effectiveness of personnel managers, there have been a few studies in recent years that throw some light on how well they are performing their functions. In a survey conducted by McFarland of chief executives, operating executives, and personnel directors, personnel managers were on the whole viewed by executives as being quite effective. The major criticism that was expressed about personnel executives was their lack of general knowledge about management and operating problems of the organization. Some of the statements made by executives in his survey were:

> I feel personnel executives should play a larger role in the total business and be broader in their outlook. [President, paper company]
>
> The personnel department is too far removed from operating problems and is not as effective as it should be. There is a decided lack of urgency when involved in plant personnel problems. [Vice-president, manufacturing equipment company]
>
> The personnel chief should be broad in experience and more of a generalist than a specialist. [President, electronics company][2]

A number of personnel directors recognized that they themselves would like to see some changes made among the members of their group, as indicated by the following statements:

> I believe that there is a great scarcity of first-class personnel leaders. There are many competent specialists but few all-around, well-informed personnel directors. [Transportation company]

[2] Dalton E. McFarland, *Company Officers Assess the Personnel Function,* AMA Research Study 79 (New York: American Management Association, 1967), p. 18.

> In general, too many personnel managers tend to think of personnel management as an end in itself rather than a major support of the profit-making capability of the corporate entity. [Building materials company][3]

In the McFarland study, personnel executives were found to discuss frequently labor relations problems, personnel procedures and techniques, and policy matters with their chief executives. Seldom discussed were public, government, and community relations; departmental planning and administration; and economic matters such as costs and efficiency. It appears, therefore, that even personnel executives by choice frequently have not become involved in the larger areas that concern top management.

Comparative Evaluation of Personnel Practices

In each of the chapters, the authors have attempted to evaluate the effectiveness of the policies and procedures that are commonly followed by personnel staff members, managers, and supervisors. Since it is often difficult for those who are part of a particular social system to evaluate it objectively, the opinions of professional personnel workers outside of our system may help to throw light on the effectiveness of the personnel function in organizations within the United States. In interviews conducted with personnel managers in European subsidiaries of United States companies, candid comments were made about the personnel practices of American companies. Only about one fourth of the managers were from the United States, the majority being foreign nationals.

Contributions of American Companies in Europe. At the outset it should be noted that any criticisms of personnel practices in United States companies were overshadowed by favorable comments about their contributions. One of the major contributions is in the area of management development. United States companies abroad have introduced contemporary programs and techniques for developing managers that are patterned after their domestic programs. Avenues of advancement have been opened for many individuals with the result that they and various organizations have benefited from the programs. Europeans who traditionally have been accustomed to autocratic leadership have learned to promote work climates that are more democratic. Since today's youth in Europe as well as in other parts of the world are less willing to accept autocratic leadership, the modern manager in Europe is becoming better prepared to provide the type of leadership that is needed. An increased degree of openness of communication and informality between employees and their superiors that is a part of American business has generally been accepted by Europeans, and it has contributed to a reduction in class barriers and to the development of a more informal work environment. The recognition that American firms have given to merit has also appealed to many Europeans, especially the younger people.

---

[3] *Ibid.*

Personnel Practices in Europe. While there has been a significant flow of new concepts and practices in personnel management from the United States to Europe, there are certain aspects of European personnel management that United States companies are beginning to adopt. Employee benefits, particularly unemployment allowances and termination payments, are much more prevalent and more generous in Europe than in the United States. Greater security against discharge or layoff that is common in European countries is now being negotiated in the United States. Europeans have long looked with disfavor at the "hire and fire" approach of many American companies, and today within the United States there are efforts, especially among management personnel, to have greater job protection. As a result of job security, Europeans do not submerge themselves in their work to the neglect of recreation and family life. They appear to be able to maintain a wholesome balance between devotion to the organization and allegiance to personal and family needs and goals. The fact that Europeans value their time off the job and attempt to utilize it in a manner that satisfies them may prove to have an unrecognized salutary effect on their job performance as well as on their own mental and physical health.

Another feature of European personnel practices is the attention given to employee representation on committees and work councils. Safety and hygiene committees are required by law in a number of European countries, and in countries where they are not required by law they may be established by the national labor agreement. While employees in the United States may be represented by a union or by some arrangement provided by the employer, neither of these approaches appears to provide the quality of upward communication that worker councils provide.

As in the United States and other parts of the world, personnel management in Europe has become increasingly professionalized. The European Association for Personnel Management (EAPM) as well as national and local associations have been very active, and many of them publish journals and hold regular meetings and conferences. European personnel managers are eager for new knowledge and are making rapid strides in applying it to their organizations. One American manager observed that European personnel management has moved from the 1920s to the 1970s in little more than a decade.[4]

Personnel Management—A Profession?

Almost every occupation in contemporary America aspires to professional status. According to at least one writer, personnel management is not presently a profession and not likely to be one for years. He concludes, however, that the occupation is indisputably an important one.[5] On the basis of their survey of personnel managers and executives, Ritzer and Trice recommend steps to be

[4] Herbert J. Chruden and Arthur W. Sherman, Jr., *Personnel Practices of American Companies in Europe* (New York: American Management Association, 1972), pp. 10-21.

[5] Thomas H. Patten, Jr., "Is Personnel Administration a Profession?" *Personnel Administration,* Vol. 31, No. 2 (March-April, 1968), pp. 39-48.

taken if personnel managers truly wish to make personnel management a profession. Their recommendations are:

Occupational Level

1. An effort should be made to unify the numerous professional personnel associations into one cohesive body.
2. Once a central national body is formed, certification could be a feasible second objective.
3. A code of ethics needs to be set forth by the national body; one which would have an impact on personnel administrators.
4. Effort is needed to define clearly what body of knowledge is the exclusive domain of personnel administrators.
5. Organization executives and the public must be educated to recognize the particular expertise of personnel administrators and their ability to handle "people problems."
6. Personnel administrators need to define their function and who their clients are.
7. Personnel administrators must recognize that they are independent decision-makers and authority-wielders.

Individual Level

1. Efforts must be made to insure that those who enter personnel in the future are well educated and have majored in personnel or related fields.
2. Public relations is needed at the college level to make personnel a more attractive vocation. This would lead to more people majoring in personnel administration while in school.
3. Increased use of the sponsorship pattern can help to inculcate neophyte personnel administrators with professional values.
4. The professional association must encourage greater activity by the members in the association.[6]

While there is still much to be done to make personnel management a profession, it should be recognized that the various personnel associations mentioned in Chapter 1 and other national, regional, state, and local organizations are devoting their efforts to the increased professionalization of the field through their various activities and programs.

PERSONNEL MANAGEMENT IN THE FUTURE

Significant changes in the personnel function are occurring rapidly as a result of the dynamic interaction of all of the forces that help to determine its role in an organization. It is exceedingly difficult, therefore, to "stop the clock" at a given moment and obtain a true assessment of the status of the function. It is even more difficult to be assured that all of the influencing forces were considered in such an assessment. Any attempts to look into the future and predict what the role of the personnel function will be presents similar difficulties. It is logical to assume, however, that the major challenges

[6] Ritzer and Trice, *op. cit.*, pp. 81-82.

confronting personnel management as discussed in Chapter 1—various social, economic, and technological forces, as well as those challenges relating to the composition of the labor market—will continue to be present in the future.

Emerging Issues

In addition to those challenges which were examined at the beginning of this book, there will undoubtedly be new ones facing the managers of the future that will demand their attention and efforts. Some of the challenges are merely variations of old problems or issues, whereas others are, or at least appear to be, new and unique to the era which lies ahead. Among those issues that are demanding increasing attention are productivity and labor costs, social responsibilities of organizations, governmental controls, and human needs and values.

Productivity and Labor Costs. Over the full post-World War II era, output per man-hour in private industry has risen approximately 3 percent a year.[7] Beginning in 1973, however, the output per man-hour leveled off and then declined as shown in Figure 24-1. At the same time, the compensation per man-hour and the unit labor costs increased in the private sector of the U.S. economy. The decline in productivity should not be interpreted as a reflection

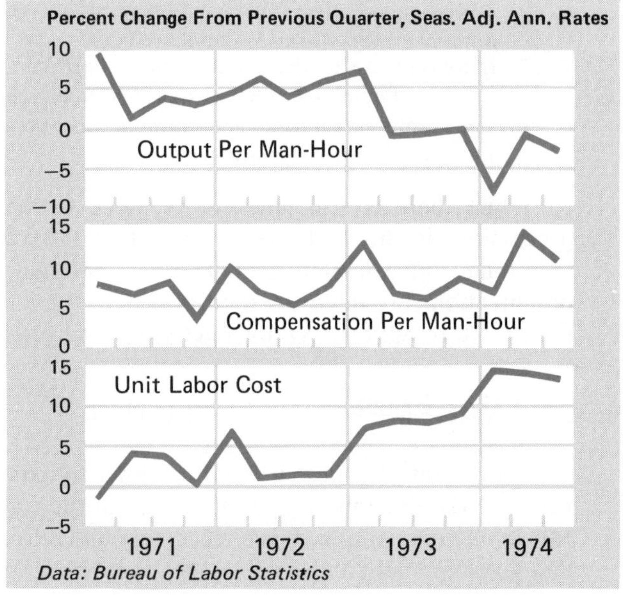

Source: Business in Brief, No. 119 (New York: The Chase Manhattan Bank, N.A., December, 1974). Reproduced with permission.

Figure 24-1 PRODUCTIVITY AND LABOR COST

---

[7] *Business in Brief*, No. 119 (New York: The Chase Manhattan Bank, N.A., December, 1974).

of changes in the ability or dedication of workers. Rather, it reflects the manner in which personnel are utilized. Some types of workers are kept on the job whether demand for their products or services is strong or weak; thus, the decrease in output per man-hour is largely due to the work being shared among more workers than are needed for efficient production. How an organization manages its work force in recessions and recoveries is thus an important factor in its unit labor costs.

With the predicted increase in public employment, attempts are being made to gauge the efficiency of employees in government jobs, particularly at the state and local levels. Since almost one fifth of the civilian work force are already employed by federal, state, and local governments, the productivity of the public-sector employees is already a matter of concern to economists, human resource planners, and others who are responsible for organizational effectiveness. Although many economists are of the opinion that it can't be done, they are trying to apply the tools of productivity analysis to the government sector in much the same way they are now applied to industry. The data from such analyses can provide governmental managers with a tool for improving the efficiency of their own operations.[8]

Social Responsibilities. The extent to which companies are meeting their responsibilities to society has become a concern of their leaders as well as those in government. This concern has led to the development of a variety of programs involving such matters as the protection of the physical environment, product safety, equal employment opportunities, employee health and safety, and others of an even broader nature such as urban renewal. According to Owen Kugel of the U.S. Chamber of Commerce, "sensitivity to social problems has become institutionalized, at least on the first two levels of management." Chief executives have accepted the need to take certain actions and have tried to make those actions a part of regular operations.[9] In a book published in 1972, 535 social action projects of 186 of the nation's largest corporations were catalogued.[10] One of the authors of that book, Diana Shayon, commented:

> I came into this thing very cynical about business. Now I still see a lot of Neanderthals at the top in many corporations, and there's still a lot of resistance. But at the same time, there are many dynamic people around who can see that things are changing and who want their business to be a constructive part of that change.[11]

Social Audits. In an effort to assist organizations that desire to improve their level of social responsibility, social audit procedures have recently been devised. The audit reflects a combination of systems analysis, economic

---

[8] "The Push to Boost Government Productivity," *Business Week* (May 13, 1972), pp. 160-164.

[9] "How Social Responsibility Became Institutionalized," *Business Week* (June 30, 1973), pp. 74-82.

[10] Stephen E. Nowlan and Diana Russell Shayon, *Profiles of Involvement,* 3 volumes (Radnor, Pennsylvania: Chilton Book Company, 1972).

[11] "Keeping Book on Social Action," *Business Week* (October 14, 1972), pp. 94-97.

analysis, social research, and management science. According to Abt, in referring to the social audit:

> At a minimum, its use will raise consciousness of social action alternatives and the likely consequences of action or inaction. At its best, the social audit can be the basis of an optimum social policy at any organizational level, yielding more of what people want and need within the resources available.[12]

Social audits may be used to reduce the risks of an equal employment opportunity violation, job dissatisfaction, high labor turnover and retraining costs, and declining morale and unit productivity, as well as to increase the effectiveness of personnel management.

Costs of Meeting Social Responsibilities. The changes that are made in organizations to meet what management and society perceive to be their social responsibilities are often done with little or no additional cost. Some changes, however, such as those required to reduce environmental pollution and to improve safety and health conditions, have resulted in enormous additional costs. A survey conducted by McGraw-Hill in 1974 showed that compared to an estimated 3 percent in 1967, nearly 10 percent of plant and equipment spending was mainly to insure that new facilities are nonpolluting and safe for employees. Slower gains in productivity are part of the price of trying to clean up the environment and make plants safer and healthier places in which to work.[13]

Governmental Controls. The first major law affecting the conduct of business was the Sherman Anti-Trust Act passed in 1890 (see page 368). Since the passage of this act, there has been legislation of all types to regulate and control industry and commerce. Some of these laws relate to labor relations, wages, working hours, and other matters related to employment, most of which have been discussed in preceding chapters. As new legislation has expanded the scope of governmental power in the area of personnel and industrial relations, employers have found it necessary to give increased consideration to the demands of government in all of their decisions. While many of the laws and regulations relating to personnel and industrial relations are necessary and desirable, employers frequently complain of having to interpret directives that are overly restrictive, poorly written, costly to comply with, and typically require excessive records and reports. It is safe to assume that personnel managers in the future will face even more legal requirements that will influence their policies and procedures, and require them to guard against the dangers of noncompliance.[14]

---

[12] Clark C. Abt, "An Introduction to Social Audit Methods," private publication, April, 1973.

[13] "A Day's Work—Real Cost of Labor Outpaces Pay Gains As Productivity Lags," *The Wall Street Journal,* October 31, 1974.

[14] "The Personnel Manager As Compliance Officer, *Personnel Journal,* Vol. 50, No. 12 (December, 1971), pp. 907-915.

Human Needs and Values. Many individuals, including the authors of this text, recognize that the organizations of the future will be those that are dedicated to providing the type of satisfactions that human beings are seeking and that function in a manner which is more consistent with the values of their members. As new generations take their places, there will be a growing requirement for organizations to change their structures, as well as their policies and procedures, so as to maintain their viability.

On the issues of human needs and values of individuals in organizations, Roeber states:

> I am going to suggest rather perversely that the direction of change has a coherence which is characteristic of a particular time, and that this coherence is given by the existence of an ''enabling'' mode of change. We intuitively feel that many of the movements which characterize social change today lean in some identifiable directions: towards individual freedom and self-realization, and away from codes of morals, social structuring, and authoritarian relationships.[15]

On the same subject, Ryterband and Bass write:

> Young people today are questioning the established structure and challenging the legitimacy of adult patterns of living. Today's students are more active, individualistic, and insistent in their demands that work be meaningful as well as productive. Self-actualization and personal freedom are of greater importance. If organizations are to attract many of the bright young people of today, they will have to accept, allow, and plan highly individual and personalized life styles for these new members of the labor force.[16]

Traditional organizational structures have become not only unwieldy and ineffective but also unpopular among those—particularly the young people—who feel dehumanized by such structures. Bureaucracy that at one time provided a suitable arrangement for routine tasks by its pyramidal structure of authority is no longer an effective type of organization. What is needed, according to Bennis, will be adaptive, rapidly changing temporary systems. Problems will be solved by task forces organized around problems and composed of relative strangers who represent a set of diverse professional skills. People in this system will be evaluated not according to rank but according to skill and professional training.[17] Toffler refers to the new type of organization replacing bureaucracy as *ad-hocracy*. He states that ''organizations now change their internal shape with a frequency—and sometimes a rashness—that makes the head swim. Titles change from week to week. Jobs are transformed. Responsibilities shift. . . . Departments and

---

[15] Richard J. C. Roeber, *The Organization in a Changing Environment* (Reading, Massachusetts: Addison-Wesley Publishing Company, 1973), p. 29.

[16] Edward C. Ryterband and Bernard M. Bass, ''Work and Nonwork: Perspectives in the Context of Change,'' in Marvin D. Dunnette, *Work and Nonwork in the Year 2001* (Monterey, California: Brooks/Cole Publishing Company, 1973), p. 87.

[17] Warren G. Bennis and Philip E. Slater, *The Temporary Society* (New York: Harper and Row, 1968), Chapter 3.

divisions spring up overnight only to vanish in another, and yet another, reorganization."[18]

Other Issues. Many of the social problems and programs for alleviating them that have been discussed in earlier chapters will undoubtedly require further attention from employees in the future. Programs concerned with affirmative action for women and minorities, special training for the disadvantaged, safety and health, and fair treatment of older and disabled persons will continue to demand the best efforts of personnel managers and their staffs. Greater attention will need to be given to the nature of jobs themselves, as well as to changing technology, so as to meet the needs of society and its individuals. Jobs should be designed so that they have meaning to the individual, provide for individual growth and adjustment, include variety, and fall into a meaningful pattern reflecting the interdependence between the individual job and the larger productive system. Using the term *sociotechnical system* to emphasize the joint operation of both social and technological systems, Davis advises that technology today is so rich in potential variations that decisions about job design can depend almost exclusively on the social side of the situation.[19] Personnel managers and others with a humanistic orientation should assume the responsibility for interpreting the human problems and for developing methods by which their organizations may contribute more effectively to the larger social system.

The Changing Personnel Function

The personnel function began as an employment and record-keeping function; later, as workers began to organize, it took on the administration of labor agreements. Increasingly, too, it was charged with carrying out programs largely developed by management. More recently it has shown signs of maturing as evidenced by more goal-oriented appraisals, better integrated compensation plans, centralized and computerized personnel records, greater attention to research, more emphasis upon planning and policy direction, greater collaboration with government in personnel matters, and more attention to identification and nurture of talent.

In addition, Fischer observes four related changes of significance:

1. *The personnel function will assume a more important role in the management of the business.* It will do more planning and policy making in the areas of manpower, organization structure, and compensation, among others. It will have more functional authority, especially in large, complex, and growing organizations. In becoming increasingly oriented toward growth and profits, instead of merely administering personnel activities, it will search out profit-improvement opportunities.
2. *The personnel function will become more creative, less mechanistic.* In the future the disparity between the paper programs and actuality will have to

[18] Alvin Toffler, *Future Shock* (New York: Random House, 1970), pp. 115-116.

[19] Louis E. Davis, "Readying the Unready: Postindustrial Jobs," *California Management Review*, Vol. 13, No. 4 (Summer, 1971), pp. 27-36.

be eliminated. The deficiencies of rigid, packaged "personnel programs" will become increasingly apparent. . . . There will be no more concern with ends rather than means, with substance rather than forms, with accomplishments rather than activities.

3. *The personnel function will be responsible for furthering the organization, not just maintaining it.* Personnel people will devote more time to proposing and promoting changes than to protecting the status quo. Instead of a miscellany of diverse specialties or activities, the personnel department will be regarded as an integrated general management function, responsible for the effective deployment of the firm's human resources. . . .
4. *Top management will become more directly involved in the deployment and development of human resources.* The chief executives of a growing number of companies are spending a good deal of time thinking about the people in the organizations, reviewing management manpower needs and resources, assessing the performance and potential of their executives, and planning their future experiences.[20]

The importance of the personnel function is reflected in part in the increases in personnel ratios since 1960. The ratio of personnel specialists per 100 employees was .15 in 1960. An estimate made in 1968 predicted that the personnel ratio for all industries and government would reach .22 in 1975.[21] In a study made in 1974 of 107 business enterprises, the median personnel ratio was .46—twice the predicted amount.[22]

The data presented above reflect the greater centralization of personnel activities that has taken place within organizations. This was predicted by executives surveyed in 1967 who also foresaw increased status for the personnel executives.[23]

Increased Status of Personnel Managers

It is being recognized more and more that the work of the personnel manager is as vital to the success of the organization as that of the line managers in such functional areas as production, finance, and sales that traditionally have received the primary attention of top management. For too long the personnel manager has been relegated to a subordinate position that provides for little voice in the extremely important area of human resources. This fact often has been the result of top management's attitude toward its employees and their role in the organization, but it is sometimes the result of the personnel manager's own inability to function as an executive. There is an increasing realization, therefore, that personnel managers must not only prepare themselves for performance of an executive quality but also be encouraged to play a more important role.

---

[20] Frank E. Fischer, "The Personnel Function in Tomorrow's Company," *Personnel,* Vol. 45, No. 1 (January-February, 1968), pp. 64-71.

[21] U.S. Dept. of Labor, Bureau of Labor Statistics, *Occupational Employment Patterns for 1960 and 1975,* Bulletin No. 1599 (Washington: U.S. Government Printing Office, 1968), pp. 86 and 283.

[22] "Planning and Budgeting the Personnel Program," ASPA-BNA Survey No. 23, *Bulletin to Management,* No. 1269-Part II (Washington, D.C.: The Bureau of National Affairs, Inc., 1974), p. 7.

[23] Dalton E. McFarland, *op. cit.*

It is quite possible that with the elevation of the personnel manager's job to a higher level within the organization some of the major problems concerned with the utilization of personnel in the business enterprise may be handled more effectively. One of the major problems is the need to motivate human beings to strive to enlarge and express their full potentialities. It was observed in Chapter 11 that there is a vast untapped source of human potential. As self-realization increases, responsibility, commitment, competence, and a respect for oneself and others also tend to increase. These qualities are important sources of productiveness and effective leadership.

Finally, in addition to being concerned with the organization and its members, the personnel executive will have to be concerned far more than before with the impact of the *external environment* on the management of the organization. There is no doubt that more will be demanded of tomorrow's personnel executive—in study, in planning, and in action.

As personnel managers attain increased status and are successful in attacking broader and more significant problems of personnel management, it will be possible for them to make even greater contributions to the organization and to society than they have made in the past. Their success and their contributions will serve to challenge managerial and supervisory personnel at all levels in their roles as managers of personnel, and will also stimulate individuals to consider personnel staff jobs as attractive opportunities for employment.

PERSONNEL MANAGEMENT AS A CAREER

Throughout this book an attempt has been made to clarify and to distinguish between the responsibilities of the line managers and supervisors and those of the personnel staff in the effective performance of the personnel functions. It is hoped that some interest concerning personnel work—in either a line or a staff capacity—has been stimulated by the discussions of its many phases. Some readers may even be giving serious thought to personnel work as a career and, therefore, desire further information about the available opportunities and how to prepare for them.

Managerial and Supervisory Jobs

While the personnel department is responsible for coordinating personnel functions within the organization and for recruitment, selection, wage and salary administration, and other specialized functions, line personnel are constantly engaging in personnel activities. Students who are interested in the daily face-to-face contacts with employees and find the building of a working team a challenge should not overlook the possibilities of achieving their goals through a supervisory or managerial position. The individual who desires to move into a personnel staff job should endeavor to obtain some experience working in a line department in order to understand the types of problems that supervisors and employees in these departments may encounter.

Personnel Staff Jobs

It was observed earlier that the ratio of personnel staff workers per 100 employees is increasing. This indicates that career opportunities will be provided for many individuals who are interested in this challenging type of work.

Types of Personnel Jobs. Among those personnel jobs included or implied in the discussions of preceding chapters are the following:

Chapter 2—Systems and Procedures Analyst
Chapter 2—Job Analyst
Chapter 3—Organizational Planning Manager
Chapter 6—Employment Interviewer
Chapter 6—Employment Manager
Chapter 7—Research Psychologist
Chapter 7—Assessment Manager
Chapter 8—Training Director
Chapter 12—Employee Opinion Analyst
Chapter 12—Safety Director
Chapter 14—Employee Counselor
Chapter 17—Labor Relations Manager
Chapter 19—Wage and Salary Administrator
Chapter 22—Employee Benefits and Services Manager
Chapter 22—Recreation Director
Chapter 23—Personnel Research Manager

This listing of jobs includes those that are typically found in larger organizations. In smaller organizations there may be fewer personnel jobs, with the result that a personnel staff worker is responsible for performing a wider variety of functions than if one were working for a larger organization. There is also some relationship between the size of an organization and the level at which a person without prior personnel experience is likely to find employment.

The college graduate without full-time experience in personnel work who is employed by the small organization or by a local branch of a larger organization may be placed in the position of personnel manager with responsibility for handling most of the personnel functions, except perhaps those concerned with labor relations. The same individual who is employed by a medium-size organization, however, would not start at the personnel manager level but would probably be placed in charge of non-technical training, employee benefits, or some other phase of the personnel program that is not dependent upon a broad background of experience. On the other hand, if one were to be hired by a large organization employing thousands of persons, an initial assignment more likely would be that of a job analyst, employment interviewer, psychological test administrator, or personnel technician. The last title is frequently used to cover a wide variety of functions including the collection, tabulation, and analysis of test scores, exit interviews, and wages.

Employment Opportunities. Opportunities for employment and advancement concern all persons who are choosing a career. The following predictions for personnel workers were reported in the *Occupational Outlook Handbook* (1974-1975)—a government publication widely used by vocational counselors and others who must have a sound basis for the information furnished to their clients:

> The number of personnel workers is expected to expand very rapidly through the mid-1980s as employers recognize the need for trained personnel to maintain good employee relations. In addition to new jobs created by growth, many openings will become available each year to replace workers who die, retire, or leave the occupation for other reasons. People trained in psychological testing and in handling work-related problems will find particularly good job prospects. Advancement to personnel positions from production, clerical, or subprofessional jobs will be limited.[24]

In another U.S. Department of Labor publication, it is estimated that there will be a growth in personnel workers of approximately 43 percent from 1968 to 1980. In that period it is predicted that there will be 6,900 openings annually with half of them needed for growth and the other half as replacements.[25]

Salaries and Working Conditions. Most students are interested in the financial opportunities in a career. Because of changing conditions, it is not possible to quote figures on salaries that will be valid for a very long period of time. Recent figures that are available, however, may be of some interest:

> Beginning personnel workers in private industry started at $9,500 a year in 1972, according to a Bureau of Labor Statistics survey in urban areas. Experienced workers earned $15,000, about twice as much as the average for all nonsupervisory workers in private industry, except farming. Directors of personnel earned between $14,300 and $24,700 a year; some top personnel and industrial relations executives in large corporations earned considerably more.
>
> In the Federal Government, inexperienced graduates with bachelor's degrees earned $7,700 a year in early 1973; those having exceptionally good academic records or one year of graduate work began at $9,500. Inexperienced workers having a master's degree and a high class standing started at $11,600 a year. Personnel workers having high levels of administrative responsibility and several years of experience earned more than $16,500; some in charge of personnel for major departments in the Federal Government earned more than $26,800 a year.
>
> Employees in personnel offices generally work 35 to 40 hours a week. During a period of intensive recruitment or emergency, they may work much longer. As a rule, personnel workers are paid for holidays and vacations, and share in the same retirement plans and other benefits available to all professional workers in their organizations.[26]

---

[24] United States Department of Labor, *Occupational Outlook Handbook,* Bulletin No. 1785 (Washington, D.C.: U.S. Government Printing Office, 1974-1975 Edition), p. 147.

[25] United States Department of Labor, *Occupational Manpower and Training Needs,* Bulletin No. 1701 (Washington, D.C.: U.S. Government Printing Office, 1971), p. 23.

[26] *Occupational Outlook Handbook, op. cit.,* p. 147.

While the above figures are useful as guidelines, it should be realized that the level of the job, the size of the organization, the nature of the business or industry, and its location, as well as the state of the economy, are all factors that determine salaries.

Personnel Consulting Opportunities

Personnel executives frequently go outside of the organization for professional assistance from qualified consultants. These consultants are utilized in connection with a variety of specific personnel problems as indicated in Figure 24-2. Specialized consulting firms—those limited to one or two areas of expertise, e.g., job evaluation and wage and salary administration—account for the majority of the consulting relationships reported in a nationwide survey conducted by the Bureau of National Affairs in cooperation with the American Society for Personnel Administration.[27]

Individuals who have received general training in personnel management and have developed special abilities in one or more of the areas for which consultants are frequently used may wish to consider joining a consulting firm or offering one's service on a self-employment basis after obtaining sufficient experience under a qualified consultant.

Preparing for a Personnel Career

In addition to understanding the occupational world and its opportunities, it is equally important that students understand themselves—their abilities and aptitudes, their interests, and their personality characteristics. Professors, faculty advisers, or vocational counselors may be depended upon to be of assistance in furthering their knowledge of the field of personnel work and in helping them to understand themselves better. Some advice of a more general nature that may be of value to students is given below.

Academic Training. Most of the personnel jobs listed on page 573 usually require that a person have training and/or experience in order to qualify for them. In recent years college training has been emphasized, although many employers still prefer work experience as a prerequisite to assignment to the personnel department. In keeping with the growing professional nature of personnel work, specialized college courses in personnel management, supervision, labor relations, and other areas are being offered. Contributions of the fields mentioned in Chapter 1, such as psychology, sociology, law, statistics, economics, and industrial engineering, also cannot be overlooked. In fact, the personnel worker who has a broad point of view can usually work more effectively with the variety of backgrounds and interests that are found among people at work.

---

[27] *Labor Policy and Practice—Personnel Management* (Washington, D.C.: The Bureau of National Affairs, Inc., 1971), pp. 251:351-356.

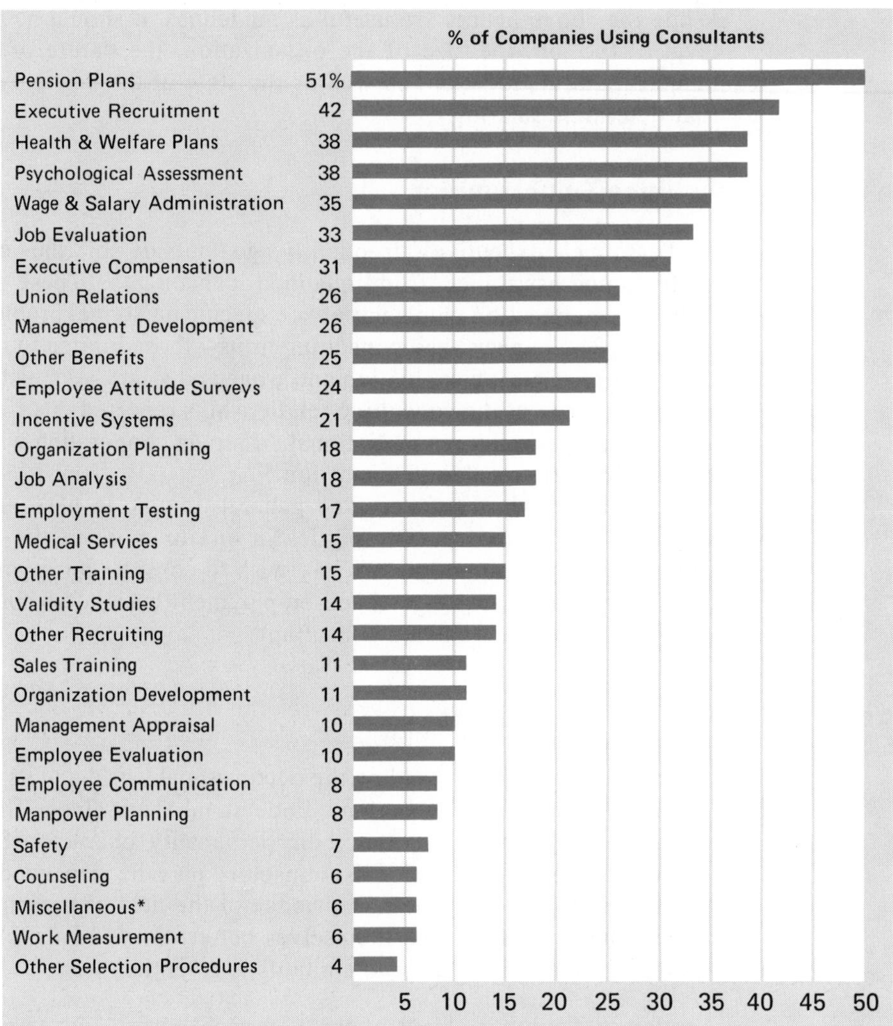

Source: Labor Policy and Practice—Personnel Management (Washington, D.C.: The Bureau of National Affairs, Inc., March, 1971), p. 251:353. Reproduced with permission.

* Includes job enrichment, security programs, data processing, personnel staffing.

Figure 24-2 FREQUENCY OF USE OF CONSULTANTS FOR SPECIFIC PERSONNEL PROBLEMS

Activities outside of the classroom and the library can provide valuable experiences for the student who is interested in personnel work. In fact, many recruiters are as interested in the extracurricular activities of prospective applicants as they are in academic success. Positions of leadership in clubs, publication staffs, and other organizations often provide the student with experiences that are comparable to those that are found on the job. Participation in organizations directly connected with one's occupational interest, such as a student chapter of the Society for the Advancement of Management, is especially valuable. During college and after graduation, participation in the local personnel association and similar professional organizations provides a means for exchanging ideas and for furthering the individual's progress as well as that of the profession.

Personal Qualifications. The academic training that the prospective personnel worker acquires should provide broad understanding of the special knowledge and skills needed for work in the field. Success, however, is dependent upon more than the training one has received and the knowledge and skills acquired. One of the most important qualifications is that the personnel worker possess good mental health. Other requirements are: a sense of humor, ability to tolerate frustrations, a flexible rather than a rigid approach to problems, ability to communicate with others, patience, and a high degree of objectivity toward other individuals. A permissive and understanding attitude toward human behavior and the ability to listen effectively are especially desirable. However, one should not assume that personnel managers are not concerned with employee performance. In a study of the values and value systems of a sample of industrial personnel managers, it was found that the group gave a higher priority to initiative and competency values and a lower priority to security and decorum than managers of other organizational functions.[28]

Employment Experiences. Employers not only attempt to make an analysis of the individual's personal characteristics and academic training but also usually look for employment experiences that may be related to success in the personnel field. While each employer has different opinions of what experiences are most desirable, many of them believe that work experience at the operating level or experience in some type of leadership position can provide a good background for personnel work. Through this type of experience the individual has probably learned something about the problems of motivating personnel and has developed some human relations skills that will make one more effective as a personnel worker.

The Challenge. An attempt has been made in this chapter to present the function of personnel management as accurately as possible. This type of work, like any other, has its rewards as well as its shortcomings. It is, however, a type of work that presents a challenge to the individual.

The individual who is interested in personnel work would do well to explore its career possibilities further. In cases where the individual needs more information, a qualified counselor is likely to prove helpful. Employees in personnel jobs may also be consulted. The important thing is that the individual's decision be made only after a careful evaluation of all available information.

---

[28] Andrew F. Sikula, "The Values and Value Systems of Industrial Personnel Managers," *Public Personnel Management,* Vol. 2, No. 4 (July-August, 1973), pp. 305-309.

Résumé

Personnel management in the future is likely to be even more dynamic than in the past. Technological developments have occurred at an increasingly faster pace, and the forces for rapid social change are clearly evident. As a result, the effective utilization of manpower in an individual organization as well as in the total economy constitutes one of the major challenges of society. Those who are engaged in the many facets of personnel management must be prepared to meet the challenge.

Studies have shown that while personnel managers as a group have been fairly effective to date, in the future they will be expected to play a larger role in the organization, be broader in their outlook, and become more involved in the larger areas that concern top management. At the same time, there is increased desire among personnel specialists to make personnel management a profession in its own right. This achievement will require efforts at both the occupational and individual levels.

The personnel function in the future will occupy a much more important role than it has in the past with greater centralization of the function. It will also be more creative and will be responsible for furthering the organization, not just maintaining it. Because of its increased responsibilities, the ratio of personnel specialists to other employees and the status of personnel executives should continue to increase. Personnel executives will have to concern themselves with the impact that the external environment has on the organization, including the influences of technological and social changes. The effect that the organization has on society and the contribution that it may make to society will also play a larger role than in the past.

There are many career opportunities for the individual who is interested in personnel work, and much like any other work it has its desirable and undesirable qualities. It appeals to some individuals but not to others. Individuals who feel that they have the required abilities and personality characteristics and whose interests appear to be grounded in reality rather than in wishful thinking should give careful consideration to a career in this field. Those who aspire to move up the promotional ladder should recognize that success in staff personnel work requires that personnel managers be good leaders. Personnel managers, furthermore, must not only be able to lead their own employees but must also be able to train and to inspire all managerial and supervisory personnel in the organization to become better managers of personnel. The future of the field is dependent upon having more personnel workers who are able to provide that type of leadership.

DISCUSSION QUESTIONS

1. In Table 24-1 on page 562, the activities of personnel managers are listed together with information about how they *do* use their time and how they feel they *should* use their time. How do you view their responses in the light of what you have learned about the personnel management function?
2. What are the criteria by which to judge whether an occupation is a profession or not? What changes would have to be made in order

to classify personnel management as a profession?

3. What recent events have you heard about that are examples of the types of emerging issues discussed in this chapter? What outcomes do you predict for these events?
4. How will the personnel function change in the years to come? How are these changes likely to affect the individuals who are responsible for this function?
5. Make arrangements through your instructor to visit the personnel department of one or more organizations. Talk with the personnel manager and the staff about their work, including its rewards and its frustrations.
6. Interview a number of people who work for different companies. Ask them to give you their opinions of personnel management as it is carried on in their companies by the supervisory personnel and by the personnel department. Summarize your findings and comment on their implications for the training and supervision of personnel workers.
7. Some authorities predict that a personnel executive will need an advanced college degree in the years ahead. If you selected personnel management as a career and you were planning to study beyond the bachelor's degree, in what subjects would you specialize? Why? In what topical area would you probably write your thesis?
8. If you are interested in personnel work, what experiences could you have now that would be similar to those that you would be likely to find in a personnel job?

SUGGESTED READINGS

Chruden, Herbert J., and Arthur W. Sherman, Jr. *Readings in Personnel Management*, 4th ed. Cincinnati: South-Western Publishing Company, Inc., 1976. Part 1.

Coleman, John R. *Blue-Collar Journal: A College President's Sabbatical*. Philadelphia: J. B. Lippincott Company, 1974.

Herman, Georgianna (ed.). *Personnel and Industrial Relations Colleges: An ASPA Directory*. Berea, Ohio: American Society for Personnel Administration, 1974.

Luthans, Fred, and Richard M. Hodgetts. *Social Issues in Business*. New York: The Macmillan Company, 1972.

Manpower Report of the President. Washington, D.C.: United States Government Printing Office. Published annually.

McFarland, Dalton E. *Company Officers Assess the Personnel Function*. AMA Research Study 79. New York: American Management Association, 1967.

O'Toole, James. *Work in America: Report of a Special Task Force to the Secretary of Health, Education, and Welfare*. Cambridge, Massachusetts: MIT Press, 1973.

Ritzer, George, and Harrison M. Trice. *An Occupation in Conflict—A Study of the Personnel Manager*. Ithaca, New York: New York State School of Industrial and Labor Relations, 1969.

Schmidt, Warren H. *Organizational Frontiers and Human Values*. Belmont, California: Wadsworth Publishing Company, 1970.

Ward, Lewis B., and Anthony G. Athos. *Student Expectations of Corporate Life: Implications for Management Recruiting*. Boston: Division of Research, Graduate School of Business Administration, Harvard University, 1972.

The Frustrated Personnel Director*

Personnel Director Greenleaf opened the interoffice envelope from F. L. Case, Secretary, and was surprised to see a copy of the Management Committee minutes enclosed. In the upper right-hand corner of the first page was penned: "Thought you'd be interested. A couple of items are yours. FLC." In his four years with the bank, this was only the second time that Greenleaf had been permitted to see or hold in his hand a copy of the minutes of the most important committee in the bank. To say that he was "interested" was an understatement. Case had promised that the Personnel Inventory and Appraisal recommendation would be considered at this meeting. They'd been holding it over for two months now. Greenleaf eagerly perused the minutes.

MINUTES

Management Committee Meeting
April

Present:

Chairman of the Board, A. B. Tateman
President, J. C. Groming
Executive Vice-President, D. L. Mentsen
Controller, C. D. Perman
Vice-President—Branches, W. H. Able
Vice-President—Operations, R. D. Framer
Secretary, F. L. Case

Absent:	None
Presiding:	Chairman, A. B. Tateman
Meeting called to order:	9:25 A.M.
Minutes of previous meeting:	Approved as submitted

1. *Statement of Condition*. Mr. Perman reported on the statistics showing the first quarter results for the bank. The committee agreed that the report reflected excellent achievements, except for the rise in interest expense as a result of increased savings account balances and the high personnel salary and benefit costs. Mr. Perman was complimented for his presentation, his analysis of the data, and the significance of his remarks as related to the bank's statement of condition.

   Chairman Tateman reviewed comparative statistics indicating that the bank now was the fourth largest in the city as compared to fifth a year ago. He commented on the merger of the Premium National and the Metropolitan Commercial, formerly third and fourth in size, into the largest bank in the city. He expressed concern about the merger trend as evidenced in other cities and stated categorically that our bank was not a merger possibility. He noted the highly satisfactory profit picture and said that it was his intention to continue his policy of providing stockholders with an attractive return on the investments. To achieve this, he called for renewed effort to reduce expenses, the addition of new services to attract new business, and improved work procedures. He also expressed concern with personnel expenses and requested that a special effort be made to hold them down.
2. *Personnel Report*. Mr. Groming read the Personnel Director's quarterly statistical report indicating a total clerical staff of 804, an official staff of 72, total annual payroll of $6,400,000, first quarter overtime in the amount of $98,000, 92 temporary employees on payroll, first quarter turnover rate of 17 percent, and 290 salary increases for $73,890 granted during the quarter. Full discussion followed and the Secretary was instructed to obtain a complete explanation for the overtime and temporary employees.
3. *Branch Offices*. Mr. Able reported that all 10 branches were performing smoothly and that applications were on file with government authorities for four additional locations in new residential neighborhoods. He noted that rapid expansion had created staffing problems which caused some of the overtime and the hiring of temporary employees reported earlier. However, he stated that he was in personal contact with a number of senior experienced people in competitive banks and that, if negotiations with them are successful, the personnel situation in the branches would be eased considerably.
4. *Check Handling Administration*. Mr. Framer indicated that all check handling now was centralized at the main office and that negotiations were continuing with two major correspondent commercial banks to determine the feasibility of having one of them perform all checking-account bookkeeping on their computers. He stressed the necessity for culminating these negotiations as soon as possible inasmuch as the volume was increasing more rapidly than anticipated. This means that present

equipment is not suitable for high-volume activity. As an alternative, Mr. Framer proposed a full study of the possibility of purchasing excess machines from Premium National to fill in the void. Such an excess exists because of their merger. Mr. Framer also thought it would be possible to hire some experienced supervisors and machine operators from both merged banks to cope with the increased check volume and the problems resulting from the centralization of check handling at the main office.

5. *New Business Activities*. A report on a recent survey of correspondent banks to determine their various customer services was made by Mr. Mentsen. Mixed reactions were given to many of the innovations now in vogue. All agreed with Chairman Tateman that the basic abilities to service checking accounts and to make loans to assist customers were the vital services for a successful banking operation. However, since there was some interest in the small loan field, Mr. Mentsen was asked to research this area more fully. No action was taken to expand the services of the Foreign or the Fiduciary Departments because an increase in services would involve additional physical facilities and personnel.

   Mr. Mentsen announced that he had obtained a new account with an opening balance of $50,000 from Kelleen Corporation. This was a payroll account for Branch #6. He anticipated that approximately 300 payroll checks would be cashed at this branch every Friday and requested Mr. Able to alert his staff for the new business. Mr. Kelleen has indicated that, if he is satisfied with the service, he will consider the possibility of moving his business account to our bank.

6. *Miscellaneous Matters*. Chairman Tateman commented on a number of miscellaneous matters including:
   a. Officer Retirements—12 officers (Executive Vice-President Mentsen, Vice-President Framer, three branch managers and seven junior officers in Foreign, Fiduciary, Control, and Operations) have indicated a desire to retire as of the end of the year. He also noted that 22 clerical staff members are 64 years old or over and that some thought should now be given to a definite policy with regard to handling retirements.
   b. Banking School Enrollment—Assistant Vice-President Caufield was registered at the State School of Banking for the three-year summer course with the expectation that the exposure would help him to assume new responsibilities in the Operations Department in view of Mr. Framer's intended retirement. The registration will be at bank expense for room, board, tuition fees, and texts. Mr. Caufield will be expected to assume any personal expenses incurred.
   c. AIB (American Institute of Banking) and College Enrollments—the AIB bill for 17 students ($780) was approved for payment. In addition, 14 employees were registered in evening college courses and all have received acknowledgments of their enrollments. In the case of Mr. Hartley Junet, an executive trainee, full refund of tuition has been paid for his college courses.
   d. Maintenance of Bank Premises—in view of their unsatisfactory performance, the contract for building maintenance with Cleaner, Inc., has been terminated and additional porters will have to be hired to properly clean all bank space.
   e. Opened and Closed Accounts—10 new commercial checking accounts with opening balances of $100,000 or over were opened (three with

proceeds of loans) in addition to the Kelleen account noted earlier. Eight accounts with average balances of $10,000 or over were closed. Reasons given were "more convenient location at another bank," "inability to provide foreign facilities," "loan application rejected," and "dissatisfaction with service."

f. Loans—the Director's Loan Committee considers the bank "loaned up" at present, and no new lines or substantial loans are to be considered without prior approval of Chairman Tateman.

g. Personnel Inventory and Appraisal Program—the Personnel Director's recommendation that the entire staff be inventoried for the multiple purposes of evaluating performance, determining individual strengths and weaknesses, and identifying areas with manpower shortages would be tabled temporarily until other pressing problems such as approval of new branch offices, correspondent bank check processing procedure, etc., were solved.

Meeting Adjourned: 10:40 A.M. Respectfully submitted,
F. L. Case, Secretary

Greenleaf slowly laid down the minutes and thought back to that day, four years ago, when he had accepted the appointment as Personnel Director, leaving a similar position at Premium National. Groming had talked about a dynamic bank, a major influence in the community, the tremendous opportunity to implement a broad and modern personnel program where none now existed, working with management as part of a team, a full vice-presidency within six years . . .

The minutes disturbed him for other reasons besides the tabling of this particular program. He saw, for the very first time, a number of new undertakings of which he had no knowledge. And there were clear-cut infringements on his responsibilities which were being approved by the committee. Further, he disliked what sounded like unethical tactics being used to recruit new personnel.

He pulled open his center drawer and removed a paper headed "Score Sheet." It was a list of all the major proposals submitted during his tenure. Opposite each proposal was noted "implemented," "pended," "rejected," or "no response." He posted "pended" against the Personnel Inventory and Appraisal Program and then reviewed the entire list.

SCORE SHEET

1. Orientation for new employees .... implemented
2. Standardized vacation schedule .... implemented
3. Employee newspaper .... no response
4. Removal of time clocks .... rejected
5. Formalized, improved tuition refund program .... pended
6. Improved hospitalization and life insurance plans .... implemented

7. Centralized personnel records ....implemented
8. Clerical recruiting and testing procedures .....no response
9. Temporary help vs. additional employees, I ....implemented (with modifications)
10. Salary budgets ....pended
11. Job evaluation program ....pended
12. Morale survey ....rejected
13. Implications of turnover statistics, I ....no response
14. Supervisors' training program ....implemented (with modifications)
15. Organization charts ....no response
16. Discontinuance of annual bonus ....rejected
17. Personnel policies manual ....implemented (with modifications)
18. Temporary help vs. additional employees, II ....pended
19. Pension program ....no response
20. Implications of turnover statistics, II ....pended
21. College recruiting and training program ....implemented (with modifications)
22. Personnel inventory and appraisal program ....pended

a. What are your reactions to the minutes of this management committee meeting? What message do they convey?
b. What would you do if you were in Greenleaf's position?

A Policy on Leaves of Absence

Belinka Zoya and her husband Ivar were employed by the Lincoln Union High School District (LUHSD). Belinka was an art teacher at Salk High School and Ivar a science teacher at Technical High School. In April, 1973, Ivar enrolled in a two-unit extension course offered cooperatively by several universities in the area. Included in the course was a field trip to Florida to witness a space lab lift-off, visit NASA facilities, and attend briefing lectures on the space program. The cost of the course including tuition, lodging, and a chartered flight totaled about $300. The course lasted from Wednesday through Sunday making it necessary for him to be absent from his instructional duties for a total of three working days.

In order to attend the course, Ivar requested and was granted permission to be absent with pay for the three-day period. He also was granted an allowance of $60 to help defray expenses. As the result of her husband being granted a leave, Belinka enrolled in the course and requested a leave of absence through her school principal Albert Sanchez. Sanchez stated that he would approve the leave request but that the final decision would be up to the administrative council. Because of this encouragement, Mrs. Zoya submitted a written request for Mr. Sanchez to forward to the district personnel office. After waiting about two weeks for approval from the council, she submitted a second request directly to Sam Stone, the district personnel officer. These two requests and the two other memorandums that followed them provide a chronological record of the leave request issue.

MEMORANDUM

To: Albert Sanchez | Date: April 12, 1973
From: Belinka Zoya | Subject: 3-Day Leave of Absence

My husband, a science teacher at Technical High School, has the opportunity to observe a sky lab lift-off at NASA in Orlando, Florida, and to participate in lectures in a class offered by California State University, which has been designed to educate the teacher to the functions of the space program and its relationships to other disciplines.

We feel this is a tremendous educational opportunity for us, in art as well as science, for art seems to play a major role in science technology. I intend to record the trip through photographs that hopefully can be used in the classroom. It will also be interesting to observe the differences, if any, in the arts and crafts of the area.

We can gain a great deal of knowledge from this experience that can be shared with our students; therefore, I request a leave beginning May 14 through May 16 without loss of pay. Thank you for your consideration.

BZ: cm (signed) Belinka Zoya

MEMORANDUM

To: Sam Stone | Date: April 26, 1973
From: Belinka Zoya | Subject: Personal Necessity Leave

I request three days personal necessity leave (May 14-16), under Ed. Code 13468.5 to be charged against my sick leave. The purpose of the leave would be to accompany my husband on an educational trip to NASA in Orlando, Florida.

BZ:cm (signed) Belinka Zoya

MEMORANDUM

To: Belinka Zoya | Date: April 30, 1973
From: Sam Stone | Subject: Leave Request May 14-16, 1973

As per administrative council meeting April 23, 1973, your request for the above leave was not approved.

In reference to your memo of April 26, present policy and administrative regulation do not permit this type of leave to be charged against sick leave as per 13468.5.

SS: rc (signed) S. Stone

MEMORANDUM

To:	Sam Stone	Date:	May 1, 1973
From:	Belinka Zoya	Subject:	Concerning Leave May 14-16

Please be advised that since my husband is definitely attending the sky lab lift-off in Orlando, Florida, May 15-16, I will accompany him on the trip.

I intend to prepare sufficient lesson plans in order that regular classroom procedures will not be interrupted.

BZ:cm (signed) Belinka Zoya

Since there was insufficient time to appeal the denial of her request through the district's formal grievance procedure, Mrs. Zoya decided, as the last memorandum indicates, to attend the course and be absent for three days without the District's approval. If necessary, she felt that she could appeal at a later date any loss of pay that she might suffer. When she received the loss of three days' pay from her May salary, she requested the Lincoln Teachers Association to initiate a formal grievance in her behalf. Failure to resolve the grievance at the first two stages of the established grievance procedure resulted in its being carried to the third stage. This stage involved utilizing the services of an outside fact finder who was to consider the evidence presented by the two sides in support of their respective positions. Based upon this evidence, the procedure called for the fact finder to present recommendations in writing to the Board of Trustees; and later, as the fourth and final stage of the grievance procedure, to discuss them with the Board in executive session. The Board, however, retained the final authority to accept, reject, or modify the fact finder's recommendations.

At the hearing conducted by the fact finder, the district personnel officer, Sam Stone, argued that the District's action was entirely justified and in conformity with the sections of the District Certified Personnel Handbook governing leaves of absence. These sections, which are based upon the provisions of Section 13468.5 of the State Education Code, are as follows:

Personal Necessity Leave

Certified employees may use their allotted days of illness and injury leave in cases of personal necessity. However, they may use no more than six days of accumulated leave in any school year for the following purposes:

1. The death or serious illness of a member of one's immediate family.
2. An accident involving one's person or property, or the personal property of a member of one immediate family.
3. An appearance in court, either as a litigator or as a witness.
4. Imminent danger to one's home which requires attention during assigned hours of service (fire, flood, etc.).

Employees must verify their absence just as for an illness and injury leave.

With the prior approval of the superintendent, an employee may take a personal necessity leave (without loss of pay) for professional, business, or personal matters that cannot be taken care of except during the school day. This leave may be used for maternity, death, or illness not covered by bereavement leave, adoption proceedings, examinations for an advanced degree, legal transactions, or religious holidays.

Leave with Pay Deduction

The cost of a substitute is deducted from an employee's pay for each personal absence not covered above, but recommended by the Principal and approved by the Superintendent.

The certificated employee's daily rate of pay is deducted from the monthly pay for each *unapproved* personal absence.

In support of Mrs. Zoya's grievance, Helen Black, president of the Lincoln Teachers Association, presented a brief supporting the position of the aggrieved party and included with it a number of exhibits. The most relevant portion of the brief submitted by Ms. Black is as follows:

The LTA believes that Mrs. Belinka Zoya's request for a personal necessity leave May 14-16, 1973, for reasons stated, should have been granted on the basis of the following:

I. Ed. Code Section 13468.5 states that any days of leave of absence for illness or injury allowed pursuant to Section 13468.5 may be used by the employee, at his or her election, in cases of personal necessity.

According to a County Counsel Opinion addressed to all school district superintendents and directors of personnel on Feb. 28, 1973: "Under general authority granted to school district governing boards to administer the schools and employees under their supervision, policies and regulations may be adopted which define the purposes for which personal necessity leave may be taken so long as the governing board does not deprive any employee of any leave of absence to which he or she is entitled by law."

To Mrs. Zoya, this leave constituted a personal necessity. As a professional teacher, she felt this would be an out of the ordinary opportunity (at no added expense to the District since monies for sick leave are already budgeted). In at least one neighboring district her request would have been honored under its personal necessity leave policy which allows personal business and defines personal business as "an event out of the ordinary and/or circumstances beyond the control of the individual."

For any teacher today to have a firsthand experience with space travel would be considered to be educationally broadening; however, since Mrs. Zoya is an art teacher, it was particularly valuable. Kennedy Space Center has the largest art facility of all the NASA installations. This provided an excellent opportunity for her to gain firsthand knowledge of the use of commercial art in the space program. She is now able to share this knowledge with her students.

Since NASA employs commercial artists in its local installation, this knowledge could provide some of her students with the necessary background to obtain this employment later on.

II. As evidenced by the policies established in neighboring districts, the reasons given for a personal necessity leave are not subject to an administrative or board judgment and should not, therefore, be a part of the rationale for the refusal of a leave. An opinion of County Counsel states that the same general approach used by districts in obtaining proof of illness may be followed with respect to personal necessity leave, i.e., a signed statement by the teacher explaining the nature of his or her illness. One would assume, therefore, that since the board and administration accept this kind of statement as proof of a short-term illness, they should do likewise for a short-term personal necessity leave.

III. The Lincoln Union High School District does not have a policy regarding personal necessity leave as provided for by the Ed. Code Section 13468.5. That the District does not have this policy was acknowledged by the fact that they brought such a proposal to the negotiation table earlier this year.

IV. It is obvious that in this case, the policy(s) under which these leaves were considered was inequitably applied. Mr. Zoya was granted a leave for the same reasons that Mrs. Zoya was denied a leave. That this was as much a case of personal necessity on the part of Mr. Zoya is evidenced by the fact (as stated by Mr. Zoya himself) that he was willing to pay the bulk of the cost of the trip for both himself and his wife because of his personal interest in space flight.

Denial of Mrs. Zoya's leave appears to be based on an unreasonable, arbitrary, and discriminatory application of leave policy. District correspondence with Mr. Zoya gives no indication of the policy(s) under which his leave was granted.

Based upon the above arguments, the LTA maintains that the LUHSD should reimburse Mrs. Zoya her full salary for the three days of her leave.

The only other section of the District Handbook having a possible bearing on the case but not mentioned by Ms. Black is the following paragraph under the heading "Conferences and Conventions":

> A representative from each school may be allowed release time to attend conferences and conventions which concern a specific subject area or the teaching profession in general. More than one teacher from each school may be approved for attendance at one- or two-day conferences which are within 100 miles of the district. Attendance is not charged against vacation time.

a. What facts, if any, support Mrs. Zoya's grievance? The District's position?
b. If you were the fact finder in the case, what recommendation would you make to the Board of Trustees?
c. What improvements, if any, might be made in the statement covering conferences and conventions to clarify it? Prepare a statement incorporating these improvements.

Working in Harmony

The job of manager in a business organization has frequently been compared with that of a symphony orchestra conductor. Both are concerned with getting each member in the organization to play his or her part and to blend each contribution into a team that work together harmoniously. In order to produce the highest quality of music for its listeners, the San Francisco Symphony Orchestra—an organization employing over 100 musicians—gives considerable attention to the recruitment and selection of personnel to fill vacancies in the various chairs. Because musicians must not only be masters of their instruments but also must be able to blend with the other members of their sections, there is no place for individuals whose musicianship is less than superior. For over 60 years, highly accomplished musicians have been striving to become a part of this organization of world fame and many of them have not achieved their goal. After an announced vacancy for the position of co-principal French horn, for example, the symphony received approximately 150 inquiries. Of the 60 musicians who appeared for auditions, only seven passed the preliminary audition. However, of this group none was considered fully suitable to fill the position.

Whenever a position in the orchestra becomes vacant, an announcement is placed in a local newspaper for musicians and in the magazine *International Musician*. Those who are interested in being considered for the position are furnished an application form that requests a résumé of educational background, orchestra experience, and other information concerning current contractual relationships, union membership, etc. Applicants are advised that all auditions will be held in San Francisco, that auditionees must appear in person at the time indicated on the audition notice, and that tapes will not be accepted.

On the date for auditions, musicians from all over the United States arrive at the War Memorial Opera House. To facilitate the process, candidates are divided into groups of 10 persons and told to appear at a designated time for the audition. Numbers are drawn for the order of appearance within the designated time period. Candidates are then provided with practice rooms so that they can warm up for the audition.

The first stage of the selection procedure is the conducting of the preliminary audition which, under the terms of the Master Agreement between the San Francisco Symphony Association and the Musicians Union Local#6, involves 10 members of the orchestra who listen to the candidates. Five of them are drawn from the principal chairs and five are members-at-large from the orchestra. When it is a candidate's turn to audition, he or she is ushered on to the stage behind a screen so as not to be seen by the members of the orchestra sitting in the auditorium. Women auditionees wearing high heeled shoes are asked to remove them before walking on the stage.

Each candidate plays the same selection designated in the repertoire for auditionees that was mailed with the application form. The repertoire typically includes a solo work designed to demonstrate the candidate's virtuosity. Immediately after a performance which usually lasts about five to eight minutes, the 10-member committee ballots on a "yes" or "no" basis. Ballots are collected and counted at once by the union steward and the symphony personnel manager. Candidates who receive six "yes" votes are advised to be available for the final audition on the following day. Those who have less than six "yes" votes are advised that they will not be considered further, and appreciation is expressed for their interest and participation.

In the audition of the finalists, the conductor joins the committee of 10 orchestra members. The candidates again appear on the stage, one at a time, and play the prescribed selection; however, no screen is used this time. In evaluating the performance of the finalists, a point system is used. Each of the 10 members has 10 points that can be given to each candidate. The committee's score on a candidate is added to the score assigned by the conductor who has 150 points for each candidate. The candidate with the highest score, which must be 200 points or more, is offered the job. Bonus points are given to local musicians (25) and to members of the San Francisco Symphony (35).

If there are several individuals who receive more than 200 points and are in the same range, and none stands out above the others, a third phase is used. In this phase the three highest candidates are called back to play with an entire section of the orchestra under the direction of the conductor. Following this tryout with the section of the orchestra, the audition committee meets with the conductor and voting again takes place. The winning candidate, if there is one, is given a letter stating salary and conditions of employment. The selected candidate is then required to give an answer immediately and state the date that he or she will be able to report for work with the orchestra.

a. Why does the orchestra have candidates perform behind a screen for the preliminary audition? Would it be advisable to use this same procedure in the typical employment interview? What would be the advantages and disadvantages of such a procedure in the interview?
b. In the audition each candidate is required to play the same musical selections. Why are they not permitted to choose their own music? How does this procedure compare with that used in evaluating job candidates in other types of organizations?
c. In the final audition the conductor is allowed more points than the entire group of 10 musicians. Is this a desirable practice?
d. Should a typical business organization be this selective when considering individuals for an executive position?

Case 4

Misplaced in a Brick Yard

The Thermal Brick Company, which manufactures refractory bricks for use in furnaces and other areas exposed to high temperatures, employs about 300 persons. Most of the jobs in the plant require only minimal skill and training and are monotonous in nature. This fact creates a safety problem since it causes many workers to become disinterested in their work and be involved in accidents. Because some of the jobs also are hazardous in nature, accident prevention is of major concern to the company. Consequently, the company has an extensive safety program which includes the usual instruction courses, as well as extensive rules governing work methods and the wearing of protective clothing.

Typical of the problems relating to morale and safety within the company was one involving Harry Moss, an employee who was hired by the company after he had completed two years of college. Harry was employed initially as a yardman and after six months became a kiln helper. This latter job consists of transferring the partially cured bricks from pallets to kiln cars on which the bricks are moved slowly through the heated kilns as a final step in the curing process. After this process is completed, the bricks are transferred by the kiln helper from the cars to the pallets on which they are shipped to customers. Kiln helpers, like the other employees, are given extensive safety instruction and are required to wear safety-toed shoes, hard hats, protective goggles, and a protective apron to reduce wear on clothing.

In spite of the safety training he had received, however, Harry became careless in the performance of his work with the result that he received two warnings and a written reprimand from his supervisor. During his third year of employment, his carelessness caused him to be injured by a moving kiln car which struck him in the lumbar region of his back.

After being absent for eight weeks as a result of the injury, Harry was cleared by the company physician to return to work. Two days after his return he complained of severe back pains and requested and received an additional 30 days' leave. On the 29th day of this leave, his supervisor received a phone call from Harry's wife requesting a two-week extension of his leave which the supervisor refused to grant without the approval of the company physician. When he failed to return at the end of his leave period, his supervisor, who had long wanted to be rid of Harry, used the continued absence as a reason for terminating him from the company. The supervisor based his action on a section of the union agreement which provided that "when an employee is on sick leave he must, before the end of the leave period, either personally notify the company that he is returning to work or personally request and receive approval for an extension of the leave." Since the request for the leave extension had been made by his wife rather than by Harry personally, and since there had been no approval of a leave extension, the plant superintendent, after noting the warning slips and low ratings in Harry's personnel file, agreed that the action taken by the supervisor was justified under the terms of the union agreement.

As might be expected, the union promptly filed a grievance demanding the reinstatement of Harry and charging that the company was being inhumane in discharging a man when he was down. The union also maintained that Harry had been in bed with the flu at the time his wife had called and therefore was unable to make the call or to come in to see the plant physician. As a result of union pressure and growing unrest in the plant among employees who believed that he had received a "raw deal," the plant superintendent rescinded the discharge and permitted Harry to have an extension of leave for the remainder of the two-week period.

When Harry reported back to work and complained of being unable to do the bending and lifting required of a kiln helper, management decided that it did not want to risk having any more conflicts with the union. Consequently, he was transferred to the job of mixer which happened to be open on the graveyard shift. The job involved operating and keeping production records on a group of mixing machines and required no physical labor, except for starting and stopping the machines by means of electric control buttons. Harry mastered the duties of the job quickly and soon was able to perform his job more competently than the operators on either the day or the swing shifts. After about six months on the job, however, Harry began to revert to his former work habits and to develop a record of excessive tardiness and absenteeism. The supervisor thus was forced to have a lengthy session with him at which time he reminded Harry that the entire shift operations were impaired when the mixing machines were idle during the time required to locate a replacement operator. Obtaining a replacement, furthermore, required other disrupting adjustments in work assignments to be made on the shift. Following Harry's next absence, his supervisor gave him a written warning in which he stated that any future absences would result in a three-day suspension without pay for the first absence and a discharge for the second absence. Although the warning served to prevent further absences or tardiness, it did not serve to increase Harry's enthusiasm for his work.

About two months after receiving the warning, Harry decided to seek other employment and informed his supervisor that he would have to leave an hour earlier on his next work period in order to be able to drive to a military installation about 50 miles away and take a civil service examination. He informed the shift supervisor that he had made arrangements with the group leader to have his job covered for the final hour of the shift. The supervisor, whose mind was preoccupied with production problems at the time, grunted what appeared to be his approval although he was not conscious of the fact. The next day, the plant superintendent arrived early to inspect the operation of the graveyard shift and discovered that Harry, now well known by everyone in management, had left early. Since Harry's request to leave early had never really registered with the shift supervisor, he was at a loss to explain Harry's absence and therefore replied, "I guess he just took off." Regarding such action as intolerable, the superintendent ordered that Harry be terminated immediately. When Harry returned the next night and was handed his discharge slip, he appealed to the union which again went to bat for him. When management refused to reinstate Harry, the union used the discharge, along with some other grievances against the company, to arouse the tensions among its members and to create a production slowdown within the plant. Again not wanting to become involved in a major confrontation with the union, management for the second time agreed to rehire Harry.

Because of its long record of difficulties with Harry and the fact that he had become somewhat of a hero in the eyes of many workers, management decided to call in a consulting psychologist to counsel Harry and see if something could be done to improve his work attitudes. The ensuing session with the psychologist proved to be quite helpful in revealing, partially at least, the basis for his attitudes. In unburdening his feelings to the psychologist, Harry revealed bitterness over the fact that he believed his education and abilities had been wasted by the company. He complained that the company had put him in jobs that could be performed by workers with far less education and ability than he possessed. Furthermore, the psychologist was able to draw from him the fact that he felt that with his education and some training he could qualify for work in the quality control lab or for some job in the office. The initial reaction of the superintendent and members of management to the results of the counseling session was less than enthusiastic. In the opinion of the superintendent, Harry was a grown man who had had plenty of opportunities to express his feelings about work and should have submitted a request for a job in the office or the lab on his own initiative. After some discussion, however, the psychologist managed to convince most of the management members that something had to be done if the company was to avoid continuing problems with Harry and with the union. Although it did so with some mental reservations, management agreed to give Harry a trial period of training for a position in the lab. When the reports on his progress and attitudes at the end of the first month proved favorable, his training was allowed to continue. Eventually Harry was given a permanent job in the lab. In the meantime he received notification that he had been accepted for a civil service position. Since by this time he had accumulated several years of seniority with the company and now was quite satisfied with his employment situation, Harry rejected the civil service position to remain with the company.

a. What lessons does the case have to offer in terms of employee selection, placement, and supervision?
b. What are the possible reasons why this problem was not resolved satisfactorily much sooner?
c. Should the services of an outside consultant have been utilized in this situation? What are some of the ethical considerations involved in the use of a consulting psychologist?
d. Based upon the facts given, how would you rate the personnel policies and practices of this company?

Career Paths

Most organizations today are aware of the importance of job satisfaction and its contribution to employee productivity and morale. Since upward progress within an organization can provide an important source of personal job satisfaction, more organizations are attempting to create career paths for their employees to indicate what advancement opportunities are open to them and thereby provide a source of motivation. In practice, however, the development and progress of many individuals, as well as their promotion opportunities, may not occur in accordance with a predetermined career path. The careers of the individuals employed by the Forest Products Corporation serve to illustrate this fact.

René Ladue's Career Path

Following graduation from the Wharton School of Finance with an MBA degree, René Ladue was hired as a management trainee. His academic qualifications appeared to provide Ladue with unlimited potential for advancement within the corporation. In order that he might gain production experience, he was assigned initially as a supervisor in a paper pulp mill. Within two years, he had advanced through two levels of management to become superintendent of the bag and converting operations. When the position of general manager became open at one of the company's smaller paper mills, he was promoted to this position.

After Ladue had been with the corporation five years, a commercial R&D (research and development) division was created within the corporate headquarters of the organization. This division was responsible for evaluating and making recommendations concerning the purchase of various product and processing patents as well as small mills and timber properties being offered to the corporation from time to time. Because of his academic qualifications and his five years of managerial experience in production work, Ladue was chosen to head the new five-member division staff with an appropriate increase in salary and rank.

Before a year had elapsed, however, the corporation's top management began to have doubts concerning the value and feasibility of such a division, and a few months later disbanded it. The major casualty resulting from this action was René Ladue, who received some of the blame for the division's failure to achieve what had been expected of it. Consequently, his career with the corporation was placed in jeopardy when the management planning committee met to consider what future, if any, he was to have with the corporation. The committee members were divided over their opinions concerning the action to be taken. Some members argued that Ladue should be terminated on the grounds that his performance as head of the R&D division indicated a lack of potential for top management. Rather than continue his employment with Forest Products where his future might be clouded by his record with the R&D division, they contended that it would be better for him to be forced to begin a new career with some other employer.

Committee members voicing support for Ladue, on the other hand, argued that the unsatisfactory record of the R&D division resulted from changes in corporate policy and the fact that the corporation probably had erred in establishing the division in the first place. They argued further that Ladue was being held responsible and made the scapegoat for the record of a division that had been destined to fail from the start. Perhaps, they argued, the committee shared some of the blame by allowing itself to be overly impressed with his academic degrees and thereby largely ignored his lack of experience with the company.

After much discussion and a thorough review of his entire record with the corporation, a majority of the committee voted to return Ladue to a position in the operating phase of the corporation as assistant manager of a large paper mill. In this position Ladue subsequently received high performance ratings and within a couple of years was promoted to resident manager.

Nathan Berg's Career Path

One management contemporary of Ladue was Nathan Berg. Upon receiving his C.P.A. certificate, Berg was hired as an understudy to the manager of a divisional accounting department that employed about 50 employees. In slightly more than a year he became the office manager and three years later became the controller of a large mill. Because of the ability he demonstrated during his three years as controller, Berg was brought to the corporate headquarters as director of pulp and paper accounting where he served for another two years. With a staff of eight personnel, his office was responsible for functional contacts between corporate headquarters and the various mills and other operating units that related to accounting. In this position, Berg showed an extraordinary understanding of accounting data and its relationship to operating problems. As a result he was able to simplify many of the accounting records and reports of the operating managers.

Because of Berg's knowledge of operating problems, he was made assistant manager of a medium-sized mill and then the manager after a little over a year. In this latter capacity he was placed in the difficult role of overseeing the reduction of the mill's workforce from 1,200 to 400 employees—a role that required him to cope with many personnel and union relations problems. His success in the latter role resulted in his being returned to corporate headquarters as director of corporate planning, a strictly staff position. After three more years he was made vice-president of employee relations and management services. The latter responsibility included corporate planning, central engineering, purchasing, and responsibility for distribution facilities and nonoperating properties such as timber lands.

Ahead of Berg now are only the positions of executive vice-president and president of the corporation. Had he chosen to progress upward through the staff positions typically open to the accounting specialist, he probably would eventually have risen from the position of director of pulp and paper accounting to that of vice-president of finance, a staff position just two levels up. As it turned out, he is now a vice-president in a line position that provides a higher salary, more authority, and a better opportunity to reach the top.

Juan Garcia's Career Path

In contrast to the careers of Ladue and Berg, that of Juan Garcia involved still a different path of progression within the Forest Products Corporation. Garcia had only a high school education and ten years of experience as a reporter and as a city editor of a small town newspaper when he joined the corporation at the age of thirty. He began as the assistant director of public relations and two years later became the director of public relations. In another three years he became manager of marketing services which included advertising, market research, and sales promotion. At the age of thirty-six, Garcia became the general sales manager of the company's pulp and paper division and, following a reorganization of the division, was made general manager of a newly created paper products division. Two years later, at the age of forty and with only ten years of service with the corporation, Garcia was appointed general manager of a geographic region containing five sawmills and two plywood plants as well as timber lands and logging operations. At this point in his career, there are still a number of years ahead for him in which to gain further advancement with the corporation.

Epilogue

The careers of the individuals just discussed represent some of the more successful ones in the Forest Products Corporation. There are other management personnel whose progress has been slower. As a result, they occupy lower positions in the corporate structure, even though they are senior to Ladue, Berg, and Garcia in terms of age and years of company service. The contrast in the career paths and progress of the three persons discussed in this case, in some instances, has been the result of being at the right place or getting the right break at the right time. Over the long run, however, their managerial capabilities, assertiveness, ability to recognize opportunities, and willingness to take the risks necessary to pursue these opportunities probably were the primary determinants of their success with the corporation.

a. In what respects did the career paths taken by Ladue, Berg, and Garcia differ, if any, from those which the management planning committee might have charted for them during their first year with the corporation?
b. What was the most critical point in the career progress of each individual?
c. Should management attempt to develop a career path for each of its members? To what extent is it possible to do so?

The Ambitious Staff Specialist

The Saline Chemical Corporation, with headquarters in the Midwest, was engaged primarily in the production and nationwide distribution of chemical products for industrial and retail markets. The company, like many others in its field, experienced very rapid growth both in its sales volume, number of products produced, and the size of its work force in the years following World War II. At the time that the problem for discussion arose, the company employed about 30,000 persons, including those in its subsidiaries.

In the process of its expansion, the company was continually on the lookout for opportunities to purchase mineral properties for future sources of raw materials. It was also considering the purchase of smaller companies that might enable it to diversify its line of products, to gain new channels of distribution, or to acquire nationally known brand names under which it could market certain of its existing products. Because of the rapid technological advances within the industry and the rapid expansion that had occurred within its work force, the company required a relatively large number of college trained personnel for both line and staff positions at the executive level. Although it had had difficulty during the postwar period in recruiting adequate personnel of the caliber desired, the company had been able to develop a technical staff composed of personnel who were extremely valuable to it.

One of the members of its financial research staff was J. Clayton Hall, who was about 38 years of age and an honor graduate with an M.B.A. degree from an eastern university. He had acquired some ten years of experience with the company and was responsible for the analysis of financial data and the compiling of reports for top management that were used in making company investment decisions. His work was extremely important because it provided the basis for decisions involving the investment of millions of dollars. Hall was regarded by his superiors as an extremely hardworking and conscientious individual who was outstanding in his type of work. His salary had been advanced rapidly and was above that being paid by other companies for similar types of work. His opportunities for advancement to positions of greater income and responsibility, although contingent upon additional years of service, were definitely assured.

In spite of his successful record and his value to the company, Hall did not feel that he enjoyed prestige within the company that was commensurate with either his ability or with that accorded to persons in supervisory positions who were much less competent and less valuable to the company. His contacts with certain of his college classmates who had risen to managerial positions of major importance caused him to be extremely sensitive of the fact that he did not have authority over anyone. Hall's failure to gain supervisory responsibility was due partly to the fact that he was more valuable to the company in the type of position in which he had been working and partly to the fact that he was totally lacking in human relations skills. Most company personnel who had any contact with him considered him to be an overbearing and extremely obnoxious individual.

Although Hall did not "rub people the wrong way" intentionally, he usually was so engrossed with the technical aspects of his work that he did not have time to give much consideration to the feelings of others. Although he had been reminded of his personality deficiencies during many previous performance rating interviews with superiors, he had never been able to improve these defects to any noticeable extent. Because of his outstanding performance in his technical field, however, Hall's personality deficiencies had not impeded his progress. Furthermore, the fact that he had relatively few contacts with other people caused his unsatisfactory traits to be overlooked.

After brooding for some time over his lack of positional status, Hall approached the head of his department with the demand that he be given a position involving supervisory responsibility or he was going to quit. His superiors were quite aware of the fact that he had received several recent offers from other companies and that he was in a position to enforce his demands. While the company did not regard any of its personnel as being indispensable, it recognized that even if it could employ another person with Hall's abilities, several years of experience would be required before the replacement could equal Hall's present contributions.

The possibility of giving Hall a position with a more prestige-lending title was considered but ruled out because it conflicted with rather rigid company policies and traditions, which caused executive titles to be reserved almost entirely for positions of a managerial nature. The few senior staff positions that did carry executive rank and status were staffed by those who had at least 20 to 25 years of company service. Although Hall undoubtedly would eventually be able to achieve one of these senior positions that carried the prestige he craved, this prospect was at least 10 years away. There appeared to be only two alternatives in dealing with Hall's demands. One was to disregard his personality and give him some supervisory responsibilities in which he could enjoy the title and prestige of a line executive position. Or, management could attempt to change his mind by pointing out his value to the company, the importance of his job, and the opportunities for status that would ultimately be available to him. There were strong indications, however, that Hall would not be satisfied with anything less than a supervisory position and that he would resign if he did not get one.

a. What are some of the possible underlying reasons for Hall's demands?
b. What action should his department head take?
c. Why is it that jobs involving authority over people traditionally carry more prestige and salary than technical jobs which may require more education but no authority over people?
d. Are the company's management development practices at fault?

Evaluating Personnel for Layoff

J. D. Robbins, the manager of a chemical research department of an aerospace company, was called into the office of the division manager and informed that two of his highest paid chemists had to be laid off as a result of cancellation of a defense contract. In order to determine which employees should be laid off, Robbins was requested to submit a new performance rating of his chemists by using the company's standard scale. The performance ratings were to include not only the eight standard items but also other items such as seniority, health, contribution to the company's growth and profit, community contacts, and value to the company in the future. The scale ranged from 1 to 10, with 10 being the highest obtainable rating, and comments were normally used with the scales to justify the ratings.

The four highest paid chemists in Robbins' department—Adams, Baker, Cooper, and Davis—were rated as shown in Table C-1 on page 605.

The comments that were included with the numerical ratings revealed the following facts and opinions about each of the four men:

> Adams, 56 years old, has been employed by the company for 20 years. He has developed a number of valuable chemicals which have been marketed by the company at a profit of over a million dollars. He, therefore, was considered to be one of the most valuable employees in the company. He also has been active in community politics. However, about nine months ago Adams suffered a severe back injury in a car accident. This injury had resulted in a poor attendance record for the past year. The value of his services to the company in the future is questionable.

Table C-1 PERFORMANCE RATINGS

	Adams	Baker	Cooper	Davis
STANDARD ITEMS				
1. Quality of Work	8	8	8	8
2. Quantity of Work	3	7	9	9
3. Dependability	9	9	9	9
4. Attendance	3	7	10	10
5. Cooperation	8	4	8	8
6. Customer Contacts	8	3	7	7
7. Skill in Report and Proposal Writing	8	9	7	7
8. Skill in Oral Presentations	8	9	7	8
NEW ITEMS				
9. Seniority	10	6	3	3
10. Health	3	7	10	10
11. Contributions to the Company's Growth and Profit	10	8	3	3
12. Community Contacts	9	4	6	6
13. Value of Services to the Company in the Future	3	7	9	9
	90	88	96	97

Baker, 43 years old, has been employed by the company for 12 years. He also has developed several valuable chemical products and processes for production of chemicals. He is considered to be an ingenious chemist of great value to the company. Baker, however, has difficulties in getting along with his co-workers, customers, and people in the community.

Both Cooper, 34 years old, and Davis, 33 years old, have been employed by the company for six years. They are considered to be outstanding chemists with no weak traits and would undoubtedly be of great value to the company in the future. Their contribution to the company's growth and profit, however, has been small as compared to that of Adams and Baker.

On the basis of Robbins' performance ratings, personnel action was taken to lay off Adams and Baker while Cooper and Davis were retained.

a. Did the inclusion of the five additional items on the rating scale increase the value of the scale as a basis for making the decision as to which persons would be laid off?
b. What assumption is made about the relative importance of the items on the scale in the method that is used by this company?
   (1) Are there any fallacies in this assumption?
   (2) Do the descriptive comments about the four men reveal anything about the problem of using numerical rating scales?
c. Do you detect any bias in Robbins' evaluation of these men?

Humanitarianism: How Far Can Management Go?

Miss Vera Baker at the age of 46 was completing her 18th year with the Department of Natural Resources when her supervisor for the past 15 years, Alex Claybourne, retired from state service. Alex was an easy-going technical specialist who spent a large part of his time drafting and redrafting memos and directives. His approach was definitely slow and methodical. Over the years that she worked for Alex, Vera received performance ratings in the satisfactory to excellent range. While the personnel officer of the department suspected that Vera's capabilities would be judged by others as being less than satisfactory, she had no difficulty in meeting Alex's standards.

Immediately after Alex's retirement the technical program with which he was associated was changed. With the reorganization of the department, Vera was placed in a secretarial pool where she served as a stenographer for several individuals who were supervised by Bob Scott. Bob and his staff of technicians were reminded by the department personnel officer that Vera had been working for Alex for 15 years and that additional time might be required to get her accustomed to the new arrangements. Bob and his staff went all out to orient and train her for her assignment, and they were patient and thoughtful in their relationships with Vera. After a period of about a year in which her work performance had been average to mediocre, Vera's output and the quality of her work deteriorated markedly to the point where she could produce only two or three satisfactory letters in an eight-hour period. In accordance with departmental personnel procedures, Bob documented this poor performance with the objective of dismissing the employee.

At about the same time that Bob was growing increasingly concerned over Vera's performance, Jerry, one of the technicians who had more frequent contact with Vera than Bob did, observed a change in Vera's manner of walking. "It appears to me," he told Bob, "that Vera drags her legs when she walks." Jerry's observation was confirmed by Bob who suggested that maybe there was something physically wrong with her.

The next day Bob talked with Vera about her physical condition. She didn't have much to say about it, except that she had not seen a physician in many years. It was then learned that her religion did not permit medical treatment of any kind. Bob explained to Vera that under the state employment regulations an employee was required to submit to a medical examination if so directed by management. Bob further explained that the fees would be paid by the department and that she would be permitted to have the examination during her regular working hours without the time being charged to her sick leave. Vera told Bob, "O.K. I'll do it if I have to."

Bob advised the department personnel officer of what had happened. The personnel officer then contacted the medical adviser for the department who furnished the names of three specialists in internal medicine. Vera was asked to select one of them, and arrangements were then made for her to have an examination at the department's expense. Shortly after the examination and before any results of it were known, Vera attempted suicide by turning on the gas stove in her apartment. Fortunately, she was not successful in this attempt and returned to work a few days later. She was still despondent and told Bob several times that her life was no good, that she was a failure, and that her whole world was caving in.

Within a few days the internist's report was received in the personnel office. The internist suspected that Vera had Parkinson's disease* and recommended that she be seen by a neurologist. The personnel officer made an appointment with a neurologist, but before Vera could keep the appointment she made another suicide attempt on her life by drinking a solution of drain cleaner. She was rushed to the hospital, and after the emergency condition was resolved she was placed under the care of a psychiatrist. At the request of the personnel officer, the psychiatrist arranged for a neurologist to examine her in the medical center where she was a patient. This diagnosis confirmed that of the internist.

By this time Vera's physical symptoms had become more pronounced. A palsy condition became noticeable and she couldn't hold a pencil steadily enough to write. She would not take any drugs to alleviate the condition because of her religious beliefs, but she did cooperate in psychotherapy which was designed to help her cope with her feelings of hopelessness, anxiety, suspiciousness, and chronic dissatisfaction. In sessions that she had with the psychiatrist it became apparent that, in addition to her physical illness and her inability to perform satisfactorily on the job, she was carrying an emotional burden of rejection by her brother who was her only relative. Vera continued to see the psychiatrist once a week for several months with considerable improvement in her emotional condition and the eventual establishment of a

* A nerve disease characterized by tremors, especially of the fingers and hands, rigidity of muscles, slowness of movements and speech, and a mask-like expressionless face.

good relationship with her brother. However, it was apparent that she would not ever be able to return to her job because of the neurological disease.

a. How far should an employer go in attempting to find the causes of an employee's ineffective performance?
b. What other types of ineffective performance may a supervisor encounter among subordinates? What effect may they have on the operations of a unit?
c. Do you believe that Bob took the best course of action in Vera's case? What would you have done if you had been in his position? Why?
d. What steps should be taken by management to terminate her employment and still provide Vera with some level of security?

Case 9

The New Broom

June Robbins, personnel officer of the state Department of Motor Vehicles, was working at her desk when a call came from the department's new director, William Sharp. Sharp requested that Robbins come to his office for a discussion. Robbins was pleased to have the opportunity to talk with the new chief—a political appointee—who had taken office only a week before at the same time that the new governor had assumed leadership of the state. She knew that Sharp had been the successful president of a large industrial corporation and that he was a very dynamic individual who had been heard to be critical of bureaucratic "red tape." This was the extent of her knowledge about Sharp, so she was looking forward to the meeting.

Sharp greeted her in a very cordial manner and put her at ease immediately. He asked her to tell him about her experiences in state government and about her role in the organization. After they became better acquainted, Sharp told Robbins that he had some plans for reorganizing the Department of Motor Vehicles so as to make it more efficient and better integrated to fit the plans that he and the new governor had for making government more responsive to the needs of the citizens. For several minutes Sharp described his plans for reorganization in detail. They involved the establishment of new units within the department, the closing out of other units, and the reassignment of many employees to new jobs. He advised Robbins that he wanted the changes implemented within two months without fail.

At this point Robbins was wondering why her boss, Sam Adams, the Assistant Director for Administration, was not called in on such an important matter. Like herself, Sam is a permanent civil service employee. He and three other assistant directors report directly to Sharp. Nevertheless, Robbins recognized that Sharp knew what he wanted. He expected her to implement his ideas for reorganization, which in her own mind she believed would be beneficial to the department in the long run. Robbins realized, however, that under civil service laws some of Sharp's proposed changes could be made without delay, others could not be made in less than 12 months, and some were prohibited by law. Rather than make any comments about Sharp's proposals, she decided that it would be more judicious to ask for one week to analyze the matter and then return a suggested plan for implementing them. Sharp found this to be quite agreeable and the interview was concluded.

a. Since Sharp bypassed Sam Adams and went strictly to Robbins, what should Robbins do before going to work on Sharp's request?
b. Why didn't Sharp present his ideas to Sam Adams?
c. If you were in Robbins' position, how would you convince Sharp that some of his proposed changes would take 12 months and that some are prohibited by law? What types of recommendations could you make to him so that he would not view you as a "red tape" expert?
d. Is it more desirable to have top jobs in government agencies filled by political appointees than by civil service employees? Explain.

A Questionable Cause for Discharge

Wheeler Motors had the dealership for a popular middle-price line of American automobiles. The company had developed a good sales staff and advertising program which enabled it to realize a fairly high profit from its new and used car departments. It also maintained a complete service department which earned a small profit and, like those of most dealers, produced its share of problems for the management. One of these problems was that of obtaining and keeping competent mechanics, supervisors, and other shop personnel who were conscientious in their work.

In July, 1975, Tony Groza, who had been the shop service manager for several years, accepted a similar position at a higher salary with another auto dealer. To fill the position the company owner, Jerry Wheeler, decided to promote Jack Bender who had worked for him the past five years as a lead man in the body shop. Although Bender did not possess any prior experience or formal training for the position of service manager, he proceeded with eagerness in his new assignment. Encouraged by Wheeler to increase efficiency and reduce the number of personnel in the shop as a means of offsetting a recessionary decline in sales, Bender began to look for workers whose termination he believed would improve efficiency. He decided that such a person was Willie Jackson, a mechanic in the shop with 18 months of service. After criticizing Jackson on two occasions for taking what was alleged to be an excessive amount of time to perform a work order, Bender mailed the following letter to Jackson's home:

Sept. 26, 1975

Mr. Willie Jackson
1212 Mesquite Road
Riverside, Texas 77367

Dear Sir

This is your first letter of warning for violation of Article 9 of the current union contract, i.e., inability to perform work assigned (R.O. P67504).

Two more violations of this order will result in your dismissal.

Very truly yours,

Jack Bender (Signed)
Service Manager
Wheeler Motors, Inc.

JB:da
cc: Mechanics Union Local

Article 9 of the contract cited in the letter stated that "Journeymen shall have acquired the necessary knowledge, experience, and ability to perform work assigned to them in a reasonable time and in a satisfactory manner. Management shall discharge for just cause." The number (R.O. P67504) represented the number of the repair order on which Jackson was accused by Bender of taking too much time. This order was for the replacement of a door handle and the adjustment of the ignition system and carburetor on a customer's car. The basis for the accusation was that the cost to the company for Jackson's labor on the order was $15.75 for which the actual value as charged to the customer was $19.50. Jackson admitted that the time required to complete the order was greater than it should have been but justified this fact on the basis that he had encountered problems in trying to remove the damaged handle. In spite of a prolonged and rather heated discussion with the service manager, Jackson was unable to obtain a retraction of the warning letter and the issue was not pursued further. During the next week or so communication between the two men occurred only when it was absolutely necessary in connection with the processing of work orders.

On October 8 Jackson received another letter from Bender, which read as follows:

> This is your second letter of warning for violation of Article 9 of the current collective bargaining agreement, i.e., inability to perform work assigned (R.O. P34000, P34021, P34165, P34245, P34366, P34408, P34458, P34511).
>
> One more violation will result in your dismissal.

An analysis of the orders revealed the following breakdown between the cost of labor and the charge to the customer:

Repair Order	Cost of Labor	Customer Charge for Labor
P34000	$ 5.71	$13.98
P34021	4.00	13.98
P34165	2.86	6.99
P34245	1.71	4.19
P34366	4.00	9.79
P34408	2.28	6.99
P34458	7.42	18.17
P34511	12.56	30.75

A conference between Jackson and Bender concerning the second warning letter failed to accomplish any greater understanding or agreement than that after the first letter. For the next two months following the conference, Jackson continued to perform his job as best he could. In spite of this fact, Bender sent a letter to Jackson's home on December 6, 1975, the contents of which are as follows:

> This is your third and final letter of warning for violation of Article 9, i.e., inability to perform work assigned. (Attached R.O. B95252 and B11235).
>
> You are hereby notified as of this date of your termination with this company. Attached is your final payroll check. This termination resulted for failure to comply with the collective bargaining agreement.
>
> (signed) Jack Bender

R.O. B95252 cited in the letter involved a charge to the customer of $4.19 for labor costing the company $1.71. R.O. B11235 involved a charge of $19.80 for labor costing $10.50. Following Jackson's letter of termination, the union filed a formal grievance which was processed without being resolved through the grievance procedure. Then it was submitted to arbitration for settlement. Before an arbitration hearing was held in January, however, Bender's services were terminated and he was not available to testify in behalf of the company at the hearing.

a. If you were the arbitrator, what would be your award in the case? Why?
b. What criticism might be leveled against both the company and the union in this case?
c. In what ways did the processing of this discharge case violate commonly accepted practices of industrial jurisprudence?

The Dissatisfied Meat Inspectors

In order to carry out the provisions of legislation governing a new joint federal-state program for meat inspection, it was necessary for the state department of agriculture to recruit and hire a large number of additional inspectors. Unlike federal inspectors with whom they frequently come into contact, those in the state department are not required to be veterinarians. They must, however, possess the ability to perform the inspection according to regulations that implement the meat inspection laws. To meet the need for additional personnel, the personnel department of the state department of agriculture determined that jouneymen meat cutters should be able to assume the responsibilities of the job with a minimum of orientation and instruction. Within a short period of time several meat cutters were hired to staff the newly authorized positions. With the size of its inspection now doubled, the state was ready to meet its responsibilities under the new joint federal-state program.

As the new personnel became more familiar with the nature of their work and observed that their jobs required knowledge and skills that were not significantly different from those required of professionally trained veterinarians with whom they came into contact, they rapidly became dissatisfied with their rate of pay and other conditions of their job. The new employees, who, until they became employees of the state had been active members of the meat cutter's union, remembered that the best way to get results was through united action. They soon convinced the other half of the organization staff that it was to their advantage as a group to organize.

Spokespersons for the group of inspectors presented their case to the meat inspector's association, a subgroup within the state employees association representing all state employees. After a series of meetings between members of the group and the state employees association leaders, a list of 15 grievances was presented to the director of the state department of agriculture and the state personnel board. The major items that were included in the list of grievances were:

1. Starting salary should be increased by $150 per month.
2. Classification and job titles should be changed.
3. Overtime should be paid on a time-and-a-half basis.
4. A work load study should be conducted.
5. In promoting personnel, more consideration should be given to seniority and ability.
6. Safety equipment and clothing should be furnished by the employer.

The director of agriculture, who agreed that there were problems, especially in the areas of job classification and remuneration, proposed that these two grievances be studied on a joint effort basis by the department, the personnel board, and the employees association. (The other grievances were resolved by the department and the employee representatives.) Representatives of these groups met together several times to discuss the substance of the classification and pay grievances and to plan a course of action. During the meetings representatives of the employees association were reminded that any changes in classification and pay would have to be acted upon by the personnel board. They also learned that there were no state funds available for special salary increases. It was decided, however, that a statewide study of job classifications of meat inspectors should be made. The grievants were asked to submit a list of the meat plants at which job studies should be conducted and to make any other suggestions that would enable the committee to do an effective job of studying their work situation. During the period in which the grievances were being studied, no specific stand was taken by the director of agriculture except that an honest effort should be made to obtain all of the facts needed to resolve the problem and recommend corrective action.

Throughout the study there was considerable communication among the representatives of the three groups on a face-to-face basis and by telephone. Special meetings were held at which elected representatives of the meat inspectors from different parts of the state were invited to attend to discuss their problems.

While the grievants were suspicious of management at first and felt that management was not on their side, they have indicated in many ways their appreciation for the thorough manner in which their grievances were being studied.

a. Did the department director handle the grievances in the best interests of the state and its employees? Would you judge his approach to be typical of most managers?
b. How does the resolving of grievances in a government agency differ from that of private enterprise?
c. What outcome do you anticipate for the requested change in job classification and increased starting salary? Why?

Retirement Benefits and Inflation

In order to provide its retirees with relief from the pressures of inflation that had steadily eroded the purchasing power of their pension annuities, the Cross Pharmaceutical Company in 1949 initiated a *Temporary Allowance Program* to supplement these annuities. Allowances made through this program increased the annuity payments to the retirees by percentages ranging from 0.5 percent to 5 percent, with the larger percentage increases going to persons who were receiving the smaller monthly payments.

As a result of increases in the benefits provided for employees retiring after 1949, the percentage increases granted to those who retired before this date were expanded to a minimum of 6.5 percent and a maximum of 23.3 percent by 1969, at which time it was decided to conduct a thorough study of the allowance program. The study was concerned not only with the program's cost to the company but also with its effectiveness in meeting needs of the retired employees. A desired outcome of the study, therefore, was the development of a formula by which the annuities of retirees could be increased in a manner that would be equitable to all of them regardless of the length of time during which they had been retired.

Since improvements in the annuity plan made in 1949, 1957, and 1965, and the adoption of a stock savings plan in 1957, served to increase the retirement income of those employees who retired during the periods subsequent to each of these dates, it was essential that any allowance formula recognize that the needs of employees who retired prior to each of these dates were proportionately greater. In particular, the company directors wanted to be certain that the allowance formula would enable those annuitants with the lower income to maintain a "moderate standard of living." Such a standard, as defined by the Bureau of Labor Statistics, "provides for the maintenance of health and social well-being and participation in community activities." Thus, this standard is intended to provide more than just a ''minimum subsistence'' or poverty level income.

In developing alternative formulas to submit to the board of directors, the personnel department recommended that any funds that might be budgeted for this purpose be used to raise the incomes of annuitants with earlier retirement dates to a moderate standard, rather than to maintain the standards of the more recent retirees whose incomes were considerably greater. The achievement of this objective required the establishment of a maximum supplement that an annuitant might be eligible to receive and thus would serve to adjust only the ''subsistence portion'' of the annuitants' incomes for inflation. Such an objective, however, would represent a departure from past practice of basing an employee's retirement income upon the traditional factors of salary, service, and age.

After several weeks of study, the personnel department submitted three formulas to the board of directors for their consideration. Each formula differed in terms of the relief that it would provide to employees in relationship to dates. Following are the formulas and the cost that each would entail for the company:

Formula A

Increase the annuity payment in the amount of 2 percent for each year of retirement completed prior to 1969. (Estimated cost: $2,350,000 for the first year and $1,000,000 for the tenth year.)

Formula B

Increase the annuity payment in the amount of 2 percent for each year of retirement from 1953 through 1968, 5 percent for each year from 1949 through 1952, and 10 percent for each year of retirement prior to 1949 up to a maximum monthly supplement of $150. (Estimated cost: $2,500,000 for the first year and $1,050,000 for the tenth year.)

Formula C

Increase the annuity payment by 2 percent for each year of retirement prior to 1966 but after 1952, 5 percent a year for each year of retirement from 1949 through 1952, and 10 percent for each year of retirement prior to 1949 applied to the first $250 of the annuity. (Estimated cost: $1,350,000 for the first year and $460,000 for the tenth year.)

a. Which of the formulas would meet most closely the intended objectives of the allowance program in providing employees with relief from inflation?
b. Why is the cost of each plan in the tenth year less than the cost for the first year, particularly when the number of retirees each year is increasing?
c. The personnel department recommended that the name *Temporary Allowance Program* be changed to *Annuitants' Voluntary Income Supplement*. Do you believe such a name is desirable? What impact, if any, would the name change have upon the program's success?

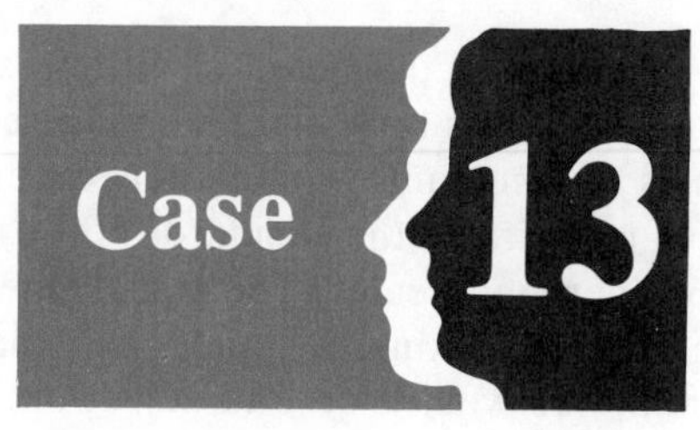

Labor Relations Overseas

For the past two years Joseph Giovani had held the position of assistant to Louis Deavoux, Vice-President of Marketing for Metal Enterprises, International, a division of Metal Enterprises, Inc. Joe, 30 years old, could be described as a "comer" who was attempting to chart a career in international management within the company. Convinced that he had reached a point of diminishing return in his present assignment, Joe sounded out his boss on the possibility of being assigned to one of the company's European subsidiaries. Deavoux was agreeable and suggested that Joe make his desires known to the Vice-President of Personnel, but also suggested that Joe contact unofficially any managers in the company's European subsidiaries with whom he might be acquainted in an effort to locate an opening for an American executive.

Since he had learned to speak Italian fluently from his Italian-born parents as a boy, Joe immediately thought of the company's subsidiary in Torino, Italy. Many of the company's managers overseas had been handicapped in their positions by their inability to speak the native language of the country. Therefore, Joe reasoned, his name and his ability to speak Italian would be an advantage to him in Italy. Besides, he had always wanted to live for a while in the country of his ancestors. Having become fairly well acquainted with Bill Shuler, managing director of the Italian subsidiary, during the latter's visits to company headquarters, he wrote to Shuler inquiring about the possibility of an assignment in Italy. In about a week he received the following reply:

Mr. Joseph G. Giovani
Assistant to the Vice-President of Marketing
Metal Enterprises, International
Rockefeller Center
New York, NY 10020

Dear Joe

Thank you for your recent letter indicating an interest in joining our organization. Although we do not have anything for you at the moment, we will have vacancies in the future as our American personnel are rotated back to Stateside assignments.

I am sure, in view of your fluency with the Italian language and your fine record with the company, you would make a valuable addition to our staff. However, there are a few things you should consider before making any move. A management position in a subsidiary, particularly in this country, certainly is no bed of roses and it is one in which you could easily stub your toe or make a poor showing through no fault of your own.

You marketing people in the home office are well aware, I am sure, with the problems we face here in sales. Trying to compete with native companies can be a real problem because we are restricted by company policies and regulations formulated some 4,000 miles away. Furthermore, not only do we have to be concerned with the antitrust and other laws of our own government but also with all of the laws and red tape established by the government in this country—which many of the native businesses often conveniently ignore. Our headaches in sales, however, are nothing compared to those we have in labor relations. Personnel management here in Italy is something else.

As you probably know, I have been at this plant for seven years in various positions as sales promotion manager, sales manager, and now general manager, and have watched a changing scene in regard to worker-employee relations. Since we have a relatively small plant (400 employees), our workers have an opportunity to see and get to know the production manager, the sales manager, and me. Furthermore, we have always attempted to have the management as close to the workers as is possible in Italy.

Union activities in Italy (for all companies) have become steadily more difficult during the last five years. Contract negotiations for companies such as ours in the metal working industry are conducted on a national level. An individual general manager can neither reject nor accept a national union's proposal.

Small problems in the plant have always been discussed with the "Internal Committee" usually made up of one or two worker-members of each of the three major national unions in Italy. During the last year, however, the decisions made by these union members are no longer being automatically accepted by the workers; and a militant, young "Committee of the Base" is now directly involving itself in all matters.

The objective of this committee seems to be more one of disruption than one of the settlement of problems. The enclosed leaflet passed out yesterday, for example, will give you an idea of the union's continuing campaign to keep the workers stirred up. Since a signed work contract has no legal validity in Italy, additional requests can be made at any time. Strikes usually are not against working conditions in our company, but are for better and lower priced government-sponsored housing, or better metropolitan transportation systems, or more schools, or a revised tax system, or occasionally against a particular political party, or a sympathy strike. Their demands are pushing in the direction of eliminating all overtime work and all incentive plans.

I have only scratched the surface on this subject but hope that these thoughts will give you some idea of the problems you would face in our subsidiary. Hopefully these observations will not prove to be overly discouraging to you because we certainly need people of your caliber on our staff who have the stamina and ability to face up to our problems. As soon as there is any information of an impending vacancy I will let you know. Meantime, be forewarned, and please give my regards to Louis and the others in your office.

Cordially yours

(signed) William Shuler
General Manager
Metal Enterprises, S.p.A.

Encl. 1

The enclosed leaflet mentioned in this letter is shown on page 621.

a. Contrast union-management relations in Italy with those in the United States as discussed in Chapters 16 and 17.
b. What message, if any, does this letter have to offer the American manager being transferred to a foreign subsidiary?
c. In Italy, unions function as appendages of the national political parties. How does this role compare with the political role exercised by unions in the United States?

TO THE WORKERS OF METAL ENTERPRISES, S.p.A.

The conditions of exploitation which exist in your factory allow your employer to increase his profit whilst your wages are not updated in comparison with the increasing costs of living, higher rents, and costs of commodities. The other side of this exploitation is the continual increase in your working rates and working hours which are becoming heavier and heavier. All of this makes you similar to a machine ready to be replaced by young workers when the continuous nervous tension, physical tiredness, and premature aging do not allow you to keep up with the pace of the machine you are working on.

The defense of your health must be a great fight of ours and must see our efforts joined together in order to safeguard it.

Workers of Metal Enterprises!

Our struggle against employers' exploitation is also the struggle meant to obtain the right to get together in meetings; to exercise, within the plant, the political and trade-union freedom; and to exercise control on rates and conditions of work.

Comrade workers of Metal Enterprises, S.p.A.! Let's stick together in our struggle in order to achieve the following goals:

- higher wages
- more favorable and human hours
- defense of health
- political and trade-union freedom within the plant

Italian Communist Party
Section "Battaglia"
Via Lorenteggio, 183

Separation with Satisfaction

Flying Tiger Line with over 3,000 employees moves freight on daily international schedules between industrial areas of the United States and the markets of Asia. Approximately one half of its employees are based at the World Headquarters at the International Airport in Los Angeles and the other half are stationed at various locations in the U.S. and Asia. Most of these employees did not share in the combat experience of the famous Flying Tigers of World War II, but the philosophy of that organization has influenced the working conditions of employees who have been with the company since its founding in 1945. Basically this philosophy stresses the importance of the welfare of the members of the organization.

One important implementation of this philosophy is found in its Outplacement Program. This program is designed to relocate employees who are leaving the company for reasons other than retirement. These employees may be good workers who are being furloughed due to business conditions or may be employees who are not effective in carrying out their responsibilities. Company policy is based on the premise that it has a social responsibility to help relocate employees, and the company believes the failure of an employee on the job may not be solely the responsibility of the employee. Furthermore, management desires to have employees who are leaving have good feelings toward the company.

The current Outplacement Program involves several steps that are designed to achieve the objectives stated earlier:

1. The terminated employee is interviewed for the purpose of understanding his or her emotional condition and to determine the individual's plans for future employment.

2. The individual may be given career counseling at a local university or by the Personnel Department.
3. Personnel department staff members assist the individual in preparing a résumé which is then printed at company expense. The terminated employee is permitted to use company telephones for making contacts with prospective employers.
4. A list of employment agencies or executive search firms is given to the individual.
5. Information regarding jobs available with other organizations is given to the individual. The personnel staff members meet to exchange information regarding job vacancies of which they have knowledge.
6. Help is provided in job-seeking skills such as interview techniques. Individuals are encouraged to get practice in being interviewed.
7. Individuals are sent to temporary employment agencies, such as Kelly Girl, if they are interested in this type of employment.
8. Individuals are referred to the Employee Benefit Department where the stock plan, conversion of group insurance to individual insurance, flight benefits, and credit union rights are explained. Individuals may remain in the credit union and borrow funds from it even though they are no longer on the company's payroll.
9. If it is advisable, individuals may be referred to a clinical psychologist who serves as a consultant paid by the company to assist those who are separated from the company.

These main features of the Outplacement Program may be supplemented to meet the needs of these individuals who may require other services.

a. What effect is the Outplacement Program likely to have on employee attitudes toward the company?
b. Do you believe that the company should share the responsibility for the employee's failure? Why or why not?
c. What impact is the Outplacement Program likely to have on society?
d. Are there any problems that may arise from the administration of this program?

Name Index

D

E

F

G

H

J

K

Subject Index

C

D

E

F

G

N

O

P